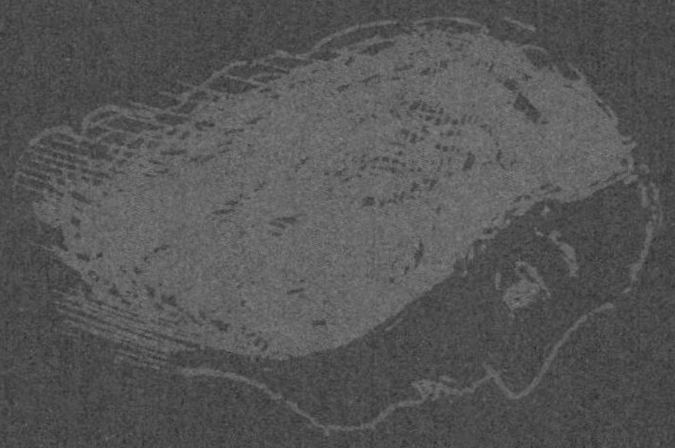

Marc Chagall

AND THE LOST JEWISH WORLD

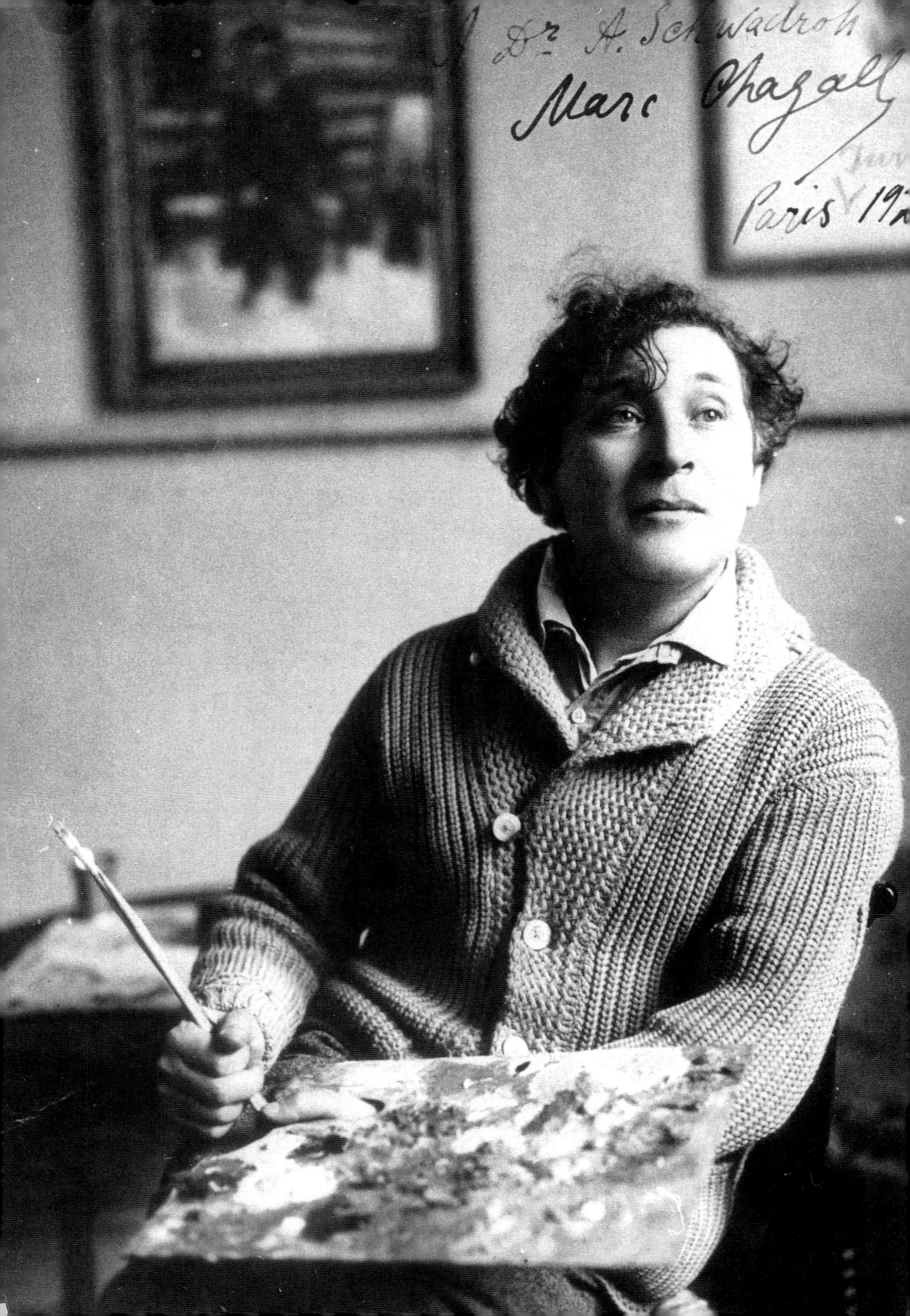
Marc Chagall
Paris

Marc Chagall

AND THE LOST JEWISH WORLD

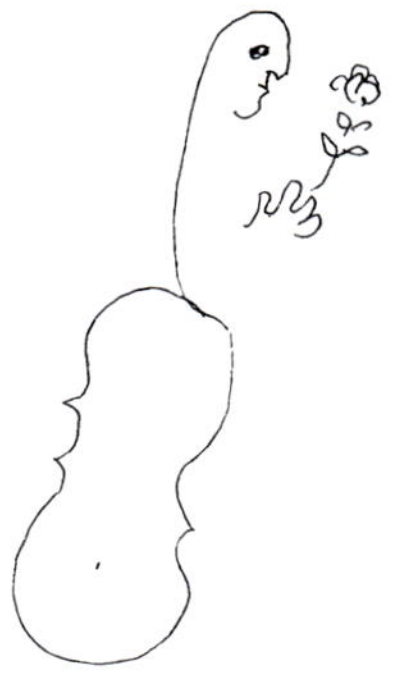

The Nature of Chagall's Art and Iconography

BENJAMIN HARSHAV

RIZZOLI
NEW YORK

Rizzoli Editor: Ellen Cohen
Design: Eric Mueller / Element Group

First published in the United States of America in 2006
by Rizzoli International Publications, Inc.
300 Park Avenue South
New York, NY 10010
www.rizzoliusa.com

2006 2007 2008 2009 2010 / 10 9 8 7 6 5 4 3 2 1

Printed in China

ISBN-13: 978-08478-2802-9
ISBN-10: 0-8478-2802-6

Library of Congress Control Number: 2005937922

Unless otherwise noted, drawings throughout the book are from Bella Chagall's memoirs *Berendike licht* ("Burning candles"), New York. Book League of the Jewish Fraternal Order, 1945.

FRONTIS: ***Marc Chagall, Paris, 1925.*** *This photograph was sent by Chagall to the collector of Jewish autographs, Dr. Abraham Schwadron, in Jerusalem at the foundation of Hebrew University. Courtesy of the National Library, Hebrew University, Jerusalem*

TITLE PAGE: ***The Fiddle-Rose*** *from A. Sutzkever's Yiddish book of poetry, by Chagall*

OPPOSITE: *From A. Lyessin's* ***Lider un poemen*** *with illustrations by Chagall, 1938*

Dear Anal
Happy Chanukah 2006 -
with all my love.
Jay
xxxx.

FOR BARBARA, MY SOUL MATE

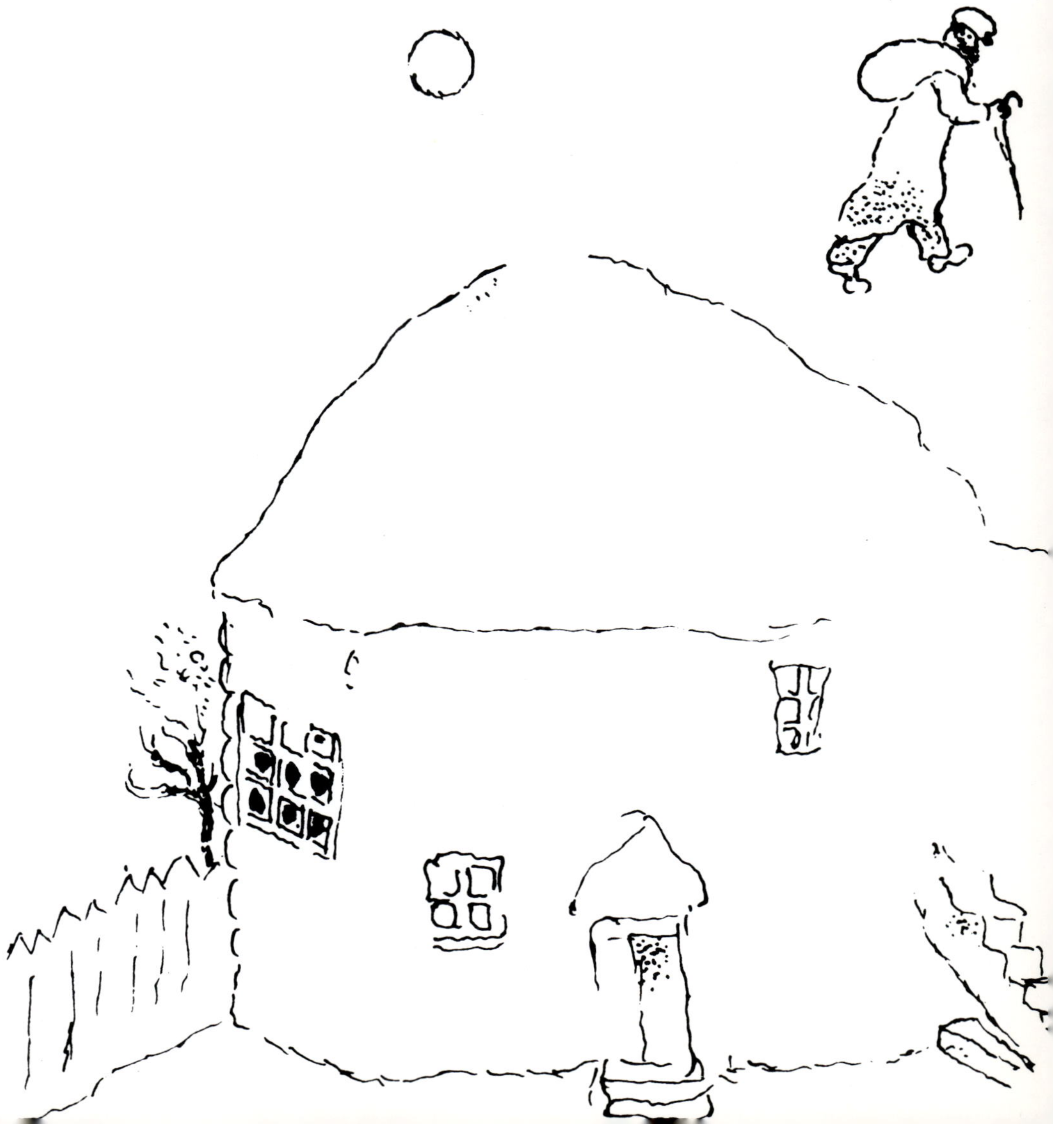

Contents

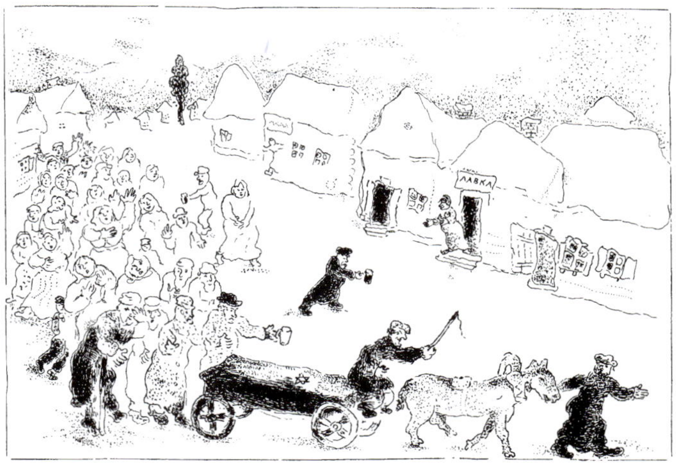

A Funeral. *Chagall's mother on the three steps of her store, giving alms.*

PREFACE

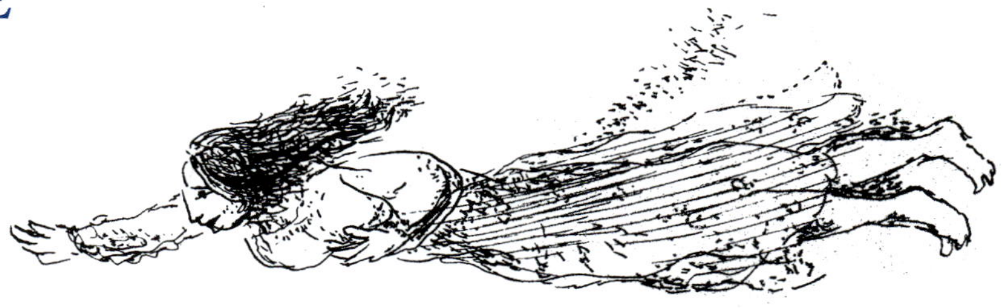

Marc Chagall (1887–1985) was an unusual figure in the center of modern art. His work is popular and alive to this day. Interest in Chagall has grown immensely with many recent publications of his early work, the so-called "Russian Period" of 1907–22—which was no less French than Russian[1]—and the many Chagall exhibitions around the globe, notably of his murals for the Moscow Yiddish Revolutionary theater.

As I intend to show in this book, Chagall's art is much more sophisticated and complex than the stereotypes about him as a childish, naïve, or fantastic painter would allow. He defined himself as "an unconsciously conscious artist," that is, intuitively he knew very well what he was doing. It is not by accident that major modern intellectuals—Guillaume Apollinaire, Herwarth Walden, Blaise Cendrars, André Malraux, Jacques Maritain, Paul Eluard, Louis Aragon, Lionello Venturi, Andrei Voznesensky—greeted him with excitement. Indeed, he was far from that sweet and sentimental optimist, which masses of people enjoyed. A proper assessment of the nature and value of Chagall's art cannot be made without uncovering and deciphering the cultural subtexts of his paintings along with his responses to the artistic trends of Modern art. He lived in several countries, spoke several languages, and was present at the unfolding of several political and artistic movements of his time. Indeed, he was a witness to the twentieth century.

This book discusses the nature of Chagall's art and its development. It observes the impulse of cultural representations in his "surreal" paintings and examines his place in the incessant dialogue on Modern art. It raises the problems of eclectic art, the polyphony of styles in one painter's work, the role of fictional worlds in painting, and the tensions between abstraction and representation. It also offers many new readings of individual paintings, their sources, aesthetics, and iconography.

The book focuses on Chagall's art, while his life and multifarious historical contexts were discussed in two earlier books of mine: Benjamin Harshav, *Marc Chagall and His Times: A Documentary Narrative* and *Marc Chagall on Art and Culture* (which I edited), both published by Stanford University Press 2004. These books include hundreds of letters and documents, illuminating Chagall's life and ideas from within. I shall rely on them for the factual support of my arguments.[2]

In the present volume, chapter one provides a brief survey of Chagall's life and cultural context. Chapter two analyzes the general principles of his art and fictional universe and his place vis-à-vis Modernism. Chapter three illuminates the foundations of his early art through a series of cultural and formal interpretations of key paintings, deciphering their enigmatic nature and aesthetic principles. Chapter four shows the depth of Chagall's engagement with "the lost Jewish world." Chapters five through seven are devoted to Chagall's most ambitious project of the Russian period, the murals he painted for the innovative Yiddish theater in Moscow after the Russian Revolution. Chapter eight looks at some developments in his later work, notably his intertwined imagery of Revolution, Jesus Christ, and Holocaust. And chapter nine provides a glimpse into Chagall's expansion into new media through a discussion of the Hadassah stained glass windows in Jerusalem.

This study grew out of my comprehensive essay, "Chagall: Postmodernism and Fictional Worlds in Painting," published in *Marc Chagall and the Jewish Theater*, New York: Guggenheim Museum, 1992, pp. 15–204; as well as my contributions to *Marc Chagall: Les années russes*, 1907–1922, Paris: Paris musées, 1995, and other publications. The studies and writings on Chagall are numerous. I learned especially from Franz Meyer, Susan Compton, Ziva Amishai-Maisels, Alexandra Shatskich, and Meret Meyer.

In many cases, the dates on Chagall's paintings were inserted later and often predated, sometimes indicating his fuzzy approach to time. Yet, unless I had clear proof for changing the date, I used the commonly accepted date as an orientation marker. For the same reason, I used the accepted names of paintings, even when I disagreed with them.

I am grateful to my friend Anthony Calnek of the Solomon R. Guggenheim Museum in New York, imaginative and far-ranging editor and publisher, for having launched me on this fascinating journey. Many persons and institutions in several countries helped me in the research. They are all acknowledged in my book *Marc Chagall and His Times*, pp. XVI–XX. Earlier versions of some of this material were published in the Guggenheim Museum's catalogue *Marc Chagall and the Jewish Theater*, 1992; my essay "The Role of Language in Modern Art" *(Modernism/Modernity*, vol. I, no. 2 (1994) and other studies (see bibliography). Finally, I am grateful to my thoughtful and precise editor Ellen Cohen, who helped bring the book to its final shape. Research funding from Yale University and Tel Aviv University were indispensable in this complex endeavor.

—Benjamin Harshav

J.& H. Blaustein Professor of Hebrew and Comparative Literature and Professor of Slavic Languages and Literatures, Yale University;

L.& S. Porter Professor Emeritus of Literary Theory and Poetics, Tel Aviv University;

Fellow, American Academy of Arts and Sciences.

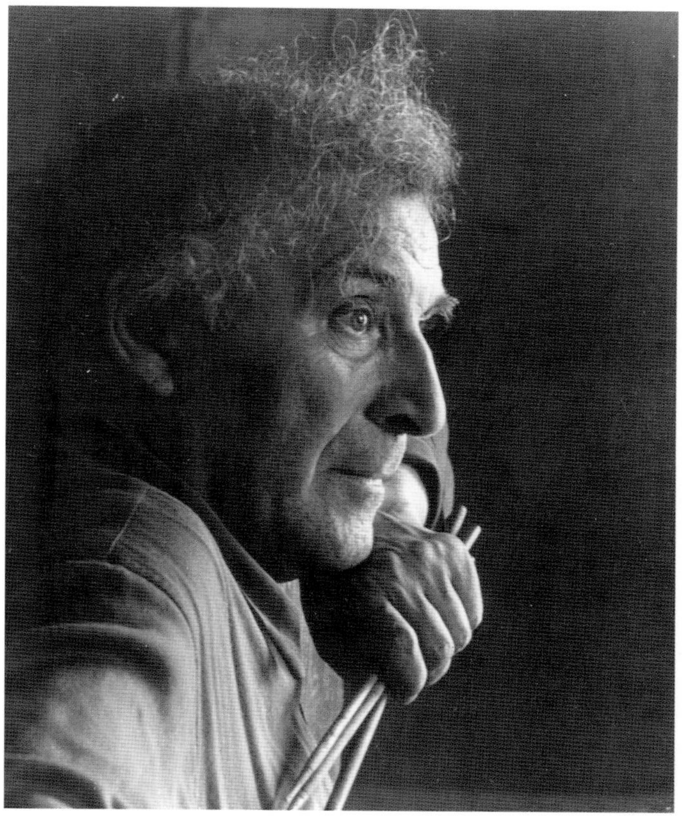

Chagall, High Falls, 1948. *Photo by Charles Leirens. Courtesy of the author*

1. In Paris, Chagall spent four years crucial to his formation as an artist (1910–14), when his individual style consolidated and asserted itself vis-à-vis French modern painting. Yet even before that, he studied with Léon Bakst in St. Petersburg in the "most European" (i.e., French) art school in Russia.

2. For my other publications on Chagall, see under Harshav in the bibliography.

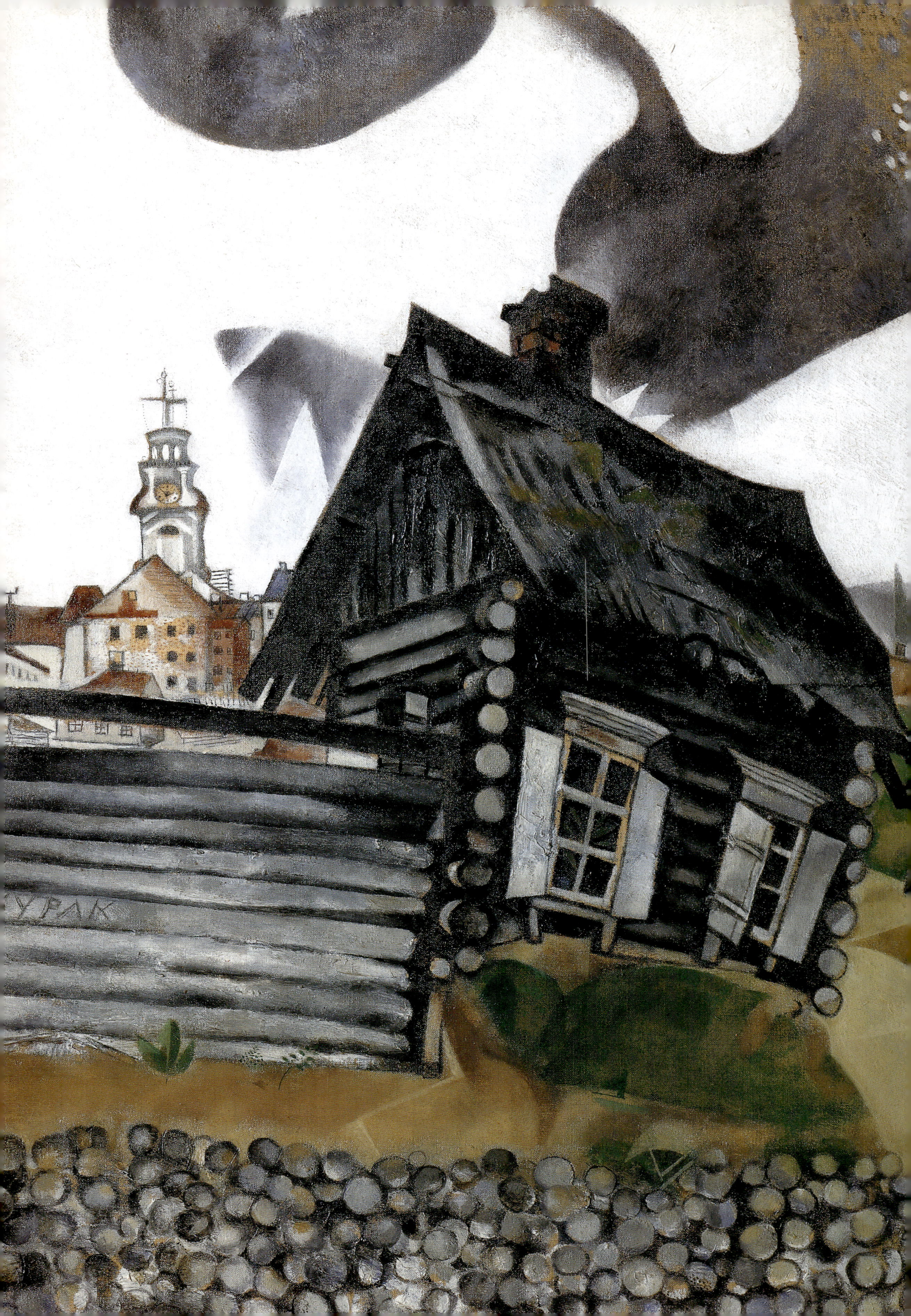
УРАК

1. Roots

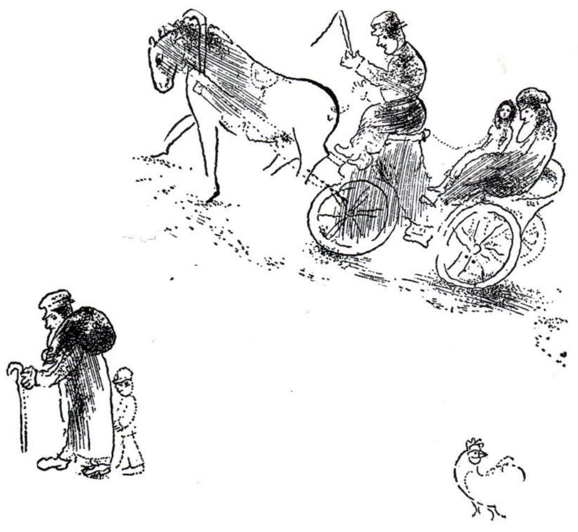

1. *The Cultural Context*

> *"If I were not a Jew (with the content I put into that word) I wouldn't have been an artist, or I would be a different artist altogether."*
>
> — MARC CHAGALL, "Leaves from My Notebook"[1]

EMPIRE WITHIN EMPIRE

The emergence of Marc Chagall as an artist was part of a powerful movement that transformed the Jews in the modern age. There seems to be a widespread assumption that a Jewish religious minority—with the emphasis both on "religious" and on "minority"—lived in Tsarist Russia, somewhat like Jews in Germany in the 1920s or in the United States today. Actually, a vast Jewish national and cultural "empire" had developed in Eastern Europe within the Russian Empire of power, especially in the nineteenth and twentieth centuries, which then fed the transformations of modernity, inside and outside the Jewish fold.

Chagall's native city, Vitebsk, is mentioned in documents as early as the eleventh century. In the Middle Ages, the city belonged to the Grand Duchy of Lithuania, which encompassed what is now Lithuania proper, all of Belarus, some areas of Latvia and Russia, as well as the Ukraine (later ceded to Poland). In the fourteenth century Lithuania and Poland united under one royal dynasty, and in the sixteenth century they merged in a full-fledged union, the "Polish Republic," stretching from the Baltic to the Black Sea. Individual Jews had lived in Lithuania at least since the earliest days of Christianity in the fourteenth century, but a significant influx came after the union of Lithuania with Poland, whose Kings lured the Jews from Germany to develop their cities. Lithuania was actually assimilated to Poland and only the Jews preserved in their memory the boundaries of the Medieval Lithuanian Grand Duchy. They kept the name Lithuania for the whole domain and called it *Litah* in Yiddish, and its Jews, the *Litvaks.* Jewish Litah is marked by a distinct Yiddish dialect, a particular Jewish cuisine, a "Litvak" mentality, and admiration for learning. Chagall always identified himself as a Litvak, even though he came from eastern Byelorussia.[2]

After the Jews were expelled from most of Western Europe in the Middle Ages, their major center shifted to Poland, the largest state in Europe. By the sixteenth century, the overwhelming majority of world Jewry resided in the united kingdom of Poland and Lithuania, where they had full-fledged autonomy with a Jewish parliament (the "Committee of Four Lands"), which assembled in central cities on major market days, collected taxes for the king and for the Jewish communities, conducted its own legal system and its own social, religious, and cultural affairs—in short, the Jews had everything a nation-state has but an army and territorial power. In 1900, 70 percent of world Jewry lived in the former territories of Poland/Lithuania and, in addition, large portions of

OPPOSITE: ***The Gray House*** *(Detail). Oil on canvas, 68 x 74 cm. Fundación Coleción Thyssen-Borneminsza, Madrid*

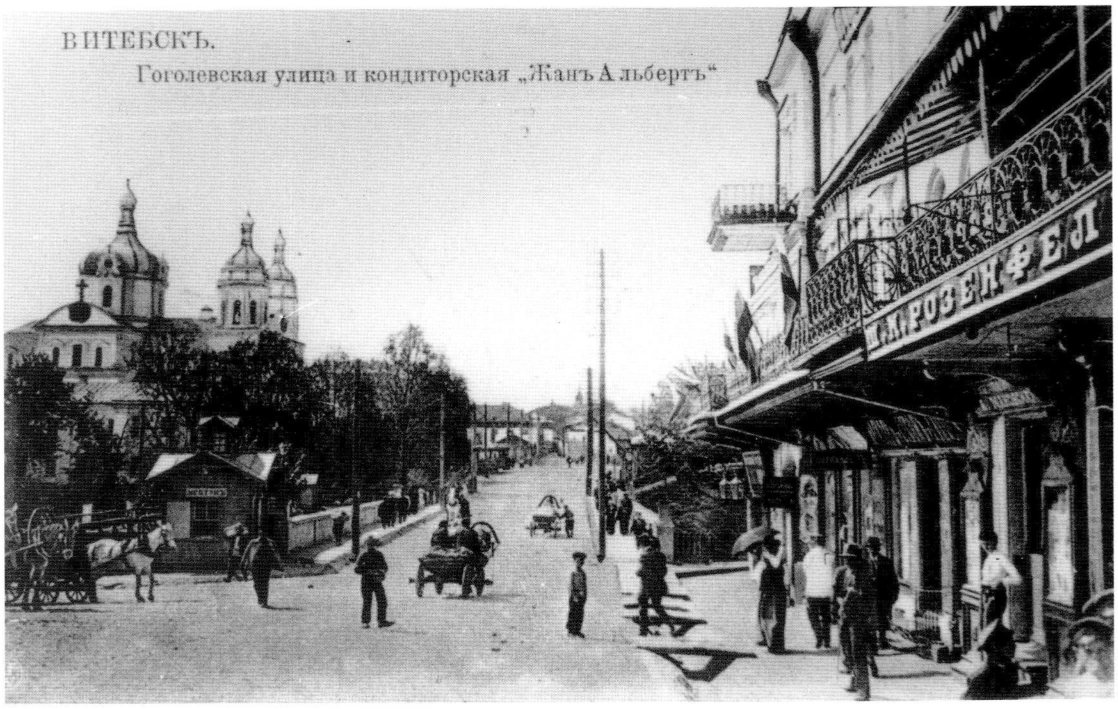

A pre-Revolutionary postcard of Vitebsk: "Gogol Street and Jean-Albert Pastry Shop." The official card does not mention the big sign under the pastry shop, on the right: "Sh. N. Rosenfeld"—the jewelry store of Bella's father. Courtesy of the author

German, Hungarian, and American Jewry were immigrants from Eastern Europe.[3]

Toward the end of the eighteenth century Poland was dismantled by its neighbors Russia, Prussia, and Austria. The Russian Empire devoured the largest chunk, including what is today central Poland, Ukraine, Belarus, and Lithuania.

The Russian Tsars had banned Jews from entering Russia proper. Now, with the annexation of a considerable Jewish population, the Jews were kept in the occupied Polish territories (as well as the new territories in the south, including Bessarabia and Odessa), enclosed in a huge geographical ghetto named the Jewish Pale of Settlement. In time, only a few thousand Jews, mostly affluent merchants and industrialists and the university educated, were allowed to live outside the Pale, in Moscow, St. Petersburg, Kiev, and other cities. Thus, in 1900, 21,000 Jews lived in St. Petersburg. In 1891–92, 30,000 Jews were expelled from Moscow, and only about 5,000 remained. The Jewish masses—over five million at the end of the nineteenth century—lived among the Empire's western minorities (Byelorussians, Ukrainians, Poles, Lithuanians, Latvians, Romanians) far from the centers of Russian culture and a large Russian-speaking population. Thus, it was easier for them to preserve their own language and culture.

In the eighteenth and nineteenth centuries there was a veritable population explosion among the Russian Jews. Between 1800 and 1880, their numbers increased four- or fivefold. Yet their demographic structure was most unusual. According to the detailed census of 1897, Jews constituted 11.8 percent of the population of Vitebsk Province as a whole, but they accounted for only 1.9 percent of the village population (mostly non-farmers). On the other hand, they constituted 66.3 percent of the population of all the twenty-eight towns in the province, as well as 52.7% of the population of all twelve cities.[4]

Thus, the predominantly Jewish cities and towns (*shtetls*) were surrounded by a sea of Christian agricultural villages. In 1897, the population of Vitebsk Province was 1,489,246, scattered over 26,590 named settlements, villages and hamlets, but only 48 places had a population of more than 500. Until 1861—just a generation before Chagall was born—the peasants were serfs, the property of Russian or Polish landowners, and could be bought and sold with their villages. Even after the serfs were nominally emancipated, their movements were limited by the village council (*obshtshina*) and by their economic dependence on their former landlords.

The distinction between three categories: city, town (shtetl), and village reflected demographic and ethnic differences and must not be confused. The Yiddish word *shtetl* (diminutive of *shtot*, "city")—like the Polish *mjasteczko*, diminutive of *mjasto*, city—was often translated in Western languages as "village" (in Chagall's own usage in French: *village*, derived from *ville*, city, meaning

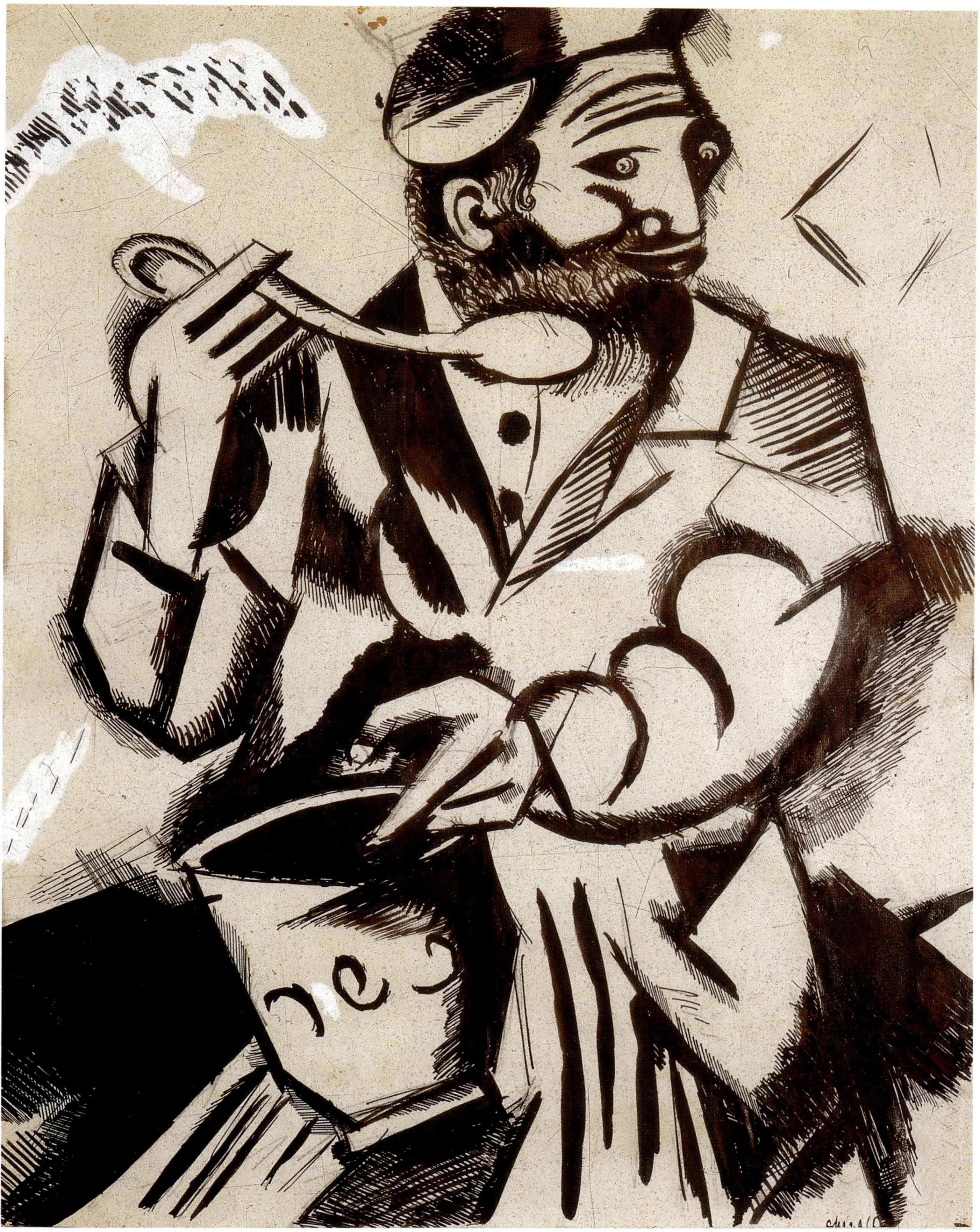

1. ***The Peasant Eating.*** *1913. India ink on paper, 29 x 22 cm. Private collection, Basel*

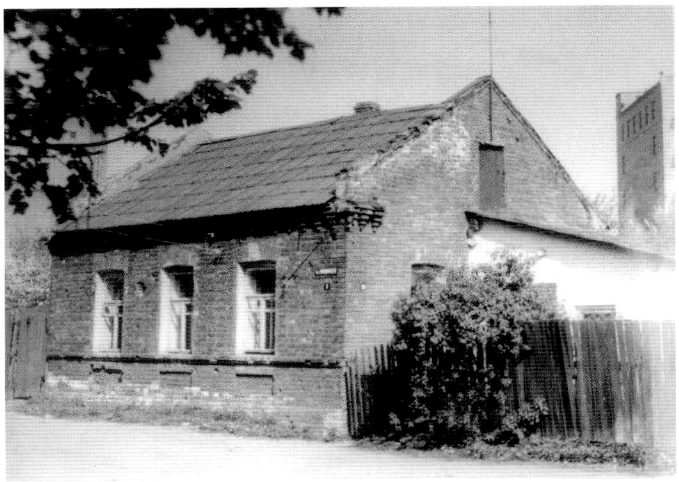

The brick house of Chagall's family on Pokrovskaya Street in Vitebsk, where he lived from age three to twenty-eight. Courtesy Comité Marc Chagall, Paris

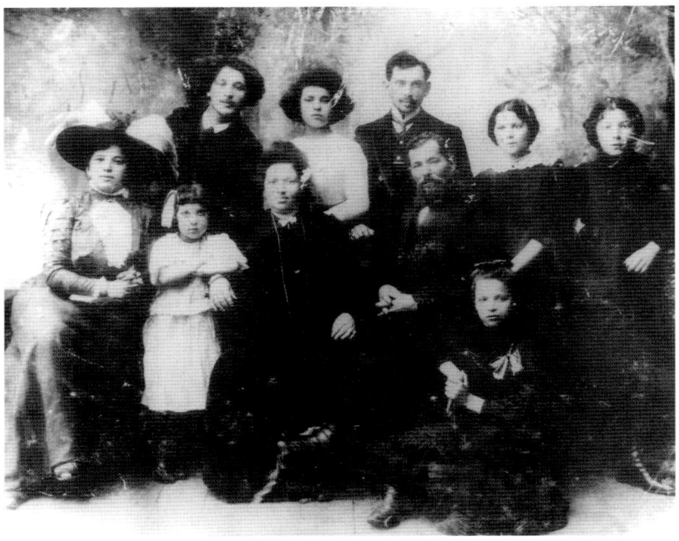

The Chagall family before Marc's departure for Paris in 1910. Top row from left: Marc, Zina, Uncle Noah, Lisa, Manya. Bottom row: Anyuta, Marussya, Mother, Father, Rosa. Courtesy Comité Marc Chagall, Paris

a small town). This is an unnecessary confusion, for villages were places where Christian peasants lived and farmed the land, whereas the towns were predominantly Jewish and had little land or peasants. In Yiddish the concept of "village" connoted something entirely different: It was a place inhabited by coarse and illiterate peasants, who would come to the town market, get drunk, and exhibit their physical prowess; or no less primitive Jews, deprived of a Jewish *minyan* (a minimal congregation of ten men) and Jewish education. Indeed, such Jews were called *poyerim* ("peasants"), i.e., ignorant and coarse, deprived of any learning, even though they observed the basic Jewish rituals as can be seen in *The Peasant Eating*, 1913 (no. 1). In spite of the misunderstood label, this drawing shows a Jew not a Christian peasant; he is wearing a hat (i.e., observing his religion) and eating from a pot with the Hebrew inscription "Kosher."

Most cities and towns were administrative centers of their regions: the capital of the province and its district capital. Here was the seat of the Russian Orthodox and Polish Catholic churches and cathedrals, memorably depicted in Chagall's work, and the Russian administrative and educational institutions. Christians constituted the ruling classes, including the Russian administration, Polish and Russian landowners, and even the dreaded *gorodovoy* (policeman on the beat). The provincial capital Vitebsk was also home to laborers who came from the surrounding villages, soldiers (mostly of peasant stock) who were stationed there, as well as bureaucrats, priests, teachers, and other representatives of the Russian power structure. While most peasants in the area spoke Byelorussian, the language of the authorities and of the dominant culture was Russian.

Among the Jewish population of Vitebsk Province, 39 percent of the breadwinners lived on trade and 36 percent were artisans. In modern terms, the *shtetl* was the shopping mall of the area; it was a marketplace and a center of artisan production, where peasants came to buy and sell, and from which Jews would go peddle their goods and crafts in the surrounding villages. Enterprising Jews also traveled to the larger cities and other lands, aided by their common language, thus casting a Yiddish-speaking commercial network from village to town to Russian cities and to Western Europe and even the Far East.

Thus, the Jews were the majority urban population; they developed banks, light industry, trade, export, and so on. Eighty percent of all artisans in the city of

Vitebsk were Jews. The masses of peasants—the overwhelming majority of the population of Russia—were still passive and depressed, coming out from their recent slavery, and had little influence on the new economic and cultural trends in the Russian provinces.[5] A good indicator of the predominance of the Jews in the economy of the Pale is the number of accredited merchants of the First, Second, and Third Guilds (an official title, bestowed by a government not particularly biased in favor of the Jews). As early as 1855, there were in Vitebsk Province fifty-eight Jewish merchants of the First and Second Guilds and only six Christians; and 161 Jewish Merchants of the Third Guild compared to thirty-four Christians.

For the first time in Jewish history after the Destruction of the Second Temple in the first century CE, here was a huge territory, a polka-dotted map, where Jews regularly constituted the majority, indeed two thirds of the population. Unlike the *Judengasse* (the "Jewish Street") in medieval German towns, often placed on the margins of the city, where the Jews were a small minority, in the Pale the whole town was basically Jewish, although power was in the hands of the Christian minority. Typically, the central church and City Hall, the tallest and most prominent buildings in town, were located at the market place, but the market itself was surrounded by Jewish homes and stores.

It is important to understand that it was not the individual ancestral, primitive *shtetl*, which its expatriates and writers remembered with contempt mixed with nostalgia but the network of *shtetls* and their new cultural institutions emanating from the larger cities that constituted the base of modern Jewish nation building as well as of the waves of Jews entering Russian and European mainstream culture. The new, secular Jews had a strong sense of being not a religion but a nation, like other nationalities oppressed in the Russian Empire. The essayist Dr. Chaim Zhitlovsky called it "Yiddishland."

Two major factors contributed to the consolidation of this network: the Hasidic movement in the eighteenth and nineteenth centuries, which spread over a large territory, connecting Jews scattered in many small towns, who would travel to congregate in the Rebbe's court in another small town and combine religion with business; and the railroads, built since the 1860s, which revolutionized the easy connections between the towns. In the first half of the twentieth century, Jews in the Russian Empire developed a dense network of social and cultural institutions of their own, including several competing educational systems, societies, synagogues and prayer houses, hospitals, cemeteries, philanthropic organizations, publishing houses, newspapers, community administrations, religious authorities, and political movements. Those were essentially secular institutions under the aegis of one religious framework, which legally separated the Jews from the Russians and the official Russian Orthodox Church. Several rich and Russified Jews in the cities outside the Pale played an important role in this renaissance. And many more moved into the dominant Russian culture.

Discourse in this autonomous world was conducted in three specifically Jewish languages: Yiddish was used for daily life, religious and secular education, and correspondence, and later for literature, newspapers, and political parties. Hebrew was the language of the Bible and most prayers and blessings, the traditional library of texts and written documents, as well as modern literature. Aramaic was the language of the Talmud, used in the judicial system and studied in the religious academies, the yeshivas. Hebrew and Aramaic together were called "The Holy Tongue" and were included in Yiddish life and quoted in Yiddish discourse. Yet writing was conducted in Yiddish or in Hebrew, with Aramaic phrases embedded.

In 1897, almost 98 percent of the 5.2 million Jews of the Russian Empire declared Yiddish as their language. Yiddish contained a folklorized universe of beliefs, stories, proverbs and jokes, as well as conventions of discourse, oral and written literature. The language separated the Jews from the surrounding world but also served as a bridge to it: Yiddish folklore absorbed many elements of German and Slavic folklore, merging them with elements of the Jewish tradition and the Jewish library. And the new Yiddish and Hebrew literature adopted the genres and aesthetic ideals of Russian and German literature.

The Yiddish language contained considerable chunks of words of German, Hebrew, and Slavic origin, often fused with each other into Yiddish forms. Yet Yiddish was also an open language, and its speakers could easily shift into any of the component languages and borrow whatever they needed. From the end of the nineteenth century, the language expanded immensely and became the main internal vehicle for the Modern Jewish Revolution,[6] as manifested in the development of modern literature, ideologies, schools, and cultural institutions.

In western Lithuania—Vilna (Vilnius) and its wide hinterland—the "rational" Judaism initiated in the eigh-

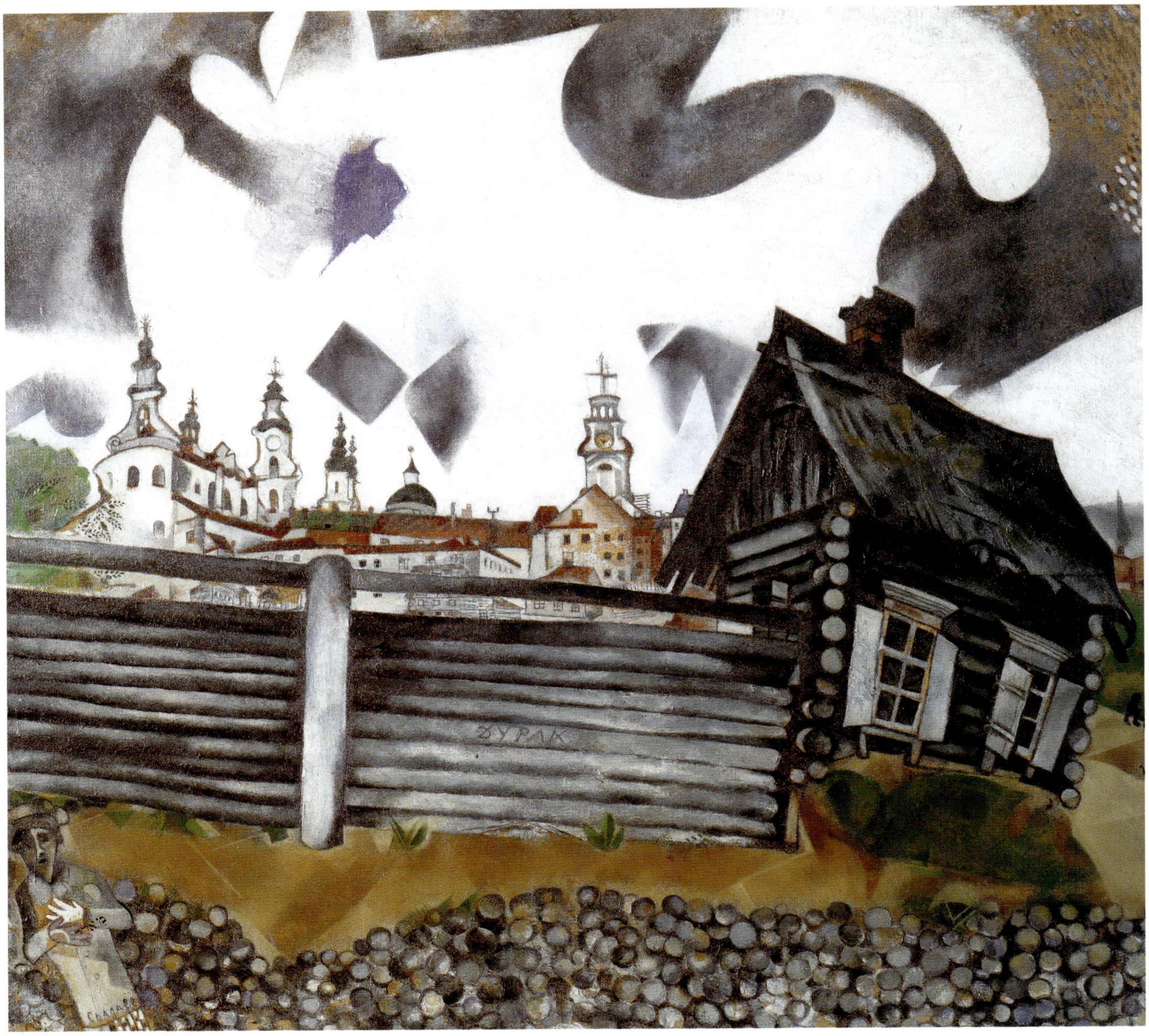

2. *The Gray House.* 1917. *Oil on canvas, 68 x 74 cm. Fundación Coleción Thyssen-Bornemisza, Madrid*

teenth century by the great Talmudic scholar the Gaon of Vilna built a fortress of learning. The adherents of this movement were called *Misnagdim*, or opponents of Hasidism. At the same time, in the eastern part of vast Jewish Lithuania (today's Belarus), where Chagall grew up, a special Hasidic movement emerged that introduced joy and optimism into the somber mood of orthodox Judaism. It fostered a revival of the emotional participation of simple people in religious experience. Being a Jewish-Lithuanian sect, however, it also stressed learning and was called ChaBaD (Chabad), a Hebrew acronym for "Wisdom, Insight, Knowledge." The founder of this movement, Shneur-Zalman of Lyady (1745–1813), was born in Lyozno, Chagall's ancestral hometown. The movement is also called "Lubavitsh" (or Lubavich), for another shtetl in that area where the Shneurson dynasty of rebbes resided before the October Revolution.

CHAGALL'S VITEBSK

In 1909, the city of Vitebsk had two synagogues and sixty prayer houses, most of them Lubavitsh. Chagall's cheerful disposition may have stemmed from Hasidism's theory of *bitul ha-Yesh*, the cancellation of, or obliviousness to, material existence in the name of spiritual elation.[7] Chagall's fictional Jewish world is a far cry from the dour descriptions of the impoverished and degenerated *shtetl* that permeated much of Jewish fiction around the turn of the century. At the end of the nineteenth century, a massive atheist movement spread among the Jews of Vitebsk. Chagall himself, who was a singer at the synagogue, left it for good at age thirteen, right after his Bar Mitzvah and at the dawn of the new century.

In 1897, the city of Vitebsk numbered 34,420 Jews, or 52.4 percent of the population, as compared to 37.9 percent of Russians and Byelorussians together. It became an important cultural center, producing such Jewish intellectuals as S. An-sky, Dr. Chaim Zhitlovsky, Yehuda Pen, and many others. The small population of this provincial capital is not surprising because even Vilna, the "Jerusalem of Lithuania," which claimed to be the cultural center of Lithuanian religious and secular Jewry, had only 64,000 Jews at the time. The Jewish population was spread throughout the towns of Vitebsk Province in a network of small communities. Only 20 percent of the Jews of the province lived in Vitebsk proper, and many cultural institutions were located in small or large towns, such as Lubavitsh, which numbered 1,660 Jews, or 67.3 percent of the population. A constant flux, cultural and economic, took place between the provincial capital, the district towns, and the smaller *shtetls*.

What, then, was the importance of Vitebsk?[8] The easternmost city of Poland, Vitebsk was annexed by Russia in 1772, more than twenty years before the final partition of Poland. It was situated in the northeastern corner of the Pale of Settlement, relatively close to both Russian capitals, St. Petersburg and Moscow. It also was home to a stratum of Russian-speaking, educated Jews, including several thousand expelled from nearby Moscow in 1891. Vitebsk was an important railroad junction, where trains passed from Odessa and Kiev to St. Petersburg, and from Riga and the West to Moscow. In his youth, Chagall took advantage of that proximity to escape to St. Petersburg, even though he often lived there illegally. And in 1919, when Granovsky's new Yiddish Theater in the recently renamed capital Petrograd sought a greater audience of Yiddish-speakers of the "people," they went to the closest Jewish center, Vitebsk.

LANGUAGES

After the Bolshevik Revolution, Anatoly Lunacharsky, People's Commissar of Enlightenment (i.e., minister of education and culture), appointed the painter David Shterenberg (whom he had known in exile in Paris) as head of IZO, the Division of Art of the People's Commissariat of Enlightenment. The art critic Abram Efros described him thus:

> Shterenberg was born in Zhitomir [Ukraine], studied in Paris, and became an artist in Moscow. He does not speak any one of the three languages, but can make himself clear in all of them. What he lacks, he substitutes with interjections and gestures. Listening to his slow speech, in which the frowning of forehead and lips, or fuzzy sounds and pauses, play the role of words and concepts—you imagine his painting as hesitant and careful. Such are the first canvases of foreigners in Paris who try to hold the brush in the French manner.[9]

Chagall could be described in similar terms. Chagall grew up in a Yiddish-speaking society, in the heartland of the Jewish masses in Russia. Vitebsk had twenty-eight Jewish schools and educational establishments, but his provincial parents sent him to a traditional *heder,* an all-male, one-class elementary "room" at the teacher's home. The first texts he learned to read were passages from the Hebrew Bible, mainly the Pentateuch with a classical commentary by the French Hebrew scholar Rashi (1040–1105) ("Chumash with Rashi") and the prayer book, but the teaching itself was conducted in Yiddish. Chagall studied such Hebrew texts from the usual age of four until the age of thirteen, with at least four different teachers. He went every day from dawn to dusk to the teacher's *heder*. When a child finished studying with one teacher, he would go to a higher class with another teacher. The average size of a *heder* in Vitebsk Province was eight children, hence the close contact between the only *melamed* (teacher) and his pupils. The young Chagall rarely saw his hard-working father, the *melamed* served as a surrogate father model as well; he conveyed to his pupil the sanctitude of The Book and the stories of Jewish history, and took the boy to the public steam bath on Fridays.

The teaching focused on reading aloud selections from the holy texts, translated word for word, embellished and expanded by an oral tradition of biblical stories, drawing on Midrash and traditional commentaries. But there was no teaching of any active, oral or written, expression in Hebrew. The Holy Tongue was not intended to be used in real-life communication. Chagall was deeply impressed by the biblical stories he heard in childhood, as retold in Yiddish, but throughout his life he demonstrated little knowledge of Hebrew. In several paintings, he copied Hebrew words from the Bible, but he never produced a single sentence or even a combination of two Hebrew words of his own. The spelling of the Hebrew words (which even a regular Yiddish reader should know) that appeared in his numerous Yiddish letters and lectures is far from perfect.[10]

At the age of thirteen, Moysey (as he was called in Russian) was taken by his mother to a Russian secondary school; she gave a hefty bribe to a teacher, who agreed to accept this Jewish student even though it was against the law. Russian was the higher language of culture and a springboard for Jews striving to enter the Russian and European world. His parents, although conventionally observant, apparently acquiesced with the new secular trends, and accepted the secularization of their children. The males in Chagall's family photos wore no hats, de rigueur for a religious person at the time. At his insistence, Chagall's mother also took him to the art school established by the Jewish painter Yury Moyseevitsh Pen, defying what was supposed to be a ban on graven images. Russian became Chagall's first language of writing; not before the mid-1920s in Paris did he write letters in his mother tongue, Yiddish.

A fellow schoolboy and budding painter introduced Moysey to the circle of affluent young people that included his future wife, Berta Rosenfeld (later called Bella), a daughter of a prosperous merchant and Lubavitsh hasid. No doubt Berta's parents spoke Yiddish at home, but the youth with whom she associated spoke Russian *comme il faut*, read Russian poetry, performed Russian theater, and discussed topics of Russian culture.

As was typical for daughters of religious and well-to-do Jews, Berta was better educated than Chagall. He later claimed that she attended a university in Moscow (Moscow University itself was not open to Jews). They apparently spoke mostly Russian, the language of the circles of Jewish youth, with each other. But Yiddish was their true mother tongue; even their daughter Ida, who grew up in Paris, understood Yiddish stories, and the Russian-educated Bella Chagall wrote her memoirs in Paris in 1939 and in New York in 1944 in Yiddish. She remembered:

> A strange thing, I wanted to write. And to write only in my stammering mother tongue, which I have almost not spoken since I left my parents' home. The farther my childhood years have moved away from me, the closer they suddenly drew up to me, as if they themselves were breathing into my mouth.

During his years in the United States (1941–48), although never politically committed, Chagall was in contact with leftist Yiddishist circles. It was with a leftist Yiddish publishing house, the Book League of the Jewish People's Fraternal Order, that Chagall published Bella's two autobiographical volumes after her death. Even when living with his non-Jewish companion Virginia Haggard in New York City or north of it, Marc read Yiddish newspapers (he did not know any English) and spoke Yiddish with the historian Max Lerner, the Yiddish novelist Yosef Opatoshu, and other friends and writers. The largest body of his extant correspondence, written in longhand throughout his life, was written in Yiddish, addressed to Yiddish writers or Israeli officials, often warm, confessional, complaining or intimate, and usually both nationalistic and critical of the Jews, as were many Jewish intellectuals at the time. The many texts inscribed on his paintings are mostly in Hebrew or Yiddish.

No doubt, Chagall read Yiddish literature. In his younger years, some stories by Mendele Moykher Sforim, Sholem Aleichem, and Y. L. Peretz made a strong impact on his worldview. Later, he read the fiction of his friend Yosef Opatoshu and the three volumes of poetry of his compatriot A. Lyessin (Walt), written in the same sonorous meters that Chagall himself mastered in his own Russian poetry. He illustrated Lyessin's poetry in the 1930s (and even understood enough to doubt their "literary," i.e., modern, quality). He also read and illustrated the modern Yiddish poetry of Dovid Hofshteyn, Abraham Sutzkever, Elkhonon Vogler, and others. Dozens of manuscripts of Yiddish speeches, articles, and poems in Chagall's own handwriting, which he read on various occasions, were preserved in archives. Many of them were eventually published in the Tel Aviv–based Yiddish literary-social quarterly *Di goldene keyt* ("The Golden Chain [of tradition]."

In 1907, when Chagall arrived in St. Petersburg to study art, the rich or learned Jews who had permission to live in the capital spoke Russian. Although his teacher Léon (Lev) Bakst (born in Grodno, in western Lithuania) and Chagall's first mentor, Maxim Vinaver (born in Warsaw), were Jews from the Pale, he apparently talked to them in Russian. Russian was the language of his formal education and reading, and in his early twenties he wrote a book of poetry in Russian (unpublished to this day).

In France, where Marc spent most of his life and had many intellectual friends, he quickly learned to speak French. But just as his Russian had a Yiddish subtext, so did his French have a Yiddish/Russian flavor. Chagall's second [common-law] wife Virginia Haggard, the daughter of an English diplomat in Paris, met him in New York after he had spent twenty-two years in France. As she

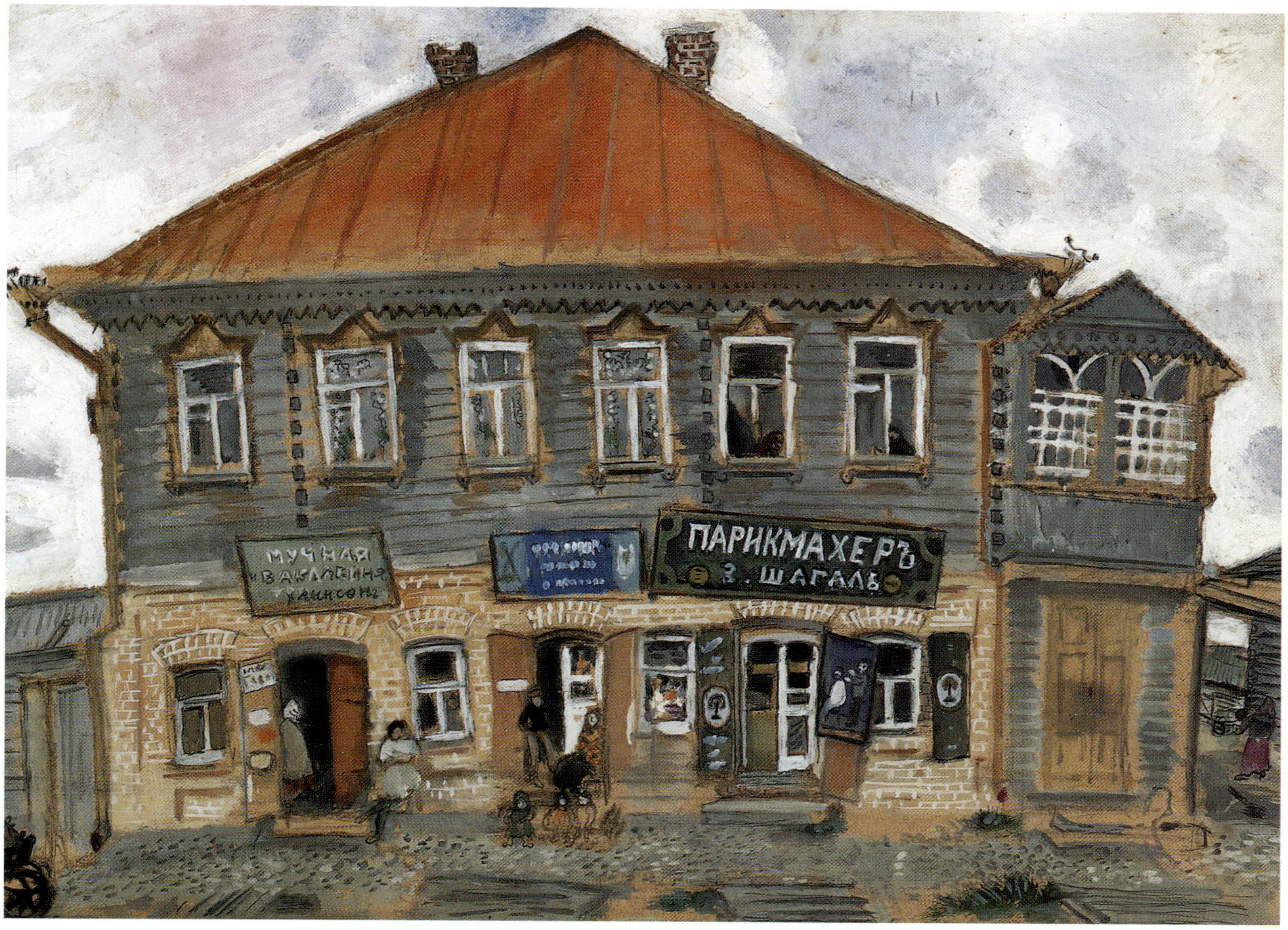

3. ***Uncle Zusya's Shop in Lyozno.*** *1914. Oil, gouache, and colored pencil on paper, 37.1 x 49 cm. Tretyakov Gallery, Moscow. The sign on the right reads in Russian: "Barber Z. Shagal."*

later recalled, "We were soon conversing in French. His Russian accent was warm and colorful, and his grammatical errors made me feel less self-conscious about my own." In a letter to Virginia, Chagall wrote, "I would like to write you a whole book, but I write French like a Russian pig."[11] Chagall was always immersed in art, not books; his language was the language of painting.

CENTER AND PERIPHERY

Chagall was born in Vitebsk. He himself had doubts about the place of his birth. His friend and art critic Abram Efros referred to him as "the painter from Lyozno," and the Israeli President and scholar Zalman Shazar himself from Jewish Lithuania (Byelorussia) addressed him as "our brother from Lyozno and Paris!" Lyozno was a large town and a prestigious place in Jewish geography, now transplanted as a symbol from a religious to a secular tradition, which embraced the religious past. Chagall's paternal grandfather moved with his son from Lyozno to the big city; when the son married a Lyozno relative, she joined them in Vitebsk, where Chagall was born. Efros recognized the impact that Lyozno images made on Chagall. In many ways he really was a provincial boy; his early images of "Vitebsk" were closer to a suburb or a small-town scene.[12] Photos of the center of Vitebsk at the time show the capital of a Russian province—a different city altogether. Yet when he married Berta in 1915 and moved to the center of Vitebsk, he painted churches and cathedrals looming above the city, as, for example in *The Gray House*, 1917 (no. 2), which shows two planes of perspective, under a cubicized sky of the artist's imagination.

The Chagall legend is anchored first and foremost in Vitebsk. As the Russian art critic Yakov Tugendhold phrased it, the formula "Zion, Babylon, and Vilna," indicating the three symbolic centers of Jewish culture in history (Bible, Talmud, and Enlightenment), became "Zion, Babylon, and Vitebsk." This is how strongly his contemporaries felt about Chagall as the symbol of what they called the "Renaissance" of Jewish culture in the beginning of the twentieth century.

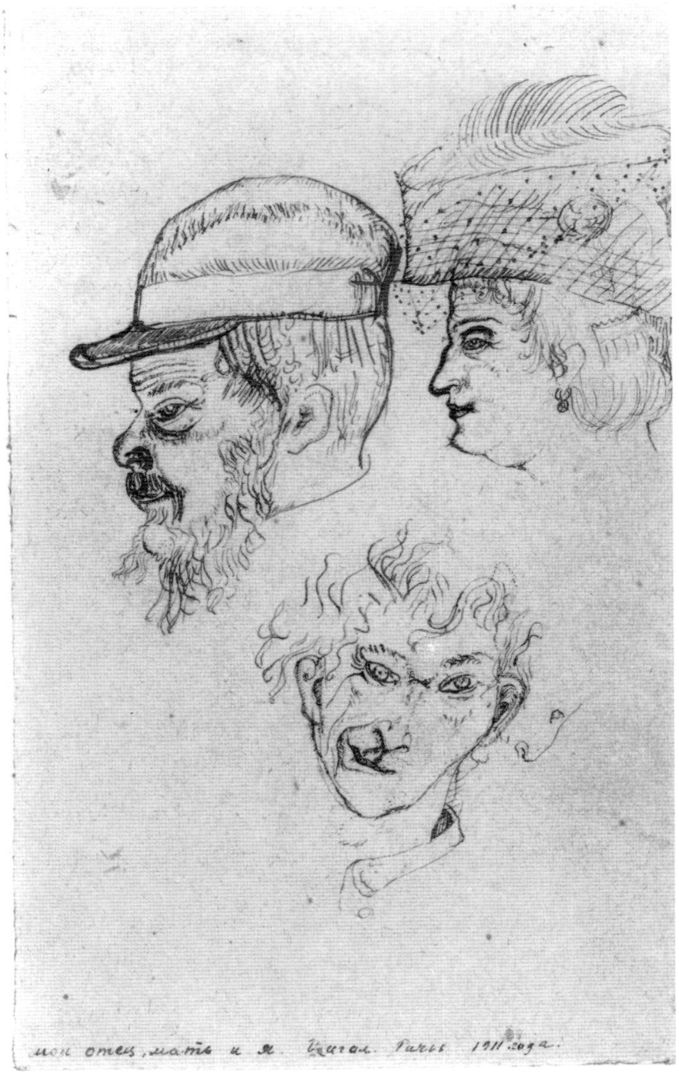

"My Father, my Mother and I. Shagal. Paris. 1911" in Russian; "Paris" in French. Religious Father is wearing a hat; Mother is wearing a wig and the fancy hat of a married woman. Marc has a twisted face, reproduced in the first book about him (1918). Courtesy Comité Marc Chagall, Paris

When he met his future fiancée in Vitebsk, Moysey Shagal was a poor boy from a provincial family, who lived near the railroad tracks. He felt ashamed of the low status of his father, who declined from the level of learning set by *his* father, a Hebrew teacher, to a laborer steeped in drudgery and smelling of herring. Berta's clan did not quite approve of the match, aspiring painter or not. Chagall developed an ambition to get into the centers of culture, prove himself as a great artist, and win his rich and intelligent bride. Paradoxically, he succeeded in the center precisely by evoking in his paintings the images of his poor, provincial past.

When Chagall first came to St. Petersburg in 1907, he boldly thrust himself into circles of Jewish high society and the best Russian art schools in the capital, simultaneously presenting the exotic images and values of "the lost Jewish world," still surviving in the Pale, and of provincial Russia in general. Those "strange" images were presented from the outside, from the viewpoint of a modern observer, including St. Petersburg's assimilated Jewish intelligentsia as well as such Russian collectors of modern art as Ivan Morozov, who bought Chagall's paintings for 300 rubles, thus making it possible for him to get married.

Chagall often depicted the past almost as an ethnographic curiosity, with a combination of nostalgia and admiration, and often as part of the multicultural scene of Russian provincial life. Kazimir Malevich in that period depicted Russian peasants, while Chagall conjured up the small town and its deep, mysterious beliefs and customs. What he offered was not a picture or a statement but a world—which appealed to the Jews of the capital, some of whom developed a pride in their past and in the authentic values of popular life and folklore.

Three years later, in 1910 or early in 1911, the ambitious Chagall moved on to Paris, the center of European art and a magnet for aspiring artists from many countries.[13] In Paris, too, he showed his fictional world to viewers recently preoccupied with form, and it was an exotic world of his constructed past. His Vitebsk—which came to include churches and cathedrals—became emblematic of Russia as well. His paintings portrayed a different cultural world, an "other," which he made vivid to his audiences in the center. In the meantime, he adopted emblematic images of the new landscape of Paris, such as the Eiffel Tower and the window of his studio. These emblems would now appear side by side with the Jewish and Christian images of Vitebsk.

RUSSIAN CULTURE

The dense Jewish culture provided a sense of a nation, yet many of the young generation aspired to belong to the general culture, which meant first of all embracing Russian language and literature. The population explosion in the Pale of Settlement produced a great deal of poverty. At the same time it begot a massive emigration from Russia. Yet it also triggered economic and cultural change and nourished revolutionary movements in art and in politics.

The early twentieth century was a time of revolutionary ferment in general Russian society and in all the arts. The Russian avant-garde interacted with the Western European avant-garde well before World War I. The two great waves of Modern art affecting Russian intellectuals were Symbolism and then Cubism and Futurism. French Symbolist poetry was echoed by Russian Symbolism with its emphasis on the musicality of verse and transcendental or religious moods. The symbolist impulse soon overflowed the limits of poetry and engulfed all the arts. It emphasized the importance of form and color and gave rise to such enterprises as Diaghilev's Ballets Russes that brought a colorful multimedia performance to Paris. Moreover, Russian art lovers were among the most important collectors of the new art of Matisse, Cézanne, and Picasso. Cubism, discovered in 1906–1908, and Italian Futurism, launched in 1909, were soon echoed in the art of the new Russian avant-garde, which was a radical as any art at the time. Indeed, the main group of Russian avant-garde poets was called "Cubo-Futurists."

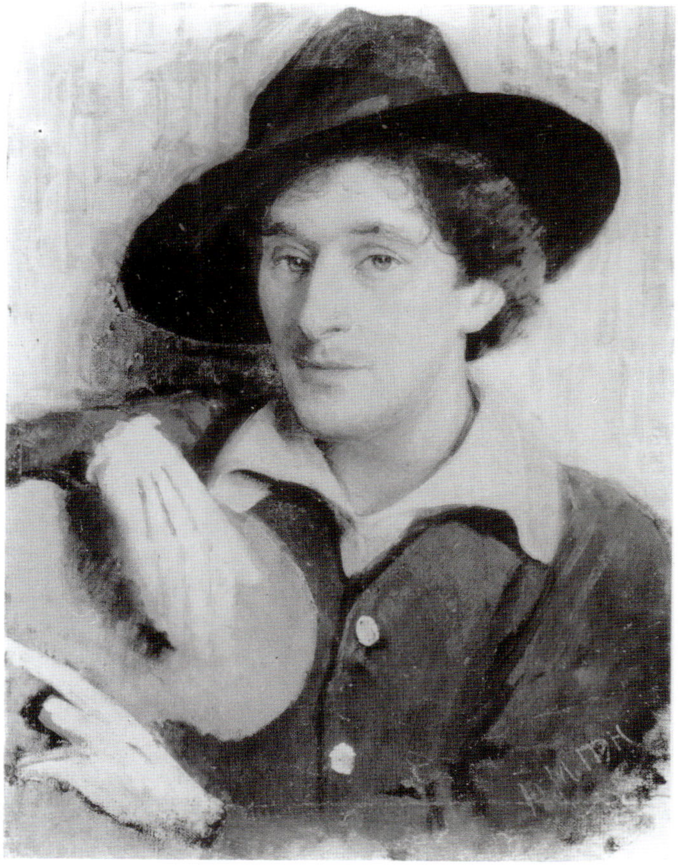

*"**Marc Chagall in Rembrandt Hat,**" a portrait of the painter by his teacher Yury Pen, 1907 or 1908. On the right is the signature Yu. M. Pen. Courtesy Comité Marc Chagall, Paris*

2. *Stations in Chagall's Life*

A knowledge of Chagall's life is indispensable for the understanding of his art and a brief survey is due here.[14]

Marc Chagall was born Moyshe (Moshka to his parents) Shagal in a Yiddish-speaking suburb of Vitebsk on the lucky day of triple seven: 7/7/87, as he believed (actually, a day earlier, on July 6, 1887). Vitebsk was the capital city of a province (called a *guberniya*, comparable in scope to an American state) in the Jewish Pale of Settlement in the Russian empire. Jews were the majority group in the population of the city, they developed and owned most of the industry, trade and artisan crafts, joined Jewish or Russian political parties and provided an alert base for Russian culture in Vitebsk.

Chagall's ancestral hometown, Lyozno, was located about 60 kilometers to the east of Vitebsk at the very edge of the Pale of Settlement, on the railroad leading to

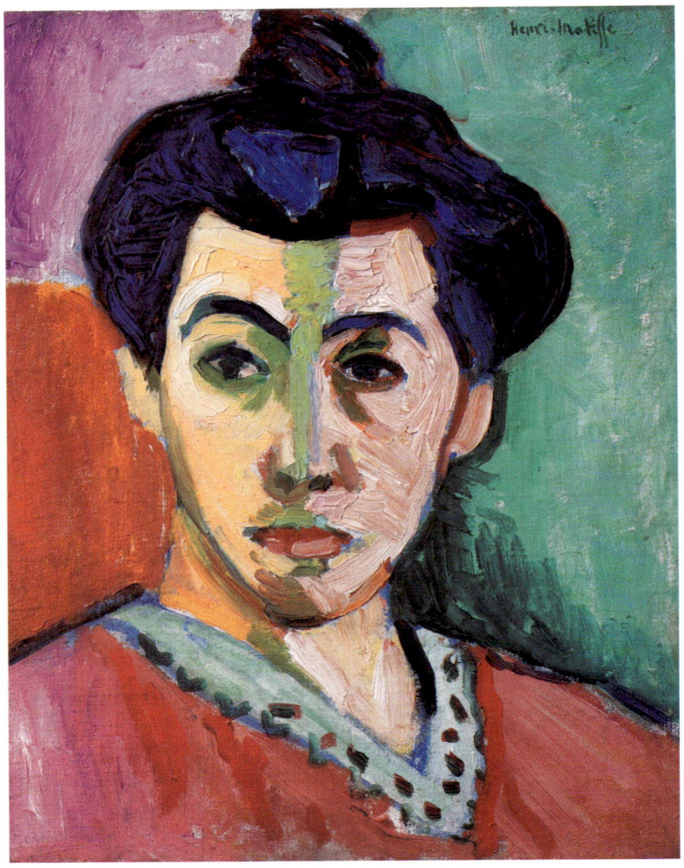

4. *Henri Matisse.* ***Portrait of Mme. Matisse.*** *1905. Oil on canvas, 40.5 x 32.5 cm. Statens Museums for Kunst, Copenhagen, J. Rump Collection*

Moscow. In 1897 it had 1,665 Jews or 67.3 percent of the population. When Chagall's grandfather and his oldest son moved from Lyozno to Vitebsk, they lived, like many provincial newcomers, in the outskirts of the capital, in a tiny shack in Peskovatik ("In-the-Sands"). When Chagall's father married a fifteen-year-old relative from Lyozno, she joined them in the same hut, where Marc Chagall was born. Three years later, after this grandfather died, they sold the house and moved to a brick house near the railroad tracks, often painted by Chagall. As a young man, Chagall liked to visit Lyozno, where his family clan remained, including uncles, aunts, and grandparents, and he painted many semi-realistic paintings there, such as *Uncle Zusya's Shop in Lyozno*, 1914 (no. 3). The sign on the right reads in Russian: "Parikmakher Z. Shagal" ("Barber Z. Shagal") in the pre-Revolutionary spelling.

Neither Vitebsk nor even Lyozno were the confined "ghetto" of Jewish literature and ideologies, a crowded *shtetl* far from any railroad and oblivious to the changes in the world, as described in Sholem Aleichem's quintessential *Town of the Little People*. The train passed through Vitebsk, bringing to it the spirits of industrialization, Russian poetry, and modern culture.

When Chagall wrote his autobiography in the Soviet Union, he wanted to present himself as a child of poverty and stressed his father's hard work, lifting heavy herring barrels. Most critics accepted this description. However, Marc's father was actually the store manager, or *podryadtshik* in Russian, of a wholesale herring cellar. There is a document certifying his long standing in the union of *podryadtshiks*. The misunderstanding arose from the Yiddish word *meshores*, which in Hebrew indeed means "servant," but in Yiddish refers to a store manager.

His mother raised nine children (one died at an early age), managed the house, built several wooden houses for rent in their yard, and kept a little grocery store. Moshka was her first child, born when she was sixteen. Between the ages of four and thirteen, the boy studied in the traditional religious elementary class, the *heder*. After his Bar Mitzvah, he abandoned religion altogether, entered a Russian high schoo,l and soon thereafter (or perhaps two years later, i.e., either in 1900 or in 1902) attended Yury Moyseevitsh (Yehuda) Pen's School of Art, where the boy studied, probably on and off, until he left Vitebsk in 1907.

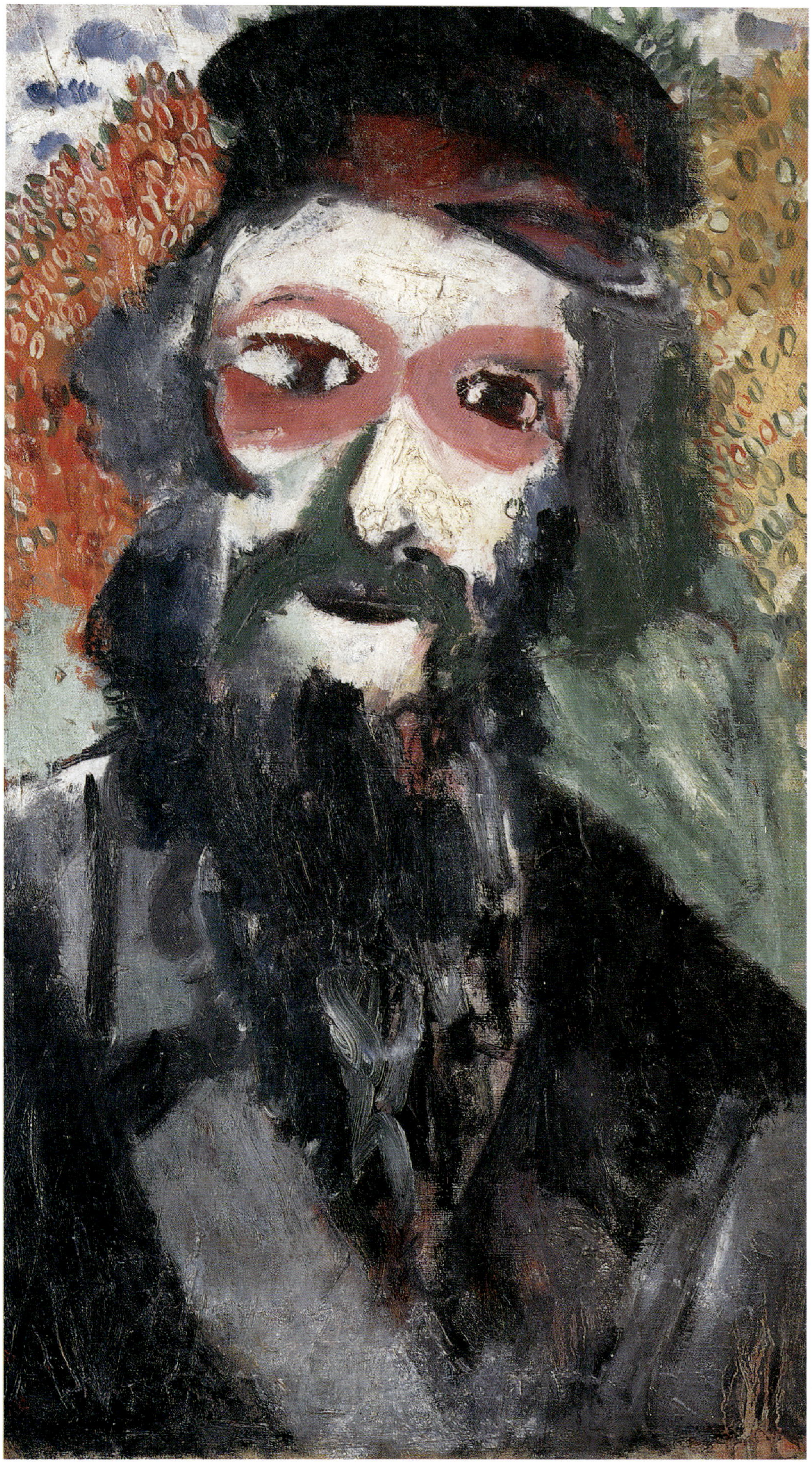

5. ***Father.*** *1910. Oil on canvas, 80 x 42.2 cm. Musée national d'art moderne, Centre Georges Pompidou, Paris*

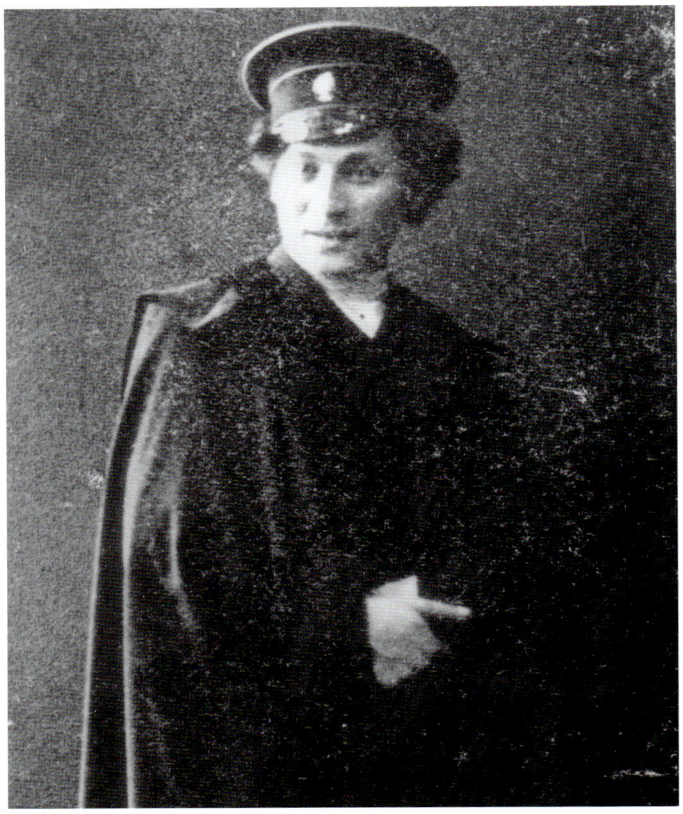

Marc Chagall in the uniform of the Imperial School for the Promotion of Art, 1907. *Courtesy Comité Marc Chagall, Paris*

FIRST TEACHER: YURY PEN

Yury Pen was a follower of the late nineteenth-century Russian school of *Peredvizhniki* ("Itinerant" artists), who moved Russian painting from a kind of academic Neoclassicism to a precise and descriptive realism and populism. In many of his paintings, Pen raised Jewish topics and symbols as well as the so-called "genre of the trivial,"[15] drawn from the mores and manners of Jewish daily life. Pen was aware of the concept of "Renaissance" in Jewish cultural ideology of the time (a term launched by both Ahad-HaAm in Russia and Martin Buber in Germany) and, in Chagall's words, "raised several generations of Jewish artists,"[16] including El Lissitzky and Osip Zadkin, who came from the neighboring Smolensk Province, just outside of the Jewish Pale of Settlement.

Naturally, in this century of Modernism and experimentation, Pen's students moved away from their teacher and his art. Chagall could never produce as meticulously detailed naturalistic paintings as Pen, nor did he see it as an ideal for his art. But he learned a great deal from Pen: the art of portraiture, a penchant for folklore and milieu, the value of small, unheroic details and mundane objects, and close observations of nature (as Chagall recalled, he and Pen would go out together to paint "fences, fences, fences"), and above all, the discipline of persistent, professional work, which he admired, as well as the interest in Jewish themes and beliefs. Here he probably acquired such basic techniques as making a sketch for a large painting and crisscrossing it with a precise geometrical grid before it is transposed to a full-size work of art, a technique he used throughout his life in large paintings, murals, and stained-glass windows as the rational frame for his free-wheeling imagination.

In 1907, ever ambitious and daring, Chagall left Pen and went to study in St. Petersburg, where Russian art was a generation ahead. He studied for a year in the Imperial School for the Encouragement of the Arts, where he was awarded the second stipend, then quarreled with a teacher and abruptly left, not even taking his stipend for the summer. As a Jew, he could not legally live in the capital without a residence permit (unless he was a student), but eventually he managed somehow and was supported by several Jewish patrons, notably the prominent lawyer Maxim Vinaver. Vinaver (was born in Warsaw in 1862, and lived in St. Petersburg. He was a founder of the Russian KaDet (Constitutional Democratic) party and was its vice chairman. He was one of the first Jewish members of the Russian Duma (parliament), was active in the Society for Promotion of Culture

Among Jews, and headed the Historic-Ethnographic Commission, which studied the history of Jews in Russia. Vinaver bought some of Chagall's early paintings. He died in Paris in 1926.

LEON BAKST

In 1909–10, Chagall studied with Léon Bakst, a key figure of the aestheticist World of Art movement. This was a real breakthrough for Chagall, which launched him on the path of his life, as he well understood. Bakst truly encouraged creativity and individuality in his students. Furthermore, he himself was an iconoclast and moved away from the World of Art aesthetics. In a paper for the Academy of Arts in 1927, Chagall's classmate Yuliya L. Obolenskaya wrote:

> No one would have guessed that under the directorship of Bakst the youth were raised on principles totally opposed to the foundations of "The World of Art": to its Retrospectivism—they opposed the naive eye of a savage; to its Stylization—the immediacy of a child's painting; to its Graphism[17]—the tempestuous, bright mishmash of colors; and, finally, to its Individualism—conscious collectivism. [. . .] Bakst taught as they used to teach swimming, by throwing you into the water and letting you scramble out on your own. [. . .] In sketches from nature, we looked first of all for an absolute combination of colors, a dialogue, even an argument between colors. [. . . Black contours were totally forbidden: they misleadingly enhanced the power of individual colors but separated the colors from each other. [. . .] The ability to juxtapose contrasting colors, balancing their mutual influences and embodying them in the simplest forms—all that helped especially those of us who later worked on murals.[18]

Color became an abstract entity with no relation to any realistic representation of figures and objects. In his theater murals of 1920 as in the Jerusalem stained-glass windows of 1962, Chagall made separate maps of colors and separate sketches for the composition of figures and then merged them in the final product. Similar color maps were made for the whole ensemble, as is beautifully demonstrated in the six stages of the Jerusalem windows.[19]

Obolenskaya remembered:

> [. . .] Marc Chagall's studies made in class were insignificant, but his works at home constantly served for analysis on Fridays. So what, after all, did Bakst's school give its students? [. . .] We trained not so much our hand as our sensibility. [. . .] We were preoccupied with the world of bright, sonorous, contrasting colors, the life of a color in its unfolding, in its clashes with other colors. We were interested in the simple and important silhouettes of objects and figures, with the unique, typical features of each object, alien to all schematism. The school gave us a childish immediacy in approaching nature. [. . .] In the dark workshops of Petersburg we had to heighten the color by juxtaposing it with the contrasting colors of the draperies. [. . .] Bakst wrote: "I tried not so much to teach as to stir up the desire to search, carefully protecting the young, searching eye from any falsehood and routine."

All this fits Chagall perfectly. In Bakst's school, Chagall learned the autonomous value of rich and unrealistic colors, the use of minute ornaments (which the art critic Yakov Tugendhold ascribed to a Jewish national ethos), and the desire to create decorations for the theater. In St. Petersburg he was impressed by the tendencies of Symbolism in painting, the value of folk art, and the interest in oriental, mystical, and legendary scenes, as represented by the pre-Symbolist Russian artist Mikhail Vrubel. Indeed the "mad genius" Vrubel was admired by Bakst and impressed Chagall as well.[20]

In this world of assimilated Jews merging with the Russian aristocratic intellectual scene, Chagall learned to fuse influences from Christian art with his Jewish motifs: elements of Christian iconography, Russian icons, and the *lubok* (a colorful Russian folk print with a narrative theme) merged in his work with images of Jewish provincial life. There were no contradictions inherent in these intersecting influences, for they all inhabited one consciousness and enriched it. Indeed, that duality was at the foundation of modern Jewish existence in general, as valid for Freud as for Kafka, for Ben Gurion as for Bialik.[21]

PARIS

Chagall came to St. Petersburg somewhat late: In 1906 the aestheticist journal *The World of Art* folded, as did *Voskhod* ("Dawn"), edited by Vinaver, a journal that had created a Jewish intellectual and scholarly forum in the Russian language. (For that reason, Chagall could stay and work in the editorial office, in Vinaver's house). Rampant anti-Semitism grew and Vinaver was not reelected to the Duma. In 1910 Chagall was due to be called for military service, and he left for Paris, and so did his patron Bakst. In Paris he lived and worked in La Ruche ("the Beehive"), a settlement of about 140 artists, many of them Eastern European Jews, among them prominent figures of the "School of Paris."

While in St. Petersburg, Chagall was influenced by the Fauves, especially as they were perceived in Russia; in his works he stressed the centrality and autonomy of color. He also learned from Bakst his lifelong opposition to "Realism," "Academism" and "routine" painting. In Paris he was confronted with the Cubist revolution and befriended several artists of the second generation of Cubists (Robert and Sonia Delaunay, Albert Gleizes, and others), who tried to combine Cubist principles with various modes of representation and deformation. He befriended the French avant-garde poet Blaise Cendrars and the poet and art critic Guillaume Apollinaire, and both wrote hagiographic poems about him. He was part of that post-Cubist scene and enjoyed a curious reception.

Yet his poetic deformations and re-creation of the world of his past also anticipated Expressionism and Surrealism; they struck Apollinaire as "surnaturel." Again, as in St. Petersburg, he came somewhat late to the birth of Cubism, and could therefore juxtapose his idiosyncratic fictional world to the formal achievements of the Cubists. In June 1914, at the age of twenty-seven, Chagall—a poor Russian in Paris—had a one-man show in Berlin, exhibiting some 240 items in the most prestigious avant-garde gallery, *Der Sturm*, directed by Herwarth Walden.

From Berlin, Chagall went to visit his family in Vitebsk. This was not a "return" to Russia, as some writers present it. If he intended to stay in Russia, he wouldn't have left all of his art in Paris and Berlin. He took his art with him in much more difficult circumstances. World War I (1914–18) broke out in August and he "got stuck" in Russia for eight years (as he wrote to Sonya Delauney). In the West, it was assumed that Chagall had died in the war, and his paintings were sold. Thus, because of his nomadic life, he lost many paintings: First, he was cheated in a framing store in St. Petersburg, where many of his early works disappeared; then he left the bulk of his work in Berlin and in Paris. Yet some of those paintings came into good hands and thus made him famous.

In July 1915, after a year's courtship, he married his pre-war fiancée Berta Rosenfeld (later renamed Bella Chagall), and a year later their daughter, Ida, was born. During the war (in 1915–17) Chagall worked in a military office in the renamed capital Petrograd, yet he had plenty of time on his hands, and he painted and exhibited in both capitals of Russia, Moscow and Petrograd. During the war, in the context of a revival of "Jewish Art," Chagall signed several paintings: MShH SGL (Moyshe Segal), thus establishing his relation to a presumed great grandfather, the eighteenth-century synagogue painter Chaim Segal of Mohilev.[22] In 1918, when he was thirty-one, the first book on *The Art of Marc Chagall* by Abram Efros and Yakov Tugendhold was published in Russian in Moscow and later translated into German.[23]

COMMISSAR OF ART

After the October Revolution, in August 1918, the Minister of Enlightenment A. Lunacharsky (who knew Chagall from the "Beehive" in Paris) appointed Chagall to the position of Plenipotentiary on Matters of Art in Vitebsk Province. Budget and power in hand, he established the People's Art College in Vitebsk, for a while the most important school of Leftist Art after the October Revolution, to which he attracted such prominent artists as Pugny, Dobuzhinsky, Lissitzky, and Malevich. Here Malevich, theoretician of Suprematism, founded the group UNOVIS ("Affirmers of the New Art"), and Chagall published Malevich's first, programmatic book.[24] Chagall also designed all the ten sets for TeRevSat (Theater of Revolutionary Satire),[25] and established a city museum in Vitebsk—two activities that were to interest him for years to come.

In 1918–19, in several manifestoes and articles, Commissar Chagall promoted the idea of Leftist Art, not as an imitation of the political revolution but as a revolution in the history of art. This brought him in conflict with the Marxist authorities of the city. The students, however, shifted to the even more radical and "Non-Objective" (abstract) art of UNOVIS and abandoned Chagall. After an inevitable clash between the two egocentric artists, Chagall and Malevich, Chagall was actually forced out of his Art College, and in the summer of 1920 he moved to Moscow.

In November–December 1920, Chagall painted the sets of the new, avant-garde Yiddish Chamber Theater in Moscow. He actually covered all the walls and the stage with his murals and sets, painted the costumes and actors' faces, and enclosed the whole theater in a "Chagallian Box."[26] Chagall's prestige in Russia was based on his fame in Paris and Berlin. The budding avant-garde Yiddish theater was proud to invite such a famous artist to design its sets. Subsequently, the theater itself became famous in Western Europe, especially during their tour of Germany in 1928, and Chagall drew on *its* fame.

Chagall, even when he became famous and rich, felt the inferiority complex of a Jewish boy from the provinces. Thus, in 1952, after major solo exhibitions in New York, Paris, London, and Bern, he wrote with amazement and pride to his friend, the Yiddish novelist Yosef Opatoshu in New York, that he was going to marry a woman from the famously rich Brodsky family from Kiev!

PARIS: MY SECOND VITEBSK

In the summer of 1922, Chagall managed to get out of closed Soviet Russia and went to Berlin, where he learned techniques of engraving and lithography. The first album of his engravings, the autobiographical *My Life, My World*, was published by Paul Cassirer.[27] In September 1923, Chagall, with his wife and daughter arrived in Paris. At this time the names Marc and Bella (rather than Moysey and Berta) were finally established. Here, too, he came somewhat late for the formal innovations in art and straight into the confusion about the goals of art that marked the 1920s and 1930s. Once again it was a ripe field for a favorable reception of his exotic and "primitive" world and his original deformations of Realism.

In France Chagall befriended many French intellectuals, traveled, exhibited, and sold paintings. He became a French artist and received formal citizenship in 1937. At the invitation of the leading Modern art dealer Ambroise Vollard, he made hundreds of engravings to illustrate Gogol's *Dead Souls*, the Bible, LaFontaine's fables, and other works of literature, all published only after World War II. In the 1930s Solomon Guggenheim bought several of his paintings, which became part of the foundation of The Solomon R. Guggenheim Museum in New York.

In 1931 the Chagalls visited the new Hebrew society emerging in Palestine, where they stayed for three months and Chagall had a major exhibition organized by a consortium of four museums. Chagall was enthusiastic about the new workers' settlements in the Land of Israel and saw them as the true revival of the Jews as a nation. He continued to visit Israel throughout his life until he reached the age of ninety.

Chagall always sympathized with his Soviet homeland, and in the late 1930s, during the Spanish Civil War, he wrote several articles in Yiddish in the Paris

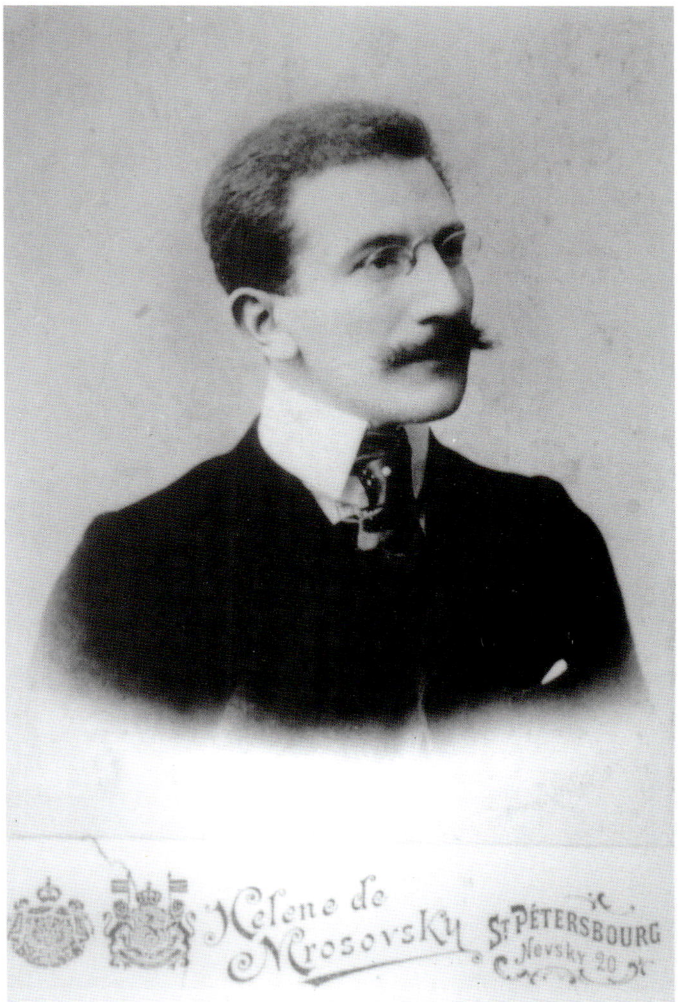

***Chagall's teacher Léon Bakst**, Director of the Zvantseva School of Art in St. Petersburg, 1907. Courtesy Comité Marc Chagall, Paris*

Communist newspaper, *Di Naye Presse*. He saw the Jewish volunteer fighters in Spain as the heirs of the Jewish national spirit. In Nazi Germany, Chagall's paintings were included in the exhibition *Entartete Kunst* ("Degenerate Art"), where he belonged both as a Modernist painter with his antiheroic, distorted figures and as a Jew. His painting *The Rabbi* was paraded in the streets of Mannheim and burnt at the stake.

In June 1940, when the German army attacked France, Chagall bought a house in Gordes in Provence, which became part of Vichy France. Chagall was stripped of his French citizenship, barely escaped from Nazi Europe, and arrived in New York on the evening of June 21, 1941, when he heard that the German armies crossed into the Soviet Union. Pierre Matisse, son of the painter Henri and owner of an important gallery for European modern art in New York, paid him a monthly stipend and held almost annual Chagall exhibitions in his gallery (twenty-six in all).

Marc Chagall's wife, Bella, his great inspiration and love, died suddenly in upstate New York in September 1944. Soon thereafter, Chagall fell in love with Virginia Haggard, an English woman born in Paris, who was twenty-eight years younger than him. This second, common-law marriage, lasted seven years, at a crucial stage in his life. In June 1946, Virginia's son, David McNeil, was born.

Chagall knew no English, spoke Russian to Bella and French to Virginia, and read Yiddish newspapers. During World War II he lectured in Yiddish at leftist assemblies in New York and was a member of the board of the Committee of Jewish Writers, Artists and Scientists, a pro-Soviet cultural organization during the war whose Honorary President was Albert Einstein. In 1949, after returning to Europe, Chagall became Honorary President of the French organization MRAP (Movement against Racism, Anti-Semitism and for Peace), a fellow-traveler organization from which he resigned in total despair in 1952, when Stalin executed his friends, the Soviet Yiddish writers. The U.S. State Department sent warnings about this organization to all its European consulates, claiming that under the guise of war against anti-Semitism it conducts anti-American propaganda, and described the honorary president Marc Chagall as a "painter and political crackpot." The FBI kept a file on Chagall and prevented him from getting a visa to reenter America between 1948 and 1958.

At the end of World War II major Chagall retrospective exhibitions were staged in New York, Chicago, and Paris, and he received the First Prize for his engravings at the Venice Biennale in 1948. That summer the Chagalls returned to France for good. Here Chagall published his prewar engravings and extended his work to new media: lithographs, ceramics, sculptures, tapestries, mosaics, and stained-glass windows in churches and synagogues. The French cultural establishment bestowed unusual honors on Chagall: an exhibition in the Louvre (granted to only one other foreigner, Picasso), two major retrospective exhibitions in three stories of the Grand Palais, and an invitation to paint the ceiling of the Paris Opera. He was awarded the Cross of the Legion of Honor and a national museum for him was built in Nice: Musée National Message Biblique Marc Chagall.

Throughout his life Chagall was close to several political and artistic movements that were in the center of European culture in the twentieth century. He remembered his days of glory as a commissar of art in Vitebsk and was sympathetic to the Soviet Union, which carried so much of the burden of fighting Hitler during World War II, yet he never joined the Communist Party, as did his friends Paul Éluard and Pablo Picasso. He was impressed by the new Hebrew nation emerging in Palestine and was emotionally involved with the events in the young State of Israel, yet he never became a Zionist. André Breton sent a messenger, inviting him to become a member of the Surrealist group, but he declined the offer and often argued against their theory of "automatic" writing. He was hailed by several German Expressionists but shook off the idea that he was one as well.

In 1952 his daughter Ida married the Swiss art historian Franz Meyer, who seven years later wrote a magisterial biography of the painter. The same year, Virginia left Chagall, and he married Vava (Valentina) Brodsky, with whom he spent the rest of his life, which was marked by an uninterrupted chain of commissions, honors, and exhibitions.

In 1973, more than fifty years after he left the Soviet Union, Chagall was finally allowed for the first (and last) time to visit Moscow. There he was asked to sign the murals, which he had made for the Yiddish theater in 1920 and which had been languishing in a cellar. But he was not allowed to visit his native Vitebsk.

In his later years Chagall was extremely productive and created numerous paintings, lithographs, tapestries, and stained-glass windows with ever different combinations of his basic modular units, which became his recognizable language. These brought him a mass audience, fame and wealth, and often provoked negative reviews from some snobbish art critics. Yet even in that period, he did some exquisite paintings and beautiful stained-glass windows.

Marc Chagall died in 1985 in his home in St. Paul de Vence, near Nice, France, and was buried in the Christian cemetery there. A lone voice read the Jewish *kaddish*. He was almost ninety-eight years old.

---

1. Published in *Shtrom* ["The Current"], Moscow, 1922. English translation in *Marc Chagall on Art and Culture*, pp. 38–40.

2. Belarus/Byelorussia (or: White Russia) could be seen as a group of dialects of Eastern Slavic, close to Russian, yet dominated by Lithuania and Poland, until it crystallized into a separate language in the modern age. Only after the October Revolution of 1917—for the first time in history—was it established as a separate nation and a Soviet Republic. Even then, Vitebsk Province remained part of Russia and was turned over to Belarus only in 1924, two years after Chagall had left the Soviet Union altogether. As far as I know, he never mentioned Belarus, and he thought of himself as a Russian Jew.

3. See Shaul Shtempfer, "Population Growth and Migration in Polish/Lithuanian Jewry in the Modern Age" [in Hebrew], in *The Broken Chain: Polish Jewry Through the Ages*, Israel Bartal and Israel Gutman, eds. Jerusalem: Zalman Shazar Center, 1997, p. 263.

4. We have detailed statistics from the census of 1897 and other sources. The figures here are based on the relevant entries in *Evreyskaya Entsiklopediya* ["Jewish encyclopedia"], St. Petersburg: Brockhaus and Ephron, 1915.

5. Compare the situation of American blacks, liberated from slavery at about the same time and carrying the memory of slavery into the twentieth century.

6. See Benjamin Harshav, *Language in Time of Revolution*. Berkeley and Los Angeles: University of California Press, 1993, Stanford University Press, 2000.

7. See Yeshurun Keshet, "Marc Chagall" in *Di goldene keyt*, no. 60 (1967), pp. 34–53.

8. On the short-lived but important Vitebsk cultural renaissance see Alexandra Shatskich, *Vitebsk: Zhizn' Iskusstva 1917–1922* ["Vitebsk: The Life of Art 1917–1922"]. Moscow: Yazyki Russkoy Kultury, 2001.

9. See Abram Efros, *Profili* [Profiles]. Moscow: Federatsiya, 1930, p. 289.

10. Chagall was aided in this by his four years in the Soviet Union (1918–22), where the spelling of Hebrew words in Yiddish was abolished in favor of a phonetic transcription.

11. Virginia Haggard, *My Life with Marc Chagall*. New York: Donald I. Fine, 1986, p. 14.

12. In a letter to Opatoshu, he wrote that he felt at home in Vitebsk only in "my own few streets," and in another, "Do I know Russia? I know just a few streets in Vitebsk, and some of [St.] Petersburg and Moscow."

13. See Yona Fisher, "Le Desire de Paris," in *L'École de Paris 1904–1929*. Paris: PARIS Musées, 2000.

14. For a detailed and documented biography, see Benjamin Harshav, *Marc Chagall and His Times*, Stanford University Press, 2004.

15. See Grigory Kasovski, "Chagall and the Jewish Art Programme" in Vitali, Christof, ed. *Marc Chagall: The Russian Years 1906–1922*. Frankfurt: Schirn Kunsthhalle, 1991, pp. 53–60.

16. Chagall's letter to Pen written in Moscow on September 14, 1921; see *Marc Chagall and His Times*, p. 302.

17. A tendency to prefer graphic design over spontaneous expression.

18. Yuliya L. Obolenskaya, "The School of Bakst." See English translation in *Marc Chagall and His Times*, pp. 183–85.

19. See chapter 9 below.

20. In his authentic autobiography, Chagall tells of a dream in which he inherited Vrubel's leading place in Russian art. See *Marc Chagall and His Times*, pp. 133–35).

21. Susan Compton sees it as a tragedy and as peculiar to Chagall. See Susan Compton, "Chagall's Auditorium: 'An Identity Crisis of Tragic Dimensions,'" in *Marc Chagall and the Jewish Theater*. New York: Guggenheim Museum, 1992, pp. 1–13.

22. Segal is a Hebrew acronym for an "Assistant Levi." The attribution stands to reason because in that area "S" would be pronounced as "Sh" "Segal" as "Shegal," but there is no other evidence of this name origin. Chagall's own story, that his father changed the name, makes no sense because his uncle's barber shop in Lyozno has a big sign: "Shagal." Nor was it simple to change a name in Tsarist Russia.

23. See A. Efros, and Y. Tugendhold. *Iskusstvo Marka Shagala* ["The Art of Marc Chagall"]. Moscow: Helikon, 1918.

24. K. Malevich, *On New Systems in Art*. Vitebsk, 1919. In his last letter from Vitebsk to Pavel Ettinger in Moscow, April 2, 1920, Chagall writes: "our publication (a little book by Malevich) will be sent you."

25. See A. N. Manteyfel, "The First Theater of the Revolution." in *Moskva*, no. 1 (1968), pp. 192–94.

26. On his work in this modern theater, see below, chapters 5–7.

27. See Susan Compton, *Marc Chagall: My Life—My Dream*. Munich: Prestel-Verlag, 1990.

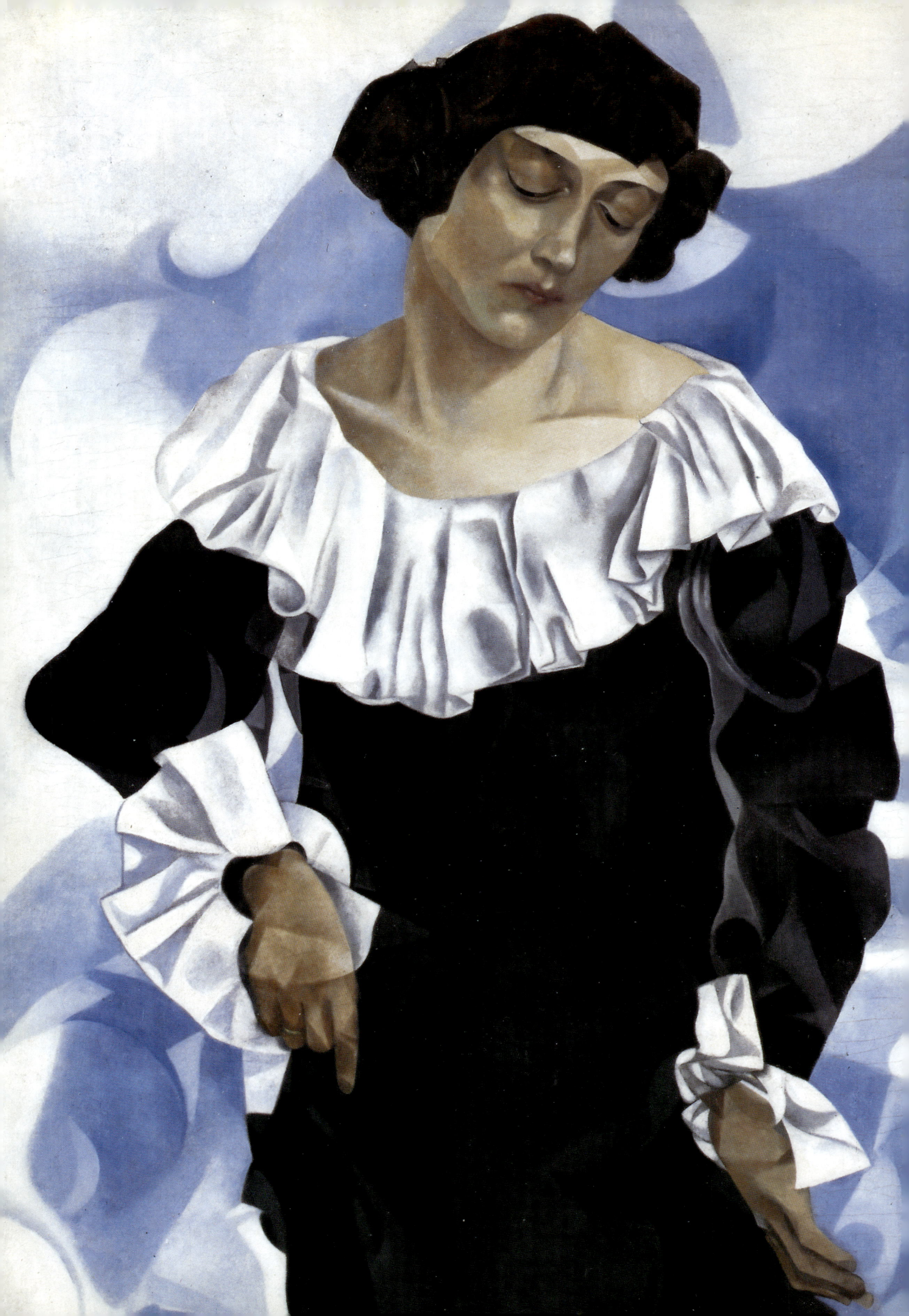

2. On the Nature of Chagall's Art

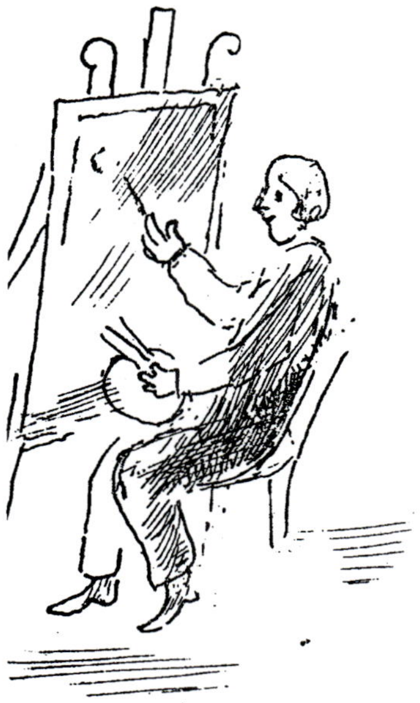

A POSTMODERNIST IN THE AGE OF MODERNISM

Marc Chagall was a conscious, even deliberate Postmodernist. Of course, not in any historical sense: the particular movement called Postmodernism emerged in the 1970s and was related to specific social and ideological trends in Western societies. But in many respects, Chagall shared with the later trend an ambivalent attitude toward the Modernist movement: an indebtedness to the revolutionary spirit, the fresh air, and the new possibilities it opened, on the one hand, combined with a rejection of the formalism and stylistic exclusivism, on the other.

Chagall was a natural relativist, free of stylistic commitment to one school or another. Like later Postmodernists, he had a wide perspective on the possibilities of art. What the Postmodernists experienced in the panorama of museums of modern art, Chagall confronted in his frequent movements from one country to another and from one center of art to another. By moving geographically he discovered the relativism of art history. Already in his youth in Russia, he intimately experienced three entirely different conceptions of art, which may be labeled in general terms: Naturalism, Post-Impressionism, and the Futurist/Constructivist avant-garde. Suddenly, he parachuted into Paris to discover the future and the past: the Cubist revolution on the one hand, and the weight of European art history as represented in the Louvre, on the other. Moving from one trend of modern painting to another, from one national context to another, Chagall absorbed new aesthetic principles and techniques, then retreated into his own world, which was largely established in his early, innovative years.

In Chagall's paintings we can find a Fauve-inspired exuberance of colors, either unrealistic or overflowing the boundaries of objects; abstract shapes and semi-geometric articulations of figures, inspired by Analytical Cubism; Orphism's predilection for colorful circles in space; the precise chromatic rectangular or triangular shapes of Suprematism; and the dynamic movement and strong diagonal lines of Futurism and Russian Rayonism. He used quasi-Expressionist deformations of human faces and figures; a dreamlike arrangement of discontinuous objects in represented space, anticipating Surrealism; and even an earlier style: the minute and multiple decorative ornaments, typical of the Russian *Mir Iskusstva* ("World of Art") movement at the eve of the twentieth century. In Chagall's work, such seemingly disparate components coexist in one painting, often in an asymmetrical, uneasy, but ultimately justified balance. Furthermore, his art always reached out beyond painting and was open to the imagery of language and cultural symbolism. Time and again, he fended off the accusation that he was a "literary" or "mythological" painter, but to a large extent both "accusations" were true.

Chagall's paintings, perhaps unfairly, have been judged from what we can identify as an implied position of purism—the pure use of a well-delimited discourse of

OPPOSITE: ***Bella with a White Collar*** *(detail). 1917. Oil on canvas with varnish, 149 x 72 cm. Musée national d'art moderne, Centre Georges Pompidou, Paris*

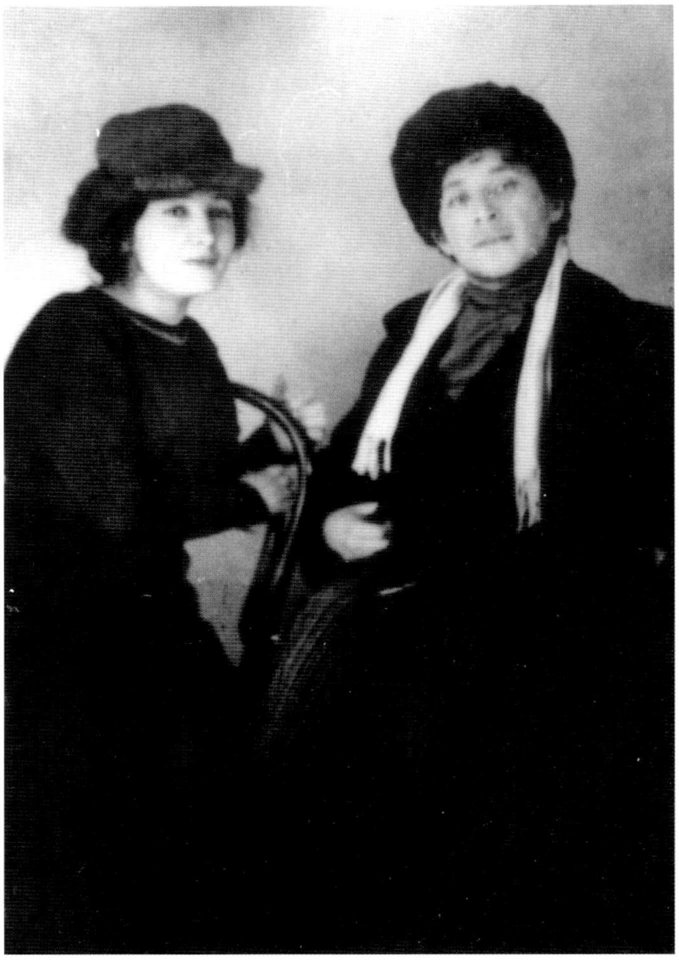

Bella and Marc Chagall in Petrograd, during World War I. *Courtesy Comité Marc Chagall, Paris*

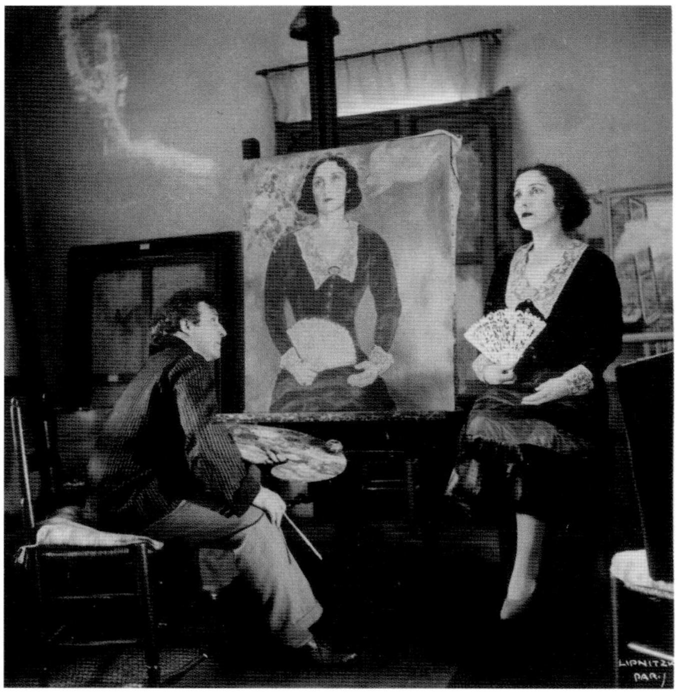

Marc Chagall painting his wife, Bella. *Courtesy Comité Marc Chagall, Paris*

art. From this perspective, as crystallized in the established narrative of the ISM's, his work may seem "eclectic." But today, in an age of Postmodernism, we can surely question the validity of a "pure" language as the highest value in art or poetry.

After the great Realist prose of the nineteenth century in Europe, poetry came back to center stage. French Symbolism, variously echoed in Russian, German and Anglo-American poetry in the early twentieth century, promoted the principle of "pure poetry," a "suggestive," "musical," "magical" art, focusing on the "language of poetry" at the expense of anything that other kinds of discourse, such as discursive prose, ideology, or philosophy, can do (statement, argument, mimesis, description, or political propaganda). The trends of art and literature that overcame Symbolism in various European countries, beginning with the French Cubists, Italian Futurists, and German Expressionists, and opened up art to the brute reality of the twentieth century; but they also promoted a pure language of their own, no matter how "impure," even "ugly," their materials may have been.

Yet this was not a consistent essentialist position; on the contrary, in Modernism, along with the promotion of a unique and monolithic artistic discourse, the purity of genres and artistic media was overruled, their boundaries deliberately broken: poetry became prosaic and dramatic, prose became lyrical, paintings reproduced words, and words were used to create graphic images. Moreover, many representatives of pure styles, such as Pablo Picasso or Kazimir Malevich, were eclectic in another sense—either in diachrony, i.e., in their development as artists, or in genre-like parallel styles. We could not say about them, "The style is the man." Think of Malevich's figurative paintings before and after his abstract Suprematism or Picasso's Neoclassical figurative drawings concurrent with Cubist portraits and sculptures. They changed their styles several times, while Chagall was open to any mixture of ingredients from the beginning. Indeed, the history of culture is to a large extent a history of eclectic combinations and cross-fertilization rather than a history of abrupt or complete changes in the style and principles of art.

The terms Modernism and Postmodernism do not denote any single idea, essence, monolithic style, or defined *Zeitgeist* permeating all artists, all works, and all aspects of art in a given period. Modernism experimented with all possibilities of the language of art; it produced a galaxy of trends, often in direct opposition to one another—some with particular labels (Futurism, Expressionism, Constructivism, Surrealism), and some embodied in the

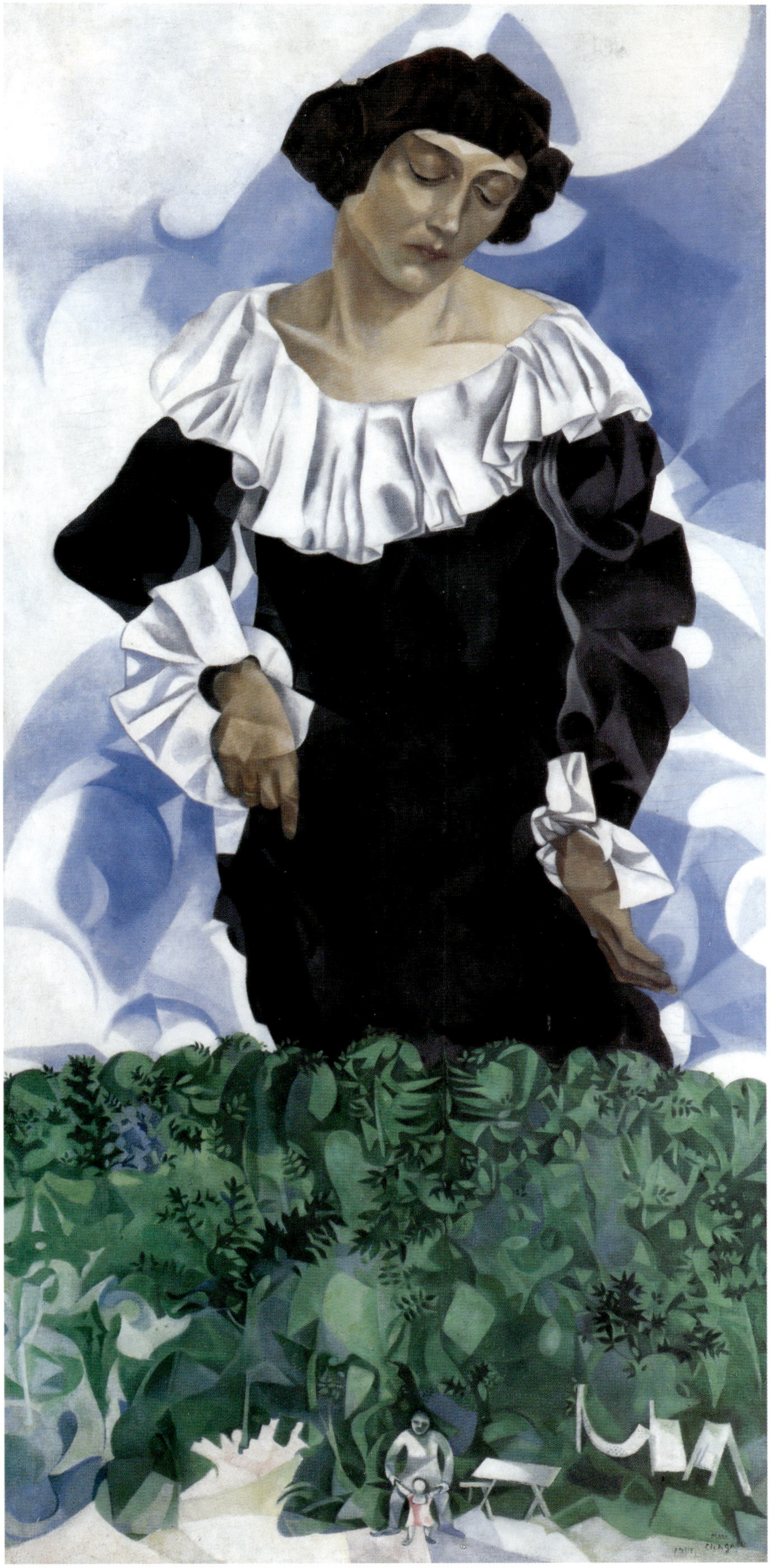

6. ***Bella with a White Collar.*** *1917. Oil on canvas with varnish, 149 x 72 cm. Musée national d'art moderne, Centre Georges Pompidou, Paris*

work of unaffiliated original artists (Paul Klee, R. M. Rilke, T. S. Eliot, Bertolt Brecht, Marc Chagall). At a certain point, the swift internal succession of Modernist trends tired of its own evolution, and the term Postmodernism emerged in the 1970s—to be sure, encouraged by wider ideological and political intellectual concerns.

Because Modernism was not one essence, expressing one ideology or one style, Postmodernism could not be a unified phenomenon either. Thus, in architecture the Modernism of the Bauhaus and the International Style exhibited streamlined simplicity, functionality of all details, rejection of ornament, cultural and contextual neutrality, and impersonality; hence the Postmodernist interest in the opposite: complexity, "quotations" from earlier styles, "impure" language, ornament, and the personal imprimatur of the architect. In literature, on the contrary, High Modernism meant elitist, difficult, metaphorical, semantically dense and obscure, allusive and impersonal poetry; while the reaction brought relaxation, less textual density, more direct and descriptive language, social engagement, and the importance of the artist's personal biography for the understanding of his or her art.

Thus, Postmodernism was a medium-dependent phenomenon—it was "post" a specific "Modernism" in each medium or genre. Furthermore, all "posts" drew on internal traditions of Modernism itself. We may describe Postmodernism as an attitude critical of, but also aware of, the achievements of many Modernist trends, styles, and breakthroughs.

The very name Postmodernism implies the use of possibilities opened by Modernism—and closed as well, for if innovation is the overriding principle of art, then those possibilities were exhausted at the moment of their discovery and first exploration. It also implies the relativization of all Modernist theories and styles, the evocation of, or quotations from earlier styles and masters, and overt eclecticism. Above all, it implies a personal voice dominating the functional integration of a work of art. The importance of form is not ignored, but rather than being an impersonal style good for all themes and places, it is made functional within each individual work of art, culturally and contextually dependent, and subsumed under the unity and continuity of the artist's personal style and world. In these respects, Chagall was a Postmodernist even as Modernism was unfolding.

Chagall himself, an ardent defender of "Leftist Art" at the time of the Russian Revolution, realized soon enough his eclectic and pan-historical position. His painting *Homage to Apollinaire*, 1911–12 (no. 44) (see description below), was still dedicated to the most avant-garde leaders of the day in his milieu: Apollinaire, Canudo, Cendrars, and Walden. Yet in 1925, on the Yiddish manuscript of his autobiography, he wrote in longhand a dedication in Russian: "For Rembrandt, Cézanne, my Mama, my wife"—promoting the great masters of art of the past over the fashions of his own age and indicating the importance of his family—no less than of art history—in the formation of his own fictional world.

Of course, Chagall was a major, visible figure in the age of Modernism. He shared some basic assumptions with most Modernist trends: opposition to mimesis in the sense of directly depicting a scene in time and space; opposition to "realism" as the main goal of art; deformation of represented figures and objects; autonomy granted to all aspects of the language of art, such as spatial form, geometric shapes, or color—outside of a direct mimetic function. Without the successive Modernist trends, there would have been no Chagall. Yet without Chagall in the general landscape, the Modernist age would lack something. As one historian of twentieth-century art put it, "We think of Marc Chagall as the painter-poet of the twentieth century. He shares this distinction only with Paul Klee."[1]

Chagall was not considered an innovator of any theoretically defined language of art. Yet his deformations of human figures, subversion of the laws of gravity, whimsical distortions of the continuities of observed reality, dreamlike compositions, and overlapping figures were all innovations—not in the language of color and form but in the formation of the fictional world presented in art—and this in itself was a new language, a language of representation. At least for this reason, he was a much more important and universal artist than his early Jewish background might indicate.

Chagall was never a group player, neither in any art coterie nor in any political party. He was never fully perceived as a Cubist, an Expressionist, a Surrealist, or anything else, but only as "Chagall"—his personality defined the uniqueness and unity of his art. He came close to several of the new waves somewhat late, absorbed some lessons and pictorial devices, and consumed anything that suited him into an all-encompassing fictional universe, unfolded by Chagall under the construct of his own biography.

FICTIONAL WORLD AS A LANGUAGE OF ART

For the avant-garde, art implied the development of one

"language" that dominated—or gave direction to—a group of works by one artist or a "school" of artists in a certain time frame, even though this language itself was in constant flux. In their period of Analytical Cubism, Picasso and Braque made paintings that met the Cubist expectations of perception and texture formation; each painting was a new variant, a new exploration of possibilities, enlarging this framework. Similarly, the early Lissitzky, when illustrating Yiddish books, was a master of stylized Jewish themes and rendered them in a stylistically pure way. But when he embraced Malevich's Suprematism and went on to transform it from the Non-Objective minimalism of Malevich to his own Constructivist "Prouns," photomontage, and politically engaged posters, his style changed entirely. The same may be said of Jean Arp, Vassily Kandinsky, Kazimir Malevich, Vladimir Tatlin, and many others who developed their various individualized styles of the avant-garde. For them, at any given moment, the poetics of their art was like a spoken language: One speaks either French or English or Russian, but not all in the same sentence.

In Yiddish, however, you *can* speak several languages in the same sentence, and you can make forays into the mainland of the component languages of Yiddish: Russian, Hebrew, German, or Polish. Chagall appropriated features of several new languages of art—or developed his own—and placed them side by side in the same painting. He used various elements of Modernist discourse as strains of texture formation included in a complex, kaleidoscopic, and contrapuntal whole. We may describe this attitude as demonstrative eclecticism or, more positively, as a polyphony of forces of various origin working in one painting.

In Chagall's work, all the strains of Modernist discourse that he encountered in St. Petersburg, Paris, and Vitebsk are intertwined with—and juxtaposed to—another discourse: the evocation of what in literary theory and philosophy is called a fictional world.[2] A fictional world (such as a novel with its fictional characters) does not necessarily mean invention or fantasy but the projection of an autonomous "world" with its own cluster of characters, events, symbols, and situations that appear in one work and have their internal relationships and coherence.

Chagall's fictional world is based on his own selection of representative items from several historical, cultural, and personal domains, as refracted through the prism of a self-constructed, often anecdotal, and mythologized autobiography. Even his illustrations to fictional worlds different from his own, such as his work on the Bible or LaFontaine's fables, are presented through the personal prism of Chagall's art and life and often carry personal vignettes or anecdotes on the peripheries of the painting. In his most ambitious work, when the collection of objects and figures on one canvas looks like an incoherent mumbo-jumbo, their unity is sanctioned not by any logical or realistic coherence but by their coexistence in the artist's mind and by their codified status as modules of his fictional universe.

Chagall's projection of a fictional world differs from its use in literature in a key sense: In literature every novel or poem may project its own separate fictional world with its own characters and situations, whereas in Chagall's oeuvre, all paintings refer to one total fictional universe, a construct outside the paintings, but to which all those paintings refer. Of course, each painting in its separate frame presents an isolated chunk of that world, a situation or a "fictional world" (in the technical sense) of its own. Hence, it may be advisable to use the term fictional universe for Chagall's work as a whole. Various individuals of that universe—from his child bride Bella to the rooster—appear and reappear in the fictional worlds of many paintings.

Chagall's universe was far removed from and strange to the eyes of his audiences in St. Petersburg or Paris, who were drawn to its primitivism, spontaneous authenticity, subconscious outpourings, irrational or "Dadaist" order, and exotic content. Chagall's achievement—using a strange world as a language of art—was understood by his friend, the French poet Blaise Cendrars, who wrote in a poem about Chagall:

> Suddenly he paints
> He takes a church and paints with a church
> He takes a cow and paints with a cow
> With a sardine
> With heads, hands, knives
> He paints with a bull's pizzle
> He paints with all the foul passions of a little
> Jewish city
> With all the heightened sexuality of provincial
> Russia.[3]

In other words, Chagall painted not just with a brush and colors but with the language of his fictional objects. Chagall himself expressed this idea on several occasions. In an interview with James Johnson Sweeney, the curator of the first major Chagall retrospective in the United States at the Museum of Modern Art in 1946, he said:

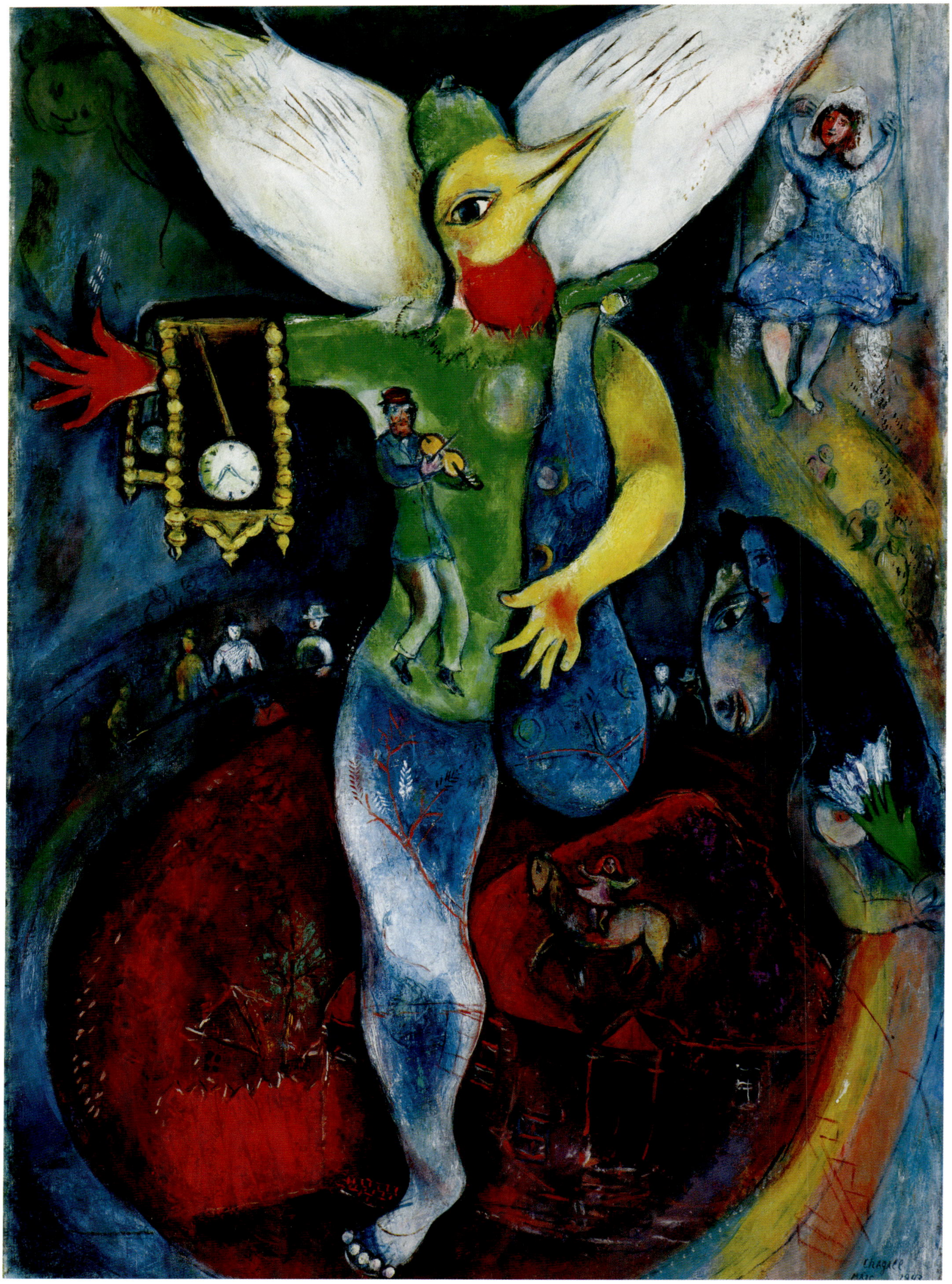

7. ***The Juggler***. *1943. Oil on canvas, 109.9 x 79.1 cm. Art Institute of Chicago, Chicago. Gift of Mrs. Gilbert W. Chapman*

Just as before the war of 1914, I constantly had the word "literature," or "literary painting" thrown at me, now I am constantly said to be a maker of fairy-tales and of fantasies. As a matter of fact, my first aim is to construct my picture architecturally, just as in their day the impressionists did, and cubists did—along the same formal paths. The impressionists filled their canvases with spots of light and shadow. The cubists with cubic, triangular, and round shapes. I try to fill my canvases in some fashion with objects and figures employed as forms—sonorous forms like noises—passion-forms which should give a supplementary dimension impossible to achieve through the bare geometry of the cubists' lines or with the spots of the impressionists.[4]

In this statement, written at the end of World War II, Chagall defines his goals not in terms of ideology, autobiography, or national nostalgia but of composition: "to fill my canvases." The "objects and figures" of his fictional universe are seen as musical "forms" that fulfill the same function as Impressionist light and shadow or Cubist cubes and cones. He continues:

In the case of the decapitated woman with the milk pails [in *To Russia, Donkeys and Others*, no. 41], I was first led to separating her head from her body merely because I happened to need [to fill] an empty space there. Inside the large cow's head [in *I and the Village*, no. 21] I made a small cow and a woman milking visible through its muzzle because I needed that sort of form there, for my composition. Whatever else may have grown out of these compositional arrangement is secondary.[5]

Chagall describes here his intuitive process of working on the canvas, filling in the space with ready-made shapes or figures, and the composition of a painting rather than the meaning of the thematic units themselves. He does not discuss the nature of his repertoire of images, the processes by which they were selected or the effects of the juxtaposition of ostensibly unrelated elements that emerged in his mind. After all, he was talking in a period when formal matters were of greatest interest. In earlier statements he would, perhaps, stress his nostalgia for "Vitebsk." Both are true at the same time: the compositional balancing of several centers of gravity in a painting is coupled with a selection of representative modules and forms—adjacent, juxtaposed, or making a counterpoint to each other.

Critics are often amazed at the wealth of topics, figures, and objects present in Chagall's paintings. As Norbert Lynton wrote:

His subjects outreach any listing: birth, death, hardship, contentment, domesticity, isolation, social events, the longings and the delights of love, rabbis and poets, family, Bella, their daughter Ida, Vava, himself in many guises, crucifixions of Christ and others, the Russian Revolution, the Old Testament, angels, The Magic Flute, Orpheus, Daphnis and Chloë, the circus, acrobats, cows, cocks, donkeys, fish, clocks, most of these with and without violins, flowers, Vitebsk, Paris, the Eiffel Tower. It is best not even to start imagining the other possible lists, of the materials he worked in, the many functions his art serves, the art and artists that he has allied himself to from early ikons to Modernists via shop-signs and ancient symbols, lest our heads spin off our shoulders in precisely the way he describes.[6]

The various items on Lynton's list are not depictions of inexhaustible individual objects in the world but representatives of several recognizable domains, repeated throughout Chagall's art: old Jews of the recent religious past, as seen from the distance of a secular generation; Christian soldiers and peasants; his own, imaginary Vitebsk as the symbolic town of a distant Jewish world; another aspect of Vitebsk, with its churches and cathedrals symbolizing Russia; animals in that world, often humanized; his young bride Bella and loving couples; Jesus Christ as the suffering Jew; Paris with the emblematic Eiffel Tower; and, later in his career, anonymous Jewish masses, crossing the Red Sea or facing the Holocaust; and the world of the Bible. All these domains were internalized in the fictional universe of one individual, carried around the globe in the artist's memory and consciousness.

Living nature, a central theme in Romantic poetry and art, was set aside in Modernism, which stressed human experience and urban landscapes. Chagall's road was the reverse. As mentioned earlier, the Jews were an urban population and had little active or productive contact with nature, even when they inhabited the smallest towns. Chagall came from this experience. Sometimes he drew an image of nature, but even then, nature was mainly a backdrop to the human experience or an ornament around the human center, as in *Bella with a White Collar*, 1917 (no. 6). In most of his work, nature was reduced to a few items, taken out of their realistic conti-

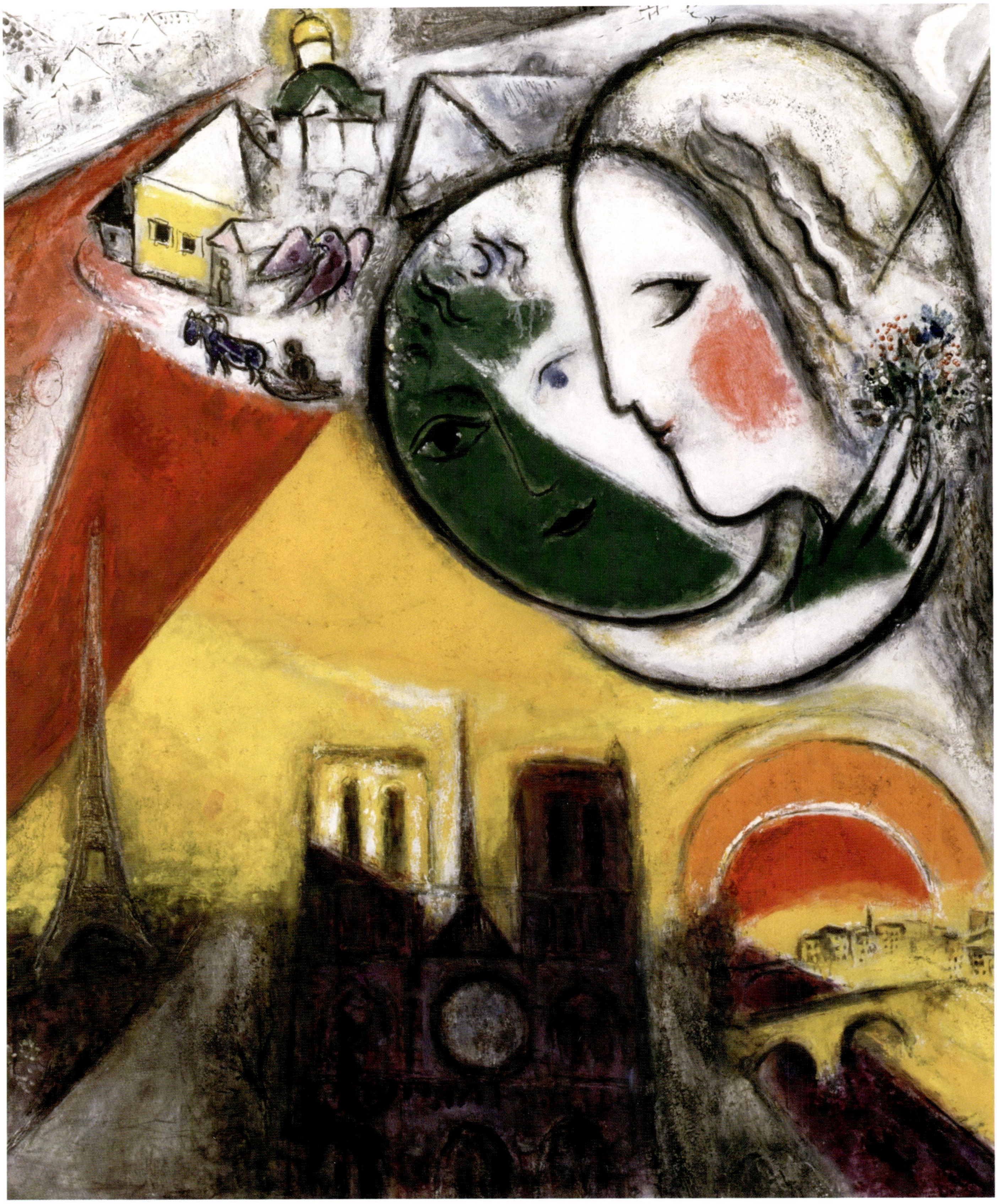

8. ***Sunday.*** *1952–54. Oil on canvas, 173 x 149 cm. Private collection*

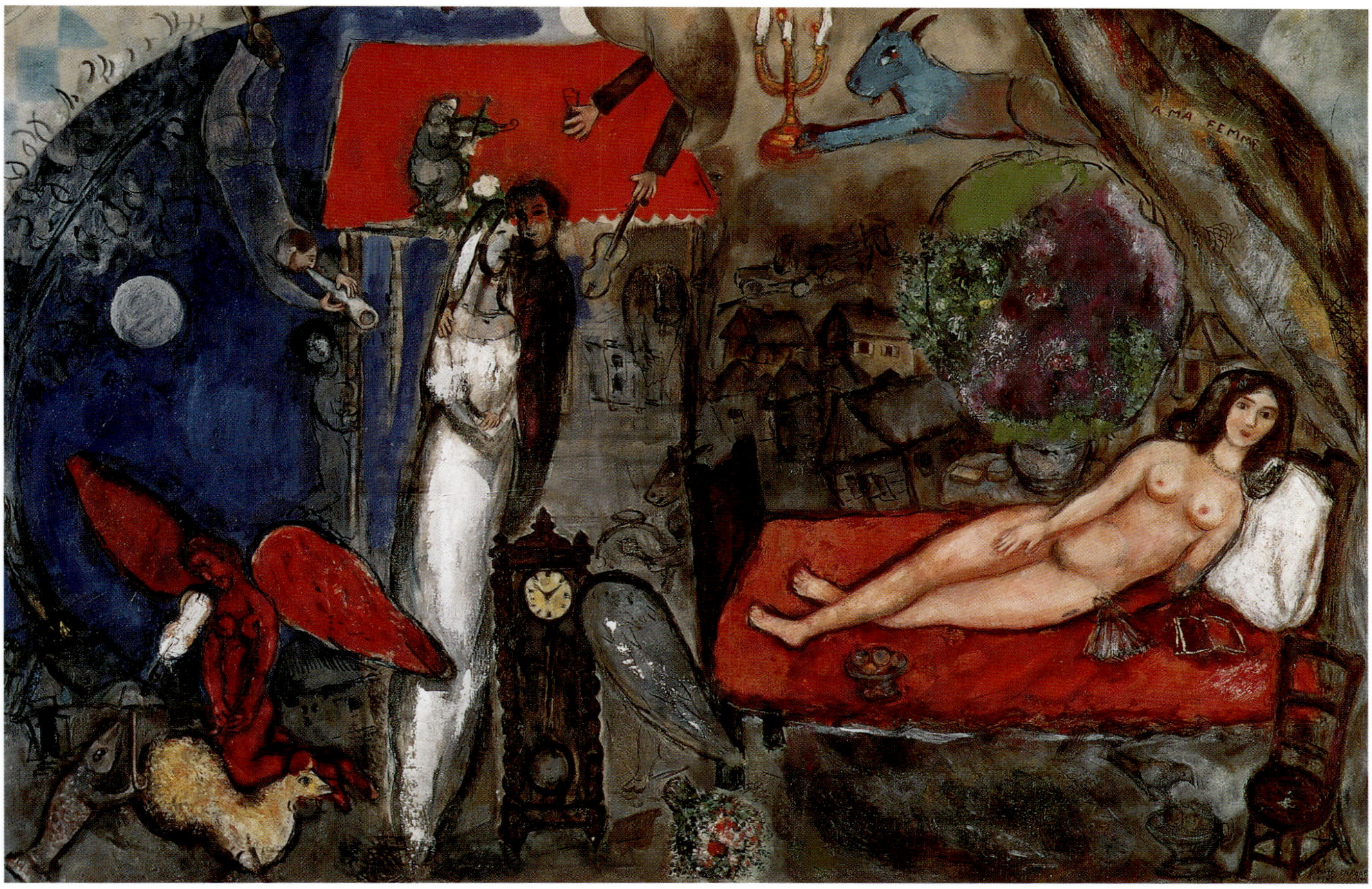

9. ***To My Wife.*** *1933–34. Oil on canvas, 107 x 178.8 cm. Musée national d'art moderne, Centre Georges Pompidou, Paris*

nuity, such as flower bouquets, a river representing time (not in a Romantic meadow, but as part of a city landscape, as in *Time Is a River Without Banks*, no. 77), and the colorful sky—all not necessarily observed at the time of painting but transferred from earlier images or from his mind and memory.

Chagall's contemporary Yisoskhor Rybak depicted synagogues of different towns in Russia in a quasi-Cubist manner; it was an act of Romantic documentation. Chagall placed all objects and persons in his imaginary Vitebsk, making them elements of the painter-poet's mythological space.

In Paris in the second decade of the twentieth century, this fictional world as a language of art attracted great attention.[7] Art, to some, seemed to have been reduced to innovations in form, two-dimensional objects in space, color, and composition. But in Chagall's paintings, an authentic, persistent world appeared, so exotic and different from the world of the spectators. The "exotic," "primitive," and "naïve" were of great interest to Modern art. And Chagall's was an exotic world not from Tahiti, Africa, or the Orient, but surviving in the midst of Europe, borne by the primitive Jews who were both detested and part of the foundations of Christian culture. This amazed reception was repeated in Berlin in 1914, in Russia during World War I and the Revolutionary period, and in France after Chagall's return in 1923.

Attention to the world he represented was reinforced by the painter's ambivalent perception of it. His images (including self-portraits) ranged from the grotesque to the sentimental, transformed through a series of drastic, anti-Realist devices. His work was often seen as a forerunner or fellow traveler of Surrealism, which shifted the goals of painting from a focus on the medium itself to the subconscious, "unsayable" mental world of the painter and the evocation of unrealistic, fantastic spaces. Chagall, the recreator of a lost world, became the "poetic" painter, the painter of a social or personal dream world, the Surrealist, the visionary, the mystic, the master of a chaotic subconscious, or the naïve narrator of a strange and colorful biography, for which he often supplied stories to any interviewer or in writing and lecturing.

Thus, in his memoirs, written in Russian in 1922–24 and first published in Yiddish in 1925,[8] Chagall wrote that his mother told him about her father, who had disappeared one day on a holiday. They searched for him everywhere, and "it turned out that in the nice weather he climbed on the roof, sat on the chimney [to warm himself], and ate *tsimes* [Jewish sweet carrot stew]." Chagall added: "Not a bad picture." Chagall domesticated the fantastic situations of his paintings in events that presumably happened in his own life. Some critics have taken him seriously and thereby made him into a Realist, defusing the surrealist effects of his work. Yet Chagall himself knew perfectly well that his grandfather in the story had enacted "not a bad picture"—the picture is primary—and added: "And perhaps I dreamt it all" (i.e., the event, the *tsimes*, and his mother's story). Chagall made a drawing of this anecdote, *Grandfather on the Roof*, 1922 (no. 13), and it was published in the album *Mein Leben* by Paul Cassirer in Berlin. In a later lithograph—*Our House in My Village*, 1947 (no. 14)—he embedded this black-and-white drawing in a blue frame, showing young Chagall in a clown's uniform, with his head half inside the white drawing, half outside in the blue frame, crossing the boundary of fiction and reality.[9] It was a fictional image after all. It is also important to note that Chagall had already placed a man on the edge of a roof (a prototype of the "fiddler on the roof") many years earlier, in *The Dead Man* of 1908 (see chapter 3, no. 27). For Chagall, his grandfather's story demonstrates the strain of positive craziness and creative freedom that ran in the family. Chagall himself wrote: "If my art didn't play any role in the lives of my family, their lives and creations, on the contrary, were very significant in my work."

Whether the story is true or apocryphal is immaterial; the salient point is Chagall's attempt to domesticate the unrealistic events of his painting in experienced "facts" or psychological attitudes. Ironically, if successful, this would explain away the very effect on which his painting depends; it would turn his *surnaturel* art into realistic recordings of reality, yet that reality itself would seem crazy indeed. Chagall kept in his mind a repertoire of the same images, which he faithfully repeated in words and in paintings at a distance of many years.

Modernist trends promoted the impersonal in art and poetry, overlooking the private emotions and biography of the individual artist in favor of the creation of independent aesthetic objects. Such was the ideal of "the poem itself," or as Archibald MacLeish put it: "A poem should not mean but be."[10] At one time, Russian Futurists did not sign their texts; Cubists emphasized the impersonal style of art. T. S. Eliot wrote of the "expression of significant emotion, emotion which has its life in the poem and not in the history of the poet. The emotion of art is impersonal."[11] Later in the century, Structuralists and Deconstructionists excluded the author from the understanding of his or her own text.

Chagall, however, promulgated the opposite view. In his art, his personal biography is at the center, and the depicted world is determined subjectively. Chagall thematized his biography in his art and made it the ostensible arbiter of his authentic style. To be sure, this individual experience contained many public, basic stereotypes about the domains he evoked: the mystery of mundane life; the transformation of the Jews; the sad decline and mental strength of the old, religious Jewry; the image of the provincial Russian town; and the depth, irrationality, and mysterious warmth of folkways and conventions.

A scholar of Chagall's art is compelled to study his biography and cultural contexts as primary sources of his language, iconography, and meaning. And so does the spectator in any Chagall exhibition. Jewish elements and subtexts, in particular those stemming from his early years, are part of the language with which Chagall forms a painting and expresses his emotions on the mysteries of life. This does not make him an exclusively "Jewish" artist any more than William Faulkner is an exclusively "Southern" writer; in both, the local specificity (*couleur local*) is the vehicle through which they see the world—it becomes the language of their universally valid art.

INTROSPECTIVISM

The theory of simultaneity in art and the interpenetration of planes was promoted in Italian Futurism. In a manifesto for a 1912 exhibition in Paris, "The Exhibitors to the Public," the Futurists stated:

> In painting a person on a balcony, seen from inside the room, we do not limit the scene to what the square frame of the window renders visible; but we try to render the sum total of visual sensations which the person on the balcony has experienced; the sunbathed throng in the street, the double row of houses which stretch to right and left, the beflowered balconies, etc. This implies the *simultaneousness* of the ambient, and, therefore, the *dislocation and dismemberment of objects, the scattering and fusion of details, freed from accepted logic, and independent from one another.*[12] [emphasis mine—BH]

The last sentence applies directly to Chagall's art—including the "dislocation and dismemberment of objects." Indeed, this manifesto transfers cubist deconstructions onto the level of a mental event. In Chagall's work, however, what motivates such simultaneity and

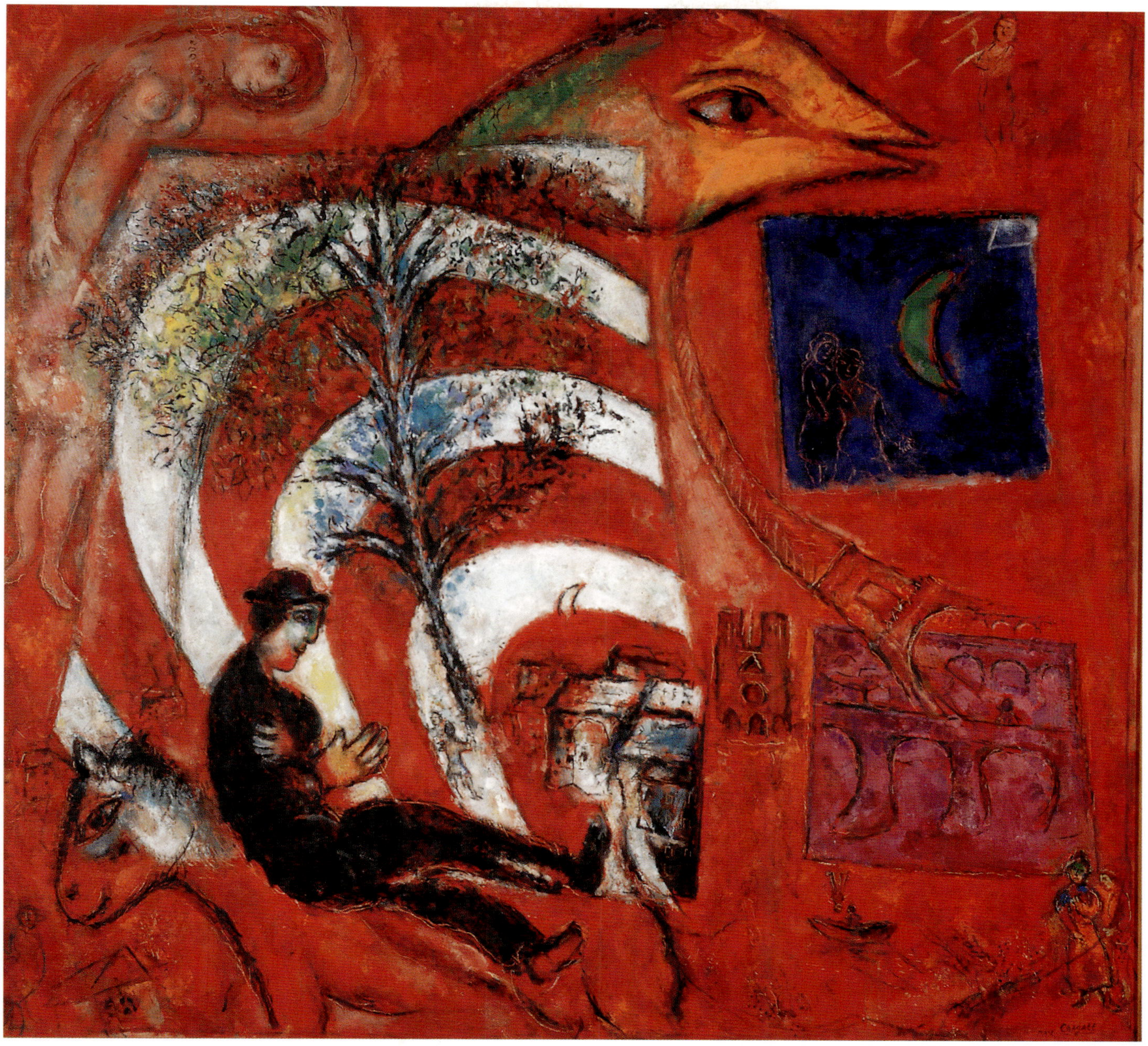

10. ***The Rainbow.*** *1967. Oil on canvas, 160 x 170.5 cm. Musée d'art moderne, Strasbourg*

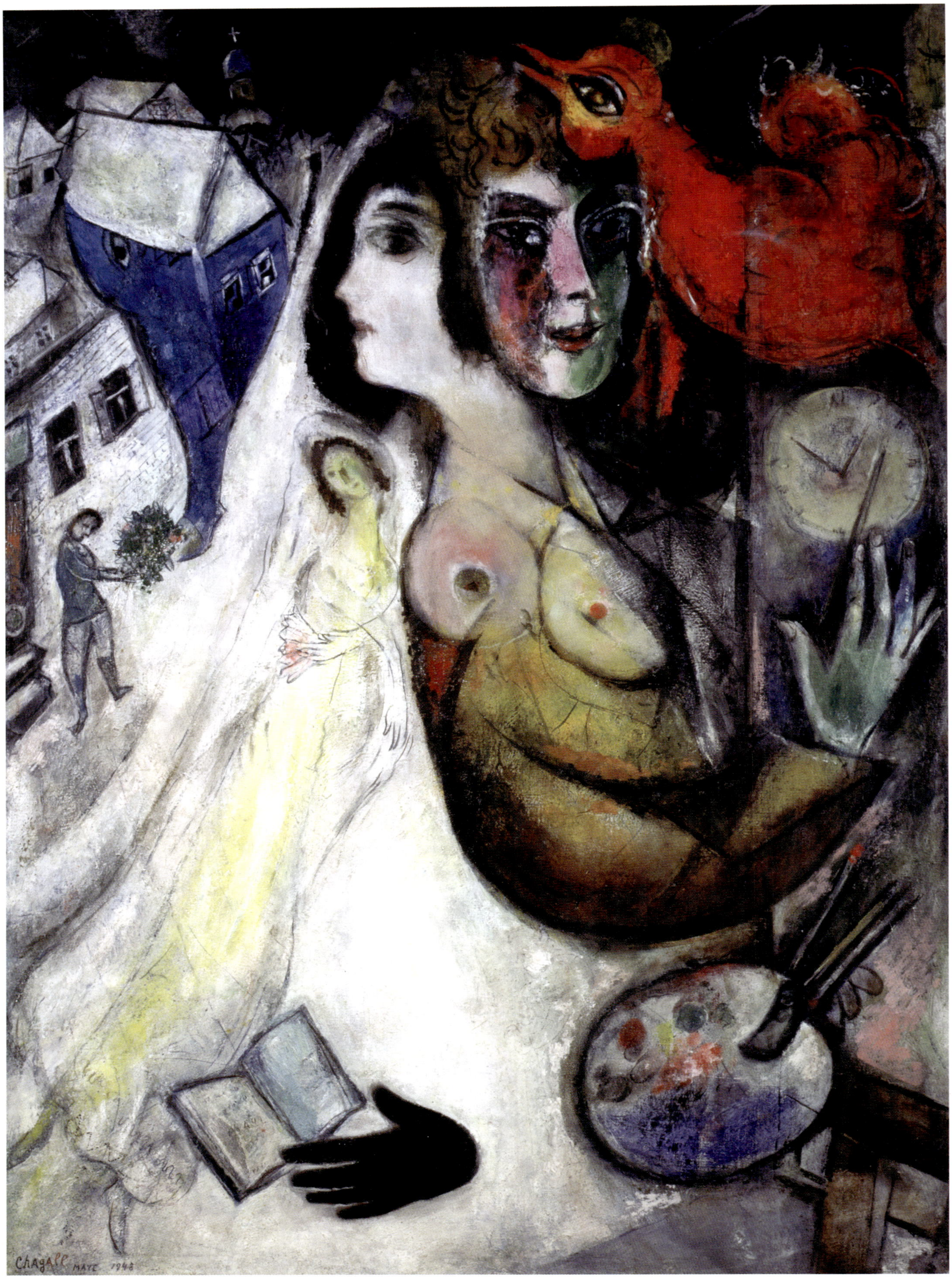

11. ***The Black Glove.*** *1923–48. Oil on canvas, 111 x 81.5 cm. Private collection*

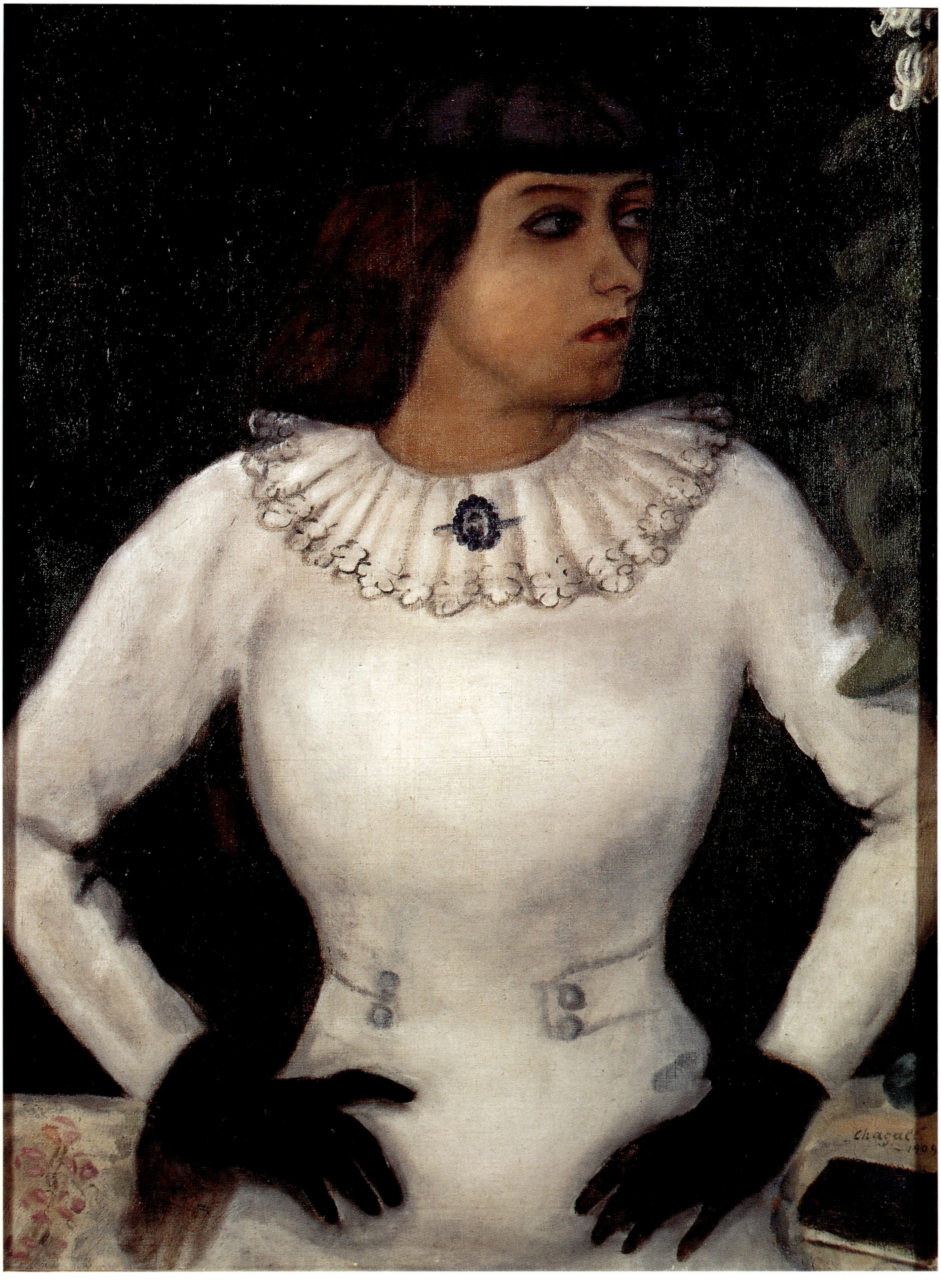

12. ***My Fiancée in Black Gloves.*** *1909. Oil on canvas, 88 x 65.1 cm. Öffentliche Kunstsammlung Basel, Kunstmuseum, Basel*

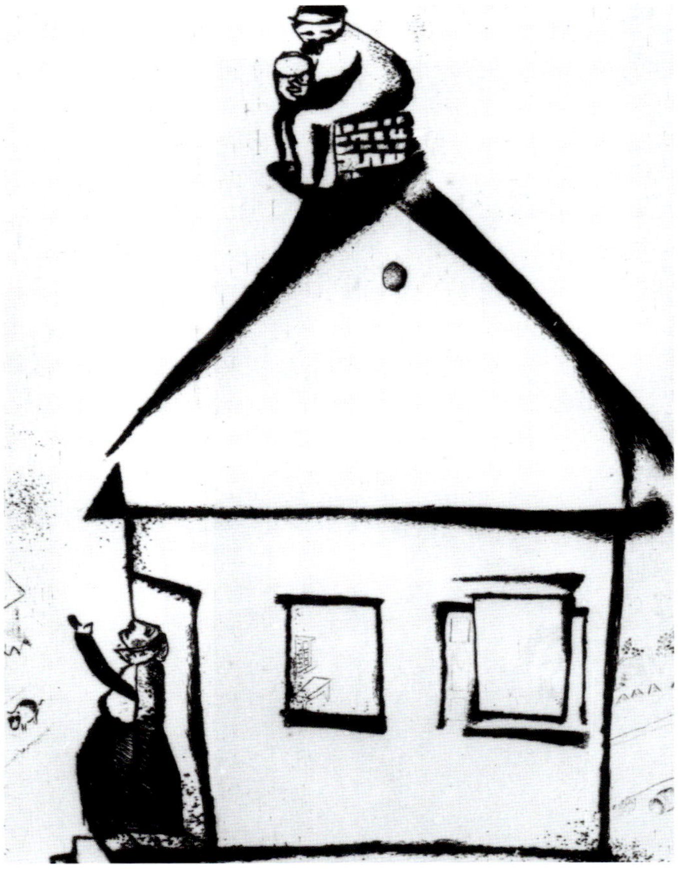

13. ***Grandfather on the Roof.*** *1922. From Mein Leben ("My Life"): 20 etchings and drypoint on paper. Berlin*

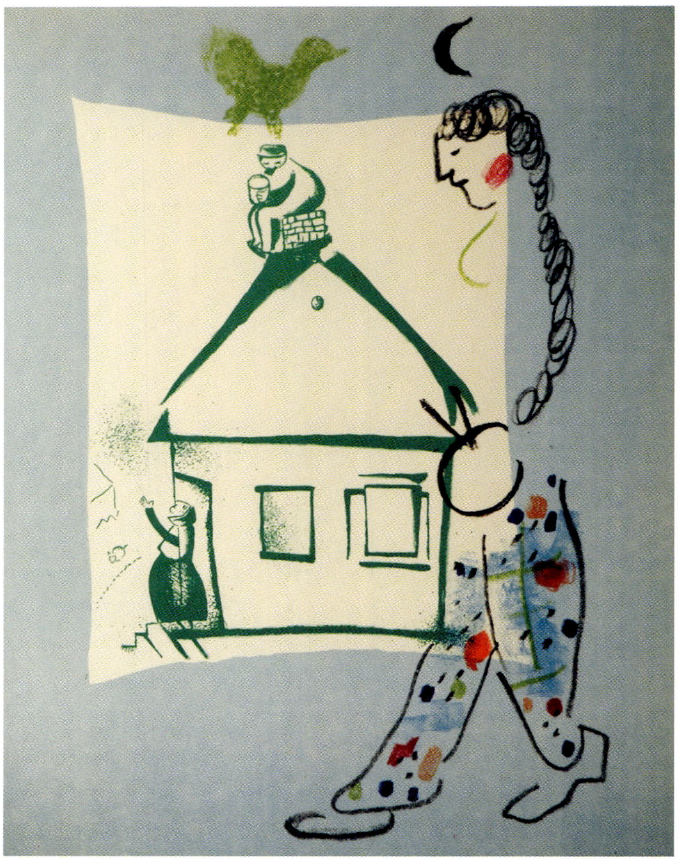

14. ***Our House in My Village.*** *1947. Color lithograph, 1960. Redrawn from Mein Leben ("My Life"), 1962*

dismemberment is not just the associative consciousness of a character depicted on the canvas but the consciousness of the artist-narrator himself, while he observes the figure and its internal point of view from an ironic distance. Thus, in the famous *I and the Village* (no. 21) the internal point of view belongs to the green face, yet "the sum total of visual sensations" represents the higher observation point of the artist himself. Furthermore, a painting by Chagall does not represent one momentary experience but involves different modules from various times and places, stored in the fictional repertoire inhabiting his mind.

Chagall's perception finds a close affinity in the theories of the Yiddish Introspectivist poets in America, whose manifesto, written in New York in 1919, proclaimed that all topics and domains of modern life and culture are legitimate subjects for poetry, provided they were presented "in an introspective and fully individual manner"[13]:

> For us, everything is "personal." Wars and revolutions, Jewish pogroms and the workers' movement, Protestantism and Buddha, the Yiddish school and the Cross, the mayoral elections and a ban on our language—all these may concern us or not, just as a blond woman and our own unrest may or may not concern us. If it does concern us, we write poetry; if it does not, we keep quiet. In either case we write about ourselves because all these exist only insofar as they are in us, insofar as they are perceived introspectively.[14]

Thus, poetry is not limited to private experience: the social and political world are part of the artist's internalized panorama. Furthermore, experience cannot be isolated or limited to the here and now of an externally observed scene:

> When the poet, or any person, looks at a sunset, he may see the strangest things which may, perhaps, appear as having no relation to the sunset. [...] This, the series of associations and the chain of suggestions, constitutes *truth* [emphases in the original], is life, much as an illusion is often more real than the cluster of external appearances we call life. [...] We insist that the poet should give us the authentic image that he sees in himself and give it in such a form as only he and no one else can see it.[15]

The Introspectivists wrote that "the poet must really listen to his inner voice, observe his internal panorama—

kaleidoscopic, contradictory, unclear or confused as it may be."[16] Although the Russian Chagall was not directly connected to the American Introspectivists, whom he met in the 1940s in New York, they all grew up in the Yiddish language in the Russian empire and were struck by the revolution of Modern art and poetry; their cultural background and perceptions were similar to his. Theirs was a generation of Jewish individualists, who abandoned the confining collective framework of their codified religious tradition, and each had to work out his own position in life and art—a feature admired in a poet or painter. Yet all this happened in the highly politicized twentieth century; poetry and art had to confront this reality, and each poet had to refract it through the prism of his own personal experience.

A major factor in all this was the Yiddish language, their common native tongue. As argued by Yiddishist linguists, especially Max Weinreich, Yiddish is a language of fusion, combining such disparate components as parts of German, Slavic languages, the Holy Tongue (Hebrew combined with Aramaic), and an international vocabulary. Historically, English was also a language of fusion, but today it appears as one integrated language to its users, who mostly live in an English-speaking environment. Yiddish speakers, however, were always conscious of the component languages because they lived in the midst of other languages and no single country was the homeland of "Yiddishland." Almost by definition, Yiddish speakers were simultaneously speakers and readers of several other languages and were well aware of the multireligious and multicultural perspective in which they lived. As I have argued elsewhere, Yiddish is not just a language of fusion but also an unusually *open* language: Speakers or writers could enlarge the Hebrew part—beyond what is ostensibly "merged" in Yiddish—and indulge in Judaic learned discourse; or enlarge the German vocabulary and shift their phonetics in order to speak and read German; or they could expand the Slavic elements and shift to speaking Russian or Polish in mid-sentence.[17]

Chagall's mind moved in the same direction. His fusion of heterogeneous components in one painting mirrors the world of Yiddish, especially of those Yiddish speakers who rapidly assimilated into general culture. Thus, he could not absorb the European masterpieces of painting without close attention to the Christian tradition in art, and he merged that tradition with the Jewish traditions of his childhood world.

Chagall's move from a provincial, ignorant Yiddish milieu to the centers of Russian and French Modernist art was part of the Modern Jewish Revolution, the secularization of masses of Jews and their entrance into general European culture.[18] He and his contemporaries entered the history of European culture from the outside and at a late moment, just as a radical upheaval—political and cultural—was upturning that very history. To the curious and eager newcomers, European history appeared as a synchronic "imaginary museum" (to use André Malraux's term): time was mapped onto space. Like Chagall in the Louvre, one could run from room to room, from century to century, and choose items regardless of their sequence or historical context. Chagall's generation began with Modernism, then recapitulated some of the very European past that had been subverted by Modernism. In a speech delivered in Yiddish in New York on June 30, 1944, Chagall observed:

> I love "contrasts" in which the harmonious truth is hidden. I think about one of many examples, in which various poles of art meet somewhere. Here is the classical Realist Pushkin with his profoundly chiseled meter and the ardent Romantic Baudelaire—veiled in dreams of enchanted, poisonous flowers—nevertheless they meet somewhere in their ultimate authenticity. I recall the last art experiments in Paris [on the verge of World War II] where, next to a painting by an old medieval primitive such as Giotto, may hang a Picasso, and next to him, the pre-Renaissance artist Mantegna; and next to our [i.e., Jewish] Modigliani can hang a Byzantine icon; and several paintings by the Naturalist artist and Revolutionary Gustav Courbet, who, during the Paris Commune, toppled the Vendôme Column to the ground, can hang along with the magic Renaissance artist Giorgione, and so on. . . . And this is not "eclecticism"—on the contrary.[19]

THE KALEIDOSCOPE

Like Yiddish Introspectivist poetry, Chagall's art was kaleidoscopic—a key terms of the Introspectivists. In his paintings he often presented a precarious but colorful balance of variegated splinters of a complex fictional universe. Any shift of the kaleidoscope created a new constellation made from the same colorful elements. Furthermore, in Chagall's best paintings, there is an internal equilibrium, a balancing of heterogeneous centers of gravity between various strata and parts of the painting. The unity of his compositions is determined neither by spatial forms, or networks of color, nor by the fictional world alone, but by the ambivalent emphasis, shifting

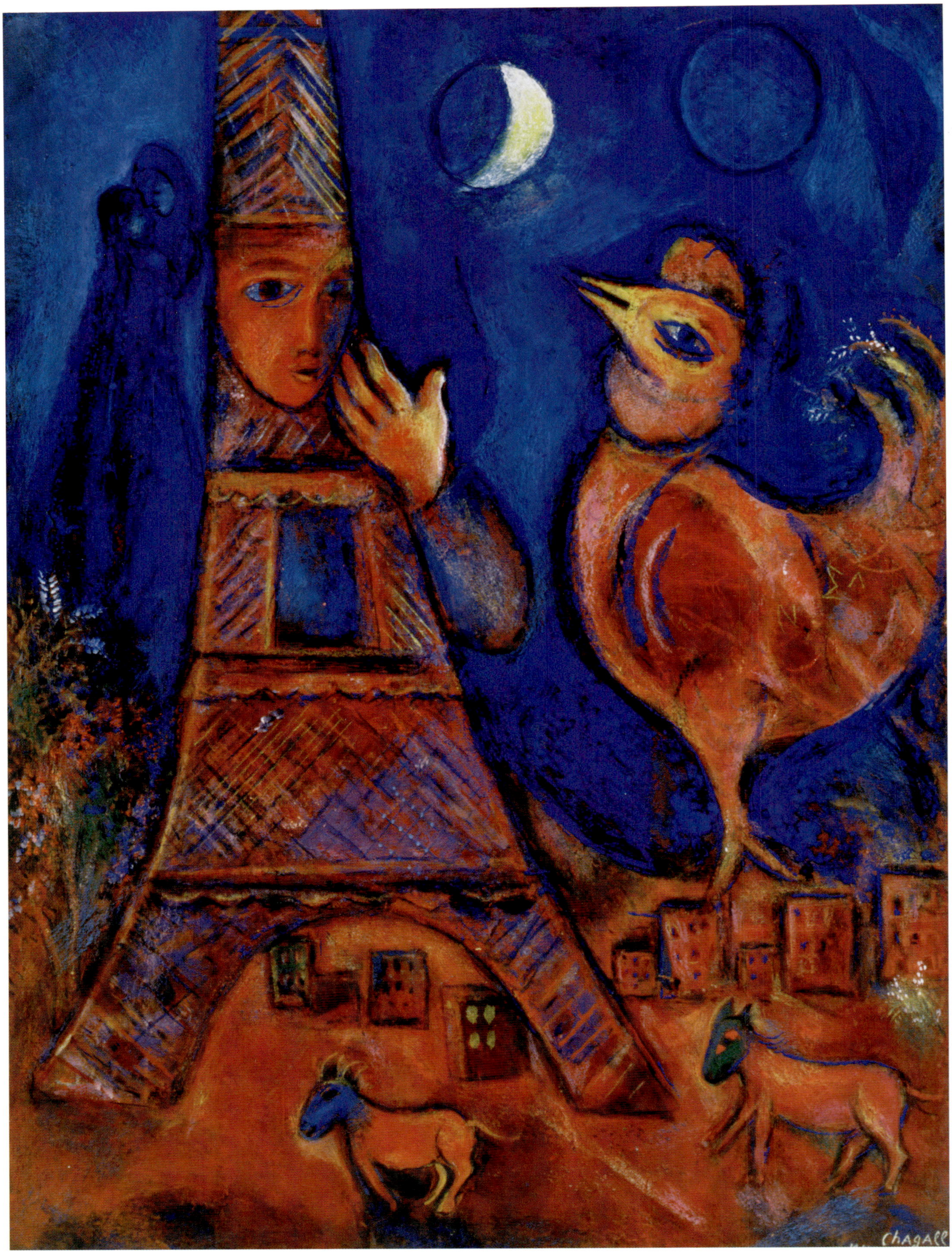

15. ***Bonjour Paris.*** *1939–42. Oil and pastel on cardboard, 62 x 46 cm. Private collection*

from one stratum to another in the space of one painting.

Chagall's attitude toward the kaleidoscope changed with time. His earlier work is usually focused on a story, a situation, or a person, while on its periphery disparate elements from his kaleidoscope appear; the whole repertoire is in his mind. But in his later work the individual painting becomes a whimsical kaleidoscope, as in *The Juggler*, 1943 (no. 7), painted in New York as a recollection of the Paris circus and, beyond it, grandfather's tiny, round hut and other Vitebsk scenes and animals; or *Sunday*, 1952–54 (no. 8), looking back from the position of Paris with the emblematic Eiffel Tower and Notre Dame, through geometric color shapes to schematized Vitebsk churches and huts, dominated by love. In *To My Wife*, 1933–34 (no. 9), we see a married couple under (and above) a red wedding canopy accompanied by a *klezmer* (Jewish musician) descending from the sky, a nude on a red sofa, a small town in the dark behind her, a bouquet of flowers above her, a nude angel kneeling greeted by a fish with a lucky umbrella, a moon, a Sabbath menorah, and so forth. There is also a winged grandfather clock—which alludes to his painting *Time Is a River Without Banks*, 1930–39 (no. 77)—although this time the wedding is in the center and the clock of time accompanies it, whereas in the original the clock is centered and the loving couple is on the margin. In the inspired *The Rainbow*, 1967 (no. 10) a soft Eiffel Tower rising from the bridges on the Seine, gently bent like one of Salvador Dalí's watches, provides a body to the bird on top, and a paradoxical white rainbow gets its colors from overlapping blue-green-yellow trees and human figures.

Many elements of the kaleidoscope are self-referential—Chagall's "post-Chagall" images. Thus, *The Black Glove*, 1923–48 (no. 11), was started upon Marc and Bella's first arrival in Paris with all the memories of his Russian images and completed when Marc and Virginia returned to Paris in 1948. The intimately dense circle—the loving couple, representing Chagall and Bella, the human-eyed rooster, and the clock of time—is placed side by side with the elongated bride, representing his "new-found love," Virginia Haggard. In a poem of that time, "The Painting," both figures merge:

> My departed love,
> My new-found love,
> Listen to me,
> I move over your soul,
> Over your belly—
> Drink the calm of your young years.

On the left, the young Chagall walks down his mother's three steps and brings a bouquet of flowers to his young bride. He quotes an early painting of Bella: *My Fiancée in Black Gloves*, 1909 (no. 12), by showing one black glove dropped on a white background.

These three principles—introspective rendering of the public world, the kaleidoscope, and the balancing of heterogeneous elements in each painting—are among the defining traits of Chagall's art.

In Chagall's numerous paintings, especially in his colorful later work, individuals from his fictional domains appear as modular units in a large mosaic. Their boundaries often melt and several individual objects overlap in what we may call overlapping (or portmanteau) figures, like portmanteau words, which combine fragments of words from several languages, partially overlapping each other, as created by Velimir Khlebnikov, James Joyce, or Vladimir Nabokov. Chagall's overlapping figures include man and musical instrument; man and animal; Christ and a praying Jew; geometric forms or patches of color and the human body; the Eiffel Tower or a lantern with human legs. (See *Bonjour Paris*, 1939–42 [no. 15], painted in New York, or *At Dusk*, 1938–43 [no. 16].) A different case is *The Bastille*, 1953 (no. 17), in which a Chagallian animal in red, mooing its longing to an entwined couple in the blue sky, becomes itself a red background for an urban scene in Paris with a couple of lovers. The surface of one object becomes the ground for another.

CHAGALL AND THE SEMIOTICS OF JEWISH DISCOURSE

In addition to the multilingual, multicultural perspective inherent in the culture of Yiddish and in the transitional and translingual existential situation of that Jewish generation, Chagall exhibits other basic features of the semiotics of Jewish discourse,[20] the signs, idioms, modes of discourse, and significant gestures of the culture.

The founding book of Jewish consciousness is the Bible. The Bible is an "encyclopedic" book (as Northrop Frye called it), encompassing all available genres of written discourse: stories, prophecy, poetry, wisdom, law, blessings, cosmology, and historiography. Those genres are embedded in a historical narrative, stretching, in the Jewish Bible, from the creation of the world to the list of generations in Chronicles.

However, with the destruction of the Jewish state and the canonization of the Bible in the first century CE, in the perception of the new, stateless Judaism, the Biblical narrative came to an end and history was finished (until the Messiah comes). Since then, in post-Biblical Judaism, the text of the Bible has been reinterpreted into a pan-historic and pan-geographic system of rules and beliefs that are independent of the country, languages, or time of their application. A major precept of interpretation has been that there is no "earlier" and no "later" in the Bible—any quote may be used for any argument at hand, detached from its place in the historical sequence of the Bible. Thus, the Ten Commandments were originally given in a very specific narrative and dramatic situation, but were later lifted from their historical and dramatic context and elevated to timeless law. While Christians have interpreted Biblical figures and events as prefigurations of the life of Jesus, rabbinical learning used Biblical texts as an authoritative source of law and language.

Accordingly, typical Jewish texts—in the Talmudic tradition of religious scholarship as well as in popular writings and sermons—do not have one unfolding logical structure or one directional narrative. Directionality gives a certain logical or narrative discipline to the unfolding of a text in the Western tradition (such as a book of philosophy or a novel), subordinating each scene or event to a continuous chain—logical or narrative—and making it functional either for the plot or for the argument. Thus, if plot is presented to us in a chain of events, e–b–d–a–c, the reader can reconstruct the chronological and causal order of a–b–c–d–e. Each event or detail depends on the earlier event and leads to the future event—both are entailed in it. The detail, image, or story is enriched by being part of the directional chain of narrative. And the same holds for a logical argument in philosophy or science.

In most Jewish Diaspora texts, however, directionality is set aside. There are no novels or Hegelian *Aesthetics* in the Jewish tradition. Each detailed observation or language is treated as an autonomous value. The detail is taken out of its linear, narrative chain and observed close up; it does not lose the reader's interest, but that interest becomes an interest in meaning rather than in the question, "what happened then?" The detail contributes to the construction of one total universe, which endows it with rich meaning, symbolic value, and depth. Each detail is not connected to a definite chain, it can be omitted without any damage to the narrative or quoted elsewhere. But it is related to a higher, universal order via symbolic representation: d -> D. Every anecdote becomes a parable.

Hence, any detail could be parallel to anything else, any textual reference could evoke any other text in the library, supporting it or arguing with it. To be sure, there are many narrative stories in the Talmud, Midrash, and Jewish folklore, but such narrative texts tend to be short, moralistic, or anecdotal. Especially associative were the structures of the oral performances by rabbis and popular preachers (such as the Magid of Slutsk in Chagall's *The Green Jew*, 1914, no. 18), for they departed from the given, fixed weekly portion of the Bible to whatever topics of the day or of morality interested them. The non-sequitur, the surprising leap, was their forte.

In the traditional Jewish milieu, talk and argument were important, for it was not enough just to know the Law, one had to understand and explain it, raising two opposite arguments on both sides of an issue and justifying the "right" one or leaving it open (*teyku*—"a draw"). This mode of religious and educational discourse, studied and practiced to some extent by every male in the family, permeated social communication and family life. A cluster of attitudes, developed in the universe of religious texts and the methods of religious teaching, was simplified, codified, and folklorized and became second nature to typical Jewish verbal behavior. This is primarily true for Eastern Europe, where there was a dense educational network, privileging dialogical teaching in the Yeshivas, and a unique, separate linguistic vehicle—Yiddish—which absorbed the basic attributes of this study and gave them the sanction of privileged communicative discourse. In the next step, various aspects of this discourse were transformed from language per se into behavioral and psychological features, which could be transferred to other languages by such assimilated Jews as Franz Kafka, Sigmund Freud, Saul Bellow, or Marc Chagall.

This semiotics of Jewish discourse can be described as a cluster of tendencies, common—though neither obligatory nor exclusive—to Jewish verbal behavior in that period, especially in Eastern Europe. Such "Jewish discourse" is talkative, argumentative, adversary, contrarian, associative. Its typical traits include answering a question with a question or with an example, anecdote, or parable rather than with a direct, logical reply; seeing the smallest detail as symbolic for universal issues; delving into the meanings, connotations, and associations of a single word; analyzing its etymology and leaping from a word or a concrete item to abstract generalizations and theories, without the need for a logical argument. In general, it was not the overall story or the logical continuity of a text but the imaginary coherence of the represented universe as a whole that guided the discourse.

It all made sense when such discourse was subordinated to one total, religious universe. But when that universe was no longer based on the certainties of a

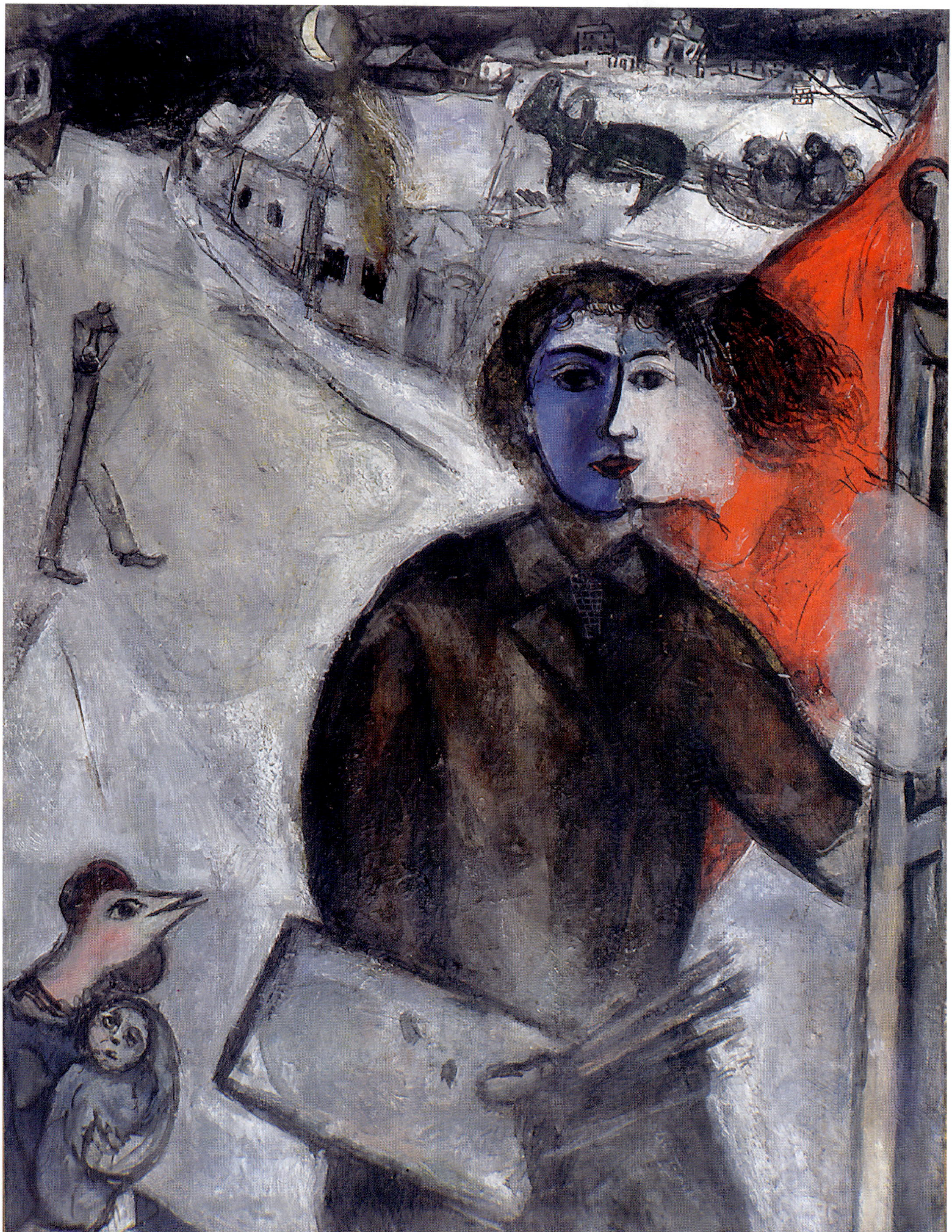

16. ***At Dusk.*** *1938–43. Oil on canvas, 100 x 73 cm. Private collection*

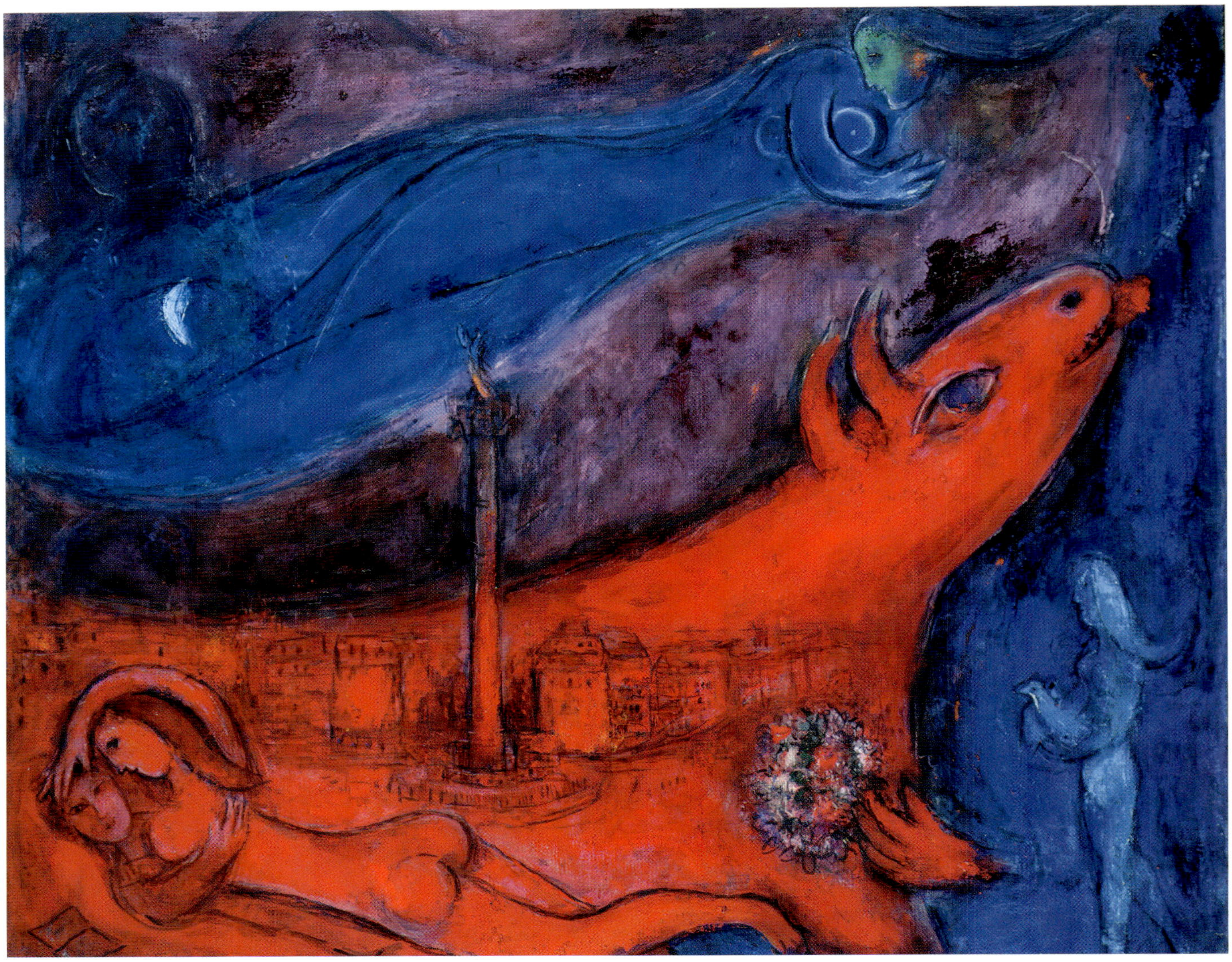

17. ***The Bastille.*** *1953. Oil on canvas, 81 x 100 cm. Private collection*

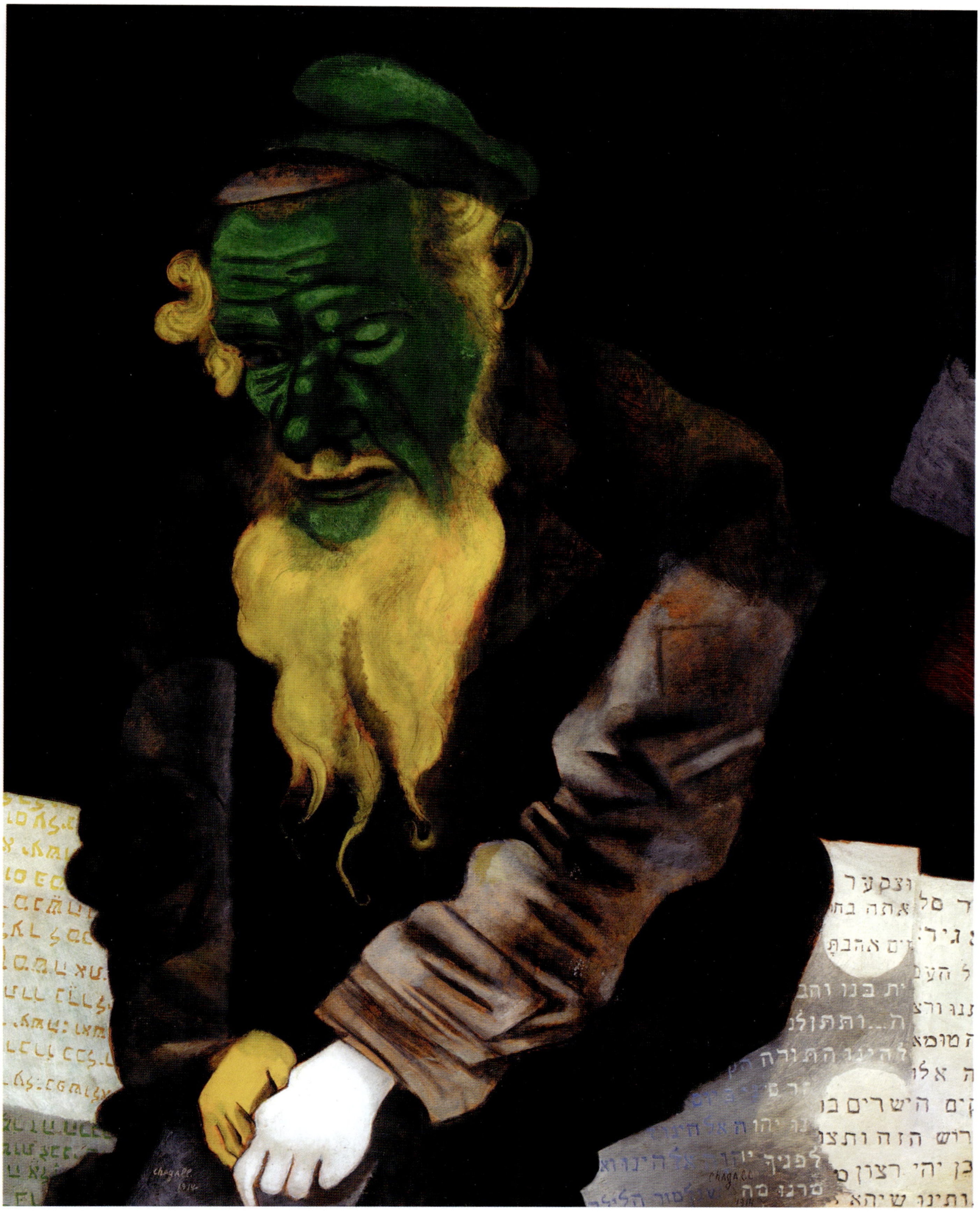

18. ***The Green Jew.*** *1914. Oil on Cardboard, 98.1 x 78.1 cm. Private collection, Geneva. Collage from Hebrew texts. On the right column:* ***"Der Slutsker Magid"*** *("The Preacher from Slutsk") in Yiddish, inserted into the Hebrew text.*

religious system, the codified and "correct" answers were discarded and only the questions remained (as Kafka understood it in his brilliant and obsessively unrelenting story "Investigations of a Dog"). Now substitute totalities were sought. In Freud's and Chagall's perceptions, that totality was one person's consciousness. Thus, in Freud, every word or detail, association or connotation, could be symbolic of the whole personality and could evoke any other detail in the individual's universe of discourse. As Peter Gay presented it, Freud's goal was "to draw the map of human experience as crisscrossed by the roads of analogy."[21]

Specific traits of that Jewish discourse were the product of an intersection of communicative habits from both the learned tradition and the traditional existential situation of the Jews. For example, the inferiority-superiority complex of Kafka's protagonists, and of Chagall's self-understanding, derived from the religious notion that the Jews are the "chosen people" in a spiritual or theological sense, on the one hand, and a fallen aristocracy of the mind, chosen for suffering, on the other. The actual precarious existence of the Jews throughout the Diaspora supported this bipolarity, entrenched in their consciousness and self-image.

In a similar fashion, the penchant for abstraction and generalization, in which a detail is unimportant in and of itself unless it can be seen as representing the "rules of the game," or as Sholem Aleichem's Tevye the Milkman put it, "the order of God's universe," has been derived from both the Jews' textual tradition and the lack of concrete contact with nature. Even when such individuals joined European cultures, they embraced first the abstract, learned language of literature and philosophy, rather than the crude, concrete, nuanced dialect spoken by real people. Trees or birds had no names in nineteenth-century Hebrew dictionaries and were dubbed "a kind of tree," "a kind of bird," and so on, because they were not relevant to daily life.

Chagall's work embodies several features of this typical cluster of Jewish discourse. His paintings are filled with many colorful details of animals or flowers, but although each figure may be drawn in a vivid, even realistic manner, the figures themselves are mostly abstractions, taken out of their normal realistic context. They serve as selected, emblematic representatives of several fictional domains and of a global perception of such general concepts as "nature," "love," or "light."

This cluster of "Jewish discourse" coincided with typical aspects of Modernism. An Italian Futurist manifesto declared, "Death to time and space!" Proust and Joyce exemplified that attitude in Modernist fiction. No continuity of space, time, and causality is required in a Chagall painting. His compositions and asides are guided by private associations. Yet the details themselves are given intensive attention, as endowed with symbolic value. Many of his paintings are "talkative"—they have a lot to say and try to say it all. There are no better examples for Chagall's folksy use of "Jewish discourse" than his associative, metaphorical, whimsical autobiography—and the tour de force of his early work, the *Introduction to the Yiddish Theater* (discussed in chapters 5 to 7).

Paradoxical as it may seem, pragmatic individualism was a prominent feature of traditional Jewish behavior. In spite of the stringent religious rules and social constraints and conventions imposed on daily behavior in the small, transparent town and the strong, folklorized stereotypes of a historical and collective worldview of the community, personal effort was the mainspring of Jewish life. The two most prestigious activities in Jewish society were learning and trade; a Yiddish proverb conjoins them in a rhyme, *tóyre iz di beste skhóyre* ("learning is the best merchandise"). For success in either of them, individual energy, talent, and effort are required. Indeed, Jews did not work in disciplined groups of people in factories or fields, and even the tailors, shoemakers, and other artisans (over a third of the Jewish population in Vitebsk at Chagall's time) had very few apprentices.

With the Modern Jewish Revolution in the nineteenth and early twentieth century, this tendency toward pragmatic individualism was transformed into an individualism of consciousness. Each person broke out of the strong chains of a totalizing religion and folklore, with their collective answers to all questions, their imposing conventions and social pressures of a small town. Hence, the high value assigned in the new Jewish culture to poetry and autobiography, genres focusing on individual consciousness. Introspection gave the individual the truth of his or her internal world and internal strength—and he or she was alone in the world. A Jewish-German writer argued that every poet is a Jew, whether he was born one or not, because Jews are the ultimate individualists in the pulverizing big city.[22] And the Russian poetess Marina Tsvetaeva wrote: "Every poet is a Yid."

Chagall's capricious and willful compositions and behavior were part of that individualism. He threw a temper tantrum when the Yiddish Theater's director Aleksey Granovsky put a real towel on his fantastically painted stage, and he broke the chairs in the Hadassah Synagogue in Jerusalem forty years later when he discovered that his magnificent Biblical windows were "buried" in a modest edifice. Nevertheless, his fame and general reception were due in part to his appeal to the most common stereotypes of Jewish and non-Jewish life.

THINKING ABOUT PICASSO

Chagall was quick to learn the languages of Modernist art and agile in distancing himself from them. This stance of independence is common in Chagall's typical style, his polyphony or demonstrative eclecticism. Below are two examples, one in black and white and one in color: *Thinking About Picasso* and *I and the Village*.

In the simple drawing *Thinking About Picasso*, 1914 (no. 22), we can see in a nutshell the full complexity of his approach—paralleling the complexity of his mind. The accepted title of this picture is misleading; the Russian text inside the painting says the exact opposite: "I am fed up with Chagall thinking about Picasso." It is a black-ink drawing, apparently made after Chagall's trip from Paris to Russia in June 1914 and the outbreak of World War I, which made it impossible for him to return to Paris and left him disoriented about the future course of his work. His friend and critic Abram Efros wrote in his book on Chagall's art (published in 1918) about the artist's current impasse, after having achieved his first triumphs at an early age. This drawing seems to reflect that dead end. Picasso was a disquieting challenge for Chagall throughout his life, and in his farewell to Russia written in 1922 at the end of his autobiography, he appeals to Picasso and a few other French artists and friends to accept him back.

In the center of the drawing, a house with separate black and white patches in simple geometrical shapes—either hard-edged or shaded in like shadows with soft boundaries—resulting in a two-dimensional, flat presentation. Indeed, it is an entirely minimalist house, a stenographic notation registering the signs of a house: a square frame, a slanted roof, one door, two windows, three steps with a rectangle for a store sign above it, and a schematic brick base (the three steps are reminiscent of his mother's store in many paintings). All those units look like letters of some elementary alphabet. Traversing the roof are two stripes with simplified shaded and white areas; one stripe bleeds from the triangle roof to the square house—a gesture indicating the autonomy of spatial forms. In the upper-left corner of the drawing is an inverted four-square structure echoing the house's geometry—it may be an abstraction of the abstraction of a house, or of a folded paper representing a house, or a hieroglyph of a home with triple "roofs" pointing downward and to the sides, uncertain of the direction of gravity, or a gesture toward Cubism.

The house itself floats diagonally; divorced from any street or ground (although embellished with a decorative bricklike base), it seems to defy gravity. Placed as it is in the center of the drawing, the house forms a diamond, capriciously challenging the rectangular paper on which it is drawn. In Chagall's abbreviated vocabulary, the house signals his own provincial home, floating unstably in space, or his return to it in an unreal world and with a topsy-turvy echo above it. Both the house and its abstraction have spiral-like doodles, perhaps indicating smoke, music, or even a snail's enclosure in his own world. A lavish tail and schematized snout are attached to the house, transforming it into a fox. Chagall seems to say that returning to his own home base, however unrealistically it is floating in the air, he "outfoxed" Picasso. The same *fiksl* from Jewish folk songs ("a sly, maverick little fox) reappears later in Chagall's illustrations to Hofshteyn's long poem *Grief*.

A text, written in a childish hand and in schematized, simplified Russian printed letters, floats like smoke above the roof. It is written out in caps, as in a caption, declaring: SHAGAL NADOEL MNE DUMAYA [O] PIKASO ("I am fed up with Chagall thinking [about] Picasso."). The "about" ("*o*" in Russian) is missing, unless we find it in the spiral protruding from the chimney; thus the text could also read, "thinking Picasso." The "o" however, does appear in the shortened version of the text below. Here it reads, *Dumaya o Pik* ("Thinking about Pik"); in a Picasso-like pun, Chagall uses the first syllable of that artist's name, "pik," which in Russian means "peak"—in this case, the summit of art. The placement of this inscription, however, suggests as a subtext a popular although vulgar Yiddish idiom, *ikh hob im in tokhes* ("I have him in my ass," i.e., I don't give a damn about him).

In the upper-right corner is a cloud, as if derived from Symbolist painting, from which a long arm stretches down (an allusion to Michelangelo?) to touch (with the famous tip of a finger) the inverted foot of the topsy-turvy artist. The soft, rounded Symbolist area in the upper right is set in opposition to the Cubist forms in the center. The representation of a person with a poet's sideburns, who looks like Picasso (or is it Chagall, with his clownish, inverted feet? or Chagall disguised as Picasso?), utilizes a third stylistic language as a gesture against Cubism. Basically, it is a simplified, realistic drawing of a human figure with a recognizable face. Rudimentary shading indicates a three-dimensional body with rounded limbs. The body is not broken down into a multitude of shards of geometric shapes, as in an Analytical Cubist portrait. But at the same time, it exhibits a drastic antire-

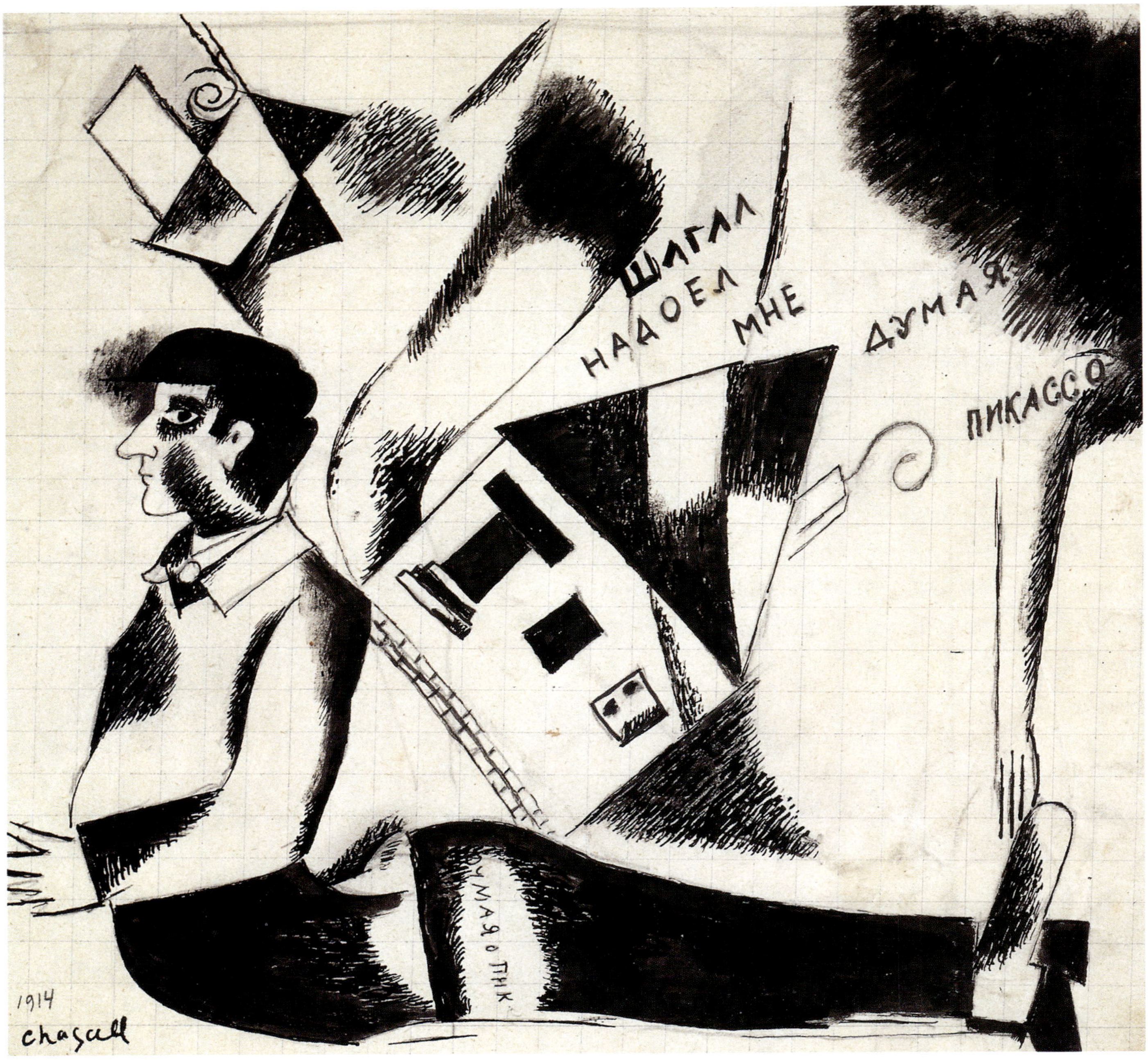

19. ***Thinking About Picasso.*** *1914. Black ink on paper, 19.1 x 21.6 cm. Musée national d'art moderne, Centre Georges Pompidou, Paris*

alistic gesture—the naturalistic outline of a human figure is suddenly bent ninety degrees backward in an entirely unnatural way. In the light of Chagall's own pronouncements, it could also be read: "I don't give a damn about reality if I have to fill a corner of my drawing."

The clownishly inverted left foot and the free-floating house placed in the artist's inverted lap indicate the willful arrangement of a fictional world and invite the spectator to interpret it and provide a context and a narrative. If Picasso's paintings ask us to rethink art, Chagall's ask us to rethink reality.

This drastic break in the naturalistic depiction of a human figure (it cannot be predicted when moving slowly your eyes along the "normal" body) can be described by the metaphor of "Catastrophe theory."[23] It is cognate to Kafka's drastic breaks of realistic credibility in the midst of an otherwise pedantic, realistic description. In his story *Blumfield, an Elderly Bachelor*, for example, two little balls pop up suddenly in a bachelor's apartment and keep bouncing up and down. In the early story *The Judgment*, Georg Bendemann commits suicide for no reason that can be discerned from what preceded it. And the first sentence of *The Trial* opens with the strange, implausible event of K.'s non-arrest arrest; then, taking that catastrophe for granted, there is a step-by-step description in realistic, almost tedious detail of an arrest (that may turn out to be a "mistake" or a "joke"). Such sudden "catastrophes"—and their smaller echoes and forerunners, strange (in Kafka) or teasing (in Chagall)—stir us to question the realism of the work of art as a whole or the different order of meaning we are invited to give the text.

One difference between fiction and painting, however, lies in the fact that literary texts are linear—we get to the catastrophe only when we get to it (for that reason, Kafka often announces the basic catastrophe in the opening), while in painting, the catastrophe may appear in the midst of a figure, and our eye finds it immediately, even before we observe the naturalistic parts of the figure. It is a perfect example of the central literary device that the Russian Formalist Viktor Shklovsky called *ostranneniye* ("making strange"), which calls the reader's attention to the text as an artificial object made by its author rather than an illusion of a "real" world. Bertolt Brecht borrowed Shklovsky's concept for his key term *Verfremdung* ("alienation"), denoting the purposeful breaking down of the realistic illusion in theater. Sometimes Chagall did not need much—just one major "catastrophe"—to call our attention to the willful strangeness of the painting, as in a figure of a woman standing on her head beside a normally standing man

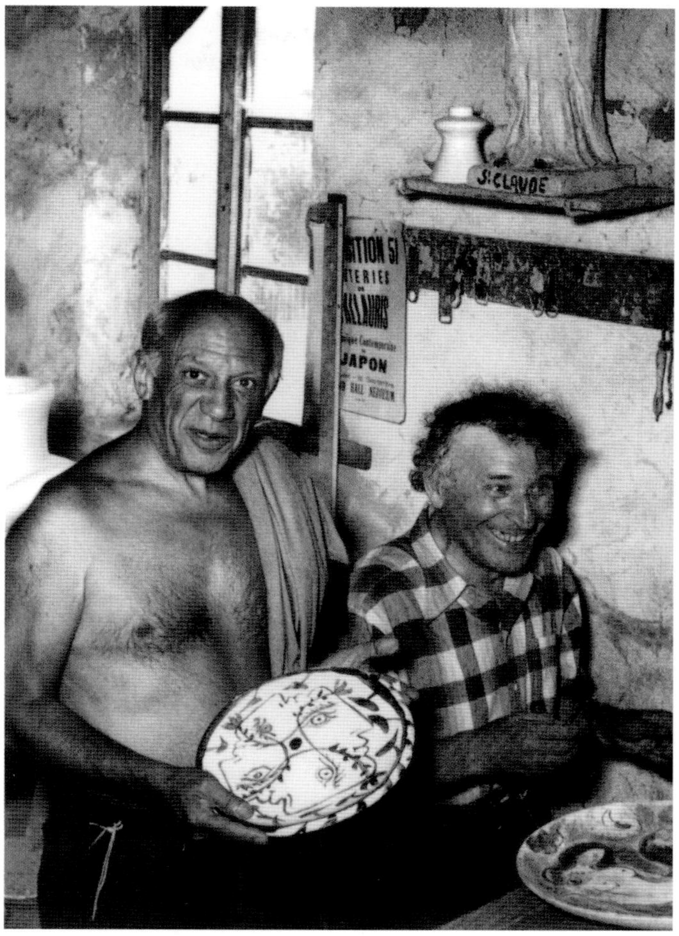

Picasso and Chagall working at the Madoura ceramics factory in Vallauris, 1951. Courtesy Comité Marc Chagall, Paris

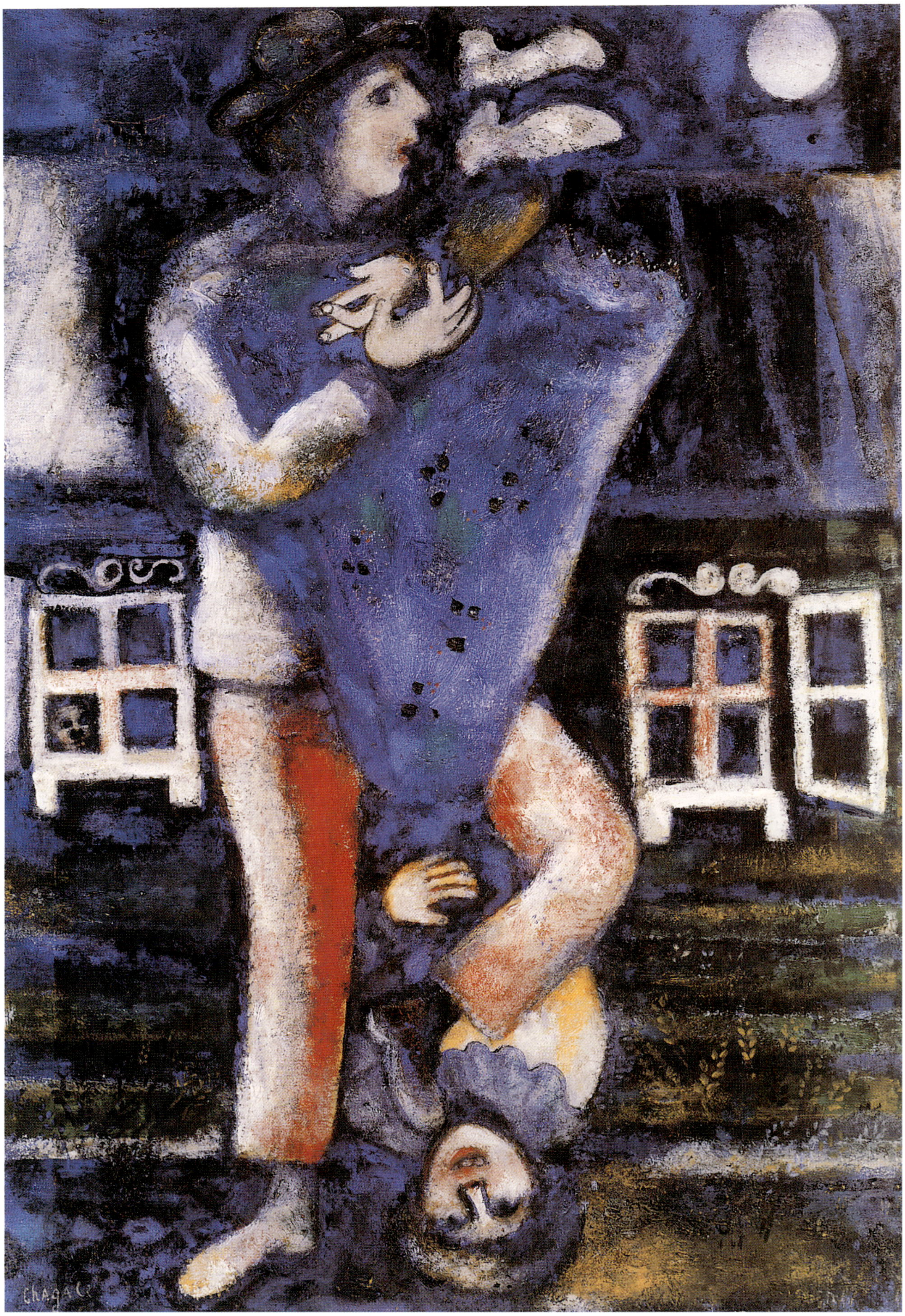

20. ***The Stroll.*** *1929. Oil on canvas, 55.5 x 39 cm. Private collection*

(see *The Stroll*, 1929, no. 20). It is very different indeed from the Cubist decomposition of the whole body or face, less systematic or comprehensive, and therefore more striking, specific, and recognizably Chagallian.

In *Thinking About Picasso*, the basic catastrophe—the defiance of normal human anatomy—is joined by a few secondary catastrophes and willful deformations such as the house that defies gravity and runs off as a fox, and the topsy-turvy abstraction of the house in the upper-left corner, looking down on it all from an inverted perspective. Such willful catastrophes, drastic breaks in a normal, realistic flow, appear in many forms and were Chagall's trademark almost from the beginning. Indeed, Chagall was a lyrical joker, an optimist of an absurdist world perception, a comedic Kafka. Chagall and Kafka's affinity is especially obvious in the realization of metaphors—a technique that is not metaphoric at all but, on the contrary, takes every metaphor literally and depicts it as a fact or a figure inside the fictional world, thereby making that world itself absurd. Such is the huge insect that Gregor Samsa actually turns into in Kafka's story *Metamorphosis*; or Chagall's depiction of a Jew with a sack on his back in *Over Vitebsk*, 1915–20 (no. 74), who actually "goes over the houses"—the literalization of a Yiddish idiom meaning "is a beggar" (see chapter 4).

The composition of *Thinking About Picasso* places a three-dimensional figure (the person) along with a two-dimensional object (the image of the house) in the two-dimensional space of the paper. No single stylistic principle is responsible for the overall order of the painting; a focus of attention at one end is not echoed but compensated for by a different focus of attention on the other end. This new kind of composition, of asymmetrical balancing of opposite centers of gravity, is a concomitant of the heterogeneity of styles and fictional domains in Chagall's work.

The modular elements assembled in a Chagall painting enter into various negotiations with each other: of metonymy, metaphoricity, analogy, inclusion, counterpoint, and composition. But why this specific selection of those modules rather than others? This question can be answered only in a Yiddish manner, with the question, "Why not?" Or better, with a Yiddish riddle:

> "What is green, hangs on the wall, and whistles?"—A herring. "Why green?"—It's my herring, I can paint it as I want. "Why hangs on the wall?"—I hung it there. "And why whistles?"—So you have something to ask.

Chagall knew a lot about herrings (his father carried barrels of them and his mother sold them in her store), and he painted the faces of his figures as he felt like (especially green). In some sense, this colloquial anecdote describes the composition of many Chagall paintings. And the artist justified even his formal devices in a similar manner. In a review of Chagall's art written in Paris in 1914, Lunatsharsky wrote:

> When at work, his caprices or his tastes, in a manner incomprehensible to himself (if you wish, subconsciously), prod him: 'Why is it forbidden? Why not? Why not make a purple cow? Why not paint a man walking on the ceiling? Why not break up the sky into several unequal triangles, and color each as the soul pleases?'[24]

The painter is the absolute authority—he is not an omniscient but an omnipotent author—and to make his whimsical personality conspicuous he must distort realistic representations. The device of colors overflowing boundaries of objects is explained in his autobiography: "Uncle Yuda always lies on the oven, doesn't even go to the prayer house, he prays at home at the window. He mumbles something quietly, and the yellow color slides down his face to the window molding, flows outside and spreads over the dome of the church. . . ."

Chagall's style of colors overflowing the boundaries of objects developed in Paris in 1911, although the story about Uncle Yuda refers to an earlier time.

COLOR AND SPATIAL FORM

Color complicates the issue immensely, and Chagall placed a great emphasis on it. (He was even dubbed the "best colorist in Paris" by Riccioto Canudo in 1914.) The liberation of color from the boundaries of depicted objects is a basic trait of much Modernist painting. Artists as diverse as Vincent van Gogh, Henri Matisse, and Vassily Kandinsky recognized color as an independent expressive force with psychological, spiritual, or musical qualities affecting the viewer in an unmediated way, which does not lend itself to verbal paraphrase. To do so it must deviate from natural colors. Kandinsky wrote in Munich in 1912, "Generally speaking, color directly influences the soul. Color is the keyboard, the eyes are the hammers, the soul is the piano with many strings. The artist is the hand that plays, touching one key or another purposively, to cause vibrations in the soul."[25]

Kandinsky, arguably the inventor of abstract painting, was influenced by the theories of Wilhelm

Worringer, a professor of aesthetics in Munich who, in his book *Abstraktion und Einfühlung* ("Abstraction and Empathy," 1908, soon thereafter translated into English), formulated a general theory about the two trends that alternate in art history: "abstraction," which generates open-ended geometrical patterns, and "empathy," depicting human bodies or nature. While abstract patterns are unlimited and timeless, empathy dwells on the living, hence mortal, men or trees in realistic situations. There is no evidence that Chagall was directly familiar with Worringer's writings, but such theories had a fluid presence in the intellectual and artistic atmosphere of the period. Robert Delauney, who included Chagall in an exhibition of young Parisian artists shown in Munich, had contacts with the German Expressionists. In his paintings, Chagall combined both poles—abstraction and empathy—and this attitude also influenced his treatment of color.

For Chagall, color fulfilled both an abstract aesthetic function, affecting the spectator directly, and an expressive function, accompanying the presented world. Indeed, he often emphasized both aspects in the same painting, with some color areas subordinated to the outlines of figures or spatial forms, and others independent and dominant in parts of the painting. Colors that are independent of object boundaries are clearly abstract art, although in Chagall they don't dominate the whole painting. And colors overlapping objects or figures can be abstract, too, if the color has no realistic relation to its object. In the first case, an abstract area in the painting is created; in the second case, the color is abstracted from the body and interacts with the other colors. This is similar to metrical poetry, in which the sound of a word interacts with other sounds to create a musical pattern. What results is a juggling act in which each painting exhibits an asymmetrical equilibrium of painterly and representational forces. Chagall treated all other strata that operate in his works in a similar dual manner.

Generally speaking, we may distinguish five major strata that interact in figurative paintings: (1) individuals (human and animal figures and objects); (2) the social functioning of those individuals; (3) continuity of a presented situation; (4) forms and shapes in space; and (5) color. The first three are aspects of the presented world, and the last two are aspects of the organized painting. Whereas the chief innovation of the Fauves lies in the fifth stratum (color), and of Cubism in the fourth (spatial form), Chagall's innovations lie primarily in the second and third: figures are separated from their normal social functioning and are taken out of any realistic continuity. He imaginatively played with color as well and used non-realistic deformations in all five strata. In different works, Chagall autonomized and deformed one or several of these strata, while simultaneously evoking their presence. Thus, perspective is suggested and then subverted; human figures are deformed or stand on their head; heads fly, legs appear in another corner of the painting, etc. Yet precisely this "making strange" device, as described by Viktor Shklovsky, brings our attention to the fictionality of the painting. The continuities of a presented situation are disrupted, yet, by the same token, foregrounded, emphasizing both the disruption as well as the disrupted figure itself.

In traditional, especially realistic, painting (admittedly, a general label lumping together a great variety of styles) all five strata basically overlap, or make believe they do under the principle of representation. To be sure, in a Renaissance painting as well, spatial form and color may create autonomous patterns. Such are the patches and traces of a given color dispersed in various parts of the canvas and echoing each other, or the semi-abstract shaping of a drapery, as well as the symmetry of the depicted world. And yet the appearance and boundaries of each color and spatial pattern are, on the whole, realistically "motivated"; that is, they are "justified" by the nature of the depicted objects. It is the selection of the objects partial abstractions.

Such coordination between strata became shaky in the age of Modernism. In various trends of Modernism, one stratum or another was subverted; in the extreme, in his *objets trouvés*, Marcel Duchamp uses real (non-art) objects separated from their normal social setting and functionality. His famous urinal, is separated from its plumbing and placed in a museum. In a fully abstract painting, there may be no represented individuals at all, and the first three strata are absent.

Paul Cézanne foregrounded semi-geometric forms in space, whose very principle seems to be in opposition to the flowing, curvilinear forms of vegetation. Nonetheless, he motivated those shapes by objects found and selected in real nature (e.g., rectangular yellow buildings among green trees) as well as—and here is a leap—by the nature of his meta-language, such as the painter's visible brush strokes overtly covering the sky. The next generation did not worry about natural motivation, but broke up a tree or a face into separate color areas (Andre Derain's trees, or Chagall's window frames in *Paris Through the Window*, no. 43), or broke up the human figure into semi-geometric independent units (in Cubism), with their autonomous shadings of lighter and darker hues. Chagall

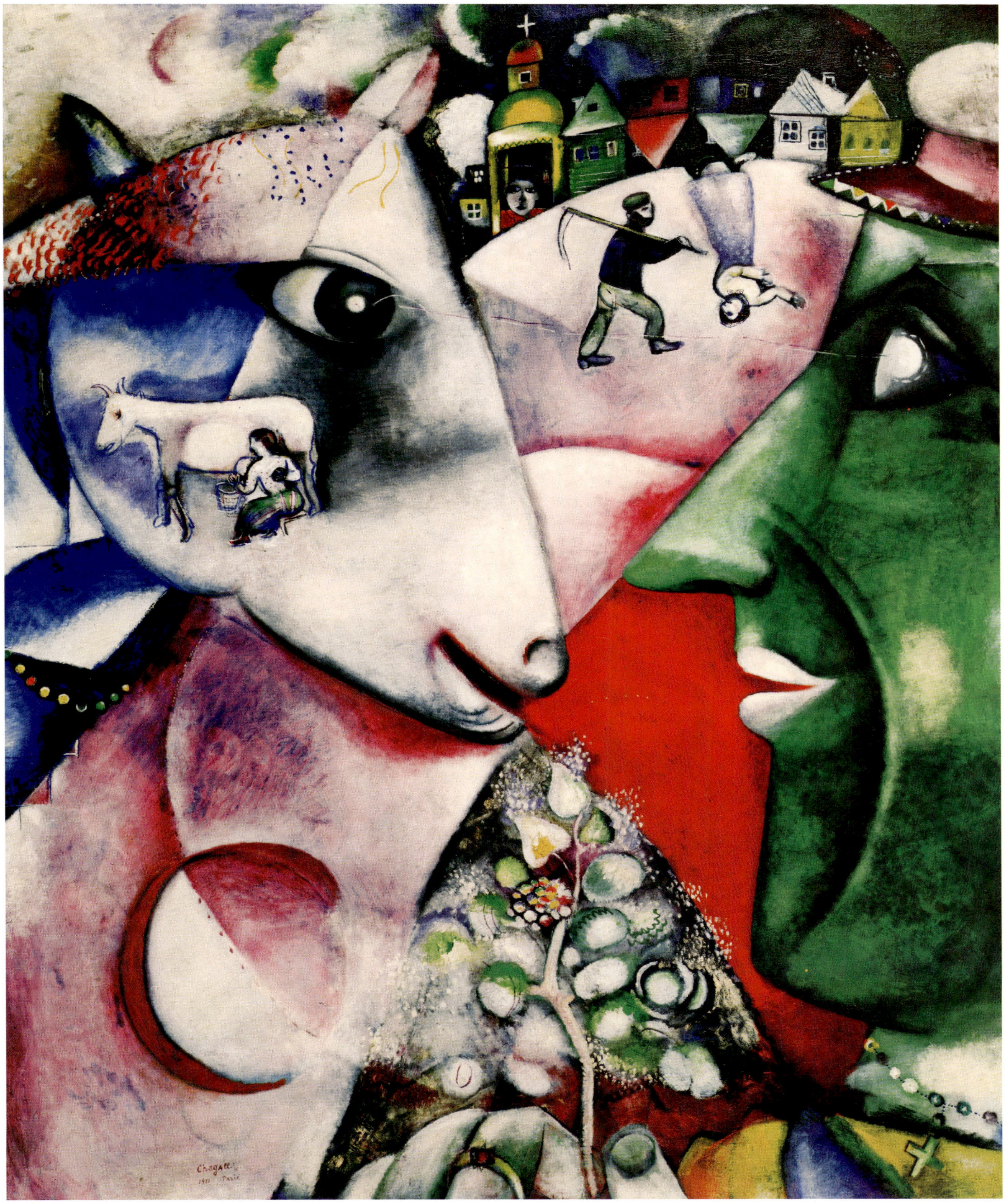

21. ***I and the Village.*** *1911. Oil on canvas. Museum of Modern Art, New York*

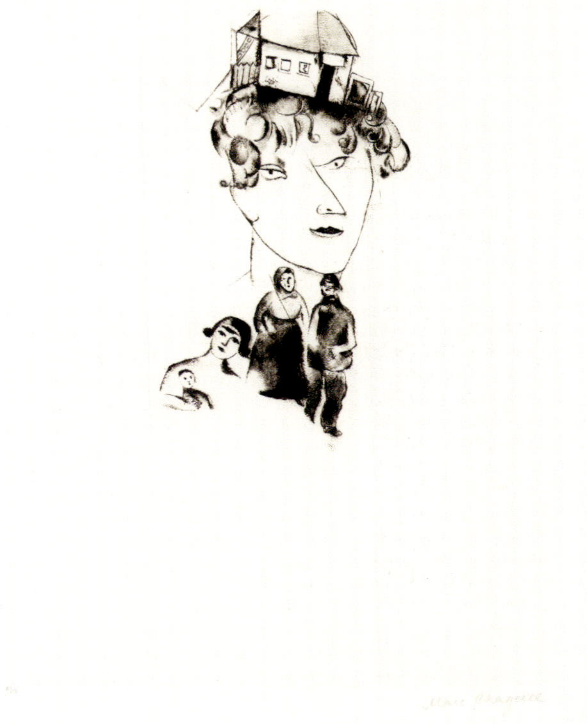

22. ***Self-Portrait.*** *1923. From Mein Leben: 20 etchings and drypoint on paper. Paul Cassirer, Berlin (also printed in* ***Chalastre,*** *no. 2, Paris, 1924, with excerpts from Chagall's autobiography in Yiddish). Chagall in Berlin, with the memory of his house, his parents, and accompanied by his wife and daughter.*

did both: He played between Realism and nonrealism in all five strata, and shifted his emphasis in mid-painting from one stratum to the other.

I AND THE VILLAGE

I and the Village, 1911 (no. 21), in collection of the Museum of Modern Art in New York, is one of the most familiar icons of Modern art, yet it still needs a full interpretation. The location is clearly in Russia, either in Chagall's mythological Vitebsk or Lyozno. Village images include a man walking back from harvest; small houses and a small church. It was created in Paris in 1911–12 but from a distance of memory. The distance is underscored by the unrealistic, impossible proportions and discontinuities between the individual figures or objects. The connections between the objects are conceptual rather than photographic.

A simple case of a conceptual composition can be observed in Chagall's *Self-Portrait*, 1923 (no. 22), an etching made for the autobiographical album *My Life, My World* (1922).[26] There is obviously no realistic transition between the house and the face or the dead parents and his living wife and daughter. Chagall seems to describe his arrival in the West in 1922, carrying his old house on his head and the memory of his family. The memory of the house has pushed aside the phylacteries on his forehead, called in Hebrew *Bayit shel rosh*, or the "house of the head," worn for prayer. Thus, the unity of the painting is conceptual rather than realistic, although each detail may be quite realistically depicted.

Similar relations determine the composition of *I and the Village*. At first glance, the painting strikes us with its strong, independent colors, intersecting with various semi-geometric forms. But clearly, the thematic aspects—the fictional world and its conceptual composition—are as strong a force in the painting as the formal aspects. This is not a Cubist guitar or still life, unimportant thematically and used as conventional motifs that would not detract attention from the formal expression. Here, on the contrary, the formal technique highlights the representation of a world.

Most of the canvas is occupied by two faces in profile, of a young man (Chagall himself as a high school student[27]) and a "Chagallian animal" (here, a calf or a cow), looking into each other's eyes with pity and love, as underscored didactically by the thin line drawn between their eyes. Indeed, the painting is the first in a series of works raising, in a painterly manner, crucial issues of Chagall's identity and ambivalence (see "Identities" in chapter 3). Young Chagall joins the

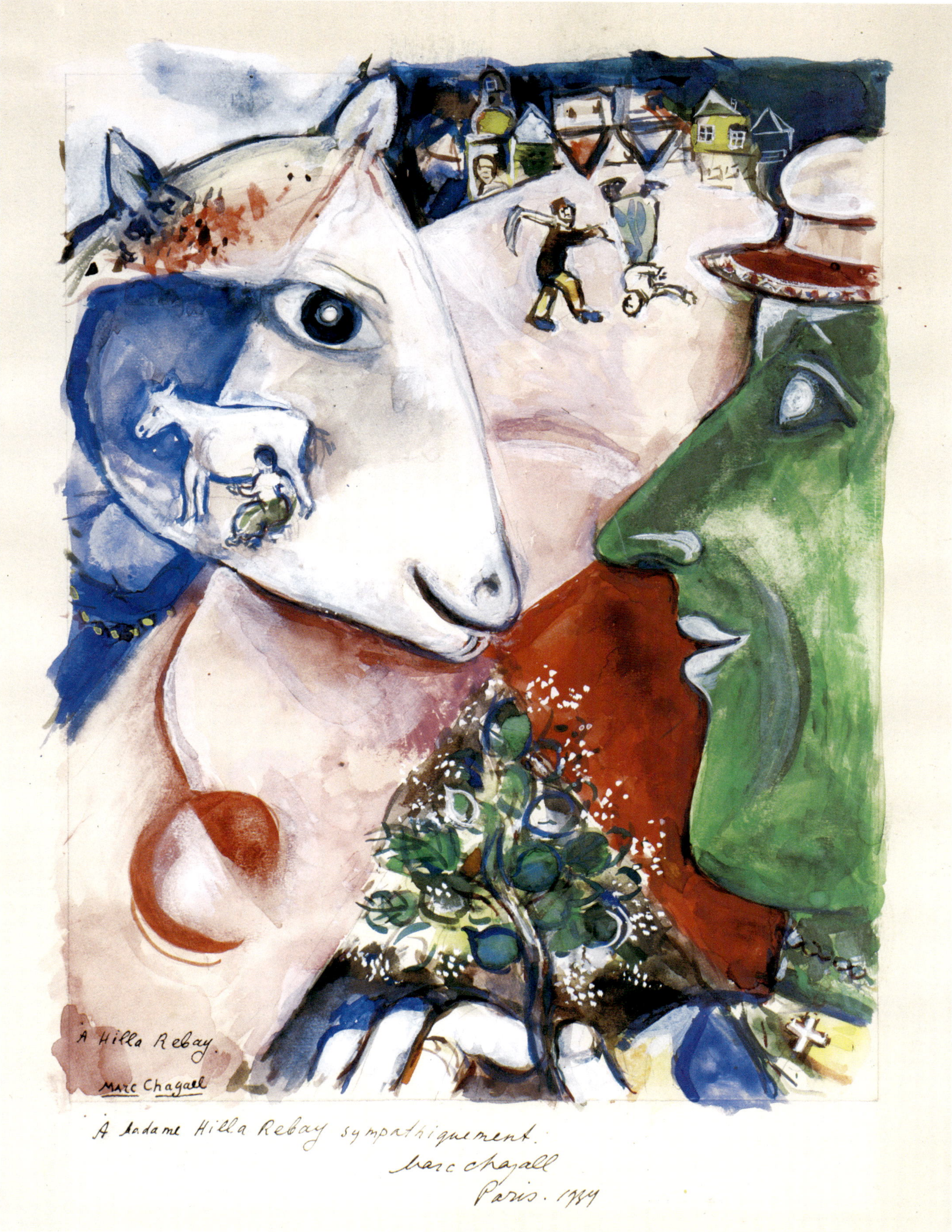

23. ***I and the Village.*** *1923–24. Gouache, watercolor, and pencil on paper, 39 x 30 cm. Solomon R. Guggenheim Museum, New York. Dedicated to Hilla Rebay, founder of the Guggenheim Museum in New York, Paris, 1934*

education and culture of the Christian world, accepts its views, symbols, and uniform, embraces its love of animals, yet he is still a Jew.

In Yiddish folk semiotics, "village" indicated the world of the *goyim,* the Christian peasants. Modern Yiddish culture, literature, and ideologies turned that stereotype into a positive value and promoted the return to nature, to an attitude of authentic people rooted in their soil and working on it, to a world of animals and sincere, sexual love.

The green man wears a cross—which shows Chagall's effort to accept and identify himself with Christian culture. He also sports a gymnasium uniform hat, which he wore proudly in several photos of his late teens or early twenties. In his autobiography he wrote: "In fact, I wanted a cockade [a uniform hat with insignia] very much. If you wear a cockade and an officer walks by you, do you salute him? Officials, soldiers, policemen, gymnasium students—we are all like one family." This is written by someone who, by his own account, as a boy hid under the bed when a *Gorodovoy* (a policeman on the beat) passed by the windows of his house!

In his St. Petersburg years, 1907–1910, Chagall was exposed to the temptation of Christianity. His admired and awe-inspiring teacher Léon Bakst was a Jew who converted to Christianity in 1903; and among the elite students of his class (the dancer Nijinsky, Princess Obolenskaya) was Countess Sofia (Dymshits) Tolstoy, the Jewish-born wife of the writer Aleksey Tolstoy. Furthermore, Chagall's role model, the sculptor Marc Antokolsky, a Jew from the Pale who successfully participated in Russian high culture in St. Petersburg and whose first name Chagall took, created a famous sculpture of Jesus Christ. In his own Russian poetry of 1909–10, Chagall imagined himself as a crucified Christ child, as in the painting *Golgotha*, 1912 (no. 40), a work proximate in time to *I and the Village* (see chapter 3). And yet in the image, as in real life, he recoils from a full conversion. On his left index finger he wears a Star of David and his flower offering is made of a branch of grapes, as in a synagogue ornament. Is it a sign of his origin? Or a challenge? Or a sincere acceptance of both cultures? Throughout his life he kept his ties with both cultures and drew on both, but religion required an either/or decision. How to interpret this ambiguity is left to the reader; Chagall provided the tension itself.

Another face of Chagall may be discovered in *I and the Village* peeping out of the black, gaping space of the church[28] and occupying the whole space, while observing it all. Thus, two internal, "naïve" points of view are established, through which the other parts of the village world are perceived: the point of view of the green-faced man in the foreground, involved in the action, his gaze fixed on the animal head with the rest of the scene in the periphery of his vision; and the point of view of the smaller face looking out of the village church onto the free scene of emotions. Simultaneously, however, an external point of view is present, that of the painter-poet, who does not hide behind his work of art but manipulates the strata of the painting at will; he is both an omniscient and an omnipotent narrator. The painter keeps an ironic distance from this charged scene. He whimsically paints a row of colorful houses, some standing upside down on their sharp-edged roofs, and places the play of emotions in a context of orchestrated colors.

In the upper center of the painting, between the two faces, we see a peasant energetically striding with a scythe on his shoulders, returning to the village from a day of harvesting the field. A young woman in a long skirt, standing on her head, is inviting him to her home with a generous gesture of her hands. Human love, indicated in the inverted man-woman pair, is the simple, healthy love of a working peasant and a sensuous village woman. Similar inverted pairs reappear in later paintings (see *The Stroll*, no. 20).

A young peasant woman, or *shikse*, is perceived in Yiddish folklore as a healthy sexual being. A straight line (though this time unmarked) leads from the scythe through the woman's arms to Chagall's invisible right eye. The allure of love includes its fulfillment in fertility: inside the calf's head (and her dream or imagination) there is a mature cow and apparently the same peasant woman is milking it (white shirt, blue skirt). The calf, or cow, may also be a substitute for Chagall's fiancée, as animals represent Chagall himself in other cases (for example, the donkey in *Dedicated to My Fiancée*, 1911, no. 61, and in *The Birth*, 1911, no. 32).

In his autobiography Chagall wrote: "I often said I was not an artist, but some kind of a cow. What's the difference? I thought of placing her on my calling card." When he was commissar of art in Vitebsk he painted a green cow to be copied and displayed around the city on the first anniversary of the October Revolution. A green cow also opens his great mural *Introduction to the Yiddish Theater*.

Why a cow? One influence was classical Yiddish literature, in this case, Mendele Moykher Sforim's Yiddish book *Seyfer HaBeheymes* ("The Book of Livestock"). Like many *Maskilim* (intellectuals) of his time, Mendele was disgusted with the mores and manners of the Jewish *shtetl* and tried to bring his readers closer to nature (earlier, he wrote a book in Hebrew, *The History of Nature*). *The Book of Livestock* can be quoted at length in this connection; cows, horses, goats, and especially the touching story of a calf, are all echoed in Chagall's universe. Whether Chagall read Mendele or not, he shared the same attitude. Mendele's introduction says:

> As I got to know my animals better, they were like humans, flesh and blood, like people with all their senses, with feelings, and as I seriously observed their situation, their miserable life, how they are in Exile, suffering from the petty humans in the world—the feeling of pity drew me toward them [. . .] and their language, as strange as it seems, is often more intelligible than the over-clever, artificial, bookish language that was intentionally invented to screw your brain and remove the slightest thing from any logic.

The animal head in this painting may be a calf (with the dream of fertility and a cow indicated in its head). Functionally, the calf is a beloved to whom the young man in green offers a bunch of grapes inside a bouquet of flowers. Chagall had little connection with animals in real life, but he remembered the shock of seeing a calf being slaughtered by his grandfather, the butcher of Lyozno; the boy was overwhelmed with empathy and promised not to touch meat (a promise not kept). The calf was a figure of wholeness and pity in stories by Mendele (in Yiddish) and M. Z. Feierberg (in Hebrew). In Yiddish idioms, it plays a similar role: *kalb* ("a calf") may connote a saintly simpleton (as in *Yoshe Kalb*), and to be in "a calf's extasis" (*kelbershe hispayles*) means to be overwhelmed with exaggerated and ignorant, but sincere, excitement. But perhaps it is a mature cow? A cow in Yiddish is a *beheyme*, which also means an idiot—someone who is stupid or speechless. Indeed Chagall often called himself a *beheyme* (cow)—someone with no rational knowledge and yet possessing warm friendliness and intuition.

Chagall constructed his animals—usually outside of their realistic context or function—as parts of his culturally stereotypical but private fictional universe, never explicitly explained and never univalent. Animals for him could represent the warmth and endearing quality of a living being, symbolize the emotional but inarticulate impact of nonverbal communication, or epitomize the ideal of humans living in close contact with nature. This was an ideal that many Jewish contemporaries saw as specifically Christian, because of the patent contrast between the Jewish urban *shtetl* and the surrounding Christian villages, situated and working in nature, and consequently an ideal that came to play a major role in the Modern Jewish Revolution—in most of its political and cultural trends—with its emphasis on a return to the land and to nature.

For Chagall there was yet another connection. He felt stifled by his poor command of language when he joined Russian culture. He described a scene in the Russian school, when he tore up a book of four hundred pages: "let the wind read it in Russian." Stammering (from social embarrassment in a Russian class) became for him the mark of a Jew in Russian society, which he ascribed to Bakst as well. His youthful aspirations were to be a singer, a dancer, a violinist, or a painter—all nonverbal, emotional arts, where communication with the other is imaginative.

Although the painting emphasizes a "world," there are several conspicuous geometric forms independent of the figures of that world, claiming a competing, semi-geometric principle of organization. Most conspicuous is the imprecise circle in the center, which cuts through and ties together the animal, the man, and his flower offering. The circle is filled in with red color, sliding into white, and its circumference is marked by white or the local color: red, green, or blue, contrasting with the immediate color context. This circle is echoed by a smaller circle on the lower left, with inverted red and white colors, intersecting the major one, but not related to any presented figures. As in other paintings of this time, it may be read as the sun and the moon, as described in the act of creation: "And God made two great lights; the greater light to rule the day, and the lesser light to rule the night" (Genesis 1:16). The pair of circles appears in several paintings of this period (see the reading of *Homage to Apollinaire* in chapter 3). Chagall could not just paint abstract circles for their own sake, and he always tried to thematize them. It would be tempting to see here the influence of his friends Sonia (a Russian Jew) and Robert Delauney, but Chagall certainly knew this image from the earliest days of his life, from the first chapter of the Bible. And if the dates are correct, Chagall's paintings preceded Robert Delauney's theory of the two lights.

This geometric form is echoed in several semicircular lines, drawn in a nonconcentric manner. It includes two intersecting ovoid lines, which dissect the cow's head, dividing color areas, the impression of the globe's surface in the upper middle, and the tangential continuation of the big circle in the lower left. Some of the outlines of the objects and figures are also involved in the geometric network; like verbal ambiguities in poetry, they participate in both systems. Two invisible crisscrossing diagonal lines symmetrically divide the great circle like spokes of a wheel in the shape of a big, imprecise X. They touch the outlines of the two faces and create four sections with different functions in the painting. But the painting is longer than this four-part area, and a fifth wedge is inserted in the upper center, carrying the burden of the broader fictional situation. This segment subdues the geometry to create a horizon, or the upper limits of a globe, where the peasant pair and the village houses are placed. This could be almost a realistic presentation—but for the woman and two houses standing on their heads and the series of houses, which are unusually colorful and lined up in a chain, without the spaces between them that would be present in a real village.

Thus, spatial figures may act as independent geometric bodies or they may be motivated by realistic objects and dependent on their shape. Competition persists between the two principles of composition as does mutual reinforcement. The overall semi-geometric organization of space compensates for any discontinuity in the fictional space of the presented village, and vice versa; where one fails, the other takes over.

The same holds for color. Several bright colors are delineated with clear-cut boundaries, yet within each color division the colors are alive, interacting and shifting as they move through areas of saturation color to paler areas and even toward zones of complete whiteness. Color deviates from the natural function of indicating an object's surface in two major ways: an "unnatural," unexpected color covers the surface of an individual object, thereby stressing the autonomy and abstraction of color; or colors create spatial areas in their own right, overflowing bodily boundaries. The first mode, the use of unnatural colors, dominates Chagall's early Russian paintings; the second, color independent of the boundaries of objects, was added in his Paris years. Both work as a different kind of reality, shifting the emphasis from the presented world to the surface of the painting itself.

An example of the first mode in *I and the Village* is the green face; the color is precisely delineated by the form of the face, but the boundaries of the face itself are guided not by a realistic portrait (which Chagall certainly knew how to draw) but, in part, by the straight, slightly curving lines of geometric shapes. The incongruity of the green face makes such a strong statement that we don't notice that most of the head is cut out of the picture. Indeed, it is the relation between the human head and the animal head that counts here, rather than the presentation of a whole human or animal figure.

The peasant houses are also painted in strong, vibrant colors, in a country where buildings and garb were usually gray, and where the poet Vladimir Mayakovsky—at about the same time—caused a scandal even in Moscow by wearing a yellow sweater for a poetry reading. The white in the upper slice would, in another painting, suggest snow, but the man with the scythe and the bouquet below suggest harvest time, and thus turn the white into an unnatural color as well, indicating vacuous space rather than physical ground.

The second mode could take on two forms: either one color overflows the boundaries of objects, as in Chagall's story about Uncle Yuda, in which the yellow color flows over his beard, out of the window, and onto the dome of the church; or several colors divide the surface of a figure. For example, the face of Chagall's father in *Father*, 1910 (no. 5), is divided into several color areas, similar to the green stripe in the face of Matisse's *Portrait of Mme. Matisse*, 1905 (no. 4), as is his hat and the background. This can also be seen in the cow's head in *I and the Village*.

The same double-directed relationship that we observe between geometric forms and the fictional world holds true of the relations between color and spatial forms: In part, colors are confined within the limits of the semi-geometric figures, and, in part, they glide outside them. Red, subordinated to the geometric form in the circles, spills over boundaries and becomes a dominant, sweeping space of its own on the lower left, echoed throughout the picture. The strong confrontation of the two opposing colors, green and red, creates the central organizing power in the color composition of the painting, and they are tied together in the center by the central circle. It is this alliance of opposites that emphasizes the dark blue and black of the sky in the background. But the colors do not organize the space as a whole either and retreat in the upper part, giving way to the dominance of the fictional world: the peasant pair and the line of houses strung in a row.

The disproportion in the size of the objects is not entirely antiperspectival. The two friends in love, young man and animal, are shown close up and large, while the smaller village is indicated in the background. But there is no transition in represented space between them (in the form of streets, roads, or fields)—just a rising white, globelike surface. A possibility of perspective is suggested and then defied and discontinued. The contours of the two frontal figures and some of the houses look almost like flat paper cutouts (although there is some hint of roundness in the middle of the faces). On the other hand, the peasants, the milking scene, the fingers, and the fruit are three-dimensional.

The result is not an overall perspective but multiple planes placed one behind the other. Yet the order of the planes is sometimes confused. Thus, the visor of the schoolboy's hat is both part of the front plane and a base of the house in the distance. To reinforce this paradox, the line continues in a line of dots climbing around the house and merging with the smoke from the chimney. And the small milking scene is placed inside the large animal head, reversing perspective and forcing a nonrealistic reading (as a hope or a dream).

Roman Jakobson stated that "every metonymy is a metaphor," meaning that contiguity implies similarity.[29] In other words, every two disjointed items, placed side by side, may evoke a metaphorical construct between them. Thus, the boy's loving look and offer of a bouquet to the calf transforms the animal into a metaphor of his beloved. This is underscored by several additional metonymies: the parallel strings of beads on the necks of the boy and the calf; the parallel between this couple and the peasant couple in the background; the motherly function of the cow in the embedded milking scene; the parallel between the marked line and the line that leads from the scythe, through the woman's gesture, to the young man's hidden eye. Thus three competing principles of composition, based on three strata—presented world, spatial form, and color—intersect, subverting or reinforcing one another.

A later gouache and watercolor version of *I and the Village*, 1923–24 (no. 23), which Chagall gave to Hilla von Rebay (the founder of the Guggenheim Museum) in Paris in 1934, has almost all the elements of the painting, including the cross, but barely a trace of the Star of David.

DEFIANCE

From time to time, Chagall skirted a new style he tried to adopt or imitate, keeping his own fictional universe. Thus, *Cubist Landscape*, 1918 (no. 24), painted at the People's Art College that he founded in Vitebsk, is an almost immaculate Cubist composition imitating a collage with an ostensible wood surface and Chagallian snails and circles and globe at the top. It is clearly influenced by Malevich (see *A Non-Stop Station: Kuntsevo*, 1913, no. 25) who came to teach at Chagall's school in November 1919 (therefore the painting should be dated in the first half of 1920). But behind, or inside the two-dimensional Cubist collage, there is a three-dimensional perspective, a precise drawing of the People's Art College (as we can see in photos of the time), and a little Chagall walking with an umbrella toward the entrance.

In Chagall's iconography, an open umbrella means luck and accomplishment. He descends with an open umbrella, like a parachute (which had not yet been invented), over Paris in *Paris through the Window* and hovers with an umbrella above his mural *Introduction to the Yiddish Theater*, 1920 (no. 137). In a late gouache on paper, *Man with Umbrella*, 1940 (no. 33), we see a happy, content Chagall next to a red sun with the French national colors and Mediterranean vegetation. We are tempted to read it as the short-lived happiness of Chagall as a French citizen saved in "independent France," just before he was stripped of French citizenship. In Yiddish, the blessing *Got zol dikh bashiremen*, "May God protect you," is literally: "May God cover you with an umbrella." It may be derived from the Hebrew-Yiddish blessing: *Zol Got dikh sheymer u-matsil zayn* ("May God watch you and save you"—as pronounced in Chagall's Lithuanian dialect), or *Got iz mayn sheymer* ("God is my guardian"). Because in Hebrew only the consonants contain the lexical stem of the word, the echoing of the two words—one coming from German, one from Hebrew—makes an anagram (with a typical inverted order of the letters, often used in Biblical interpretation): ShiReM—SheyMeR (umbrella/guardian: ShRM/ShMR).

And on the left, on what looks like a simple, Cubist, yellow slab, Chagall surveyed his languages in their chronological order, climbing upward, in a multilingual recording of his name:

> שאגאל шагал шагал шагал шагал шагал // шагал шагал шагал chagall chagall chagall chagall шагал шагал шагал шагал художественное училище

The word *Shagal* in Russian means "he/you/I walked" (in a striding step, which Chagall often represented as striding upward on a diagonal), and Mayakovsky rhymed Chagall with *Shagal* ("and he strode / like Marc Chagall"). Hence, it could also be interpreted as: "Chagall walked and walked, through many languages, until he got to his triumph: The People's Art College." He apparently wrote the number of repetitions in each language as the number of years spent there, and in the same order. The basis is Yiddish (in small, printed and stylized letters), then eight (ten?) years in Russian (1900–10),[30] then four years in French (1910–14), then again four years in Russian (1914–18), culminating in the "Art College" (only the first word of

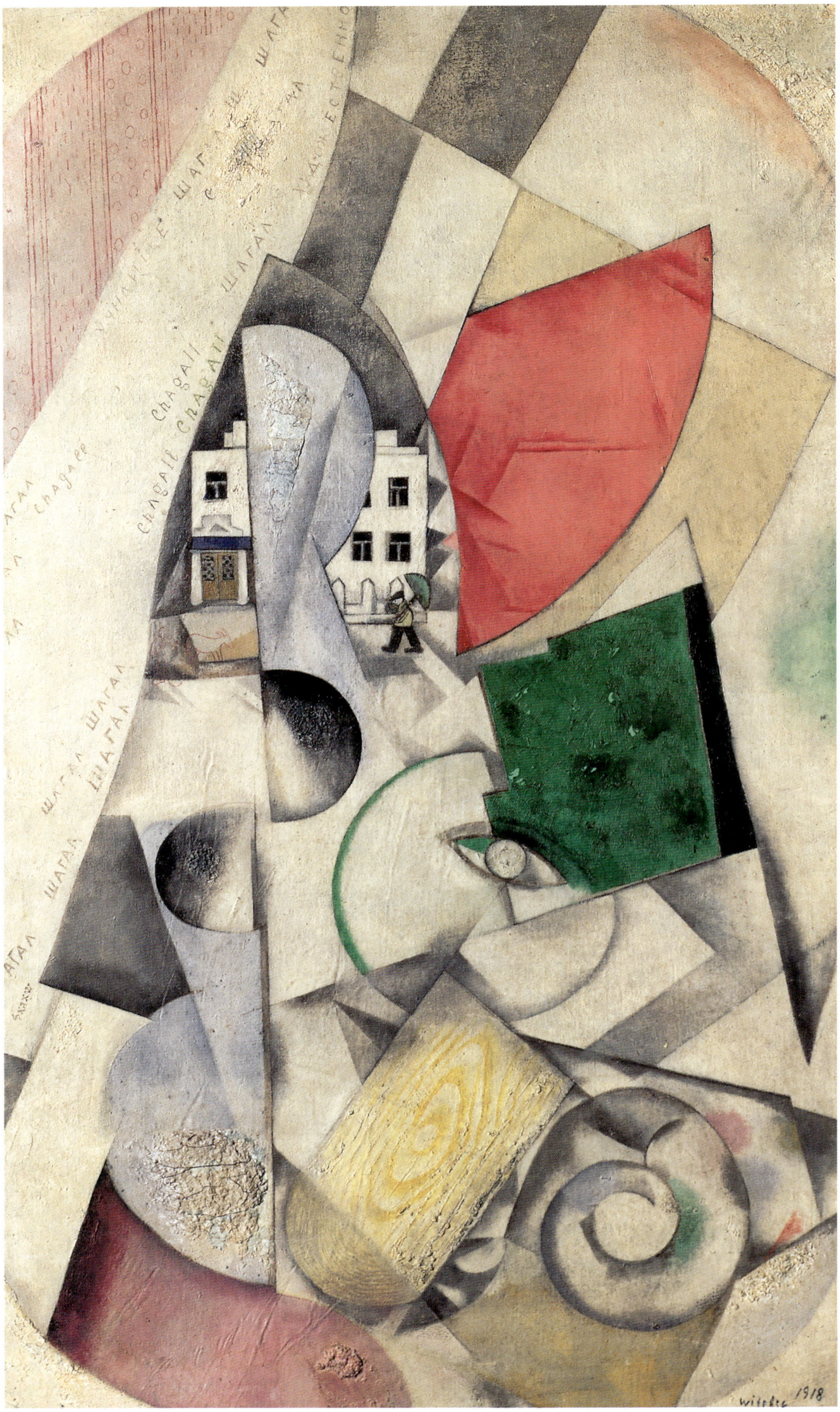

24. ***Cubist Landscape.*** *1918. Oil on canvas, 100 x 59 cm. Musée national d'art moderne, Centre Georges Pompidou, Paris*

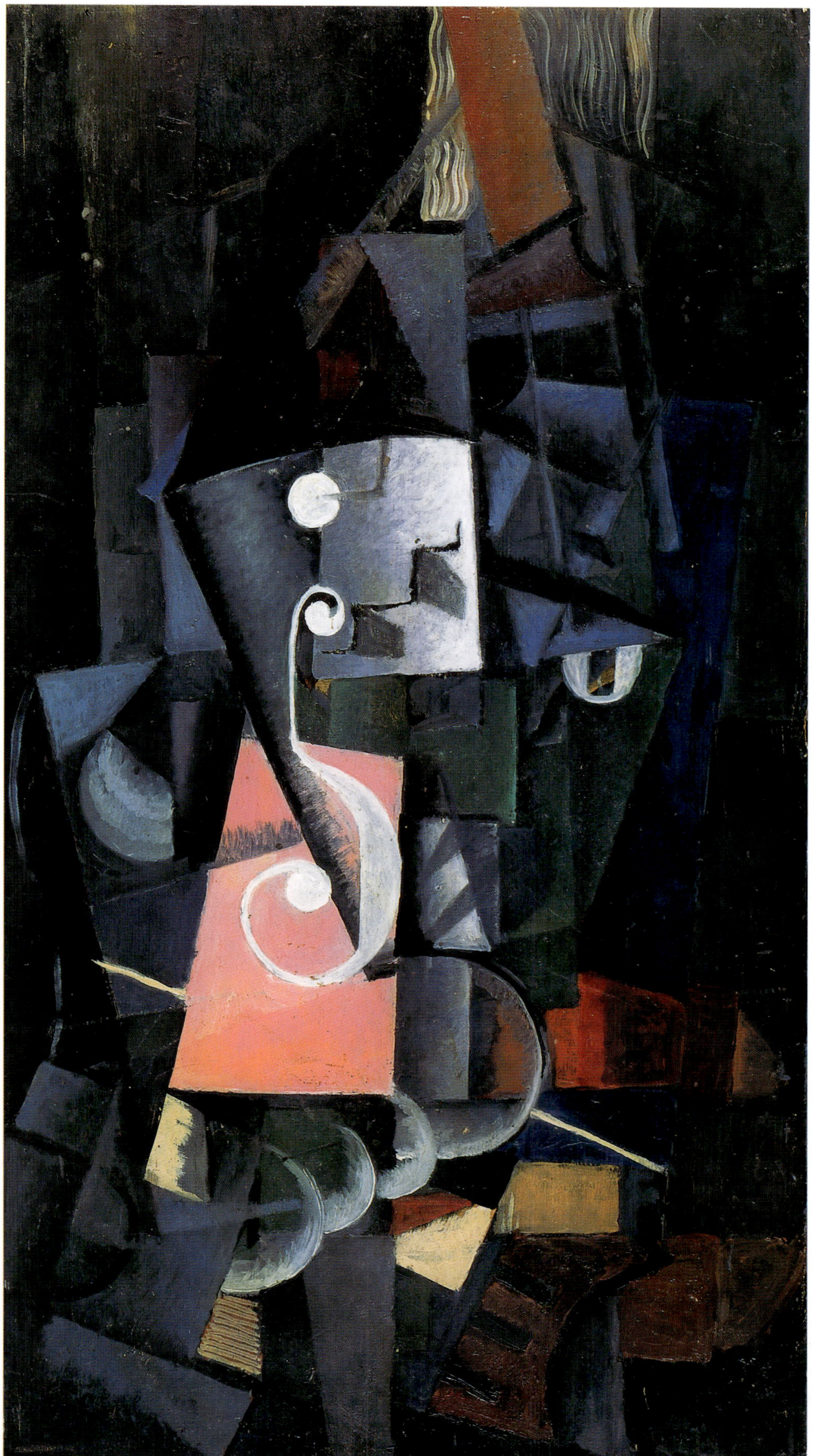

25. *Kazimir Malevich.* ***A Non-Stop Station: Kuntsevo.*** *1913. Oil on canvas, 49 x 25.5 cm. Tretyakov Gallery, Moscow*

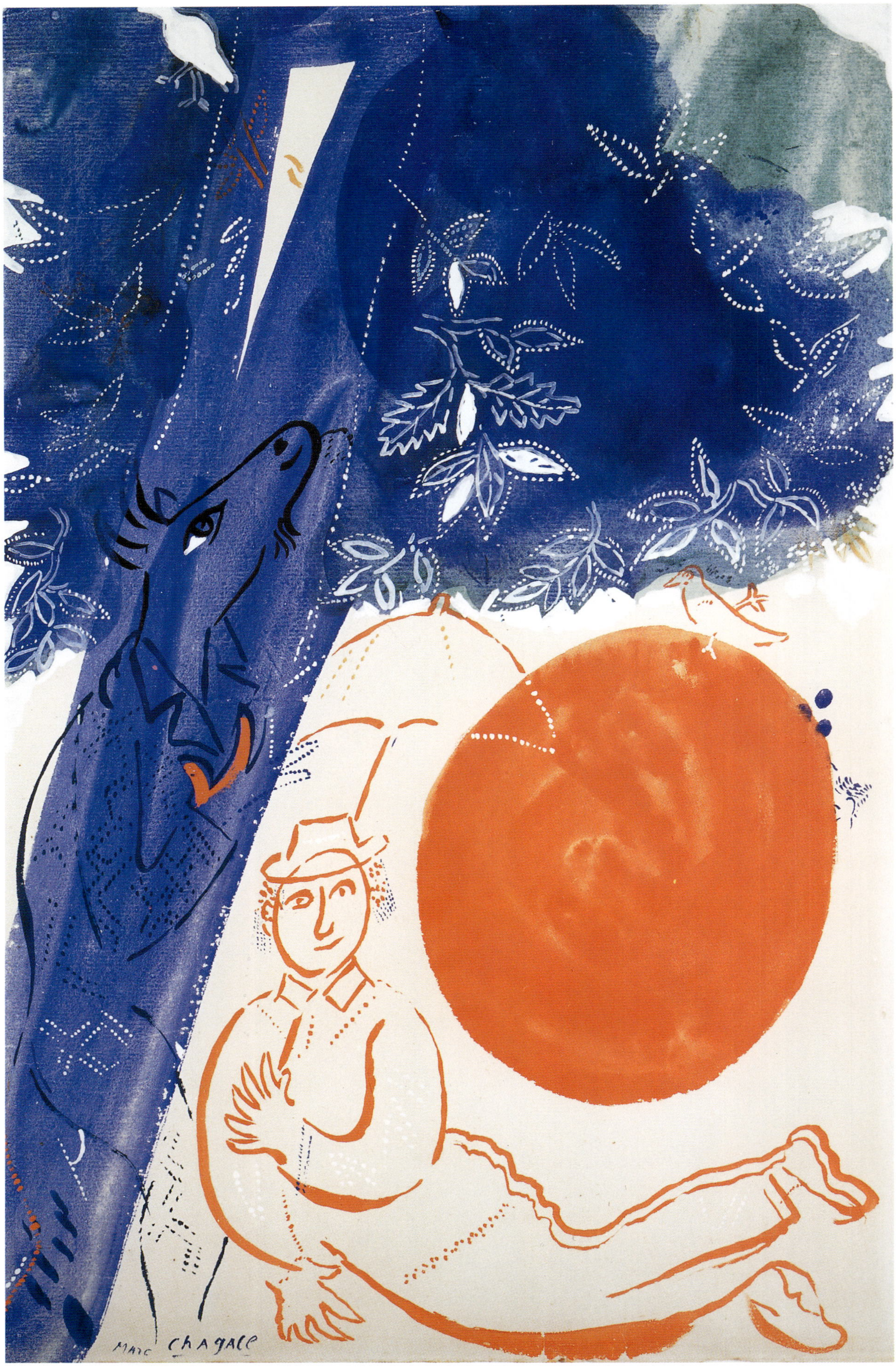

26. ***Man with Umbrella.*** *1940. Gouache on paper, 45 x 28.3 cm. Private collection*

the name "Art College"—*Khudozhestvennoe*—got in at the end of the ladder, the second word was placed earlier, on top). Now there is a place for the umbrella.

In the midst of the tensions between them, Chagall accepted Malevich's (and Picasso's) challenge and showed that he could work in the same mode, but immediately subverted it through stories from his personal odyssey and his fictional universe.

---

1. Werner Haftmann. *Marc Chagall*. New York: Harry Abrams, 1973, p. 7

2. On the theory of fictional worlds, see Thomas G. Pavel. *Fictional Worlds*. Cambridge, Mass.: Harvard University Press, 1986. Also, see my essay: Benjamin Hrushovski [Harshav]. "Fictionality and Fields of Reference: Remarks on a Theoretical Framework," in *Poetics Today*, vol. 5 (1984), no. 2.

3. Cendrars, Blaise. "Portrait," Oct. 1913, in *Selected Writings of Blaise Cendrars*, ed. by Walter Albert. New York: New Directions, 1966.

4. James Johnson Sweeney. "An Interview with Marc Chagall," in *Marc Chagall on Art and Culture*, p. 81.

5. Ibid, p. 43.

6. Norbert Lyton. "Chagall 'over the Roofs of the World,'" in: Compton, Susan. *Chagall*. London: Royal Academy of Arts, 1985.

7. See Viviane Tarenne. "Chagall et la fortune critique, la presse des années dix et vingt," in Musée d'Art moderne de la Ville de Paris. *Marc Chagall: Les années russes, 1907–1922*. Paris: Paris musées, 1995, pp. 150–56.

8. See "From My World" in *Marc Chagall and His Times*, p. 100.

9. See Julian Cain. ed., *The Lithographs of Chagall*. Monte Carlo: Andrè Sauret, 1960, p. 27.

10. In his poem, "Ars Poetica."

11. T. S. Eliot."Tradition and the Individual Talent," in *The Sacred Wood*. London: Methuen, 1960, p. 58.

12. See Herschel B. Chipp, with Peter Selz and Joshua C. Taylor, *Theories of Modern Art: A Source Book by Artists and Critics*. Berkeley and Los Angeles: University of California Press, 1968, p. 295.

13. In Yiddish, their journal was called *In zikh* ("in oneself") and the trend, *Inzikhism*. This was in direct opposition to the social and political slogans of the time.

14. Translated in *American Yiddish Poetry: A Bilingual Anthology*, ed. and trans. Benjamin and Barbara Harshav. Berkeley and Los Angeles: University of California Press, 1986, p. 779.

15. Ibid., p. 776.

16. Ibid., p. 774.

17. See Benjamin Harshav. *The Meaning of Yiddish*. Stanford: Stanford University Press, 1999.

18. See Benjamin Harshav. *Language in Time of Revolution*. Stanford: Stanford University Press, 1999, esp. part I.

19. "Two Kinds of Art-Poetry" in *Marc Chagall on Art and Culture*, p. 96.

20. See Harshav, *The Meaning of Yiddish*, pp. 89–116.

21. Peter Gay. "Sigmund Freud: A German and His Discontents," in *Freud, Jews and Other Germans: Masters and Victims in Modernist Culture*. New York: Oxford University Press, 1978.

22. Alfred Wolfenstein. "Das neue Dichtertum der Juden," in *Juden in der deutschen Literatur*, ed. Gustav Krojanker. Berlin: Welt-Verlag, 1922.

23. The French mathematician René Thom developed such a theory to be applied to psychology, economics or semiotics of language and culture. It offers a series of models representing unpredictable breaks, "catastrophes" in an otherwise regular process and graph. I am not using it here in any precise mathematical sense, but merely as a suggestive metaphor.

24. Anatoly Lunacharsky. "Marc Chagall," in *Kiyevskaya Mysl*, May 14, 1914, no. 73. The article was written in Paris and published in Kiev. English translation in *Marc Chagall and His Times*, pp. 213–16.

25. See *Theories of Modern Art*, p. 154.

26. See Susan Compton. *Chagall*. London: Royal Academy of Arts, 1985, p. 15.

27. The title *I and the Village* was presumably given by Chagall's friend Blaise Cendrars, but that does not change Chagall's intention. He must have provided the story and, in any case, he accepted the name of this seminal painting throughout his life.

28. See Susan Compton. "Chagall's Auditorium: 'An Identity Crisis of Tragic Dimensions,'" in *Marc Chagall and the Jewish Theater*. New York: Guggenheim Museum, 1992, pp. 1–13.

29. See his seminal paper, "Linguistics and Poetics," in Roman Jakobson, *Language in Literature*, Harvard University Press, 1987, pp. 62–94.

30. Apparently, he counts here the time since he first studied with Yury Pen, either in 1900 or 1902.

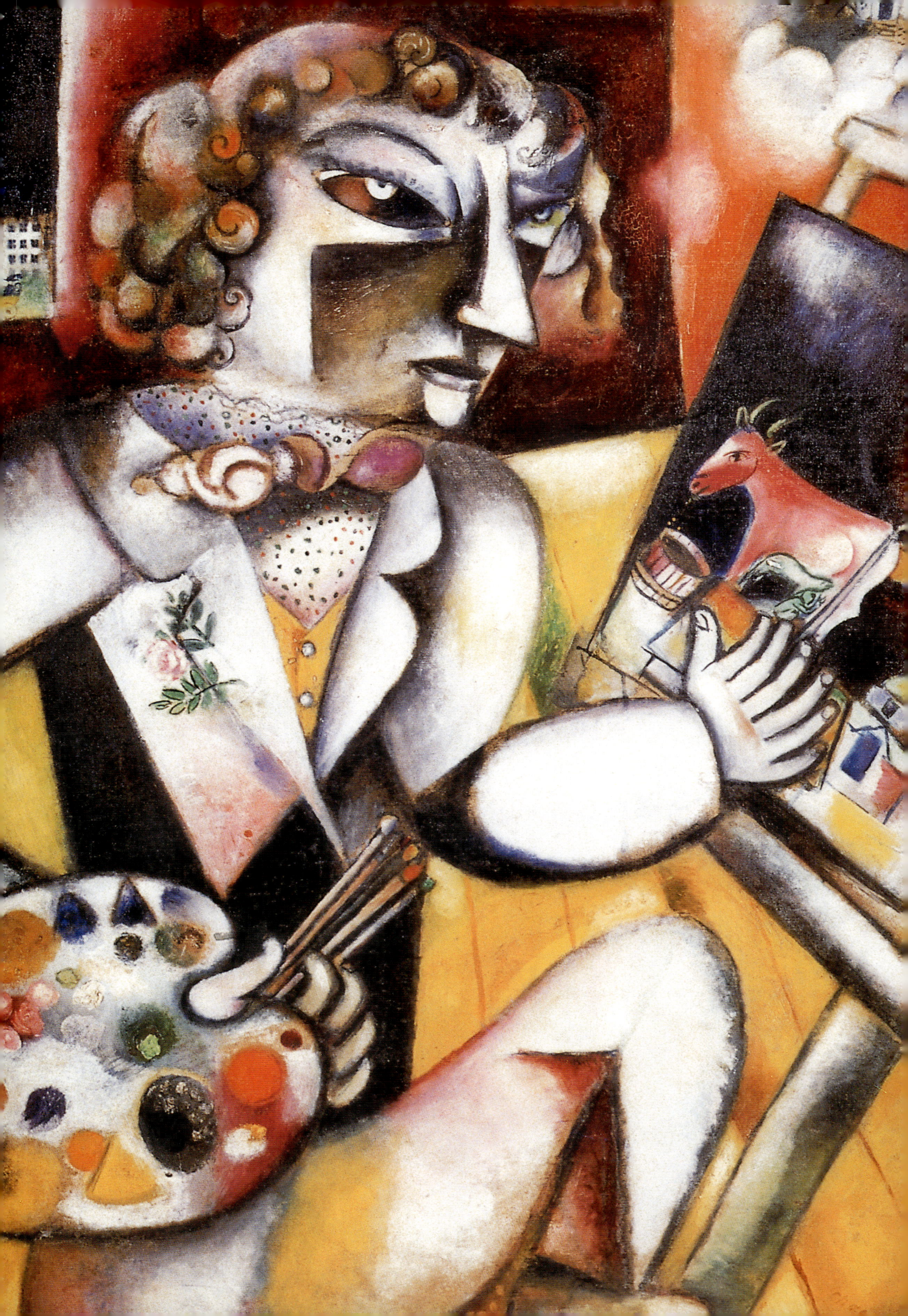

3. Early Masterpieces—The Foundations of Chagall's Art

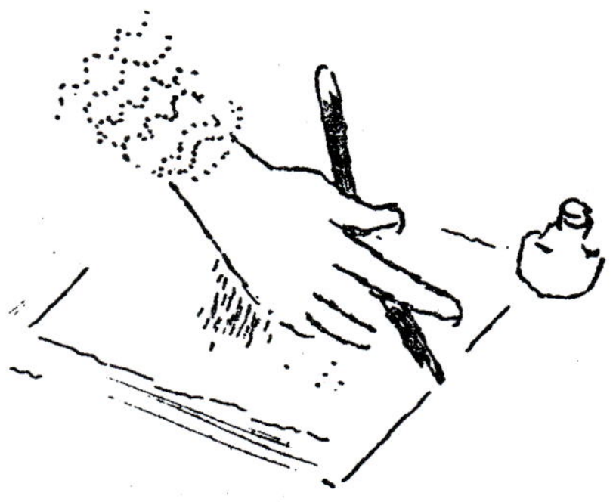

Chagall knew that "thirty thousand artists of all countries and nations" lived in Paris and tried to exhibit their work. He burst onto the art scene with his original and "crazy" work that generated as much consternation and rejection as excited approval. Chagall worked spontaneously and developed several intertextual genres of paintings related to or quoting each other. He used the materials and memories that he brought from Russia but tried to learn from his new environment and respond to his early fascinated reception. Here I shall analyze some key paintings of Chagall's early years, when his artistic conceptions were crystallized.

1. *Stations in Man's Life*

DEATH

The Dead Man, or *The Street*, 1908 (no. 27), is the first of a series of mysterious, enigmatic and suggestive, "primitive" paintings made in St. Petersburg in 1908–10, or perhaps in Vitebsk and Lyozno, where Chagall went on vacations, to escape the formal framework of school and (in the summer of 1909) pursue his difficult love affair with Berta Rosenfeld. The painting is dated 1908; Chagall left it in Russia when he went to Paris in 1910 or 1911, and asked Berta to send it to the exhibition of the Russian avant-garde in Moscow in 1912. Throughout his life, Chagall saw *The Dead Man* as his first mature work and scheduled many anniversary exhibitions related to this date. At other times he used 1907 as his starting point, when he left Vitebsk and Yury Pen for St. Petersburg.

The Magritte-esque incongruity of dark in the street and light in the sky, the disproportionate size of the human figures in relation to the houses and the street, and their incoherent composition are all antirealistic features, further subverted by an indication that the whole is mere fiction—a stage scene, or a dream image.

The theater metaphor is exposed when we compare the painting to the gouache sketch of *The Dead Man*, 1911 (no. 28).[1] The houses on the right can be seen as a cardboard stage setting, for the man who fled from the scene (only his legs are still visible) shook the right-hand house so that the flowerpots fell into the street (simultaneously creating a symbolic gesture of dying). The human figures, although placed inside the street, are so large that the houses become a mere externalized set, a frame for their emotions.

Leonid Andreev's play *Zhizn' Tsheloveka* ("The Life of Man") seems to have had a decisive impact on this and related paintings. It gave them direction and created a genre. "Man" is the name of the play's protagonist, implying both the generic man—"The Life of Man"—and this particular man—"The Life of *a* Man"—because Russian has no articles. The play, staged by the famous avant-garde director Vsevolod Meyerhold in a transitional, Symbolist-Expressionist style, was first produced in St. Petersburg in February 1907, shortly before Chagall's

OPPOSITE: ***Self-Portrait with Seven Fingers*** *(detail). 1913–14. Oil on canvas, 128 x 107 cm. Stedelijk Museum, Amsterdam*

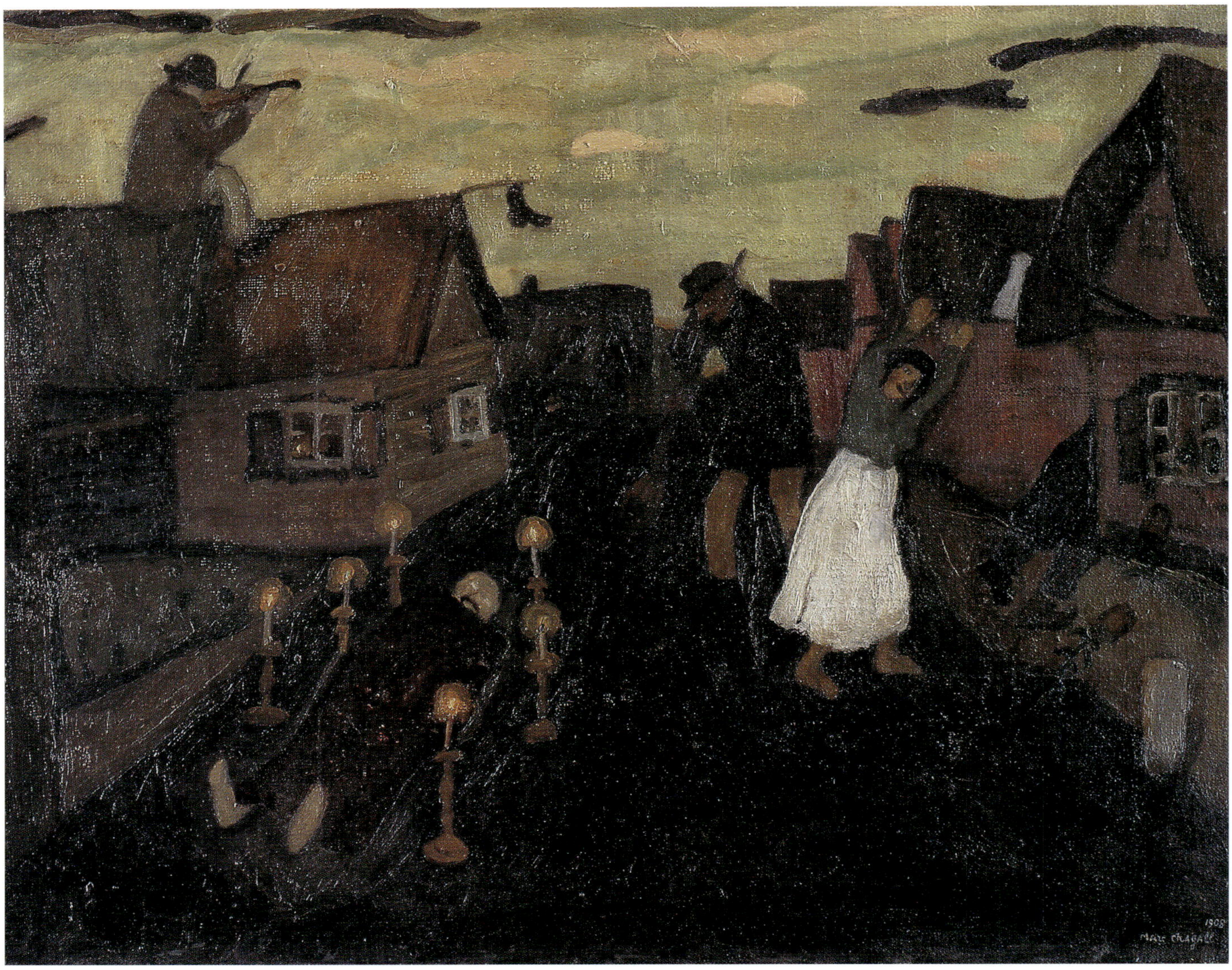

27. ***The Dead Man.*** *1908. Oil on canvas, 68.2 x 87 cm. Musée national d'art moderne, Centre Georges Pompidou, Paris*

arrival in the capital. Apparently, the affluent Viktor Mekler, Chagall's close friend and admirer at the time, who took him to St. Petersburg, who spoke Russian at home and would have been interested in a sensational new play, went with him to see it.

The Life of Man is an allegorical play; the characters have no proper names and are called: "Man," "Wife," or have group designations with no individuality: "Old Women," "Drunkards," and the like. There is a non-narrative frame: the play starts and ends with Man's death. The prologue is followed by five scenes: Man's Birth and Mother's Suffering, Love, Wedding, Catastrophe (the loss of a child), and Man's Death. In the Prologue, the narrator, "Someone in Gray," talks to the audience about Man's life, as it will unfold not in reality but on stage: "Here, the whole life of Man will pass before your eyes, from its dark beginning to its dark end." Man's death is invoked even before he appears: "Thus Man will die. Coming out of night, he will return to night." The stage is a large, empty, gray room; in the "night of non-existence," a candle burns bright, providing the source of light on stage; its flame symbolizes Man's life. Man challenges his nemesis: "Hey, You, whatever your name, Destiny, Devil, or Life." Andreev's source here was found in the German writer L. Boerne: "On the world stage, Destiny is the prompter, reading the play calmly, whispering, with no gestures, no declamations, paying no attention to whether it is a tragedy or a comedy."

In the scene "Man's Ball" *(Wedding)*, a trio plays a fiddle, a flute and a double bass—and the musicians look like their instruments: the Fiddler looks like a fiddle, etc.—such are the overlapping images in Chagall's work (see *Musician*, 1922, no. 29). The play ends with the words: "Hush! A Man died!"

All the features of Andreev's play highlighted here are easily applicable to Chagall—this could hardly be an accident, especially if he was exposed to his first theater experience at the impressionable age of twenty. Chagall

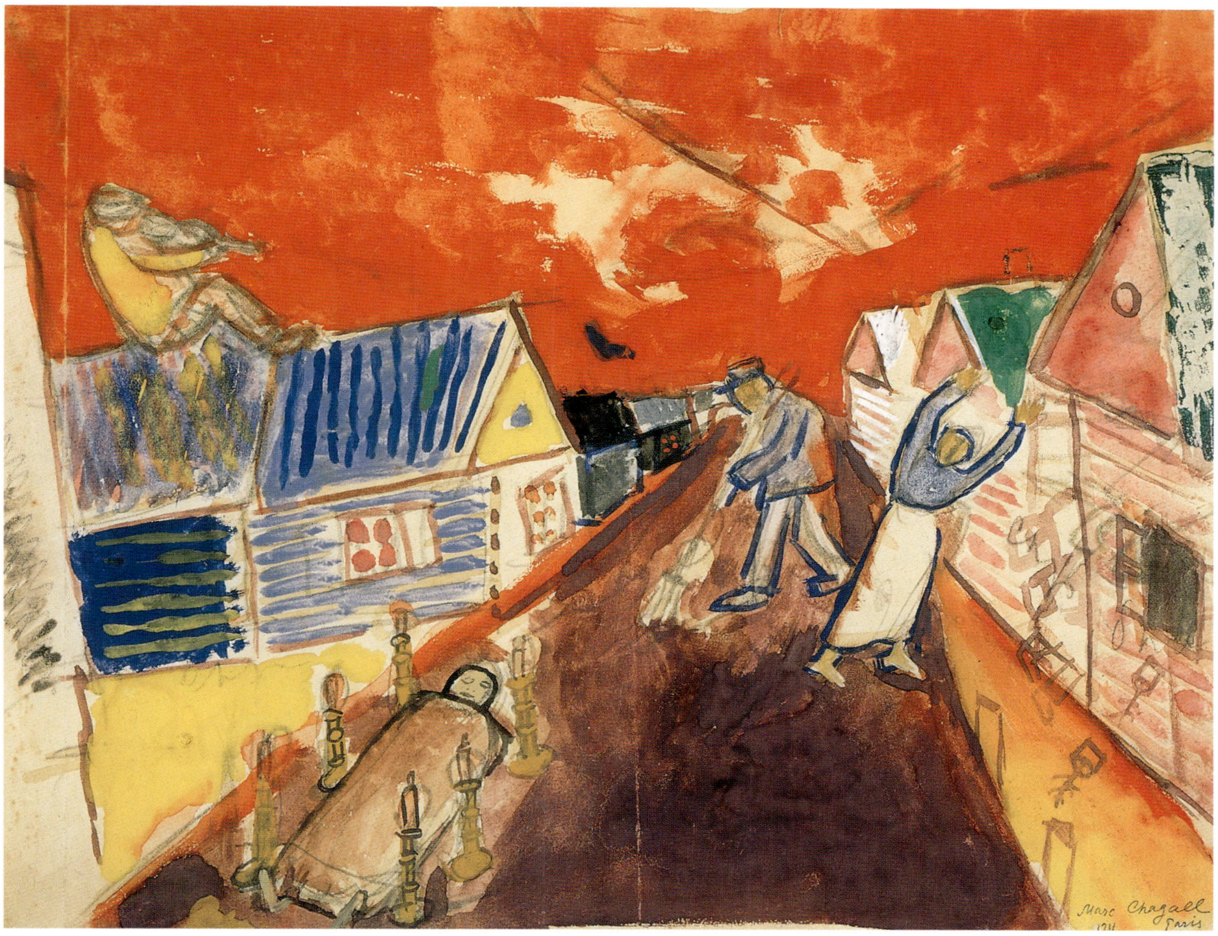

28. ***The Dead Man.*** *1911. Gouache on paper, 24.1 x 31.1 cm. Private collection, Basel*

may have had different sources for the same images as well (such as an actual group of Jewish klezmers) but the similarity of many details to Andreev's play is evident.

The premiere in St. Petersburg, staged in Meyerhold's provocative manner, took place on February 22, 1907; and in December the veteran establishment theater director, Konstantin Stanislavsky, produced it in Moscow. A critical controversy ensued. The key to Meyerhold's conception was, in his own words: "Everything as in a dream." Although professional theater critics didn't like it, some prominent intellectuals did. The major Symbolist poet and playwright Aleksandr Blok admired the play and wrote: "Meterlinck never achieved such cruelty, such coarseness, such crudeness and naiveté in posing the questions." Blok was Chagall's favorite poet and "crudeness and naiveté" could describe Chagall as well. Andreev himself felt that the director gave the play an unnecessarily "mystical character," which we see in the Chagall paintings. Meyerhold was a brilliant young director at the time, and the theory of theater was in the focus of public attention. The critic N. E. Efros wrote about the production: "The theater moved one more step forward into the unknown future, rife with splendid possibilities."

From Léon Bakst, Chagall learned the importance of autonomous color and color juxtapositions, but he always needed a fictional world of his own. Andreev's play and the atmosphere created around it gave him a legitimate thematic thread, a genre unusual in Russian painting of his time. It also inspired the mystical mood, the "dreamlike," proto-Surrealist composition, and the blurring of the boundaries between tragedy and comedy in Chagall's world.

Chagall produced a series of paintings—in what may be called a Symbolist-Expressionist manner with a mystical aura—on crucial turning points in man's life, translated into concrete images of his own world of Vitebsk and Lyozno, and shifting between Jewish and Christian motifs: *The Village Fair* (no. 30), several versions of *The Birth* (no. 31, no. 32), *Circumcision*, *The Pregnant Woman*, *The Holy Family*, *The Wedding* (no. 35), *Russian Wedding* (no. 33), *The Procession*, *Crucifixion*, and their variants, many of which he took with him to Paris in 1910–11 and finished there. Chagall absorbed Andreev's detached, protoexistentialist stance, but he was not as gloomy as Andreev. The ChaBaD Hasidic mood injected cheerful optimism in him, no matter what. He made the turning points in man's life enigmatic and

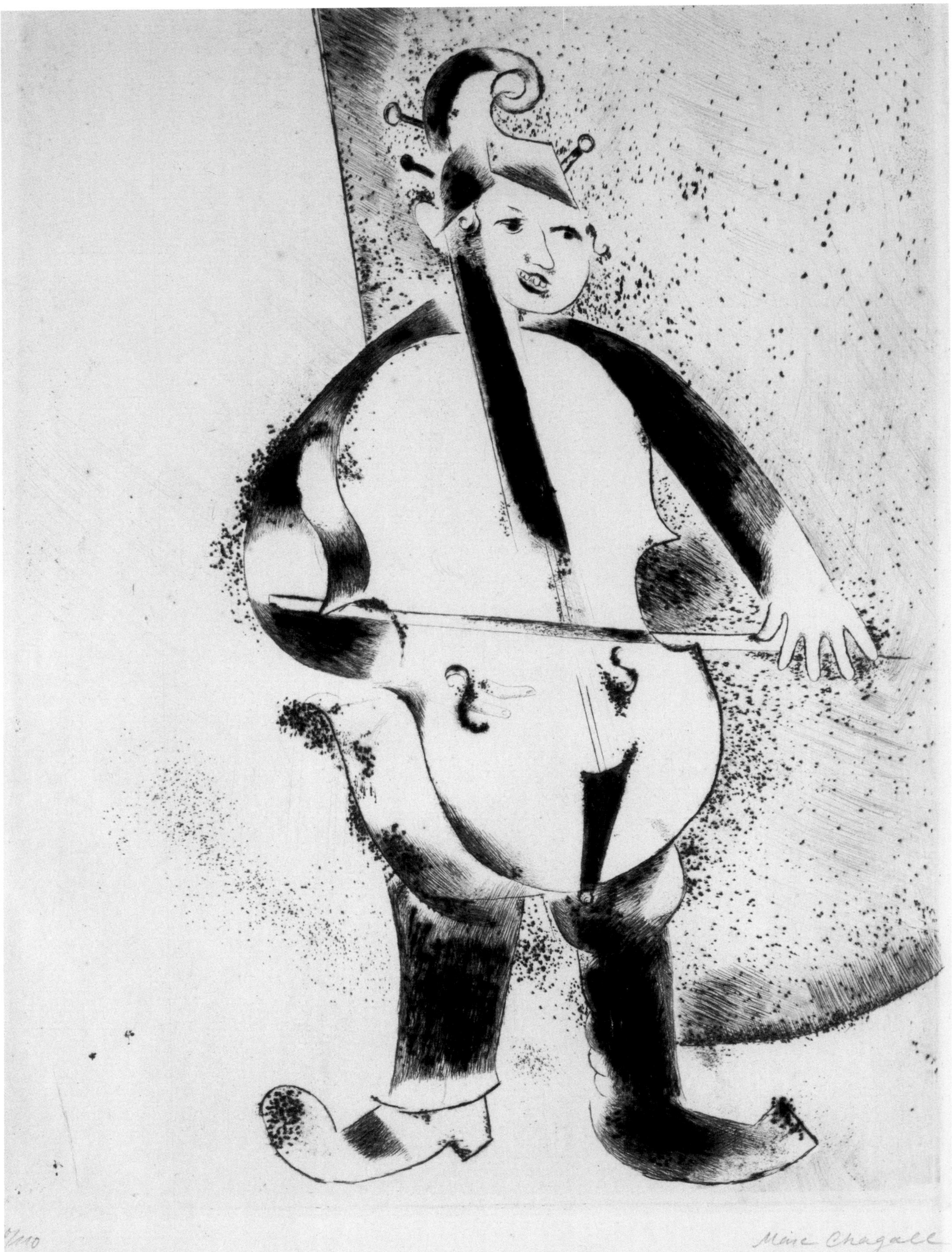

29. ***Musician***. *1922. Supplementary sheet to* ***Mein Leben***, *(30/110). Etching and drypoint on paper, paper: 44.1 x 34.9 cm, plate: 44.5 x 34.9 cm. Solomon R. Guggenheim Museum, New York*

injected them with irony and intimations of carnival (in Mikhail Bakhtin's sense).

In an interview in 1959, Chagall explained how *The Dead Man* came about. According to Franz Meyer, "On glancing out of the window he was struck by the view of the empty, strangely deserted street. But how could he paint that air of desolation, of impending tragedy? Naturalistic methods alone were quite inadequate [. . .] 'How could I compose a street as black as a corpse but without symbolism?' he asked himself."[2] His solution was typical: represent absence through the presence of concrete figures, through the realization of metaphorical descriptions.

In Yiddish, an empty, deserted street is called a *toyte gas* ("a dead street").[3] The street is still a street and "dead" (in the sense of "lifeless," "objectless") is a mere metaphor describing the darkness. In the actual painting, however, the metaphor becomes an object; the corpse in the dark street is a realization of that idiom: it turns the language metaphor "dead" into a visible fictional figure. Thus, the metaphor gets stripped of its metaphoricity and what was a secondary image becomes a figure in the fictional world of the painting. Yet as a result, that world itself becomes an unreal, fantastic world. To indicate that it is a corpse, the artist surrounded the body with six candles, which also provide a source of light in the dark street, as in Andreev's play. Jewish corpses do not lie in the street and have to be buried promptly; candles do not surround a dead man on the ground, only one candle is lit in his home (as seen in the window) for seven days after the burial.

Instead of using the adjective "dead" the candles are placed in the street as real objects. We have three stages of metaphoricity: the candles are a substitute for a "dead corpse," which is a substitute for a dark street, which is a symbol of the artist's anxiety. As in many cases, when Chagall uses language in art, the mere immaterial adjective "dead" is turned into a noun: a dead man. A further pointer to death is the shocked, screaming, and fleeing woman, made conspicuous by Chagall's favorite central patch of bright green juxtaposed to her white skirt in the dark street; and so are the legs of a fleeing man on the right. In *My Life* Chagall retold the story as a recollection from his childhood, as if it actually happened, but as Franz Meyer pointed out, the autobiography was written fourteen years later than this painting. Indeed, it is similar to other verbal reconstructions of his past based on earlier paintings (see the earlier discussion of *Grandfather on a Roof).*

This painting also has the first image of a fiddler on a roof, perhaps accompanying the dead with a mournful melody. Jews in Eastern Europe were proud of their fiddlers, who played at weddings and on mourning days, and eventually produced world-famous violinists. Music was a transcendental, nonsemantic art, the only art accepted by Judaism that had no language boundaries; a violinist could move beyond the Jewish Pale, for the gentiles also enjoyed Jewish violin music. In a children's story, *The Violin,* by Sholem Aleichem, the narrator tells the child:

> A violin, you understand, is an instrument older than all instruments. The first violinist in the world was Tuval-Kain, or Methuselah, I don't remember precisely. . . . The second violinist was King David. And there was a third one, Paganini was his name, also a Jew; all the best violinists in the world were Jews.[4]

Sholem Aleichem, of course, mocks the ethnic-centered Jewish folk beliefs. Like the child in the story, and under the influence of an uncle, Chagall aspired to play the violin until he switched to another nonverbal art, painting. And King David became a central figure in his later work, especially in his Biblical paintings. (Both his beloved deceased brother and his own son were named David.)

This is perhaps Chagall's earliest image of a man sitting on top of a roof; indeed, it is a realization of the Yiddish idiom: *meshugener, arop fun dakh!*—"You're crazy, get off the roof!"—which is said to someone who is not physically on a roof but who pursues an unrealistic, unattainable, or absurd idea. *Meshuge* ("crazy") in Yiddish can be used not only literally and pejoratively but as an affectionate, admiring appellation, indicating idiosyncrasy, unpredictability, and creativity. It is derived from the Biblical phrase, *meshuga ish ha-ruakh* ("The prophet is a fool, the spiritual man is mad," Hos. 9:7). Indeed, in Yiddish, "genius" (*góen*) is even phonetically embedded in "craziness" (*shigóen*). The "crazy man" sitting on a roof is a creative genius; his music is above the tragedy of life.

Another enigma is the dark boot hanging above the center, in the bright, lemon-green sky of dawn. It recalls a Yiddish anecdote:

> A man came to a town and needed his shoes repaired. He saw a sign with a boot and walked in, but the owner said, "How can I repair your shoe? I am not a shoemaker." "So what are you?" "A *mohel* [a performer of ritual circumcision]." "So why did you hang out a boot as your sign?" "What else should I hang out?"

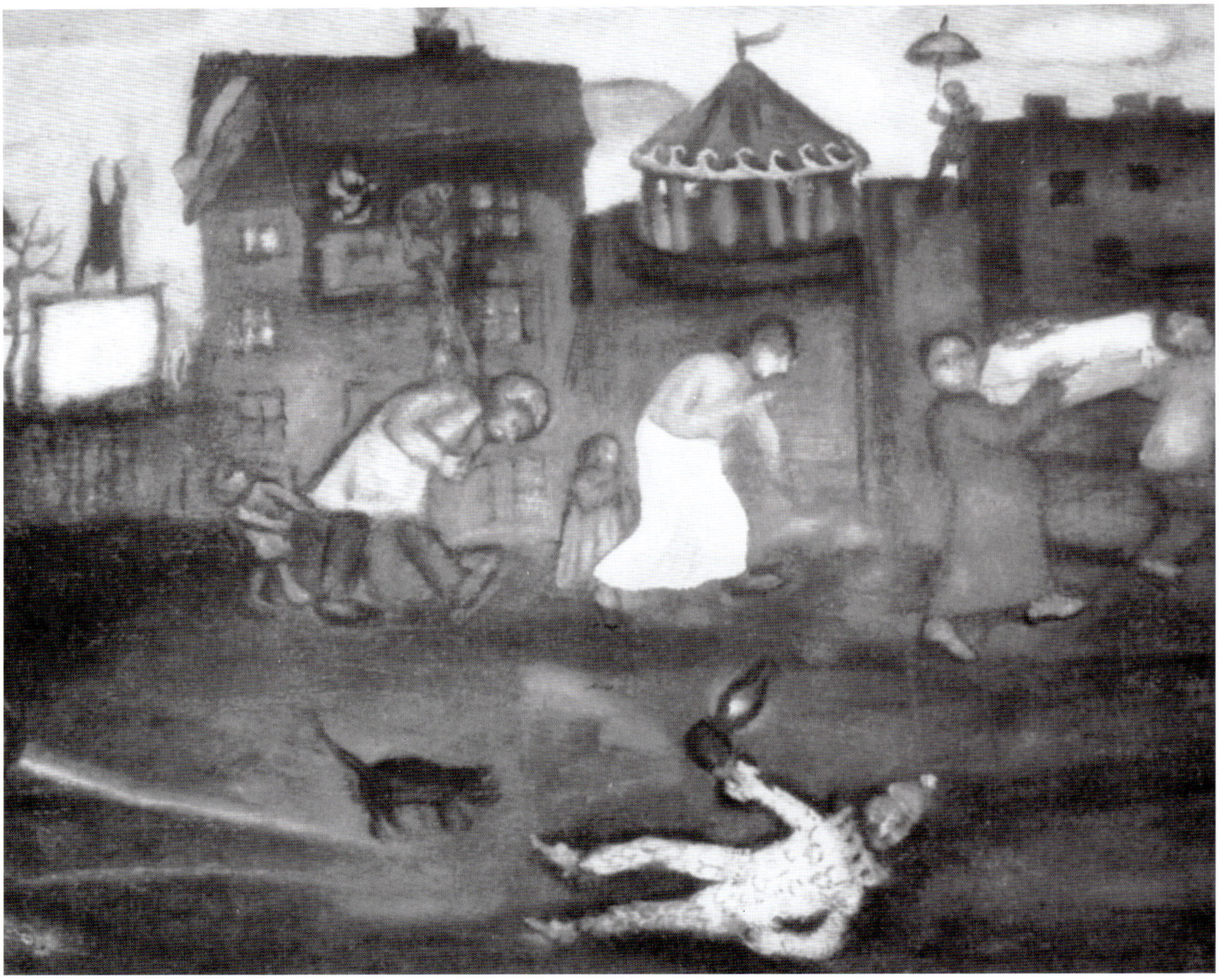

30. ***The Village Fair.*** *1908. Oil on canvas, 68 x 95 cm. Private collection, New York*

Thus, between circumcision on the eighth day, the name-giving and beginning of a man's life, and death—the "life of a man" passed. The white milestone in the lower right is a symbolic reminder of the road. And the sweeper in the middle of the street and the middle of the painting, indifferent to all the excitement, the people, and the music, sweeps out the life that was (or sweeps the stage clean). But Chagall is not Andreev: the music soars, the sky is bright and moody—"the dancing wind that howled over the sullen sky," as the art critic Abram Efros described it, and the boot above the dark street ironizes it all.

The sketch in gouache on paper, signed *Paris 1911*, (no. 28) was painted in Paris from recollection (the original was left in Russia). It translated the tragedy of *The Dead Man* into bright colors with a red sky, as a jolly celebration.

THE CIRCUS OF LIFE

At about the same time, Chagall painted a different death, which he later called *The Village Fair*, 1908 (no. 30). It is less famous, perhaps less striking and focused, but more complex and ambivalent. The scene recalls Andreev's *Catastrophe* (the death of a child). Again, as in *The Dead Man*, the human world is steeped in dark under a bright sky. A funeral procession passes by along the front of the painting. The coffin of a child is carried by two people, followed by the parents of the dead child, bent in their grief (in an exaggerated posture), accompanied by two children, who don't know what to do. The leader of the procession hysterically complains to God—his gesture means "Why have you done it?" or "Why hast thou forsaken me?" And in the center is a woman in a white skirt, a focus of light, as in *The Dead Man*.

A woman on the third floor pours her slops into the street (as was done in provincial towns before water closets). The dirty water falls on the bent man's head, suggesting further degradation and adding an ironic, folkloric dimension to the serious topic. Like the street sweeper in *The Dead*,

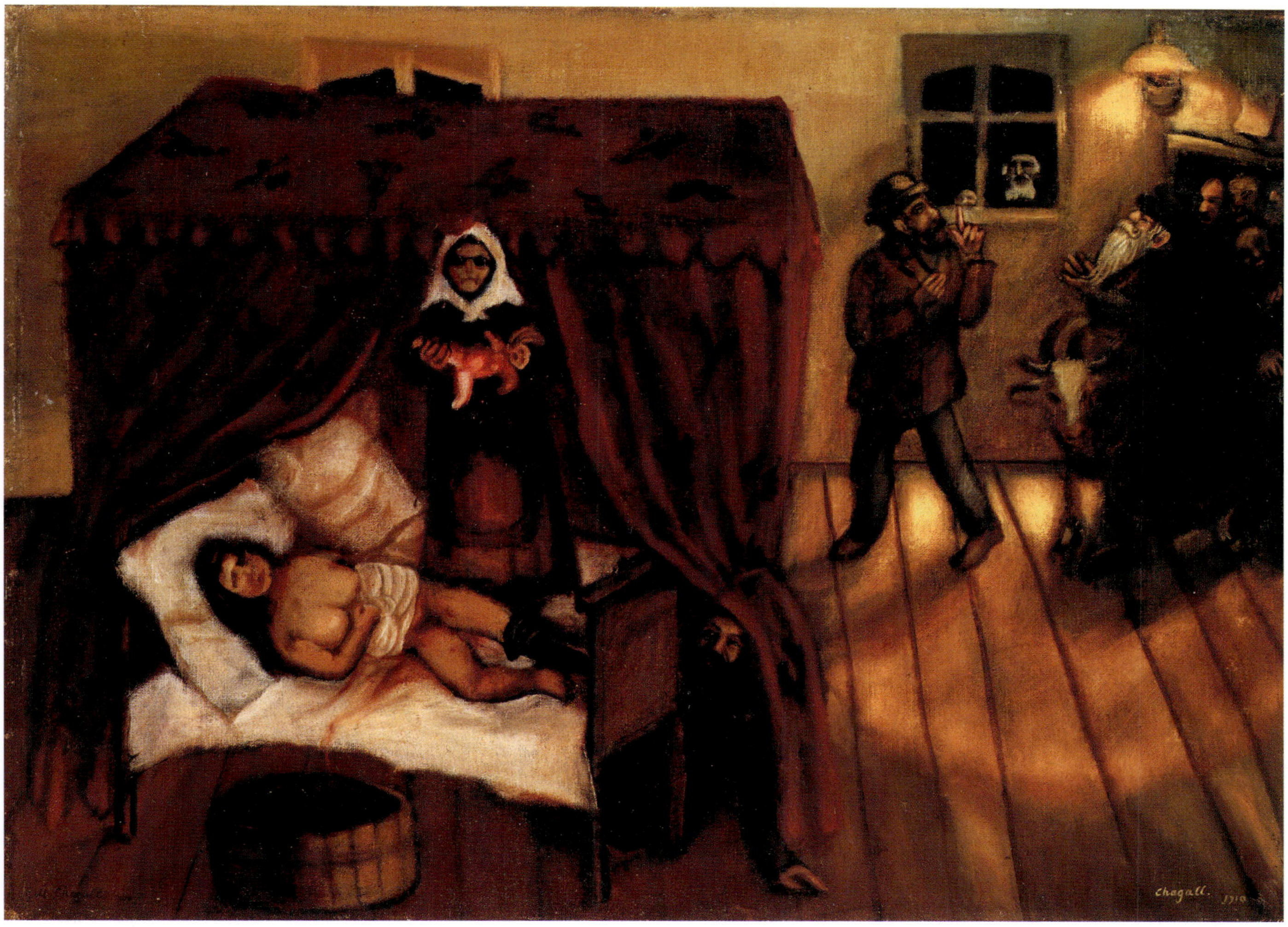

31. ***The Birth.*** *1910. Oil on canvas, 27 x 40 cm. Kunsthaus Zurich*

this gesture belittles the importance of the death event. It cancels, at the same time, any perspective: the figures are as tall as the three-story houses not because of the distance between them (there is none) but rather to highlight the centrality of the human dimension. In a similar way, Chagall shortened the distance between the front and the back panel with his uniform school hat in *I and the Village*.

Other mocking gestures, lowering a serious topic through a coarse anecdote, can be seen in the vignettes of a bare-assed little boy defecating at a fence, that appear in many paintings as well as in the unexpurgated autobiography.[5] For example, in *Over the Village*, (no. 64) a painting of romantic lovers, soaring above the city, a little boy is doing his thing at a fence; or in the theater panel *Music* (no. 110), a hymn to the soaring music of a fiddler, a little boy is crouching bare-assed above him.

But the death topic is not just ironized, its seriousness is overruled by the Luna Park that came to town on an annual fair day. Not candles but rather a clown lying up front illuminates the central objects in the dark scene. An acrobat on the left stands on his head; the world as a carousel in the middle; and little Chagall on the top right, carrying his protective umbrella.[6] This is a double-directed metaphor: either life and death are a circus or the circus is overruled by the human catastrophe and the human condition, or both. Two forces, two domains of reality balance each other and vie for centrality in the interpretation of the painting. Andreev's philosophical stance is overruled by Jewish irony, the comic gesture of "low" or coarse behavior, which mocks the serious, unbearable topic.

As everyone knows, in the 1930s, Ambroise Vollard sent Chagall to a circus in Paris, which resulted in a series of circus paintings. But the frolicking circus acrobats appeared in Chagall's work almost from the beginning. Along with many writers and artists of his time, including Pablo Picasso and Rainer Maria Rilke, he shared the interest in this profession, marginal to settled society and rather magical in its subversion of gravity.

BIRTH

In his autobiography Chagall tells a complex anecdote: At the age of four, his mother sent him one Sabbath to his teacher's house to learn Wisdom of the Fathers. The

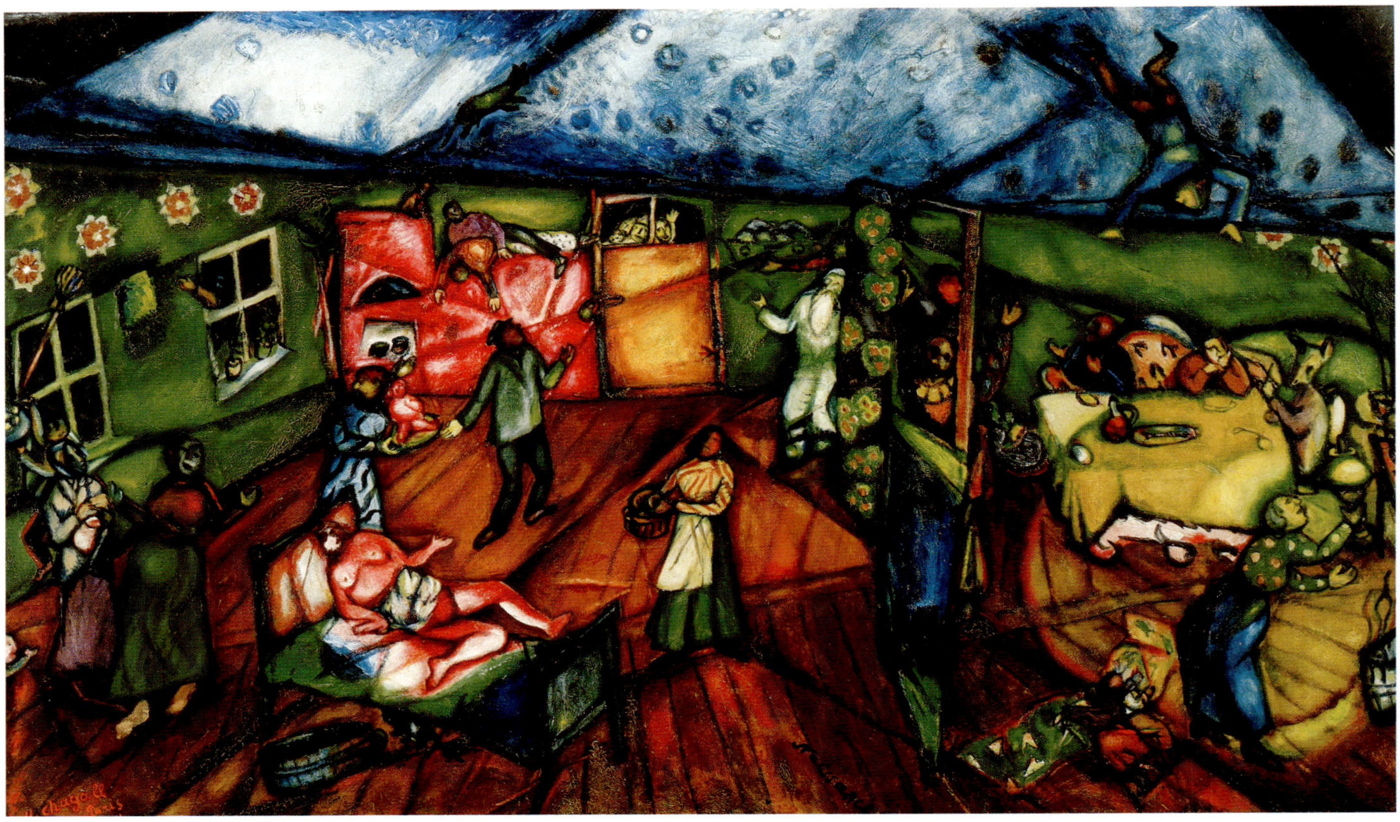

32. ***The Birth.*** *1911. Oil on canvas, 113.3 x 195.3 cm. Art Institute of Chicago, Chicago. Gift of Mr. and Mrs. Maurice E. Culberg*

child knew that on a Sabbath his teacher sleeps naked with his wife (probably for the same reason that his mother sent him out) and was patiently waiting at the door. But suddenly from the upper floor, where the landlord lived, a big dog emerged and bit the little boy. The dog had rabies, and it was chased and killed. The little boy was taken immediately by his uncle to a hospital in St. Petersburg (where normally Jews could not go, but perhaps this uncle had special rights). Young Moshka spent four days between life and death and when he came back home he saw his mother giving birth to a little boy (his brother David). The several paintings called *The Birth* (nos. 31, 32) present the scene from the eyes of a four-year-old child.

In his memory, Chagall may have conflated several incidents and mingled his early erotic curiosity with his fear of dogs and births. Twice he fled from home: When his daughter was born in Vitebsk in 1916, and when his son was born in America in 1946 (Chagall went to Paris and his friend in New York attended at the circumcision). When he himself was born, he claims, he was born dead:

> I didn't want to be alive. Imagine a pale bladder that doesn't want to live in the world. . . . As if it were glutted with Chagallian pictures. They pricked it with pins, revived it, threw it into a bucket of water, and finally it gave out a squeal. But what's important is that I was born dead. I certainly don't want the psychologists to draw any unfavorable interpretation for me. . . . Please!

—of course, calling attention to the psychological problem.

His autobiography starts with the sentence:

> The first thing that struck my eye was a trough. A simple, rectangular, half-eroded trough. A trough you can buy in the market. My whole body disappeared in it.

This is the trough where the newborn baby was washed and revived. And there is plenty of red and fear in the story:

> I don't remember who—my mother, I think—told me that when she was giving birth to me in Vitebsk, on the Pyeskovatik ("in the sands"), behind the prison, in a little hut next to the highway—there was a big fire in the city. The town was in flames. The section inhabited by the Jewish poor. The bed and mattress, with me at Mama's feet, were carried off to safety in another part of the city.

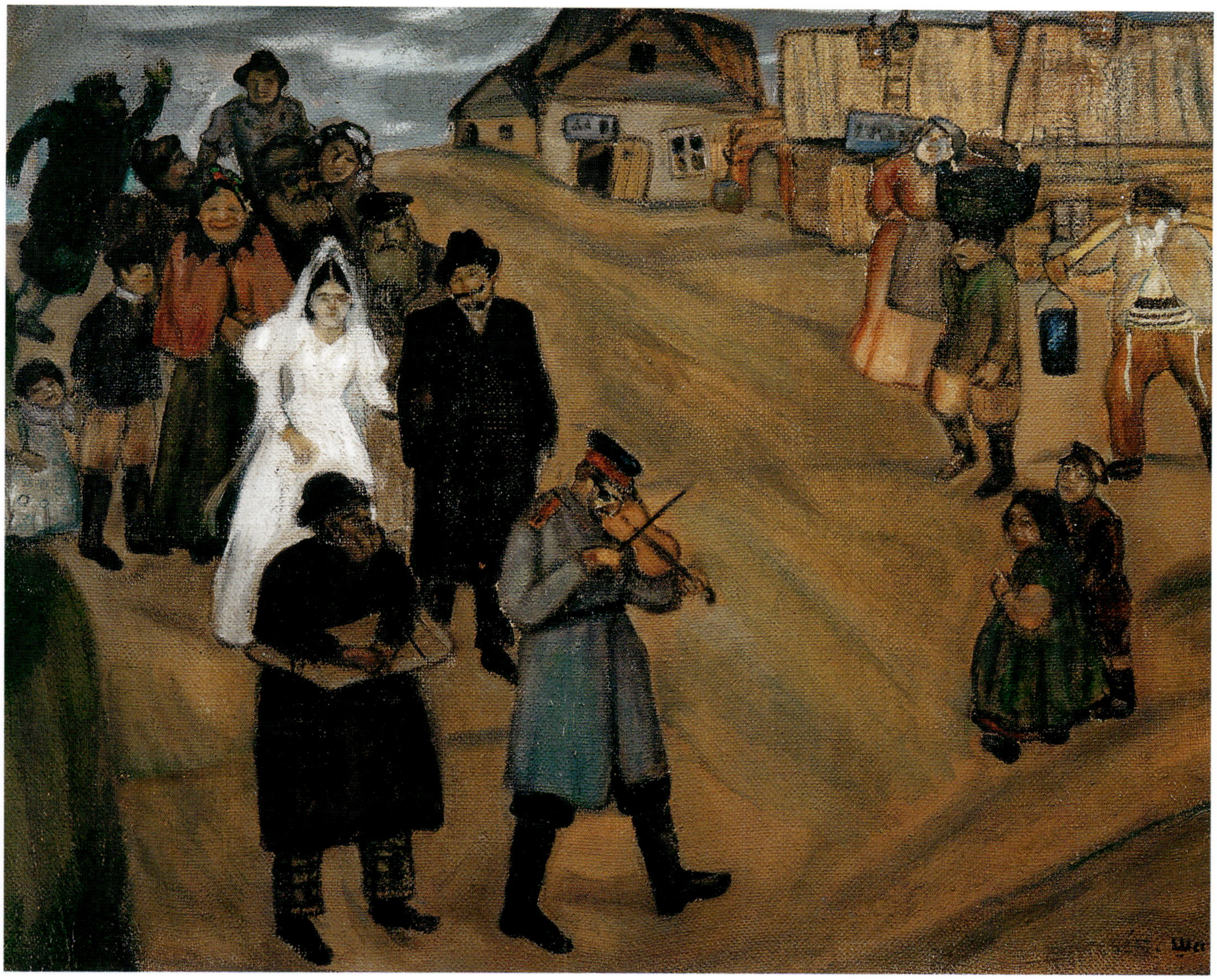

33. ***Russian Wedding.*** *1909. Oil on canvas, 68 x 97 cm. Foundation G.G. Bührle collection, Zurich*

All those perceptions and memories reverberate in the background of the paintings.

The Birth, 1910 (no. 31), is a striking, focused painting, suffused in red. Chagall's mother once entered his room in her courtyard and saw a painting of a naked woman giving birth (probably this very painting) and said: "at least cover up her belly." So he did, thereby accentuating the genital area even more. The woman lies in a Russian wooden double bed, under a red canopy, one sock on and one off (Chagall's whimsical asymmetry). The midwife stands behind her, holding the baby, still covered in blood. Father is hiding under the bed, scared of the momentous event. A group of Jews debate the miracle of birth with talmudic gestures; the one on the right is making an argument, the one on the left points upward with his finger, making a decisive counterclaim (or evoking God). And the cow they bring in is a symbol of fertility (as in *I and the Village*, no. 21).

A much more elaborate, Breughel-esque scene unfolds in *The Birth* of 1911 (no. 32). As the windows indicate, it is not clear whether we are outside the house or inside, probably both. The peacock's tail eyes are a metaphor, to say: "this is beautiful" (rather than appear as beautiful). We see again the birth-giving woman, the midwife with the baby, and the obligatory trough. The center is red. In the back, there is a big, well-heated Russian oven, such as Chagall's mother baked bread in (the fire is lit in the rounded entrance on the left side); a couple is making love on top of it—to explain how the miracle came about, as in a narrative painting. Up front, in the lower right, two little children are imitating the act. A man in the center, lost in the colorful carousel around him, tries to puzzle out the miracle, negotiating an argument with the man to the right. And behind the door on the right, there is the festive meal, presided over by a donkey (possibly a substitute for Chagall himself).[7]

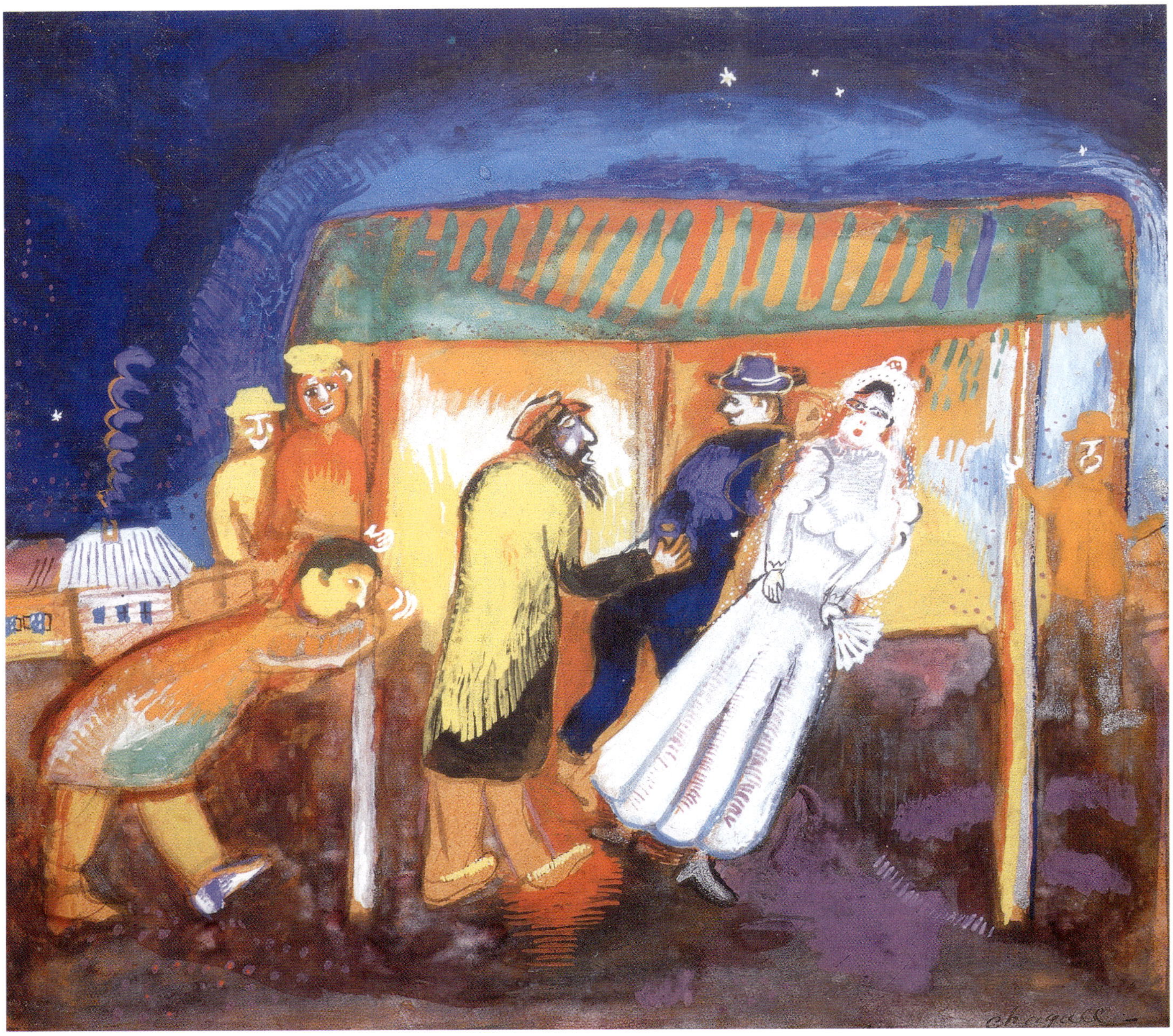

34. ***The Canopy***. *1912. Gouache on paper, 21.5 x 23.5 cm. Private collection*

Above it, there is a triangular, sloping roof, blue and transparent as the sky. And above it all, the clown stands on his head, a joyful prankster overriding the solemn occasion, as in *The Village Fair* (no. 30).

WEDDING

Several paintings depict a wedding, including *Russian Wedding*, *The Canopy* (no. 34), and *The Wedding*. In *Russian Wedding*, 1909 (no. 33), it is not clear whether it is a Jewish or a Christian procession. The violinist at the head of the procession wears a Russian military uniform, and the bearded men may be Russian as well. Among the onlookers some look like Russian peasants. Yet the "holy" water carrier wears a *tallis* (Jewish prayer shawl).

A water carrier was among the lowest professions in the social ladder of Eastern European towns; he needed no language or professional skills, just physical strength to carry water from the river uphill to the houses. But in the new, populist atmosphere in Jewish political life and literature, which Chagall also shared, something holy could be seen in his work, for the Bible said: "hewers of wood and drawers of water for the house of my God . . . and for the altar of my Lord." (Joshua 9: 23/27). The *Lamed-Vov*, the "Thirty-Six Just Men" who will save the world according to legend, are hiding among us, disguised as simple hewers of wood and carriers of water. Carrying water is like performing a prayer, a communion with God, according to the Hasidic worldview that you can serve God through any, indeed the lowest activity. A woman meeting a water carrier with full buckets will be blessed with good luck, and for a bride it is an omen of fullness, pregnancy, and fertility.

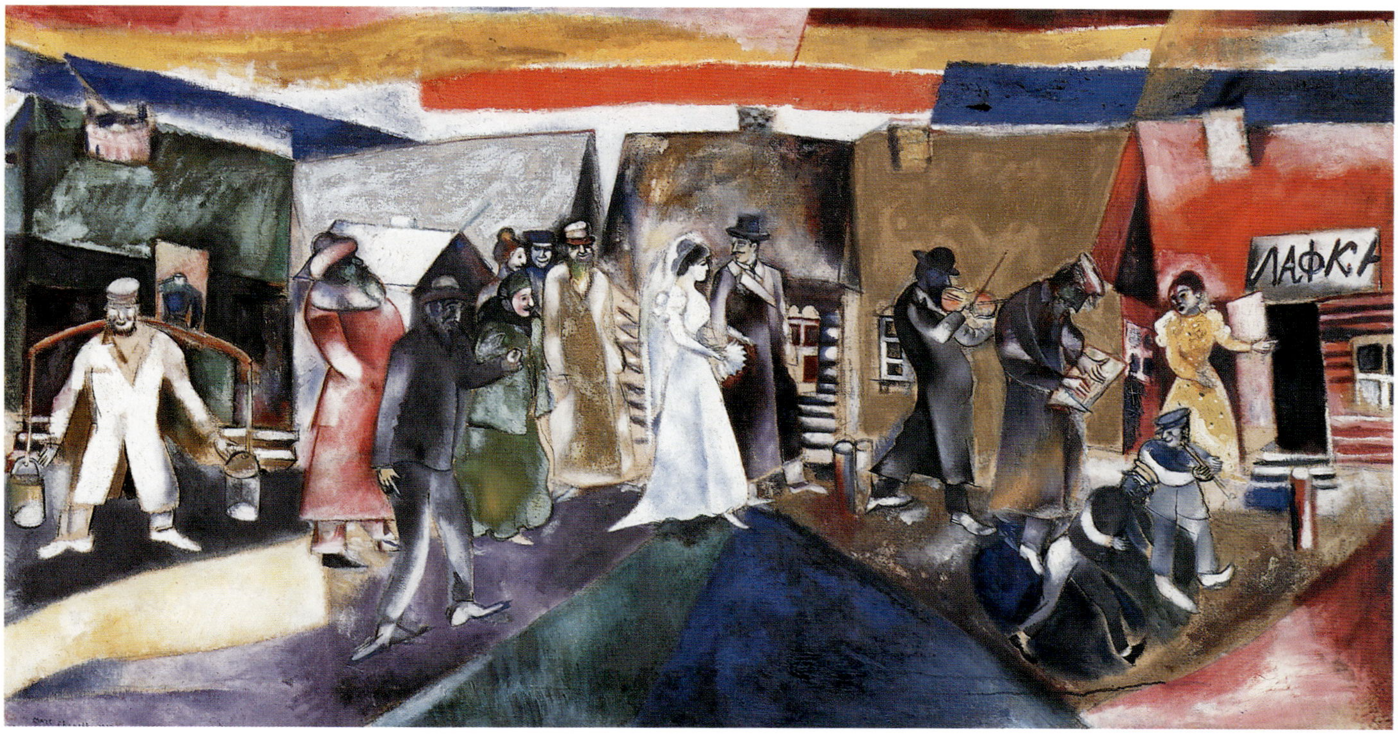

35. ***The Wedding***. *1911. Oil on canvas, 99.5 x 188.5 cm. Musée national d'art moderne, Centre George Pompidou, Paris*

The same couple appears in the colorful *The Canopy*, 1912 (no. 34), under a Jewish wedding canopy *(Khupa)*, and here there is no question any longer what cultural ritual is involved. Hence, in the earlier "Russian Wedding," the adjective may simply mean: "in Russia." Nevertheless, a transposition of such modular units from one cultural frame to another is common for Chagall, and so is his vacillation between emphasizing and subduing the Jewish attributes of his painted world.

The Wedding of 1911 (no. 35), painted in Paris and cognate to the work of Robert Delaunay and the post-Cubist searches of the day, accentuates Chagall's interest in primeval, pivotal points in the human life cycle, as embodied in his own fictional universe, clashing and interacting with the purely stylistic concerns of the time. To be sure, there is a celebration of colors and the construction is tighter, less folkloric or naturalistic. The cortege is drawn together, consists just of representatives of the major groups attending the wedding, and is placed directly before the background houses, creating a counterpoint between the poor physical setting and the colorful human celebration. The dwellings are also crowded tightly together, almost overlapping one another, like a catalogue of multicolored houses (as can be seen on a small scale in *I and the Village*, no. 21).

It is a multicentered painting. The saturated colors in hard-edged spaces compete with the fictional representation for dominance of the painting. In part, the forces overlap, as in the colorful houses (no such colors are found in Russian villages); and in part, each force has its own pure areas, which mirror and symbolically reinforce each other. In the center band (the human procession and the houses behind it), the colors are still motivated by the forms of the stylized houses and human attire. But above them, instead of a sky, there are monochromatic stripes of many colors (no relation to a rainbow), such as those which appear in the works of American minimalist artists of the 1950s and 1960s (e.g., Adolph Gottlieb's *Units #2*, 1965). And in front, there are quasitriangular color segments of a rotating ground. This looks like abstract painting, but the abstraction is located in the marginal areas of the painting (below and above) and can be translated onto the level of meaning: life as a rotating stage and a colorful celebration.

On the right, Chagall's mother invites the procession into her store with the familiar three steps. The large sign in Russian in caps: LAFKA indicates the colloquial pronunciation (rather than the correct spelling: *lavka*, which appears in some other paintings). The bride and bridegroom in the center, at the axis of the wheel of destiny, are clad in European, modern clothes; the musicians in front and the accompanying older people wear traditional Jewish garb, as does the stereotypical rich man with a protruding belly in fur hat and red coat. The procession is led by a *klezmer* band carrying the instruments of Andreev's *Man's Life* (violin, flute, and double bass) with an added cimbalom. At the left, a water carrier in full view shows his full buckets—for good luck and fertility. Behind him is

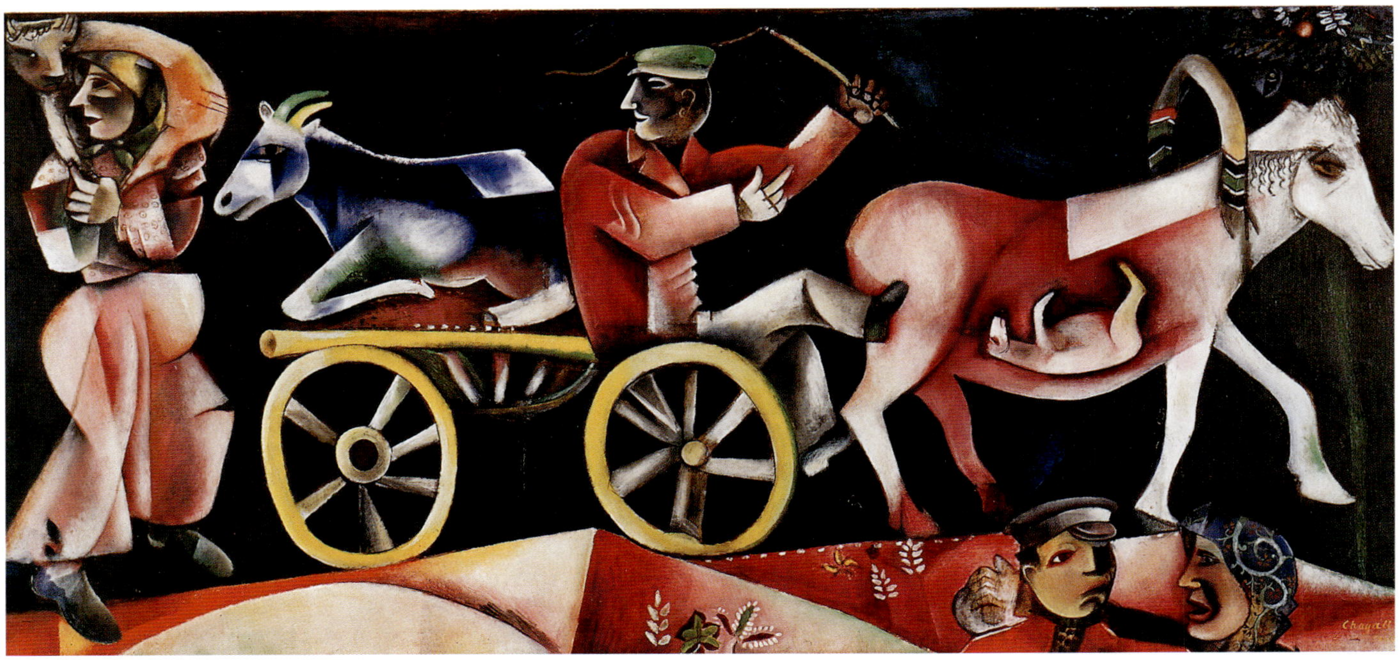

36. ***The Cattle Dealer.*** *1912. Oil on canvas, 97 x 200.5 cm. Öffentliche Kunstsammlung Basel, Kunstmuseum*

a sign of a tailor, as if advertising the colorful exhibit. And on the roof, a bucket with grandfather's pot of carrot stew.

•

Chagall could only paint things he personally experienced; love itself came only after his return to Russia. Of Andreev's five stations, real catastrophe appeared for Chagall only during the Holocaust, but he did not experience it personally. After the Holocaust he developed his large scenes of anonymous masses (first explored in the painting *The Revolution*, no. 127) and became fascinated with the crucified figure of Christ as an individualized symbol of Jewish suffering (see chapter 8).

PREGNANCY

After the *Birth* paintings, Chagall was attracted to painting pregnant women and animals, and in Paris he made many quasi-expressionist, often erotic drawings of nudes. In *I and the Village* the animal is pregnant in its dream or imagination. In *The Cattle Dealer*, 1912 (no. 36), the artist's X-rays see the fetus in the horse's belly. The colors have nothing to do with reality and have no realistic shading or nuances; they simply demarcate lines in each body. Chagall's green faces are here again. Some of the bodies are cubicized, yet at the same time folk ornaments appear on the woman's shawl, on the horse's mane, in the lower, "abstract" margin, and even as a line of little dots under the body of a cow. A schoolboy and a peasant woman in the lower right (is it Chagall and his grandmother?) supply an internal point of view.

The theme of pregnancy was also extended to human figures. *Maternity*, 1912–13 (no. 37), has all the Chagallian features discussed in chapter 2. The free-wheeling color areas, especially the strong red and warm yellow, interacting with the geometrical shapes, create a mood that conveys the excitement of this cosmic moment. The color areas in the mode of shared abstraction are often overruled by putting, for example, birds on a red area, thus turning it into a sky. And all human participants point in the direction of the grown-up fetus. The double-faced woman enhances the irrationality of the miraculous event (as we saw it in the *Birth* images, no. 31, no. 32).

2. *Identities*

In Paris since 1910, Chagall appeared as a Russian artist. But he had to explain his identity to others and to himself. Following the genre of "Stations in Man's Life" (*The Dead Man*, *The Birth*, *Russian Wedding*, etc.), he launched a new genre, a series of conceptual paintings on his relations to Russia, echoing each other yet shifting in a new direction. An intertextual chain takes us from *I and the Village*, 1911 (no. 21), to *To Russia, Donkeys and Others*, 1912 (no. 41),[9] to *Self-Portrait with Seven Fingers*, 1913 (no. 42), to *Paris Through the Window*, 1913 (no. 43), thus shifting from a Russian definition of self to a window on Paris. A parallel line evokes his interest in Christianity, as in *Golgotha* (no. 40) and *I and the Village. Homage to Apollinaire* (no. 44, also known as *Adam and Eve*) ties both genres—the Stations and the Identities—together.

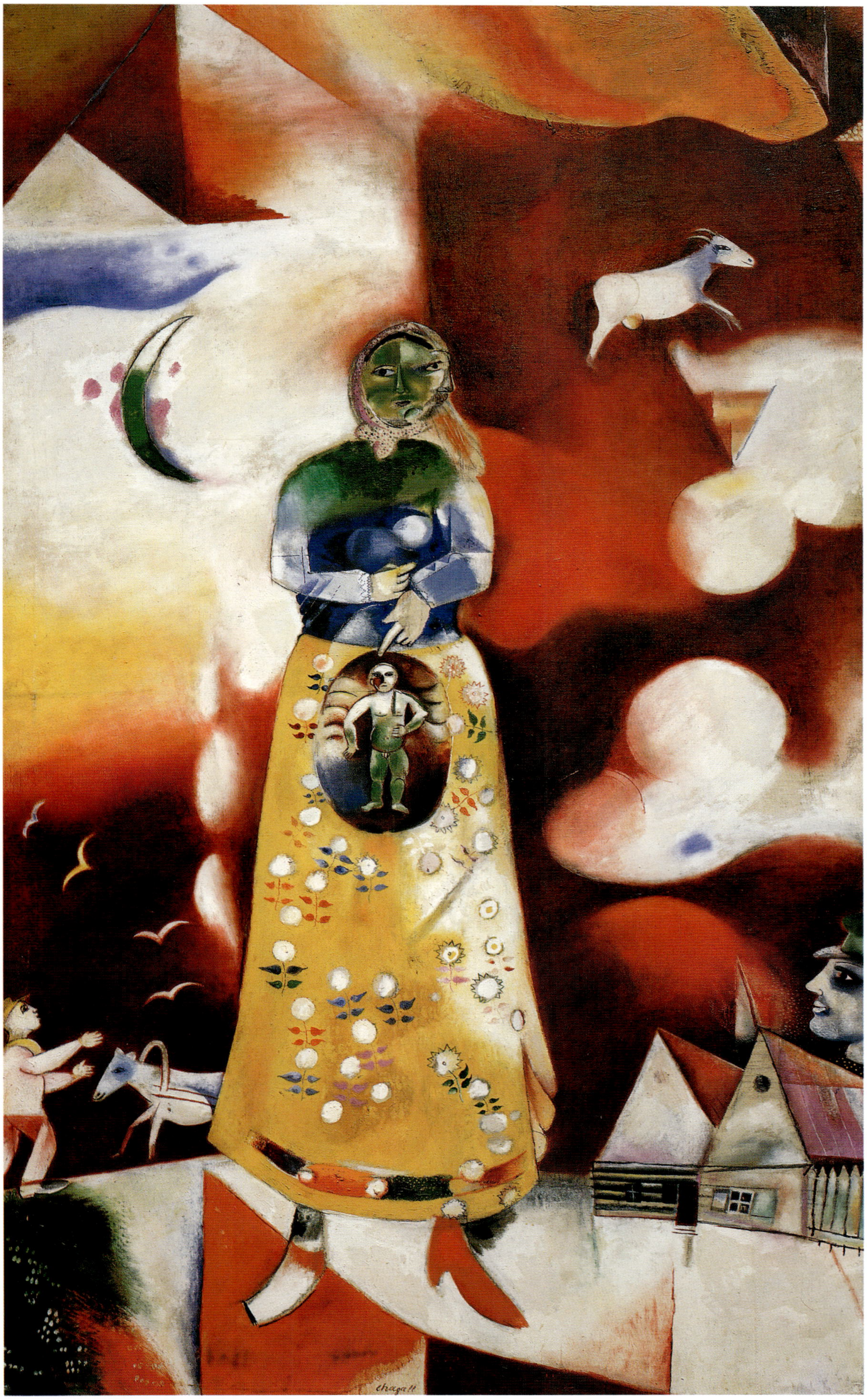

37. ***Maternity.*** *1912–13. Oil on canvas, 193 x 116 cm. Stedelijk Museum, Amsterdam*

The conceptual works are painterly manifestoes on Chagall's multicultural perspective. As we saw in *I and the Village*, the tensions are unresolved, as good literature would leave it. At the same time, those are self-examinations of his relation to the tensions between post-Cubist or other abstract styles, on the one hand, and representational functions, on the other.

ABSTRACTION AND REPRESENTATION

As we saw in *The Wedding* of 1911 (no. 35), Chagall was one of the early painters interested in abstraction, notably in geometrical figures painted in strong, saturated colors. A typical painting of this style is *Russian Village Under the Moon*, 1911 (no. 38).

Of Cézanne's oracular, dictum "treat nature by the cylinder, the sphere, the cone," Chagall developed a special interest in the sphere, always disrupted in one way or another and cut up by semi-triangular shapes or slices. In these paintings, abstract shapes and colors share space with representations of figures and objects. Pure abstraction was just beginning to appear in the work of Kandinsky, Balla, and others but was not yet known or pronounced as a goal of art.

The style of these paintings may be called shared abstraction, whereby true abstract areas share space on the canvas with (re)presentations, as we saw in *The Wedding* of 1911 (no. 35). It is related to the work of his friends at the time, such as Robert Delauney or Albert Gleizes, but in their work, the abstract elements appear as aspects of "cubicized" figures and objects (such as Delauney's *Eiffel Tower*) or on the painting's margins, subordinated to the thematic parts; while Chagall assigns them to independent abstract-color parts of the canvas. And whereas Picasso, in his "cubicized" figures, uses a narrow range of colors, with each small geometrical shape shaded separately from light to dark, Chagall makes exuberant use of bright, saturated colors, which cover semi-geometrical shapes and are juxtaposed to each other.

The *Russian Village Under the Moon* is constructed as a series of independent areas, each with its own principle of structure—either abstract or representational, or both. Most elements are repeated twice: two moons, two houses—one with unfolded walls—two locks, two yellows, two greens, etc. Self-reference of the painting to itself as a painting is central to this style. It is further emphasized through undermining the autonomy of the sphere and other color areas as independent objects by cuts into them or otherwise "dirty" intrusions—see the black, white, and blue dissolving triangles cutting into the green areas in the center right. Cutting into a sphere makes the three-dimensionality of the sphere more palpable, as Henry Moore demonstrated in his sculptures.

Beyond the autonomy of the two forces of this painting, abstraction and representation, they also enter each other's domain and adopt parts of the opposite side. Thus, the beams of the wooden house on top and the unfolded house at the bottom can also be seen as parallel stripes and circles. And vice versa, the green areas above the lower house on the left can be read as a triangular, sloping roof. Furthermore, the moon is echoed in the large red sphere, creating a pair of spheres, small and large, that appear in many of Chagall's paintings and can be read as the sun and the moon, the two lights of Genesis, thus placing the whole event in a cosmic perspective. Slices of the red sphere are cut out like slices of apples and lie in the upper part of the green grass (if it is grass). Indeed, when related to the house on the top right, the green area seems to be grass, but when related to the house below, it can be read as part of a steep roof. Yet, when related to the overall interplay of colors and geometrical shapes, it is a green rectangle in tension with triangular shapes cutting into it, and the slices are events in the body of an abstract shape.

The yellow and white/brown stripes at the bottom can be seen as a road and perspective or a revolving stage (as in *The Wedding*), or as a cluster of minimalist monochromes. The yellow, blue, and white shapes at the top would naturally be seen as the sky, although these colors have no relation either to reality or to painterly conventions of representing the sky. And so is the dark green adorned smoke, like a peacock's tail, on the top right. Only the representational insert (a flashed-out segment of a sphere) in the upper left has a dark blue sky of the night. That scene, often repeated in Chagall's work, is derived from Sholem Aleichem's story "The Enchanted Tailor" (published in the book *Stories for Children*, which Chagall clearly knew). It is a story about a poor little tailor, whose wife sends him out to a distant village to buy a goat, to have milk for the starving children. On the way back he stays overnight in an inn, where his acquired she-goat is exchanged for a worthless he-goat, and when he arrives with the goat at his home, the wife cannot milk the goat. He takes the goat back to the distant town, but on the way back he is tricked again and the reverse exchange happens: he shows the seller a perfect milking goat. The enchanted tailor believes he is cursed. He is apparently naïve about sexual signs, a topic suppressed in Jewish religious discourse. The tailor, as the vulgar Russian saying goes, is "left with his prick" (*s khuyem ostalsya*, i.e. useless). The tailor in the painting

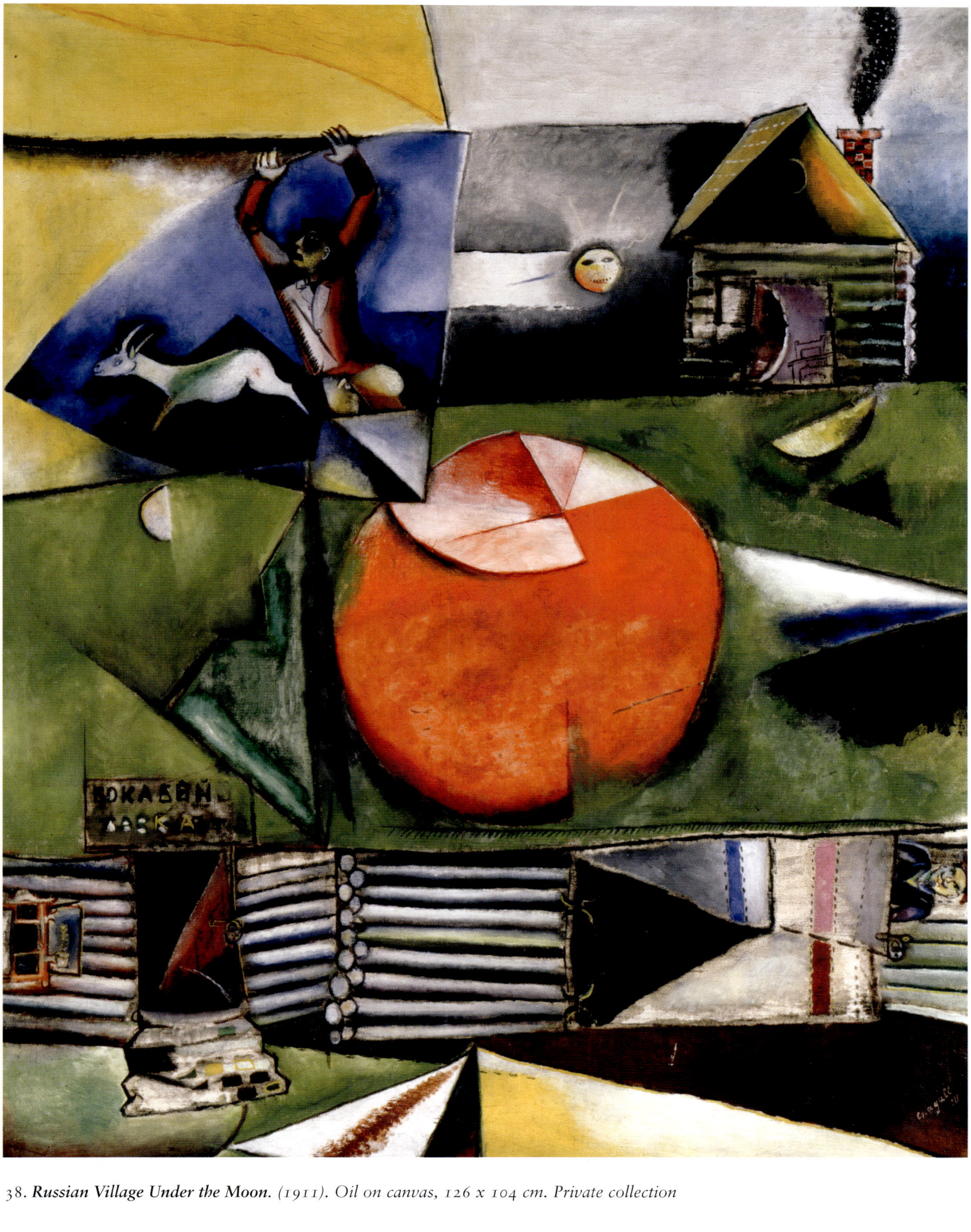

38. ***Russian Village Under the Moon.*** *(1911). Oil on canvas, 126 x 104 cm. Private collection*

has no beard, as a religious Jew would have, and is rather a boy in Chagall's boyish imagination.

At the bottom left, we again see Chagall's mother's store with the three steps, familiar from many paintings and drawings. This time the steps are divided into little rectangular colored shapes, in Chagall's whimsical ornamentation and asymmetry. The sign has another variant of inscriptions in Russian: BOKALEY [NAYA] LAVKA ("grocery shop"). This time *Lavka* is spelled correctly, but the first word has Chagall's own mistake, writing an O instead of an A (the correct spelling is: *Bakaleynaya*). He pronounced an O anyway as A, but the spelling is overcorrecting his Russian. The store is locked up, and so is the man standing horizontally on the right, who looks like Chagall's brother-in-law in images of the wedding. Thus, anecdotes from Jewish literature and from his private life, some known only to Chagall, help create that dreamlike or poetic mood—the enchanted atmosphere of the painting "under the moon" (the moon is a patron saint of romantics and lunatics). Although the store and the three steps are the same, the text of the sign changes from one painting to another, because it was made in Paris as an evocation from memory. In sum, the painting can be seen either as an interplay of abstract shapes and colors, where thematic anecdotes are part of the modular elements, or as an evocation of an incoherent dream world, supported by the colorful texture, or an interplay of both.

GOLGOTHA

In this style of shared abstraction Chagall made a major programmatic painting with himself as the crucified Christ child. The images echo Chagall's Russian poetry, written in 1909–10 and never published[10], when he was a student in Léon Bakst's art school in St. Petersburg. Most poems were written in Vitebsk and Lyozno during Chagall's self-banishment from the school, in a Russian Symbolist, semi-religious style. The poems are filled with Symbolist and Christian imagery and suicidal overtones of a desperate love. Was the addressee his "fiancée" Berta? It is difficult to know.

Why Christ? Art in Chagall's world at the time was a Christian tradition. His admired teacher Bakst converted to Christianity in 1903 (and returned to Judaism in 1912). Bakst's school was located on the first floor of Vyacheslav Ivanov's "ivory tower," the symbolic stronghold of Symbolist poetry. Chagall once claimed that Aleksandr Blok himself read and liked his poetry. True or not, Blok's poetry of those years had an impact on the style of young Chagall's poems, and the figure of Christ was an important image in it at the time.

Chagall's Russian poems are filled with metaphors of nature and religion, the temple of love or of life. The mood is decadent: He writes of death and suicide, her silences, their self-tortured nights till dawn. In several poems he presents himself in the image of Christ: "I walk toward you [my beloved]/ Through the thread of [your] yesterday's silence/ On the path of momentary hesitations/ Here I am sad.// The blue cupolas [of the sky]/ As above Christ/ I am his high pupil/ [Hanging] in tandem, we are alone/ Forever;" "From the morning I was assigned/ My early destiny on the Cross."

This sentiment of a Chagall/child identifying with Jesus hanging on the cross was clearly influenced by Aleksandr Blok, notably Blok's poem "Autumn Love" ("*Osennyaya lyubov,*" October 1907).[11] Indeed, Chagall's unusual painting *Golgotha*, 1912 (no. 40), is almost an illustration of Blok's poem: "When above the leaden ripple of rivers,/ In the humid and grey height,/ Before the countenance of my terse homeland/ I shall swing on the Cross,—// Then—far and wide/ I look through the flood of tears before dying,/ And I see: in a wide river/ Christ sails to me in a boat.// Christ! The homeland expanses are sad!/ I grow faint on the Cross!/ And your boat—will it moor/ at my Crucified height?"[12]

Chagall's painting has all those images, yet without an overtly tragic tone. His parents, perhaps pleading with him, are veiled in Oriental garb, representing the Jews as an Oriental people, in the ideologies of the time; and perhaps under the influence of Bakst's Oriental imagery. Both his mother's dress and his loincloth are sprinkled with peacock eyes to indicate beauty. And the man who takes away the ladder (an image from Christian iconography) wears a Jewish *tallis*.

On an abstract level, the semi-geometrical shapes and strong color areas, the quarrel of spheres and triangles, dark and light, create an asymmetrical balance of powers, with the human cluster dominant on the lower left. The three individual figures separate the overwhelming upper green from the lower red—a reversal of the expected green ground and perhaps red sunset. The green with its unsettled geometrical shapes and disruption, moving from light to dark, embodies a stormy movement in the sky. Christ on the cross and in the boat repeats the same blue-and-white pattern that occupies a conspicuous role between the two color powers. Green and red are also the central color juxtaposition in *I and the Village* (with a blue-and-white element between, no. 21), but here it is a total dominance of abstract color shapes in the painting.

Chagall's self-image as Christ was echoed in the words of his contemporary friends, both in Canudo's observation that Chagall looked like Christ (quoted by Chagall himself) and in Cendrars's poem about him: "He's Christ/ He spent his childhood on the Cross/ he commits suicide every day" (from the poem "Portrait"). The connection of Christ and suicide could only derive from Chagall's poems, which Cendrars apparently read. Obviously, both Canudo's and Cendrars's notions came from the same source, Chagall himself. Chagall's *Self-Portrait* of the same period, dated 1914, seems to express a Christ-like face. On the other hand, Chagall's later Christ images in his Holocaust paintings are quite different—there, Christ is the suffering Jew, wrapped in a loincloth made of a Jewish prayer shawl—and is inspired by internal, Jewish literary sources (see chapter 8). But here he came as close to identifying with the Christ figure as ever.

A Drawing of 1923 (no. 39) (if the date is correct) with the same composition as *Golgotha* is still very Christian, for the crucified and the parents have saintly halos around their heads. It is a realistic and symmetrical scene without the color explosion in *Golgotha* itself. And above Christ's head there is an inscription in Hebrew letters (undecipherable). These unambiguously Christian elements are blurred in *Golgotha*.

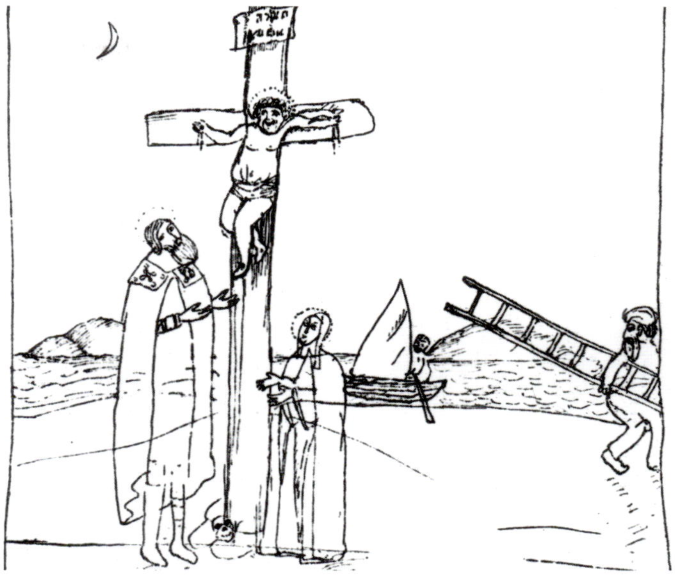

39. ***Drawing***. *Published in Sturm Bilderbücher, Berlin, 1923*

TO RUSSIA, DONKEYS AND OTHERS

From *I and the Village* (no. 21), Chagall moved to another painting, *To Russia, Donkeys and Others*, 1912 (no. 41). In March 1912 the provocative "Donkey's Tail" exhibition of the Russian radical avant-garde was opened in Moscow. Laryonov and Goncharova, developing Russian Cubo-Futurism into their own "Rayonism," advocated a Russian national style, independent of Western fashions; they embraced a "Primitivist" manner, inspired by Russian icons and peasant art. Malevich and Tatlin joined the show, and Chagall asked his fiancée Berta (who remained in Russia) to submit his *Dead Man*. *To Russia* was supposed to be sent from Paris to Moscow but apparently was not. It was exhibited the same month in the Salon des Indépendants in Paris. The painting carried Chagall's "greetings" and a challenge to the Russian artists, a manifesto of what we may call Magical Avant-garde.

A study for this work and the much more sophisticated painting itself refer to the eclipse of the sun in 1912,[13] hence it must have been painted early that year. The painting includes allusions to *I and the Village* of 1911 and continues Chagall's self-examination of his relations to Russia and the nature of his art. At first glance, there is nothing overtly Jewish in this painting; it is authentic, Christian Russia with its small church (foregrounded by a blue cupola radiating in the dark), an icon-emblem on the roof before it, and a peasant woman close to nature. Yet Chagall placed in the dark sky on the left two little Stars of David and two decomposed stars in the form of triangles—a little Jewish presence in big Mother Russia.

In *I and the Village* (see description in chapter 2) young Chagall wears a Russian school hat and a cross, lovingly looking at authentic, peasant Russia. Facing the calf like a lover, he sees in her the future cow, a symbol of nature's fertility and plenitude, milked by a healthy peasant woman. Now the figures of cow, woman, and bucket, transplanted from *I and the Village*, are magnified; what was an embedded scene inside the cow's head is brought to center stage, a symbol of Mother Russia elevated above its churches and rooftops. Yet the woman with the bucket, on her way to milking the cow, is awestruck by the sun's eclipse. The ray of the Russian Rayonists or the "power lines" of Italian Futurists penetrate the scene, but here it is an oxymoron: a powerful band of unmitigated black light, reinforced by the colorful cosmic lights beyond it.

The woman wears peasant garb and coarse wooden clogs, but her beauty is expressed conceptually (and metaphorically) by the "eyes" of a peacock tail covering her body. In shock and revelation, her head is "flying in the sky" (the Yiddish idiom, meaning carried away by fantasy). A well-known nostalgic Yiddish folk song, *"Iz gefloygn di goldene pave"* ("When the Golden Peacock Flew"), which he couldn't have avoided hearing in his milieu or reading in the famous Ginsburg-Marek collection of Yiddish folksongs published in St. Petersburg in 1901,[14] combines the peacock with love and longing for parents and homeland. The song opens: "The golden peacock flew/ over all the seas./ Oh, carry my regards to my dear father/ and my beloved mother." It ends: "As it is bitter, my beloved mother,/ a little bird without a ground,—/ So it is bitter, my beloved mother,/ When you are stranded in a foreign land."

The Yiddish expression "a cow flew over the roof" (*a ku iz gefloygn ibern dakh*)[15] is said to a person who imagines unreal, impossible, fantastic things. Yet the big cow here is calmly ensconced above the roofs, unlike the soaring music of the hovering Jewish fiddlers in later paintings.

To indicate the cow's fertility, two calves are sucking its milk; yet, as appears often in Chagall's work, the same image is used for additional functions and allusions: The green, young calves turn into Romulus and Remus, founders of Rome. This apparently refers to the idea of Russia as "The Third Rome," an idea widespread in the Christian Orthodox ideology and poetry at the beginning of the twentieth century. Yet the one on the right looks like a human child and may allude to young Chagall being nourished by Mother Russia. The trough on the left is mentioned in the first sentence of Chagall's autobiography as the first thing he ever saw. It serves to wash the newborn baby, still covered in blood and as a drinking vessel for pigs and calves.

SELF-PORTRAIT WITH SEVEN FINGERS

Self-Portrait with Seven Fingers, 1913–14 (no. 42), is a manifesto of what Chagall perceived as his bifocal mental world. The two worlds dominating his mind are Russia and Paris, placed in the two upper corners. Several scholars have speculated about the inscriptions, but an early reproduction in the book *The Art of Marc Chagall* by Efros and Tugendhold (Moscow 1918) reads clearly in Yiddish: ROSIYE (on the right) PARIZ (left), supplied with Hebrew vowel markers, as in old Yiddish books. The first is not the usual Yiddish name "Rusland" but the Russian name "Rossiya," slightly Yiddishized (an unstressed e in the end), thus representing a trilingual culture. When the painting was created in La Ruche he still had Yiddish-speaking artist friends, and Yiddish still represented his own mental world; but when the language disappeared from his milieu, he painted over the word endings. The words are still readable but now fulfill mainly a graphic function as well as an emblem of a culture. Russia (on the top right) is represented by the small church and little houses, carried on a cloud, as a dream or a memory.

Paris is represented in a painting hanging on the red wall, a precursor to *Paris Through the Window*, 1913 (see below, no. 43), including the Eiffel Tower, the multistoried buildings around it, and little Chagall hovering above Paris with his triumphant green triangle-umbrella (see the reading of *Cubist Landscape*, no. 24, page 66). In the actual painting *Paris Through the Window*, the standing couple is lying on the ground and the car is transformed into a train turned upside down. Furthermore *Paris Through the Window* is inverted, as if seen in a mirror: Chagall with his umbrella and the

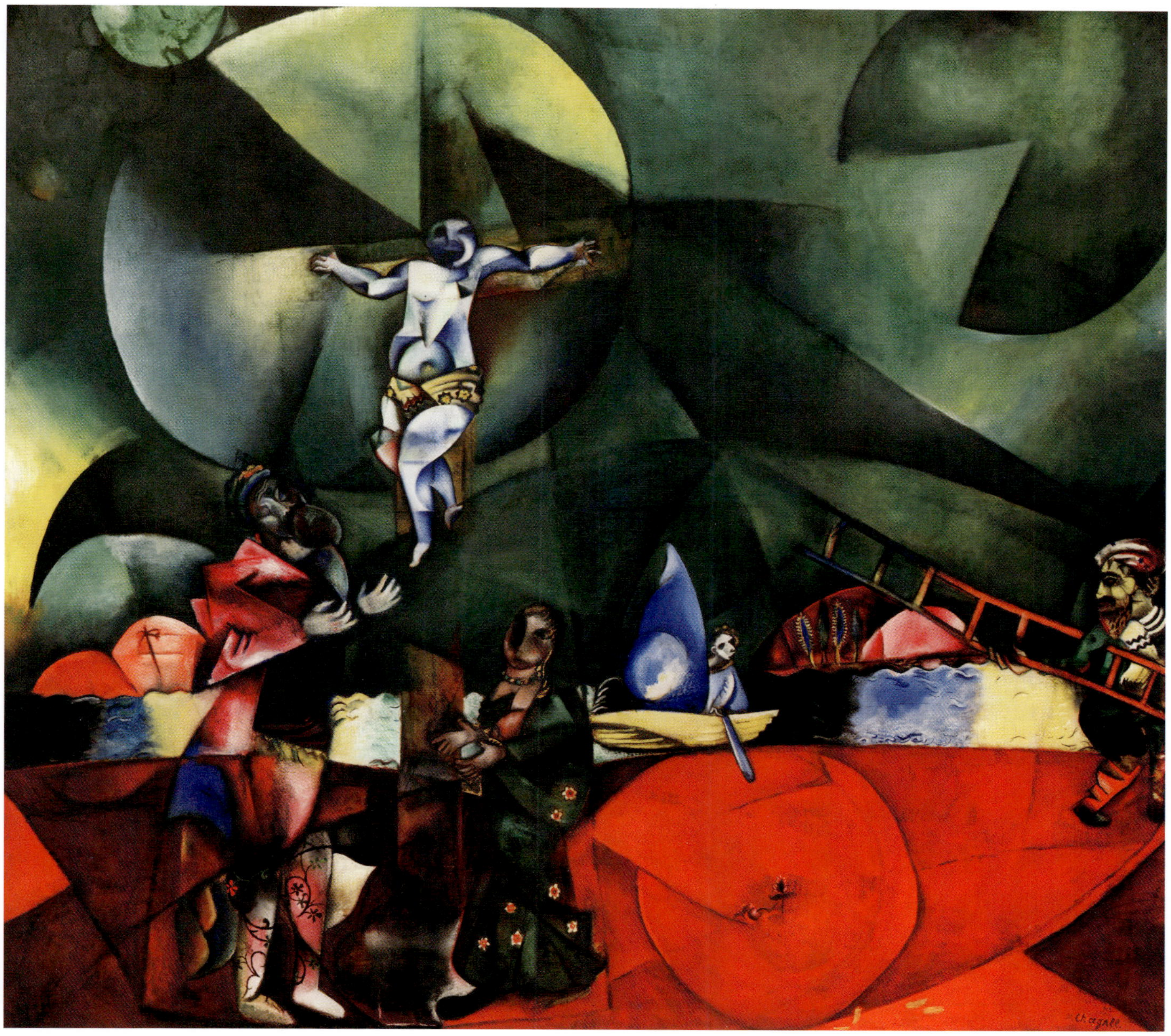

40. **Golgotha.** *1912. Oil on canvas, 174.6 x 192.4 cm. The Museum of Modern Art, New York*

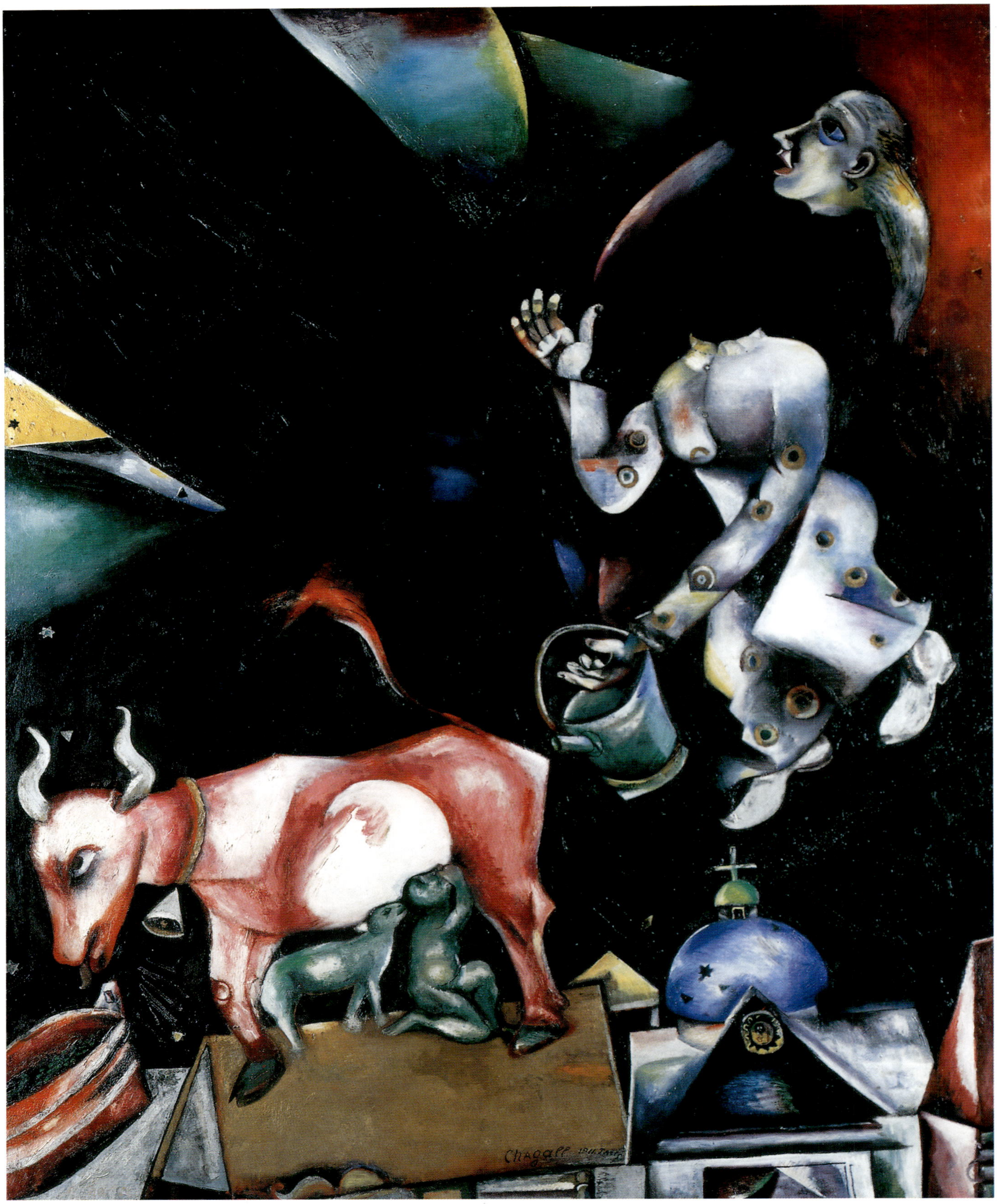

41. ***To Russia, Donkeys and Others.*** 1912. *Oil on canvas, 157 x 122 cm. Musée national d'art moderne, Centre Georges Pompidou, Paris*

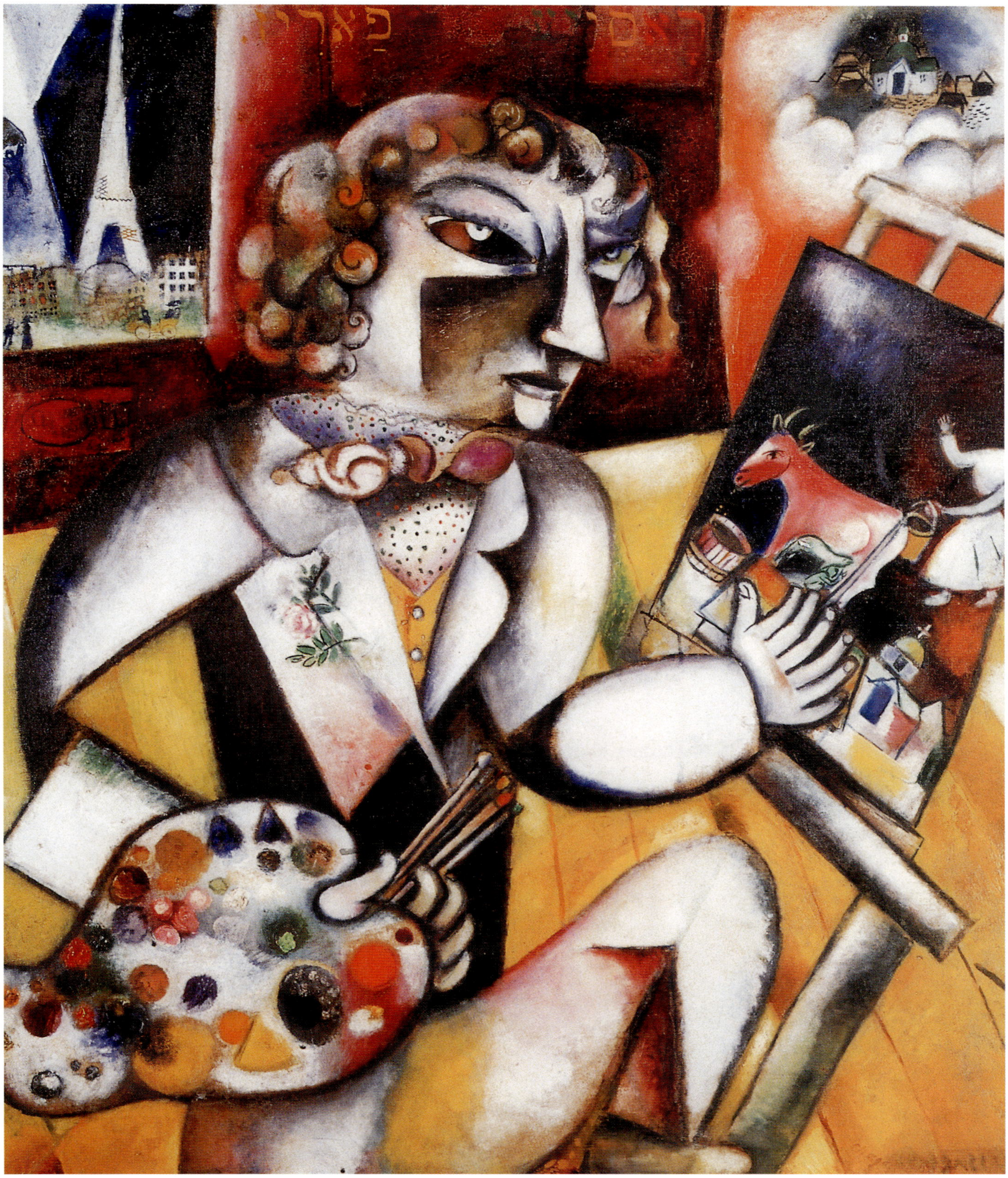

42. ***Self-Portrait with Seven Fingers.*** *1913–14. [Reproduction: 1918]. Oil on canvas, 128 x 107 cm. Stedelijk Museum, Amsterdam*

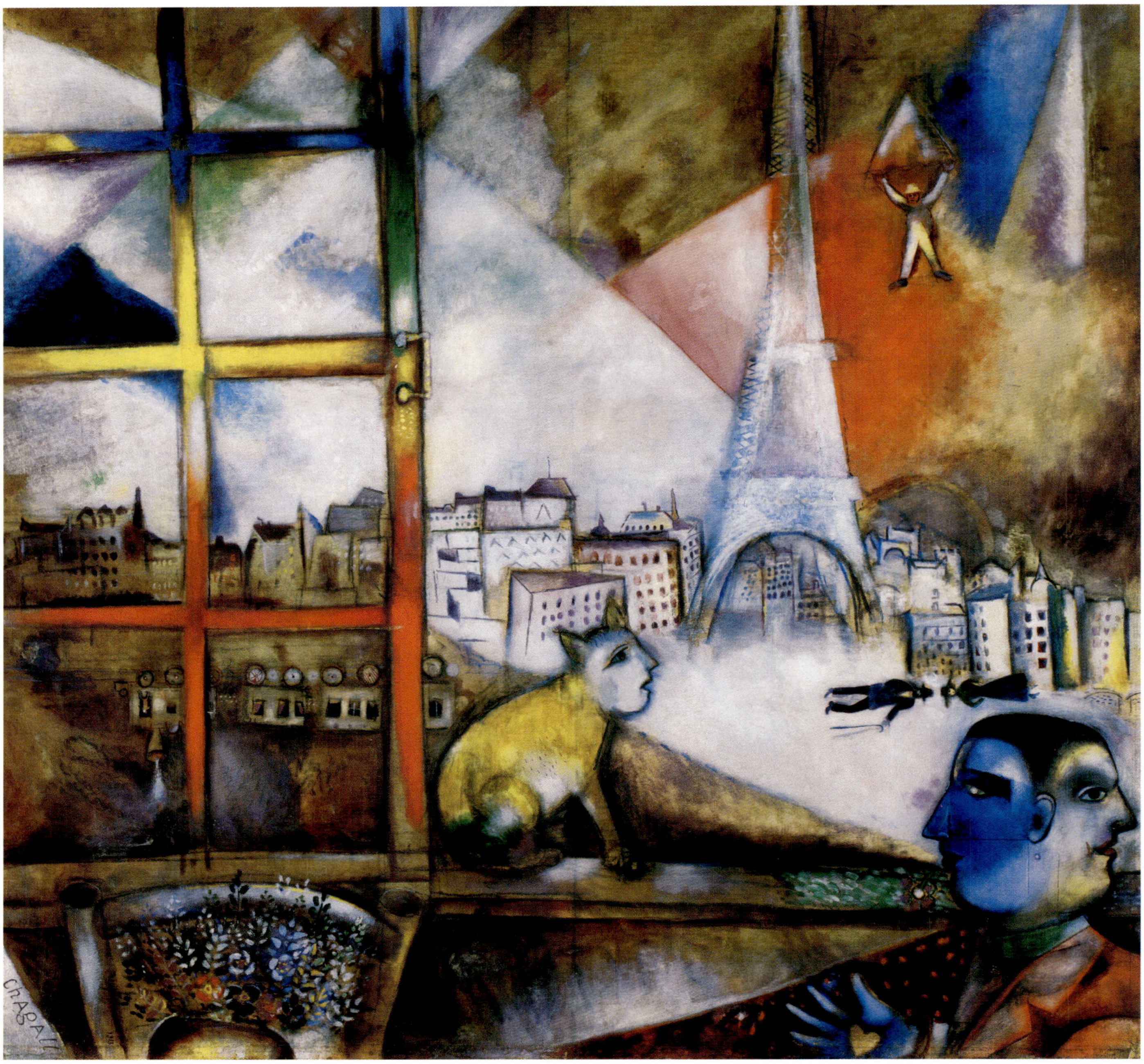

43. ***Paris Through the Window.*** *1913. Oil on canvas, 135.8 x 141.4 cm. Solomon R. Guggenheim Museum, New York*

couple in black are on the left side, and the window with the cat does not yet exist.

With those two worlds dominating his mind, Chagall created a magic painting "with all his seven fingers," as if playing a piano to activate the music of colors. Seven is a magical number in the Bible and the Jewish tradition, indicating an exaggerated or maximal figure: seven years, seven skies, to look with seven eyes (intensely); in Yiddish, *mit ale zibn finger* ("with all seven fingers") means doing something "with all seven senses," investing in a work one's whole being, one's rational and irrational powers. The artist shows himself painting *To Russia, Donkeys and Others* (no. 41)—a manifesto of what I called his Magical Avant-garde. Thus, the *Seven Fingers* portrait is intertextually related to both the paintings preceding and following it.

PARIS THROUGH THE WINDOW

The Janus-like figure in the lower right corner of *Paris Through the Window*, 1913 (no. 43), cannot be understood unless it refers to *Self-Portrait with Seven Fingers* (no. 42): He is looking at his two cultural sources, Russia and Paris, simultaneously. He embodies the point of view observing the whole scene and also the artist with the spread fingers, playing his palette like music. And he is facing the emblem of Paris, the Eiffel Tower, as well as his past, illuminated by a brownish ray in the Rayonist style, emanating from his face and cutting across cat and houses, directed toward the train. And a broad white band of light brings him the light of Paris, as described in Chagall's autobiography.

Koshka (kitty) is a common nickname for a beloved woman in Russian and refers to Berta in Vitebsk; the train, however, is turned upside down, and he cannot return to Russia. The black couple on the white ground is also separated, going in different directions. And the window frame is colored in a rainbow of colors, like trees by Derain: an artist's view. The canvas is divided by diagonal stripes and hard-edged patches of color with no relation to reality (although the colors are often "dirty" with intruding dissipations of "alien" colors). But the (re)presentations overrule this color autonomy and tell their own story. And on the upper right, little Chagall is descending on Paris with his God-given protective umbrella. The Yiddish verb *bashiremen* (to protect, to guard, as God would) appears as derived from *shirem*, umbrella (see *Cubist Landscape*, no. 24, page 66). And he carries the French national colors: red, blue, and white.

Chagall seems to have worked on both paintings at the same time, for *Self-Portrait with Seven Fingers* has a partial reproduction of *Paris Through the Window*, yet inverted as a mirror image. The Eiffel Tower, the Paris houses, and parachuting Chagall are there, but the couple in black is still standing and arguing (on the left side). There is no trace yet of the kitten Berta, the painter, and the view from a colorful window.

ADAM AND EVE

Homage to Apollinaire, 1911–12 (no. 44), offers a striking, quite non-Chagallian image. Yet Chagallian it very much is. Three forces interact, creating tensions and counterpoints with each other: semi-geometrical shapes, colors, and representations. These are key foci of attention vying for the organization of the painting.

The geometrical lines sometimes overlap color boundaries or borderlines of figures, only to part again. Thus, the pelvis of the woman begins on the left as a circular shape, yet the circle, changing color as it moves to the right, becomes an autonomous, nonrepresentational shape, the incomplete innermost circle in four concentric (often unfinished) rings. The straight lines demarcating the legs intersect just above the feet in Chagall's whimsical asymmetry and cut off the feet in a way no body could survive. The big circle is divided into several color areas, with triangular segments and just "dirty" flows of color disrupting the neat shapes. The big circle is close to the Orphism experiments of Robert and Sonia Delauney, but rather than a precise circle it looks like a Chagallian squeezed potato. Furthermore, it is quite orderly in the north-west and rather colorless in the south-east.

Yet Chagall is not interested in the abstract for its own sake, he thematizes the circle. He did so since his earliest days. When he learned Hebrew at the age of four, he was told to memorize the first Hebrew letter and vowel: *kometz alef* O (the zero consonant "a," marked by the vowel "o"). Yet he immediately turned the abstract letters into painterly shapes: he saw the **א** (A, Alef) as an outhouse seat to squat on, and the diacritical mark komet (ָ as in **אָ** which is read O in Ashkenazi Hebrew) as a platform to sleep on.

Due to the added little sphere on top, the two circles become the sun and the moon, as in several other paintings of the time (see *I and the Village*, no. 21). Thus he places the specific events in a cosmic order and, in this case, in the act of Creation in Genesis: "And God made two great lights; the greater light to rule the day, and the lesser light to rule the night" (Genesis 1:16).

Chagall often disliked leaving monochromatic spaces "empty" (as he himself explained in his lectures). Here he filled in the dark lower left corner with clouds and little birds, turning the dark into a sky. What looks like time

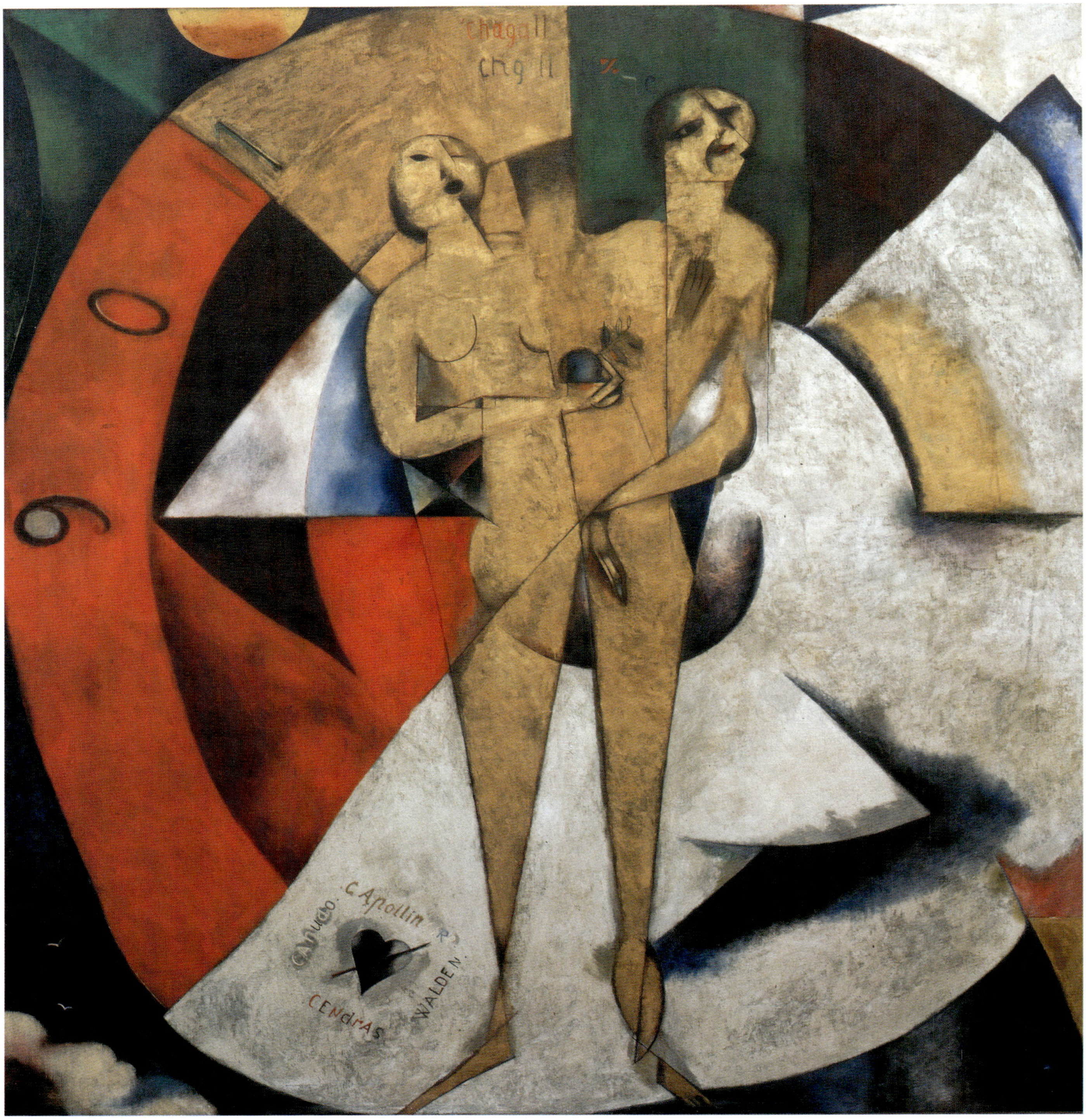

44. ***Homage to Apollinaire.*** *1911–12. Oil on canvas, 209 x 198 cm. Collection Van Abbe Museum, Eindhoven, The Netherlands*

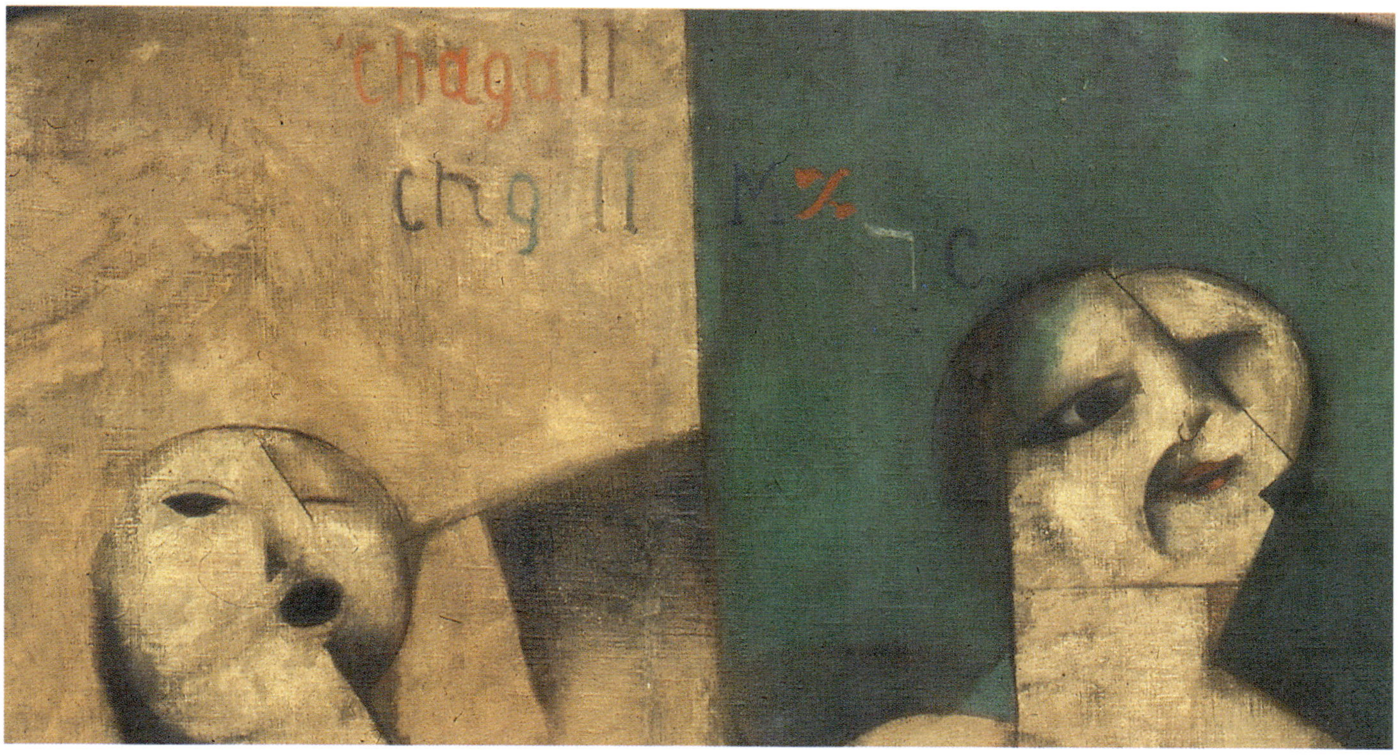

45. ***Homage to Apollinaire*** *(detail). 1911–12. Oil on canvas, 209 x 198 cm. Collection Van Abbe Museum, Eindhoven, The Netherlands*

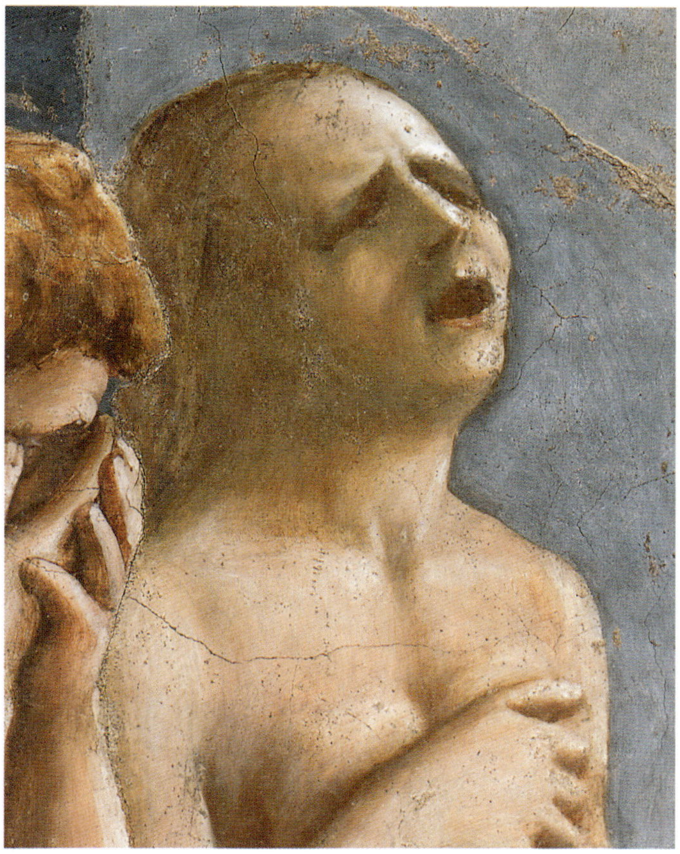

Masaccio (1401–1428). ***Expulsion from Paradise*** *(detail), Brancacci Chapel, S. Maria del Carmine, Florence*

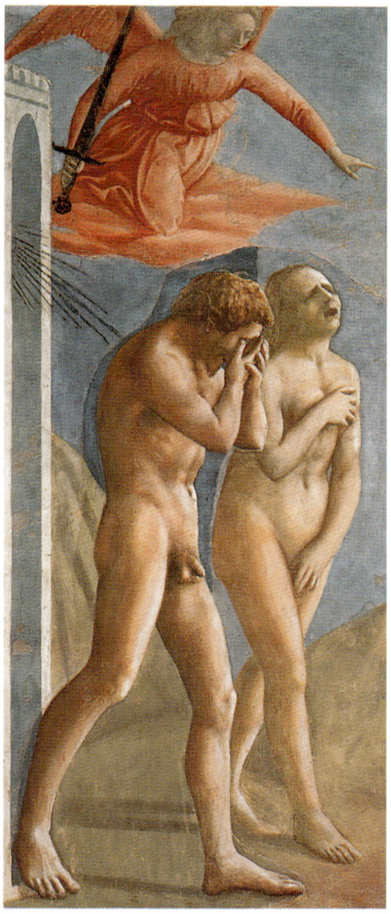

46. *Masaccio (1401–1428).* ***Expulsion from Paradise****, Brancacci Chapel, S. Maria del Carmine, Florence*

on the red segment indicates a clock, thus representing the wheel of time or the Clock of Eternity. Yet, the 10 is given only as a zero. Indeed, the numbers here can be read as the year of the painting, 1911, for Chagall in his personal correspondence (and often in signatures on his paintings) did not use the 1 for one thousand and wrote "911." This is based on the Russian oral language: whereas in English we say "nineteen eleven," the Russians omit the thousand and say "nine hundred eleven." This is the form Chagall adopted here.

Chagall's signatures on top (see detail no. 45) are used as multicolored lines, changing their colors unpredictably (like the window frame in *Paris Through the Window*). The "ll" in Chagall repeats precisely the 11 of the clock. Yet underneath it he writes again: **Chgll**, his name written with only consonants, as in Hebrew, but with Latin letters. And then comes his first name, written in two interlaced languages: M̲ אְר C. The two external letters are French, yet the internal letters "a" and "r" are in Yiddish, and both languages get Hebrew vocalization signs: an "a" is placed under the French M and *shewa* under the Hebrew R. Chagall is reading the Hebrew vowels in the Latin direction, from left to right. Furthermore, each letter has a different color, the Alef is turned 90 degrees lying down, and the two last letters descend a step. This seems to be a small point, but it too reflects Chagall's functional use of every detail, his meticulous and whimsical attention to ornament as well as his cultural ambivalence.

Within all this textural complexity, the thematic force looms. The bodies of Adam and Eve grow out of only one pair of legs and one place of genitalia, and it is not clear whether Eve was born out of Adam's rib [or side, according to a Jewish traditional interpretation] (see Genesis 18:25) or Adam grew out of Eve's rib. The gender ambivalence of Chagall's youth has not yet been discussed, but it is evident in various effeminate self-portraits and textual expressions indicating either latent homosexuality of youth or his playing with a feminine self-image (attributed in his paintings to the image of Christ as well). Adam's hand moves to cover the genitals, but by doing so it only calls our attention to and substitutes for them. Are there any male genitals here? Rather, the hand turns into the snake of the Bible and Eve's apple is a replica of the two breasts nearby.

But the book of Genesis also offers a second theory of the creation of genders: "So God created man in his own image, in the image of God created he him; male and female created he them." (Genesis 1:27). *Him* or *them?* The early Jewish interpreters in the Midrash were puzzled by this contradictory use of singular and plural. Several explanations were suggested, which can be reduced to two major ideas, as explained in the midrash Genesis Rabba:[16] Said Rabbi Jeremiah ben Elazar, "When the Holy-One-Blessed-Be-He created the first Adam, he created him as an androgyne," for he had both signs of masculinity and signs of femininity; and Rabbi Shmuel ben Nahman said, "When the Holy-One-Blessed-Be-He created the first Adam, he created him as a Diprosaphon," that is he created him with two faces, then he sawed him up in half and made him with two torsos. Chagall combines both biblical theories.

Chagall probably never read the Midrash, but his teacher could certainly convey to him this knowledge, especially since the boy had a pronounced sexual curiosity and a fantasy world of his own. Moreover, the classical and popular commentator Rashi of twelfth-century France, a must in studying the Torah in *heder*, referred to the debate: "There is a Midrash legend that He created [Adam] with two faces in his first creation, and later divided them." Jewish education from age four on included *Humash with Rashi*, i.e., the Torah with this twelfth-century commentary. Thus, a painting with nothing overtly Jewish relies on a Jewish interpretive tradition.

The central circle is held together by four spikes, four diagonal lines, meeting in the exact center, the "center of procreation" (as R. M. Rilke called it). The basic structure is reminiscent of Leonardo da Vinci's famous drawing of a man, which might have influenced Chagall's composition.

But a more pertinent influence seems to be one of the foundational paintings of the Italian Renaissance, Tommaso Masaccio's *Expulsion of Adam and Eve* (no. 46) in the Brancacci Chapel in Florence. Chagall transposed the places of the two figures and merged their legs. Eve's scream (which a Masaccio scholar recently described as the loudest scream in art history) is almost the same; instead of her left arm covering her genitals, now Adam does the same gesture for the merged genitalia; even the color of the bodies is similar. Thus, in his allusion to Masaccio, Chagall conflated the birth pangs of the creation of genders with the anxiety of expulsion, exile, and human existence. Indeed, for all its colors, there are in this painting no serious modulations of color related to the variations of the human body, except for the "dirty" effect of the texture. Indeed, this too may be based on a Biblical description: "And the Lord God formed man of the dust of the ground, and breathed into his nostrils the breath of life; and man became a living soul" (Genesis 2:7). The bodies are simplified, "primi-

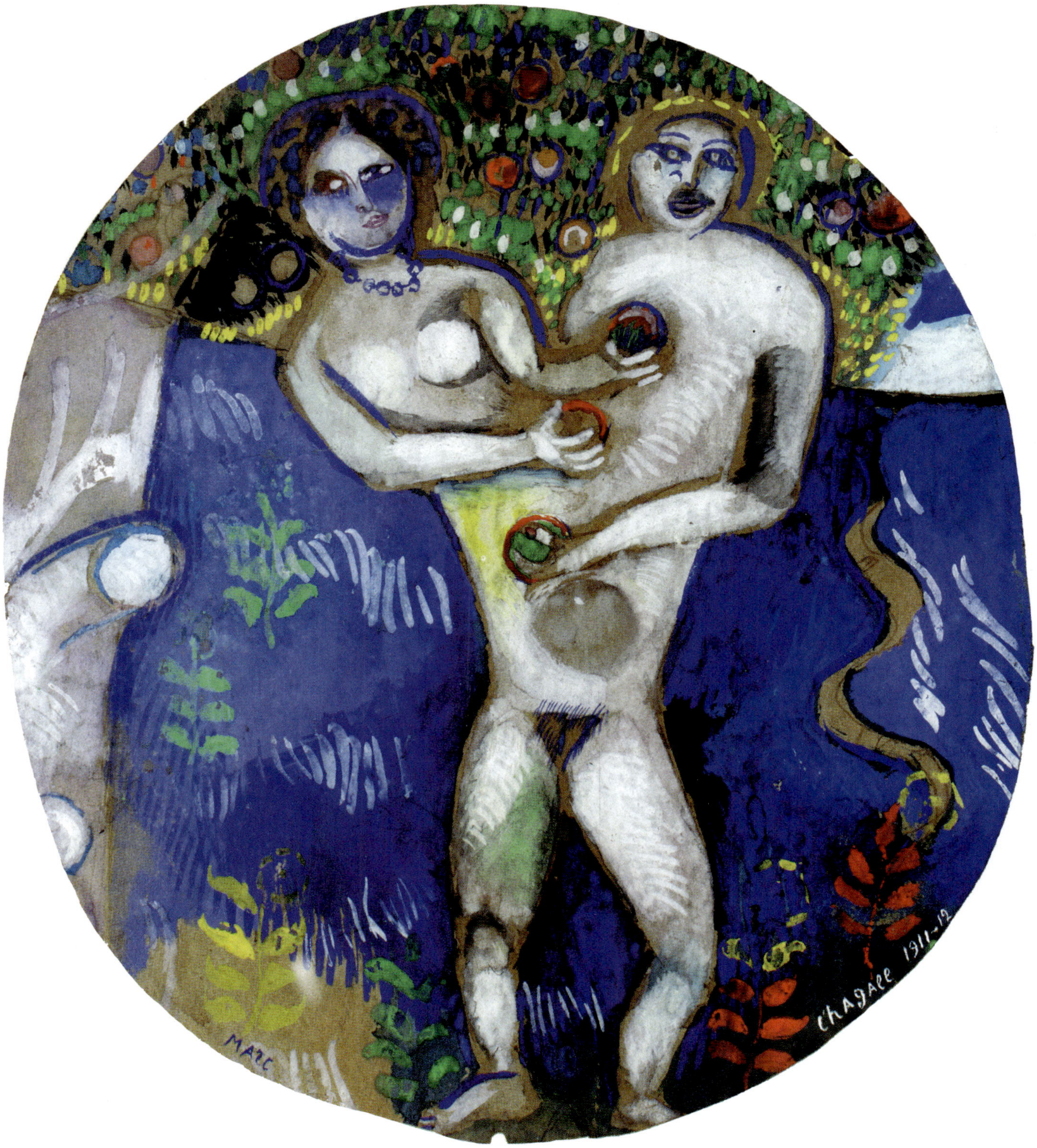

47. ***Study for Adam and Eve.*** *1910. Gouache on paper, 27.5 x 24 cm: oval. Private collection*

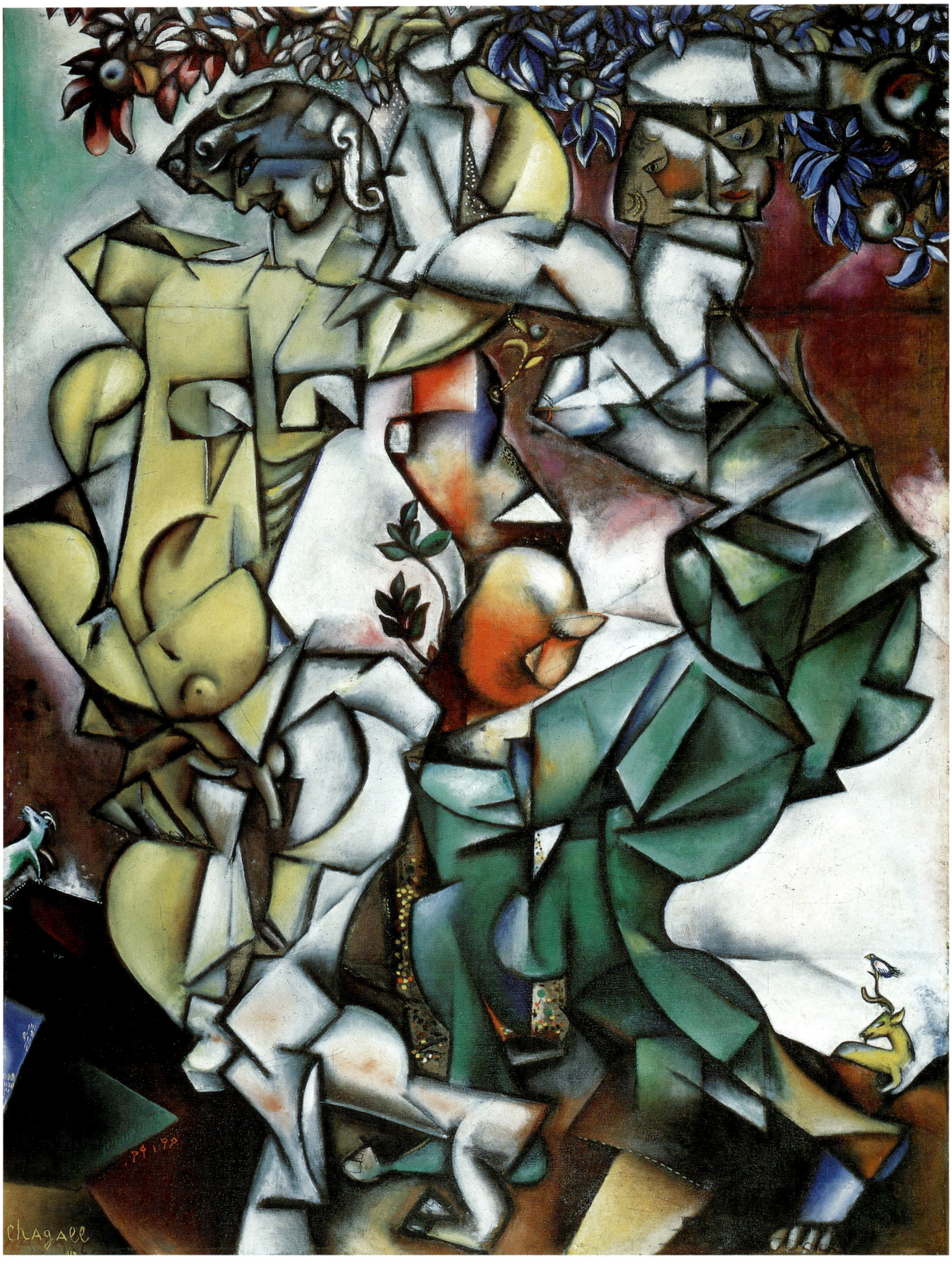

48. ***The Temptation.*** *1912. Oil on canvas, 166.4 x 118.7 cm. Saint Louis Art Museum, Gift of Morton D. May*

tive," and almost as flat and two-dimensional as the geometrical shapes.

As far as I can tell, no critic has looked at this possibility because of the title "Homage to Apollinaire" and the Modernist associations of the painter. Here again Chagall's ambivalence plays, this time between Modernism and the Christian tradition of painting. And here again Chagall is much more sophisticated and conscious of his work than his public image would allow.

Thus a series of ambivalences is expressed in this painting: between Latin and Hebrew letters, between Jewish and Christian traditions, between letters as transparent signs and letters as graphic shapes, between male and female genders, between Modernist and traditional styles, between birth and existence. This must not be seen as a derivative and eclectic work; on the contrary, it is so much stronger for all those tensions. Indeed, its style is the demonstrative eclecticism I mentioned before or, in a positive term, the polyphony of contradictory forces.

To what extent this stylistic polyphony contributes to the strength of the painting can be seen if we look at two different attempts by Chagall on the theme of Adam and Eve: one, *Study for Adam and Eve*, 1910 (no. 47), in the folk tradition of the Russian Lubok—a straightforward illustration, which remains as naïve as its genre; and the other, *The Temptation*, 1912 (no. 48), a Cubist tour-de-force imitating Picasso in a more sensuous vein—a road which Chagall experimented with but ultimately did not take. In either case, there is one dominant stylistic principle, whereas in our painting Chagall plays with several. The pluricentered *Homage to Apollinaire* is so much stronger and holds our attention to the ambiguities of the painting. The formal explorations in shapes and colors give a dimension of depth to the mere thematic elements. Indeed, he moved here from an influence of Picasso to Delauney and the second generation of Cubists.

The title "Homage to Apollinaire" is an abbreviation; the painting is dedicated with love to four avant-garde artists who recognized Chagall's unique talent early on: [Guillaume] Apollinaire, [Ricciotto] Canudo, [Herwarth] Walden, and [Blaise] Cendrars (misspelled in the painting). But the inscription is the only verbal element not integrated with its context and it looks like a later addition. Because Cendrars met Chagall only after his return from America late in 1912, and Chagall met Walden only in 1913, the dedication could not be written earlier than 1913. The painting itself could still be a product of 1911, as traditionally dated and as indicated on the clock circle.

Homage to Apollinaire combined both earlier series; it is about a major station in life and about Chagall's own identity problems. But it is basically a cosmopolitan painting. This station in life—a merger of man and woman—is not folklorically determined, it is neither Jewish nor Russian, but is a universal human predicament. The input of Jewish cultural elements is merely an infrastructure of the image, without changing the theme itself. Ambiguity, a basic issue in modern thought, emerges not from reading Kerkegaard, but from Chagall's own experience as a multicultural person with conflicting identities, a person who abandoned the monolithic doctrine of religion, opened up to contradictory trends in the world and opened his eyes to a great variety of possibilities in art.

At the same time, *Homage to Apollinaire* opened a third series, images from the Bible, which preoccupied him throughout his life, up to the "Biblical Message" of the French National Museum Marc Chagall in Nice and the stained-glass windows he created for various churches and synagogues. The Bible was universal in European culture, and Chagall lived with its stories from his earliest years. He could combine the reading of the Bible as a classical text with its associations in the world of his childhood and still present it as a universal, Judeo-Christian message.

3. *Documents*

The flights of imagination and original, enigmatic fictional worlds that informed Chagall's Paris works were to a large extent supported by the freedom Chagall had from the concrete objects of his Vitebsk surroundings, and the enthusiastic reception of Chagall's world by some avant-garde artists. Much in his Paris work referred to the Vitebsk landscapes and people, for it was a reconstruction of his family and typical scenes from the distance of memory, perhaps with the aid of some drawings and paintings Chagall brought with him from Russia. Yet the compositions were fantastic and dreamlike and not bound to any demands of realism.

Back in Vitebsk in July 1914, he embarked on a new series that he called "documents" or "my Vitebsk series of 1914" as if to fill his arsenal with fresh images from life, which could later be used in imaginative recollection. Here the basic realistic descriptions were preserved and the Modernism was curbed, confined to limited deformations, foreshortening of perspectives, and unreal colors.

The Vitebsk documents returned to the sanctity of

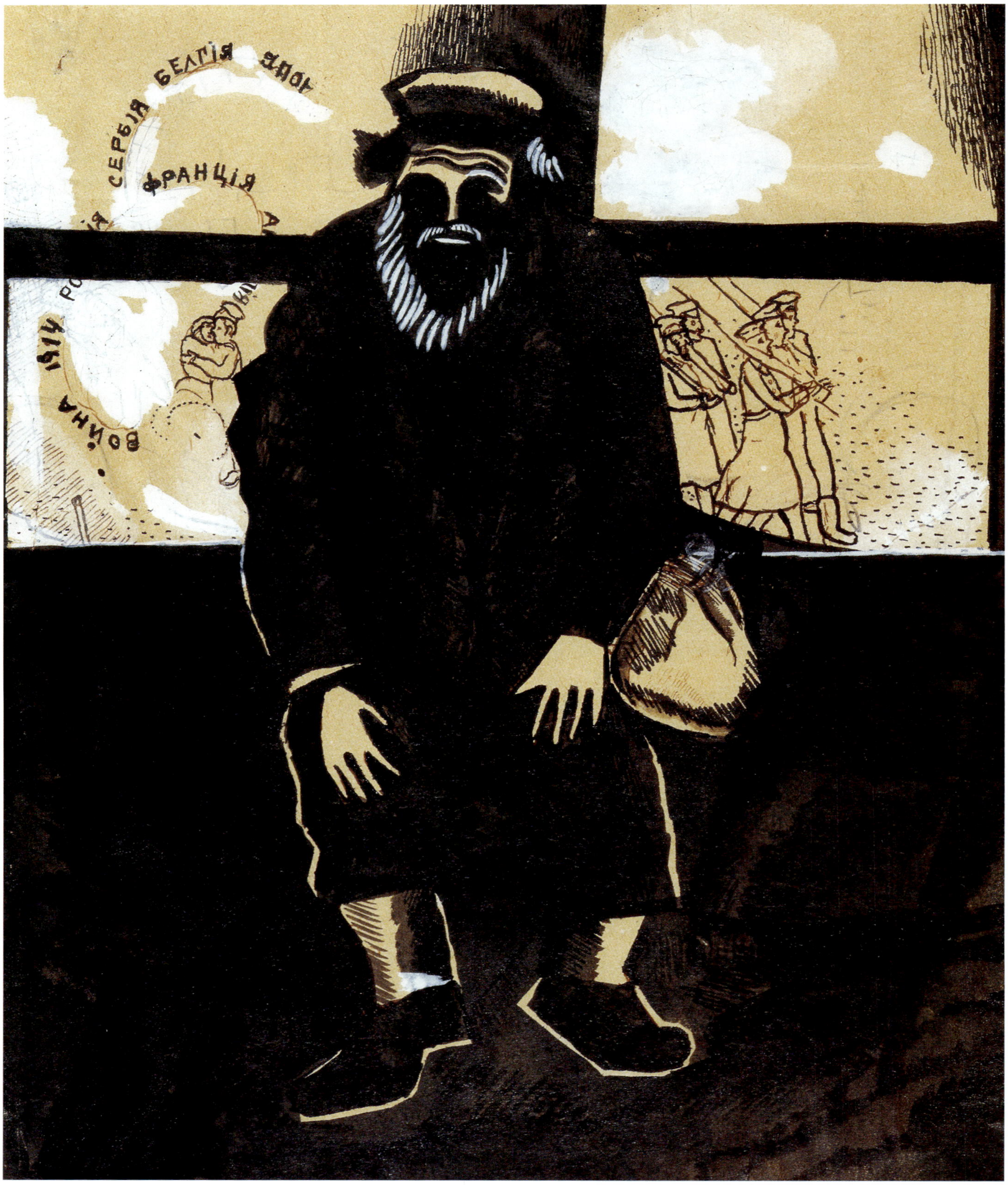

49. ***War.*** *1914. India ink and opaque white with pen and brush on paper, 22 x 18 cm. Kovalenko Art Museum, Krasnodar*

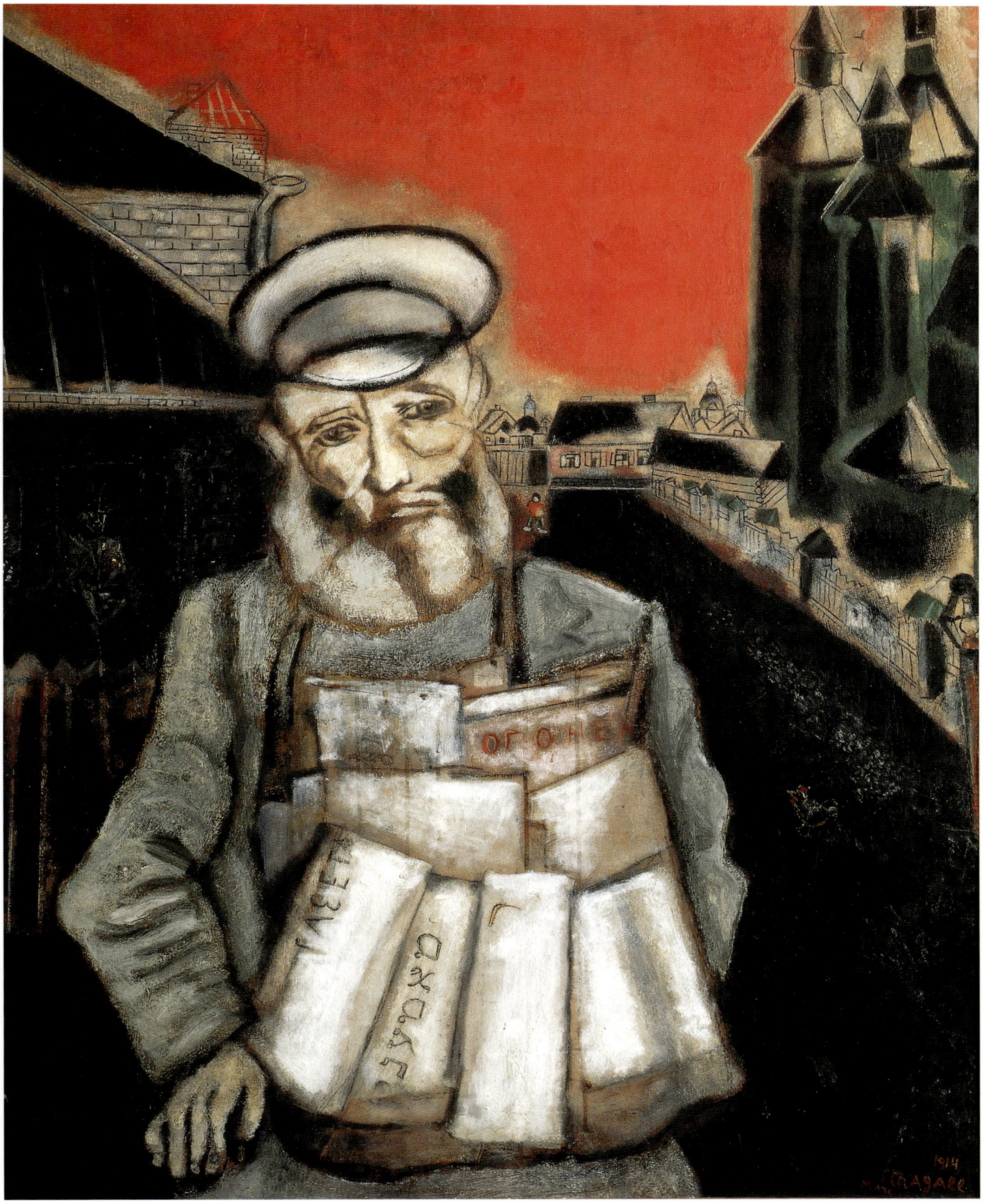

50. ***The Newspaper Vendor.*** *1914. Oil on canvas, 98 x 78.5 cm. Paris, Musée national d'art moderne, Centre Georges Pompidou, Paris*

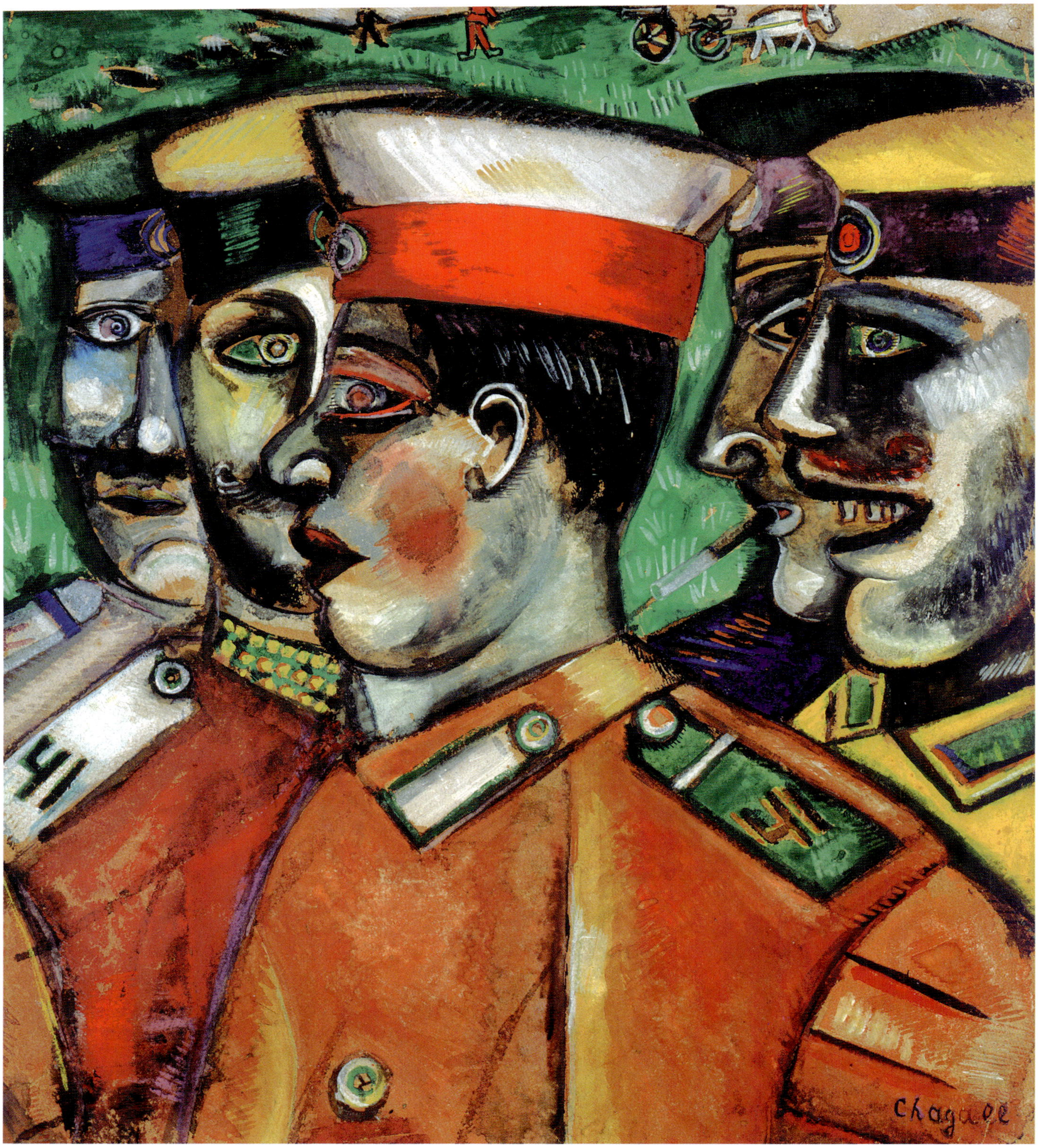

51. ***Soldiers.*** *1912. Gouache on cardboard, 38.1 x 31.7 cm. Private collection*

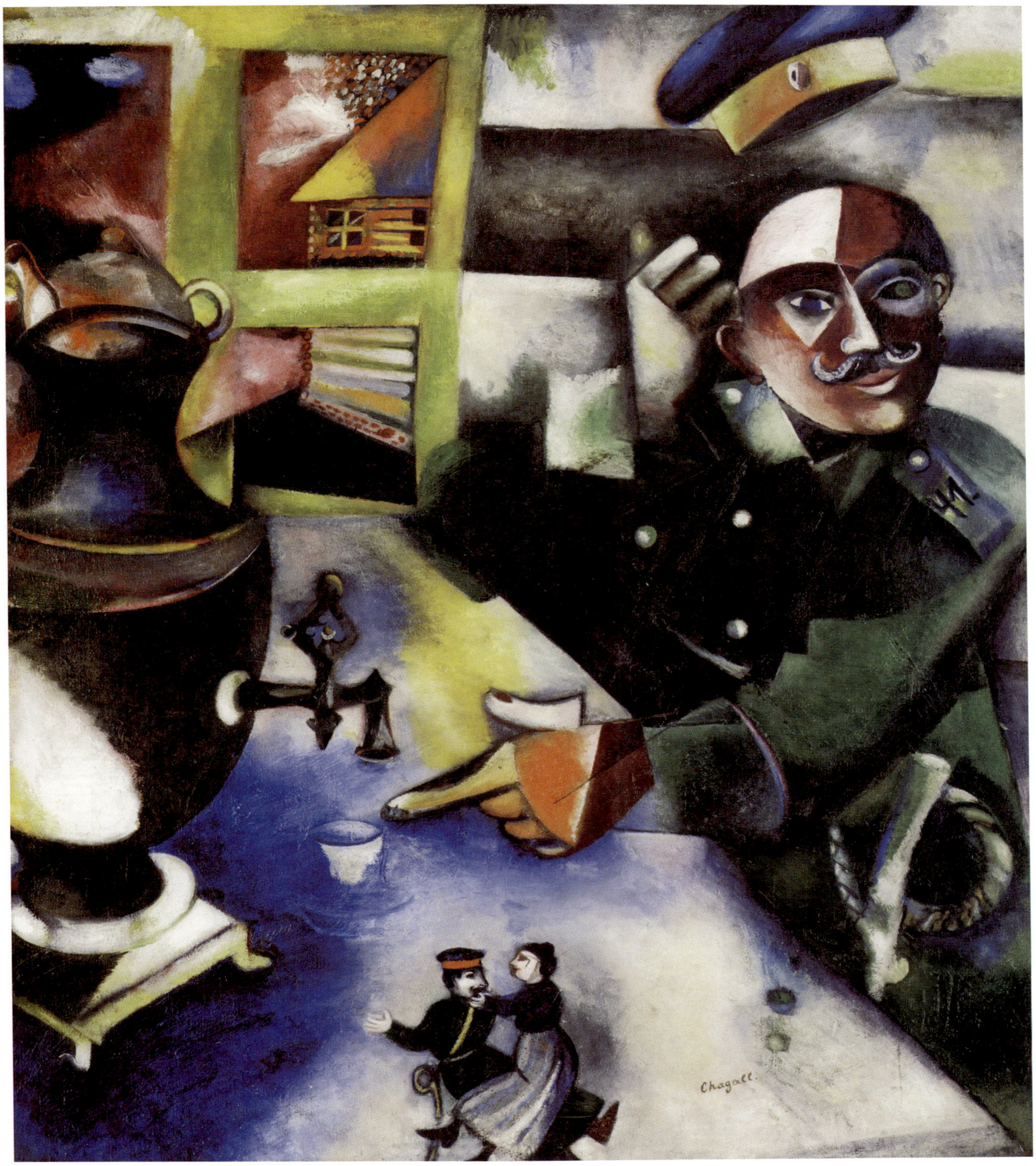

52. ***The Soldier Drinks.*** *1911–12. Oil on canvas, 109.1 x 94.5 cm. Solomon R. Guggenheim Museum, New York*

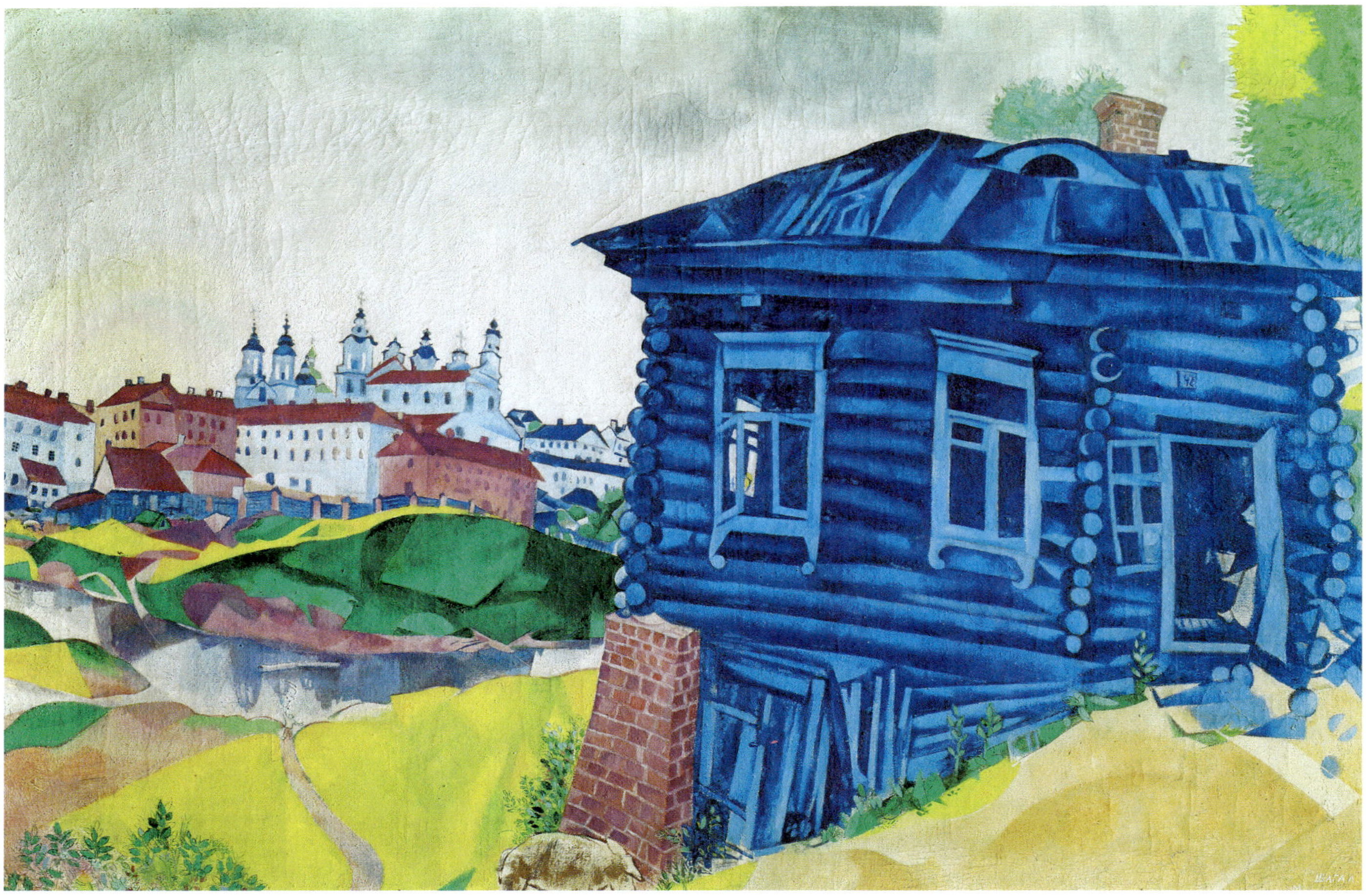

53. ***The Blue House.*** *1917. Oil on canvas, 66 x 97 cm. Liège, Musée d'Art Moderne et d'Art Contemporain, Liege, Belgium*

objects: no more Cubist decompositions of figures, as in *Dedicated to My Fiancée*. Colors did not cross any boundaries of objects and figures, and only occasionally was a figure divided into several color areas. It seems that Chagall did his drawings and drafts in nature but painted later at home. What remained of the Modernist impulse can be seen in some cubicized folds—such as the magnificent, phantasmagoric white sky with geometrical color intrusions, which add a halo and a flying mood to the image of cathedrals in *The Gray House* (no. 2); some foreshortened perspectives, and most notably the willful selection of bright colors that may have no relation to the colors of the real objects. The symphony of colors had its own, autonomous structure, akin to the sound patterns of poetic meter.

The "documents" started with the outbreak of World War I and first depicted the general Russian wartime atmosphere; yet suddenly in 1915, with the expulsion of a million Jews from the front areas, Chagall shifted to Jewish topics, as if documenting "the lost Jewish world" (see chapter 4). Both topics are then quite intermingled, reflecting a multicultural perception of provincial Russia.

War, 1914 (no. 49), depicts a bearded peasant, perhaps waiting to be drafted and ready with his little bag. Through the window we see a couple parting and a Russian inscription: "War 1914 Russia Serbia Belgium Japan France England." In front of them (to our right) a military unit is marching off. *The Newspaper Vendor*, 1914 (no. 50), sells to a bilingual audience: the upper right-hand paper is *Ogone[K]* (*The Little Flame*), a Russian weekly; by dropping the last letter Chagall emphasizes *ogon'* ("fire"), written in red letters and reflected in the solid red sky background and on the margins of the houses around the black "dead street" (a Yiddish idiom for a deserted place). The other titles are: the Yiddish newspaper *Moment*, with the T obfuscated so that it reads *Mameni[u]* ("Oy, Mama," like "Mama mia!"); the Yiddish R (perhaps for the newspaper *Radio*); and the Russian *Gazeta* (perhaps *Smolenskaya Gazeta*, "Smolensk Gazette," which he reproduced elsewhere).

During the war, the headquarters of the central front and war hospitals were in Vitebsk; now the soldiers come into focus in Chagall's "documents." The painting *Soldiers*, 1912 (no. 51), shows almost Picasso-like double

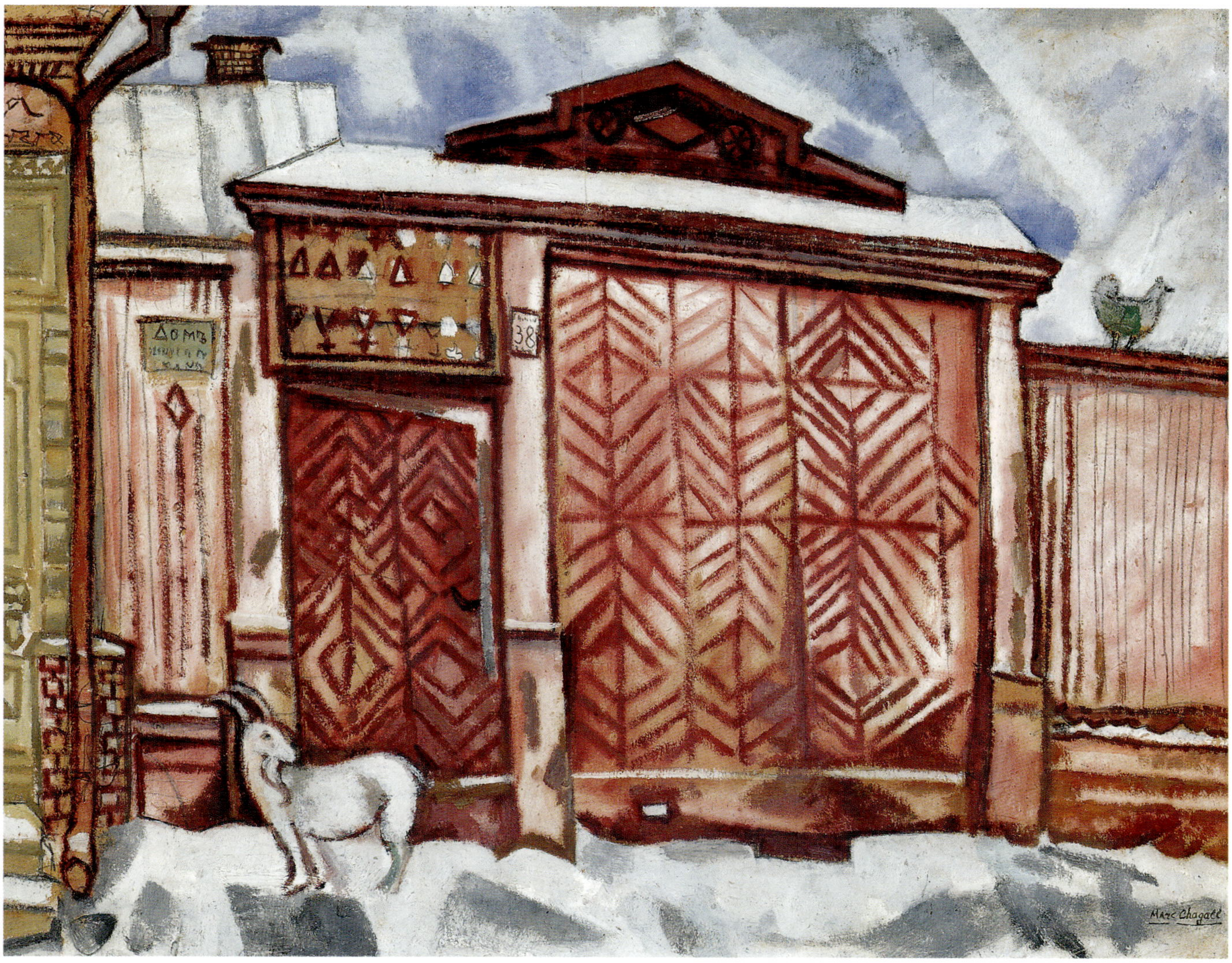

54. ***The Red Gate.*** *1917. Oil on cardboard, 49.4 x 66 cm. Staatsgalerie Stuttgart*

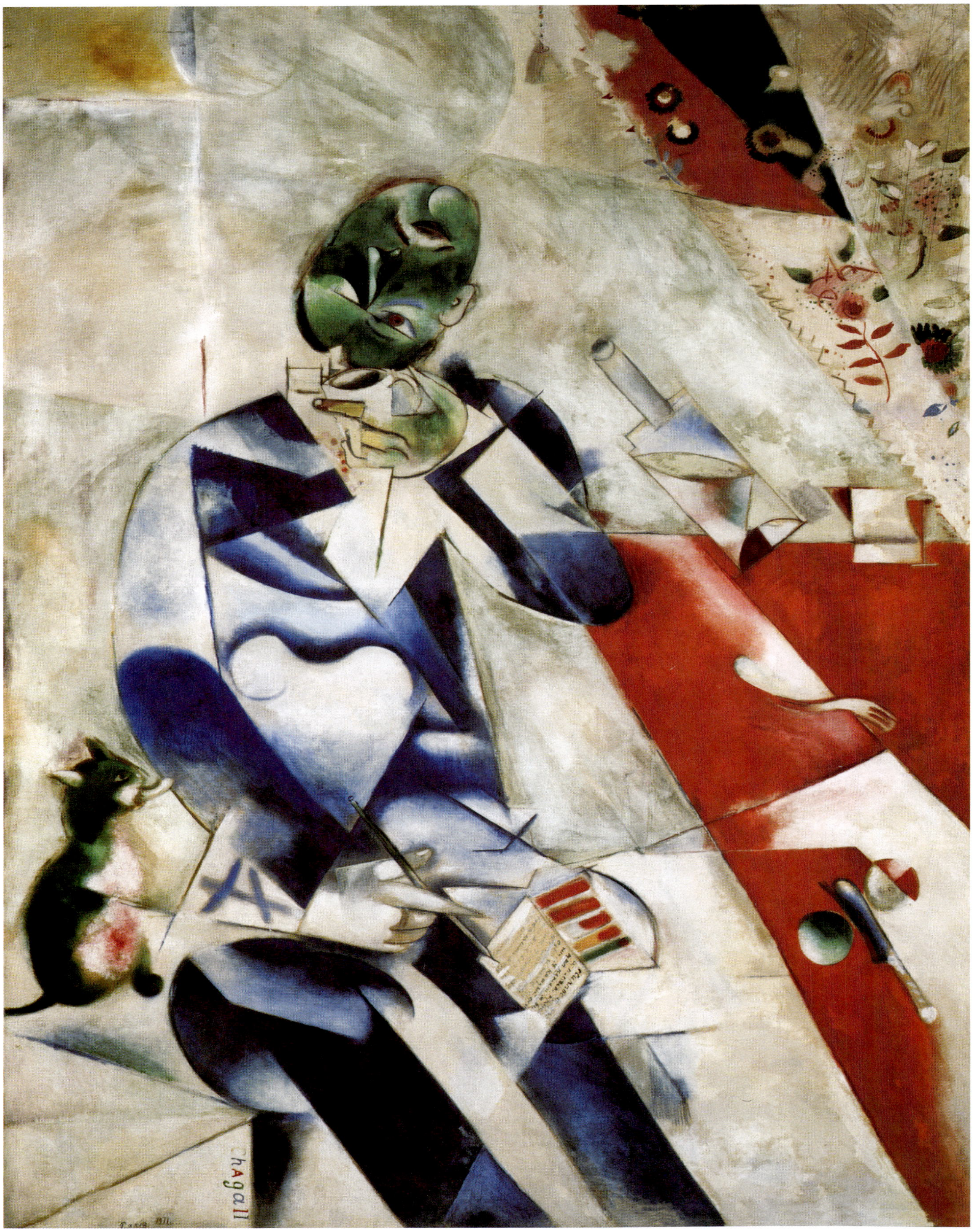

55. ***Half Past Three (The Poet).*** *1911. Oil on canvas, 195.9 x 144.8 cm. The Louise and Walter Arensberg Collection, 1950, Philadelphia Museum of Art, Philadelphia*

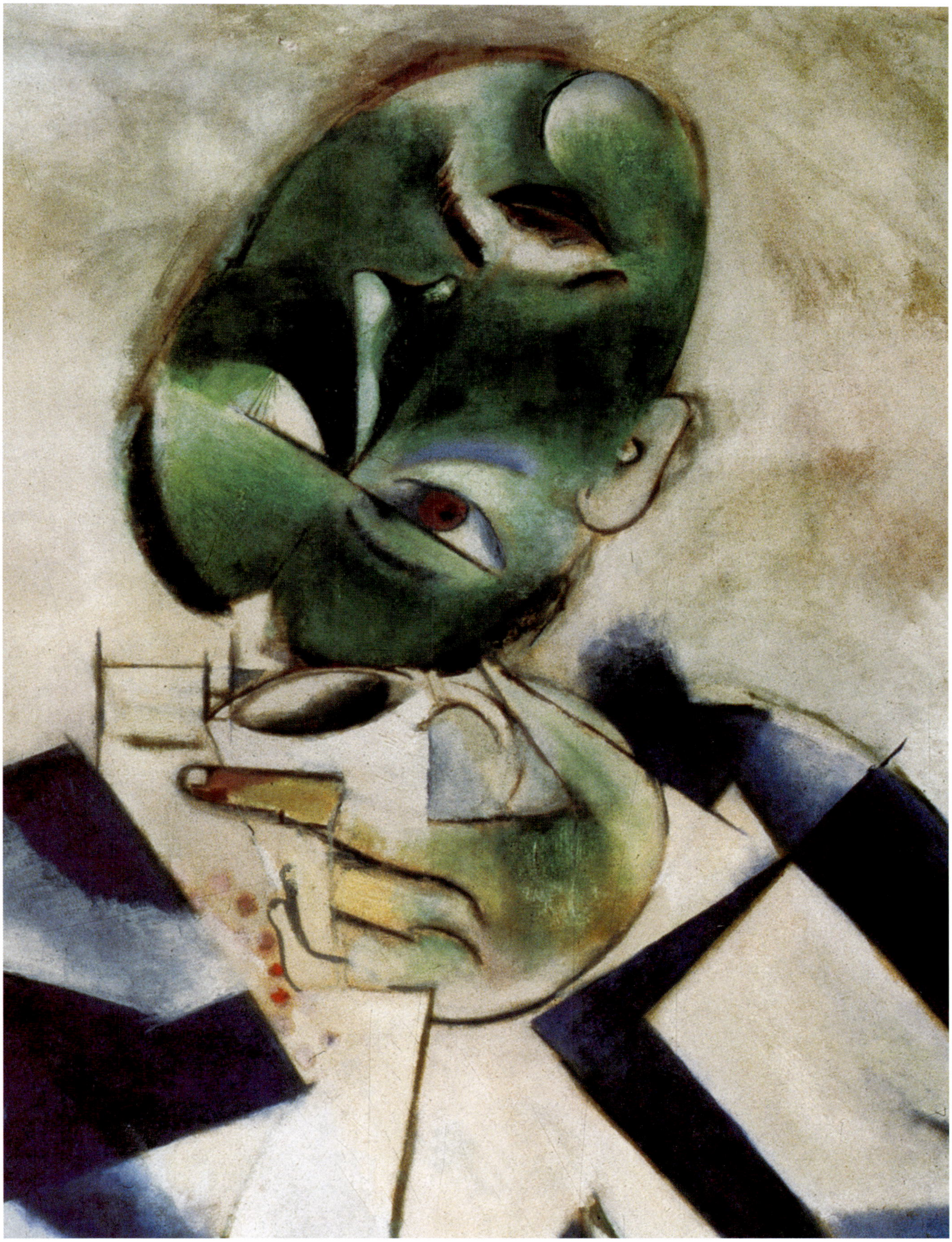

56. ***Half Past Three (The Poet)** (detail). 1911. Oil on canvas, 195.9 x 144.8 cm. The Louise and Walter Arensberg Collection, 1950, Philadelphia Museum of Art, Philadelphia*

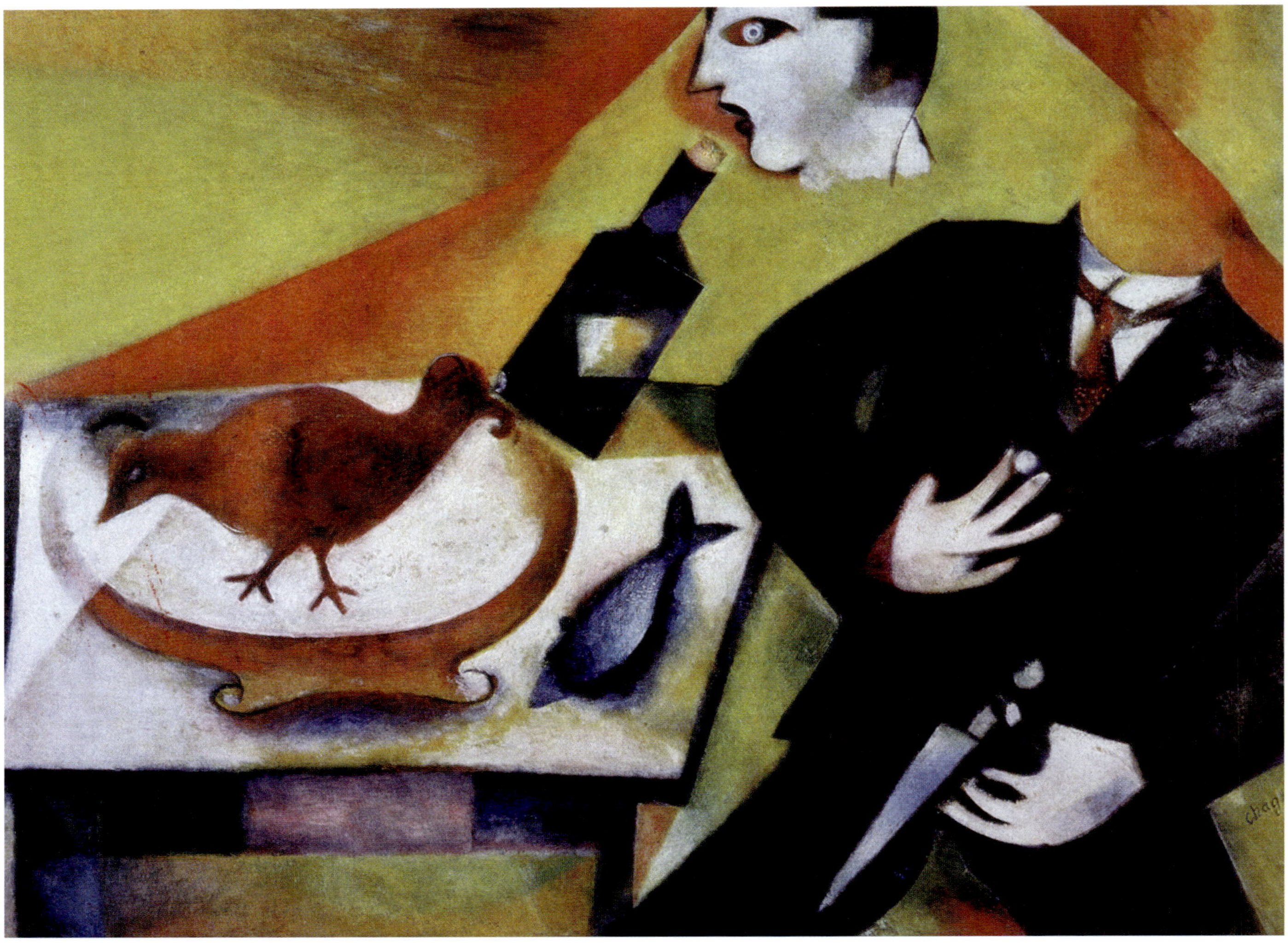

57. ***The Drunkard.*** *1910–12. Oil on canvas, 85 x 115 cm. Private collection*

faces. The soldiers are from regiment No. 41 and the date "1912," which refers to a time when Chagall was still in Paris, cannot possibly be correct. The same is true for *The Soldier Drinks*, 1911–12 (no. 52), which features a soldier from the same regiment. In this work Chagall uses the stereotype of a soldier flirting with a woman and getting drunk, although overtly it is tea from a samovar that he is drinking—another stereotype of Russia. His drunken hat flies off his head.

A more ambitious and monumental "document" is *The Blue House*, 1917 (no. 53), showing the Vitebsk cathedrals in their majestic stature, underlined by the red roofs in front of them. There is a strong juxtaposition of unrealistically colored objects. Outside of the houses the terrain is stylized to the point of cubicized abstractions (the green and yellow areas). The water reflects the cathedrals, but the yellow bridge is displaced to the green area.

The Red Gate, 1917 (no. 54), is the gate of the Chagall house at Pokrovskaya 38 (which certainly was not painted red). The painting is entirely devoted to the force of color. Here Chagall found a realistic basis for his geometrical ornaments, rendered with shades of color in areas that are sometimes blurred and sometimes intense. The three steps to his mother's store, the Chagallian rooster on top, and the goat below are almost de rigueur. The framing on the left and the abstract formations of light colors above and below the gate help create the full impact of the work.

4. *From Eroticism to Love*

The erotic nudes of 1911 and 1913 (nos. 58, 59, and 60) have simplified features and exaggerated gestures, reminiscent of some German Expressionist woodcuts, along with counternatural twists of the body. Diagonal and triangular shapes further distort and sharpen the feminine body. And sometimes circles or spheres fulfill a similar function (see no. 60). The striking painting *Dedicated to My Fiancée*, 1911 (no. 61), was first called *The Ass and the Woman*. It contains three hands and three legs. The Chagallian overlapping man/ass (usually an emblem of himself, "the stupid

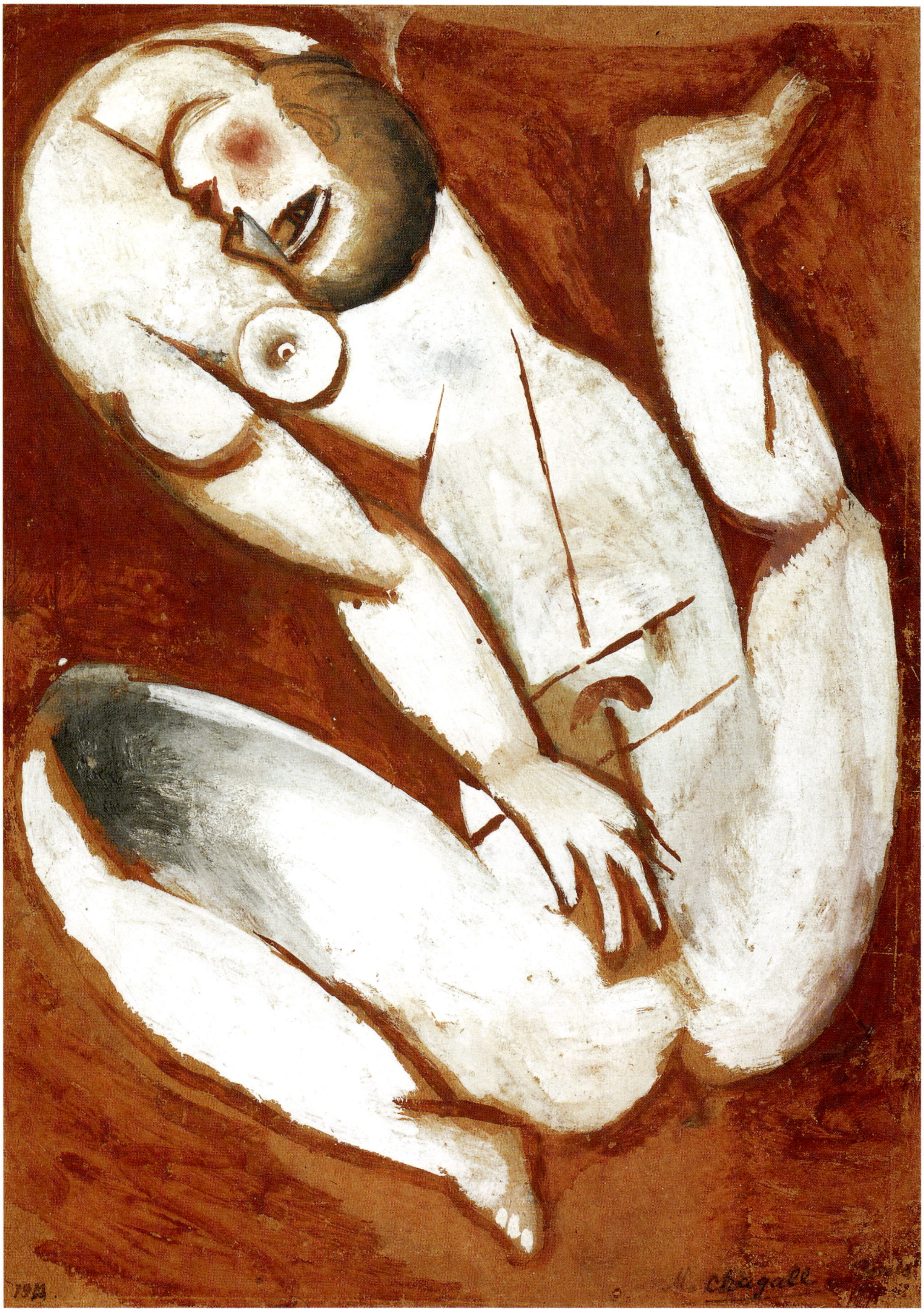

58. ***Nude in Movement.*** *1913. Gouache on brown packing paper, 34.7 x 23.9 cm. Musée national d'art moderne, Centre George Pompidou, Paris*

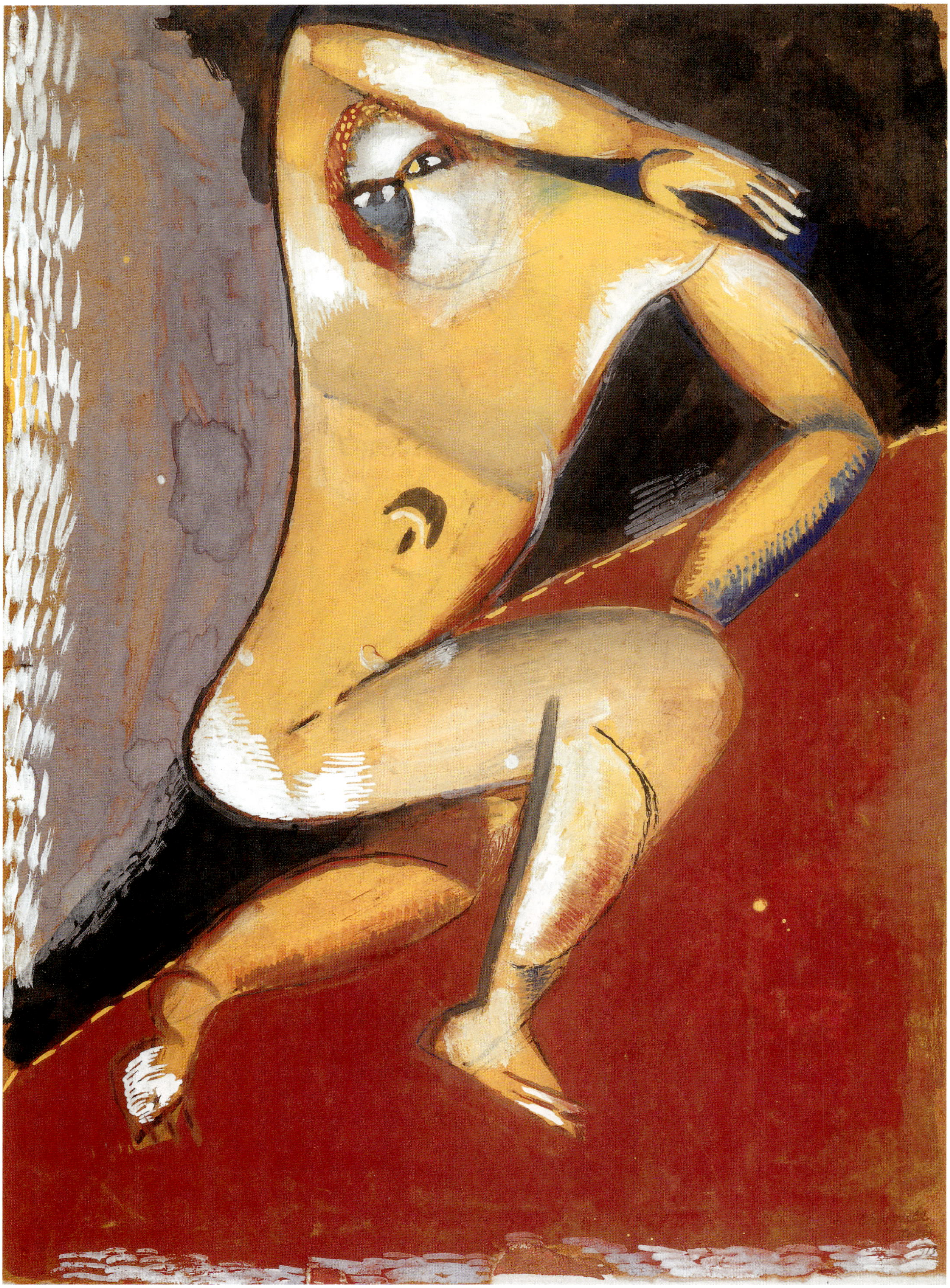

59. **Nude.** *1913. Gouache on paper, 34 x 24 cm. The Thyssen-Bornemisza collection, Madrid*

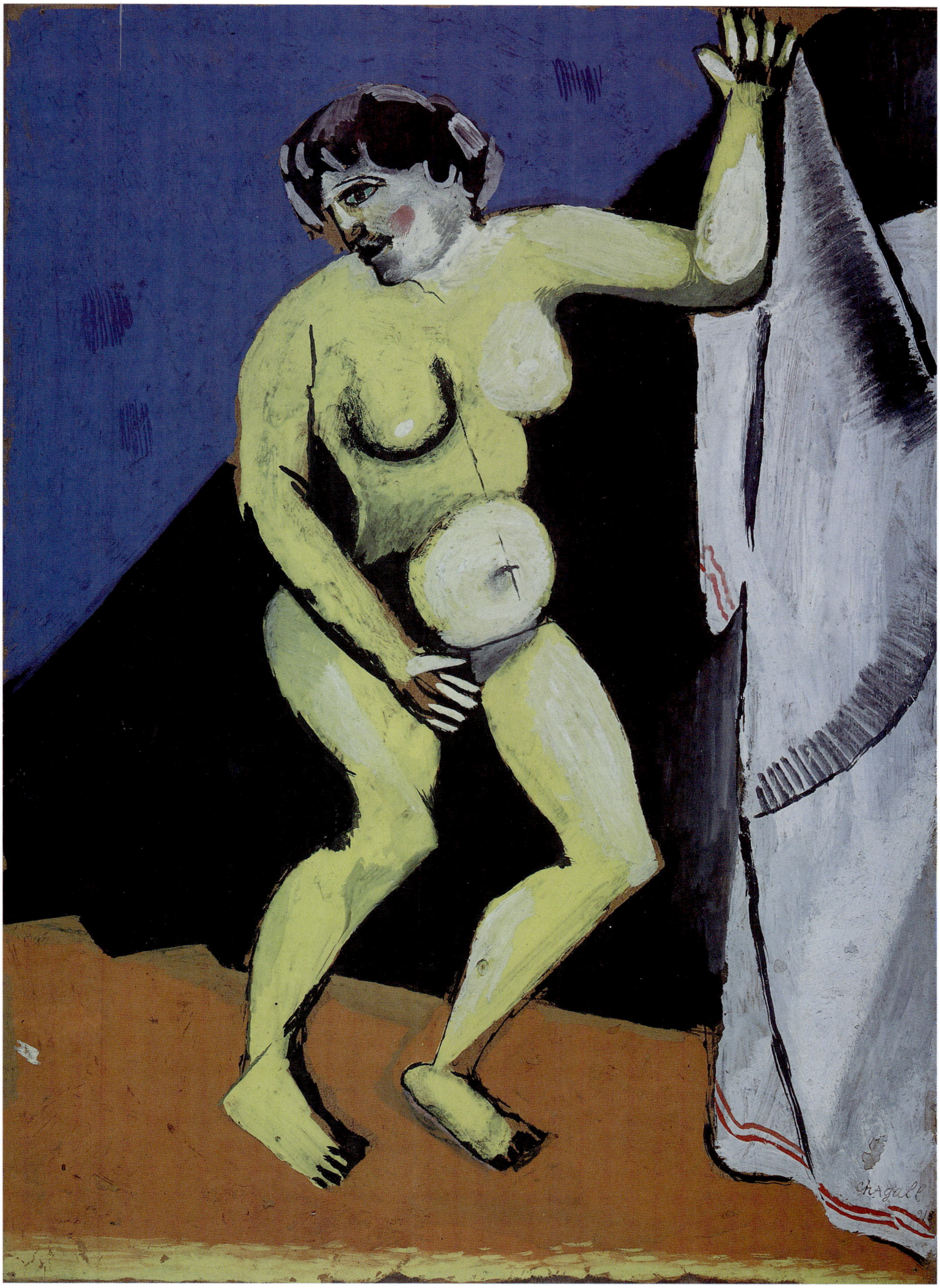

60. ***Standing Nude.*** *1913. Gouache on paper, 34 x 24 cm. Collection of E.W. Kornfeld, Berne*

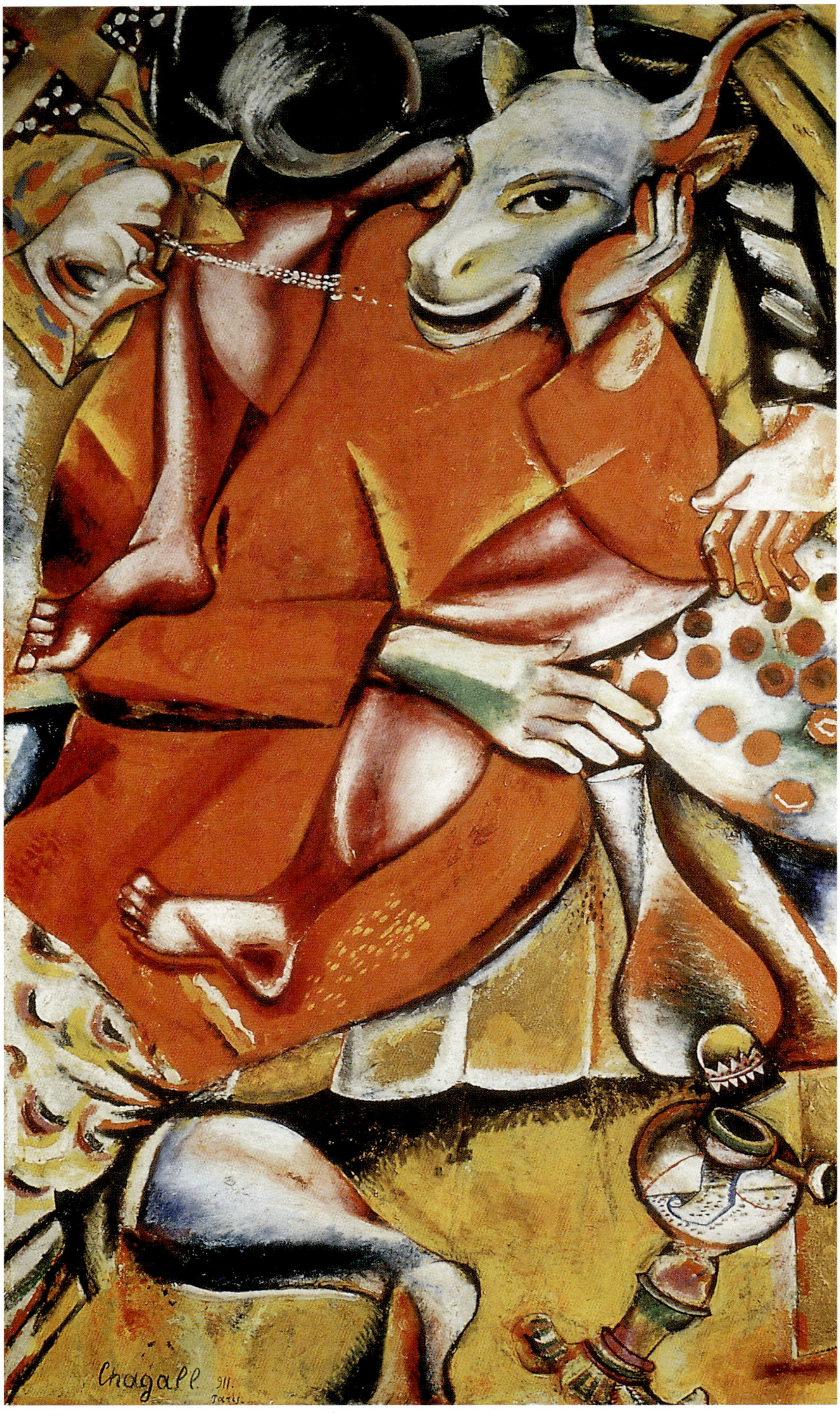

61. ***Dedicated to My Fiancée.*** *1911. Oil on canvas, 196 x 114.5 cm. Kunstmuseum, Berne*

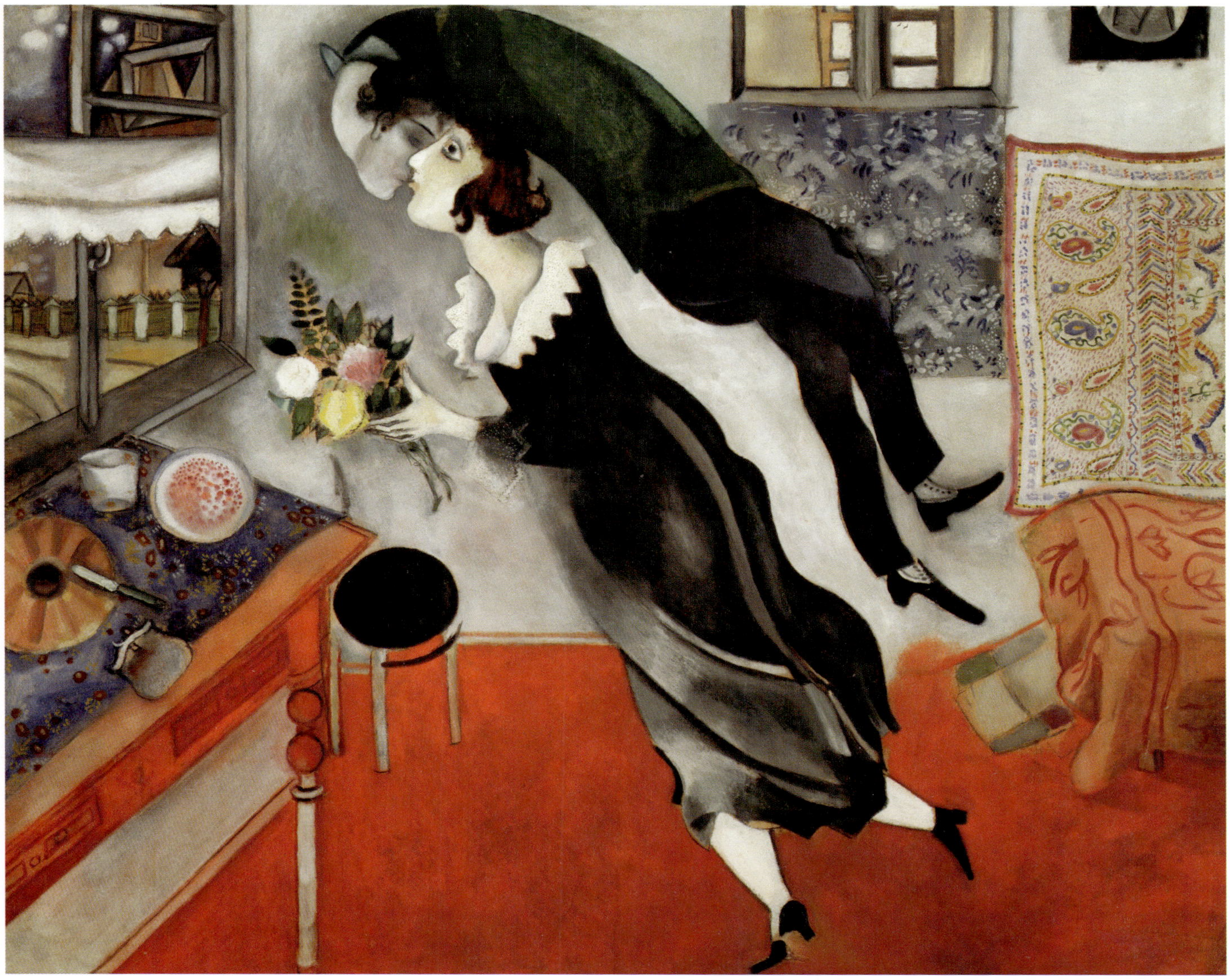

62. ***The Birthday***. *1915. Oil on cardboard, 80.5 x 99.5 cm. The Museum of Modern Art, New York*

ass") sits comfortably in the wide lap of a woman, marked by her two red legs. Apollinaire saw it as "a golden donkey smoking opium." The third leg and hand on the right may represent yet another woman, enormously encircling the man/ass and spitting in his face. The oil lamp represents folk culture and its glass is shaped like the calf of the third leg. The ornament seems to represent Russian folk art. "I spit on you" (*naplevat'*) in Russian means: "I don't give a damn about you / I don't need you / I despise you," as if communicating to Berta in Russian about his erotic debauchery. If this is a portrait of his fiancée, it may indicate the crisis in their relationship. Chagall wrote in his autobiography:

> This fourth and last love [with Berta] could have come to naught in my four years in France. At the end of my stay in Paris, all that remained of it was a heap of letters, which didn't even have a sign of an ending. One more letter with a few interesting words, and I decided everything was over between us.[8]

From the later vantage point of love and marriage, Chagall might have wanted retrospectively to attribute such images to his "fiancée," yet his Russian poetry of 1909–1910 and the notation in the autobiography betray a doubtful love relationship. Indeed it took them a year after his return in 1914 to get married.

Only after their marriage did Chagall's paintings celebrate the exaltation of love through broad gestures of lightness, flying, and defying gravity. *The Birthday*, 1915 (no. 62) has Marc unnaturally bending over in midflight to kiss his birthday bride. The meticulous decorations, including a wall rag with Indian patterns, are reminiscent of Matisse's Morocco paintings. The open pomegranate is a recipe for a woman's fruitfulness. The strange buildings in the window may indicate the Rebbe's headquarters in Zaolshe, the place of Marc and Berta's honeymoon.

The Promenade, 1917 (no. 63) has some of the same ornamental features, such as the red carpet with a samovar for a picnic. The ground, the fence, and the sky are cubicized. Bella's purple dress echoes the color of the church, and the whole view is not one of his familiar Vitebsk landscapes. The dividing fence fulfills the function of the Vitebsk river.

Double Portrait with a Glass of Wine, 1917–18 (no. 67) is suffused in Chagall's favorite scarlet red, including the bridge and the Vitebsk cathedral, the wine, and the little angel blessing the couple, who reappears in the theater mural *Music*, 1920 (no. 154).

The freest expression of all is seen in *Over the Village*, 1914–18 (no. 64) (the correct hame would be "Over the Town"), in which both lovers are actually flying in the sky. A Yiddish idiom *er flit in di himlen* ("he is flying in the sky") means: he is carried away by his fantasy and excitement. This image is cognate to (and probably follows) *Over Vitebsk* (no. 74), which employs the same defiance of gravity for a different theme altogether. The impressionistic lightness of the pastel colors in parts of the city is in striking contrast to the previously discussed love images. Everything is airy here, except for the goat and the little boy defecating at the fence, which ironize the romantic message (see detail, no. 65).

5. *On Chagall's Evolution*

The "Stations in Man's Life" series was started in Russia, yet Chagall presumably took those paintings with him to Paris and finished them there. The works finished in Russia, such as *The Dead Man*, 1908 (no. 27), *Russian Wedding*, 1909 (no. 33), or *The Studio*, 1910, show distorted proportions of reality and an unrealistic and conspicuous use of bright colors, based on Bakst's esteem of the centrality of color in painting and his encouragement of anti-routine, anti-academic creative freedom. But only in post-Cubist Paris did Chagall's colors overflow the boundaries of objects and abstract, formal, and geometrical shapes assumed equal value in the painting. That difference can be clearly seen in the change from *The Russian Wedding*, 1909, to *The Wedding*, 1911 (no. 35), or from the folkloric *Study for Adam and Eve*, 1910 (no. 47), to *Homage to Apollinaire*, 1911 (no. 44).

In the Stations of Man's Life, there are unrealistic colors, continuities, and dimensions of figures relative to Chagall's settings. But only in Paris did Chagall discover the possibilities of dismembered bodies and detached limbs. In *The Drunkard*, 1910–12 (no. 57), the head of the central figure flies off, indicating the drunkard's confusion. It evokes the Yiddish idiom, *Der kop is im farfloygn* (literally, "his head flew off him," meaning, "he lives in a fantasyland," "he overreached himself"). In *The Poet (Half Past Three)*, 1911 (nos. 55 and 56), the poet depicted may well be Chagall himself. The green head is not just detached from the body, but also turned around. In Yiddish, the cognate idiom *der kop is im fardreyt* (literally, his head is turned around one turn too many, or "screwed up") means something like: he is discombobulated—indeed Chagall selected this image for the cover of Efros and Tugendhold's *The Art of Marc Chagall*, 1918 (no. 66). The titles of the book are written upside down: the author is on top, while the name of the book, inverted, is on the bottom. Yet of the two cultural domains that influenced Chagall (as seen in *Self-Portrait with Seven Fingers*) only Vitebsk remained. Indeed, Chagall himself referred to his paintings when explaining his state of mind.

In *To Russia, Donkeys and Others* the woman's head flying upward is a realization of an ecstatic experience. Yet elsewhere, Chagall explained that in this painting, the head was separated from the body because he needed to fill out the space in the upper right. Indeed, while the first cases of this device are specifically motivated by the theme of the painting, it later becomes an independent device and a trademark of Chagall, used time and again, especially in the great mural *Introduction to the Yiddish Theater*. Back in Russia in 1914 he developed further devices of deformations of the human body: bending backward, as in *Thinking about Picasso*, or flying above the ground, as in *Over Vitebsk* and *The Birthday*.

The Stations series was based on his own world; Chagall was bringing images of provincial Russia, Jewish small towns, and his own "crazy" family, to the educated and assimilated Jews in the capital. He used folklore and ethnography in a joyful and mystifying frame of mind. He brought the strength of his periphery to the center, to which he aspired, and this audience admired the genius from the "people" and bought his first paintings. Alisa Berson paid a large monthly tuition (30 rubles) for his studies at Bakst's school. Maxim Vinaver, a leader of the Russian KaDet (Constitutional-Democratic) party and past editor of *Voskhod*, the Jewish intellectual journal in

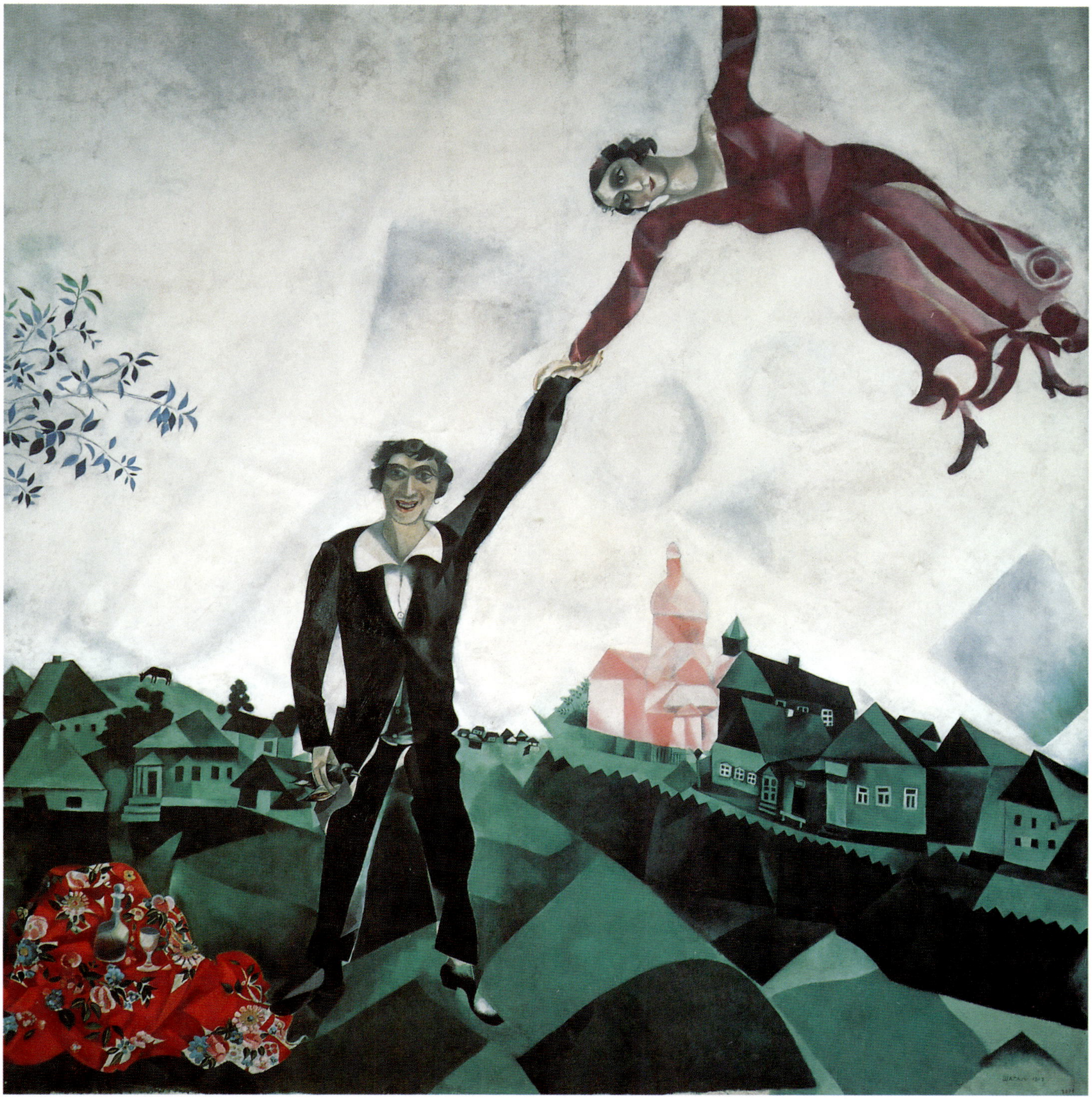

63. ***The Promenade.*** *1917. Oil on canvas, 170 x 163.5 cm. State Russian Museum, St. Petersburg*

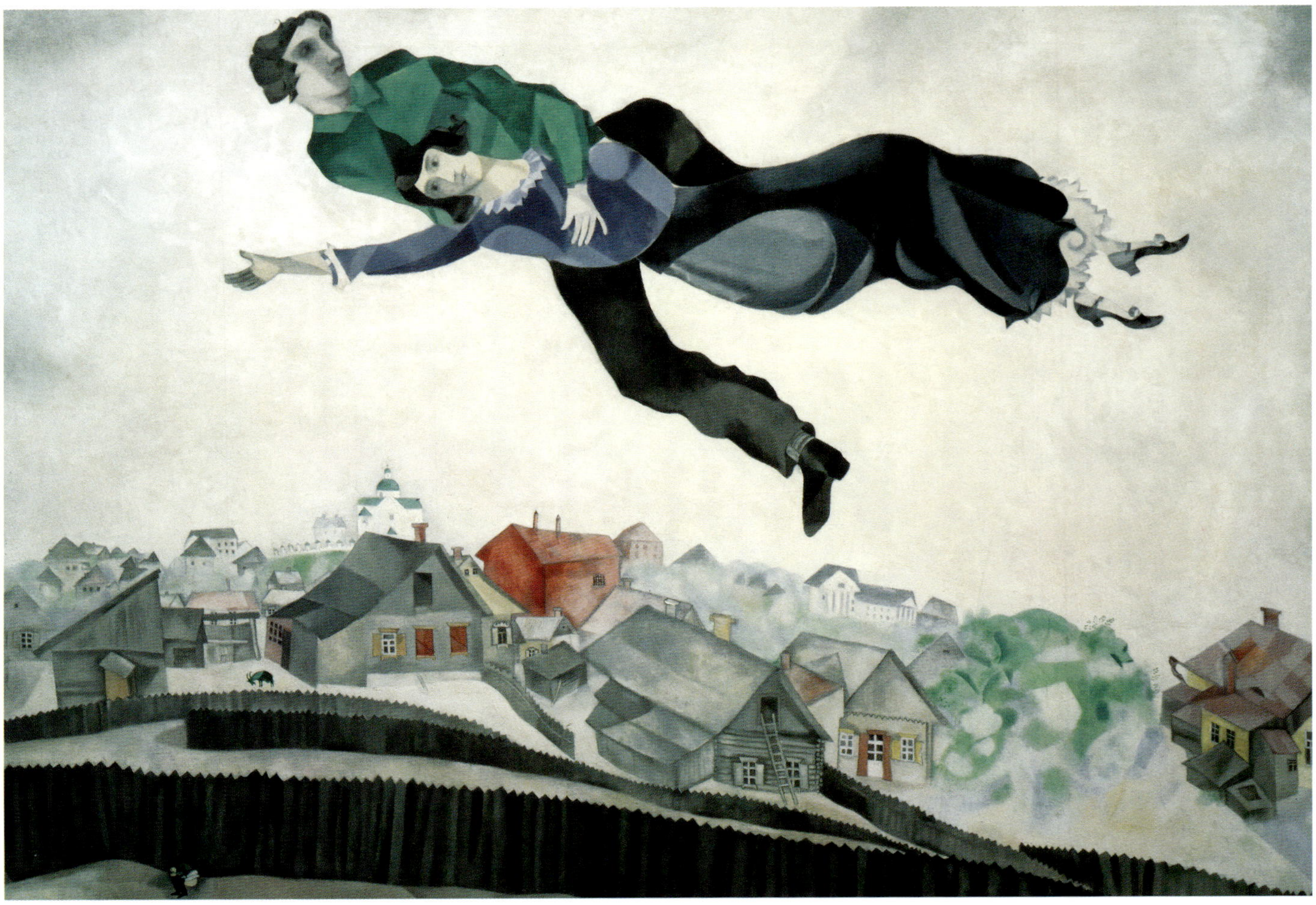

64. ***Over the Village.*** *1914–18. Oil on canvas, 141 x 198 cm. Tretyakov Gallery, Moscow*

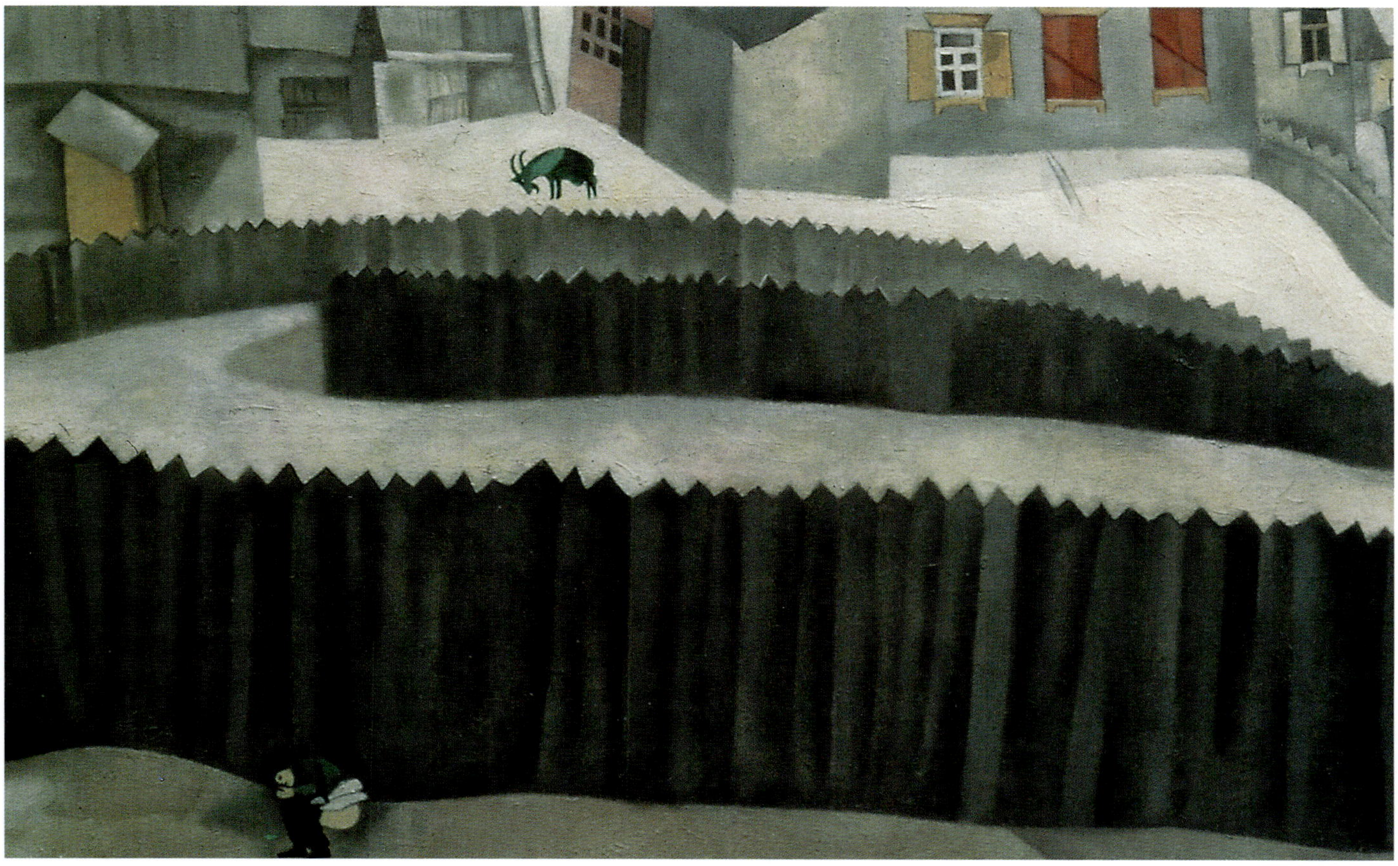

65. ***Over the Village*** *(detail). 1914–18. Oil on canvas, 141 x 198 cm. Tretyakov Gallery, Moscow*

the Russian language, bought his *Russian Wedding* probably in 1908 and gave him a stipend to live in Paris.

The "Identity" series was his introductory card to French art circles. Much more sophisticated than his earlier work, these paintings were influenced by the formal problems that preoccupied Parisian art of the day, and were appreciated by some of the most advanced artists and critics. Chagall was now conspicuously concerned with questions of form. The paintings of this period demonstrated the art and artificiality of painting, in the sense of Roman Jakobson's "poetic function," which he defined as "a set toward the message," or what we would call today "orientation toward the text itself." But Chagall never gave up the idea that representations are also part of the form, provided they undergo strong deformations. Indeed, it is only in his first Paris period that heads in his paintings were turned around or detached from their bodies.

Chagall never forgot the images of his early work; he transformed their functions while repeating them in numerous variations. His rooster—meaningful or devoid of any meaning—appears with no thematic invitation, for example in *Introduction to the Yiddish Theater*. Yet in the first decades of his career, most paintings had a theme or a story and only in the periphery of the painting did he scatter unrelated modules, perceived as ornaments or signatures of his authentic world. The kaleidoscope was an inventory of modules in Chagall's head, to be used at liberty in many variations. Only in his later years did he create individual kaleidoscopic paintings with no obvious dominant narrative center.

---

1. As suggested to me by Didier Schulman.

2. See Franz Meyer. Marc *Chagall: Life and Work*. New York: Harry N. Abrams, 1963, p. 64.

3. As observed by Ziva Amishai-Maisels.

4. Sholem-Aleichem, "The Violin," in *Stories for Jewish Children*, vol. 1. (New York: Sholem Aleichem Folksfond, 1918), p. 42.

5. See *Marc Chagall and His Times*, Chapter 2.

6. On the image of the protective umbrella and its linguistic sources, see Chapter 2, in the interpretation of *Cubist Landscape*.

7. The donkey leaning on his human elbow, as a thinking man, is central to the painting *To My Fiancée*.

8. See *Marc Chagall and His Times*, p. 147.

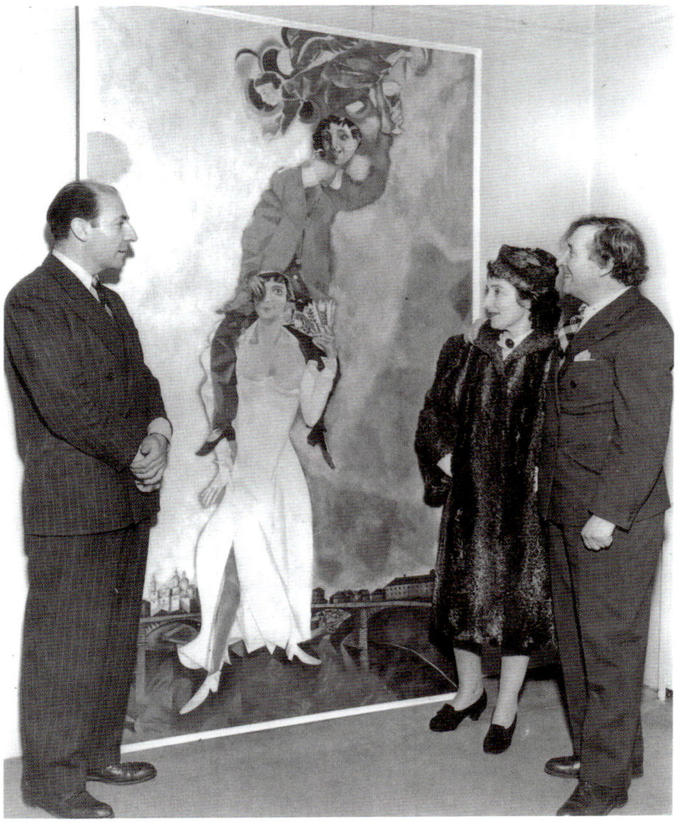

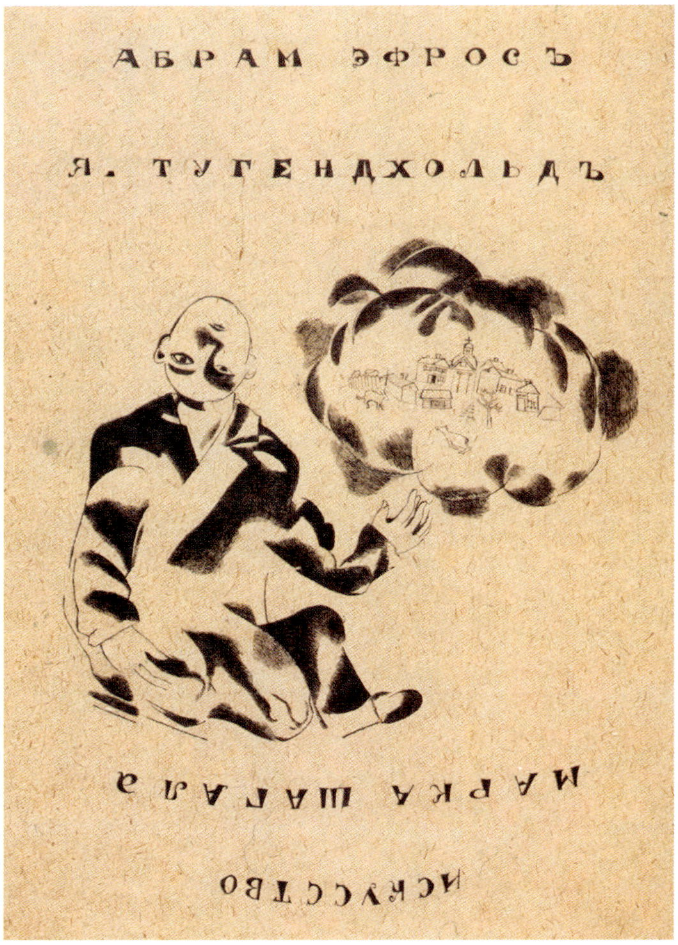

66. *Cover of **The Art of Marc Chagall** (1918) written by Abram Efros and Yakov Tugendhold, Moscow*

9. Some scholars tend to post-date *I and the Village*, but their arguments can easily be reversed. In any case, the intertextuality and the generic connection of the two paintings remain.

10. I am grateful to Miriam Cendrars in Paris for letting me read the unpublished manuscript.

11. I am grateful to Nina Rudnik for this reference.

12. Aleksandr Blok, *Sobraniye Sochineniya v vos mi tomakh* ("Collected works in eight volumes"). Moscow-Leningrad, Vol. 2, p. 55.

13. See Susan Compton. "Chagall's Auditorium: 'An Identity Crisis of Tragic Dimensions,'" in *Marc Chagall and the Jewish Theater*. New York: Guggenheim Museum, 1992, pp. 1–13.

14. See the new edition: S. M. Ginzburg, and P. S. Marek, *Yiddish Folksongs in Russia*, photo reproductions of the 1901 St. Petersburg edition. Edited and annotated with an introduction by Dov Noy. Ramat Gan: Bar-Ilan Univer sity, 1991.

15. The full version is: "A cow flew over the roof and laid an egg" (*a ku iz gefloygn ibern dakh un geleygt an ey*), and there are more vulgar variants.

16. I used the edition of *Bereshith Rabba* interpreted by Moshe Arye Mirkin.

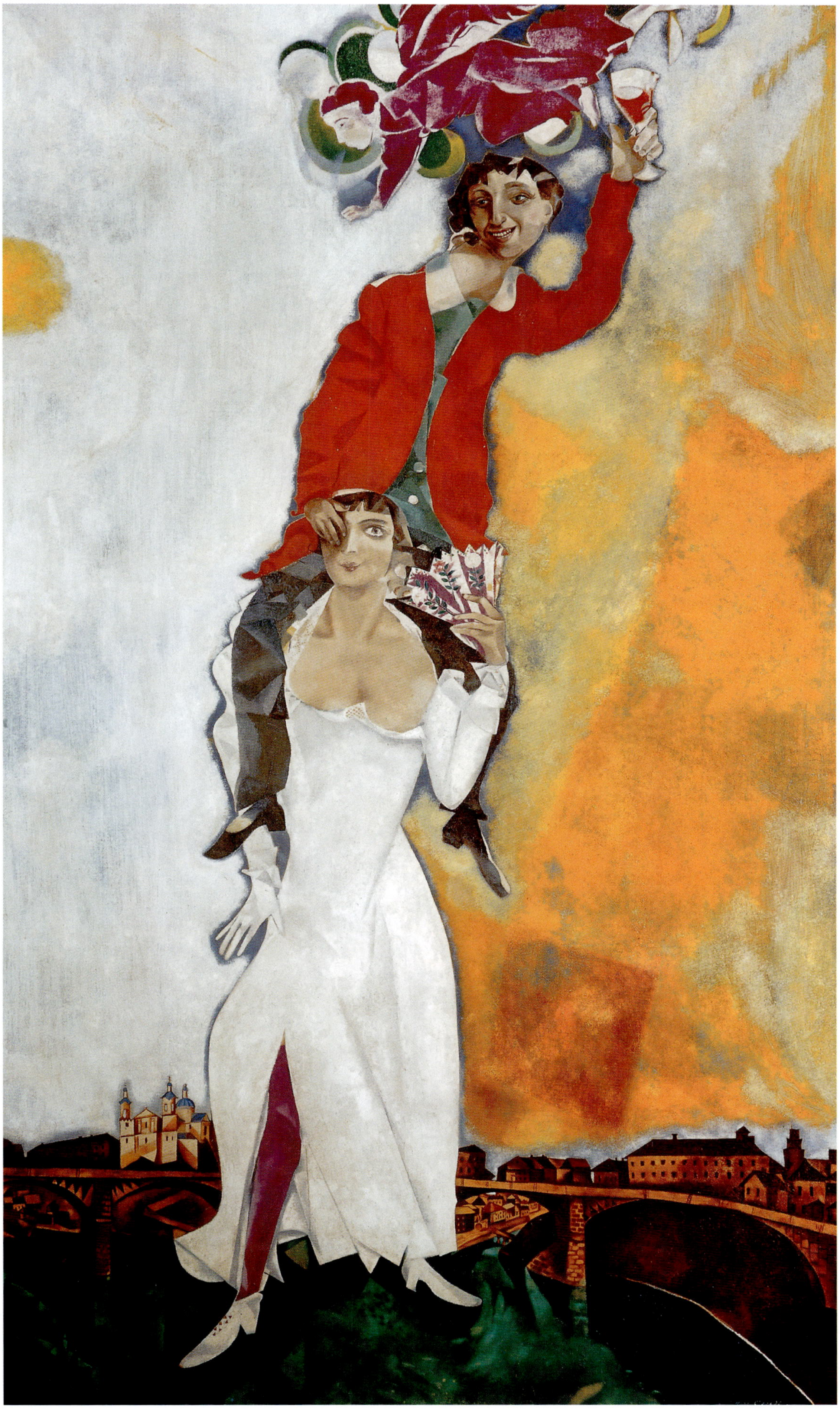

67. ***Double Portrait with a Glass of Wine.*** *1917–18. Oil on canvas, 233 x 136 cm. Musée national d'art moderne, Centre Georges Pompidou, Paris*

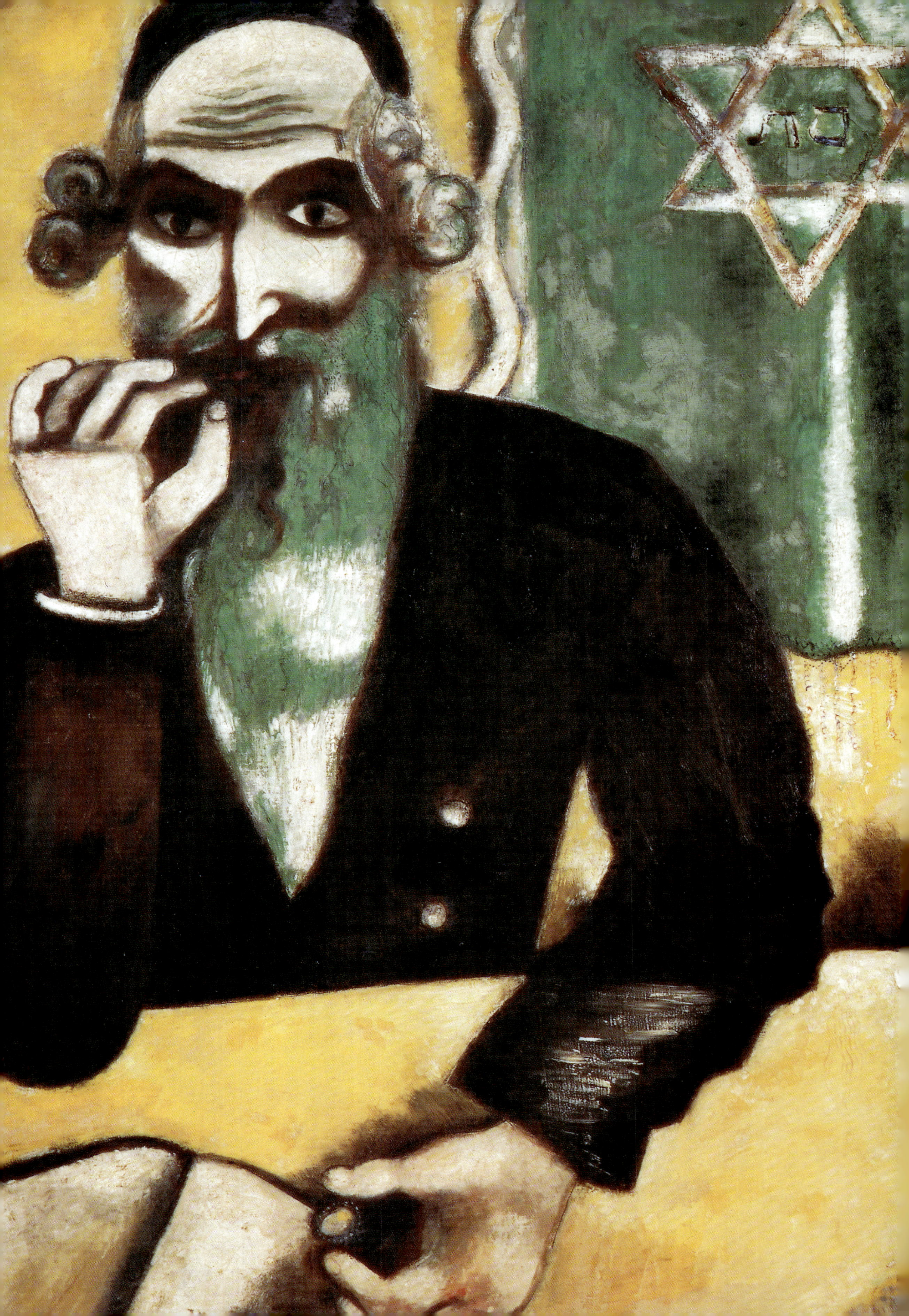

4. The Lost Jewish World

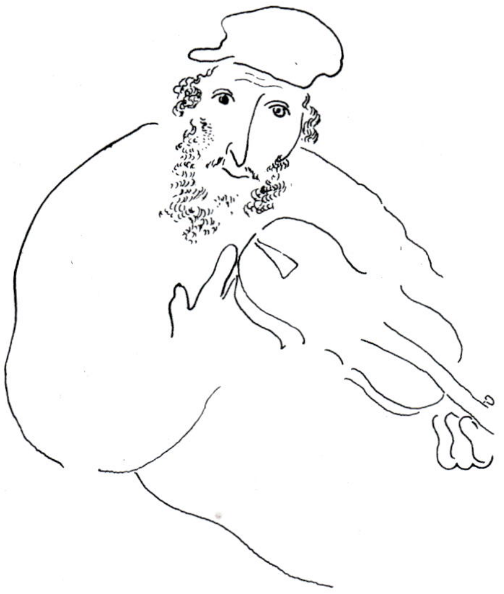

Marc Chagall was not a representative of the *shtetl* world. On the contrary, he and his generation, who became secular and accepted Russian culture, looked back with criticism and love at the world of their parents and grandparents. It is they who established the patterns of nostalgia a century ago in one great, reconstructed myth. Nevertheless, as we saw on many occasions in other chapters of this book, images of that Jewish world permeated the consciousness, the painterly and fictional worlds of Chagall and his contemporaries in several important ways.

THE WANDERING JEW

The Wandering Jew or the Eternal Jew[1] is a key figure in Christian imagery, often with anti-Semitic connotations. It is based on the figure of Ahasver, who refused to help Jesus carry the wooden cross in Jerusalem and was condemned by Jesus to an eternal life of wandering. It fit well the secular mythology of the awakening Jewish historical consciousness that saw the existence of the Jews as a history of wandering from exile to exile and eternally surviving. Simon Dubnov's multivolume *History of the World People* matches the Hebrew phrase *Am Olam*, which means both "World People" and the "Eternal People." The Yiddish and Hebrew prophetic poet Uri-Zvi Grinberg identified in his poetry with both Ahasver, the eternal wanderer, and Jesus, the suffering Jew. Modern Jewish literature appropriated and internalized this image. A play in Yiddish by Dovid Pinsky, *The Eternal Jew*, was performed by HaBimah in Hebrew in Moscow. Chagall too adopted this image.

In August 1914 World War I broke out. Russian Jews were suspected of spying for the Germans (especially as Yiddish was considered akin to German) and were blamed for the Russian defeat in the war. The Russian army ordered large-scale expulsions of Jews from whole areas of the retreating Russo-German front, to be carried out within twenty-four hours. From the fall of 1914 to the summer of 1915 large parts of the heartland of Russian Jewry were uprooted, hundreds of towns were banished, or fell under German occupation. In May and June 1915, 200,000 Jews were expelled from the Lithuanian provinces of Kurland and Kovno and moved to the east; Vitebsk absorbed many of the refugees. A massive aid activity mobilized the Vitebsk Jews, and thousands of refugees were lodged in all the synagogues and many private homes. Russian Jewry was again shaken by the specter of Jewish exile. "The Section of Banishment" (*parshes lekh-lekho*) in the Bible was topical again. In a literal translation it reads, "And God said to Abram: Go you, out of your land and out of your homeland and out of your father's house"—a triple incantation of banishment—and only then God syas, "to the land that I will show you" (Genesis 12:1). In the Bible, this section promises a Zionist vision of going to the Promised Land, but in Yiddish folk semiotics the first part of the sentence is decisive and heartfelt, it symbolizes

OPPOSITE: ***The Rabbi (The Pinch of Snuff)*** *(detail) 1923–26. Oil on canvas, 117 x 89.5 cm. Kunstmuseum, Basel, Switzerland*

the expulsion of the Jews from their own paternal land and their own homes throughout the ages. Indeed, *Lekh-lekho* is the name of the last chapter of Sholem Aleichem's *Tevye the Milkman*, referring to the expulsion of the Jews from all the Russian villages in 1892. It even has an ugly, guttural sound repeated within it as in a magic formula: LeKH-LeKHo. In *The Red Jew*, 1915 (no. 68), Chagall inscribed parts of this text in printed Hebrew letters on a yellow circle, like a halo or a sinking sun framing the old Jew's world.

A weary, ancient Jew with a fiery red beard, clad in dark green, sits with his back to a red house, much like Chagall's home, with the three or four steps of his mother's store on the left. His towering figure, half-rising, suggests that he may have to leave his home and the town behind it. The cluster of houses in the back represents not Chagall's usual Vitebsk street but Sholem Aleichem's prototypical *shtetl* Kasrilevke, with its houses "huddled together, one on top of the other, like the gravestones in an ancient cemetery." Chagall's text in the yellow halo quotes, on the right-hand side, the opening and closure of this Biblical section: from the banishment moving to a prophecy of consolation, that the Jews will become a great nation, and closing with the symbolic assertion of identity by circumcision. And on the left-hand part of the circle, the story of Isaac going back to *Paddan Aram* to marry his wife, and she, the barren woman, becoming pregnant. The last part may perhaps echo Chagall's own return from France to Vitebsk, his marriage in July 1915 and Bella's pregnancy, but it is immaterial to the basic message. Toward the end, interlaced in the Biblical text and written in caps, as if it were part of it—and just preceding Rebecca's pregnancy—is Chagall's newly discovered Jewish name: Moyshe Segal, written in Hebrew: MShH SGL (see *The Pinch of Snuff*, no. 82).

More condensed and symbolic is a drawing in gouache, India ink, and pencil on paper, titled *Remembrance*, 1915 (no. 69). Although the Guggenheim Museum catalogue marks the date as ca. 1918, it seems to be better placed in 1915 (or completed in 1922 in Berlin). The drawing has an inscription in Chagall's handwriting, "Erinnerung 1914" (in German), on top of an earlier pencil mark, "Chagall 914." No doubt the inscription was made when Chagall was in Berlin in 1922–23 (German is rare in Chagall's texts), and Chagall's date 1914 refers to the expulsions, and perhaps to the inception of the painting. This is amply confirmed by the painting's subject, which shows a banished Jew who takes his mother's home with him on his back. The Jew wears a traditional hat, has a full beard, and is old: There is no iconography symbolizing Jewish destiny for Chagall's own generation—young and secular.

A related drawing is the work often misleadingly called *The Walking Village*, 1921 (no. 70), which depicts a whimsical superimposition of a series of houses on a body with human legs, reclining backward. This was, in fact, an illustration in a collaborative work, a book-length poetic cycle entitled *Troyer* (*Grief*) by the young Yiddish poet Dovid Hofshteyn, published in Kiev in 1922 with "cover and illustrations by M. Chagall." *Grief* is an avant-garde poem, written in response to the 1919 pogroms in Ukraine, which explores the paradox and absurdity of the twin births: of world renewal in the October Revolution and the Jewish tragedy. It adopts a hyperbolic tone, modernist imagery, avant-garde graphics, and Futuristic rhythms. One poem of the cycle reflects the poet's visit to the recently devastated Jewish towns of Ukraine. Destruction and emptiness are covered with the lucid air of autumn, and the poet concludes, "What do I need it, the transparent lucidity/ that leaks into the cracks of ruins?"[2] In Chagall's *Walking Village*, a tiny figure pops out of a window with an accusing finger and hurls Hofshteyn's memorable iambic pentameter line into the empty world: *vos toyg zi mir, di loyterkayt di klore* ("What [= why] do I need it, the clear, transparent lucidity?"), while the reader and the text supply the next line and the full context. In the original drawing itself (reproduced here), we see something like male genitals between two big legs, evidently a popular conception of the psychoanalytic version of the irrationality of this world. This was erased in the Soviet printing of the book. The drawing piles on a series of empty, blank houses. Ironically, they look like Suprematist white squares and triangles. Yet there is a sign of life: smoke in the last house. Human legs create an overlapping image: The body of houses may be seen as a human body leaning unnaturally backward, smoking a pipe. It may also be the reverse—a town acquired legs and is walking.

The received title of this drawing, *Walking Village*, is rather misleading. As I explained previously, in translating the term *shtetl* people often confused two very different administrative and ethnic concepts, "village" and "town." In the context of the poem it is safe to assume that the title is *The Town Is Walking*, which is a Yiddish idiom, *di shtot geyt* ("the whole town goes"), meaning that all the Jews are leaving their hometown, fleeing from pogroms into exile. Indeed, the book opens with an illustration of a carter and his wagon leaving a home (or carrying it away?), depicted on top of a child's head, where we read the inscription, in a child's longhand: "To all

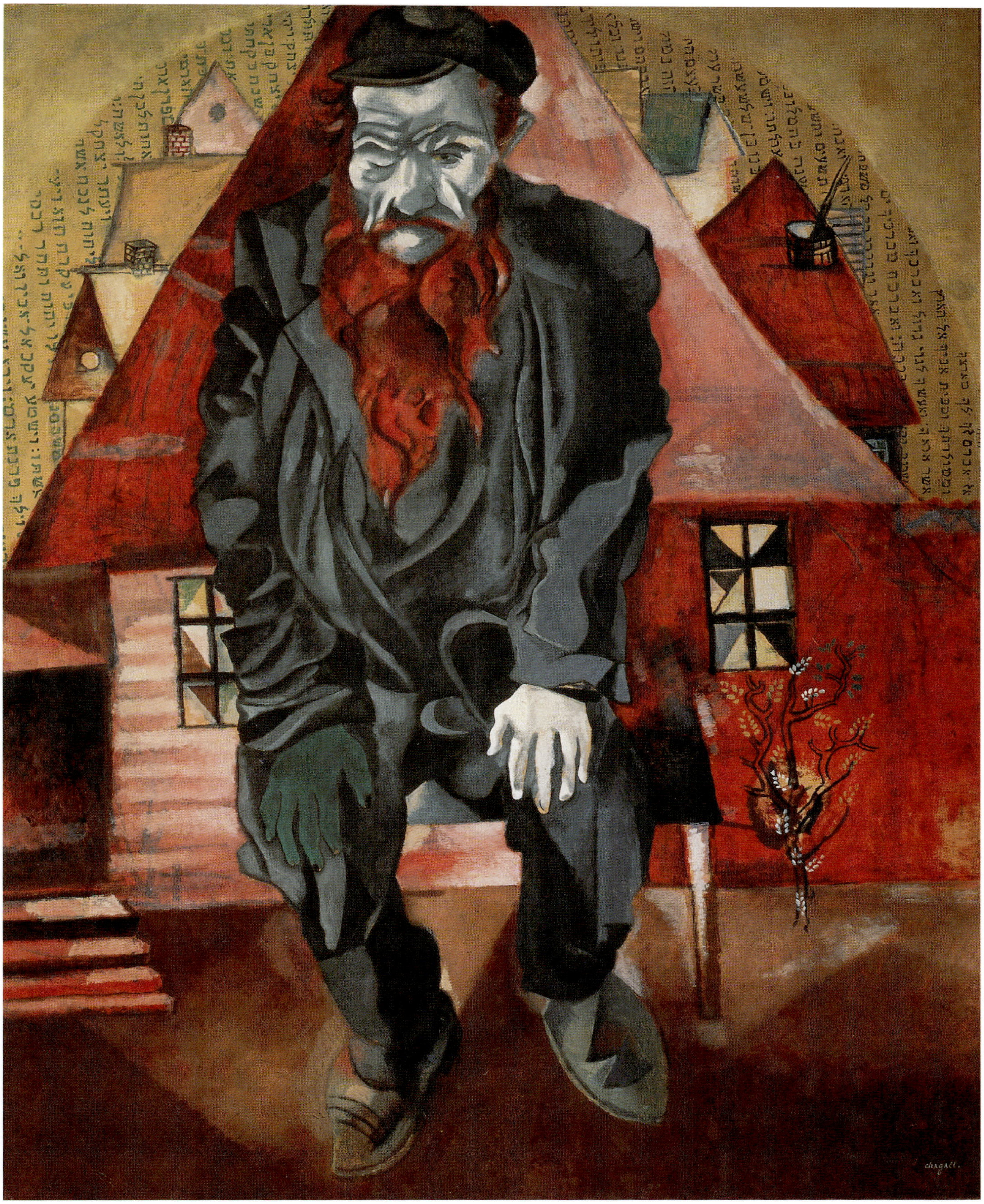

68. ***The Red Jew***. *1915. Oil on cardboard, 100 x 80.6 cm. Russian State Museum, St. Petersburg*

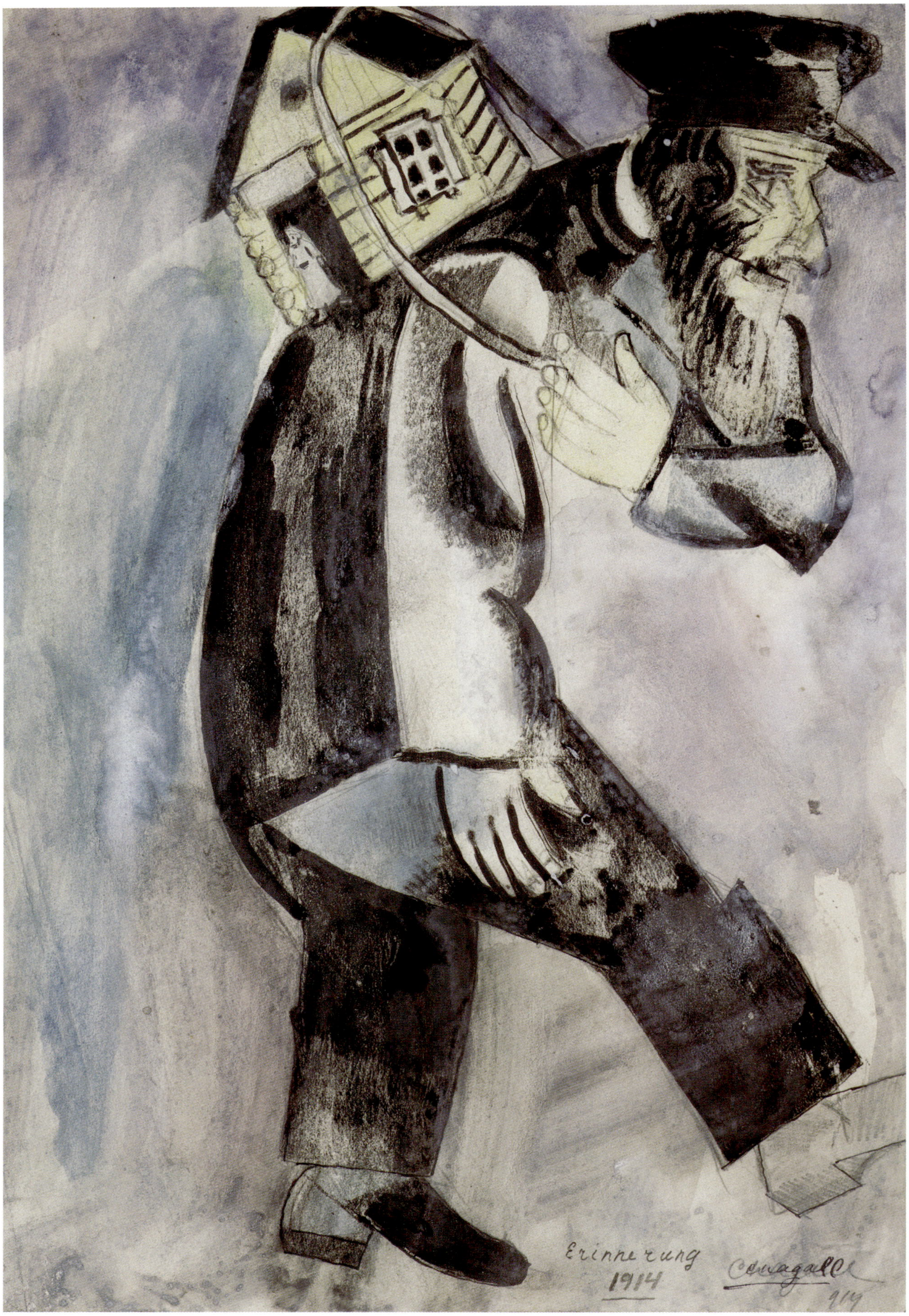

69. **Remembrance.** *c. 1915 [the inscription in German* **Erinnerung** *("Remember") and the date 1914 were added later when Chagall came to Germany in 1922]. Gouache, India ink, and pencil on paper, 31.7 x 22.3 cm. Solomon R. Guggenheim Museum, New York*

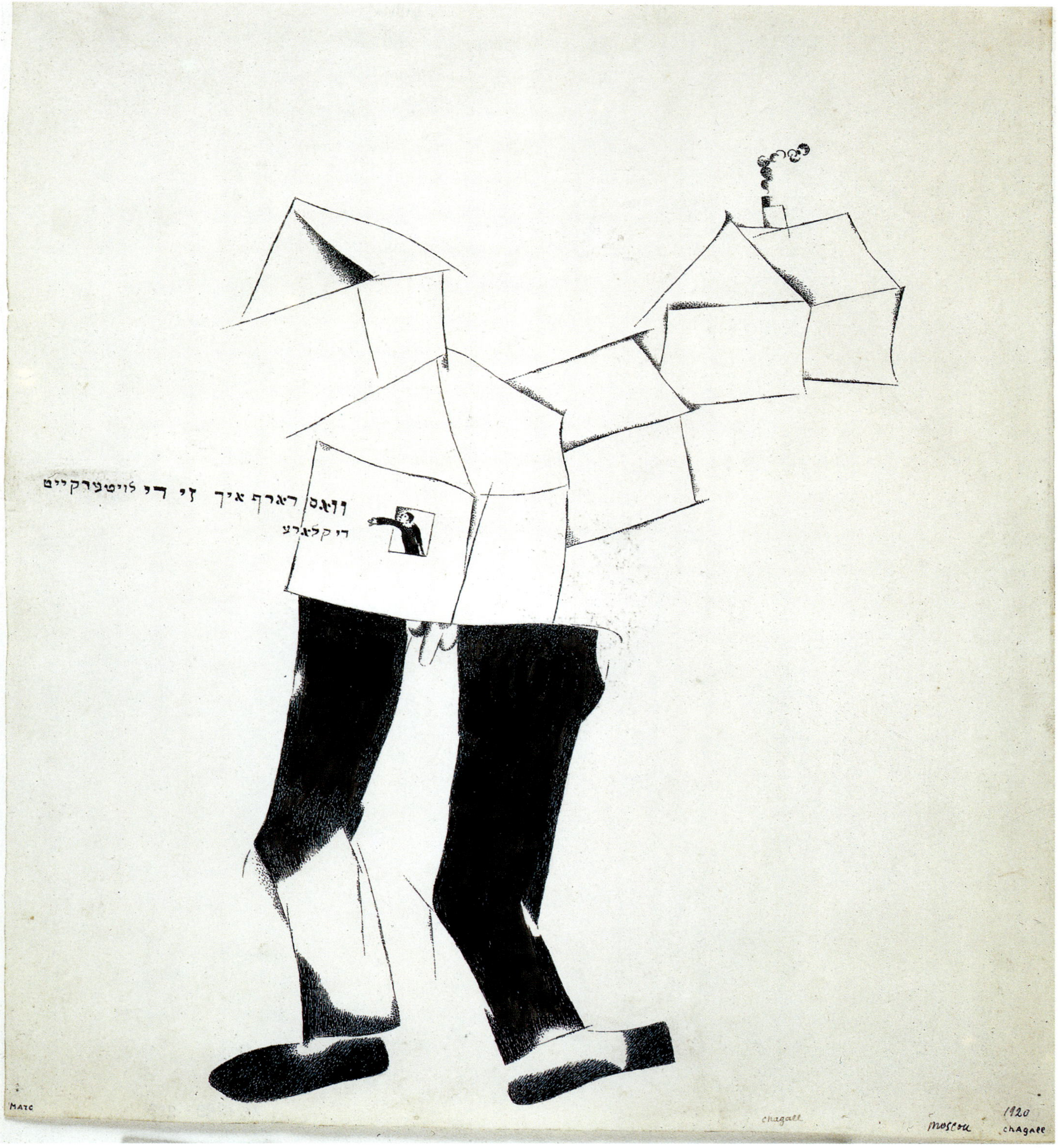

70. ***What do I need it, the transparent lucidity [that leaks into the cracks of ruins]?*** *or* ***The Walking Village.*** *1921. Illustration for* ***Grief (Troyer)*** *by D. Hofshteyn. Ink on vellum paper, 32.6 x 29 cm. AM 1988-217. Musée National d'Art Moderne, Centre Georges Pompidou, Paris*

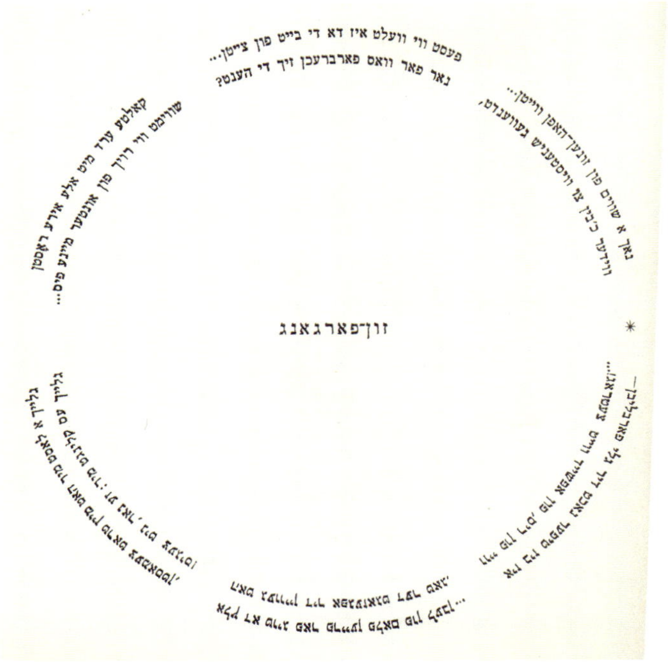

71. *Page XI,* **TROYER**. *Courtesy Yivo Institute for Jewish Research, New York*

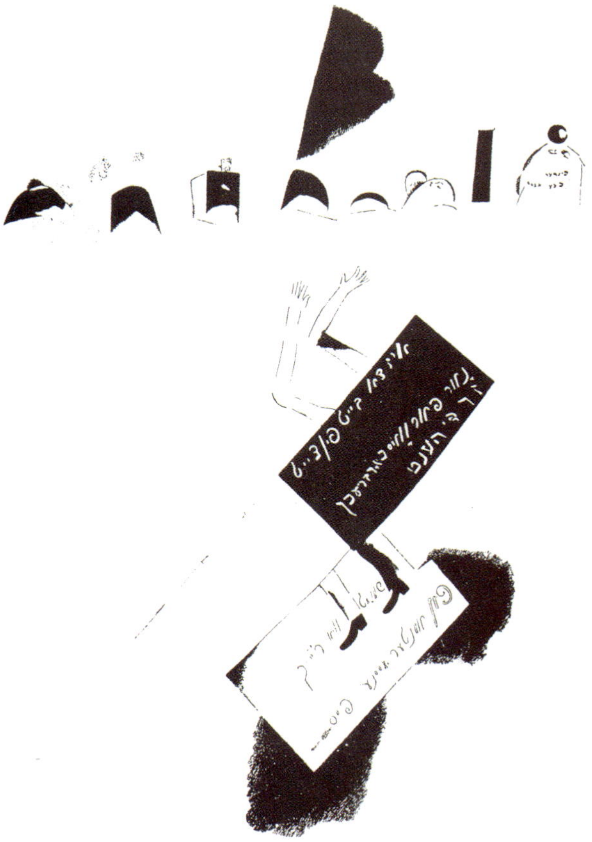

72. *Illustration across from page X,* **TROYER**. *Courtesy Yivo Institute for Jewish Research, New York*

those slaughtered before their time." The usual translation is: "To those who departed before their time." However, *farshnitene* means literally cut down, as wheat is cut down with a scythe, or slaughtered with a knife.

The poem "Sunset" (no. 71), which is typographically arranged in an iconic form in the shape of the sun, states:

> "The change of Times here is as sturdy as the globe.
> But why are my hands wringing?" [. . .]
> "Cold earth with all its rust
> Floats away like smoke under my feet. . . ."

In another illustration (no. 72), parts of the same four lines are inscribed in rectangular tablets that cover a body. The hands of that body stretch in despair toward the graves of recently slaughtered children.

An unusual illustration (no. 73) quotes a line from the poem in children's longhand, thinly drawn through the images: "A thin thread of drops of blood, bright and pure. . . ."

On the right, dogs are smelling blood on the ground; on the left, an upside-down woman is apparently menstruating in an outhouse. Chagall overlaps a childhood memory of thin threads of fresh blood with the images of slaughter depicted in the poem.

NATURAL LANGUAGE IN MODERN ART

As must be clear by now, the effect of a painting is dependent not just on the immediate sensuous impression produced by its own painterly language and the scenes and objects presented in it, but also on natural language, narrative knowledge, and the semiotics of culture reflected in it. Some of these elements are indicated in the painting itself, while others are part of its wider context. A painting is created in a cultural, and yet at the same time private, chamber of resonance. When that chamber of resonance is no longer common to our whole culture, we have to reconstruct the particular chamber of resonance for each artist in order to "read" his work. The role of natural language in the reading of painting can take on several different forms:

1. Language as mediator, describing the nature of the represented world. In the works of Chagall, our understanding is guided by his own constructed biography and those domains of Eastern European life he evokes.

2. Language describing the ideology or poetics of a specific artistic trend. The dependence of the reception of art on the manifestos and other writings of artistic

coteries became crucial in the various trends of Modernism: We have to read the theoretical writings of the painters and their peers, or the theories constructed from these texts, to be guided in our mode of "reading" the actual art objects. The same holds for an individual artist, such as Marc Chagall, for whom his writings and correspondence are crucial to the meanings of his works, even though his own verbal texts may themselves have derived from the intuitive paintings. It is a bidirectional interdependence.

3. Language as a secondary medium or subtext attached to specific paintings or their details. Marcel Duchamp's *The Bride Stripped Bare by Her Bachelors,* Even makes little sense without the specific notes he jotted down for this work.[3] It is a two-tiered work of art, where the primary medium, appealing directly to our senses, is painting and the secondary is a specific written text, including its variants, crossed-out versions, and accompanying drawings. Although these secondary signs operate only behind the scenes, as it were, they guide the signification of the visual, sensuous signs and determine the meanings of the entire work of art. In Chagall's art, subtexts of this kind are provided by idioms, proverbs, dead metaphors, and literary images, primarily of the Yiddish language and literature. His fictional world draws on collective stereotypes, and Yiddish culture represents that collective consciousness; his private world draws on his own self-constructed and self-explained biography.

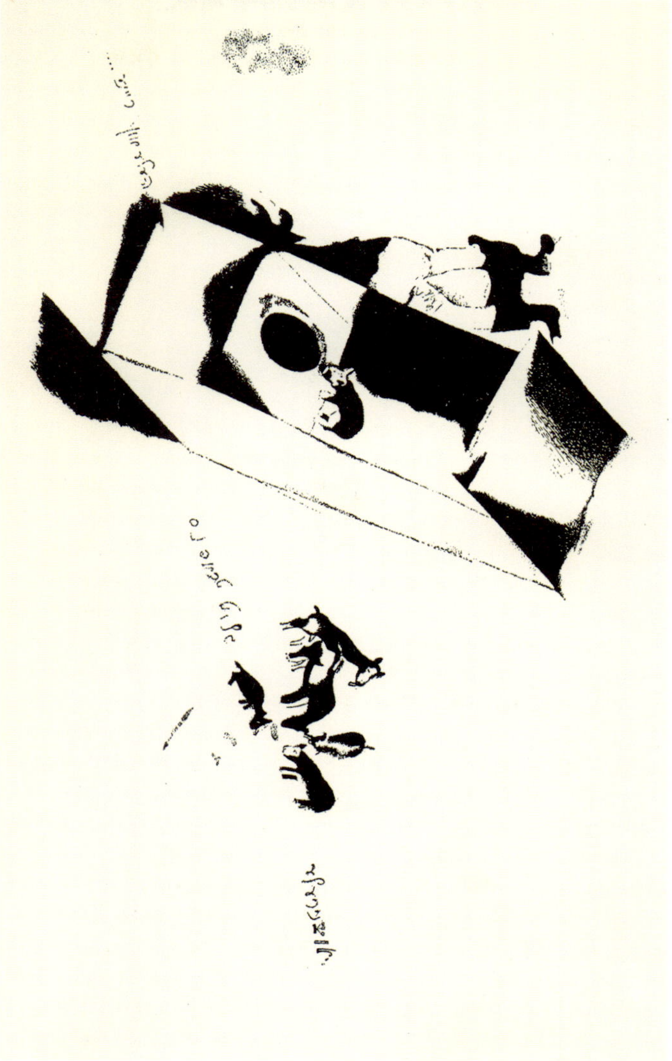

73. *Illustration across from page XIV,* **TROYER.** *Courtesy Yivo Institute for Jewish Research, New York*

4. Language incorporated in the paintings themselves. In many Modern paintings, various texts, even pieces of words appear, often deformed or extracted from their normal context and everyday purposes. These fulfill many functions: They represent the textual nature of modern culture in general, the plethora of words surrounding us; they signal the crossing of the boundaries between visual art and art in language, painting and textuality; they represent two-dimensional surfaces, thus motivating the foregrounding of the two-dimensional canvas; and they serve well in collages, representing the daily, journalistic, practical, or political world, as tram tickets do in Kurt Schwitters's work. They may also serve specific thematic functions in each concrete case, either referring to another object on the canvas, providing a title for the painting as a whole, teasing its topics with contradictory meanings, or alluding to another text and its denotations.

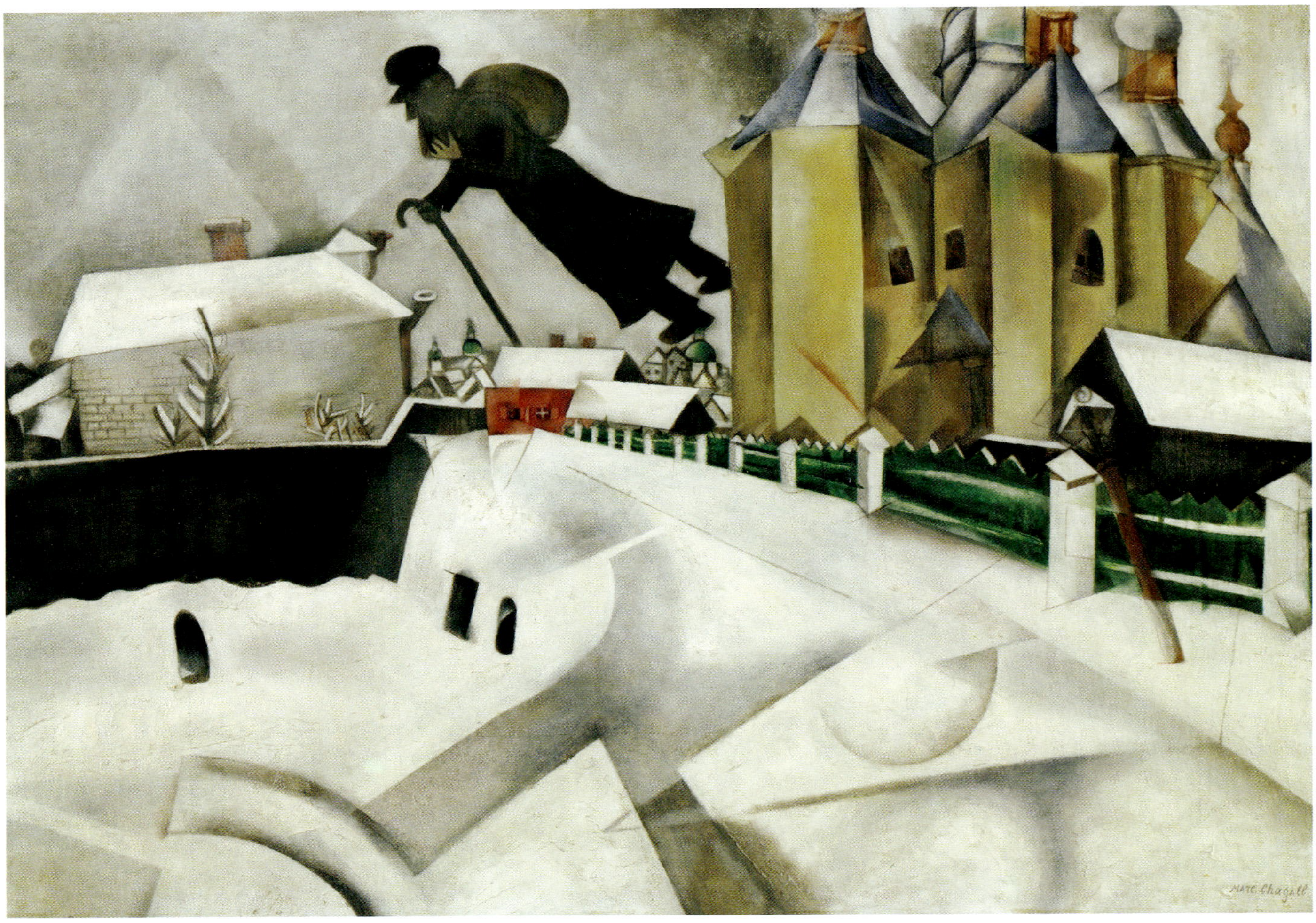

74. **Over Vitebsk.** *1915–20 (after painting of 1914). Oil on canvas, 26 3/8 x 36 1/2". Acquired through the Lillie P. Bliss Bequest. (277.1949) The Museum of Modern Art, New York*

Chagall was an early practitioner of language use in modern paintings, and a variegated and prolific one. The earliest instances of text in his artworks appeared during his first Paris period—for example, in *The Poet (Half Past Three)*, no. 55. From the time of his late teens Chagall tried to assimilate the Russian language and culture, and later also the French. Yet he lived in a Yiddish-speaking world at least until the age of twenty, and then again in Moscow in 1920–22, and in New York in 1941–48. He also communicated and corresponded in Yiddish with Yiddish writers throughout his life, and wrote poems, essays, and speeches in Yiddish. From an early age he absorbed its imagery in his conscious and subconscious mind, and with it, the foundations of his fictional world. He read the classics of Yiddish literature, and he read the Bible exclusively in Yiddish. These cultural sources combined in his work with his subsequently acquired Russian and French languages, themes, and painterly models, yet the linguistic base of his formative years was in popular Jewish culture.

YIDDISH IDIOMS AND STEREOTYPES

An idiom is a fixed cluster of words, some or all of which have lost their independent meaning when entering this cluster, while the whole means something more and often very different from the sum of its components.[4] Like a dead metaphor, an idiom incorporates a frozen figurative situation or its derivative, as we saw in the idiom "crazy man, get off the roof" in chapter 2. It implies that only a crazy man would sit on a sharp-edged roof; hence, if you think or say such and such, you must be crazy—get off the roof! But there is no actual roof. When we use an idiom, we may even visualize or contemplate its figural aspects or imagery beside the new, composite meaning, yet such images have no ontological status in the real or fictional world: There is no roof in these words. In contrast, a realization of an idiom in literature or painting inverts this relationship: What was a mere expression in language becomes a real object or event in the presented world—a man actually sits on a roof. The image now denotes, while the idiomatic meaning ("he's crazy") has become merely a potential connotation. Figurative language is replaced by immediate objects. But when placed

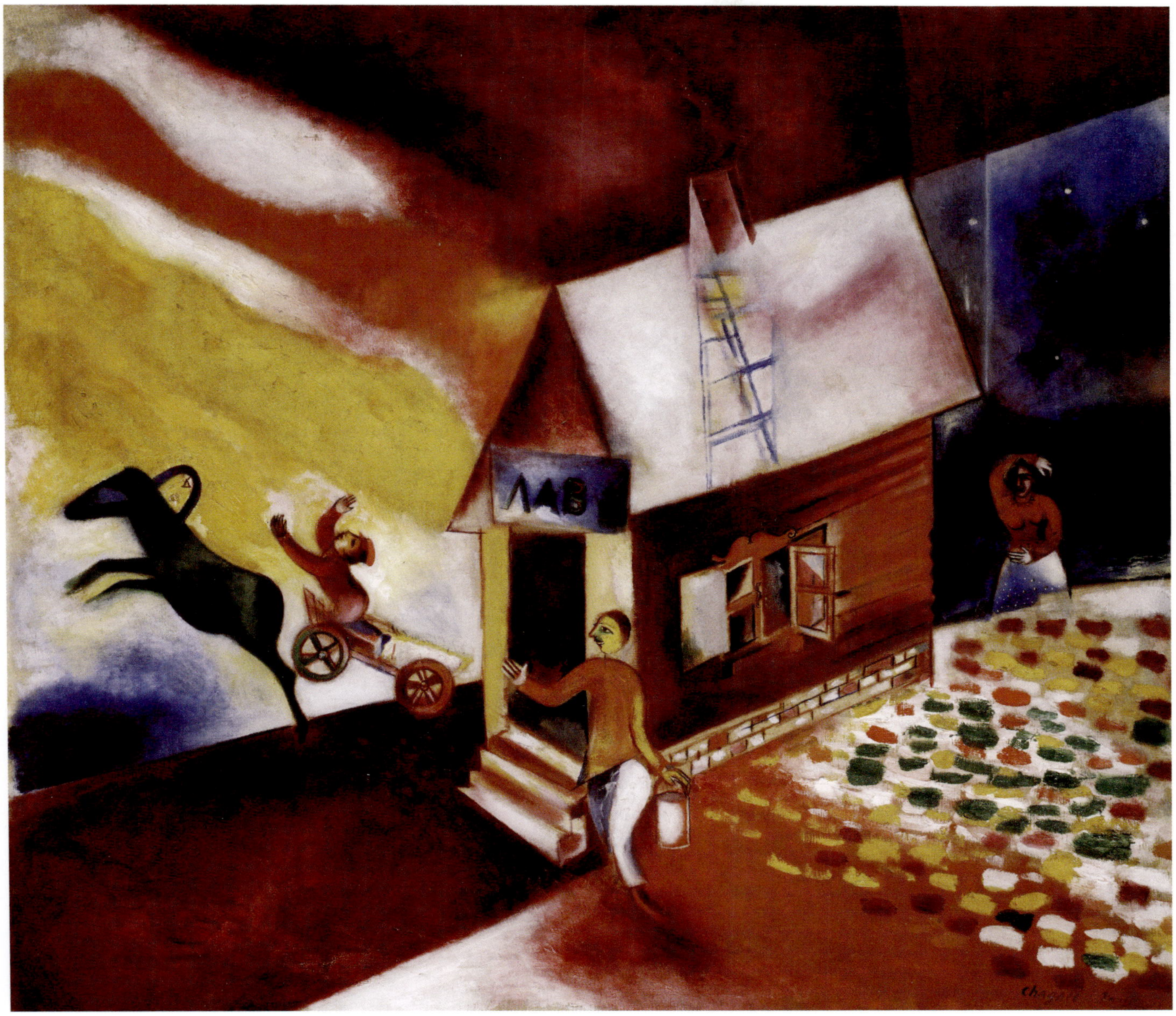

*75. **The Flying Carriage** or **The Burning House**. 1913. Oil on canvas, 106.7 x 120.1 cm. Solomon R. Guggenheim Museum, New York*

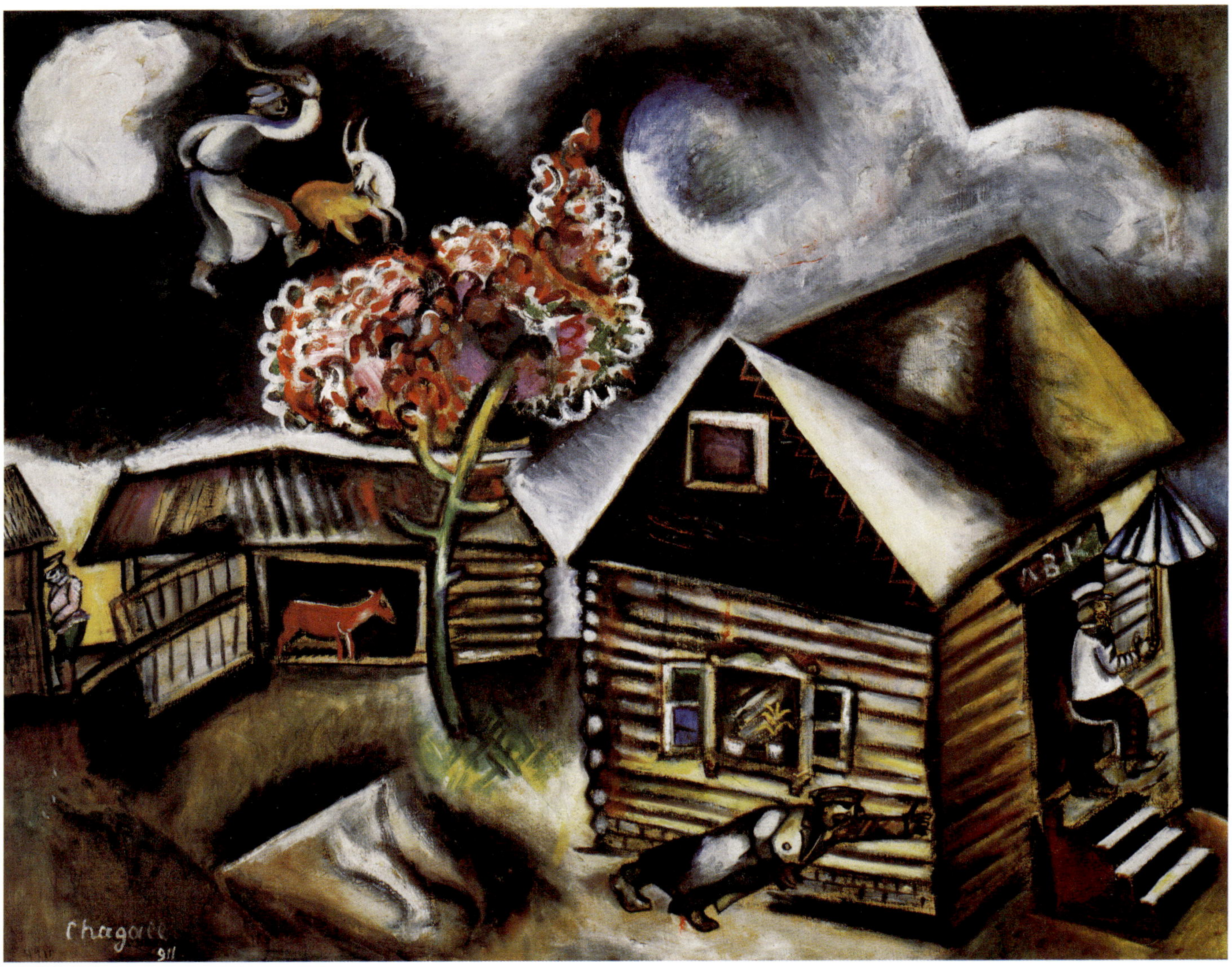

76. ***Rain.*** *1911. Oil on canvas, 86.7 x 108 cm. The Peggy Guggenheim Collection, Venice*

in the presented "reality," such objects or events are often out of place, creating an unrealistic, grotesque, or poetic fictional world, as in Kafka's famous realization of a metaphor of a person becoming a monstrous insect. Literature and art of this sort are not metaphorical; they transfer metaphoricity from the level of style to the fictional world itself, and by so doing, make it "irrational," "surrealistic," "fantastic."

We saw such realizations of metaphors in *The Dead Man* (no. 27): A creative fiddler is "crazy" and actually sits on a roof, and on a "dead street" we find an actual dead body on the ground, surrounded by memorial candles. The several variants of the painting *Over Vitebsk*, 1914/1915–20 (no. 74), feature a Jew hovering above the buildings and churches of the city. He is the embodiment of the fantastic *luft-mentshen* (people of the air), created in Yiddish literature by Mendele Moykher Sforim and Sholem Aleichem: These are people who have no income from productive work and live "on air" as well as "in the air," with no ground under their feet, unlike a healthy nation rooted in its own soil. This expression became a key image of self-criticism of the Jewish Diaspora existence in most Jewish ideologies, from Zionist to Socialist, as well as of Western Jews in Berlin or New York vis-à-vis their Eastern brethren. In his story "Investigations of a Dog," Kafka described them as a special race of miraculously surviving "soaring dogs."

The image itself is a realization of the idiom *er geyt iber di hayzer* (literally, "he walks over the houses"), which simply means in Yiddish, "he is a beggar or a pauper." It is often used as a euphemism to describe somebody's profession or state of affairs. *Iber* (literally: over) here means to walk from house to house, from door to door (as in the English expression, "to go over some papers"). But literally, the word means over or above; hence the image of a man walking above Vitebsk. In Chagall's painting, the worn-out or "dead" spatial metaphor of "over" was returned to its original literary sense and visual image. The massive cathedral looms above this world.

Yet this is only the beginning of an interpretation; other literary and cultural images are grafted onto the idiom. The so-called "grandfather of Yiddish literature," Mendele Moykher Sforim (Mendele the Book Peddler, pseudonym of Sh. Abramovitsh, 1837–1917; nicknamed Méndele), wrote one of the seminal books of modern Jewish self-understanding, *The Short Travels of Benjamin III*. A Jewish Don Quixote, Benjamin the Third, guided by fantastic books and numerous Hebrew quotations, departs with his Sancho Pancha, Senderl the Woman, from their backward *shtetl* to find a way to Eretz-Israel. A grotesque clash between imagination and reality ensues: They mistake a swamp for a great sea; they cannot even communicate with their Slavic neighbors; eventually, they are caught and conscripted into the Russian army, only to be released as good-for-nothings. The world is topsy-turvy, reality doesn't match the quoted texts, and the Zionist dream is a flop. In his mock introduction, the narrator tells us that every person has his guardian angel:

> The angels hit all kinds of beggars, pushing them: grow, beggars, paupers, poverty-stricken, born, arrived, open, concealed, sprout like grass, like nettles! Go, Jewish children, go—over the houses! . . .[5]

On the road, when Benjamin realizes that they fled their hometown without taking any food, the practical Senderl the Woman retorts:

> What do you mean, Benjamin, to eat? Do you intend to carry a kitchen with us? What for? Are there no inns, no houses on the road? . . . And if there are houses, we can, at the same time, go over the houses. For what are all other Jews doing? Today some go to others' houses, and tomorrow, those will go to yet others' houses. It's a Jewish thing, just a grace. . . .[6]

The symbol of this voyage is the ubiquitous *tórbe* (sack), and the similar *pekl* or *pékale* (nomad's pack). It is not just a beggar's sack he carries on his back, but a mishmash of various and sundry peddler's merchandise, tailor's tools, books to sell or to guide him on the road, dry bread, and whatnot. It is a symbol of the "unproductive" existence of the Jews, their beggars' predicament, their essentially parasitic and "unreal" peddler life, overlapping the image of the "Wandering Jew" going into exile. Mendele coined the phrase *kol Isroel—eyn torbe* ("all [the children of] Israel—are one sack"), i.e., the quintessence of Jewish existence is the *torbe*: You are a beggar, a *shnorer* and a nomad, whether you are poor or "rich." Yet whereas Mendele foregrounded degrading poverty and lack of productive work, Chagall stressed the connotations of exile and Jewish destiny.[7]

The "eternal Jew" is a mythical figure, condemned to exile, yet eternal. A popular song at the time, "A Goles Marsh" ("A March of Exile") by the American Yiddish poet Morris Rosenfeld (1861–1923), begins thus:

> With the wanderer's staff in hand,
> With no home and with no land,
> No friend or savior on the way,
> No tomorrow, no today,
> Chased, not suffered in our plight,
> Ne'er a day where spent a night,
> Always pain will knock, knock, knock,
> Always walk, walk, walk,
> Always stride, stride, stride,
> While your strength can still abide.[8]

Chagall's painting has the legendary image, but without the pity. Indeed, this was a key image throughout Chagall's life and work. On July 28, 1948, before leaving New York to return to France, he writes in a private letter to his friend, the Yiddish novelist Y. Opatoshu:

> How are you dear Opatoshu. Ever closer to our voyage to the abysses–perhaps of Europe. I feel like dancing. You are toiling now and I am toiling on the *peklakh*[9] together with the little, thin, young Virginia, who must also taste a bit of what it means to be a Jew with the sack on his back.[10]

This was neither exile from America nor a tragic trip to Europe, where major exhibitions and fame awaited him, but simply a stereotype, a central symbol of Chagall's self-perception as a homeless Jew.

Here the realization of an idiom is a direct bridge that links the painting with a whole cultural conceptual world. Without that cultural cluster—in our case, the movement above the houses, the religious garb, the stick and sack—the defiance of gravity may have a different meaning altogether. The painting *Over the Village* (no. 64), ostensibly similar to *Over Vitebsk*, does not include the element of walking, indispensable for the idiom, or any other attributes of the Eternal Jew; instead it features two lovers flying weightlessly above Vitebsk. In the theater mural entitled *Music* (no. 110) the towering figure of

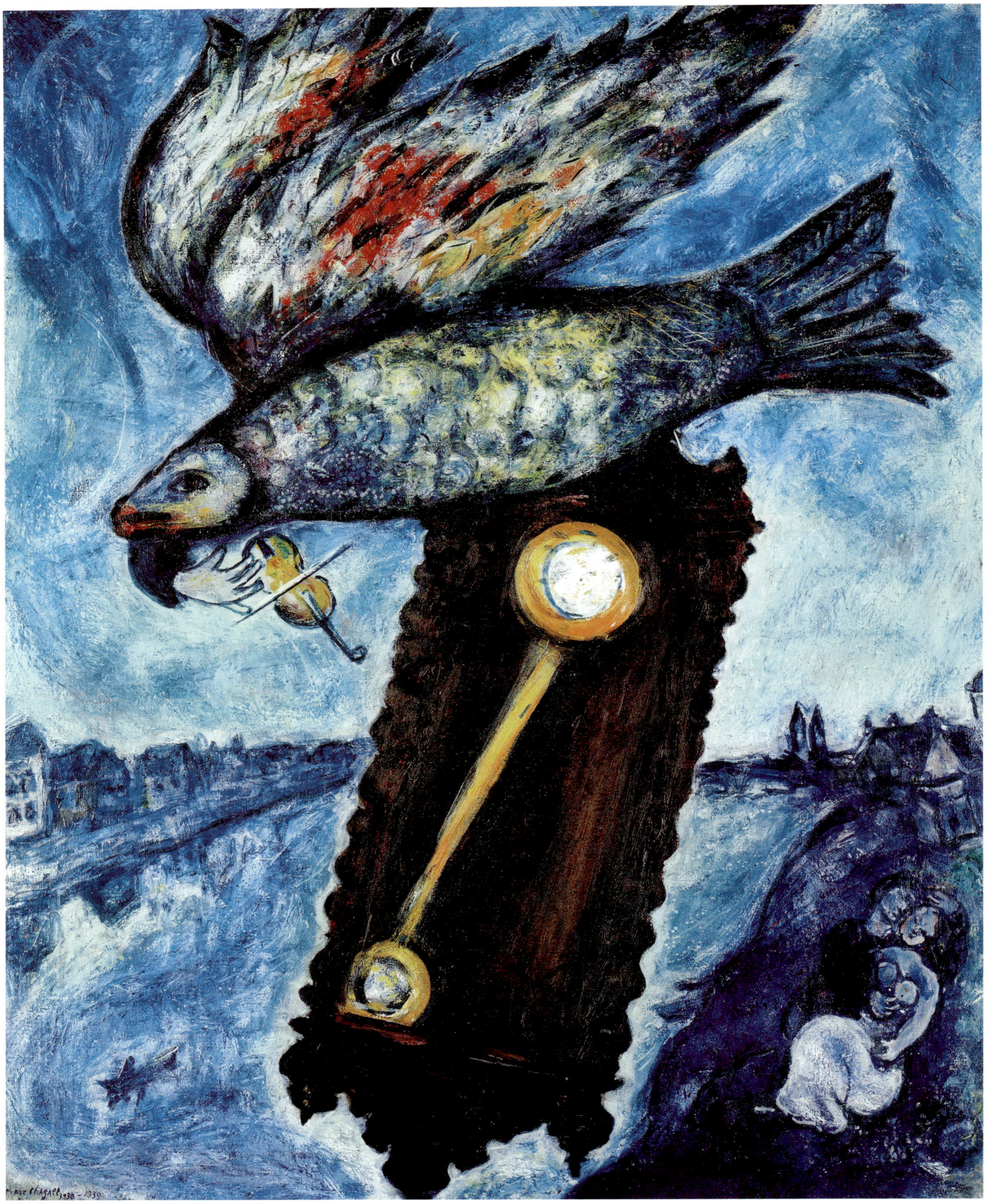

77. ***Time Is a River Without Banks.*** *1930–39. Oil on canvas, 100 x 81.3 cm. Private collection*

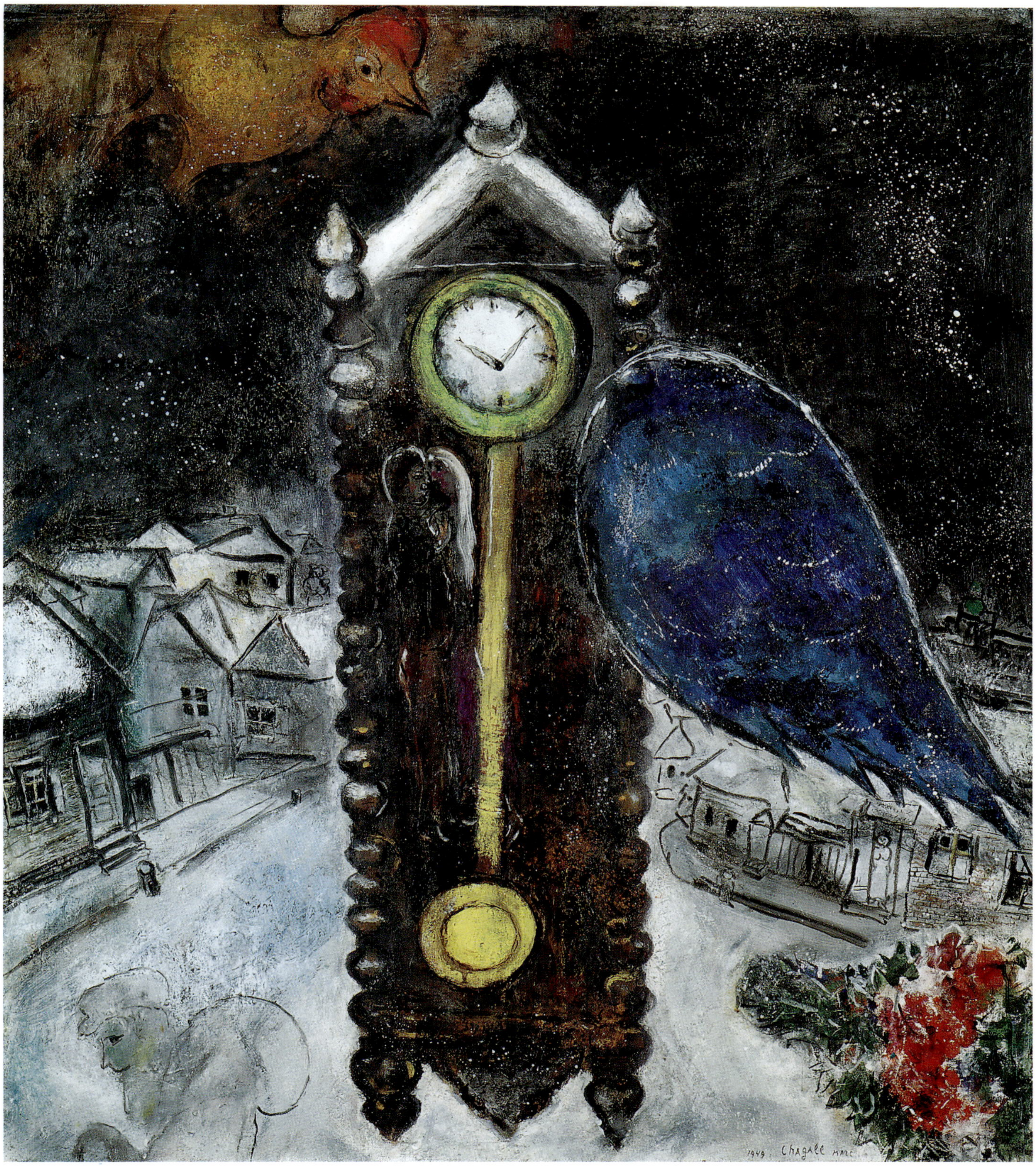

78. ***Grandfather Clock with a Blue Wing.*** *1949. Oil on canvas, 92 x 79 cm. Private collection*

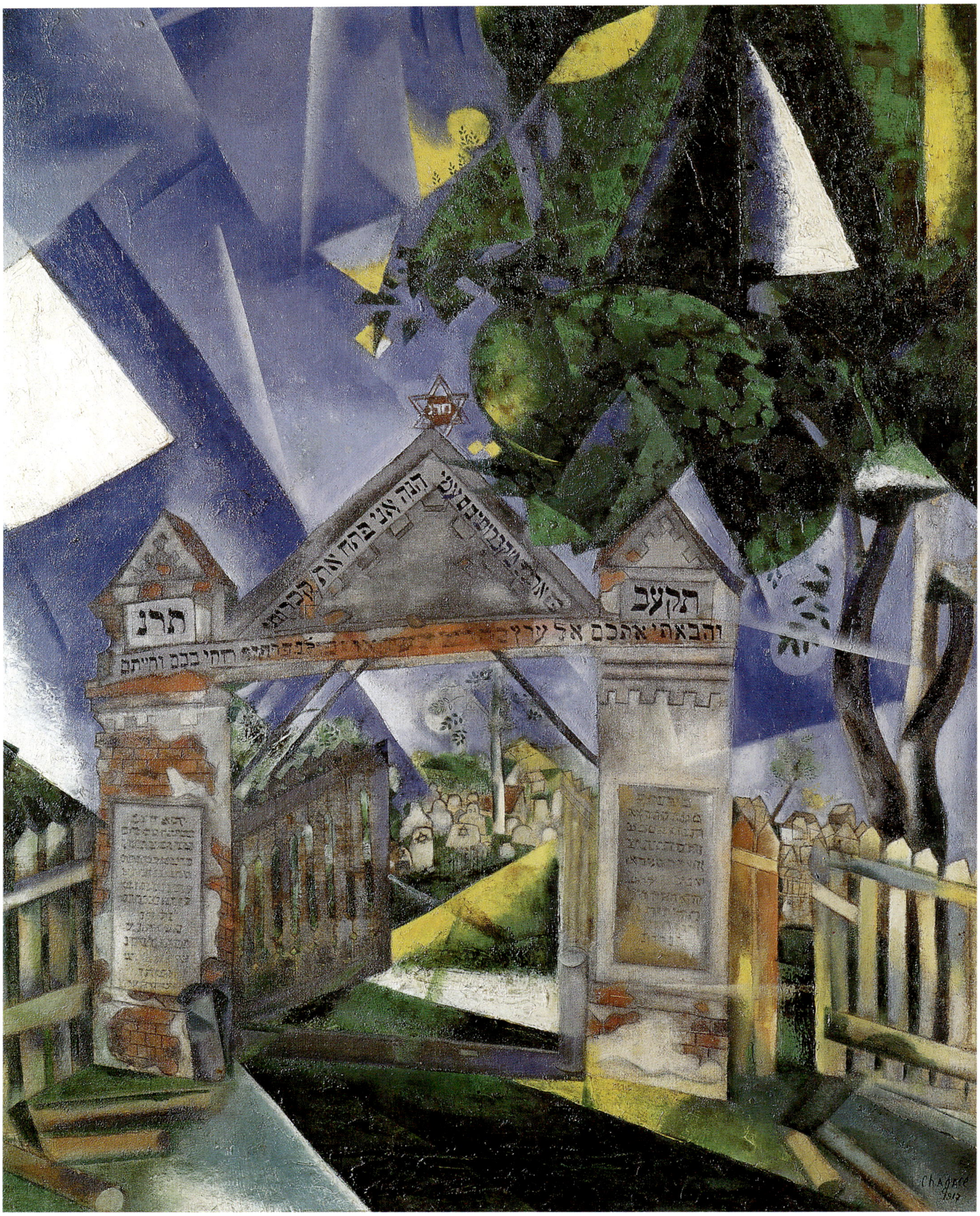

79. ***The Cemetery Gate.*** *1917. Oil on canvas, 87 x 68.5 cm. Paris, Musée national d'art moderne, Centre Georges Pompidou, Paris*

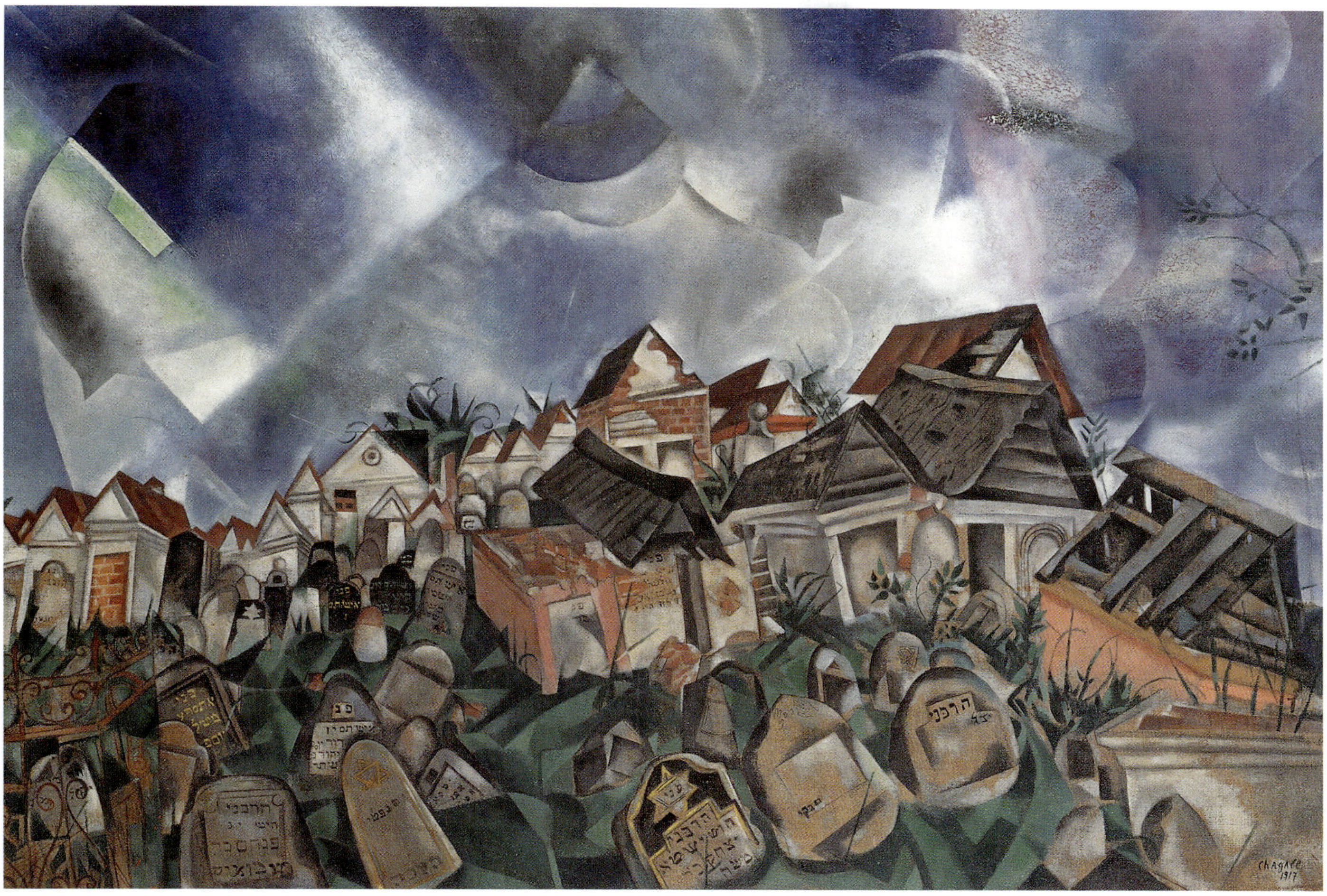

80. **The Cemetery**. *1911. Oil on canvas, 69.3 x 100 cm. Musée national d'art moderne, Centre Georges Pompidou, Paris*

a Jewish fiddler looms above the little houses and church—evoking not the Eternal Jew but the soaring power of music that is not bound to mundane reality.

In some of Chagall's soaring characters, the idiom loses its relevance; in others, we observe realizations of various expressions, not exclusively Yiddish, that lift people or objects against the force of gravity.[11] As soon as he discovered the principle, Chagall turned it into an unmotivated device that signals the irrationality of his fictional world, using it almost anywhere. It is a device for making familiar objects strange, as well as an imprint of Chagall's authority over the painting. Thus, the fantastic, absurd, or poetic world in the painting, even though it may be derived from Yiddish idioms and literature, is perceived both as a departure from reality and as its most authentic expression. Chagall himself, for example, wrote that Lenin stood Russia on its head like figures in a Chagall painting and depicted Lenin standing on his head in the painting *Revolution* (see chapter 8).

Another use of a double idiom is *The Flying Carriage*, 1913 (no. 75), also called *The Burning House*. "Flying" means running fast or driving by. Chagall saw carriages flying by his house from the time of his childhood. The simple expression to slow them down is: "What [why] are you flying? What's burning?" which gets a full realization in this painting, and serves as a good excuse for the flood of red that Chagall cherished (see the two paintings entitled *The Birth*, nos. 31 and 32)

YIDDISH LITERATURE

A major influence on Chagall's perception of the Jewish world was Sholem-Aleichem (1859–1916), ostensibly a good-natured humorist, who exposed the irrationalities and absurdities of Jewish life and—through it—life in general. For Sholem-Aleichem, irrationality lies both in the dangerous unworldliness of Jewish existence and in the endearing quality of the true folk person, who sees the abyss yet does not want to see it, glossing it over with a smile and a quotation. Chagall adoped this stance in his depiction of reality in his early paintings.

We find many traces of Sholem-Aleichem's children's stories in Chagall's worldview. I discussed the motif of "The Enchanted Tailor" in *Russian Village Under the Moon* (no. 38) (page 85). The tailor and his goat appear again in *Rain*, 1911 (no. 76) and other paintings. And the goat is ubiquitous in Chagall's work, especially since it is proverbially the most elementary bread-earner in Jewish poverty. Typically, the sign on the store: *LVK* in Russian (for Lavka) is spelled in the Hebrew way with consonants only. The man on the left is peeing in an outhouse.

No less ubiquitous is the image of the violin, which also may be derived from Sholem Alechem's short story "The Violin." In the story, a child recounts, "The desire to play the violin grew together with me" (as it grew with Chagall when he was a boy). The violin was the most widespread and prestigious instrument of music in traditional Jewish society:

> A violin, you understand, is an instrument older than all instruments. The first violinist in the world was Tuval-Kain, or Methuselah, I don't remember precisely. . . . The second violinist was King David. And there was a third one, Paganini was his name, also a Jew; all the best violinists in the world were Jews.[12]

The animal and the violin—both nonverbal communicators—merged in his imagination, and there is a close empathy between the painter and all these characters.

The big grandfather clock is also a conspicuous figure in Chagall's world. It is reminiscent of Sholem Aleichem's story "The Clock," which begins thus: "The clock rang thirteen . . . " and continues somewhat later, "I swear, it's a crime that a clock is not a living thing, a mute tongue, speechless: he would have had to tell and tell! . . ."—just like an animal. In the story, the clock dominates the life of the town: The father tries to prevent it from ringing thirteen, and hangs more and more weights on it, until the clock collapses with an unbelievable noise, and everyone mourns it as a dead person. The boy internalizes the experience:

> The whole night afterward, clocks crowded my head. I imagined: our old clock lies on the floor, wearing a white shroud. I thought the clock was alive, but, instead of the pendulum, a long tongue, the tongue of a human being, swings back and forth, and the clock does not ring but sighs, and each sigh takes away a piece of my health. . . . And on the face, where I am used to see a twelve I suddenly see thirteen, truly thirteen—believe me![13]

The dominating clock appears, with its enigmatic, blurred face, swinging diagonally, along with a flying fish playing a fiddle (alliterative in Yiddish: *fish, flit* [flies], *fidl, fligl* [wing]) and a pair of lovers on a riverbank, in Chagall's *Time Is a River Without Banks*, 1930–39 (no. 77). This is, of course, a paradox: There are two banks to any river. In the painting we see indications of a town on both banks, and we are reminded of Chagall's early encounters with Berta on the bank of the Dvina River, as described in Bella's memoirs.[14] It has been suggested that the idea came from Ovid; but Ovid states only "time is a river," an idea from Greek philosophy, without the decisive clause that creates the paradox: "a river with no banks." And would Chagall have known Ovid?

In this painting, too, Jewish proverbs are at work. There is a Hebrew expression, widely used in Yiddish, *yam ha-talmud*, "the sea of the Talmud," or better, "the sea of learning," which indicates an inexhaustible, endless body of knowledge. You can swim in it—a related metaphor, describing a learned person and astute scholar, is "he swims in the sea of learning"—but you cannot reach or see the other shore. Several additional proverbs are related to it: (1) the rhymed couplet: *der yam on a breg, di toyre on an ek* ("the sea has no shore, learning no end"; (2) *di toyre hot nit keyn breg* (literally, "learning has no shore").[15] Indeed, *breg* (shore, riverbank) and *ek* (end) rhyme in Yiddish and are interchangeable; dictionaries translate the word *breg* (shore) also as *ek* (end). Thus, "a river with no shore" actually means "with no end," and in our context, "timeless." Yet Chagall revives the primary meaning of *breg* and thus paints two shores. Hence, the paradox of the pictorial and verbal aspects of the picture: The river has no shore, yet in order to be read as a river in a painting, it must have two shores. The young love scene is placed in the shadow of this paradox; the tune is played by Chagall/fish, the artist/fiddler; and the rest is in the hands of color. This image was recycled several times. Thus *Clock with a Blue Wing*, 1949 (no. 78), has a pair of lovers sheltered inside the clock. The clock, and thus time itself, is looming above Vitebsk, and the Wandering Jew (lower left) goes into exile.

TEXTS AND QUOTATIONS IN PAINTINGS

Writing plays a conspicuous role in Chagall's art. To be sure, words or parts of words were used by Picasso and his followers in France and in Russia (notably, Malevich). Chagall, however, often used long texts, especially Biblical quotations, and the textual engagements of his paintings are usually complex. This was clearly a function of Chagall's origins and interest in Jewish culture, which had been a profoundly textual culture. The Jews had no cathedrals filled with art objects (even though synagogue art—limited as it is—was discovered and extolled in Chagall's generation). Their "otherness" was

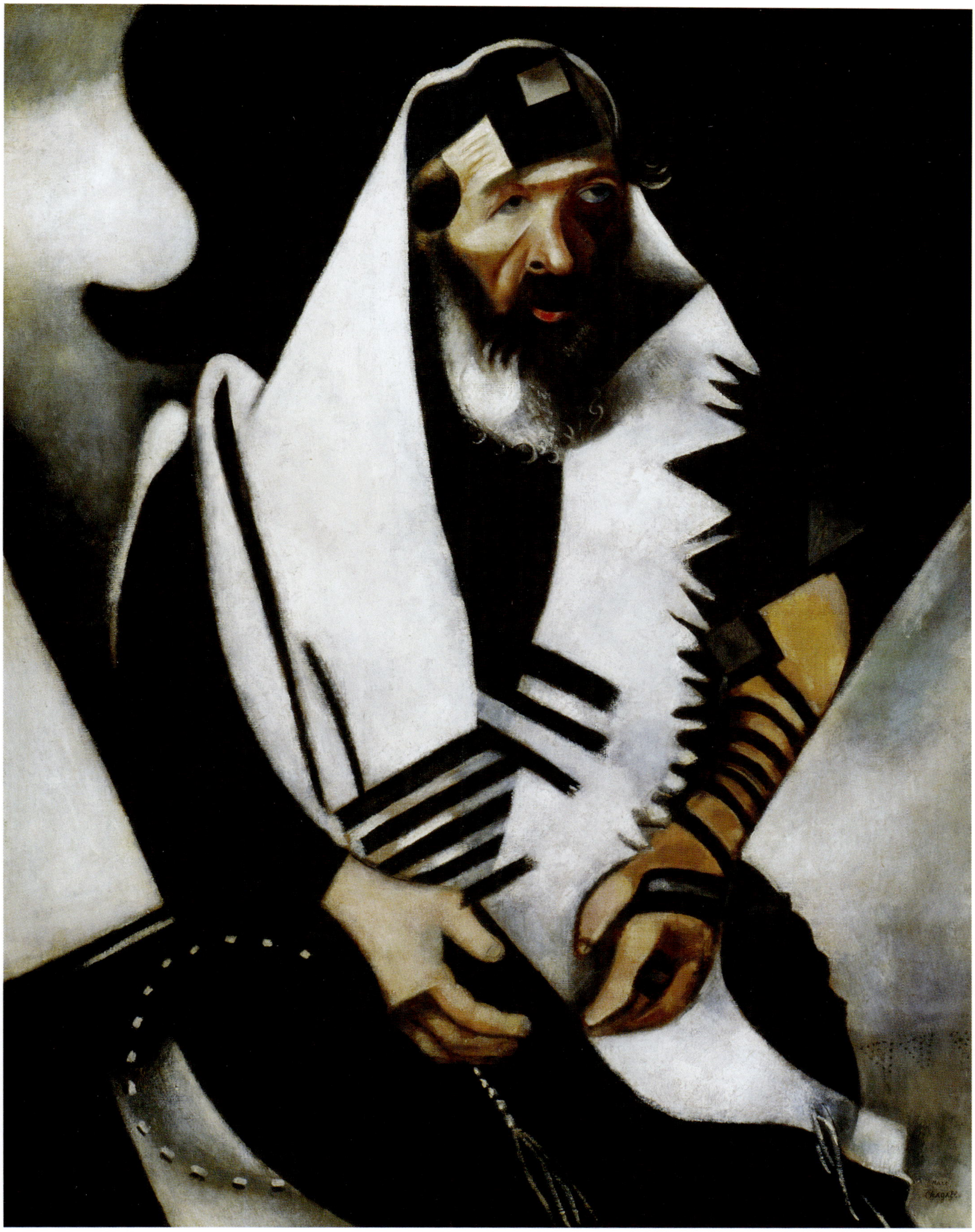

81. ***The Praying Jew.*** *1923. Oil on canvas, 116.9 x 88.9 cm. Chicago, The Joseph Winterbotham Collection, 1937.188, The Art Institute of Chicago*

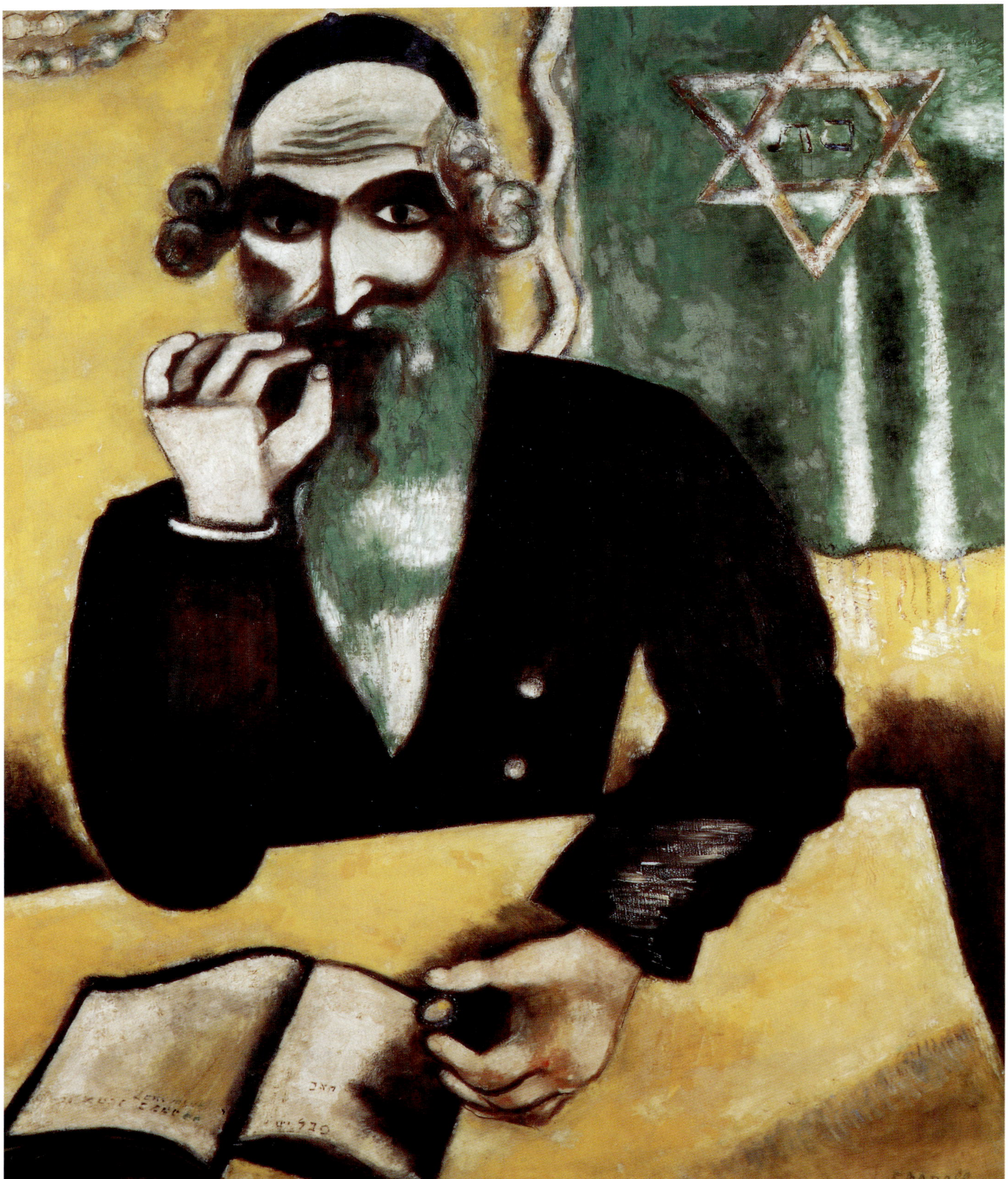

82. ***The Rabbi (A Pinch of Snuff)*** *1923–26. Oil on canvas, 117 x 89.5 cm. Kunstmuseum, Basel, Switzerland*

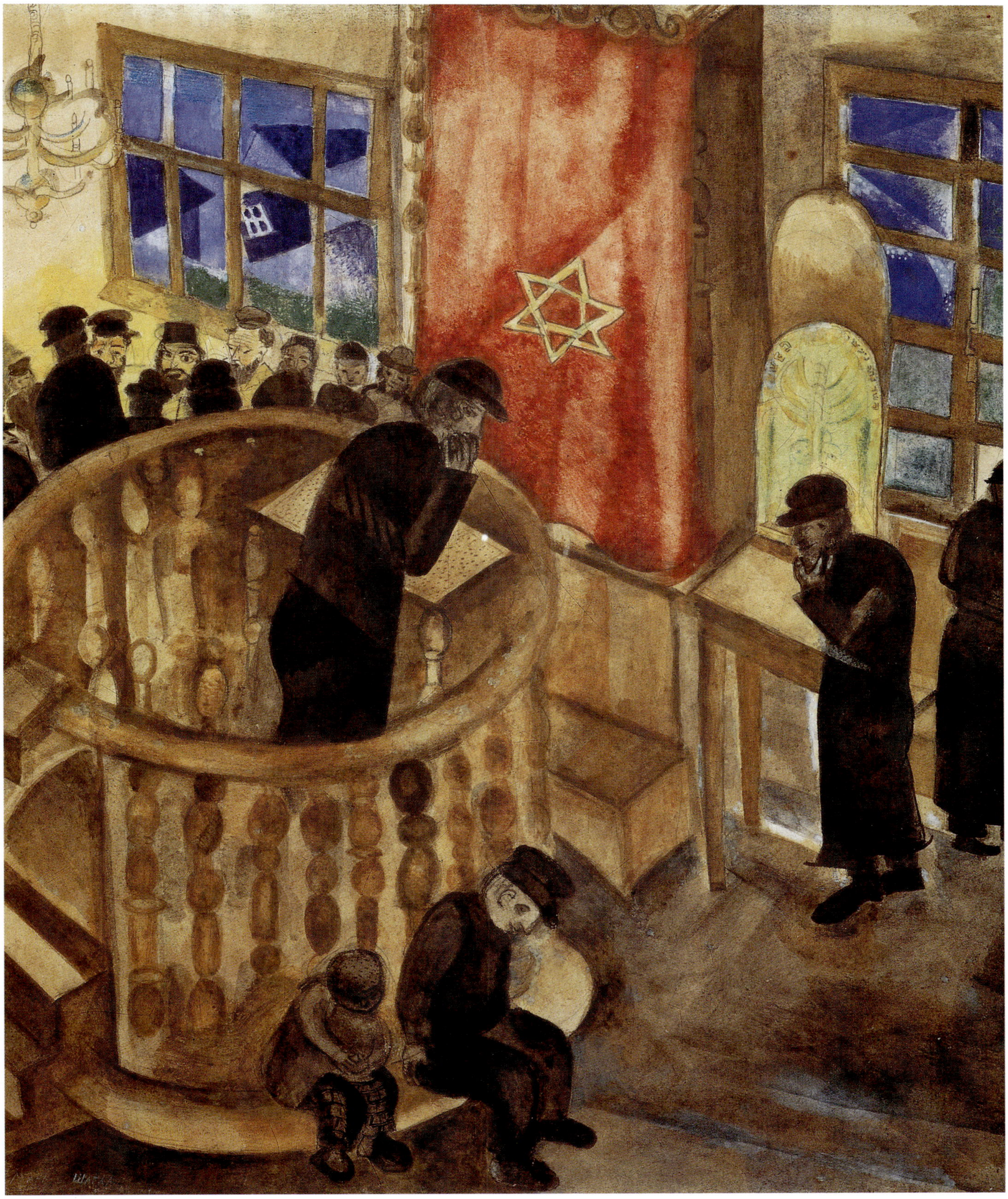

83. ***The Synagogue.*** *1917. Gouache, watercolor and crayon on paper, 40 x 35 cm. Private collection, Basel, Switzerland*

vividly embodied in their "other" letters, their writing in the "opposite" direction, and mainly their "other," and essentially private, religious library.

In Chagall's work, texts fulfill first of all a global function, representing the very culture of his world. The quoted words also fill numerous specific functions, often simultaneously. They serve as synecdoches, a part of an object in the represented world (for example, inscriptions in a cemetery); they issue multimedia signals, suggesting nonvisual aspects of the represented frame of reference (referring, for example, to the song "Bridegroom's Voice, Bride's Voice" with an image of a dancer in the theater mural *Dance*); they offer titles for some of the other material in the painting; they evoke allusions that bring in additional frames of reference that are otherwise indiscernible in the painting proper (Biblical quotes and references to Biblical events); they serve as a metalanguage that shows the artist's interference in his presented world (such as the tiny names of his family members inserted in longhand on a geometrically embellished pair of paints in the *Introduction to the Yiddish Theater* [no. 95]); and they fulfill a compositional function within the painting.

Chagall often wrote a text and subsequently erased part of it, leaving the full content as his own private knowledge: a mystifying gesture that appears on other levels of his paintings—figures and colors—as well. He deforms words and texts, just as he does other represented objects, perhaps because he originally had in mind two different audiences but increasingly lost the audience that could read the Hebrew and Yiddish inscriptions. In spite of his acculturation and his shift to speaking Russian and French, most of the texts in his paintings are in Hebrew letters, whether the language is Hebrew or Yiddish. Russian rarely appears as an independent text, but as an object within a represented reality: a sign on a store, a newspaper headline ("War!"), or a quotation from a revolutionary slogan in the early Soviet years (such as Lenin's slogan "War on the Palaces!").[16]

One example of a Hebrew text appears in *The Cemetery Gate*, 1917 (no. 79). Chagall combined here his new interest in Jewish folk art (primarily expressed in religious functional objects) with his genre of major stations in man's life. The Hebrew Vitebsk memorial book uses Chagall's picture as the authentic gate of a Vitebsk Jewish cemetery.[17] The colors, however, are not realistic at all. The upper part is treated in a Cubist manner, while the lower half seems almost photographic. Yet it is precisely the "realistic" part that offers an unrealistic textual collage. At the heads of the two pillars, in large letters, are Hebrew dates: תקעב–תרנ, equivalent to 1812–1890. These cannot indicate the opening and closing dates of a real cemetery (certainly not of an ancient cemetery, as Vitebsk had), but must refer to a person's life. Chagall has apparently transferred them from an individual gravestone. When he was back in Vitebsk in 1914, his grandmother—who was first the wife of his father's father, and after his death the wife of his mother's father—pointed it out to him: "*That* is your grandfather's grave. Your father's father and my first husband." It was the gravestone of his paternal grandfather, whom he admired for his learning, and was happy to place his date of death, 1890, on a triumphant Star of David set upon the peak of his imaginary gate. We know that the paternal grandfather from Lyozno, who had a house in Vitebsk, had died when Chagall was a child, whereupon the family sold his house "in-the-Sands" and moved to a neighborhood in Vitebsk proper. If the dates indeed refer to this grandfather, Marc was three years old when David Chagall died.

On each of the two pillars there is a long Hebrew text, precisely written out and then obscured, as if worn away with time. And on the central triangle above the gate, there are phrases from the prophet Ezekiel's Vision in the Valley of Dry Bones. Here it may speak as much of the resurrection of his grandfather as it does of the resurrection of the Jews, according to a Zionist interpretation. The absent context is: "Then He [God] said unto me, Son of man, these bones are the whole house of Israel: behold, they say, our bones are dried, and our hope is lost:[18] we are cut off for our parts" (Ez. 37:11). The text on the gate reads, from midverse (Ez. 37:12): "Behold, I will open your grave[s] [and cause] you [to come up] out of your graves, my people / And bring you onto the land [of Israel] [here verse 13 is missing and some text is obfuscated] [and shall put] my spirit in you, and ye shall live"[19] (the parts in brackets were omitted by Chagall). The text is written in Hebrew, however, the first two clauses are placed in the reverse direction, as if in Russian: the first half of the text on the left side, the second on the right.

There is only one change in the biblical text and it is significant: on the horizontal plank, instead of אדמת ישראל = *admat Israel* ("the soil of Israel"), he wrote *eretz* ("the Land"), as the Zionists affectionately referred to Palestine. Furthermore, he misspelled *eretz*, as if it were Yiddish (ערץ, beginning with an *ayin* instead of an *alef*). Finally, one may see in the soaring blue sky the Zionist colors. Chagall hid his Zionist leanings during the Revolutionary period, and he revived it during the thirties and forties. In the murals for the Soviet Yiddish theater he paints "Carmel" wine from Eretz-Israel, a Zionist gesture. It is plausible that *The Cemetery Gate* refers

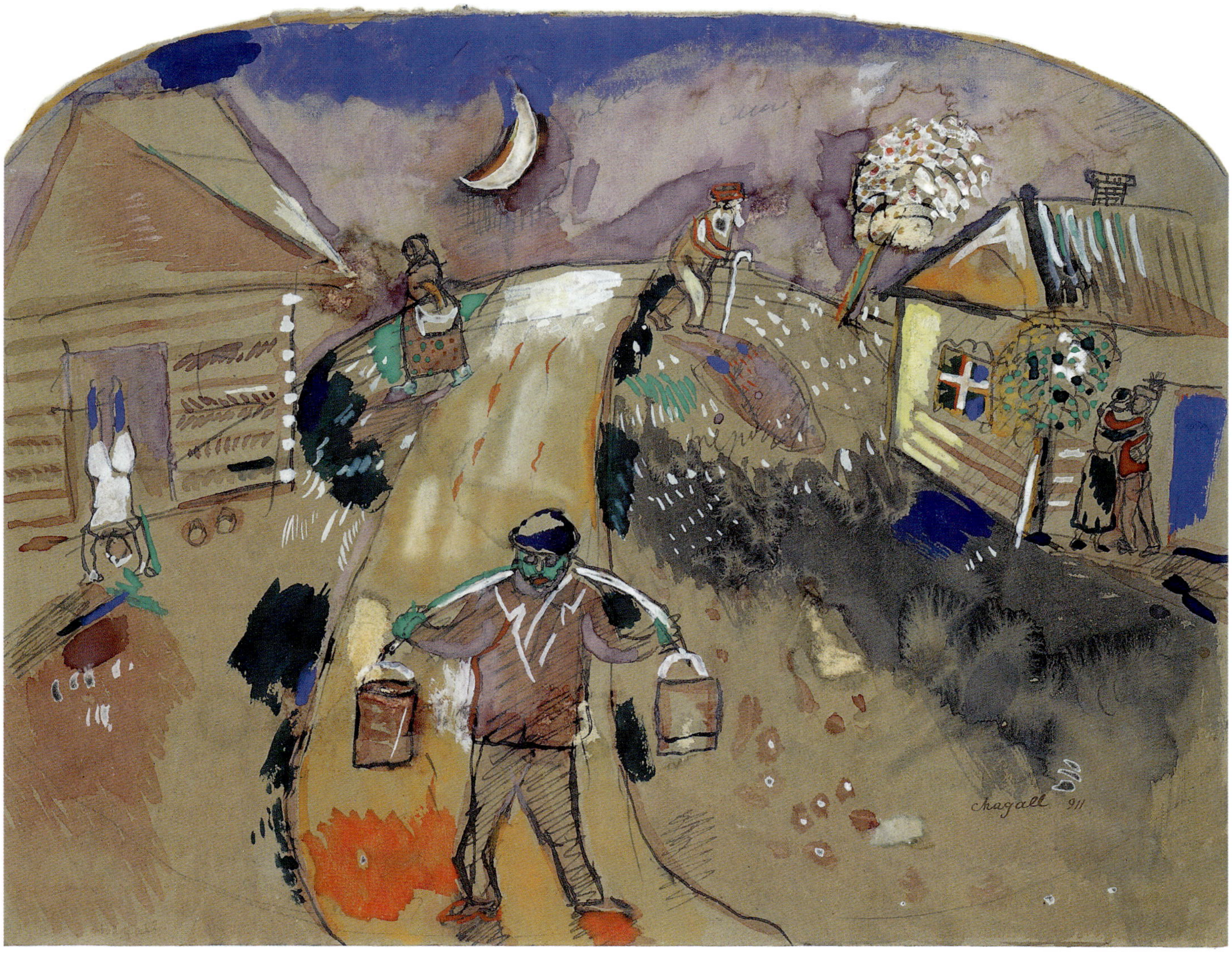

84. ***Water Carrier by Moonlight.*** *1911. Watercolor, gouache, crayon and fountain pen on paper, 24.1 x 31.1 cm. The Metropolitan Museum of Art, New York*

to the Balfour Declaration of November 2, 1917, promising a Jewish homeland in Palestine. The painting was postdated "1917" and certainly does not refer to the October Revolution.

The Cemetery, 1917 (no. 80), shows dilapidated sinking graves, most of them with the inscription: *HaRabani* ("The Rabbinical"), meaning a learned sage. But this is too formulaic a label to be true, especially as the graves appear, ironically, on a slope off of which dirty water runs.

RELIGIOUS SITUATIONS

Chagall often portrayed the ritual icons of a spiritual world. His *Praying Jew*, 1922 (no. 81), is an awesome image of a Jew in the solemn moment of prayer, wearing his white prayer shawl and his phylacteries: black straps on his left arm and a black box on his forehead. The moody, stylized, semi-geometrical background (compare to the sky in *The Gray House*, no. 2) with a white-black-green sky underscore the towering strength of the praying man. Chagall couldn't explain to the West that every single Orthodox Jew prays like that three times a day, and so he called it *The Rabbi*. But the painting was actually done using a beggar, who sat for him for a few kopecks. As in *Music* (no. 110) of the theater murals (see chapter 7), the patterns of the ritual attire merge with the geometrical patterns, as if they were one continuum—as if the Jewish ritual entailed an authentic Cubism. The parallel black stripes in the middle of the figure, unattached to any object, conduct a dialogue with the black straps on the left arm. And the white dots floating in a semicircle on the lower left are made to continue the fringe of the "four-corner" undershirt (*arba-kanfes*).

The painting *A Pinch of Snuff*, 1912–15 (no. 82), depicts a religious Jew (not necessarily a rabbi, as some have assumed) leisurely studying a *seyfer* (religious book)—a holy duty for a Jewish man, not to be disturbed by mundane matters or talk. He has changed his hat for a *yarmulke* (skullcap) and is enjoying a pinch of snuff to keep his wits alert—a proverbial bourgeois pleasure. Behind him is the Holy Ark containing a Torah scroll covered with a curtain (*paroykhes*), and on the left, we see the edge of a rich seven-branched candelabra, the Jewish national symbol. The scene is in a synagogue or a study house; the same two objects can be seen in *The Synagogue* of 1917 (no. 83) and may have been painted in the same place (the Jew is sitting behind the stage, to the left, where the conversational circle was seen). The Hebrew letters inside the Star of David on the curtain read: *ST* (*Seyfer Torah* = Torah Scroll), possibly corrected to or from *KT* (*Keser Torah* = Torah Crown). Yet the open book is not a holy *seyfer* but a secular *bukh* with a text in the secular language, Yiddish (perhaps with some Hebrew inserts). Individual words can still be read, but the syntactic continuity has been erased. The text is signed: "Segal Moyshe" in Hebrew (i.e., consonants only): SGL MShH—last name first, in the order of a Russian roll call. This signature, "Moyshe Segal," appears only combined with Hebrew texts in several thematically Jewish paintings of his Vitebsk years, dated 1914–15, such as *The Red Jew* (no. 68) and *The Green Jew* (no. 18). In his letters of the thirties, Chagall mentioned that his parents called him "Moshka" (from Moyshe). Yet now he discovered that Shagall (ShGL) was a distortion of Segal (spelled SGL, a Hebrew acronym), for the Jews in his region pronounced "S" as "Sh." He was also proud of the possibility that the eighteenth-century synagogue painter Chaim Segal of Mohilev was his ancestor (Chagall's family's hometown, Lyozno, belonged to the Mohilev Province). Yet this could not have happened before 1915–16, when the painters El Lissitzky and Nathan Rybak discovered the paintings in the Mohilev synagogue.

Reading the signature "Moyshe Segal" changes the date and place of the painting and our whole perception of Chagall's periodization. It is attributed to 1912, when Chagall was in Paris, but it could not have been done then. In Paris Chagall primarily appeared as a Russian painter, while the directly Jewish religious thematics were foregrounded after the persecutions of Jews in Russia in 1914–15 and the national revival of Jewish art in 1916–20. Furthermore, the Jew is similar to the almost realistic portraits of religious Jews of those years (*Jew in Red*, *The Green Jew*); the portrait is probably painted from a model; and the scene looks like the Vitebsk Synagogue. The argument that Herwarth Walden had the painting, thus dating it before the "Der Sturm" exhibition of Chagall's work in Berlin 1914, has no support: It does not appear in the list of this exhibition. And it is easily explainable: Chagall came again to Berlin in May 1922, and Walden offered the second version of this painting to the *Dial* in November 1922, which could have been brought from Russia then.

For a period of his childhood Marc Chagall was a singer at a synagogue, but he abandoned religion after his Bar Mitzvah, as did most of his generation. The revived interest in Jewish religious objects and customs, shared by several cultural activists, writers, and artists at the time, was entirely secular, turning the religious world into expressions of folklore, folk art, wisdom, and vitality—thus supplying roots of a culture in the past. In *The Synagogue*, 1917 (no. 83), we see the stage where the Torah is read; the Holy Ark closed with a red curtain, where the Torah scroll is kept; on its right, a relief of a seven-branched candelabra, as is the chandelier with candles hanging on the left. This synagogue is colorful but hollow, not performing its authentic functions. The man on the stage is supposed to read the Torah scroll, but he looks embarrassed and lost with no Torah in front of him. No one pays attention to the reading: The circle around the rich man (in fur coat), their backs to the East, are doing business or chatting about politics and gossip. Similarly frustrated are the solitary characters to the right and the two children. The elder one is probably Marc, who clearly doesn't belong here, and next to him is his brother David. It is an exotic, old, and weary world, however vivid the memories about it may be. Through the window are seen a blue sky and a romantic *shtetl*, which Chagall preferred to his grandfather's *shtot* (the permanent seat at the Eastern wall).

WATER CARRIERS AND CARTERS

In Eastern European Jewish folklore, tailors and cobblers were considered the lowest class, "thick heads," and uneducated; yet these were the most widespread artisan professions among Jews, in Vitebsk and elsewhere. The new literature raised their dignity, showed the nobility of the "simple people," as did Chagall. Yet water carriers and carters were even lower, for they needed no skill to perform their job; indeed, they were outside the social scale altogether. Now, in the populist perception shared by Chagall, and in a typical reversal, the lowest became revered.

The low status of water carriers derives from the Bible; some alien people in Canaan were enslaved and degraded: "Let them live; but let them be hewers of wood and drawers of water unto all the congregation" (Joshua 9:21). We can see the woodcutter bringing a bundle of cut wood at the top left of the work. In a Jewish small town in Eastern Europe, the water carrier fulfilled an important function: For pennies, he brought water from the river to the houses uphill, rich and poor. Now one could see something holy about his service, for the Bible also said: "hewers of wood and drawers of water for the house of my God . . . and for the altar of my Lord." (Joshua 9: 23,27). Indeed, the *Lamed-Vov*, the "Thirty-six Just Men," who according to legend will save the world, are hiding among us disguised as simple hewers of wood and carriers of water. Yet there were no Jewish hewers of wood.

Jewish carters (*balegoles*) were known for their cursing, their coarse language, and strong hand. Here their physical strength and healthy language are idealized: They are "real" people, without the Jewish frailty and fear, without the intellectual complexes and the *luftmentsh's* detachment from reality. Water carriers and carters, like circus people, were on the margins of regular, stratified society, thus bearing the fascination of the "free" outsider. In a child's fantasy, carters could also "fly" (drive fast) in their wagons way beyond the local community, skipping spaces and boundaries.

The holiness of the water carrier is evident in *Water Carrier by Moonlight*, 1911 (no. 84). Encountering full buckets of water is believed to bring good luck, and the two moons caught in the buckets have a magical effect. This is a night of magic and love, as we can see in the couple embracing on the right, the figure in her long underwear on the left, standing on her head, the man-goat above, and the water carrier's white road floating above the surreal mound and the earthy shadows. An early moon, connoting monthly periods and fertility, illuminates it all.

TYPEFACES AND SPELLING

Accounting for all the language elements in Chagall's paintings would require an annotated edition that deciphers all the texts and allusions and explains their different cultural levels. Apart from the referential function exemplified above, Chagall was a sophisticated user of the language material itself. He treated language as he treated other representational elements in his fictional world and formal elements on his canvas: Deformation and polyphony of voices were his guiding principles, allusion and whimsical twists his constant devices.

Chagall used Hebrew, Yiddish, and Russian texts in his graphic work, but often confounded their respective spellings and direction of writing in a multicultural manner. Hebrew is basically spelled with consonants,

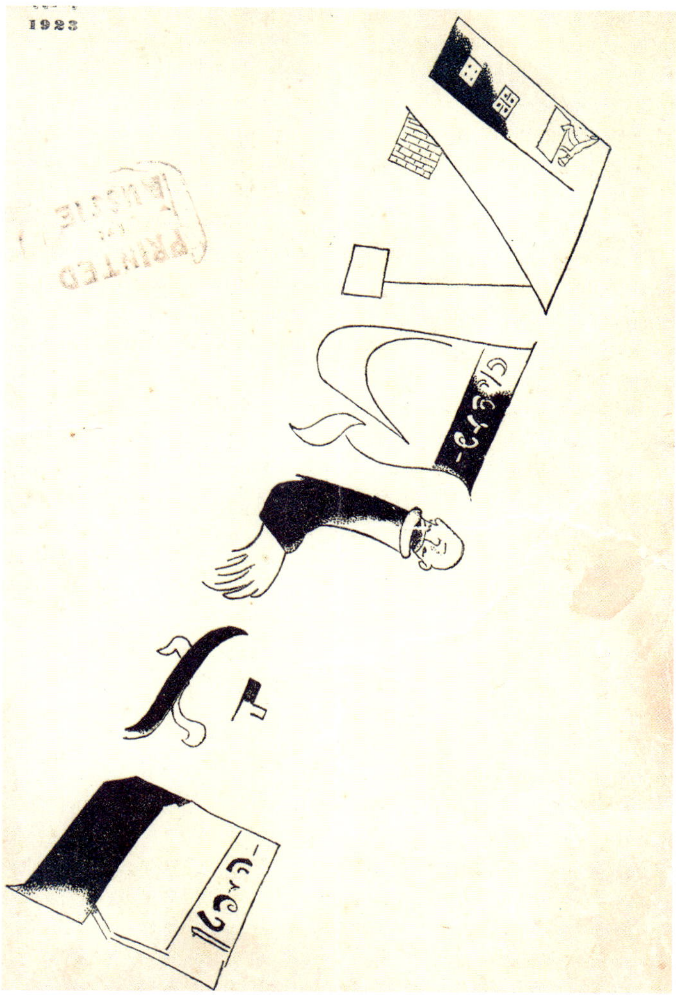

85. *Cover illustraton of* ***Shtrom****. 1922. Courtesy Yivo Institute for Jewish Research, New York*

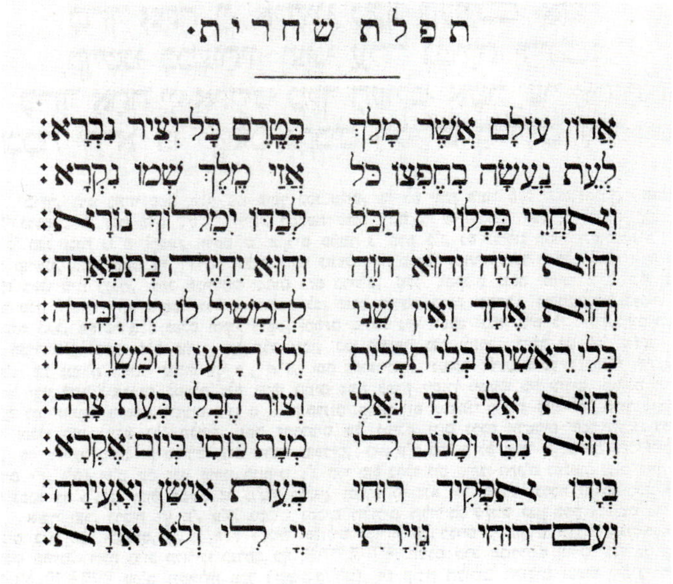

תפלת שחרית.

אדון עולם אשר מלך בטרם כל־יציר נברא:
לעת נעשה בחפצו כל אזי מלך שמו נקרא:
ואחרי כבלות הכל לבדו ימלוך נורא:
והוא היה והוא הוה והוא יהיה בתפארה:
והוא אחד ואין שני להמשיל לו להחבירה:
בלי ראשית בלי תכלית ולו העז והמשרה:
והוא אלי וחי גאלי וצור חבלי בעת צרה:
והוא נסי ומנוס לי מנת כוסי ביום אקרא:
בידו אפקיד רוחי בעת אישן ואעירה:
ועם רוחי גויתי יי לי ולא אירא:

86. *Page 35 from* ***Seder Avodat Israel****, edited by Yitzhak ben Ayre Yosef Dov, Seligman Baer, new edition, Schocken, Berlin. 1937. Courtesy Leo Baeck, New York*

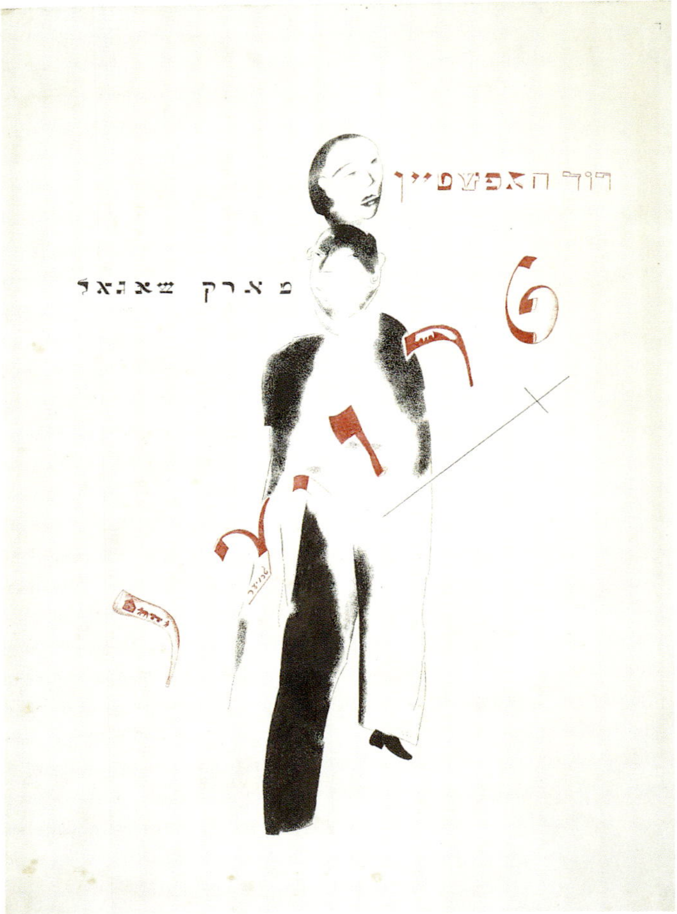

87. ***Grief (Troyer).*** *Illustration for the cover of* ***Grief*** *by D. Hofshteyn. 1919. Ink on paper, 47.2 x 33.7 cm. AM 1988-213. Musée National d'Art Moderne, Centre Georges Pompidou, Paris*

whereas Yiddish evolved a European-type spelling system, including all vowels. Hebrew words inside Yiddish, however, use the Hebrew consonantal spelling, to separate the holy tongue from the mundane language. After the Communist Revolution, the Hebrew (or "religious") spelling of Yiddish words was abolished and all words acquired vowel letters. Thus, in *My Life* the inscription on his mother's tombstone reads in Hebrew: **שגל** = *ShGL* (capitals represent the actual letters; Sh is one letter in Hebrew) while in the same book his father's tombstone reads **שאגאל** = ShAGAL, with all vowels filled in.[20] The reason for this is simple: His mother died in 1916, and his father died after the Revolution, in 1921. The artist adopted the Soviet spelling and used it throughout his life for his own name and in private correspondence.

In the Bible, in children's books, and in other special cases, Hebrew uses signs of vocalization above, below, and inside the letters. But normal Hebrew texts make do without them. Paradoxically, Yiddish, a language that does not need them, used Hebrew vocalizations in addition to its normal vowel letters. In his paintings, Chagall played with the differences and their cultural connotations.

On several occasions Chagall signed his paintings in consonants only: **משה סגל** = *MShH SGL* (pronounced: *Moyshe Segal*), invoking the Jewish art pedigree of an eighteenth-century synagogue painter, Chaim Segal. In the painting *Rain* (no. 104), a Russian word is even spelled in consonants: ЛВК = *LVK* (for *lavka*, "store" in Russian), perhaps to indicate Jewish ownership. In the same way, in *Homage to Apollinaire* (no. 44), Chagall spells his French name: ChGL, to indicate his Hebrew identity. On the other hand, in the midst of a holy text in *The Green Jew* (no. 21), we find a Yiddish insert, *der slutsker magid* ("the preacher from Slutsk"). "Preacher" is a Hebrew term for a religious profession, spelled in both languages: **מגיד** = *MGID*. By inserting a vowel, *MAGID* **מאגיד**, Chagall indicates the preaching was done in Yiddish.

The interactions between Hebrew and Cyrillic letters often hinged on direction: Hebrew and Yiddish read right to left, while Russian goes from left to right. Sometimes Chagall changed the direction of parts of a Hebrew text, as we saw in *The Cemetery Gate* (no. 79). In one case he even changed the order of the two tablets of the Ten Commandments, indicating his double-directed culture. He signed a painting: Marc **לאגאש** = *MARC* [*LAGASh*]. When read in reverse, continuing the direction of "Marc," the Yiddish letters sound *ShAGAL*. On the stage design of a train for Sholem Aleichem's *Agents* (no. 91), he wrote: III פאר ר״יכער לק = *FAR REYKHER[ers] LK III* (for smokers lk III). The last, enigmatic part, when read in the reverse direction, says: "III cl[ass]" in Russian. Here he has adapted the Russian of the official train to the Yiddish of the travelers.

An interesting case appears in the mural *Introduction to the Yiddish Theater* (no. 95), which depicts Efros, the literary director of the theater, bringing Chagall to the stage director Granovsky. In a preliminary study for this painting (no. 108), the Yiddish inscription above the figures, reads: יקסוואנארג לאגאש עפראס = *IKSVVONARG LAGASh EFROS*. Efros, a name traditionally spelled in Hebrew as אפרת *(APRT)*, receives an "outrageous" Soviet spelling: *EFROS*. The other two names are inverted; if read in the Russian direction, they read "Shagal Granovsky." This is similar to the reversible rhymes (*perevertni*) in Russian Futurism, but it also expresses the multicultural symbiosis of Chagall's generation. In the actual painting, moreover, Chagall deletes a letter in both his and Efros's names and inserts miniature drawings of a literary critic and a painter instead, thus achieving a double-media denotation. In the actual mural this gets even more complex (see chapter 7).

Similar close attention to cultural details can be seen in the use of typefaces in Chagall's paintings. In the Ashkenazi religious tradition, which he knew from his childhood, Hebrew letters appeared in several socially determined categories of typefaces: (1) The so-called *"square" letters*, which were mostly based on straight lines or rounded backbones but which had their thickness elaborated in curvaceous forms and additional ornaments. These were obligatory in handwritten Torah scrolls and in printings of the Bible, having an aura of "holy text." (2) *Moderate "square" letters* were used as normal typefaces in printed Hebrew and Yiddish, usually printed without the vocalization markers. Typically, in engravings on a tombstone, the curvaceous embellishments could be moderate, as imitated by Chagall in *The Cemetery Gate* or as later developed by him in casual biblical names in his stained-glass windows. (3) *Rashi letters*, which possess a shape similar to that of longhand letters, were used for commentaries printed on the margins of a Bible or Talmud: A commentary must never be confused with the holy text itself. (4) *Vayber-taytsh* ("women's typeface")—special scripts between printed and cursive—were used for books for women on religious topics in Yiddish. All Hebrew words within the Yiddish, however, are printed in Hebrew square letters and placed in parentheses in midsentence between the feminine words, so as not to mix the feminine and the masculine, or the Yiddish and the Hebrew. (5) *Written letters* (cursive) were used for writing in longhand: for personal correspondence, manuscripts, and the like (with "childish" and "adult" varieties).

Examine the page from a traditional book of Joshua (no. 86), printed 1862–66.[21] In the center is the text of the Bible in "square" letters. The letters are accompanied by markers of vocalization and syntactic-musical reading accents, in the form of tiny dots, dashes, and other markers below, above, and inside the letters. To the right, with small letters, i.e., of a second degree of importance, is an Aramaic translation of the same text. Around these two rectangles there are three classical commentaries in *Rashi* letters; and at the bottom, there are additional commentaries by modern scholars, in even smaller *Rashi* letters.

Chagall used square letters to indicate textual quotations from religious texts, and moderate square letters for other "serious" purposes. He—and the whole secular movement—would rarely use the second-class *Rashi* or the women's scripts. He often used "written" letters for his own personal message (e.g., the list of his siblings and parents written-in on a pair of paints in *Introduction to the Yiddish Theater*) or to indicate a character's personal statement ("I am an acrobat," "I am frolicking," written on the belts of the clowns standing on their heads).

Yet he also used the following types: (6) *Modern printed letters*, which were developed in Yiddish and Hebrew secular literature. (7) *Geometrical letters*, which reduce all letter shapes to straight strokes, stripes, or semicircles, as developed in the modern movement. Such letters were used in Constructivist designs of book covers and in secular Yiddish schools and institutions—for headlines, front pages, invitations, posters, and so on, and were often given fancy geometrical forms and three-dimensional bodies.

One example is the cover of the Soviet Yiddish literary journal שטראָם = *ShTROM* (no. 85) ("stream" or "torrent," connoting both the torrential stream of the Revolution and the slogan of "going with the 'stream,'" accepting it). The title is drawn on a diagonal base, a favorite device of Chagall. The first letter *Sh* (at the top right) is fully geometrical, but inverts the traditional manner: In "square" letters, the base is thick and the three diagonal strokes are thin; here the base is just a line, whereas the right side is thick. The body of the side stroke and the heads of the two others are of a precise, rectangular form, rather than the traditional curving sides and ornamented heads. The geometrical bodies are used as a background for "construction" themes. The second

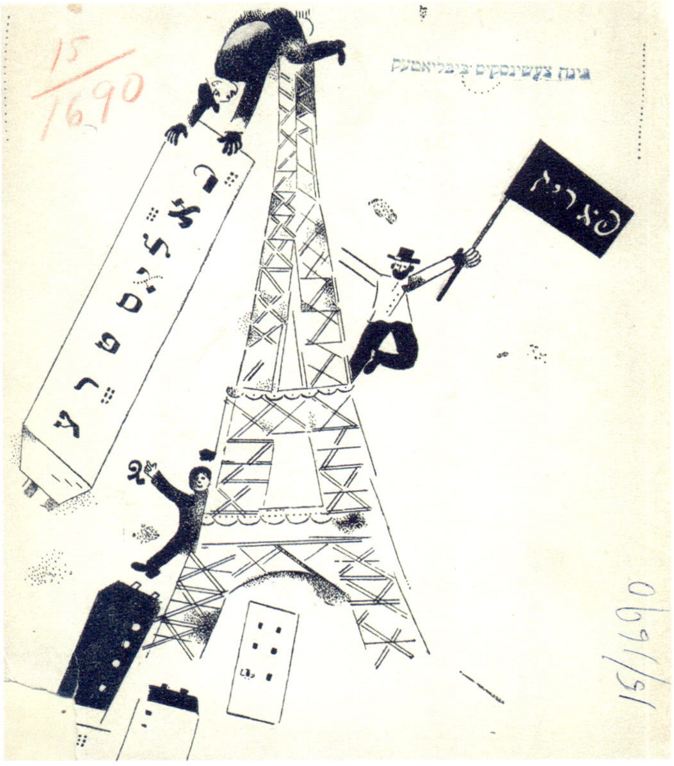

88. *Cover illustration of* ***Khalyastre****. 1924. Courtesy Yivo Institute for Jewish Research, New York*

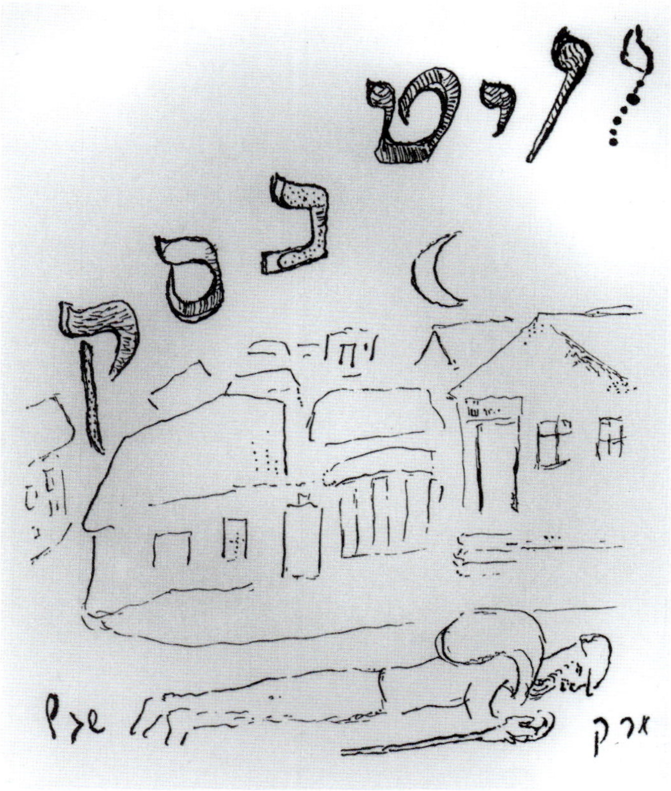

The cover of ***Vitebsk****, a collection of memoirs and historical studies in Hebrew, published by the Association of Immigrants from Vitebsk and Vicinity, Tel Aviv, 1957. Chagall signs his names in the Hebrew (not the Yiddish) spelling (MRK ShGL), yet hints at Yiddish by adding a tentative second V in the name of the city (VViTBSK). Courtesy of the author*

letter, *T*, has a geometricized imitation of the traditional rounded upper part. The third and fourth letters (*R*, *O*) are modern, simplified, and stylized imitations of square letters, whimsically Chagallized with anthropomorphic bodies. The fifth letter, *closing M* (used only at the end of a word), is again geometrically rectangular in its sides and in its overall closure—yet the horizontal parallel lines move slightly apart, making the whole body dynamic. The rectangular head has a symbolic dollop on top. Thus, Chagall uses his "demonstrative eclecticism" repeatedly to evoke juxtapositions and surprises inside each letter and between the letters. The allusions to the distinct typefaces and their cultural connotations are not lost on the reader.

Furthermore, as in many other cases, the wide sides of the letters can be used as backgrounds for Chagallian little figures and shaded spaces. In the rectangular base of two of the geometrical printed letters, written letters announce in Soviet spelling: "monthly journal."[22] The written letters, however, have an unusual thickness that is rendered sometimes as a white and sometimes as a dark surface. These provide an intimate, casual feeling to the Constructivist *ShTROM*, like a personal letter to the reader; yet the Constructivist part itself has been softened and humanized in the middle three letters—which El Lissitkzy, taking Constructivism seriously, would never have done—through the portrait of the head of a Russian high school boy, one of Chagall's emblems indicating general (Russian) education.

The cover for *Troyer* ("Grief") (no. 87) has the effective red-black-white graphic design that El Lissitzky later developed into his book designs and agitprop posters. The poet David Hofshteyn and Marc Chagall overlap within a single figure that has two heads, with Hofshteyn's on top. Their names are written next to the heads, and Hofshteyn's name, in almost purely geometrical letters, shifts between line and body, as it does between black and red. The diagonal title *Troyer*, which blurs the boundaries between printed and written letters, is softer than the title we saw in the cover for *ShTROM*. The written *T* looks like a *b*. The first *R* has a fox on its body, and the last *R* includes the image of a house and a wagon departing into exile. Also, the *E* has the word *troyer* in red, written in a child's handwriting upon its base. The date, 1919, in Chagall's signature indicates the time of the pogroms in Ukraine, although the poem itself was written in 1921.

A very different cover was made two years later in Paris for the Yiddish Expressionist literary journal *Khalyastre* ("Happy Gang"), no. 88. To indicate "the

Khalyastre ("Happy Gang"), no. 88. To indicate "the Jews (Yiddish literature) conquer Paris," his atheist friends are made to wear emblems of religious garb. The Eiffel Tower and the rectangular leaning houses of his Paris paintings are here, as are the lines and clusters of tiny dots. The "beautiful" (with his thick, "feminine" lips) Peretz Markish hangs down the top of the Eiffel Tower, holding the title *Khalyastre* (which turns into a building), and the climbing Oyzer Varshavski on the right proudly holds a banner that reads "Paris." A boy, Chagall himself, holds out the number of the issue, 2. The text is in simplified, square letters, mocked and disrupted: The *A* wants to walk away, the second *A* turns its foot backward and has dots instead of its central diagonal backbone; and in *Paris* the first letter is written and the others printed, yet rounded and moving in a written direction. By juxtaposing typefaces, subverting and mixing them, Chagall turns them into malleable graphic bodies. He uses their social functionality, ironizes it, and foregrounds its problematic nature.

---

1. See Musée d'art et d'histoire du Judaïsme, *Le Juif un Témoin du temps Errant*. Paris: Société Nouvelle Adam Biro, 2001.

2. Dovid Hofshteyn, *Troyer* (Kiev: kulter-lige, 1922). The two lines were translated in Franz Meyer's Chagall biography as, "What do I need her for,/ the sincerity, the purity?" which does not convey the real meaning of this text. Franz Meyer, *Marc Chagall: Life and Work*. New York: Harry N. Abrams, 1963, p. 742.

3. See Richard Hamilton, *The Bride Stripped Bare by Her Bachelors, Even: A Typographical Version*. New York: Jaap Rietman Inc., 1960.

4. An excellent study of the theory of idioms, including many Yiddish examples, is Uriel Weinreich's "Problems in the Analysis of Idioms," in his *On Semantics*. Philadelphia: University of Pennsylvania Press, 1980, pp. 208–64.

5. Mendele Moykher Sforim, *Kitzer masoes binyomin ha-shlishi* [The Short Travels of Benjamin III]. Vilna: Widow and Brothers Romm, 1878, p. 4.

6. Ibid.

7. The expressions "going into exile" *(geyn in goles)* and "conducting exile" *(praven goles)* are also used for a man who leaves his town and family to repent for his sins, or goes to places of study, or leaves to seek his fortune, sleeping in prayer houses on the road, with no place to rest. For a powerful example, see I. J. Singer's novel *Yoshe Kalb*.

8. Morris Rosenfeld, *A Goles Marsh*, in *Shriftn*, vol. 1. New York: A. M. Evalenko, 1908, p. 100. Translated by Benjamin and Barbara Harshav.

9. Bags and packages—the symbol of a Jewish nomad.

10. See *Marc Chagall and His Times*.

11. The "elevated mood," "ecstasy," or "trance" of love lift the lovers off the ground; a fast moving carriage is said to be "flying by" *(farbaygefloygn)*; *er flit in di himlen* ("he is soaring in the heavens") means elation or fantasy and delusion; *zayn kop flit in himl* ("his head is flying in the sky") implies unsubstantiated fantasy.

12. Sholem Aleichem, "The Violin," in *Stories for Jewish Children*, vol. 1. New York: Sholem Aleichem Folksfond, 1918, p. 42.

13. Ibid., pp. 63, 75.

14. Bella Chagall, *Brenendike likht* ("Burning Candles"). New York: Book League of the Jewish Fraternal Order, 1945, passim.

15. Ignaz Bernstein, *yudishe shprikhverter un redensarten,* pp. 130, 290.

16. See the half-effaced slogan in "Peace to Huts—War on Palaces" (1918) in *Marc Chagall: The Russian Years, 1906–1922*, ed., Christoph Vitali. Frankfurt: Schirn Kunsthalle, 1991, image 134.

17. See Vitebsk. *Sefer Vitebsk* ("The Book of Vitebsk"), ed. Barukh Karu (Krupnik). Tel Aviv: The Organization of Immigrants from Vitebsk and Environs, 1957, p. 238.

18. The Zionist hymn "Ha-Tikva" begins with a verse stating, "Our hope is not yet lost."

19. Authorized King James Version.

20. Images of the tombstones are reprinted in *My Life*, facing pages 10 and 146. *ShGL* is perceived as variant of *SGL* (Segal), a Hebrew acronym, hence spelled with consonants only.

21. *Mikraot Gedolot, Neviim u-ktuvim*, new edition. New York: Schocken Books, 1946, p. 5.

22. Literally, "monthly notebooks": *khoydesh* (month) is a Hebrew word spelled *HDSh*, here Sovietized; *heftn*, "issues," like the French *cahiers*.

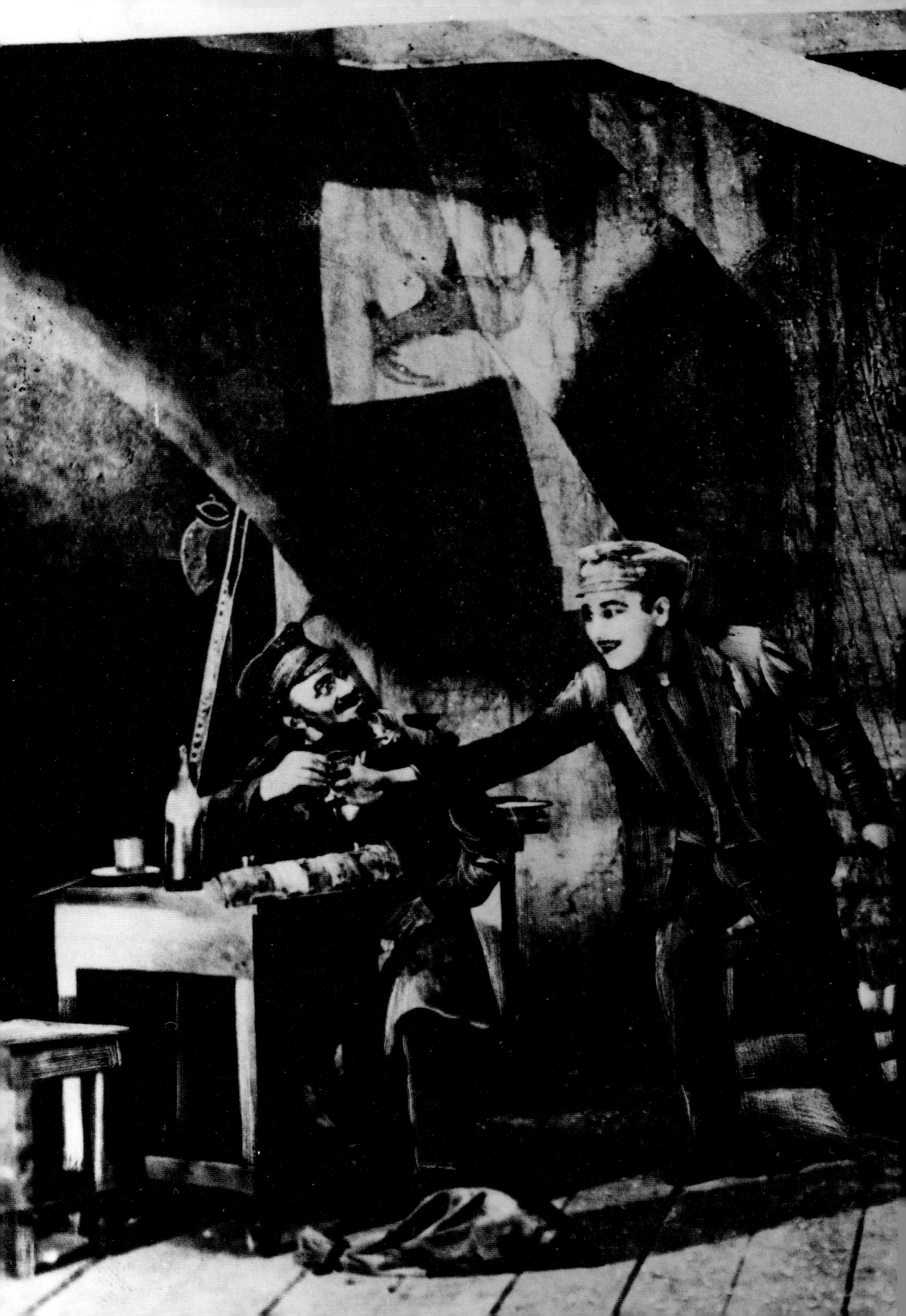

5. The Yiddish Art Theater

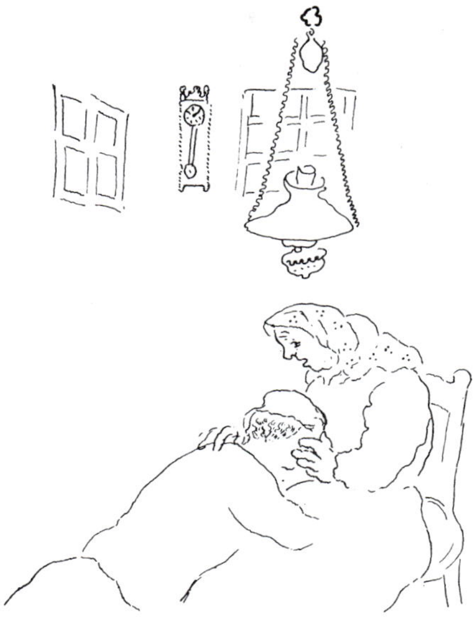

THE FAME OF THE YIDDISH AVANT-GARDE THEATER

The Moscow Yiddish theater—"Yiddish" and "Jewish" are the same word in Russian and in Yiddish—later known as GOSET (*Gosudarstvenny Evreysky Teatr*, "State Jewish/Yiddish Theater") began as a modest actors' studio in Petrograd in 1919 and moved to Moscow toward the end of 1920. By the mid-1920s it was considered one of the most exciting companies in Russia and, indeed, in Europe. On a visit to Russia, the English theater critic Huntley Carter, who wrote several books on the Russian avant-garde theater, said, "The work of GOSET has no equal in Europe."[1] The German theater critic Alfons Goldschmidt, after visiting Moscow in 1925, wrote, "The Moscow State Yiddish Theater, directed by Granovsky in ensemble with the actors, embodies at least the beginning of something entirely new, while the Western European theater, in its degeneration, looks in vain for new forms."[2]

When the Yiddish theater came to Berlin's Theater des Westens in 1928, the awe-inspiring theater critic Alfred Kerr began his essay with these words:

> This is great art. Great art.
> External image and soul-shaking. The sound of words, the sound of blood, the sound of color, the sound of images. There are calls, voices, questions, shouts, choruses. It is enjoyment and horror . . . and in the end, human communion.
> That is, of course, pantomime with movement into eternity.
> Something wonderful.
> Great art.[3]

OPPOSITE: *A scene from* ***Mazel-tov*** *by Sholem Aleichem, 1921, setting by Chagall, including a long-lost curtain with an upside-down goat. Sitting: Shloyme Mikhoels as Reb Alter. Courtesy Natalia Vofsi-Michoels and the History of Theatre Archives, Tel Aviv University*

These were not usually sentimental or nostalgic intellectuals but highly critical, cosmopolitan theater critics. Similar superlatives were expressed both by visitors to Russia and by other German theater critics during the troupe's tour of Western Europe in 1928. After all the formal inventions of the first quarter of the century, it seemed that the avant-garde theater had exhausted its innovations, and this new company seemed to fulfill a need at a moment of crisis. It also exemplified both the new culture created in the wake of the Russian Revolution and the miraculous rebirth of the oppressed and primitive Jews.

YIDDISH CULTURE AND YIDDISH THEATER

Toward the end of the tsarist regime in Russia, new ideas were coalescing among the new class of Jewish intellectuals concerning the organized creation and promotion of a full-fledged national culture for the more than five million Jews in Russia. After the democratic revolution of February 1917, when Jews were granted civil rights and could freely move to the centers of Russia, it was only natural that they tried to implement those ideas and continued doing so after the October Revolution, under the

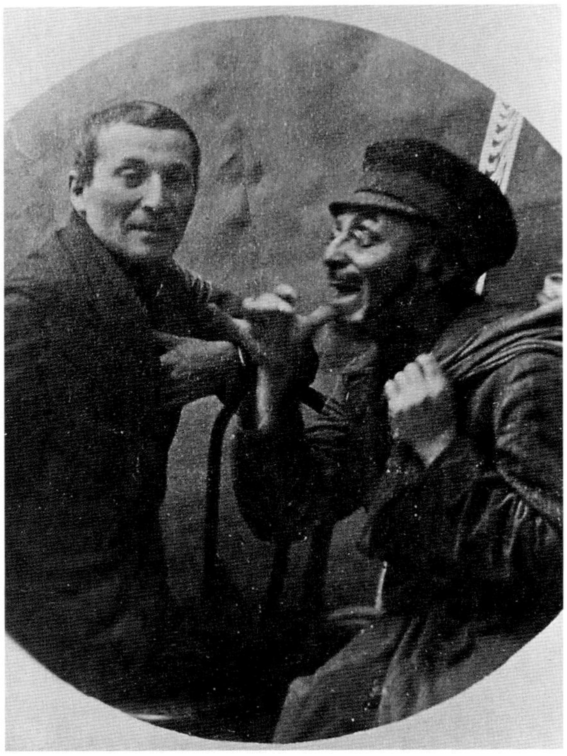

Chagall and the actor Shloyme Mikhoels as Reb Alter in ***Mazel-tov****, a one-act play by Sholem Aleichem, performed by the Yiddish Chamber Theater in Moscow, January 1921. Courtesy Comité Marc Chagall, Paris*

new Communist regime. In 1918, in Ukraine's capital Kiev, there emerged an umbrella organization, Kultur-Lige ("Culture League"), devoted to Yiddish national culture. Their program declared:

> Kultur-Lige stands on three pillars: Yiddish education for the people, Yiddish literature, and Jewish art. The goal of Kultur-Lige is to make our masses intelligent and make our intelligentsia Jewish. . . .
>
> The goal of Kultur-Lige is to help create a new Yiddish secular culture in the Yiddish language, in Jewish national forms, with the vital forces of the broad Jewish populace, in the spirit of the Jewish working masses, in harmony with their ideal of the future.
>
> The working field of Kultur-Lige is the whole field of the new secular culture: the child before the school and in the school, education for the young and adult Jew, Yiddish literature, Jewish art.[4]

The stamp issued by Kultur-Lige bore the inscription "Mendele, Peretz, Sholem Aleichem"—the three great Yiddish fiction writers, all of whom died during World War I, and thus secured their status as the three "classical" writers of modern Yiddish literature. Theirs was a sophisticated, language-sensitive and precise prose that reached the highest European standards and yet was rooted in the world of Eastern European Jewry. Deeply involved in understanding Jewish existence, their work formed a dignified foundation for a modern, secular, authentic Jewish literature and culture. Chagall was influenced by these three classical writers and included their names in his mural, *Introduction to the Yiddish Theater* (no. 137).

Kultur-Lige emerged during the Civil War, when Kiev itself was shifting from one power to another. The war, and the exterminating pogroms of 1919 (when about 100,000 Jews were slaughtered in Ukraine and several hundred thousand were exiled from their towns), were hard on the Kiev center; but its ideas were shared by other centers in Russia and in the newly reestablished Polish Republic.

In the same spirit that led to Kultur-Lige's formation, on November 9, 1916, with Russia still under the tsarist regime, a Jewish Theater Society was founded in Petrograd. The revolutions disrupted all work in the capital, but the emerging cultural powers supported the rehabilitation of the Jews as part of the new policy of elevating those oppressed by the Tsarist regime. On

November 29, 1918, the journal *Zhizn Iskusstva* ("The Life of Art") announced the establishment of a "Yiddish workers' theater" in Petrograd, affiliated with the theater and performance department of the People's Commissariat of Education. The prerevolutionary Jewish Theater Society implemented that decision. In February 1919, a theater studio was established, and Aleksey Granovsky, who had studied in Germany and was a disciple of the celebrated theater director Max Reinhardt, was appointed director of the Artistic Division. After five months of intensive studies, the studio was transformed into the Yiddish Chamber Theater and began performances on July 3, 1919.

But Petrograd was not the best place for Yiddish theater. Its small Jewish community before the 1917 revolutions consisted of largely Russified, privileged Jews, with no Yiddish-speaking masses. Thus, between July 7 and August 22, 1919, the company gave performances in the nearest Jewish center—Vitebsk, where Chagall was then Commissar of Art and director of the People's Art School. Chagall showed no special interest in this Yiddish theater when it visited Vitebsk, for he was immersed in making the sets for the Theater of Revolutionary Satire in the Russian language. The Yiddish theater's designs were heavily Symbolist, and its artists impressed him as uninteresting or epigones.

During its Petrograd period, the cosmopolitan Yiddish Chamber Theater included the works of Yiddish and non-Yiddish authors alike, producing such plays as Maurice Maeterlinck's *The Blind*, Karl Gutzkow's *Uriel Acosta*, Scholem Asch's *Sin* and *Amnon and Tamar*, and A. Vayter's *Before Dawn*. It was an art theater that happened to perform in the Yiddish language. For lack of heating materials in Petrograd, the theater was closed for the 1919–20 season, yet rehearsals continued, giving Granovsky the chance to train, educate, and form a well-trained and integrated troupe of an entirely new kind.

A parallel, smaller initiative was taken in Moscow. In September 1918, the Jewish Commissariat of the Russian government founded a theater section as part of its Education Department. According to its head, B. Orshansky, the call for actors met with little response because the Jewish intelligentsia did not support the Soviet power and "sabotaged" the enterprise. For that reason they gathered some young and politically trustworthy people, with no theater experience. Thus, an independent actors' studio was founded in Moscow in 1919, which included actors from a similar theater studio in Vitebsk.

In 1920 the Soviet capital moved back from Petrograd to the old capital Moscow. On April 1, 1920, the government authority chaired by Anatoly Lunacharsky decided to transfer the Yiddish Chamber Theater from Petrograd to Moscow. When Granovsky's theater arrived in November 1920 (with only eight of the original students), it merged with the Moscow actors' studio as well as with some actors from the Vilna Troupe, a recently established Yiddish art theater in Vilna. Performances in Moscow began on January 1, 1921, in a hall with ninety seats, surrounded by Chagall's murals. A year later, the theater moved from "Chagall's box," as it became known, to a larger auditorium, containing 500 seats.

In 1921 Granovsky's theater was renamed GOSEKT (State Yiddish Chamber Theater). Its name changed several times: "Studio of the Yiddish Workers Theater," "Studio of the State Yiddish Chamber Theater," "State Yiddish Chamber Theater" (GOSEKT), and finally, in 1924, it was renamed "State Yiddish/Jewish Theater" (GOSET). It also appeared in the West as the "State Yiddish Academic Theater." Chagall's murals stayed behind in the old place, turned into an actor's studio, but after 1925 they were displayed in the foyer of the new auditorium.

Two magical slogans guided the new Yiddish theater and gave it immense prestige: "theater as art" and "theater of the State." Finally, Jews could have an "art theater" (in the tradition of Stanislavsky's "Moscow Art Theater"), connected with the most advanced of the other arts—graphic art, literature, dance, music—and separate from the kitschy Yiddish entertainment stage. And this theater was supported by the State itself—the foreign State that had been the enemy of the Jews for 2,000—almost a Zionist vision! The Yiddish name for the theater sounded even better—Moskver Yidisher *Melukhisher* Teatr ("Moscow Yiddish *Royal* Theater"). It is hard to imagine the dignity and pride its supporters felt. Their tangible hope for a new secular and elite Jewish national culture and the revolutionary spirit that inspired this enterprise made those involved open to the trends of political revolution and the artistic avant-garde.

In his Yiddish productions Granovsky wanted the Jewish subject matter to represent general human values. Yet as director of the Yiddish Theater he felt a special mission, which included both raising the Jewish masses to a high cultural level and creating a national Jewish secular culture. In the archives of the theater is a document dating from 1920 or 1921, handwritten in Russian, which looks like points for a lecture by Granovsky, describing the goals and organizational structure of GOSEKT. The first section reads:

General Principles

- GOSEKT is the first and only attempt to create a permanent performing-arts theater for the Jewish nation.

- Because of political conditions, it was hitherto impossible to establish such a theater.

- Geographically, Moscow was selected as the cultural and artistic center of the life of the whole Republic.

- Unlike all other nationalities inhabiting Russia, the Jews are the only ones who have no territory of their own.

This was the succinct ideology of a political-cultural program, from which the organizational framework followed. To keep a theater of such importance alive, one needed to train personnel at all levels. As Granovsky saw it, there were to be three separate units: a School of Stage Art, to "train the personnel of actors and directors, who are totally lacking in the Yiddish theater"; a Studio, "a laboratory to develop the forms of the Yiddish theater"; and the Theater itself, "for the broad masses."

GRANOVSKY AND THEATER AS ART

Aleksey (or Aleksandr) Granovsky was born Abraham Azarkh in Moscow in 1890. Moscow was out of bounds for most Jews, thus his parents must have been well off, probably well-educated, and certainly Russian-speaking (it was said of Granovsky that he knew no Yiddish before he heard it from his actors[5]). In 1891 most of Moscow's Jews were expelled. His family settled in Riga, then the third-largest city of Russia. Riga has a long German tradition but had been under Russian rule for over two centuries. There, he imbibed both the Russian and German languages and culture, and through them, the culture of Western Europe. Riga produced such contemporary intellectuals as the film director Sergey Eisenstein (who was two years older than Granovsky), whose Jewish father converted to Lutheranism and became the city architect of Riga, whose Art Nouveau buildings stand in Riga to this day, and the Yiddish actor Solomon (Shloyme) Mikhoels, who, like Granovsky, was born in 1890.

In 1910 Granovsky began his theater studies in St. Petersburg, and from 1911 to 1914 he studied in Germany at the Munich Theater Academy, where he worked for a season as an assistant to Max Reinhardt. In 1917 he studied film directing in Sweden. Back in Petrograd in 1918, he joined the new Theater of Tragedy, which was supported by prominent Russian intellectuals such as Maksim Gorky and Aleksandr Blok and was devoted to promoting classical drama for the masses. There he directed Sophocles's *Oedipus Rex* and Shakespeare's *Macbeth* in Russian. He also directed two operas, Charles Gounod's *Faust* and Nikolai Rimsky-Korsakov's *Sadko*, and the famous German-language production of Vladimir Mayakovsky's avant-garde play *Mystery Bouffe*, which was performed for the Third Congress of the Comintern. Then he strove to create a theater of his own in Yiddish.

Granovsky and his mentors believed in the creation of Yiddish theater as *Art*. The Jewish cultural renaissance of the preceding forty years had been concentrated in literature and ideology; they believed that to become a full-fledged culture, the nation needed music, art, and theater. Since theater was accepted as an art only in the most modern sense, they recognized no earlier Jewish theatrical tradition. Granovsky was to begin from absolute zero.

Since the Greco-Roman period in Palestine, theater was banned in Judaism, probably because it epitomized the joys and debauchery of heathen culture. Naturally, there were a few exceptions: Some Hebrew plays were written and performed in post-Renaissance Italy and in the Haskala period, the Jewish "Enlightenment," which emerged in Berlin in the late eighteenth century and spread to Central and Eastern Europe. For centuries there were also popular theatrical entertainments in Yiddish, notably the *Purim-shpil*. Nevertheless, theater in the modern, European sense was almost nonexistent in Yiddish or Hebrew. Avrom Goldfaden launched a Yiddish theater to provide entertainment in 1876, but in 1883 the Russian government banned all theater in "jargon" (Yiddish). The ban was lifted between 1905 and 1910, then renewed until the 1917 Revolution. Yiddish popular theater, primarily low-class melodrama (such as Kafka saw and admired in Prague in 1910), blossomed in London and New York, but Granovsky, like most Yiddish highbrow writers and cultural activists of his time, would have nothing to do with it. Among Yiddish intellectuals, New York's celebrated Second Avenue Yiddish theater was considered terrible, kitschy, and degrading to Yiddish culture in America.

During the 1905–10 period, when Yiddish theater was legal in Russia, there were important beginnings: Good literary and theatrical plays were written by Peretz Hirshbeyn, Dovid Pinsky, and others; celebrated actors emerged, notably Ester-Rokhl Kaminsky, who made a strong impact on young Mikhoels during her performances in Riga; and plays by Gorky, Gerhard Hauptmann, Shakespeare, and Friedrich von Schiller, translated into literary Yiddish, were performed. Granovsky and his contemporaries rejected that theater as well because it was individualistic, psychological, and literary rather than social and theatrical. The new regime, certainly, saw those Yiddish playwrights as "petit-bourgeois" writers, and young, Russian-speaking Granovsky probably knew little about them; they were too parochial for this snobbish disciple of Reinhardt. Like Chagall did in the art world, Granovsky absorbed the most recent developments in theater technique in Europe, while simultaneously reaching back to the most sophisticated classics of Yiddish literature.

GRANOVSKY'S SYSTEM

In 1918, when Granovsky undertook his mission, he announced the search for candidates to train as actors for the new theater. There were only two preconditions: The candidates—men and women—must have no previous experience with theater and could not be older than twenty-seven. (Granovsky himself was twenty-eight.) This selection process coincided with the political selection process in the Moscow group, barring anybody with "Old World" conventions or habits. As for age, Granovsky made an exception for Shloyme Vovsi, an intellectual who studied law at Petrograd University but was Granovsky's age. Vovsi had a "monkey-face" so ugly that Granovsky found him beautiful. From the beginning—and under his new stage name, Mikhoels—he was Granovsky's righthand man and his conduit to the other, Yiddish-speaking actors.

In the first programmatic publication of the Yiddish Theater in Petrograd in 1919, Mikhoels described the situation:

> Outside, the revolutionary wave raged, and human eyes and too-human thoughts, scared and scattered, were blinking in the chaos of destruction and the chaos of becoming. . . . At a time when worlds sank, cracked and changed into new worlds, a miracle occurred, perhaps still small, but very big and meaningful for us, Jews—the Yiddish theater was born.[6]

Granovsky trained his actors from zero, utilizing the best resources of the European and Russian avant-garde theater. In the starving capital he could get the best Russian teachers to instruct them in music, rhythm and dance, gesture, "plastic movement," and acting techniques. They also intensively studied Yiddish literature, language, folklore, and folksongs with specialists. Each actor was to be a master of all theater arts and in precise command of his or her body and voice. The system was similar in part to Meyerhold's "Biomechanics": It prepared the actors to be as agile as acrobats (the circus was an inspiration for the theater, as it had been for Meyerhold and Eisenstein). The stress fell on language, music, and folklore as related to the Jewish fictional world they reenacted. A rich, modern Yiddish language was an avant-garde achievement in itself.

Mikhoels described the state of the students:

> Two feelings struggled in our heart: the great will to create on the stage in the Jewish domain and the internal doubt in our own powers. . . . Indeed, who were we—lonely dreamers with unclear strivings; what did we bring with us—except for oppressed and bound limbs and internal tightness, complete ignorance and helplessness in stage work and stage technique—nothing. . . . Yet one thing each of us had—fiery will and readiness for sacrifice. . . . And our leader told us it was enough.[7]

For Granovsky, "Man" was but one of the elements of a stage production, along with the script, the music, the sets, and the lighting. But, as Mikhoels wrote, "We could only give ourselves, the Jew . . . to give the stage *Man* with a capital "M"—this became our goal." The teaching and rehearsals were conducted in Russian, although the texts were in Yiddish, and Granovsky learned some Yiddish from the actors' speech. A typical *yekke* (Eastern European nickname for a German Jew), he was assimilated to what Jews understood as high-culture German manners. Granovsky's ideal was silence—a state that was alien to the talkative Eastern European Jews who were his actors and audiences. He taught:

> The word is the greatest weapon of stage creation. Its value lies not only in speech but in silence. . . . The normal state is silence. . . . The word is a whole event, a super-normal state of man. . . . The intervals of silence between utterances of phrases or words are the background from which the great, meaningful word emerges. . . .

> The normal state is static. . . . The movement is an event, a super-normal state. . . . Every move must start from the static state, which is the gnarled background from which the meaningful move emerges. . . . A movement must be logically articulated into its basic elements as a complex algebraic formula is broken down to its simple multipliers.[8]

The theater performance was a work of art, a radical, densely orchestrated multimedia event that had nothing to do with Stanislavsky's realism. When all this was drilled perfectly, rehearsals began. Eventually, Granovsky devoted between 150 and 250 rehearsals per production, chiseling every move and every word and half word. No wonder the actors who remained with the troupe admired their director; Mikhoels called him "our leader." "For us," the actor wrote, "he is the highest authority and the last word," for "only we, the students, see what is still hidden from every other eye . . . the work of self-sacrifice, the love of art and the people, the rich content, filled with ideals, which his activity breathes!"[9]

The State Bakhrushin Museum in Moscow has in its collection Granovsky's handwritten key to the scores for actors and for the director's exposition of the play; it dates from the early 1920s:

I	pause
II	long pause
I:I	long pause and change of mood
→	merging
word underlined	foregrounding
⌒	modulating a word
↓	end of mood
↑	beginning of mood
Mus	music
- - - - -	music continues
F. M.	end of music

Modulation of movement and voice, and shifts of mood and dynamics, gave life to the ensemble. It was between words and movement that the art of the ensemble was located. The text, like the actor, was treated as a means to the goal, and the shorter the text the better. Granovsky sought a total effect, involving every move of a multimedia polyphony, and involving every spectator in every move. Performances were so rich because they articulated each separate medium into a myriad of tiny steps, each one foregrounded and meaningful. The Yiddish Theater did not stage many productions, but almost every one was a true cultural event. Mikhoels noted his director's programmatic statement (made at the early studio stage):

> I see the ensemble performance, the stage action, as a choir action. . . . Every type, everybody's movement, everybody's acting, playing, painting, every individual action in the play is only a part of the architectonic whole. . . . Our artistic goal is the play as a whole. . . . And the value and significance of the smallest role is great in its relations to the whole dramatic construct. . . . One false performance of a word, or a move, not just of the central figure in a play but of the smallest and most overshadowed, can corrupt and cheapen the whole artistic image.[10]

In short, a play was to become a multilayered, internally cohesive, autonomous and ideal object of art. This was Granovsky's theory in the first months of molding his studio. He refined this vision throughout his tenure at the Yiddish Theater. Granovsky choreographed a polyphonic and dynamic, constantly surprising stage. He was "mathematically" precise and pedantically meticulous about every detail.

A prominent Soviet drama critic and theater professional observed:

> When one sees this "Jewish acting," one cannot fail to be struck by the emotional appeal and rapidity of movement, the intensity of speech and vigor of the gestures. In its early productions, when the old repertory was being revised, poor Jews in tattered garments and comical masks of rich Jews—in frock-coats and stately, old-fashioned robes with colorful trimmings—would dart and dance about on the curious platforms and crooked staircases, in an ecstasy of delight. They were the Jews of the poorer slums. They would stand for a moment in solemn stillness, like monuments, before dashing away into the hum of the marketplace, or springing from one platform to another, or rushing down a flight of stairs and away.[11]

The importance of language was diminished (or condensed) in the context of the polyphonic productions. The greatest successes of the theater occurred with audiences who hardly understood Yiddish; many Russians attended its performances in Moscow, and German audiences perhaps understood only some of the words. There is a story about HaBima, the parallel Moscow theater in Hebrew, directed by Vakhtangov, which used similar sources of Yiddish folklore. The actor and director Mikhail Chekhov once visited a rehearsal directed by Vakhtangov. Chekhov, who did not know Hebrew (neither, for that matter, did Vakhtangov), said to him, "I understood it all except for one scene." Vakhtangov continued to work on that scene, and on his next visit Chekhov understood it perfectly. The scene was not effective if you needed the words. The lack of a common language among the audience members encouraged Granovsky's virtuoso treatment of the nonverbal aspects of this Wagnerian *Gesamtkunstwerk*.

For the same reason, ideology was unimportant as well. Like Mayakovsky and Meyerhold, Granovsky was willing to incorporate a Socialist propaganda message in whatever play he staged—what counted to him was not the message but the effectiveness of the play's impact on the spectator. Indeed, ideology was almost an excuse for producing a play. As soon as the troupe performed in Western Europe in 1928, Granovsky was accused by the Commissar of Enlightenment Lunacharsky of neglecting Socialist ideology and the theater was summoned back to Moscow. (Granovsky remained in the West.)

The theater's greatness, however, did not rest solely on Granovsky's polyphonic approach, nor on his mathematically calculated scores and directing. It derived rather from the fusion of his ideas with a Jewish fictional world created by modern Yiddish literature, and elevated to a level of art by Chagall. As in Chagall's work itself, another language was superimposed on the languages of avant-garde theater: a powerful, time-forged, fictional world, with a series of generalized but unique types. That world was deformed, made grotesque, stood on its head—and thus revitalized in a new, theatrical mythology.

Other Russian directors of the time merged leftist art with ideological slogans, but ideology is flimsy and transient, while a fictional world with unique prototypical characters remains in the imagination of the spectator. The ideologies that were attached to GOSET's productions were easily forgotten: "They went out to curse and found themselves blessing," as one critic put it. Indeed, such estranged Jews as the poet Osip Mandelshtam and the Formalist critic Viktor Shklovsky saw in this theater's productions the vitality—and the tragic end—of the *shtetl* world, and paid no attention to the obvious Soviet propaganda message.

This fictional world was raised to the level of a timeless myth through Granovsky's rhythm of "spots," which broke down the continuities of character and plot as if they were the subject matter of an Analytic Cubist painting. It was Chagall who taught him to depart from realism and continuity of space and time, and to embrace simultaneity of action on several levels—for which not Chagall himself, but his Constructivist followers, built multilevel stages.

THE FICTIONAL WORLD

Chagall and Granovsky were polar opposites: The former was emotional, "childish," "crazy," the very embodiment of the awakening folk type from the Jewish Pale of Settlement, whereas the latter was rational, Europeanized, Russian-speaking, and German-trained. They met at the very beginning of the Yiddish Theater in Moscow, for a production of three negligible skits, yet the collision of these two willful originals changed the course of the theater.

One critic bluntly asked about Granovsky: "This alien Goy will build a Jewish theater?" The printed program for a Petrograd performance of the Yiddish Chamber Theater carried a notice, written in quasi-German, yet in Yiddish letters, that exemplifies Granovsky's attitude: *Das publikum wert gebeten entzagen zikh fun aplodismentn um tsu behalten di gantskeyt fun ayndruk*. ("The audience is requested to refrain from applauding to preserve the wholeness [totality] of the impression.")

Granovsky's productions in Petrograd might have been perfect, but no one remembered them. It was only after Chagall's influence on the theater that its stunning effect was achieved—the *Sholem Aleichem Evening* was performed 300 times. After Chagall's departure, Granovsky revived another (thematically Jewish) play, first performed in Petrograd, the nineteenth-century German playwright Gutzkow's *Uriel Acosta*, but in Moscow too it was a boring flop that endangered the very existence of the theater. Only a return to Sholem Aleichem, as seen through Chagallian eyes, put the Yiddish Theater back.

The vital link between Granovsky and Chagall was Mikhoels. Shloyme Vovsi-Mikhoels was born in Dvinsk, midway between Chagall's Yiddish Vitebsk and Granovsky's Russian Riga. Before the Revolution, Dvinsk belonged to the Vitebsk province, and after 1918 it was incorporated into Latvia. Thus, it came to be affiliated with two different cultural worlds and shared features of both. Hence Mikhoels's closeness to emotive, rich Yiddish folklore, on the one hand, and admiration for Europe's precise and sophisticated culture on the other. Mikhoels found a common language with and admiration for both

Chagall and Granovsky. As one of eight sons of a rich merchant he received a traditional Jewish education until the age of fifteen, and was steeped in Jewish learning and literature.

Like Chagall's parents, Mikhoels' family adhered to the Byelorussian brand of Hasidism, ChaBaD, typified by emotionalism, warmth, and joy. However, in Western Lithuania, where Mikhoels was born, a rich man's home was influenced by the Haskala (Enlightenment) and by an admiration for Russian and German culture. When his father went bankrupt, the family moved to Riga, where Mikhoels went to a science-oriented Russian high school. He married a daughter of Yehuda-Leyb Kantor, a rabbi, doctor, *maskil* (secular intellectual), Hebrew poet, and editor of a Russian newspaper in St. Petersburg, *Russky Evrey* ("The Russian Jew").

After being rejected by St. Petersburg University because he was a Jew, Mikhoels studied in Kiev. Finally, in 1915, he was admitted to the Law School of Petrograd University. In 1918 his attraction to acting and his commitment to Jewish culture led him to Granovsky's budding studio. As an actor, Mikhoels combined his intellectual powers, a restrained emotionalism, and the skills he had learned under Granovsky's tutelage to create one celebrated role after another. The essence of his art, however, came from Chagall: The painter was the source of the tragicomic perception of the absurdity of Jewish (and general human) existence, evoked through a demonstrative antirealism.

Almost from the beginning, the aloof Granovsky charged Mikhoels with conducting the daily work of the troupe. Mikhoels was the stage director, and before each production he announced a competition for each role. Mikhoels read to the actors from the recently published multivolume *Evreyskaya Entsiklopediya* ("Jewish Encyclopedia") in Russian. Mikhoels's enthusiastic "conversion" to Chagall led to the conversion of the theater as a whole. Under Mikhoels's guidance, the actors—all of whom came from various towns in the Pale—retrieved from their childhood memories the gestures, movements, intonations, and sensibilities of the Jewish *shtetl* world. Mikhoels and his counterpart Benyomin Zuskin (another Western Lithuanian) worked together to bring to light the subtle connotations and gestures of the disappearing Jewish world. This was knowledge that no teacher could provide; it was the source of the emotive depth that the actors brought with them, and which was then stylized and refined by Granovsky's system. Granovsky embraced the Jewish fictional world, its gestures and characters, and integrated it into his polyphonic conception, creating theater productions that were closer to a mythological happening than to a formalist performance.

The *Sholem Aleichem Evening* was based on character types familiar from Yiddish literature and folklore. The central character of the one-act *Agents* is Menakhem-Mendel, mirrored fourfold, a symbolic character based on Sholem Aleichem's book by that name, and as proverbial and popular in Yiddish discourse as Hamlet is in English. Menakhem-Mendel is the prototype of a *shlemiel*, who seesaws between soaring fantasy and searing failure. A *shtetl* type, he attempts all Jewish *luftparnoses* (professions of the air), such as matchmaking (shlemiel that he is, he brings together "a wall with a wall," a bride with a bride) and stock-market speculation (with much the same success). *Agents* provides only abbreviated glimpses of Menakhem-Mendel riding a train, but it needed no full-fledged presentation—just an evocation of the type, which the spectators were expected to know. Menakhem-Mendel, acted by Mikhoels, was also the central figure of the Yiddish Theater's *200,000* (based on Sholem Aleichem's *The Great Winning Ticket*), and the later version, titled simply *Menakhem-Mendel*. In 1925, he became the hero of the film *Jewish Luck*, which boasted Granovsky as director, Lev Pulver as composer, Isaac Babel as screenwriter, Edward Tisse (Eisenstein's cameraman) as cinematographer, and Shloyme Mikhoels, Benyomin Zuskin, and the cast of the Yiddish Theater as actors; even the train compartment used for the stage production was adapted and became the trademark of the film.

Other variants of the same fictional world were liberally and brilliantly conceived for plays based on Goldfaden's *Sorceress*, Peretz's *At Night in the Old Market Place*, and Mendele's *Travels of Benjamin the Third*. The texts were treated nonchalantly, shortened and augmented with other works by the same authors.[12] What Granovsky kept intact were the grotesque and "philosophical" characters and the symbolic situations.

In an interview given in Berlin in April 1928, the now Soviet actor Mikhoels formulated "the method of scenic social analysis":

> Instead of the individual's moods, half words, half tones—explicit, burgeoning social feelings; instead of isolated heroes with private, purely subjective, limited experiences—joyful mass movements, with their noise, their dancing on the ruins of the old, their great social hopes and rational activities; instead of types—social figures that convey the breadth of large human masses, of human collectives: instead of family

conflicts, instead of "Chekhovism," instead of sadness and melancholy—large social contradictions which create the background for the whole action on the stage.[13]

No doubt, part of this language was due to the fact that Mikhoels toed the Communist Party line; yet part of it was a true theatrical vision, which had excited European audiences. Indeed, the "crazy," unreal characters of classical Yiddish literature were social types representing a codified, stereotypical society; they were quintessential prototypes of a world rather then psychologically refined individuals. This is why the theater went back to the classics rather than dealing with the early twentieth-century Yiddish literature of individualism and impressionism. The ideological conflict was described by Mikhoels thus:

> Looking for the means, how most sharply and conspicuously to uncover the tragic content of past Jewish life, condemned to disappear in our country, the theater showed a great diversity in evoking new stimulae in its development. To hone the characters, to perfect the stage devices, uncover new social kernels hidden in the atrocious, often-anecdotal classical figures—this was our continuing path. Isn't tragicomedy one of the phenomena typical of our contemporary epoch?[14]

This ideological conflict, combined with the artistic tensions within the polyphonic art, produced new, hybrid genres: *At Night in the Old Market Place* was dubbed "A Tragic Carnival"; *The Travels of Benjamin the Third*, "A Touching Epic"; *200,000*, "A Musical Comedy"; *Trouhadec*, "An Eccentric Operetta."

Granovsky did not mind being eclectic. He harnessed any and all means of the contemporary Russian and European avant-garde theater for his new concept: a "surrealist" perception of the fictional world of Jewish literature, refracted through the tragicomic and polyphonic, kinetic and musical, rationally calculated, multimedia event. A historian of the avant-garde theater in Soviet Russia wrote:

> At the same time it is obvious from early accounts of their work that while they borrowed much from Meyerhold—his system of biomechanics, for instance—they had nothing in common with his intellectualization of theatrical form. They held his theories but expressed them with more drama and play of mood. Particularly is this seen in their stage settings. They believed that the decor should evolve images in the minds of the audiences—but they approached the mind through the senses. Their settings were always highly functional—look, for instance, at the settings for Goldfaden's *Sorceress*, three-dimensional combinations of planes, ladders and platforms arranged in a staccato picture that stabs the mind into an awareness of incoherent pain. The idea of the structure is pure Meyerhold—the carrying out of the idea has the stamp of ecstasy, mystery and unfathomable sadness. A great contribution was made by such expressionists as the artists Chagall and Rabichev, and later by Nathan Altman, Rabinovich, and Falk. They lit up the stage with a series of vivid pictures, always three-dimensional and mobile, which seemed to have a life of their own, which harmonized with and enhanced the grotesquerie of the stylized movements and which underlined the inherent colour and richness in the Jewish character.[15]

This conception could almost be a description of Chagall's art. Chagall left the Yiddish theater after its first production, yet the artists that succeeded him were his admirers and disciples. Moreover, the conception of the theater as a whole was influenced by him, as various accounts report. An unexpected witness was David Ben-Gurion, who came from Eretz-Israel to visit Moscow in 1923. In the "war of the languages," the Palestinian David Ben-Gurion came down on the side of the Hebrew HaBima rather than this acting, which is both Yiddish and "leftist." Of the Yiddish Theater's production of *200,000* he recorded in his diary: "They sit on roofs, ledges and stairs, they don't walk but hop, don't go up but clamber, don't come down but tumble and leap—Sholem Aleichem is unrecognizable." The set was Rabichev's, yet this is clearly the description of a Chagallian placement of characters and his conception of "groundless" space. Of course, Chagall's reading of Sholem Aleichem's topsy-turvy world was absolutely correct. Ben-Gurion was never known for his appreciation of literature or art, but he recorded what he saw.

The German critic Max Osborn also visited Moscow in 1923, and on his return he wrote an essay on Chagall. He described Sholem Aleichem's *200,000* in this way:

> The curtain goes up and you see a strange chaos of houses, intertwined in a Cubist manner, rising one above the other on different levels. Intersecting one

> another at sharp angles, they either stand below wide roofs or suddenly appear without a roof altogether, like a man taking off his hat, and display all their internal secrets. Here and there, bridges and passways are drawn; wide streets rise and fall diagonally. Meyerhold's Constructivist stage is embodied here in original variants. The Cubist, linear play of these forms is complemented and enriched by Cézanne colors. Your eye perceives a fantastic interpretation of a Jewish-Russian small town, presented in the narrow confines of a stage in an unusually joyful and charming formula. Before the spectator's eye, everything can happen simultaneously: the events in the tailor shop, scenes among the populace of the shtetl who accompany the play and the experiences of the main characters as their own—a picturesque, machinelike, mimic-acrobatic choir.
>
> When the news arrives about the tailor's unexpected great win of a huge sum, setting the whole town into an unusual excitement, suddenly, high above the roof of one building, appears the figure of a Jew with a red beard and a green greatcoat, with a sack on his back and a staff in his hand. Instinctively I said aloud: "Chagall!" And suddenly everything became clear: this is the world of Chagall. From him, everything emerged: the young artist-decorator Rabitshev's creations, Granovsky's constructions, and the accompanying music of the composer Pulver. The latter, with unusual expressiveness, embodied Oriental motifs, ancient Jewish images, and Russian songs in operatic melodies, with trumpets and kettledrums.[16]

Later, in Mikhoels's dressing room, Osborn learned that, indeed, "Marc Chagall had played a decisive role in the development of the whole stage art of the Yiddish Chamber Theater; that, in this circle, he was considered the great originator and inspiration." He also learned that "Chagall's box" was preserved like a temple in the "House of Yiddish Theater Art" (as the former small theater was called). Osborn explained:

> It is no accident that painting exerted such an influence on the stage, no whim of a theater director attracted by the work of an artist. It was a stronger force, an inner necessity. Always, when the personality and the school of a master truly find a clear and strong expression for the cultural spirit of the time—the stage is captivated by it—and only then it is captivated. . . . Like no one else in the young Russia of our days, Chagall has the stunning power of transforming the elements of an exceedingly rich and profound artistic folk culture into colorful, dreamy visions, striking our imagination.[17]

HABIMA

At the same time, a Hebrew theater was established in Moscow. Monti Jakobs, the theater critic of the prestigious German newspaper *Vossische Zeitung*, began his review of the Yiddish Theater's *200,000* thus: "Like HaBima, the same *furor judaicum*, it is a play that pulls the spectator out of his seat and draws him into the strong rhythm emanating from the stage." This is not the place to discuss HaBima at length, but a few words are in order, for the two theaters are often mentioned together.

A group of young people gathered before World War I in Bialystok to create a new kind of *bima* (the Hebrew word for "stage"; *ha* is the article) in order to perform in the budding spoken Hebrew language. In 1918 they arrived in Moscow and received the patronage of the great Stanislavsky, the teacher and master of Realist-psychological theater. HaBima became one of the four studios attached to Stanislavsky's Moscow Art Theater. The young Vakhtangov, Stanislavsky's most famous disciple, became HaBima's director. In November 1918 HaBima was recognized as a Soviet State theater. With *The Eternal Jew*, *The Dybbuk*, and other plays, HaBima entered general theater history; its 1926 tour of Europe was a great triumph, especially in Germany, then the center of European theater.

Hebrew was the language of the holy books and the Jewish religious library (as Chagall said of HaBima: "they don't act, they pray"), but during the Modern Jewish Revolution it rapidly expanded its genres into secular literature, politics, and science. It was not easy to turn a language of religious texts into a spoken language, dealing with mundane and secular topics, yet toward the end of the nineteenth century such a language began to crystallize, and between 1906 and 1913 the first Hebrew-speaking social cells emerged in Palestine. The launching of HaBima was an early attempt at speaking the Biblical language on stage (most of its own actors knew no Hebrew beforehand). Thus two Jewish theaters in two different languages were established in Moscow as Soviet State theaters in the first years after the October Revolution.

Soon the "war of the languages" was raging. Those who wanted to revive Yiddish culture in Russia saw Hebrew as a religious vestige of old times, not the language of the masses. Kultur-Lige's programmatic

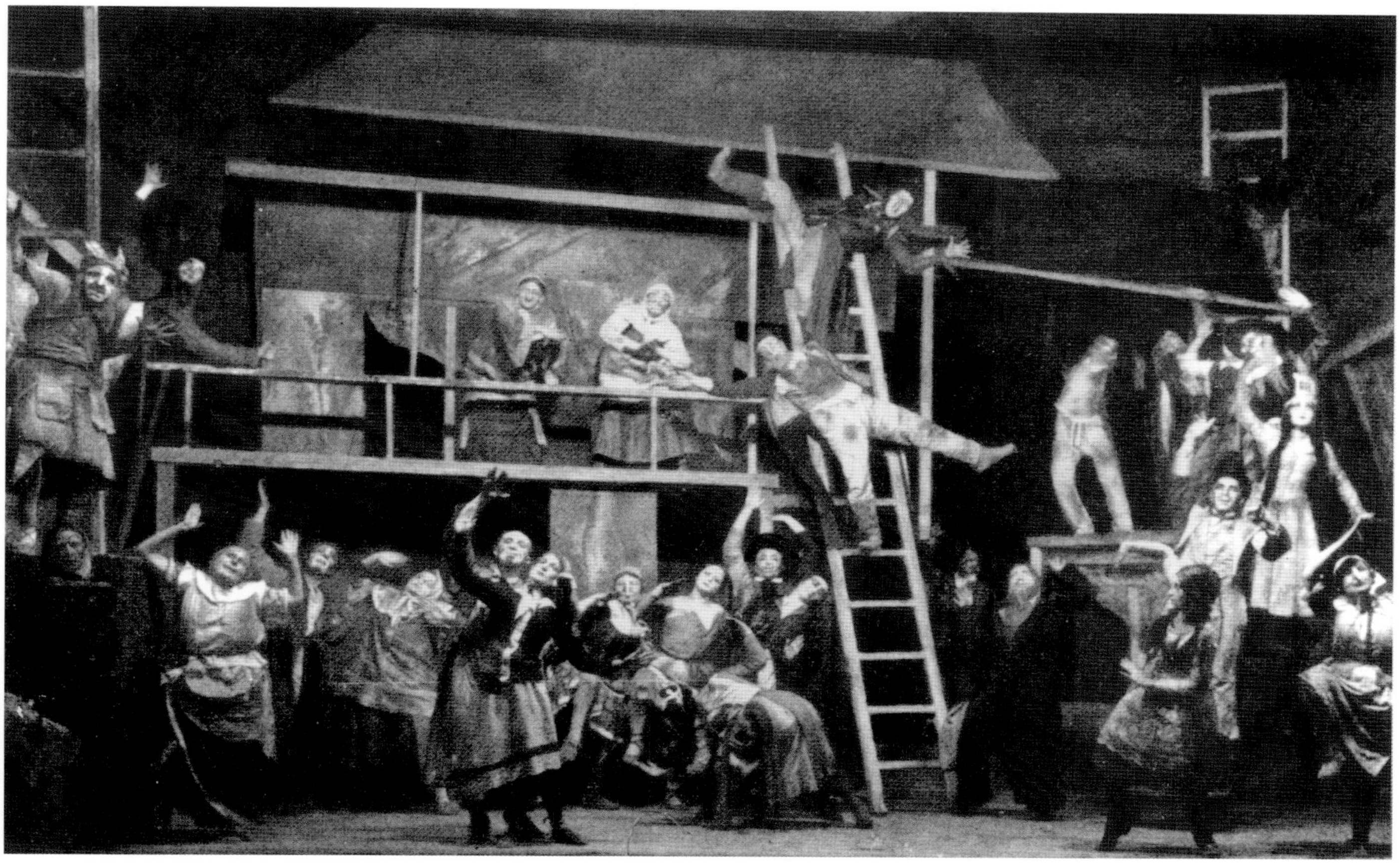

A scene from ***The Witch*** *by Goldfaden, 1922. Director: Granovsky. As Chagall said, "They Chagallized after Chagall." Courtesy Natalia Vofsi-Michoels and the History of Theatre Archives, Tel Aviv University*

brochure exemplifies the conflict. It attacked the parallel Hebrew school organization Tarbut as being "Zionist-Rabbinical" and promoting Eretz-Israel: "A land where Jews don't live they call our land, a language Jews don't speak they call our language." The Evsektsya (the Jewish Section of the Communist Party) battled the recognition of HaBima; its leader, Dimandshteyn, claimed that HaBima was "a whim of the Jewish bourgeoisie; the money of the Revolutionary power should not be allowed to support a theater the peasants and workers don't want." But some of the most illustrious, non-Jewish Russian intellectuals of the day (and, as Efros put it, the anti-Semites) supported the new phenomenon in the lofty and pure Biblical language. The great proletarian writer Maksim Gorky and the world-famous singer Fyodor Chalyapin wept during its performances. Leaders of the Russian intelligentsia wrote a letter to Lenin on its behalf, and the Commissar of Nationalities—Stalin himself—overruled the Yiddish Evsektsya and saved the Hebrew HaBima.

In January 1926 the Moscow State Theater HaBima departed on its spectacular tour of Western Europe and the United States.[18] Most of the troupe did not return to Russia, and HaBima was reestablished in Tel Aviv, where it eventually became the Israeli National Theater.

Both HaBima and GOSET drew on the achievements of the Russian avant-garde theater, although HaBima, still in the Stanislavsky tradition, was more conservative and expressionistic. Both derived their strength from the same collective Jewish folk tradition, expressed in mass ensemble scenes and the multimedia polyphony of music, dance, sets, and stage scenes. The Hebrew HaBima, too, drew on the Yiddish literary tradition (Dovid Pinsky's *The Eternal Jew*, An-sky's *The Dybbuk*), translated into Hebrew. However, the solemn language of the still far from colloquial and Biblical Hebrew influenced the pathos and the elevated, heroic style of HaBima; it did not have the humor, irony, or flexibility of moods typical of popular Yiddish. Although emanating from the same national milieu, HaBima fostered the Hebrew genre of high tragedy, oriented toward a utopian dream, while GOSET showcased the Yiddish genre of comedy, looking the tragic end of a culture straight in the eye.

EPILOGUE

In 1927, in recognition of their artistic contribution, Granovsky, Mikhoels, and Zuskin were awarded the title of People's Artist of the USSR. In the Soviet Union, GOSET had to bend over backward to adapt to the ideological and political demands. Indeed, it served propaganda purposes in the USSR and abroad. The degree to which the Jewish tradition was merged with the so-called Soviet "internationalism" and political engagement can be seen, for example, in the program of the spectacle *Carnival of Yiddish Comedians*. According to the playbill of May 12, 1923 (still under Granovsky!), it included:

> Thieves' songs from Odessa and Warsaw; a Negro performance, *Java Celebes*; the Jewish *King Lear* in Pensa; klezmer songs; three loves—Negro, American, Hasidic; street songs from Vilna; Hasidic songs and dances; *Matchmaking*—an unusual operetta; American songs in Jewish style; six Jewish acrobats; the Marseillaise.

What the Jewish comedians in Russia knew of "Negro love" and "Java Celebes" is hard to imagine; and the Marseillaise is a rather comical ending to a Jewish folk carnival.

Finally, the theater was allowed to go abroad. On April 7, 1928, GOSET performed *200,000* in Berlin, where it received more than forty reviews. Its reception surpassed anything other Russian theaters experienced, and a book about it was published in German with the participation of such prominent writers of the time as Ernst Toller and Joseph Roth.[19] Berlin was the center of innovative theater at the time. As many reviews indicated, "Granovsky was received in Berlin as a new theatrical messiah, a more innovative and revolutionary director than Meyerhold, Reinhardt, and Piscator."[20]

GOSET traveled throughout Germany and visited Vienna and Paris, but toward the end of the year Lunacharsky scolded the apolitical direction of the theater and it was forced to return to Russia. Granovsky stayed in the West; after several unsuccessful attempts, he had considerable success directing Arnold Zweig's *Sergeant Grisha*, produced in Berlin in 1930, and he also made several German films. Apparently, he fled Germany with the rise of the Nazis, and faded into oblivion. On March 11, 1937, at the age of forty-seven, one of the original theater directors of the century died in Paris. At about the same time, the great innovator Meyerhold, who had sold his soul to the Communists, was tortured to death in a Soviet prison.

In 1928, when Granovsky remained in the West, Mikhoels became the director of GOSET. He enjoyed great fame in Russia and was accepted to Moscow's high society. He continued performing Jewish plays, insisting that this was the task of the Yiddish theater—classical and Russian plays were better performed in the Russian Chamber Theater next door. But pressures and criticism were incessant. During the purges of the 1930s, Stalin's righthand man, the Yiddish-speaking Lazar Kaganovitsh, came to a performance. He inspired terror in the director and actors, screaming that it was a shame to show such crippled Jews: "Look at me, I am a Jew, my father was also like this: tall, broad, healthy."[21] Mikhoels immediately started rehearsing a drama about a strong type from the people, Moyshe Kulbak's *Boytre*; but soon enough Kulbak himself was arrested and liquidated and his plays were forbidden.

During World War II, Mikhoels was appointed Chairman of the Jewish Anti-Fascist Committee, seeking international help in the war against Hitler. In this function he visited the United States in 1943 and saw Chagall again. But in 1948 he was lured from Moscow to Minsk and brutally murdered on Stalin's orders. Most Yiddish writers, actors, and activists were arrested; some were shot, others tortured. The theater was closed, along with the Yiddish newspaper and publishing house.

Chagall (in 1922) and Granovsky (in 1928) left Soviet Russia for Western Europe and were unmentionable in the Soviet period. During the purges of 1937, Chagall's murals were hidden under the stage. Eventually, they found their way to the Tretyakov Gallery in Moscow. One version has it that the Liquidation Commission (of the Yiddish theater) gave the murals to the gallery in 1950;[22] another version, prevalent in Moscow art circles, is that the last artistic director of the theater, the painter Aleksandr Tyshler, when he saw that all was lost, carried the canvases there on his back. The murals were hidden in a cellar of an inactive church, a closed storage area of the Tretyakov Gallery, and were opened only in 1973 for Chagall's signature. The canvas was restored in 1989 and was shown in many exhibitions around the world. The Tretyakov conservators did a careful job in preparing the canvases in 1991 for "the long-distance transport first to Germany, and then at a later date to other countries."[23] They did not attempt to restore the original colors, as explained to me by Mr. Kovalev, consciously "letting time do what time did [does]." Except that "time" here had a human face.

Production designs from throughout the theater's brief history were placed in the State Bakhrushin Museum in Moscow. There they were sealed in a special room along with the archives of Tairov's Chamber Theater (a Russian theater with a Jewish director), which was also liquidated. A fire, presumably, broke out at the Bakhrushin—only in this room—and the set designs, packed in a tight ball, were burned around the margins. The documents also suffered a layer of water damage: Somebody must have tried to extinguish the fire with water. To this day, the causes and facts of that destruction have not been disclosed.

---

1. *Leningradskaya krasnaya gazeta*, Aug. 30, 1926.

2. "Das jüdische Theater in Moskau," in *Das Moskauer jüdische akademische Theater* (The Moscow Yiddish Academic Theater). Berlin: Die Schmiede, 1928, pp. 17–21.

3. In *Mit Schleuder und Harfe: Theaterkritiken aus drei Jahrzehnten*. Berlin: Hensche Verlag, 1981.

4. *Kultur-Lige: A sakh-hakl* ("The Culture League: Results"), Kiev, Nov. 1919, pp. 1–3.

5. That may be an exaggeration for a Jew who grew up in Riga; Granovsky didn't talk much anyway. To claim "I didn't know Yiddish" was bon ton among assimilated Jews, implying: I am a man of the larger world.

6. Mikhoels, "In Our Studio," in *Dos yidishe kamer teatr* ("The Yiddish Chamber Theater"). Petrograd: Jewish Theater Society, 1919, p. 22.

7. Ibid.

8. Ibid.

9. Ibid., p. 17.

10. Ibid., p. 24.

11. P. A. Markov, *The Soviet Theatre*. New York: G. P. Putnam's Sons, 1935, pp. 165–66.

12. For one Soviet version of *Benjamin the Third*, see *The Travels of Benjamin the Third* by Mendele Moykher Sforim, adapted for the stage by Yikhezkel Dobrushin (publication by B. Harshav and Y. Schein), *DiPen*, Nov.–Dec. 1996, no. 28 (29, pp. 1–40).

13. S. Mikhoels, "Mikhoels Vofsi on the Theater," interview, *Literarishe bleter*, April 27, 1928.

14. Ibid.

15. Andre Van Gyseghem, *Theatre in Soviet Russia*. London: Faber and Faber, 1943, p. 174.

16. Max Osborn, "Marc Chagall," *Zhar-ptitsa*, no. 11 (1923), p. 13.

17. Ibid.

18. In *The New York Times*, December 14, 1926, influential drama critic J. Brooks Atkinson wrote, "The effect is astonishing, as unreal as the mystic legend of the play."

19. *Das Moskauer jüdische akademische Theater.*

20. Faina Burko, *The Soviet Yiddish Theatre in the Twenties* (Ph.D. diss., Southern Illinois University, Carbondale, 1978), p. 81.

21. Yosef Schein, *Arum moskver yidishn teater* ("Around the Moscow Yiddish Theater"). Paris: Les éditions polyglottes, 1964.

22. The papers of the commission were kept in CGALI (Central State Archive for Literature and Art), Moscow, Fond. 2307, Opis' 1, Unit 81: "Acts of Documentary Control of the Financial-Economic Activity of the Liquidation Commission of the Moscow State Yiddish Theater" (1950, 66 pp.); and Units 82–83: "Acts and Powers of Attorney for the Transfer and Acceptance of Property of the Moscow State Yiddish Theater" (1950; vol. 1, 206 pp., vol. 2, 179 pp.). In 1976, however, these files were extracted from the archive and sent to *vydeleny v makulaturu* (scrap paper). Unit 3 is also missing. According to some sources, they must be preserved somewhere, perhaps by the KGB (the fate of similar files sent as "scrap paper").

23. See Aleksei Kovaliev. "Report on the Restoration of the Murals for the Jewish Kamerny Theatre in Moscow," in Vitali, ed. *Marc Chagall: The Russian Years 1906–1922*. Frankfurt: Schirn Kunsthalle, 1991, p. 134.

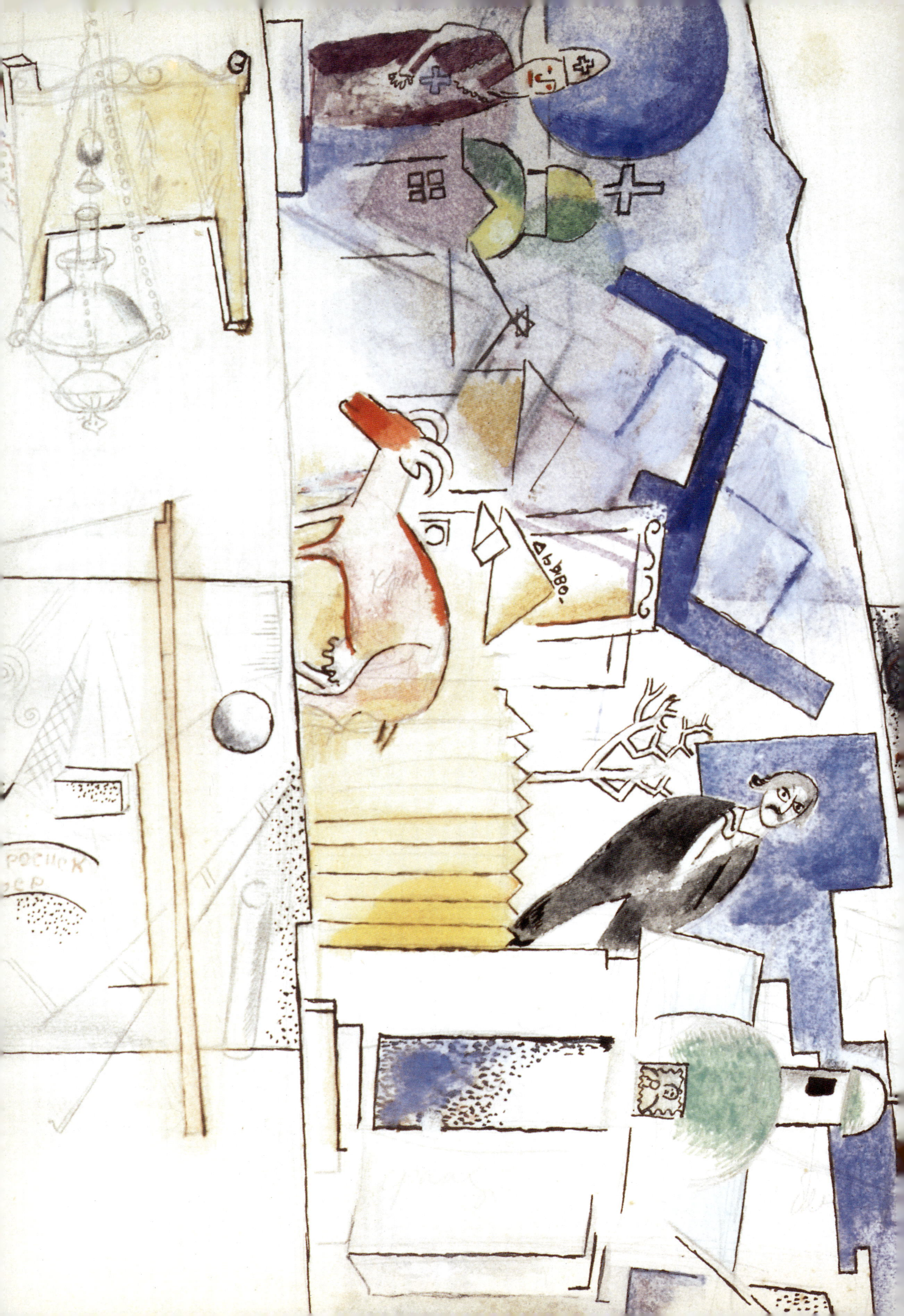

6. Chagall's Theater Murals

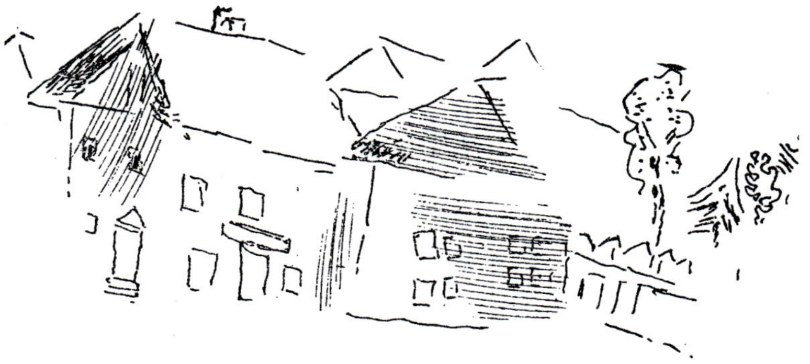

The murals Chagall made for the State Yiddish Chamber Theater in Moscow were a landmark for both the painter and the theater. The theater was transformed from a small actors' studio, producing traditional literary plays to one embracing Chagall's imaginative, anti-Realist conception of Modern art, combined with his vision of Sholem Aleichem's world and the totality and vitality of topsy-turvy Jewish existence. In a few years it became one of the most celebrated theaters in Europe. This success seemed to have eclipsed Chagall's earlier work in the theater, which began in St. Petersburg before 1910 and was renewed after his return from Paris to Russia in 1914. Furthermore, probably for later political reasons, Chagall never discussed his revolutionary activities of 1918–19 and covered up the names of some theater designs.

EARLY WORK FOR THE STAGE

In his memoir on Léon Bakst, Chagall mentioned a dialogue with the master, just before both of them left Russia:

> Stammering, I said to Bakst: "Couldn't I, Lev Samoylovitsh. . . . You know, Lev Samoylovitsh, I want . . . to Paris." "Ah, of course! Listen, can you paint stage decorations?" "Naturally!" (Couldn't do a thing). "Here are a hundred rubles. Learn some techniques of making decorations, and I shall take you with me."[1]

OPPOSITE: ***The Little Goat*** *(detail). 1920. Pencil, ink, gouache, watercolor on paper, 29.2 x 35.6 cm. AM 1988-230, recto, Musée National d'Art Moderne, Centre Georges Pompidou, Paris*

(Stammering represents his Jewish embarrassment in a Russian society, as it happened in the Russian high school, as well as his solidarity with Bakst.)

As in many details of his autobiography, Chagall plays here the poor, reverend, and modest boy. Actually, he did have some theater experience and was ambitious about it. It is doubtful whether Bakst would have just handed him 100 rubles (the high tuition in Bakst's elitist school was 30 rubles a month, paid for Chagall by a philanthropist) if he didn't believe in his pupil's abilities and originality. Indeed, Bakst himself invited Chagall to work as his assistant in creating the sets for the Russian ballet *Narcissus and Echo* by Nikolay Tsherepin, which was to be performed in Paris.

When Chagall returned to Russia in 1914 and did his clerical service in the army in the newly renamed Petrograd during World War I (1915–17), the Northern capital was the center of theater experimentation and avant-garde opposition to the "aesthetic" and decorative stage backdrops of the World of Art painters. It was a time of avant-garde defiance in all the arts. Innovations were spurred by a new wave of little theaters that emerged in the decade before the Revolution. As the art historian Aleksandra Shatskikh has pointed out, "in the period of 1908–17 small theaters of a semiclub semistudio character developed everywhere—the so-called cellars, pubs, cabarets, and 'little stages.' The most famous of them were House of Interlude, Flying Mouse, Vagabond Dog, Comedians' Resting Place."[2]

Chagall's first successful production design was for one of three miniplays, *A Thoroughly Joyful Song*, staged

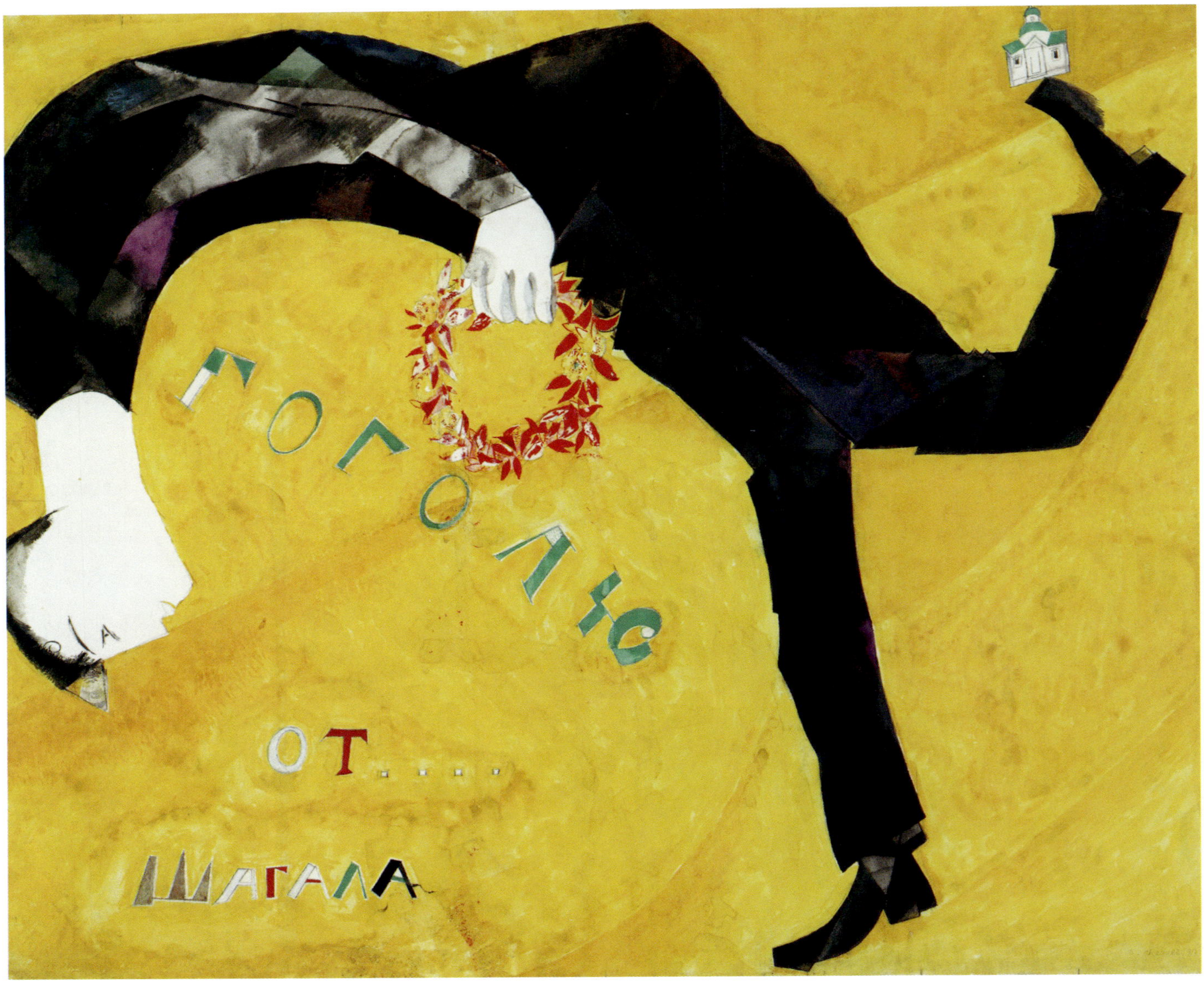

89. ***Homage to Gogol.*** *Design for curtain (not executed) for Gogol festival, Hermitage Theater, Petrograd (Leningrad). 1917. Watercolor on paper, 39.4 x 50.2 cm. Acquired through the Lillie P. Bliss Bequest. (71.1944) The Museum of Modern Art, New York. In whimsical Russian letters: "For Gogol from Chagall."*

by the famous director Nikolay Evreinov, which opened at the cabaret Comedians' Resting Place on January 23, 1917. Chagall painted the faces of all the actors green and their hands blue. In this establishment, the stage and auditorium were fused in one "unified decoration," made by S. Yu. Sudeykin and others, which might have influenced Chagall's perception of the artist's total role in the theater.

When appointed Plenipotentiary on Matters of Art in Vitebsk, Chagall plunged into revolutionary artistic initiatives, including founding a People's Art College and a city art museum and organizing mass decorations around the city for celebrations on the first anniversary of the October Revolution, November 7, 1918. In early 1919, while still a commissar of art in Vitebsk, he was invited to prepare the decorations and costumes for two plays by Nikolay Gogol for the Petrograd theater Hermitage. Chagall's *Homage to Gogol*, 1919 (no. 89), carries an inscription in Russian: "For Gogol from . . . . Chagall." The four dots before his name express something like "surprise surprise." In the painting, Chagall plays with the shape of the body and with the geometrical, simplified shapes of his whimsically colored letters. Gogol, master of humor, anecdotes, and grotesque and fantastic distortions, with his profound and hilarious comedy of life, was a major literary influence on Chagall. Chagall's design, however, was not accepted.

Chagall was also the sole artist of a new kind of Russian political theater that emerged in Vitebsk, TeRevSat (an acronym for Theater of Revolutionary Satire). Vitebsk was close to the front line of the Civil War, and TeRevSat supplied entertainment and propaganda for the army as well as the city. It combined political agitation with antibourgeois satire in a popular review based on traditions of the Russian folk theater, wrapped in Communist slogans. Its stylistic direction may be compared to Vladimir Mayakovsky's satirical propaganda in his caricatures and rhymed couplets for the ROSTA Windows (Russian Telegraphic Agency posters) in the same period. The Vitebsk TeRevSat became a model for similar theaters in other cities.

TeRevSat opened on February 7, 1919, with a performance in the square before the Vitebsk railroad station, and Chagall was its only artist for the 1919–20 season. He designed all ten productions,[3] including costumes, makeup, and various stage props. In April 1920, TeRevSat moved from Vitebsk to Moscow; Chagall came a month later.

Shatskikh argues that TeRevSat's move to Moscow, and not an explicit expulsion from his own Art College by the Suprematist Malevich, was the cause of Chagall's going to the capital. Indeed, Chagall wanted to resign his administrative duties and leave the Art College several times before, but the students who opposed it, prevailed. Now he was traveling back and forth from Vitebsk to Moscow and all the students of his master class shifted to Malevich, either influenced by the radical, antimimetic avant-garde art or exasperated by Chagall's absences and crises, or both. He himself claimed that his enemies expelled him from the College "within twenty-four hours," but that must not be taken literally: With Chagall it was rather a code word for anti-Semitism, alluding to the expulsions of masses of Jews from the front areas during World War I "within twenty-four hours." Chagall tended to ascribe any opposition to his art to anti-Semitism, real or imagined. True, Lissitzky was also a Jew, but the more was he seen as a "traitor."

In Moscow, Chagall prepared the sets for a revolutionary propaganda play, *Tovarishtsh Khlestakov* ("Comrade Khlestakov"), alluding to the hero of Gogol's play *Revisor* and placing it in the new, revolutionary setting. Several costume designs by Chagall have names from works by Gogol, apparently carried over to the new play (the text of the play did not survive). The journal *Ekran* announced: "In December [1920] the play *'Khlestakov'* by D. Smolin will be performed, director D. Gutman, decorations from set designs by Marc Chagall." But by December 1920 TeRevSat folded due to a lack of money. The play was not staged, and Chagall was immersed in his work for the Yiddish theater. The shift from Russian to Jewish culture and back was almost self-understood.

Much later, in June 1922, Meyerhold became director of TeRevSat and this Vitebsk theater was renamed Theater of the Revolution at the Moscow Soviet. For political reasons Chagall later attributed whatever remained of his revolutionary designs either to Gogol himself or to Sholem Aleichem, and so they are labeled to this day. One conspicuous mislabeling is the "Set Design for *The Inspector General (Revisor)*" by *Gogol*, 1919. This title, repeated in many books on Chagall,[4] is absurd, as one can see from the Russian texts depicted in the painting. Chagall himself caused the confusion. On a later occasion, at the bottom of the drawing, he wrote in Russian: "For Gogol Revisor (Inspector General) Theater 'Terevsat' Moscow"; then he signed his name in French and added in parentheses in Russian: "(not performed)." Typically for his multilingualism, inside the Russian sentence he wrote "Gogol" in French.[5]

As the "Set Design for *The Inspector General*" shows, in front of the domestic, petit-bourgeois room furnished on the stage, two huge rectangular panels were to be erected. One is the "Old World"—with its churches and priests (as in Blok's famous poem "Twelve") and Chagall's Jewish goat. And the other one is the "New World," busy with construction, under banners and slogans in Russian, referring to the Communist Party organs and even to the dreaded yet rhapsodized CheKa, the first Soviet secret police. The slogans are: "[Proletarians of All] Countries Un[ite]," "Cooperat[ive]," "All[-Russian] ChKRKP" (CheKa, Special Committee for security of the Russian Communist Party), "TsKRKP" (Central Committee of the Russian Communist Party), "All-Russian RSFSR" (Russian Soviet Federation of Socialist Republics). The binary opposition: "Before—and After the Revolution" was a key image of Soviet propaganda and window displays, developed in those years. Very far from Gogol.

Another piece ascribed to Gogol's *Revisor* is a "Set Design that Contains a Little Train" (no. 91), signed "Moscow 1920." In a Constructivist stage setting for "Comrade Khlestakov," the Old World appears. On the round shield in the square panel, it is stamped with a cross as on a grave. Horizontally and vertically there is an inscription in Russian, *K CHERTU!* ("to hell!" literally: "to the devil!"), repeated in scattered letters at the top right, and obviously addressed to the Old World. The little train was later repeated on a circular frame in the setting for Sholem Aleichem's *Agents* made for the Yiddish Chamber Theater, December 1920. Also, a companion set design on the same stage, with new constructions on the triangular platform, seems to represent the New World instead of the stamped-out Old World.

In a similar fashion, Chagall lumped together some costumes and attributed them to Sholem Aleichem. One example is the "Costume for a Sailor." There is no such figure in the plays performed in the *Sholem Aleichem*

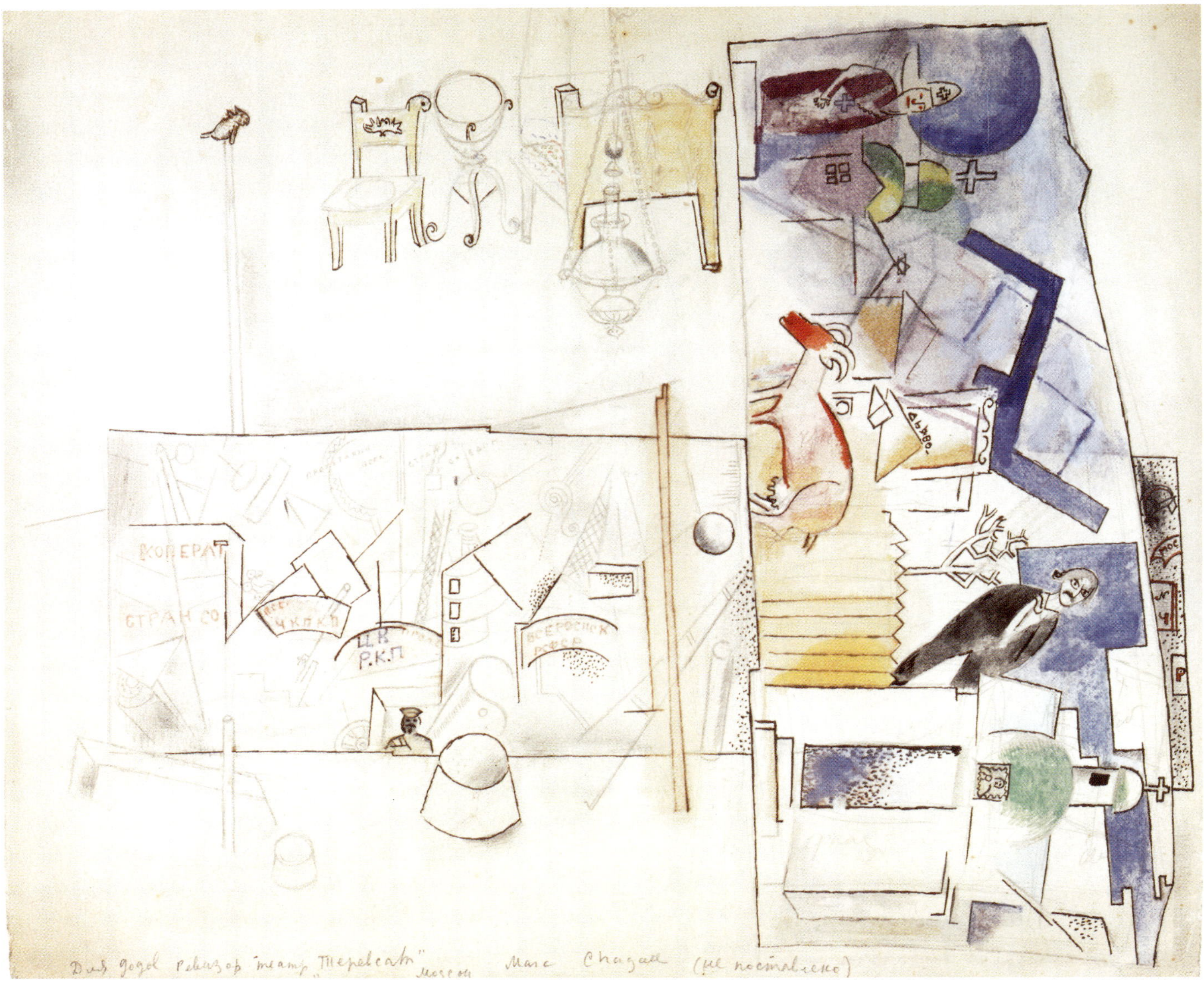

90. ***The Little Goat.*** *1920. Pencil, ink, gouache, watercolor on paper, 29.2 x 35.6 cm. AM 1988-230, recto, Musée National d'Art Moderne, Centre Georges Pompidou, Paris. On the right, the Old World with religious symbols (Christian and Jewish); on the left, the New World. Russian acronyms are referred to on page 165.*

Evening (was there a Jewish sailor?). The hat says *matros* ("sailor" in Russian) and is, no doubt, or a piece by the Theater of Revolutionary Satire in Vitebsk. Thus, the date "1919" may be correct. And the same is true for other costumes attributed to Gogol or Sholem Aleichem.

Another imaginative design is the set design for Synge's *Playboy of the Western World*, 1920–21 (no. 92). It has a suspended child / Christ figure on the cross with Hebrew letters above his halo. The first letter, **ש** (Sh), is the name of God (*Shadai*), as on a *mezuzah*, but it is hard to decipher the connections of the other letters. The inscription in Latin letters "TRINK ID BAR" seems to substitute the Yiddish *Trink* for the English *Drink*, and the "ID" may similarly indicate the word *It* (for "drink it").

A TOTAL PAINTING ENVIRONMENT

Founded in Petrograd in 1919, the Yiddish Chamber Theater moved to Moscow near the end of 1920, where its second birth occurred. Abram Efros, the art critic who coauthored the first book about Chagall's art, was appointed artistic director of the theater. He persuaded the director, Aleksey Granovsky, to commission Chagall to design the stage sets for the first production in Moscow. Chagall had just been defeated by the radical abstractionists Malevich and Lissitzky in his own People's Art College in Vitebsk and was stranded in Moscow when TeRevSat folded. Thus, a commission in Moscow was welcome, even though it was for a separate, Jewish (rather than general) institution. While working as a teacher in a Jewish orphanage colony outside Moscow, he made a detailed study for *Introduction to the Yiddish Theater* (see photo, no. 93).

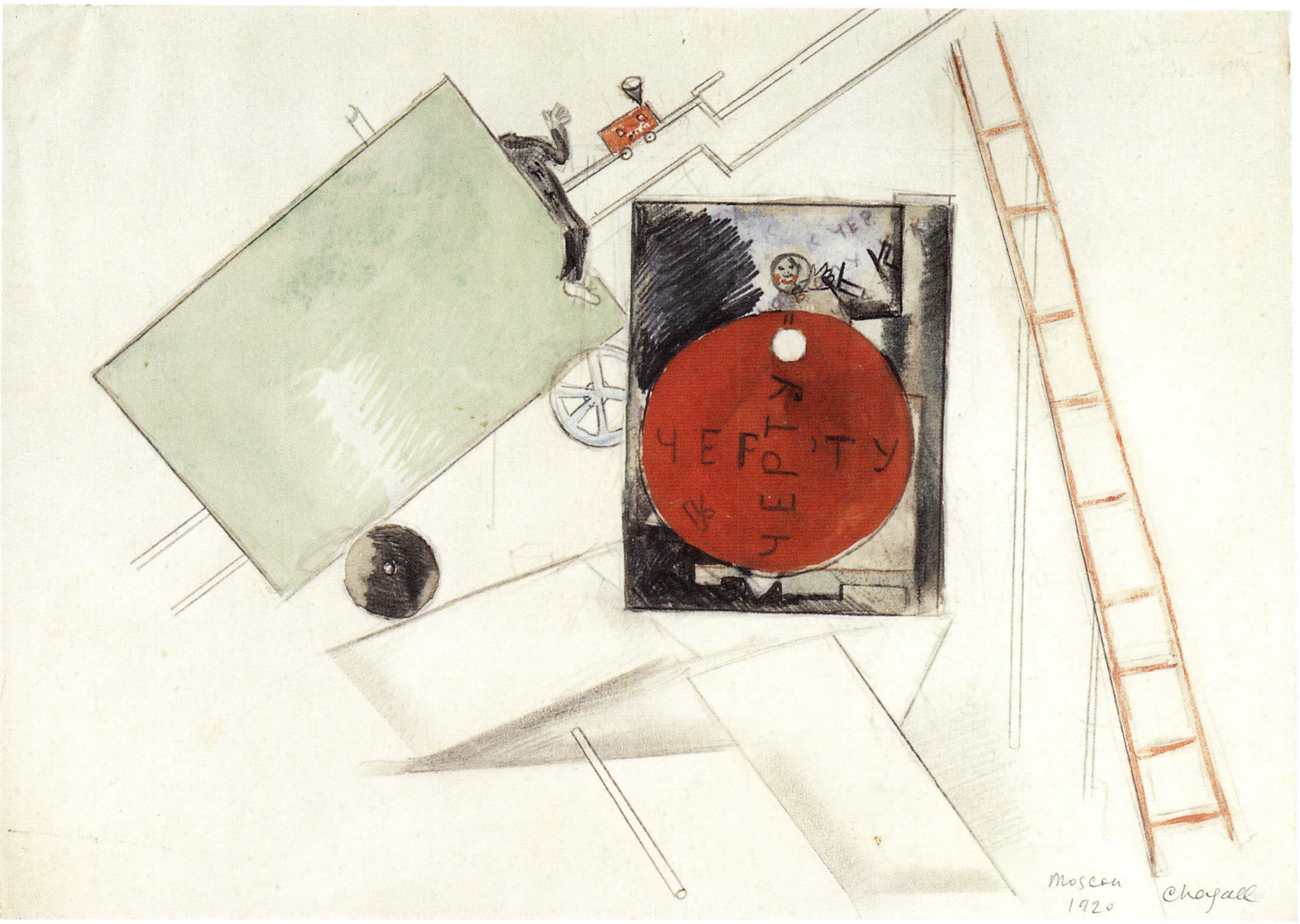

91. ***The Little Train.*** *1920. Pencil, ink, gouache, watercolor on paper, 25.5 x 34.4 cm. AM 1988-229, recto. Musée National d'Art Moderne, Centre Georges Pompidou, Paris*

The opening production was the *Sholem Aleichem Evening*, with two one-act plays by that Yiddish classical fiction writer—*Agents: A Joke in One Act* and *Mazel Tov: A Comedy in One Act*—as well as his dialogue in prose, *It's a Lie*. Because these were light pieces—almost caricatures—Granovsky could fill in the texts with elements of all other media, according to the theatrical conception of the *Gesamtkunstwerk* ("total work of art") he had brought from Germany and perfected into a meticulously choreographed multimedia event. Simultaneously, Chagall used the opportunity to impose onto the theater his vision of a grotesque, tragicomic Jewish world, disappearing yet brimming with vitality. The result was a new, condensed, tragic, and hilarious mythology.

In the cold winter of 1920, as civil war raged in the Soviet Union and food was scarce in the capital, rehearsals went on and Chagall painted like obsessed. The Yiddish Theater was located on Bolshoy Chernyshevsky Lane in central Moscow, in the nationalized house of a Jewish businessman, L. I. Gurevich. Gurevich, who apparently fled Russia after the Revolution, had built the three-story mansion in 1902 and lived with his family on the second floor. Now the second floor, including the large reception room, was turned into a theater auditorium that held ninety seats. The adjacent kitchen was turned into a stage, and the actors were given living quarters on the third floor of the same building.

Aleksandr Tairov, the director of the Russian Chamber Theater in Moscow, had promoted a new conception of the artist's function: Rather than painting only the backdrop decoration, the artist constructed the whole, three-dimensional stage. But Chagall went beyond even this radical notion, embracing the entire auditorium in a Chagallian painting ensemble. Within forty days,[6] working single-handedly, he painted a twenty-six-foot-long canvas, *Introduction to the Yiddish Theater* (no. 95), on the left, continuous wall; four tall images of the "Four Arts" that contributed to the new total theater according to Granovsky's conception—*Music* (no. 110), *Dance* (no. 114), *Drama* (no. 116), and *Literature* (no. 117)—between the windows on the righthand wall; a long frieze above them, *The Wedding Table* (no. 118), unifying the Four Arts; and in the back, facing the audience leaving the theater, an almost translucent and cosmopolitan square

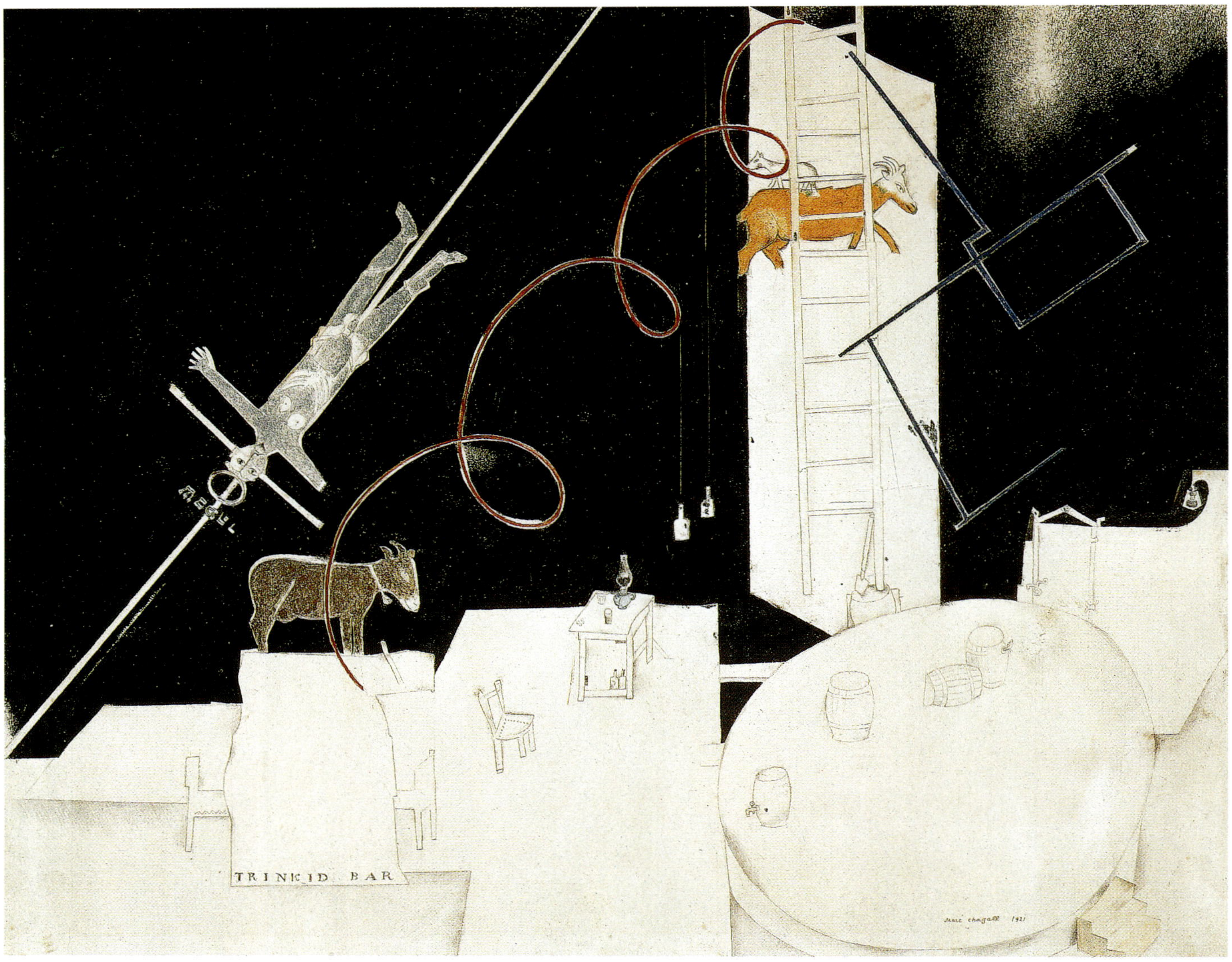

92. ***Playboy of the Western World.*** *1921. Pencil, ink, gouache, gold and silver paint on paper, 40.7 x 51.1 cm. AM 1988-255. Musée National d'Art Moderne, Centre Georges Pompidou, Paris*

painting, *Love on the Stage* (no. 119). In sum, the murals covered all the walls (see diagram, no. 94). And, of course, Chagall designed the stage, the furniture, the curtains, and the costumes as well. Thus, instead of seeing a painting in a theater, the audience experienced a theater performance within a Chagallian four-wall space. It was soon nicknamed "Chagall's box." A critic described the impression:

> The task that confronted the artist—to paint the auditorium of the theater—challenged him to a dialogue between the auditorium and the stage. The auditorium, presumably embodying life itself, life standing against the stage, speaks in Chagall's *Introduction to the Yiddish Theater* about the ever-theatrical nature of mundane life itself, about life itself being drunk on the elixir of theatricality, about Chagall's paintings connecting the ties between the Harlequinade of the stage and the Harlequinade of mundane life.[7]

Chagall hated any naturalistic disturbance and pitched a temper tantrum when Granovsky, in the Stanislavskyan tradition, hung a real towel on the stage. Chagall even painted the rags that were bought in the market to make costumes, and covered the actors' bodies and faces with colorful dots and miniature drawings. As Efros tells it:

> He obviously considered the spectator a fly, which would soar out of its chair, sit on Mikhoels's hat and observe with the thousand tiny crystals of its fly's eye what he, Chagall, had conjured up there. . . . On the day of the premiere, just before Mikhoels's entrance on the stage, he clutched the actor's shoulder and frenziedly thrust his brush at him as at a mannequin, daubing dots on his costume and painting tiny birds and pigs no opera glass could observe on his visored cap, despite repeated, anxious summonses to the stage.[8]

The actors were thus perceived as moving Chagallian figures. This coincided with Granovsky's theory that the normal human state is silence, and actors should pop up out of silence and go back to it. Efros wrote of the production:

> The best places were those in which Granovsky executed his system of "dots" and the actors froze in mid-movement and gesture, from one moment to the next. The narrative line was turned into an assembly of dots.

But this was contrary to the usual conception of theater as a three-dimensional, dynamic art. Efros shrewdly understood the problem:

> The wholeness of the spectator's impression was complete. When the curtain rose, Chagall's wall panels and the decorations with the actors on the stage simply mirrored each other. But the nature of this ensemble was so untheatrical that one might have asked, why turn off the light in the auditorium, and why do these Chagallian beings move and speak on the stage rather than stand unmoving and silent as on his canvases.

The stage and the walls mirrored each other because Chagall used images of the actors for his painted carnival. Chagall wouldn't abide by the traditional three-dimensionality of the theater any more than he would limit himself to two dimensions in painting: on his long murals within a demonstratively two-dimensional surface he rendered figures as both two- and three-dimensional. We may call it: two-and-a-half dimensional art. The images are often presented in a mutiplanar perspective; that is, individual figures or groups and geometric forms appear each on their own plane, sometimes two- and sometimes three-dimensional, and the planes are stacked one behind or beside, or on top of each other, with no realistic continuity between them. If some figures seem to move in and out of this painted world, it is a fulfillment of his larger conceptual vision: His own wife and child peep out from between two flat color stripes in the *Introduction*, and the major figures of the painted theater leap above geometric space altogether. In his early work, Chagall often used geometrical shapes in his paintings, especially flat monochromatic rectangulars, but he always tended to see geometrical forms or flat surfaces as real objects in a three-dimensional world, which one can climb under or fly above.

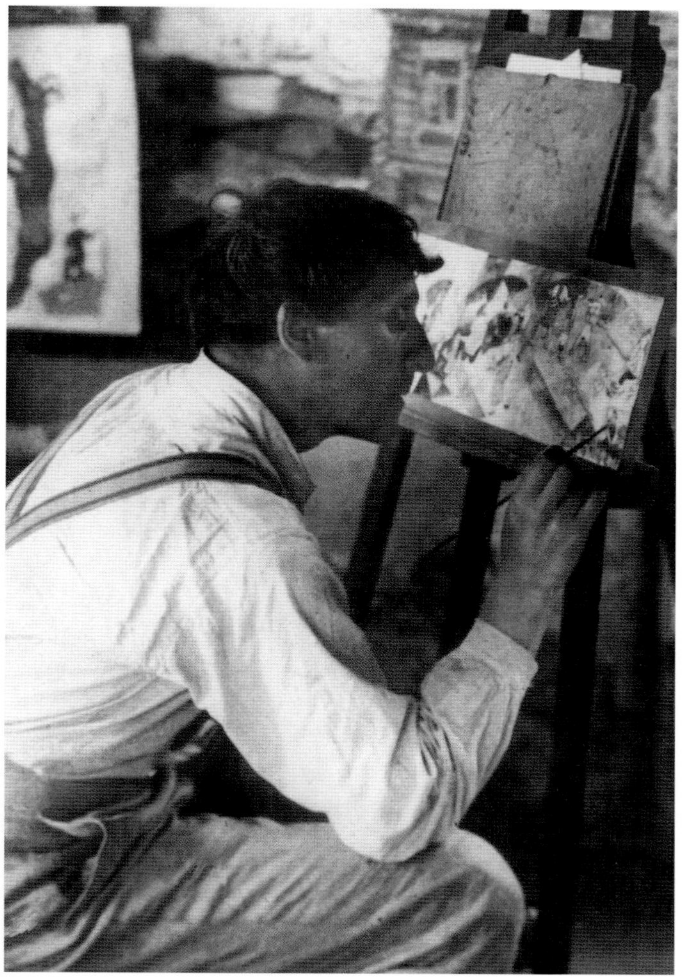

93. Marc Chagall painting the study for the ***Introduction to the Jewish Theater****. 1920. Courtesy Comité Marc Chagall, Paris*

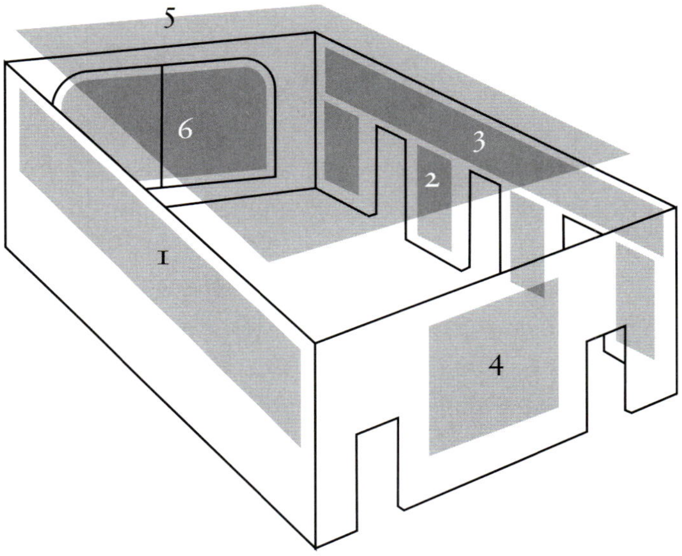

94. ***Diagram of the Theater***
1. ***Introduction to the Jewish Theater***
2. *Between the windows:* ***Music, Dance, Theater, Literature***
3. *Frieze:* ***Wedding Feast***
4. *Exit wall:* ***Love on the Stage***
5. *Ceiling*
6. *Curtain*

Thus, to Chagall, the actors merely provided another degree of animation in a two-and-a-half-dimensional space. Nevertheless, Efros concluded, "[Chagall] never understood that he was the clear and undisputable victor, and that, in the end, the young Yiddish theater had struggled because of this victory."

For years, Chagall himself did not recover from the exhilarating experience of having created a huge object of public art, a panorama and summation of many of his figures of art. Still in Vitebsk, Chagall concluded one of his manifestos with the call: "Give us a wall!" assuming that this was the best way to communicate art to the people. Now that dream had materialized, incorporating most elements of his painterly achievements. After that, he kept repeating, "Give me a wall!"—until he made his great stained-glass windows, tapestries, and ceilings in churches, synagogues, and opera houses after World War II.

THE MULTIPLANAR CANVAS

As we enter the theater and look at the huge mural on the left wall, *Introduction to the Yiddish Theater*, 1920 (no. 95), a powerful, sweeping movement carries us forward and upward; yet the movement is constantly impeded by groups of figures, bizarre activities, and ever-changing painterly events, making it a long journey indeed. In many of his authentic paintings, Chagall's figures hover over the depicted scenery, but here there is no such setting at all, no houses, streets, town, or stage. They are simply floating in mid-air. The authority of space is transferred from the fictional world to another stratum, the geometric areas formed by Suprematist-like stripes and Orphic-like circles. Colorful figures float on this spaceless canvas, brought together in three functional groups: the management of the theater, the musicians, and the comedians.

The whole painting is framed on each side by a cow and a human figure in a red shirt, and many smaller groups, individuals, and vignettes appear throughout the painting. Within each human grouping there is no realistic space but rather a conceptual conjunction that unites them. We cannot imagine, for example, an actual scene in which Chagall, touching Granovsky with his palette, is carried in Efros's arms while a midget serves milk to the trio. It is rather a realization of the dead metaphor, "Efros brought Chagall to Granovsky."

Basically, the composition is organized in three circles with margins on either end. The circles increase in diameter from left to right, and their upper arcs rise from a distance of about one quarter below the top of the canvas to the very top. In addition to the circles, there are conspicuous stripes and triangles, with well-defined, hard-edged boundaries, as well as lines, segments, and radii, all of which overlap the circles.

From the Suprematists, Chagall learned the value of abstract, pure geometric shapes, defined in sharp outlines as if made by a ruler, and usually monochromatic. The geometric forms he used in the *Introduction* enabled him to hold such a large work of art together. For years afterward, he was proud and jealous of this achievement. He attempted another massive composition in the sample painting toward a long "political" mural, *The Revolution*, 1937 (see chapter 8, no. 127), made on the twentieth anniversary of the October Revolution and aimed at the World Exhibition in Paris (where Chagall participated in the Jewish/Yiddish section). But this was never put into a large painting, and eventually he had to divide his design into three parts, for he could not handle the unity of a painting larger than the length of his arms. This dilemma found its solution later in life, in the grills of his stained-glass windows, which were executed by masters of the craft.

The use of Suprematist elements in the midst of this lively work is, of course, a profanation. Malevich sought to achieve "a 'desert' in which nothing could be perceived but feeling," the rediscovery of pure art "not obscured by the accumulation of 'things' [or human figures]," hence called "Non-Objective Art."[9] (A better translation of Malevich's *bez-predmetroe iskusstvo* would be "Objectless Art.") And along comes Chagall, using a complex structure of geometric forms as a floor to climb under and as a ground for his human figures to walk on and to float above!

One of the first things that strikes us is the strong black diagonal stripe at the center of the canvas, moving forward and upward. We recognize this gesture in other post-Revolutionary paintings by Chagall as the realization of his name in Russian: *Shagal* means "he strode." To the left of this black diagonal, and parallel to it, is Efros's footless black leg, as a premonition of the big diagonal. In the right half of the painting we have a parallel move: The faint, pastel stripes, although oriented downward, are stacked so that as a band of colors they also move upward in a parallel diagonal. Indeed, if we look at all the precisely organized diagonal stripes and lines, we see that a huge flattened W underlies the composition, uniting the canvas—circles, people, and all.

The movement upward and forward is further reinforced by the band of human figures that occupies precisely half of the height of the mural and moves slowly from its lower to its upper half. This colorful band represents the story of this theater, whereas the paler images and vignettes in grisaille all around it represent Chagall's fictional and personal worlds.

Some parts of the individual figures look like flat paper cutouts (for example, Mikhoels's blue shirt in the center of the mural—#22 in the diagram), but most human figures have three-dimensional characteristics, either through their rounded bodies or through Cubistic formations of body and clothing (for example, Chagall's yellow suit—#7). From group to group, perspectives are often inverted—for example, some miniature figures (implying that we are seeing them at a distance) appear not beyond but before the larger figures.

The same ambiguity permeates Chagall's treatment of time. Preparations for the theater, the performances themselves, as well as reminders from the Jewish religious and folkloric past are all presented simultaneously. In a typical Postmodernist gesture, Chagall thus blurs the boundary between object-language (describing the presented objects) and metalanguage (describing the painter's language and himself).

In sum, space, time, and perspective are all evoked in the painting and are presented in discontinuous, disrupted bursts. The spectator's position is not taken for granted either. Chagall was furious that chairs were placed in the auditorium, thus fixing the place of the spectators. Apparently, he wanted them to go back and forth from mural to mural. The spectator's distance needs to be variable: to grasp the whole, one must stand at a distance; to understand the activities of the social groups, one needs a middle view, far enough to absorb one third of the canvas but close enough to recognize the figures; and to read the minute inscriptions and ornaments, one must press one's nose up to the canvas.

An important issue was raised by Avram Kampf, who argued that a "perspective of sentiment" governs the picture: "that which looms large in one's memory appears huge on the canvas."[10] Perhaps such a principle helps the writer rationalize Chagall's programmatic antiRealism, but it does not really work. Can we say that any of the actors loomed larger in Chagall's memory than his own parents, wife, and child, who are quite small on this canvas? In the case of the *Introduction*, it is thematic foregrounding rather than a "perspective of sentiment" that governs the scale, and even that is not a constant relation. The topic of his painting, the theater, is represented by large, colored figures, while Chagall's personal world and conceptual perspectives are inserted in the margins and interstices of space, often in grisaille. Small size makes things no less important or less close to the artist's sentiment; on the contrary, it betrays his love for minute

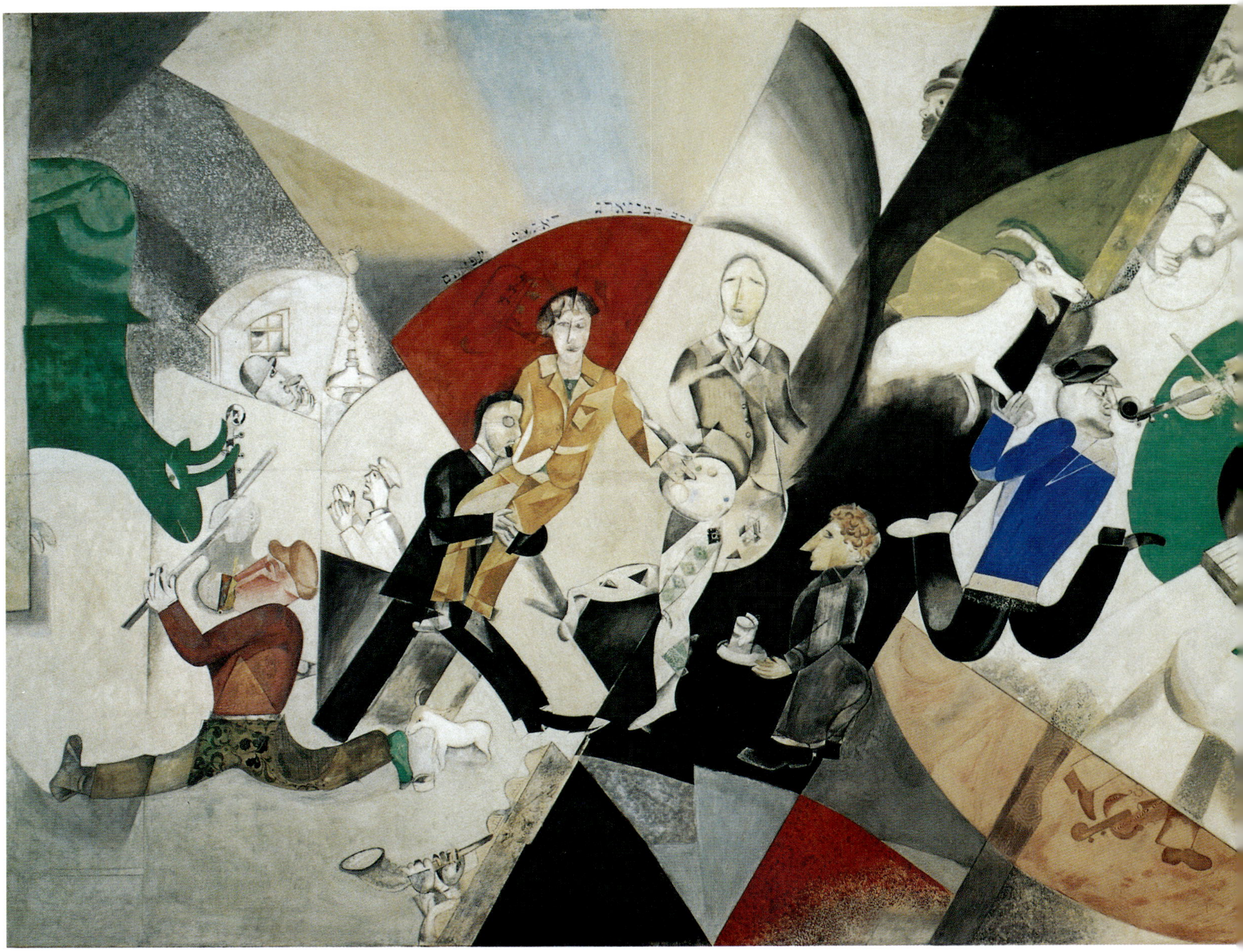

95. ***Introduction to the Yiddish Theater.*** *1920. Tempera and gouache on canvas, 284.2 x 784.2 cm. Tretyakov Gallery, Moscow*

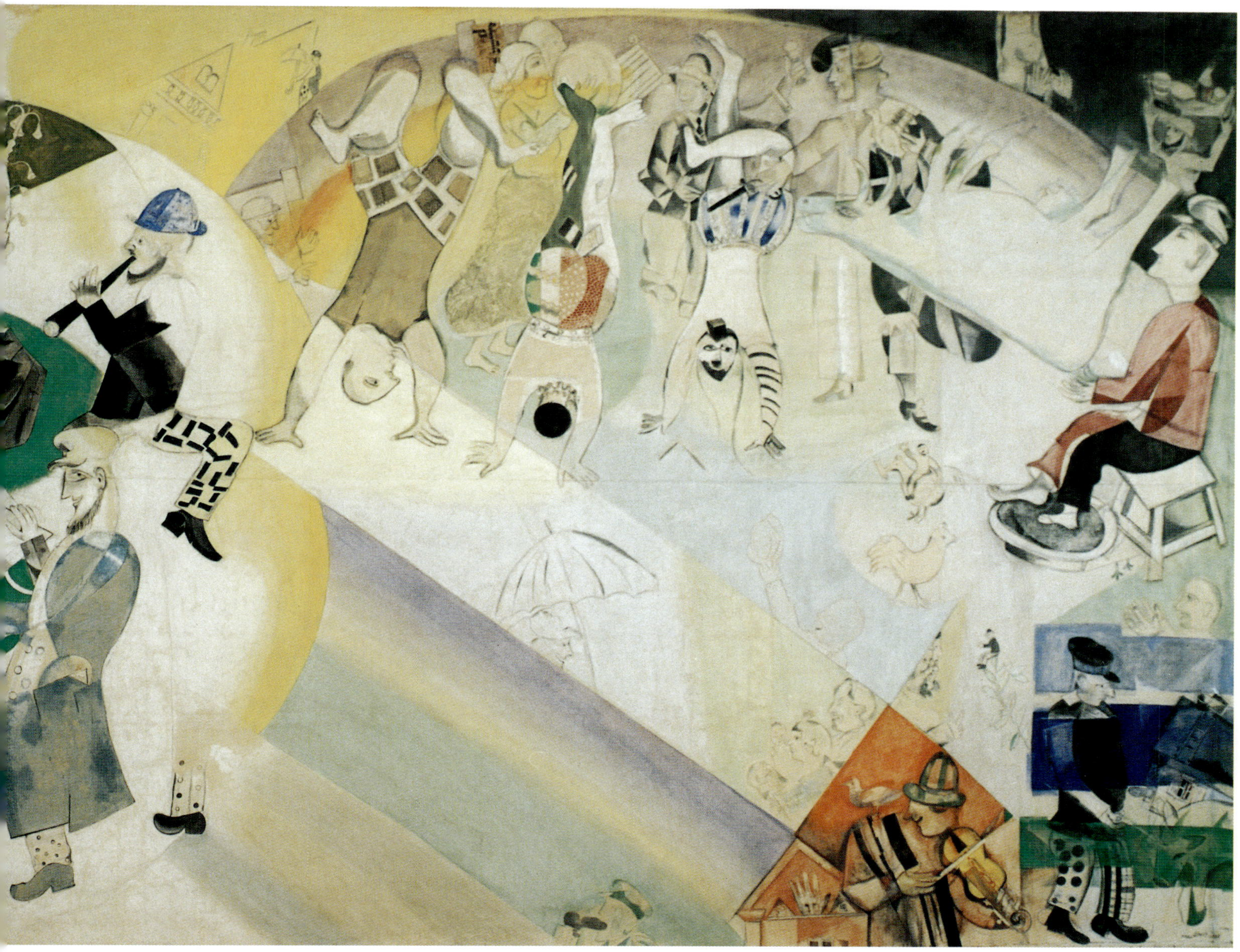

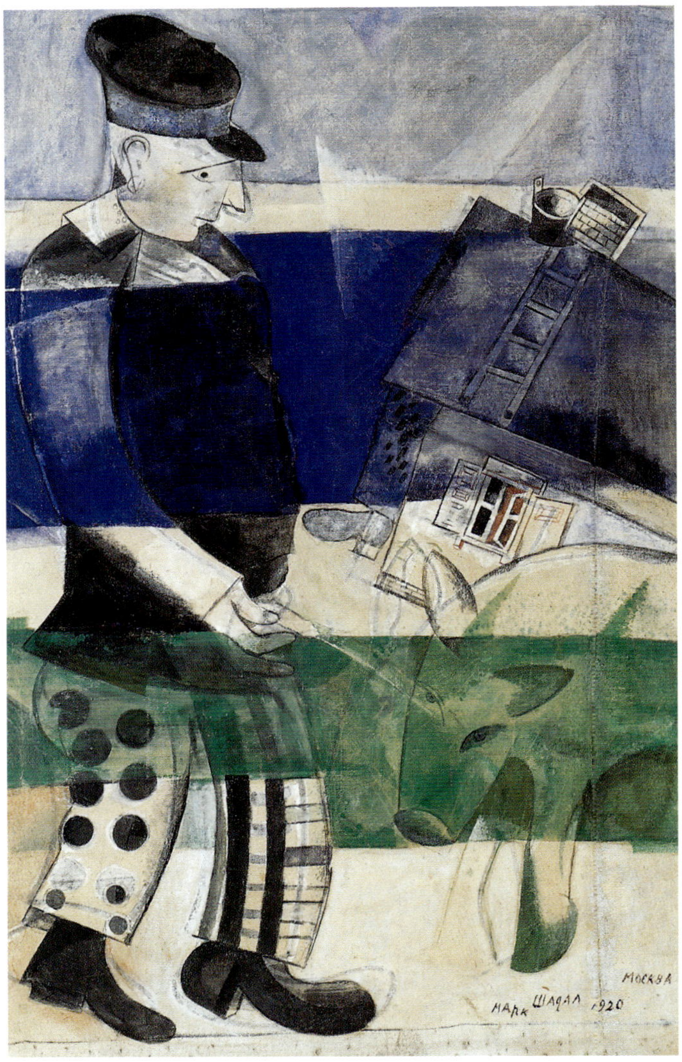

96. ***Introduction to the Yiddish Theater*** *(detail). 1920. Tempera and gouache on canvas, 284.2 x 784.2 cm. Tretyakov Gallery, Moscow*

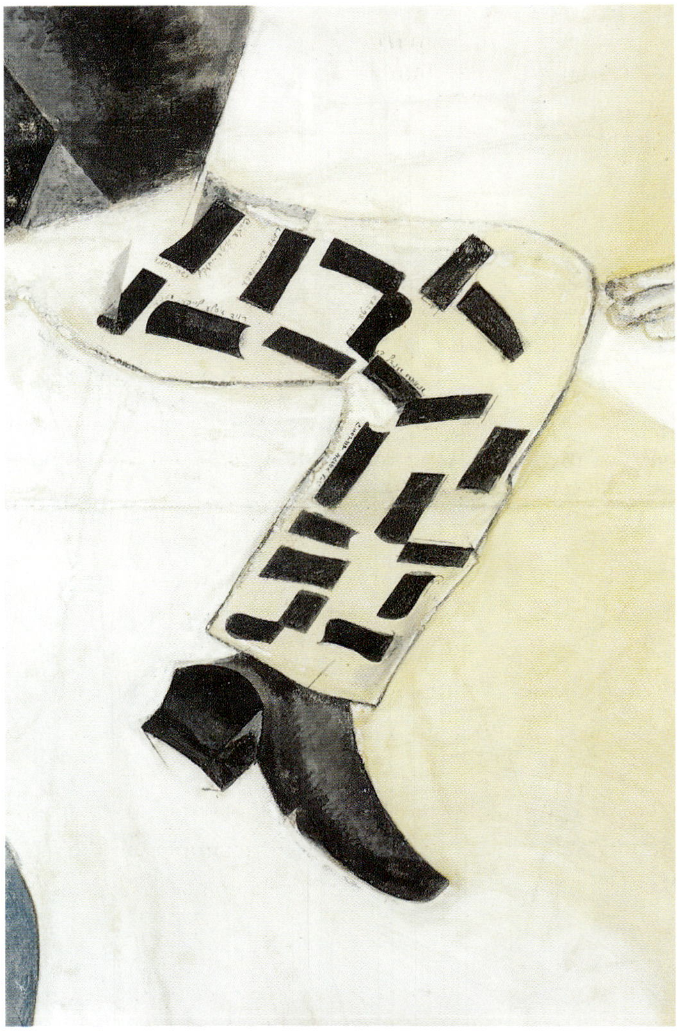

97. ***Introduction to the Yiddish Theater*** *(detail). 1920. Tempera and gouache on canvas, 284.2 x 784.2 cm. Tretyakov Gallery, Moscow*

details and reveals his personal world. We also see this in the small insertions of the world of his fictionalized "Vitebsk" at the bottom and on the margins of the panels representing the Four Arts.

The *Introduction* is characterized by a happy celebration of colors: Some are bold and saturated (in the left half of the painting), some are pale and ornamented (mostly toward the right[11]), some are subtle. Color, though by and large subordinated to the boundaries of figures and geometric bodies, occasionally revolts against the domination of spatial form. Thus, the yellow on the margins of the middle circle flows over the geometric boundary into the space above, where it becomes a background for the little sketched figures; similarly, in the lower-right triangle, the diffuse orange, although contained in geometric boundaries, permeates the fiddler, bird, and synagogue in the background, as if merging all the disproportionate objects in one level of color and depth; and in the lower-right corner, several colored stripes cover up the indecent scene of a boy urinating on a pig.

Thus, each major stratum of the painting (such as color, spatial shapes, human figures, social continuity) is subordinated to other strata in parts of the canvas and asserts its dominance in some other parts. Where one stratum is interrupted, another takes over. The general principles of Chagall's early art apply to the murals: Several stylistic strains may interact in one figure or texture; several figures and objects may overlap, fully or partially; deformation or distortion may act on any established figure or artistic stratum; disproportion of the sizes of figures is universally accepted; and any surface of one thing may become the background for another.

The paucity of means available to Chagall in the winter of 1920 is obvious, but he used anything he could lay his hands on. The mural was painted on thin "Dutch bed sheets" (whatever that means[12]) sewn together, with a poorer lining behind it. He used gouaches as well as kaolin with paint and water[13] (in several cases, he left the dripping or mopped-up paint stains as part of the texture), sawdust, and pencil; he dipped lace in paint, pressed it to the canvas, and then removed it, leaving its impression in some areas of the canvas (for example, on the dress of the female dancer), and drew similar tiny patterns with a brush.

THE ART OF COMEDY

Chagall's "surrealist" perception of both art and life, his turning away from the realism, psychologism, and individualism that still reigned in the Russian theater, his unsentimental emphasis on the vitality of traditional Jewish folk culture—these traits infected the spirit of the theater and influenced its later achievements.

The Yiddish writer Dovid Bergelson wrote that he welcomed the Russian Revolution but did not know how to write "proletarian" fiction: Although he knew exactly how the Jewish bourgeois puts his slippers under his bed, he had no idea what the proletarian would do (indeed, there were no Jewish proletarians yet, and if there were, they had no slippers). This was a general problem of the new Soviet Russian theater and of literature as well; plays that promoted the new society were sloganeering and vacuous, for they did not embody any real society, any specific, concrete world. The importance of Chagall's role in the theater lay in his embracing the genre of the carnivalesque (as later formulated by the Russian cultural critic Mikhail Bakhtin[14]), the topsy-turvy world that had reigned in medieval fairs. It was precisely through the carnival that Chagall was able to introduce the old, abandoned, and subverted world as a real, tangible substance of a work of art. This enabled the theater to fill its productions with a fictional world populated by rich archetypes, flesh-and-blood popular characters, widely shared jokes, and an inimitable and endearing language to its readers. And although these characters were grotesque and out of touch with reality, they also were inspired by flights of fantasy and poetry and by an ahistorical sense of an absurd and comic human dignity.

By turning that fictional world upside down, Chagall saved it from empty Soviet slogans. Later the Yiddish Theater could be either sentimental or politically obnoxious and rudely critical, even anti-Semitic (showing the "Yid" in full bloom, as Efros described it); yet the tangible existence and vitality of the lost Jewish world was preserved and resounded in the minds of the spectators, including gentiles and assimilated Jews in Russia and in Western Europe.

There was no significant narrative here, only a "world"—and it could be reproduced with plotless plays, or the stereotypical plots of a joke; characters with no psychology or grounding in reality; and dialogue with no psychological subtlety. The leap that Jewish literature, art, and theater made from a medieval carnivalesque or comedic art to the age of Revolution—leapfrogging Realism and psychology—made it seem fresh, Modernist, and Constructivist. In this sense Chagall learned a great lesson from his new understanding of the master. Chagall wrote, "I was angry at the small town guys who read Sholem Aleichem and laughed all the time just for the sake of laughing. I, on the contrary, didn't laugh so much and thought that Sholem Aleichem was a 'Modernist' in art."[15]

Entertainment and folk literature are fragmentary, anecdotal, joking, melodramatic, with no narrative or continuous structures; this is the mode of comedy. The traditional Jewish world, fictionalized in Yiddish literature, could be resurrected on the Soviet stage as an entertainment only in the genre of comedy.

Chagall's perception prevailed. In 1919–20, the Yiddish players still called themselves "actors" and attempted serious drama; after Chagall and Sholem Aleichem, they called themselves "comedians."[16] For fifteen years they did not approach serious tragedy. Mikhoels's stunning success as King Lear in 1935 was the victory of a comedian turned tragic actor. In the early years of the theater, Mikhoels had recognized the tragic depths encompassed by comedy, and had described the theater and the contemporary human condition as "tragicomedy." In 1924, on a tour of Jewish Ukraine just a few years after the wave of terrible pogroms in the Jewish towns all over Ukraine, Mikhoels had written an article in the playbill titled: "The Comedians on the Ruins of Ukraine." In 1935, Mikhoels performed one of his greatest roles—King Lear; he inverted the relationship and brought all his comedic experiences to bear on this tragic role. And this was true Shakespeare. To all witnesses, the power and scope of the impact on the Russian theater was unforgettable.

Unlike graven images, theater is not forbidden in the Bible. Rather, the prohibition against it in Jewish tradition stems from a ban against the Hellenistic theater entertainment enjoyed in Palestine in the early centuries of the Common Era. But comedians and clowns were not considered part of theater in Jewish folklore. Indeed, the European Renaissance concept of "comedians" enjoyed a long tradition. In Yiddish, they were called *Purimshpiler*, *komediantn*, or the self-derogatory *Komedyanshtshikes*. A later version of the *Sholem Aleichem Evening* was titled *A Spectacle of Comedians*. Chagall's *Introduction* is a manifesto for that antirealistic and antitragic art. The tragic vision of Modernism hardly touched him.

The *Introduction* is, in general, a celebration of Jewish culture and a vindication of Jewish dignity. As Chagall proudly wrote in his *Leaves from My Notebook*, "I am too shy to say what this little nation can show," implying primarily that it could produce great, universal Art with a capital A (through Chagall himself), as earlier it had produced Christianity and Marxism.[17] Radical Jewish vignettes appear at the end, on the right margins of the mural. In the upper-right corner, an adult is being "Jewified"—we can clearly see the circumcision tool. In the lower-right corner a circumcised (and therefore Jewish) boy urinates on a pig—a gesture of defiance against the Christian world (see detail, no. 138). It is as though Chagall were saying, "We will produce art in spite of all our enemies" (in Yiddish, a triumphant stance, meaning "we shall overcome," has this formulaic addition, *oyf tselokhes ale sonim*, "in spite of all our enemies"). Having painted this scene of defilement, he covered it over with three bars ("I cannot say aloud what this little nation can achieve").

Chagall was extremely ambivalent about the Jewishness of his art, and he caused a small scandal when the management of the theater refused to open the auditorium as an exhibition to the general public; he argued that his art was being seen only by the one hundred Jews who came to the theater, while he wanted a wider audience composed of many nationalities.[18] His wish was fulfilled.

CHAGALL'S "INTRODUCTION" AND PICASSO'S "GUERNICA"

In many ways, the *Introduction to the Yiddish Theater* plays a role in Chagall's oeuvre similar to that of *Guernica* (no. 98) in Picasso's. Both are murals, made at the invitation of a central cultural body of their respective cultures, both of which were in "Diaspora" (Picasso's was commissioned in Paris in January 1937 by the Spanish government-in-exile). Both were made for a public purpose, expressing a political and cultural position. Neither Chagall nor Picasso were overtly political artists, yet both eagerly responded to a public invitation and mobilized their entire stock of images for this new purpose such that the commissions became quintessential encyclopedias of their previous work.

For Picasso, in the midst of a period of stylistic hesitation, the commission gave new motivation for the use of his techniques. What had been mere formal elements of his art became thematized and politicized. For Chagall, after a brief and stormy period of propaganda painting in Vitebsk, this new opportunity also came at a crossroads.

Picasso's mural was a summation of the major artistic trends of the twentieth century, notably Cubism, Futurism, Expressionism, Surrealism, and political art. In Chagall's mural, various contradictory trends are also brought together, but in a pluralistic balance; whereas in Picasso's painting they are fused within each figure. Picasso's painting is almost monochromatic, while Chagall's is a celebration of many colors and hues.

Both artists use the irrational, nonverbal, primitive and empathic power of animals: In Picasso's vision it is the Spanish bull (representing Picasso himself) and the heroic horse-cum-statue, while in Chagall's it is the green

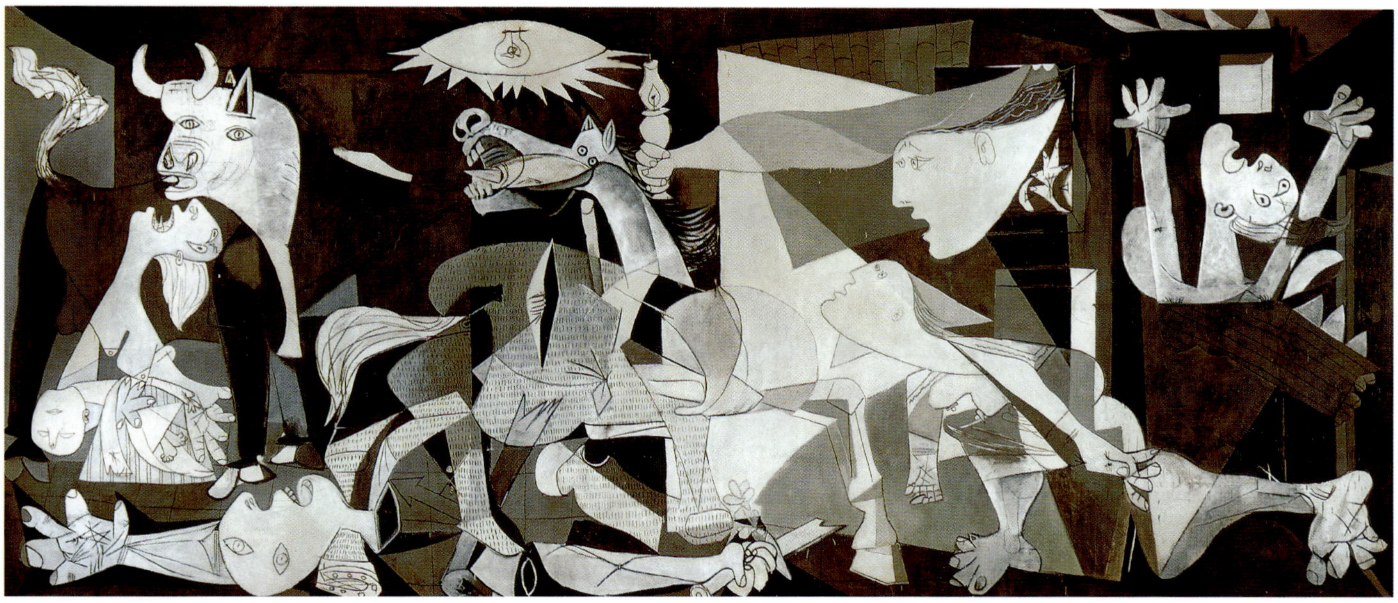

98. Pablo Picasso (1881–1973). ***Guernica.*** *Paris, June 4, 1937. Oil on canvas, 349.3 x 776.6 cm. Museo Nacional Centro de Arte Reina Sofia, Madrid © ARS, NY*

cow (also self-representative) and such domestic *shtetl* animals as goats, chickens, and fish.

Both artists confronted a similar task of organizing a large, unwieldy mural. Picasso's is slightly more than twice as long as it is high, whereas the length of Chagall's is almost three times its height. As Rudolf Arnheim has pointed out, "Picasso prevented the composition from falling to pieces by the symmetrical correspondence of the flanks—the bull at the left, the falling woman at the right—and the roughly equilateral triangle culminating in the oil lamp."[19] Chagall's mural was longer and could not be integrated in one pyramid; hence his use of the "W" and the three semicircles as underlying structures.

There are additional devices to unify the murals. In both, a dynamic move pulls the viewer with it. As Arnheim noted, "Any compositional movement toward the left . . . runs against the tide, because for psychological reasons the observer's glance proceeds freely from left to right whereas it is impeded in the opposite direction."[20] In Picasso's mural, there is a "movement of the wave of figures . . . directed toward the bull" (on the left), counteracting the normal, rightward current. In Chagall's mural, on the contrary, the basic movement is from left to right. But Arnheim did not explain the reasons for his psychological rule. It is plausible that the rule applies only to cultures writing from left to right; the Jewish viewer, however, who writes from right to left, would have felt a tension while viewing Chagall's mural, moving in the opposite direction.

There are similar images bracketing both works: A powerful cow or bull dominates the leftmost parts of the canvases, while a person at the right summarizes the mood of each painting—a scream in Picasso's and relaxed acceptance in Chagall's.

The difference between Picasso and Chagall may be compared to the difference between tragedy and comedy. In *Guernica* Picasso presents the Aristotelian unities of time, space, and action; Chagall displays a plurality of all three. The genre of comedy does not require one purposeful action, but rather prefers anecdotes, a string of immediate effects following each other. It is the heroic gesture of a Spaniard and a political leftist versus Jewish utopian hope and self-irony.

The different social purposes and cultural backgrounds of the two artists account for the different conceptions of the whole, yet in both murals we can see the artist taking stock of several waves of Modernism and the political urge to go beyond the problems of art itself. Both plunged into the work with extreme intensity. There was also a practical difference: Picasso had time and could afford to make dozens of sketches and choose any materials that suited him, while Chagall had a paucity of time and materials at his disposal.

AN ART OF THREE TIMES

One might look at the whole room, "Chagall's box," in light of Efros's understanding of Chagall and the Yiddish theater as an art sprung from nowhere, with no history or tradition—an "art of three times," encompassing its own present, past, and future. Indeed, the large *Introduction* is a summation of Chagall's work as a whole, but without the dark, mystical visions of his early years and without the figures of old, pious Jews. It is a celebration of Chagall's and the actors' generation as they try to enact

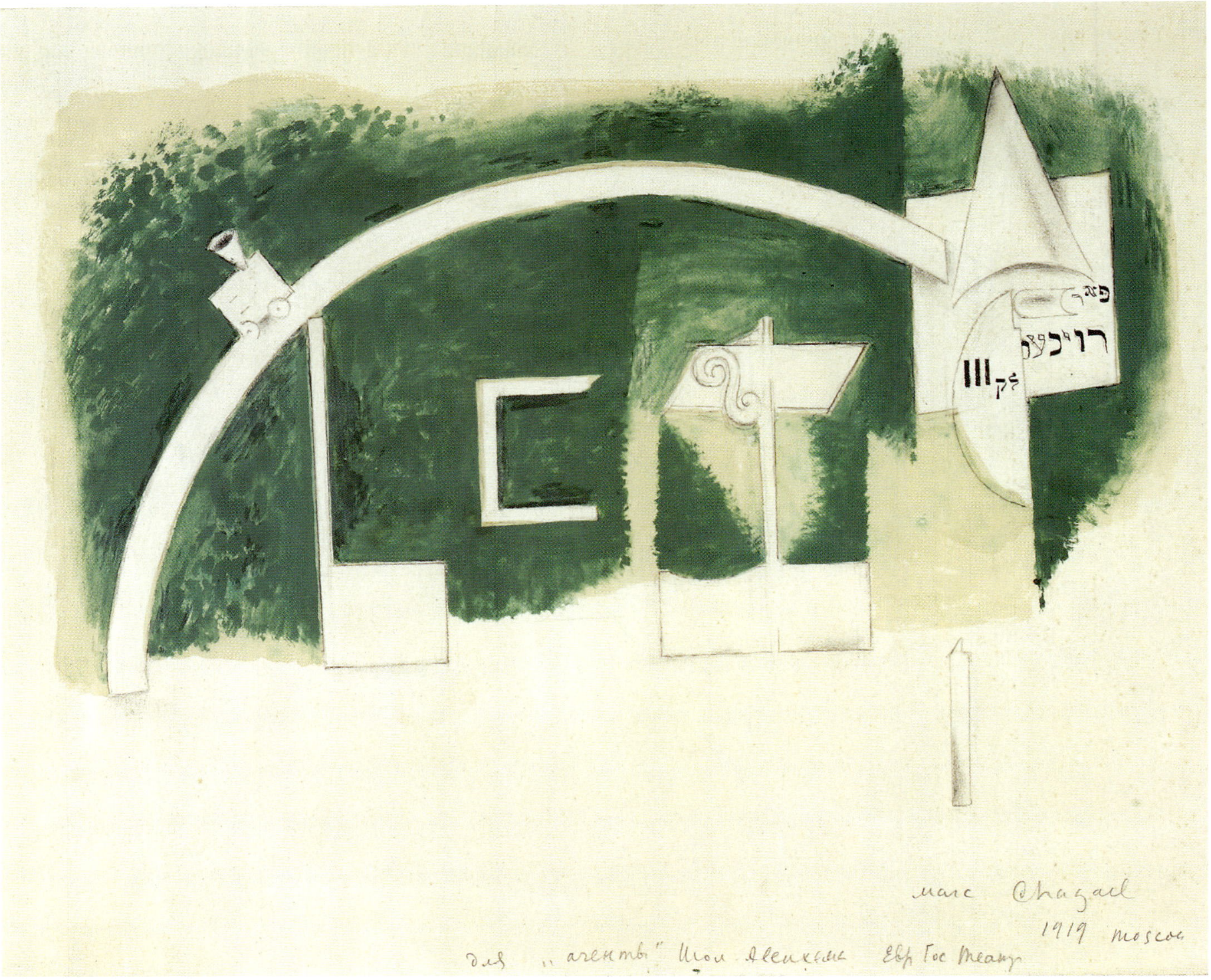

*99. **The Agents** by Sholem Aleichem. 1919–20. Pencil, gouache, ink on paper, 25.6 x 43.2 cm. AM 1988-253. Musée National d'Art Moderne, Centre Georges Pompidou, Paris. Signed **Marc Shagal** (in Russian) 1919 **Moscou** (in French).*

the past, to extract its folk spirit, joy, and artistic values for the present. It is a procession onward and upward, to an unknown future, which they will reach by turning their world upside down. Yet the figures in the last group on the right of the long wall are not looking to the future but back to the present, to the performance itself. On the righthand wall, the past is presented in full bloom, the four towering figures of the Four Arts, looming large above their *shtetl* world. And on the back wall, an image of universal Love, with no specifically Jewish attributes, evokes a cosmopolitan, veiled vision of the future.

Chagall's art, in general, developed in this direction: from a fictional world grounded in the past and reclaimed by a secular generation by means of deformation, to the abstract notion of human love—as diffuse as the colors of his later paintings. He came to embrace the ahistorical world of the Bible, as a humanistic vision created by the Jews that will save the world from a nuclear disaster, as he argued in his Yiddish lectures in the 1950s and 1960s.[21]

This perception of Jewish culture entailed a foreboding of its own disaster. Secular Jewish culture, to which Chagall, Efros, and the new Yiddish Theater contributed, was imported from general European culture. It was a utopian effort to create a culture of "three times," encompassing past and future in the present, in one great burst of art. But secular Jewish culture had no true past, so it had to borrow one from the religious tradition; and it had no true future of its own, so it borrowed one from the Russian Revolution. In Russia, it was wiped out by that Revolution itself. What remains is a heroic art that captured the moment of transformation.

CONSTRUCTIONS OF THE STAGE

The Yiddish Theater planned to perform Sholem Aleichem's *Agents* while still in Petrograd. The artist Schildknecht in Petrograd designed a realistic background of middle-class

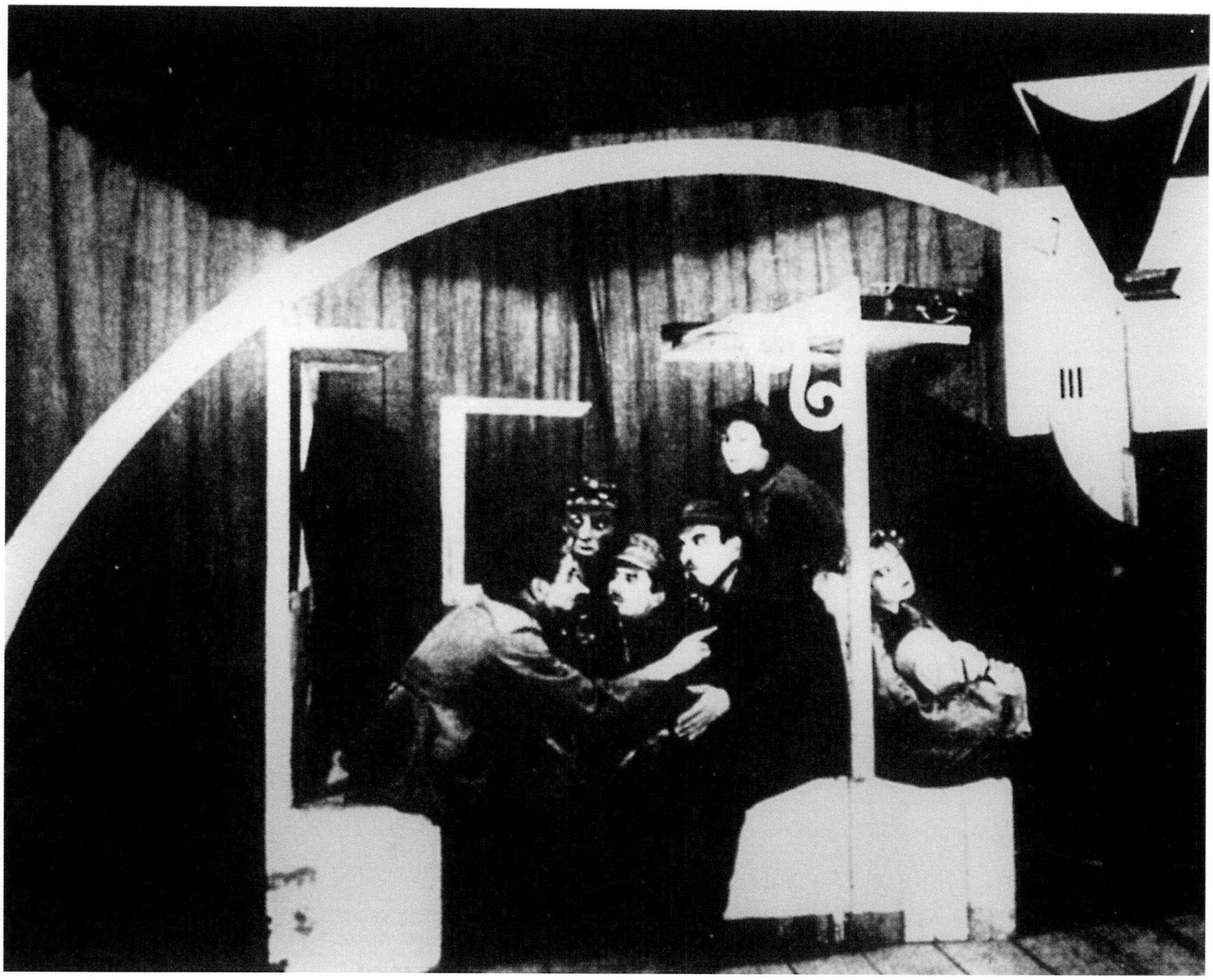

100. *Photo of actors from **The Agents**. Courtesy Natalia Vofsi-Michoels and the History of Theatre Archives, Tel Aviv University*

living, rich in details and colors, in the style of the World of Art. When Chagall was assigned the production design in Moscow, the only aspect of Schildknecht's design he took was a compartment and a half of a railroad car standing at the center (see design, no. 99, and photo, no. 100). He presented the double compartment furniture with minimalist detail and unified the scene with a sweeping asymmetrical arch, breaking the realistic illusion. On top of the arch is a tiny locomotive train and a whistle, to indicate that the action of the play occurs during a journey around the globe.

The minimalism and financial poverty of that first production of *Agents* can be seen in a list of costumes and props required for the performances:

> Vovsi [Mikhoels]/ for Agents / 1. Valise, hard. 2. Coat. 3. Briefcase. 4. Matches. 5. Letter with envelope. 6. Paper, white pages.
> Krashinski [another actor] / for Agents / 1. Small valise. 2. Briefcase. 3. Cigarette case. 4. Cigarettes. 5. Pages of white paper.

As late as January 1, 1922, the required inventory for the stage consisted of the following:

> Green curtain (left side, right side); wooden window on stand; wooden moon; wooden board with painting of locomotive smokestack, on stand; white bench (of railroad car); valise with cover for Yakenhoz, same for Lanternshooter; big doll (for Davidka); whistle (wooden instrument).[22]

In his set design for *Mazel-tov* (no. 101), Chagall utilized a similar rounded arch and a minimalized kitchen, as well as his emblematic goat (turned upside down) painted on the wall, minimal furniture, and several Constructivist patterns. A plate above the stove has a former Yiddish inscription, disintegrating into vertical and horizontal lines. The legible beginning reads *ELEY*, which could be

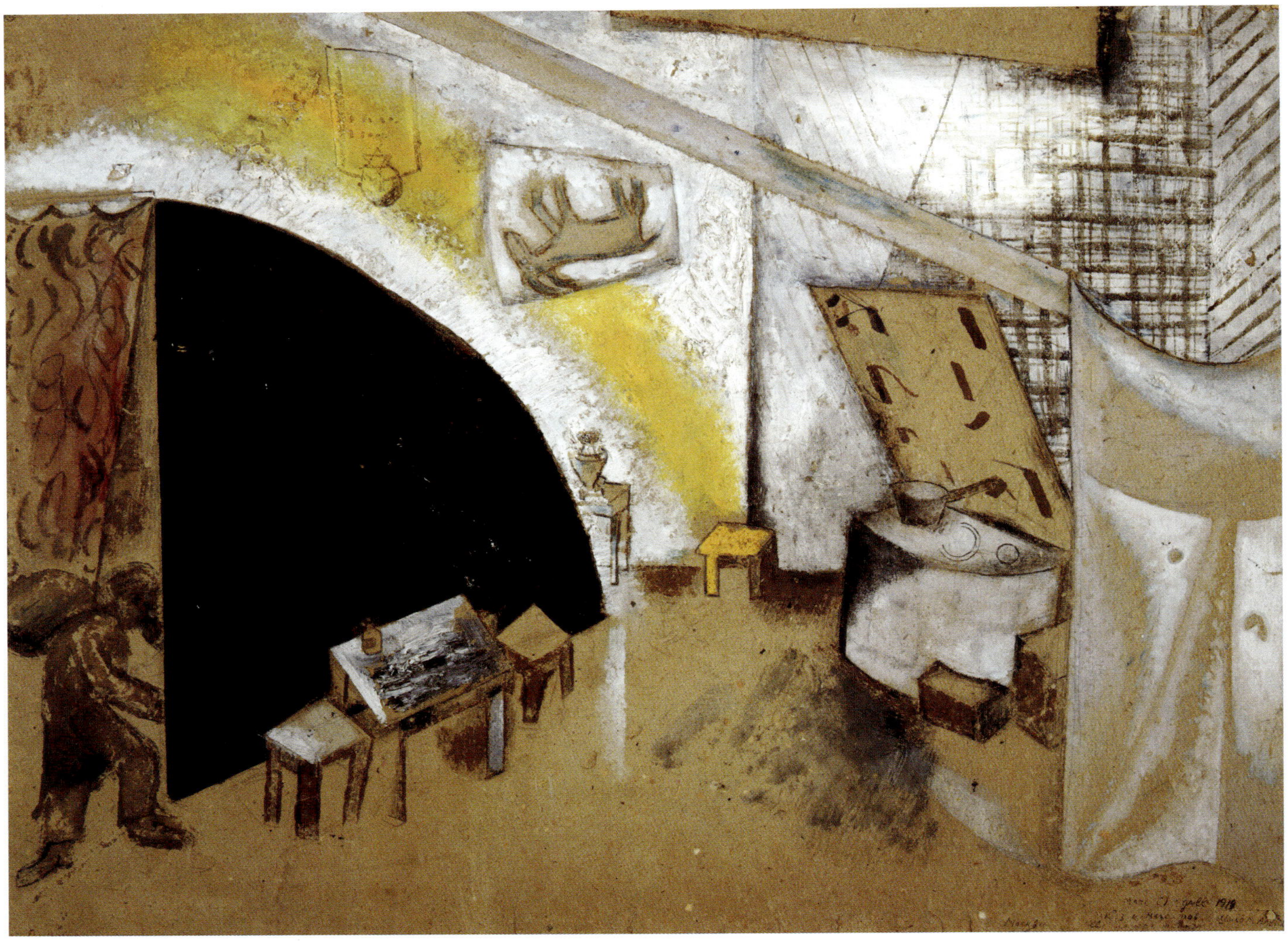

101. ***Mazel-tov***, *set design. 1920. Pencil and watercolor on paper, 25.5 x 34.5 cm. Collection of Ida Chagall, Paris*

either the beginning of "Alei[chem] [Sholem]" or the inverted name of the cook, [B]eyle.

An even more conceptual and abstract stage was designed by Chagall for *S'A Lign* ("It's a Lie"), a dialogue that takes place on a train. An ugly story about corruption is revealed little by little, as the narrator keeps protesting "It's a lie" before uncovering another ugly detail. Apparently Chagall's design (no. 102) for the work was so minimalist and abstract that it was replaced with a set by Natan Al'tman.[23] Chagall included a home in which the roof was half removed, a boot was hanging out, and a huge pencil was leaning from the ground to the ceiling. Looming above it was a ten-story-high piece of paper and a huge pen, turned lamp, illuminating the scene. The top of the paper was imprinted with tentative headline letters, *HGSh* (a distortion of *LaGaSh*, the inverted "Chagall") and *S'ALIGN S'ALIGN* ("it's a lie, it's a lie"). One of the costumes portrays a popular bluffer, with partially obscured Yiddish inscriptions on his pants; on them, we can read *s'align* several times, *sheker* (Hebrew and Yiddish for "lie"), parts of *sidur* and *tallis*, and perhaps the name of the corrupt rich man in the play, *Shia* [Finkelstein].[24]

•

Chagall was never paid for his murals, and they remained in the Yiddish theater until its liquidation. The murals now display Chagall's signatures, which he applied to them on his visit to Russia in 1973. Chagall, accustomed for so long to signing his name in French, confused the two languages: On the large *Introduction*, his signature is in printed Russian letters with the exception of the "G" written in the Latin rather than Cyrillic alphabet. Perhaps he did it as yet another sign of his multicultural personality.

---

1. See *Marc Chagall and His Times*, p. 189.

2. Aleksandra Shatskikh, "Marc Chagall and the Jewish Chamber Theater," [unpublished manuscript]. On Chagall's early work for the stage, see her "Marc Chagall and the Theater" in Vitali, ed. *Marc Chagall: The Russian Years 1906–1922*, 1991, pp. 76–89.

3. For a list of productions, see A. N. Manteyfel, "The First Theater of the Revolution," *Moskva*, no. 1 (1968).

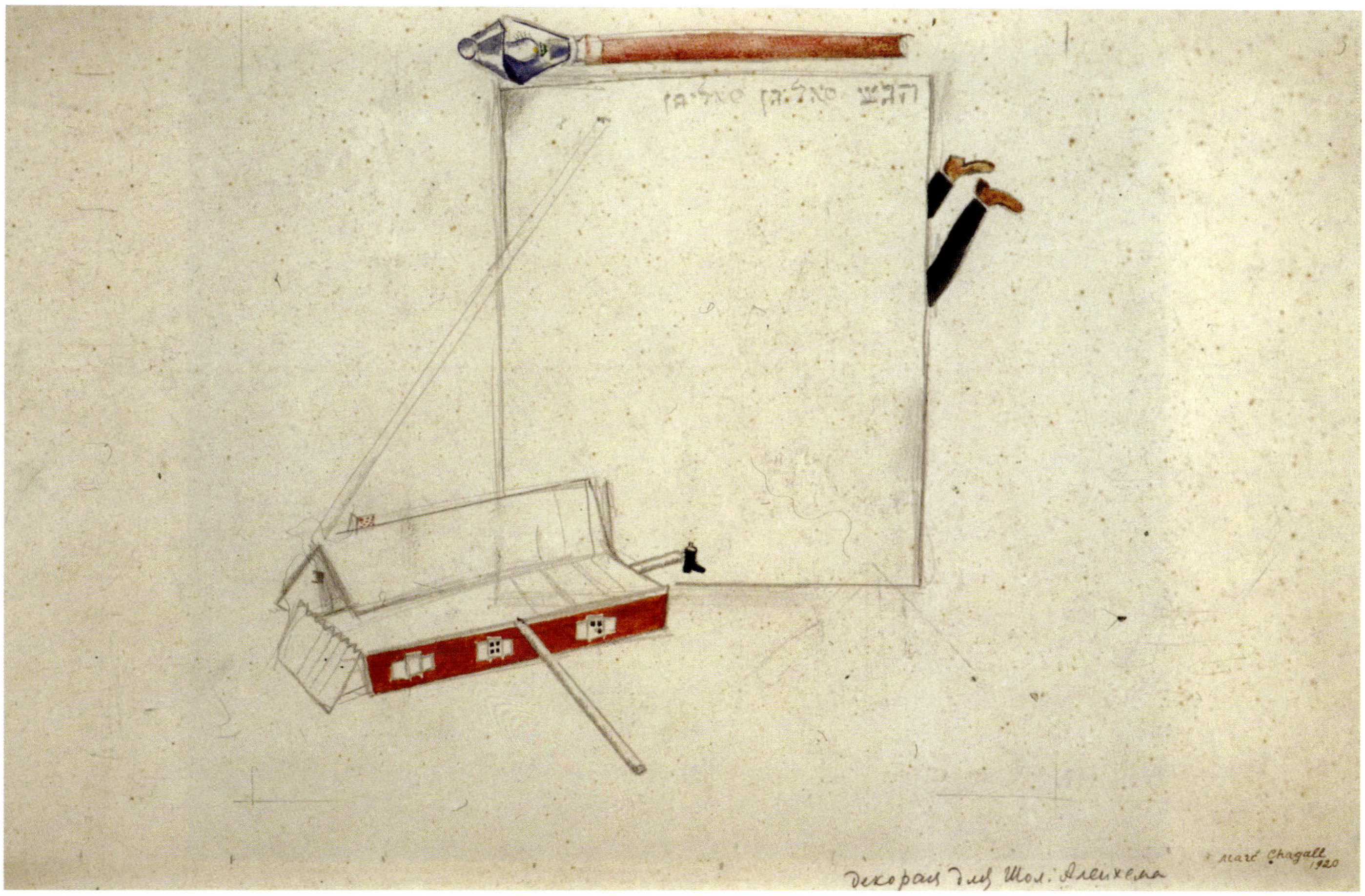

102. ***It's a Lie****, set design. 1920. Pencil and gouache on paper, 22.5 x 30 cm. Collection of Ida Chagall, Paris. On top of the empty page:* ***HGSh*** *(distorted from LAGASh, Chagall in reverse)* ***S'align S'align*** *("It's a Lie, It's a Lie").*

4. See Kamensky, Aleksandr. *Chagall: The Russian Years 1907–1922*, trans. from the French by C. Phillips. New York: Rizzoli Publications, 1989, p. 343.

5. Chagall seems to have trouble remembering the Russian "G": when he signed the theater mural at the Tretyakov Gallery in 1973, he wrote Shagal in Russian with a French "g."

6. See "Marc Chagall and the Jewish Chamber Theater."

7. A. Vetrov, "On Chagall," *Ekran*, no. 7 (1921).

8. Abram Efros, "The artists of Granovsky's Theater," *Iskusstvo*, Moscow, vol. 4, 1928.

9. Kazimir Malevich, "The Non-Objective World," in Chip, et. al., *Theories of Modern Art*, pp. 341–42.

10. "Chagall in the Yiddish Theater," in Vitali, ed., *Marc Chagall: The Russian Years 1906–1922*, 1991, p. 98.

11. Chagall apparently ran out of paint, as he argued years later, explaining to his Russian hosts in 1973 why he left the Soviet Union in 1922.

12. Unless the sheets were really brought from Holland, it may have a pornographic and pejorative connotation in Russian, based on expressions such as "a Dutch prick."

13. Conversation with Aleksei Kovalev, Director of the Restoration Department, State Tret'yakov Gallery, in New York, July 30, 1992.

14. It is interesting to note that at the time Bakhtin lived in Vitebsk, and his pupil Pavel Medvedev was head of the city culture department. The concepts of carnival, polyphony, even dialogical discourse fit Chagall very well.

15. Similarly, Vladimir Mayakovsky, in his radical essay "Two Chekhovs," reread the sentimentalized Chekhov as a great and funny master of language. See Vladimir Mayakovsky. *Polnoe Sobranie Sochineny* ["Complete Collection of Essays"]. Moscow: Gosudarstvennoe izdatel'stvo Khudozhestvennoy Literatyry [State publishing house of Artistic Literature], 1955, vol. 1, p. 294.

16. See S. Mikhoels. "The New Jewish Comedian" and "Our Comedians Parade in the Ukraine" (see bibliography).

17. See *Marc Chagall on Art and Culture*, pp. 38–40.

18. See his letter "To the Management of GOSEKT," in *Marc Chagall and the Jewish Theater*, p. 173.

19. Rudolf Arnheim, *The Genesis of a Painting: Picasso's Guernica*. Berkeley and Los Angeles: University of California Press, 1962, p. 26.

20. Ibid., p. 26.

21. See *Marc Chagall on Art and Culture.*

22. State Bakhrushin Museum, Moscow, Fond. 584, files 20, 21, 87.

23. The early announcements list Chagall as the designer of all three plays, while later ones mention Al'tman.

24. For examples of Chagall's costume designs for the *Sholem Aleichem Evening*, see *Marc Chagall and the Jewish Theater*, cat. nos. 18–20.

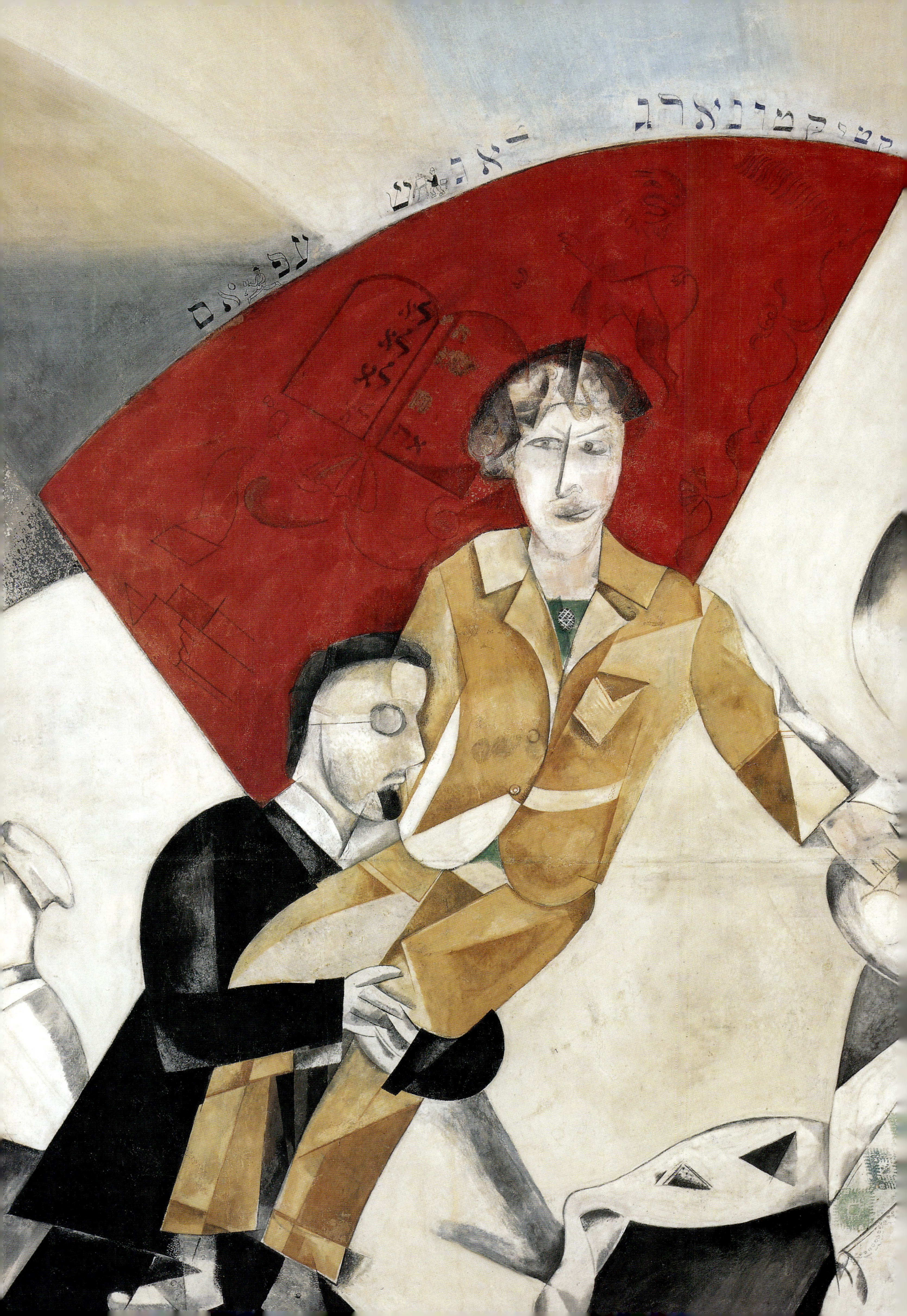

7. A Guide to the Iconography of Chagall's Theater Paintings

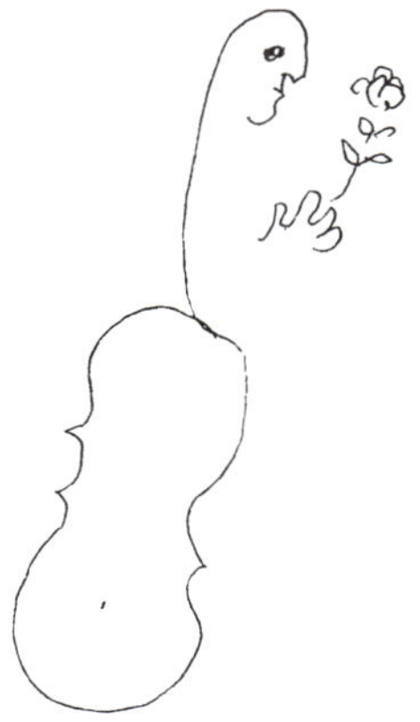

THE LONG MURAL *INTRODUCTION TO THE YIDDISH THEATER*

The following explanations refer to the numbered locations on the map of *Introduction to the Yiddish Theater* (no. 104).

1. In gray, the beginnings of the new Yiddish Workers' Theater in the white nights of Petrograd in 1918–19. Realization of two metaphors: The director (or actor) drinks light, enlightenment, but he "talks to the lamp" (*redt tsum lomp*)[1] —Yiddish idiom meaning: has no response, no resonance. Indeed, there were no Jewish masses in Petrograd and no Jewish proletariat, a necessary prerequisite for a Revolutionary institution.

2. The isolated proletarian audience (wearing workers' caps) of what was called the "Yiddish Workers Theater" is eagerly waiting to applaud. Yet it encounters a void (according to the Yiddish idiom, *redt tsu der vant*— "talk to the wall"). Into this gray background area, a colorful theater narrative is introduced.

3. A green Chagallian animal ("cow") bursts onto the scene and takes on the play with its horns. For the October celebrations in Vitebsk, on November 8 (according to the new calendar), 1918, Chagall supposedly painted a green cow, indicating the new, revolutionary, and useful art. His students copied it and hung it all over the city (note the split in the middle of the cow, as if painted on two cardboards). Whether the story is true or not doesn't matter. Chagall retold it as part of his private mythology. The Communist bosses did not like it: "Why is the cow

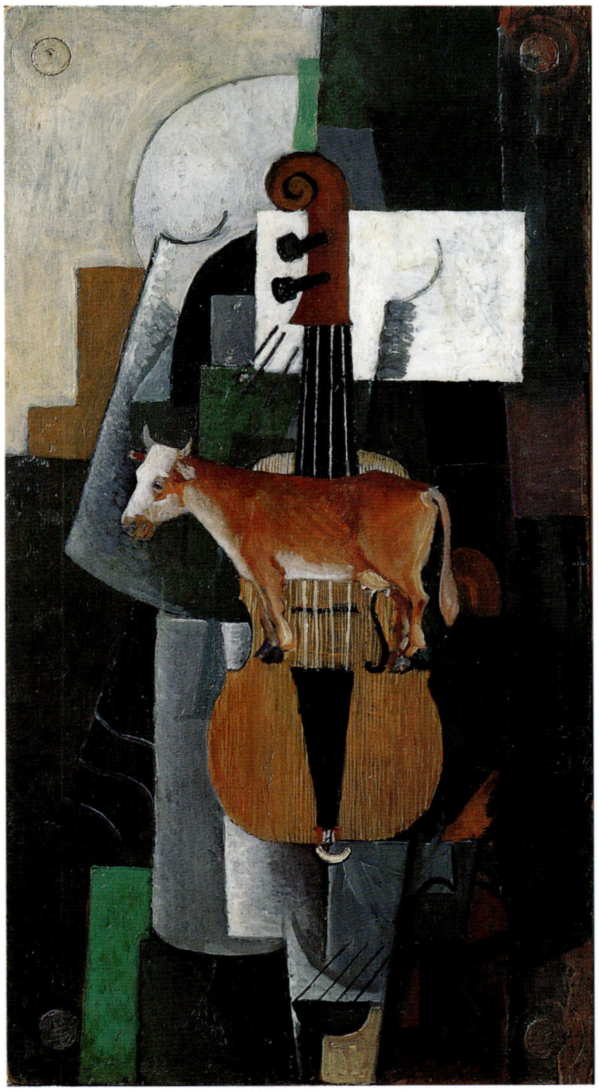

103. *Kazimir Malevich.* ***Cow and Violin.*** *1913. Oil on wood, 48.8 x 25.8 cm. Russian State Museum, St. Petersburg*

OPPOSITE: ***Introduction to the Yiddish Theater*** *(detail). 1920. Tempera and gouache on canvas, 284.2 x 784.2 cm. Tretyakov Gallery, Moscow*

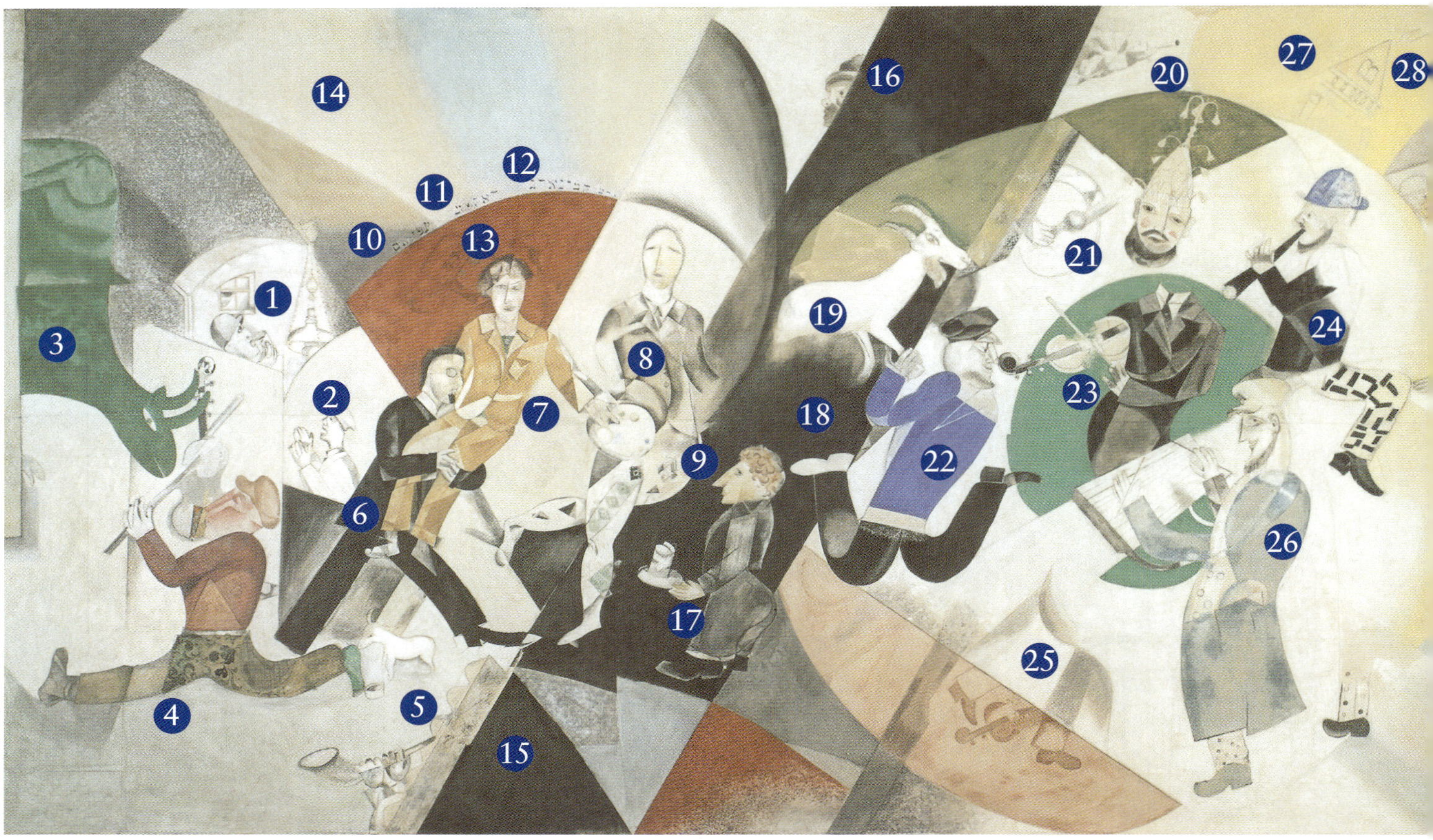

104. *Map of* ***Introduction to the Yiddish Theater****. 1920. Tempera and gouache on canvas, 284.2 x 784.2 cm. Tretyakov Gallery, Moscow*

green? What has that to do with Marx and Lenin?" (as repeated in *My Life*). Chagall often used bright green as a challenge to realism: in his first theater work, in the Petrograd cabaret *Comedians Resting Place*, he painted the faces of all the actors green; his own face is green in *I and the Village* (no. 21); and so are the faces of *The Green Jew*, 1914 (no. 18) and the violinist in the panel *Music* (no. 110) on the opposite wall of the theater. The argument that the cow represents Malevich[2] is untenable: Malevich's *Cow and Violin* (no. 103) has nothing to do with Chagall's scene. Also, in his autobiography Chagall wrote: "I often said that I was not an artist, but some kind of a cow. I thought of placing her [the cow] on my calling card."[3]

4. The leading actor, Shloyme (Solomon) Mikhoels, came to Chagall to learn the nature of Modern art (see detail, no. 106). In Yiddish, Russian, and in some other languages, to play the violin and to act on a stage take the same verb, "to play" (*shpiln*), hence the violin is a metaphor for acting: if you cannot *"shpil"* (play) you cannot *"shpil"* (act).[4] The broken fiddle indicates the impasse Mikhoels saw in the old acting and the gesture of offering it to the animal implies his willingness to learn. Chagall's avant-garde art transformed Granovky's theater and helped Mikhoels and the entire group to overcome what Chagall called "the familiar psychological realism." The folk ornament on his pants indicates Mikhoels's link to popular culture and fondness of Yiddish folklore, which he taught to the actors.

5. The goat kid may indicate that Mikhoels is a "baby"; the popular Yiddish lullaby starts, *Unter shloymeles vigele/ shteyt a shney-vays tsigele* ("Under little Shloyme's [or whatever the child's name is] cradle/ stands a snow-white goat kid"). It is sniffing the new, green, unrealistic art.

6. Abram Efros, coauthor of the first book on Chagall (Moscow, 1918), was artistic director of the Yiddish Chamber Theater in Moscow; he brought Chagall to the Director Granovsky—here he brings him literally, a realization of the metaphor. Efros strides determinedly, left foot forward (as in Mayakovsky's "Left March"), as Chagall himself used to stride in his Revolutionary paintings (in Russian *Shagal* means "to stride"—see *Cubist Landscape*, no. 31).

7. Marc Chagall, in semi-Constructivist working clothes, pointing out to Granovsky the palette of his new art.

8. Aleksey (Aleksandr) Granovsky, Director of the Yiddish Chamber Theater. Assimilated to Russian and German culture, he wears formal attire and a tie; but he

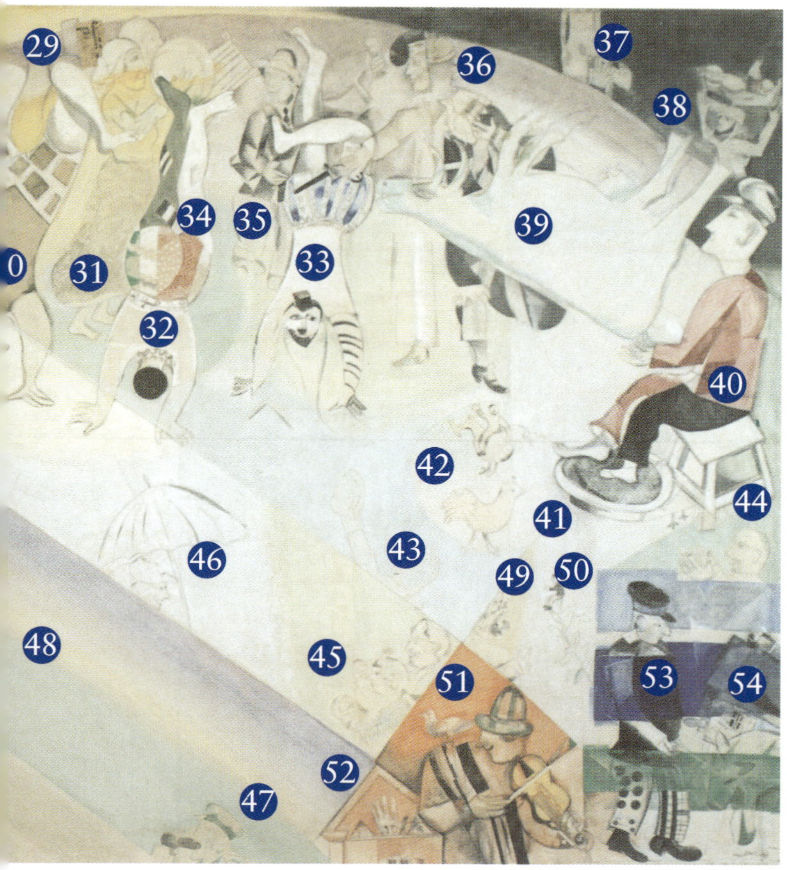

dances a quadrille, and has folk ornaments on his legs and a Star of David (see #9).

9. Star of David, representing the Jewish national mission Granovsky undertook. The triangles on his left leg are shards of decomposed stars of David, as can be seen in the *Sketch for the Introduction to the Yiddish Theater*.

10. A Yiddish inscription appears on top of the first circle, written with solemn,"square" Hebrew letters. It is conspicuously placed above the red arc that brings together the three dominant figures of the theater: artistic director Efros, painter Chagall, and theater director Granovsky (see detail, #150). The study for *Introduction* (see below, no. 137) reads unambiguously: *EFROS IKSVONARG LAGASh*.[5] In the completed mural, however, this becomes more complex. The first surprise is Efros's name, which in Yiddish texts is usually spelled as it is in Hebrew (consonants only): *APRT*, **אפרת**; but here we have the new Soviet Yiddish spelling, with all its vowels: *EFROS*, **עפראס**. His revolutionary stride underlines the message: Energy! Move with your left leg forward! (as in Mayakovsky's "Left March") Revolution! (In the state? In the theater? In art?). The other two words look like total gibberish, a collection of Yiddish letters; only if we read the text letter by letter, in the opposite direction (as if it were Russian), can we decipher the names *ShAGAL GRANOVSKY.*

On the final canvas, however, the names are distorted further than on the study. Of *LAGASh*, all that remains is . . . *AG* . . . *Sh*, with vestiges of letters in between; and even *EFROS* has only *EF* . . . *S*, with paler outlines of the rest. Inside the words, however, in place of the missing letters, there are tiny drawings: of Chagall painting at his easel and the professorial Efros reading a book. Thus, Chagall combined two systems, letters and ideograms, to represent his protagonists.

11. *LAGASh* **לאגאש** "Chagall" inverted, as if to read the Yiddish letters in the Russian direction, from left to right. Here the name is presented with dual media: instead of the second "A" we get an iconic representation of the painter, his body in the form of the missing letter A, *Alef*.

12. The inverted name of Granovsky. In the study, when read in Yiddish from right to left, it appears in full: *IKSVONARG*, **יקָסוָואנָארגְ**,and includes Hebrew vowel markers, as in traditional Yiddish books. When read in the inverted, "Russian" direction it reads: "Granovski."[6] In the final mural, however, the name is "distorted": *IKTIKTUNARG*, **יקטיקטונארג**. When read in the inverted direction, we get "Granu..." and, seeing the figure, we know who it is, the rest is redundant. When, however, we read in the Jewish direction (from right), we get twice IKT (in Yiddish, the graphic shape of a printed S **ס** is easily changed into T **ט**). IKT are the Russian initials of the "Jewish Chamber Theater" when spelled in Yiddish: *Ievreysky Kamerny Teatr*, **קאמערני טעאטר יעווריעיסקי**, the name of the theater at that time. Again, a kind of dual naming: the man, and the acronym of his theater, mirroring the linguistic duality (or should I say: trilingualism, including the Hebrew vowels).[7]

Inversions and mirror-images of words were in fashion; the Russian Futurists boasted of having invented *perevertni* (inverted rhymes). Yet Chagall's unusual spelling, with most Yiddish letters arranged from left to right, indicates the direction of the reader's walk along the canvas toward the stage. It may also indicate the new, European direction Yiddish culture was taking, symbolized in the shift of the direction of writing.

13. Behind Chagall, on a red, revolutionary background, appear the tablets with the Ten Commandments (abbreviated) and various synagogue objects and ornaments: on the upper right, a lion; on the lower left, a Constructivist rendering of the synagogue bimah (reading stage). Those indicate the tradition of Jewish ritual art that stands behind him, as symbolized by his "great-grandfather" Chaim Segal, the eighteenth-century painter of the Mohilev synagogue. Under the tablets, Chagall's ubiquitous umbrella, in Yiddish: *shirem*, as if saying: *zol undz got bashiremen*, "may God protect us" (see *Cubist Landscape*, no. 24).

14. Areas of autonomous colors, as if radiating from the event, a huge rainbow after the Flood; yet representing neither the sky nor the order of colors in a rainbow (see also the dove in #39 and the rainbow in #48).

15. Man blowing a *shofar* (ram's horn), emerging from a wooden synagogue ornament, as if heralding the new year, the new time.

16. Half a head peeping out from under the black stripe, to observe this new scene. As in other missing limbs in this mural, it may be the head of the *shofar* blower (#15).[8]

17. According to Chagall's autobiographical accounts, the janitor, Efraim, served him milk mixed with water while he was working on the murals. Both strains may be seen in the glass.

18. Black stripe in a Suprematist shape, paralleling Efros's rectangular leg, and marching upward and toward the stage. Yet its two-dimensionality is undermined and ironized, from above and beneath.

19. The goat, the cheapest milk-giving animal, is a symbol of Jewish *shtetl* poverty. Like the goats Chagall painted on both sides of the theater curtain, the goat opens the show.

20. Winged angel with trumpet, announcing the event.

21. Drummer. The play begins: playing music as a metaphor for playing on a stage (acting), in the form of a *klezmer* band, the traditional Jewish musicians (see *The Wedding*, no. 35). Here: drum, violin, clarinet, and cymbalom. The musicians are elated and defy realism; their limbs are scattered, above and below the geometrical planes.

22. Mikhoels performing his acrobatics, his right hand holding and leading Chagall's goat. On his white belt are subtle drawings of *shtetl* images; a lace pattern below it. Little figures drawn by Chagall are also on his chest and throat.

23. Violinist in formal dress with clown hat. His head flew off to the sky and his legs may be in (#25).

24. Clarinet player. On his pants, above all the black stripes, Chagall's most intimate personal signature, unrelated to the theater: Yiddish inscriptions in written letters. It is a list of Chagall's family, mostly using the Yiddish rather than the Russian forms of their names: *feyge ite* [mother], *yhzkl* ["Yikhezkel," in Hebrew—father], *mshe* ["Moyshe," Marc's Hebrew name], *blanh* ["Bella-Anna"—Anyuta], *roze mariyaske* [sisters], *zisle* [sister Zina], *leyke mane* [the twin sisters Liza and Manya], *berte* [his wife], *ide* [daughter Ida] *mnahem mendl* ["Menakhem-Mendl," grandfather, spelled half-Hebrew, half-Yiddish],[9] *ba* [unfinished], *basheve* [grandmother], *avrhm neyah* [uncles Avrohom, Noyak, or Abraham and Noah as pronounced in Chagall's Yiddish dialect].

25. Violinist in tailcoats, like in *The Wedding* (Paris, 1911), climbing under the square surface.

26. Cymbalist (playing a cymbalom), as in *The Wedding* (Paris, 1911). Some identify him as Lev Pulver, major composer and musical director of the Moscow Yiddish Theater, but in 1920 he was not yet around.

27. Facade of Petrograd synagogue where Chagall was invited to paint murals for a school.

28. Little figure with umbrella, representing Chagall in his satisfied state (see also #46 and the description of the painting *Cubist Landscape*). Umbrella in Yiddish: *shirem*; the figure is *bashiremt*, protected by destiny (literally, "covered with an umbrella").

29. A collage of newspapers or posters with headline letters. In pale: *BAVEGUNG* (cultural or political "movement"); in bold: *IDISHE K[ultur]* ("Yiddish culture") and perhaps *[tea]TR*.[10] Chagall refers apparently to the cultural movement Kultur-Lige, which organized Yiddish schools, literature, art, and so on. Chagall joined its Moscow chapter (see also #34).

30, 31, 32, 33. The three clowns still wear religious insignia but stand the old Jewish world on its head, topsy-turvy, as in Sholem Aleichem's fiction. The old, religious Jew drawn in on the left seems to chastise them with a pointing finger.

31. Religious Jew in skullcap, turned clown. On his belt, a Star of David ornament and an inscription in Yiddish written letters: *ikh bin akrob[at]* ("I am an acrobat").

32. Jew in the most solemn moment of prayer, standing on his head (see detail, #151). Stars of David appear among the geometrical figures on the clown's pants. Around his waist, in written letters, a Yiddish inscription: *ikh balavezekh ikh* ("I frolic I," or: "I play pranks, am mischievous, have fun").[11]

33. Between the middle clown's legs (see detail, #152), a printed message, listing the three classical Yiddish writers, as celebrated by Kultur-Lige and printed on their stamp: *Mend[ele-] Abramovitz Peretz Sholem Aleichem*; as well as two younger writers, friends of Chagall: *Bil [Bal-Makhshoves?] [der] Nis[ter]*. It was modern Yiddish literature that showed the vitality of Jewish folk life and saved its images in a secular age by turning the austere religious world into a source of folklore and culture. Rather than a coarse gesture, the note seems to be a banner raised above the overturning of the old, religious world. Or maybe Chagall had no other place to stuck it in on top of the acrobatic show.

34. Two actors, playing the tambourine and the lyre. The first, dancing barefoot, was identified as Sara Rotboym.

35. Figure in formal dress, toasting the performance. Sometimes identified as Benjamin Zuskin, the second most important actor of this theater, but Zuskin apparently joined the theater later.

36. Dual figure probably representing Uriel Acosta. The German playwright Karl Gutzkow's drama *Uriel Acosta* was performed by Granovsky's theater in Petrograd and was being prepared for a new production in Moscow. Acosta (1585–1640) was a Converso ("Marano," a Jew forcibly converted to Christianity) born in Portugal who moved to the Netherlands, returned to Judaism and had himself circumcised in his twenties. He wrote a philosophical book against religion and was excommunicated and persecuted by the rabbis in Amsterdam. He recanted, and eventually shot himself with a revolver. His dilemma of how to be a free and thinking Jew without being religious was close to the situation of Chagall and the secular Yiddish theater. The revolver, the Spanish attire, and the circumcision scene (see #37) support this hypothesis. The duality and ambivalence are also expressed in the double face, male/female shoes, black/white half-figures, classical-aristocratic/modern-folkstyle dress, and the gender ambivalence of a "feminine" figure undergoing circumcision (see #37).

The two half-faces of Uriel Acosta are of the painters Nathan Al'tman and probably David Shterenberg (including his bulbous nose and little moustache). Shterenberg was head of IZO, the Section for Graphic Arts of the People's Commissariat of Education, and Al'tman was a member of the board. They organized a branch of Kultur-Lige artists in Moscow (and later, an exhibition of the three, including Marc Chagall). Chagall saw them all as ambivalent between Jewish and general culture.

37. Two hands hold an instrument of circumcision. This fits the hypothesis of Uriel Acosta, who underwent circumcision in his twenties. It could also indicate the Jewification of the new art. The body, seemingly of a pregnant woman, appears later in Chagall's portrayals of Jesus Christ (e.g., *Resurrection*, 1937–48) and may contribute to the ambivalence expressed in Acosta's figure (see #36).

38. The waiter, bringing food to the celebration, looks like photos of El Lissitzky at the time. Chagall, furious with Lissitzky's "betrayal" by joining Suprematism, teaches him a lesson in real art. It is a realization of the idiom *Er meg undz badinen* ("He may serve us"), meaning, "he is not of our class."

39. Chagall's cow is happy, frolicking upside down, like the inverted Jewish world. It ran out of its green "blood" (or Chagall ran out of paint, as he later complained when asked why he left the Soviet Union) in 1922. Its avant-garde mission is fulfilled, and its horns are crowned with a dove, signaling that the Flood is over (see also the rainbow, #14 and #48).

40. The identity of this figure is disputed. It is probably the director Granovsky, resting satisfied after the performance. Soaking feet in a bowl of cold water is both a way of resting after long work and a means to keep alert (practiced by religious Jews while studying all night).

41. In spite of the joy, the whole thing stands "on chicken legs" (*oyf hinershe fislekh*), i.e., on a shaky foundation.

42. Yet chickens are domestic animals, one of Chagall's emblems of the Jewish world. In the enclave connected to the chicken feet, we see a Jew riding on a rooster with another Chagall emblem, a fish, in his mouth.

43–44. Ovations from the audience, echoing #2, #3.

45. Bella Chagall and daughter, Ida, along with Yikhezkel Dobrushin, Yiddish writer and literary dramaturge of the theater, come to greet Chagall.

46. Happy Marc Chagall, protected by destiny (*bashiremt*, covered with a *shirem*, see #28).

47. Perhaps, in view of the new art, the enemies may shut up (literally, "stop their mouth," *farshtop zey dos moyl*—a Yiddish idiom). It seems to be Malevich, paralleling Lissitzky in #38.

48. Another area of the rainbow after the Flood (see #14 and #39).

49. Chagall's parents, emerging from the past to greet Marc, who climbed a treetop.

50. Marc Chagall, as a religious boy in a hat, greeting his parents. He sits like a free bird on a tree (the Yiddish idiom, *fray vi a foygl*, "as free as a bird").

51. Is it Chagall himself as a happy boy playing his art, and preoccupied with music/art (Yiddish idiom: "his head is in the music") with the dove descending to his shoulder after the Flood (see #39)?

52. Emblem of Jewish architecture, as in a synagogue (see #27) or on a gravestone monument; a hand inscribed *PN* (*po nikbar*, "Here is buried") as on Jewish gravestones. It may also mean the end of the old religious world (Lissitzky used this hand with *PN* in a famous poster). In triangles on both sides, the letters *AT* (Yiddish Theater) placed in the Russian direction, symbolize the new "Temple of Art" that Granovsky planned to erect in the Yiddish theater.

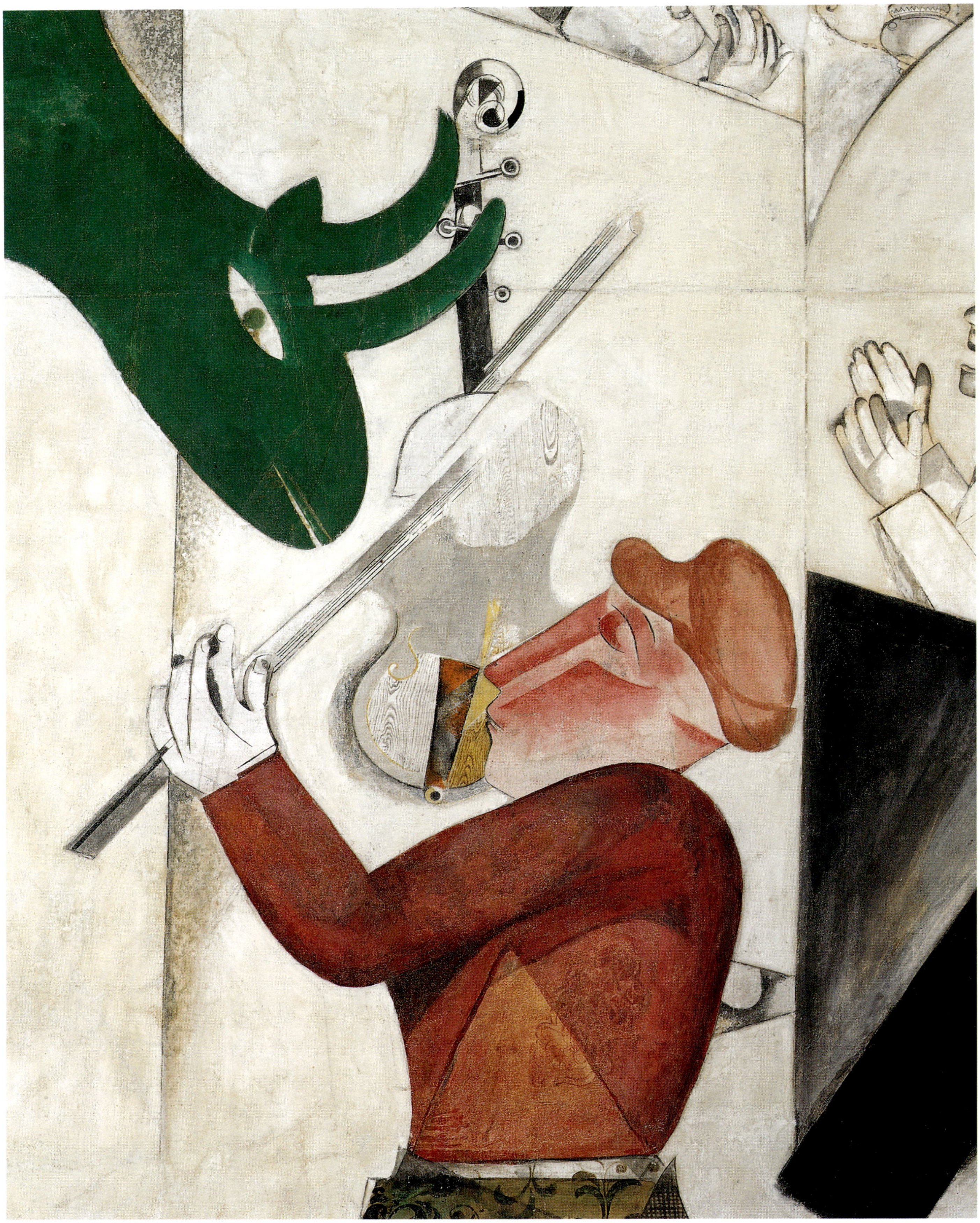

105. ***Introduction to the Yiddish Theater*** *(detail). 1920. Tempera and gouache on canvas, 284.2 x 784.2 cm. Tretyakov Gallery, Moscow. See Guide's note #4.*

53. Circumcised boy peeing on a pig at the shaken Old World. (A pig is "unclean" and a taboo, non-Jewish animal, representing the gentile world). The high school uniform hat (as in *I and the Village*) and the clown's pants apparently represent the boy Marc himself, dreaming to excel even though he is a mere Jew, as the Yiddish idiom says: *oyf tselokhes ale sonim* ("in spite of all the enemies [who are denigrating the Jews]"). This is not an anti-Christian statement, as some suggested, but an expression of Jewish pride and achievement, using folk stereotypes of a divided world.

The *Introduction* is a celebration of the new Jewish art, both in painting and in theater. In his manifesto *Leaves from My Notebook* (published in Yiddish in Moscow, 1922), Chagall wrote: "For myself I know quite well what this little nation can achieve. Unfortunately, I am too modest and cannot say aloud what it can achieve. . . . When it wanted—it showed Christ and Christianity. When it wished—it gave Marx and Socialism. Can it be that it won't show the world some art? It will! Kill me if not."[12] Because of the chauvinistic message, he cannot say it aloud (i.e., only publish in a Yiddish journal), hence the images in the corner of the painting are painted over or crossed out with blue and green stripes. Yet, as a true cosmopolitan, in the manifesto he speaks not of Jewish but universal art.

54. Family house in Lyozno, where his grandfather climbed on the roof and ate sweet carrot stew (*tsimes*), according to the idiom: *Meshugener, arop fun dakh*—"crazy man [creative genius], get off the roof!"—a repeated emblem in Chagall's paintings. The ladder is there, but the crazy/creative man, clearly, left the roof to create great art.

STUDY FOR THE INTRODUCTION TO THE YIDDISH THEATER

The small *Study for the Introduction to the Yiddish Theater* (no. 108) maps out the *Introduction* (no. 95) in the greatest detail (see interpretations above). It clearly shows the well-planned and precise work Chagall made toward his seemingly chaotic or "surreal" effect. The geometrical background shows two strong movements of straight lines from lower left to upper right, toward the stage, while the final product exhibits more of an open W structure. In the finished mural, the colors are more elaborated and somewhat changed, and the upper left corner is filled in. In the sketch, however, the names of the three protagonists (#10, #11, #12) are written in full, in Yiddish with Hebrew vowel markers, as in old Yiddish texts. As the markers show, Chagall did write what is in Yiddish: *IKSVONARG* in the opposite, Russian direction, despite the Yiddish letters: יקְסְווְאנֶארֵגְ (i.e., "Granovsky" spelled from left to right, as in Russian). But he called himself: LAGASH, here and in other places, and wrote it in this order. Unlike the murals themselves, Chagall succeeded in getting the study out of Russia. Although later dated "1919," it could obviously not be made before the fall of 1920, when Chagall worked for the Moscow Yiddish theater.

THE FOUR ARTS, OR THE FOUR JEWISH MUSES

The director of the Yiddish Chamber Theater, Aleksandr Granovsky worked with Max Reinhardt in Germany and, in that tradition, developed a conception of the theater as a *Gesamtkunstwerk*, a polyphonic, multimedia event encompassing all the arts and precisely choreographed by the director. The actors had to be musical acrobats and, indeed, were called "comedians" in the medieval tradition. As one historian of Soviet theater observed, "while they borrowed much from Meyerhold—his system of biomechanics, for instance—they had nothing in common with his intellectualization of theatrical form"; they rather expressed "the inherent color and richness in the Jewish character."[13]

While still in Petrograd, Granovsky provided his actors with the best Russian teachers of music, rhythm and dance, "plastic movement," literature and song. Chagall's contribution was to bring to this polyphony of arts the vibrant expressions and images of the Eastern European Jewish world, thus providing the formalistic avant-garde art and theater with a fictional world, a "myth" of its own. Although Jews did not have formal painting, drama, or music in the European sense, the argument went, they had intensely meaningful and deeply experienced, authentic expressions of such artistic sensibilities.

The four arts that Chagall painted for the righthand wall of the theater hall, inter-framed with three windows, represent such folkloric traditions—the Jewish popular equivalents to *Music*, *Dance*, *Drama*, and *Literature*. These traditions were linked to significant events in Jewish ritualized life and were conducted in the mundane language, Yiddish, on the margins of the Hebrew sacred texts. Indeed, in his memoirs, which were written in Russian but published in Yiddish, Chagall does not refer to the Four Arts by their general names (as listed in the Russian invitation to the exhibition) but by the names of their traditional Jewish professions: "*klezmers*, a wedding jester, women dancers, a Torah scribe."

Music (nos. 110, 112) ["Klezmers"] is a transformation of the fiddler on the roof in *The Dead Man* via *The Violinist* of 1912–13 (no. 111). It is the same creative "craziness" in the most universal, non-lingual art—music—yet oblivious of mundane and trivial reality altogether. The central figure in *The Violinist* rises from a black stool and stands tall above the houses, the globelike glass, and the Polish *kościol* (the Russian cross has two bars, one placed diagonally). The white ground stands vertical, again stretching to a globelike surface, as in *I and the Village* (no. 21), with footprints in the snow. Only the black shadow behind the house on the right looks like a road with a perspective. A little angel in the clouds blesses the music, and three children climb on top of each other to see the miracle of the music. On both sides of the fiddler's shoulders there are little white and black cubes; they reveal Chagall's fondness of ornament. These are painted before the black square, taken from Malevich, which appears in *Music*.

Whereas the fiddler of 1912–13 is a stalky, Chagall-type figure, in *Music* he is tall (adapting to the high wall of the mural) and is truly looming above the little houses and the church of the Russian provincial town. The two rows of houses create horizontal depth between them, yet, in its vertical rise, the towering figure connects the front and back rows in a perspectival paradox. The patterns of the musician's *tallis* (prayer shawl) under the coat are translated into geometrical forms and are continued in the checkered pants (see detail, no. 113): In Chagall's eyes, Jewish tradition provides geometrical forms, thus religious form and Cubist invention are one continuum. On the upper left, Malevich's famous black square is quoted, stood on its edge among the clouds, and the Chagall-child (see map of the *Introduction*, no. 104, at #42 and #50) is hovering above the music, like a little angel. A Chagallian animal on the lower left is enchanted by the music and a little man on the upper left is praising it between the houses, while a tiny boy is defecating behind a fence. Like the musician himself, so are many of the vignettes here quotations from earlier works and verbal images by Chagall: the abandoned ladder, the free bird on the treetop, mother in the window, the little Lyozno church, etc.

Dance (nos. 114, 115) ("Women Dancers") presents a wedding dancer in a Russian peasant dress, accompanied by the instruments of a Jewish *klezmer* band. At her feet, a man stands upside down, stressing the carnival atmosphere. Outside the yellow ring and inside it are the words of the Hebrew wedding song: *kol khosn, kol kale* ("The voice of the groom, the voice of the bride"). In the upper left triangle, a worker collects the folded-up *khupa* (wedding canopy).

Drama (no. 116) ("Wedding Jester") presents a *badkhn* (wedding jester), again immensely larger than the surrounding figures. His task is to amuse the audience by reciting improvised and topical rhymed couplets in Yiddish: satirical, humorous, and often bawdy. Behind him is the purple *khupa,* and on both sides of it stand mother and father. One verse says: "Cry, bride, cry!" Indeed, the bride and groom are pale, and the women on the right bemoan the loss of the virgin. Yet the purple *khupa* (a canopy held on four pillars, only one of which is seen here) is waiting with the rabbi (or father) behind it. The painting is rich with ornaments and cubicized shapes.

Literature (no. 117) ("Torah Scribe") shows a scribe, a traditional sacred profession dedicated to the careful copying of Torah scrolls, which must be copied without a single error or blemish. He wears a prayer shawl at his holy work; yet he is writing not a Hebrew sacred text but a Yiddish folk story: "once upon a time" (*amol iz [geven]*). Yiddish literature takes over the role of religion. Above, behind the blue space, the same yearning animal, as in *Music*, moos, "ShAGALL" in Yiddish, with the last two letters A and L inverted to the Russian side. And the chair, carried by a boy in the back, as if behind the globe of this universe, has a sign: *DER T[eatr]* ("The Th[eater]").

Above the Four Arts hung a long frieze, *The Wedding Table* (no. 118), connecting the Four Arts murals. It consists of two halves, painted as mirror images (the painter literally stood on the other side of the canvas, stretched out on the floor). It may mirror the two weddings in Sholem Aleichem's sketch *Mazel-Tov* ("Congratulations!"), which closed the *Sholem Aleichem Evening* for which Chagall was commissioned to produce this work. It presents the best of Jewish traditional food without regard for any religious requirements (for example, Jews cannot have a Sabbath bread, *Khallah*, on Passover). The inscriptions read: *koshe[r le-pe]sakh* ("kosher for Passover") and Carmel (Carmel is a wine from Eretz-Israel, a Zionist gesture). Yet along with food, we are served a Chagallian living rooster, a humanized fish, soda water for digestion, and a boy in a school uniform (Marc himself, as a boy).

LOVE ON THE STAGE

The unusual painting *Love on the Stage* (no. 119) was placed in the back of the theater hall, faced by the spectators after the play. Painted in airy hues, mostly shifting between gray and silver (perhaps faded or yellowed with time), it represents a cosmopolitan dance with no overt Jewish features, an early embodiment of Chagall's universal concept of "Love": the message of the theater as art. The man and woman dancing, their faces close to each other, are interlaced with rounded geometrical bodies:

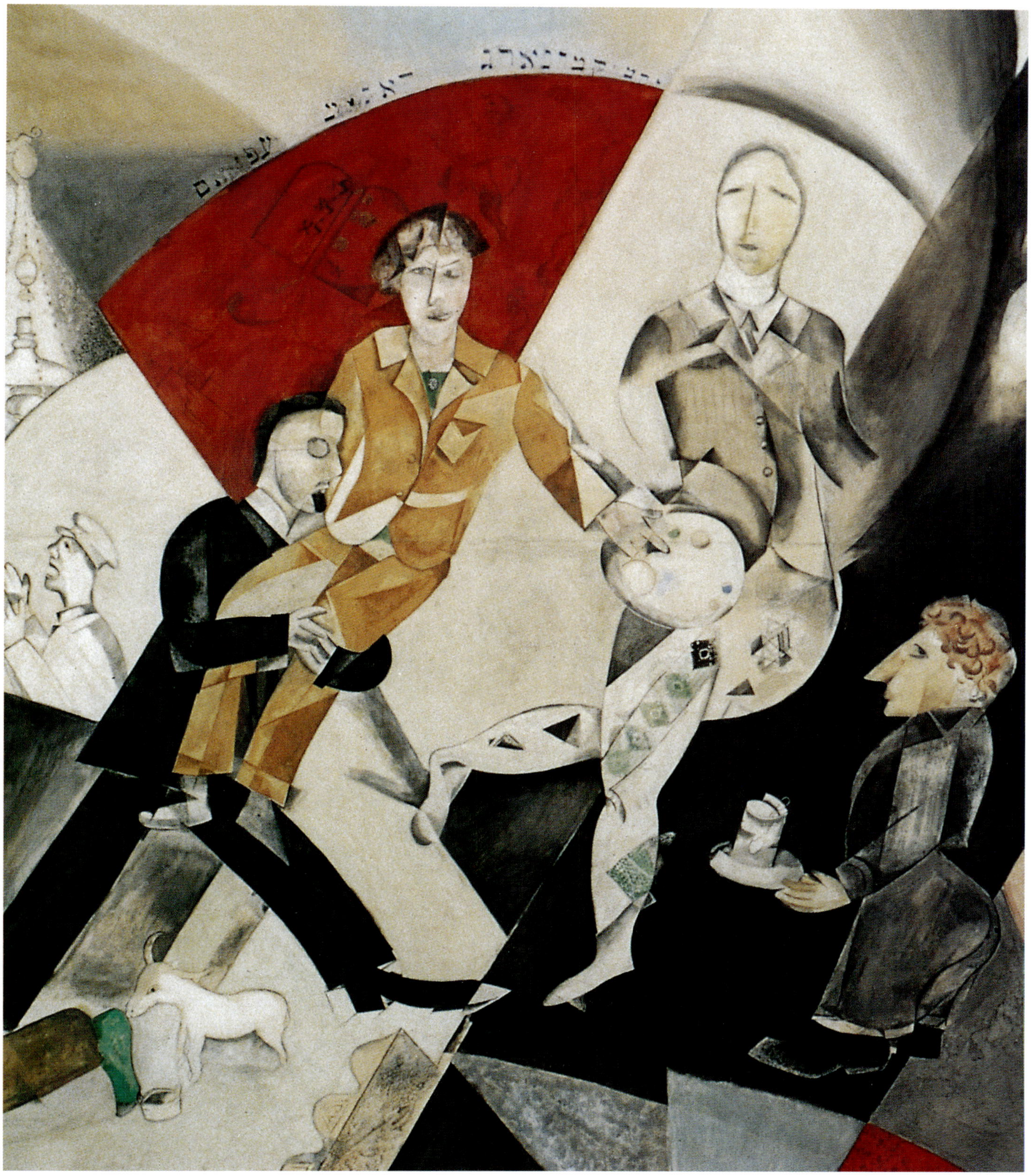

106. ***Introduction to the Yiddish Theater*** *(detail). 1920. Tempera and gouache on canvas, 284.2 x 784.2 cm. Tretyakov Gallery, Moscow. The leaders of the theater. According to Chagall, Efraim the janitor served milk mixed with water.*

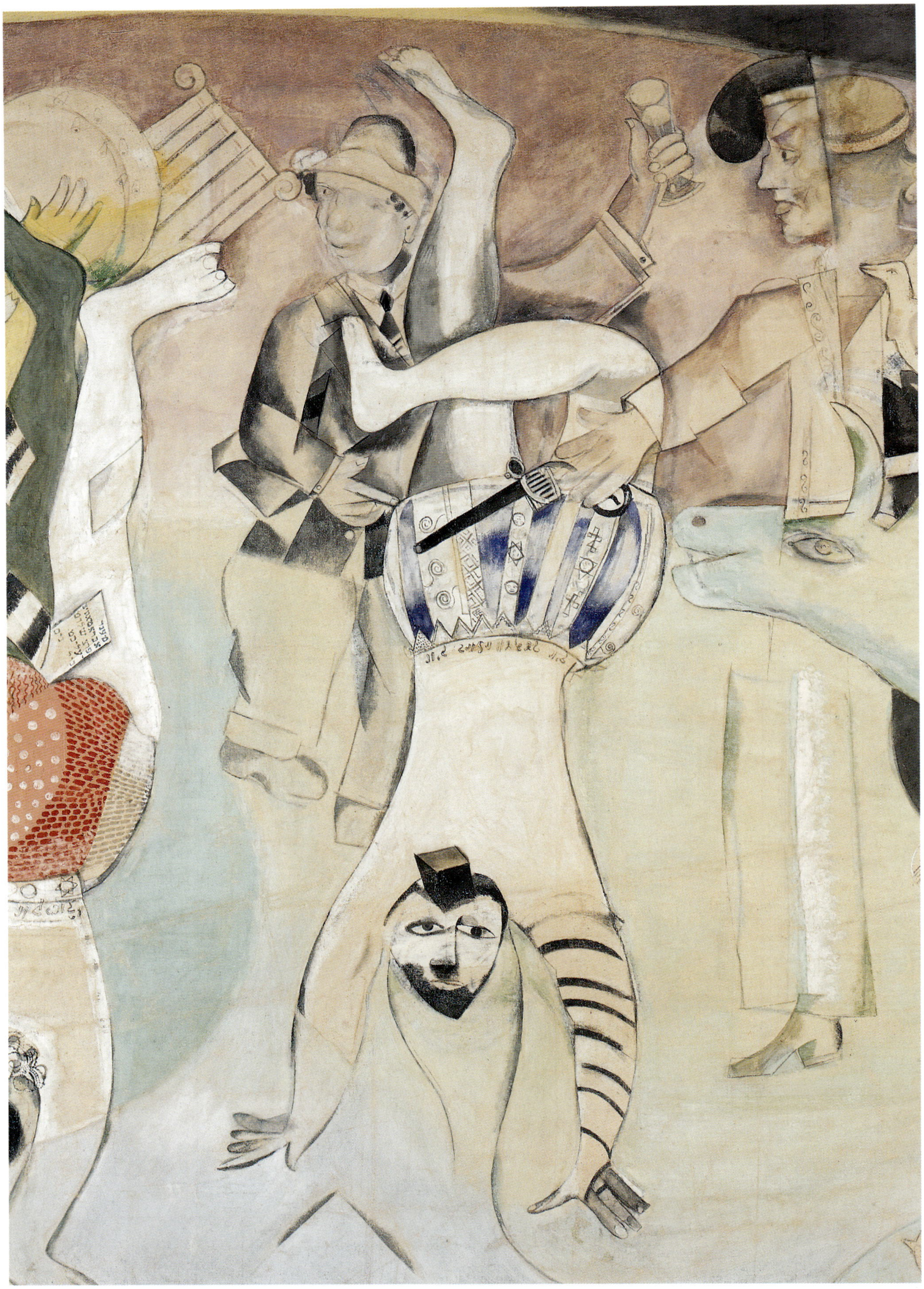

107. ***Introduction to the Yiddish Theater*** *(detail). 1920. Tempera and gouache on canvas, 284.2 x 784.2 cm. Tretyakov Gallery, Moscow*

Both kinds of figures are transparent, so it is hard to tell which is below or above. The man stands (on his legs, brown socks), embracing the woman, while her lower, disproportionately long body moves in a huge swing under a transparent dress, ornamented with whirling spirals and marked by blue socks. They float in the air although their feet are on the stage. In the lowest part, before the ramp, two Jews (iconographically wearing hats and holding a primitive kerosene lamp) are watching this cosmopolitan show. The dance is surrounded by wings of the stage and various Constructivist objects or props; in the proscenium we can see a fiddle hovering in the air and, perhaps, a piano in the lower left.

This is the modern, secular Yiddish theater, as indicated on the man's socks (see detail, no. 120). The sock on the right foot reads: *K[amer] AIDISh RTAET,* **רטאעט ק אידיש** ("Chamber Yiddish Theater"); *Yiddish* is written in the correct direction, *theater* in the reverse, and in the Russian spelling (TEATR).

On the left foot, in little vertical columns, are the names of two classic Yiddish writers:

[Y]	L						
	P	Sh	M	L	Kh	A	T
	R	L	[A]	[E]	M		
	Ts	O					

When we read the text on the socks from top to bottom and from right to left (here copied in the English direction) and interpolate the missing letters, we get: *Y. L. PERETS SHOLOM ALEKHEM A T* (Yiddish Theater).

The most striking feature is the unusual three-dimensional geometrical bodies, rounded and shaded, reminiscent of Fernand Léger or early Malevich, yet abstract and occupying most of the space. A closer look reveals Chagall's name in three huge Hebrew letters, written from right to left: *Sh, G* (occupying the upper half of the painting), and *L* (in the lower half, on the right), culminating in music. These transparent bodies both emerge through the human figures and appear on top of them (see diagram, no. 121).

Chagall was one of the major creators of the modern Jewish secular geometrical style of typefaces, deviating sharply from the traditional, holy, so-called "square" letters. He played whimsically with ever-changing calligraphic forms of the letters, freely moving from printed letters to handwritten cursive. The first letter, a large *Sh* (ש)—occupying the right part of the upper half—is like the *Sh* of *Shaday*, God's name, as written on the little box a Jew puts on his forehead for prayer, and on the *mezuzah* that is fixed on every Jewish door frame. The red tongue calls our attention to the letter. The second letter, *G,* (ג), is transformed into a person, stepping with a shoe on top of the dance. The third letter, *L,* (ל), is closer to a written form, swinging between several geometrical bodies (triangle, circle), and is also the initial letter of *libe* ("Love" in Yiddish). All this is freely framed by the wings of the stage in the back and moving toward the audience below. The critics overlooked this farewell that Chagall took from the Yiddish theater, leaving his imprint on its avant-garde stage.

UNTITLED COLLAGE

Chagall painted the murals for the Yiddish State Theater in Moscow, which opened on January 1, 1921, but he was not invited to continue. According to Efros, an impossible situation arose: Either the artist takes over the whole performance or the director regains domination over his show. In an emotional letter of February 12, 1921, to the theater management, he demanded that his work be opened, as promised, to the wider public: "The works appear to have been placed in a cage and can be seen, crowded, by at most a hundred Jews [the theater audience]. I love Jews very much . . . but I also love Russians and various other peoples and am used to painting serious work for many nationalities." He succeeded in this struggle, and the exhibit was officially opened in June 1921 as "The XXIII Exhibition of the Central Section of IZO NARKOMPROS" (Department for Art of the People's Commissariat for Education), headed by David Shterenberg. Chagall's *Collage* (no. 122) includes part of the official Russian invitation to the exhibit and is crowned with a triumphant triangle (as on Jewish graveyard monuments, e.g., in his cemetery paintings and in the lower right corner of the *Introduction to the Yiddish Theater*, no. 95). A brown triangle is pasted on another piece of the invitation paper, and on top of it, in Hebrew printed letters, the Hebrew and Yiddish word *TsDK* (*Tsedek*, "Justice")—Chagall's statement that his murals were exhibited to the public and justice prevailed.[14] The collage, a rare medium for Chagall and perhaps (as suggested by S. Compton) echoing collages by Rodchenko and Stepanova, combines geometrical cut-outs with Chagallian dotted ornaments in brown ink. The diagonal wallpaper cutout—in a 70-degree swing from lower left to upper right—represents Chagall's typical gesture of energetic striding, or marching forward. Marching was a positive, avant-garde, "leftist" act. Here, as in *Cubist*

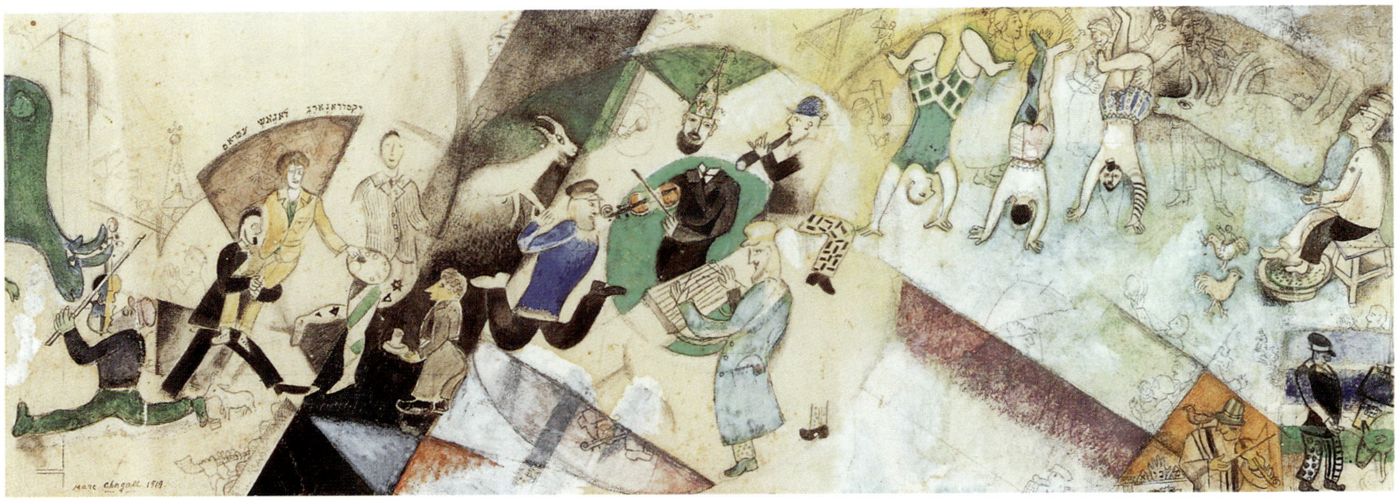

108. ***Study for Introduction to the Yiddish Theater.*** *1919–20. Pencil, ink, gouache, watercolor on paper. 17.3 x 49 cm. Musée National d'Art Moderne, Centre Georges Pompidou, Paris*

Landscape, he attempts a move toward the avant-garde art of his time, and here too, he superimposes his personal message. The date "1920" is incorrect—the work was completed in 1921.

REMEMBERING THE MURALS

The Harlequins, 1922–44 (no. 123), is a remarkable example of Chagall's "recycling" or transformation of earlier paintings in later works, whereby he remembered the exact composition of a painting, including many significant or anecdotal scenes, and yet filled it with entirely new images. He did it with such large compositions as *Revolution*, 1937 (no. 127), a later adaptation (*Resurrection*, no. 132) of which puts Jesus Christ in Lenin's place, and with *Introduction to the Yiddish Theater* (no. 95), transformed in *The Harlequins* into a different context altogether. Here a cosmopolitan scene of the secular and avant-garde theater management became sentimentally "Jewish," based on *shtetl* scenes.

This painting reproduces slightly more than the left half of the theater *Introduction*. The date 1922 probably indicates that it derived from the original theater murals, but one could hardly imagine such a small-town Jewish nostalgic scene painted in Berlin or in Paris in the twenties. The later date, 1944, seems more appropriate: It was painted or finished in America in 1944, during the Holocaust, when his audience was largely Jewish and he wanted to preserve the memory of the vanished Jewish world in Eastern Europe.

Instead of the procession of actors floating in space provided by geometrical forms (hard-edged stripes interacting with large circles) that we saw in the *Introduction*, here he supplied a semi-realistic ground under their feet, with some perspectival depth; most sharp lines have disappeared, and the figures have mellowed. Even the *shofar* blower regains his head (and is clearly a Jew in a *talis*). In the background, Chagall painted the dark houses of a small Jewish town on an early moon night where there had been no objects at all, but rather a rainbow of colors. We can see his mother's store in the center, and in front of the houses, an "outside" for the human circus to unfold; Chagall even put tables and chairs in the street.

The two lonely figures to the left (#1 and #2 in the *Introduction*—just heads and hands) now have full bodies and a table to sit at; instead of a man "talking to the lamp," a woman makes a blessing on Sabbath candles (in Yiddish, the same word, *likht*, refers to both a "candle" and "light" or "lamp") and the man drinks the blessing wine; their positions on the canvas, even the gestures of the hands are preserved, yet their functions and represented world are totally changed. Now all the figures (except for Marc and Bella) are of the old religious world. The former secular Efros wears a hat and brings Chagall not to Director Granovsky but to the symbol of love, Bella. Bella is placed in the center of the painting, at the crossing of two diagonals that form two white, semi-diamond-shaped spaces on both sides. Instead of the forward procession, marching toward the right on a very long wall, here we have one marketplace of images, with the musicians turning to the new center. Up front, an intersection of geometrical figures was transformed into a table, at which a lonely mother sits at a kerosene lamp (emblem of the Old World), glancing at the reflection of Bella's red sweater on the table.

Instead of the disjointed avant-garde mural, with competing formal and representational elements, announcing a sweeping, optimistic celebration, we have now a confined world, crowded in a narrow space of a

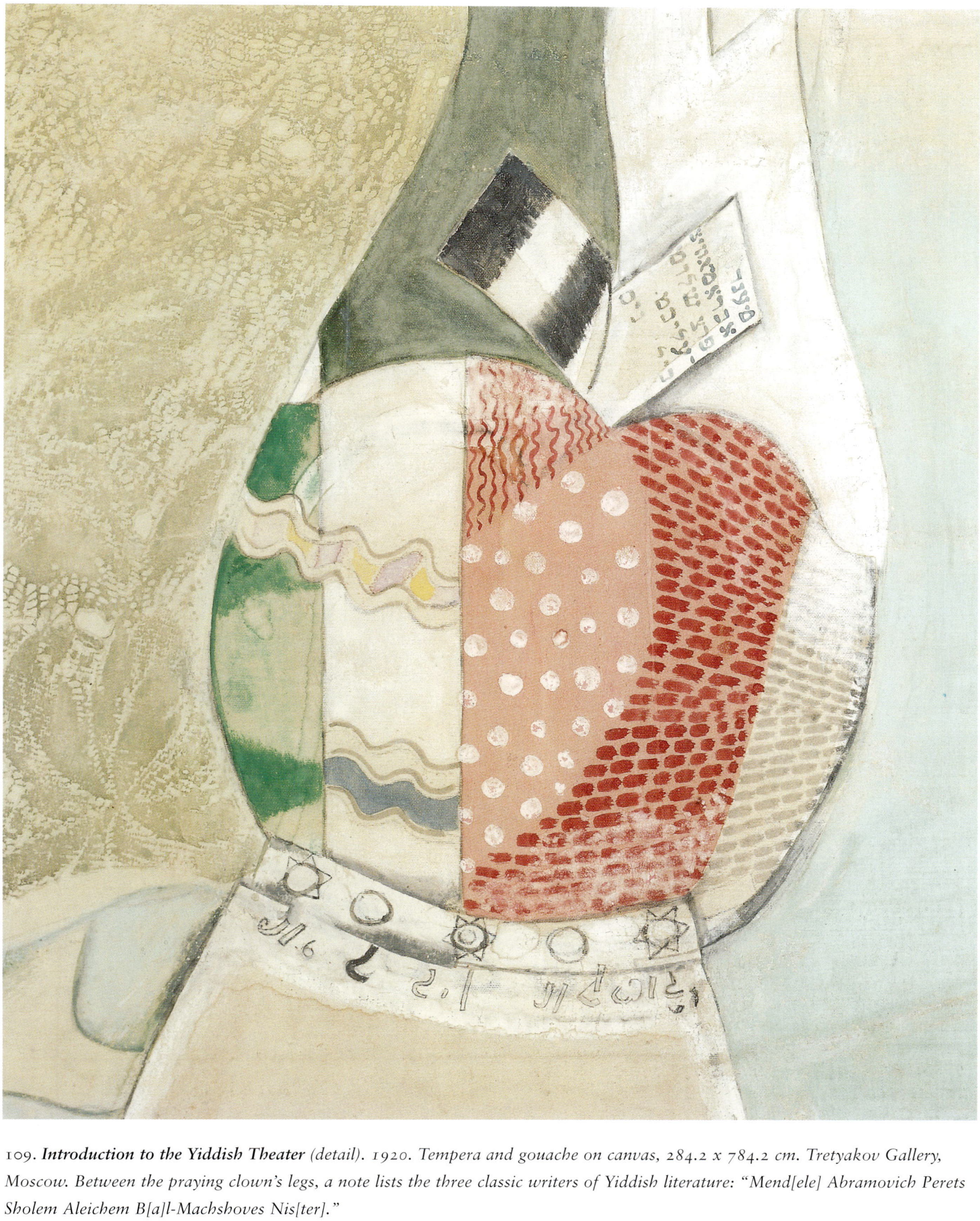

109. ***Introduction to the Yiddish Theater*** *(detail). 1920. Tempera and gouache on canvas, 284.2 x 784.2 cm. Tretyakov Gallery, Moscow. Between the praying clown's legs, a note lists the three classic writers of Yiddish literature: "Mend[ele] Abramovich Perets Sholem Aleichem B[a]l-Machshoves Nis[ter]."*

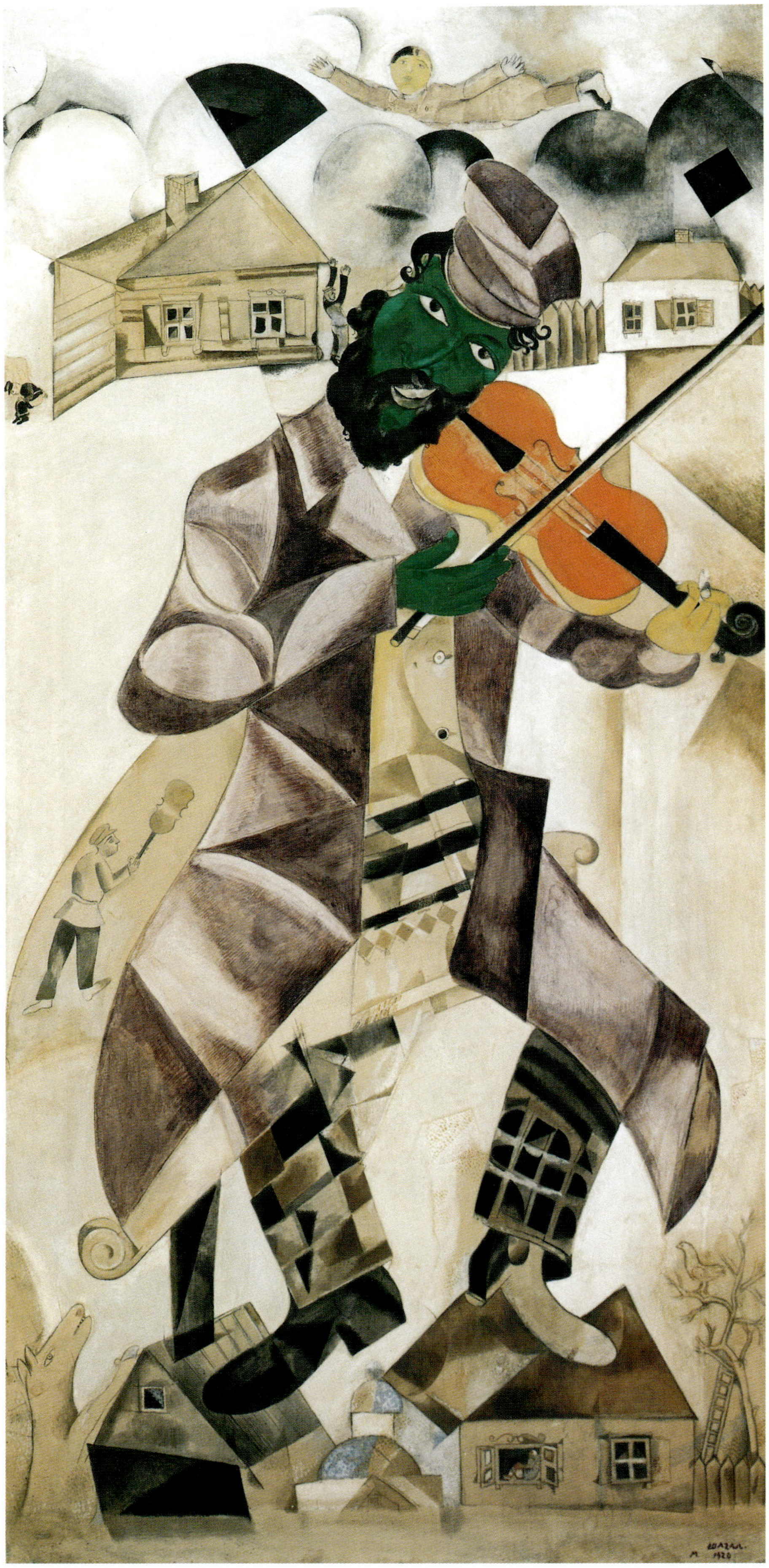

110. ***Music.*** *1920. Tempera and gouache on canvas, 212.4 x 103.5 cm. Tretyakov Gallery, Moscow. Kazimir Malevich's* ***Black Square*** *appears on the upper right.*

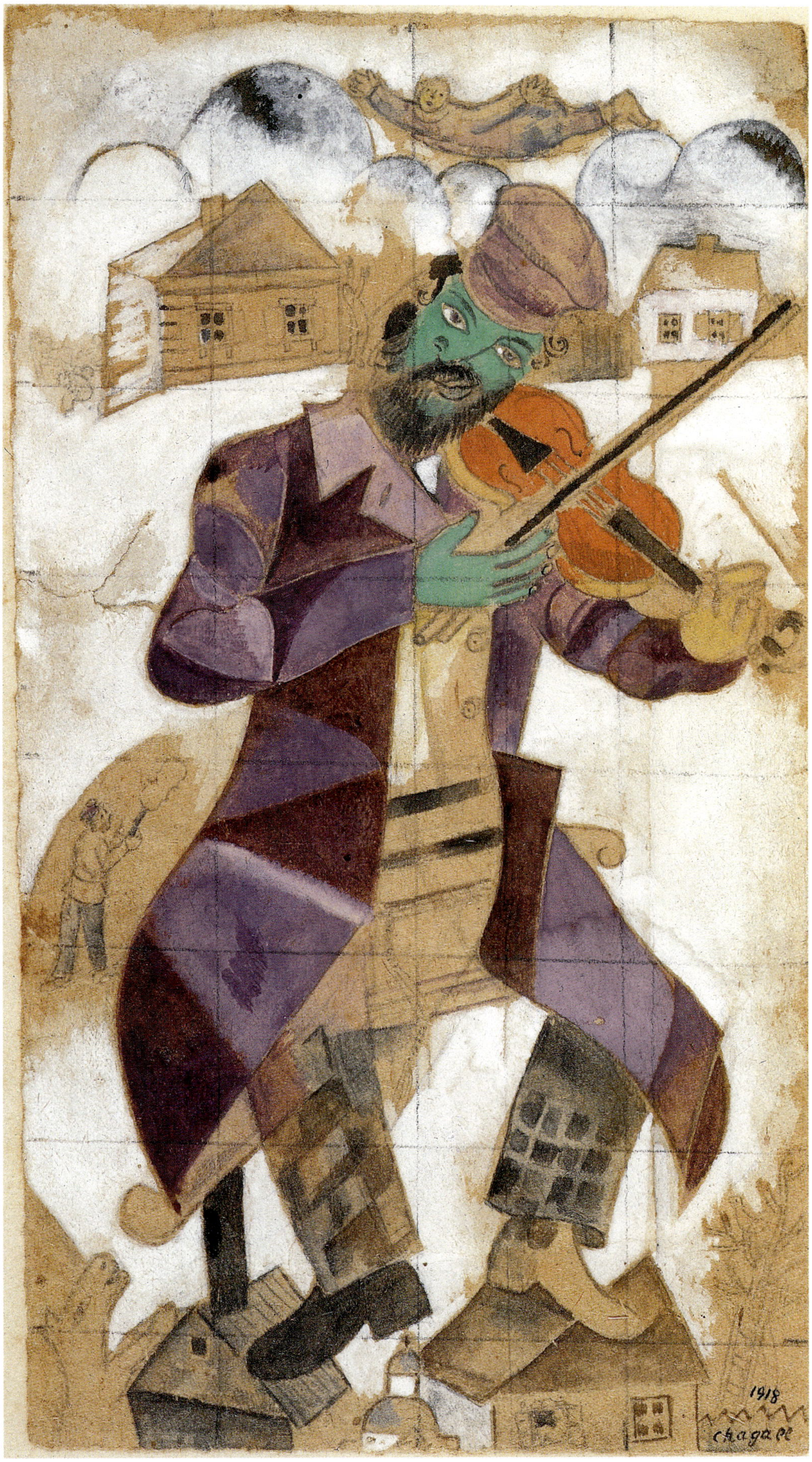

111. ***The Green Violinist.*** *c. 1923–24 [the date 1918 was added later]. Pencil, gouache, watercolor on brown paper, 24.7 x 13.3 cm. Musée National d'Art Moderne, Centre Georges Pompidou, Paris*

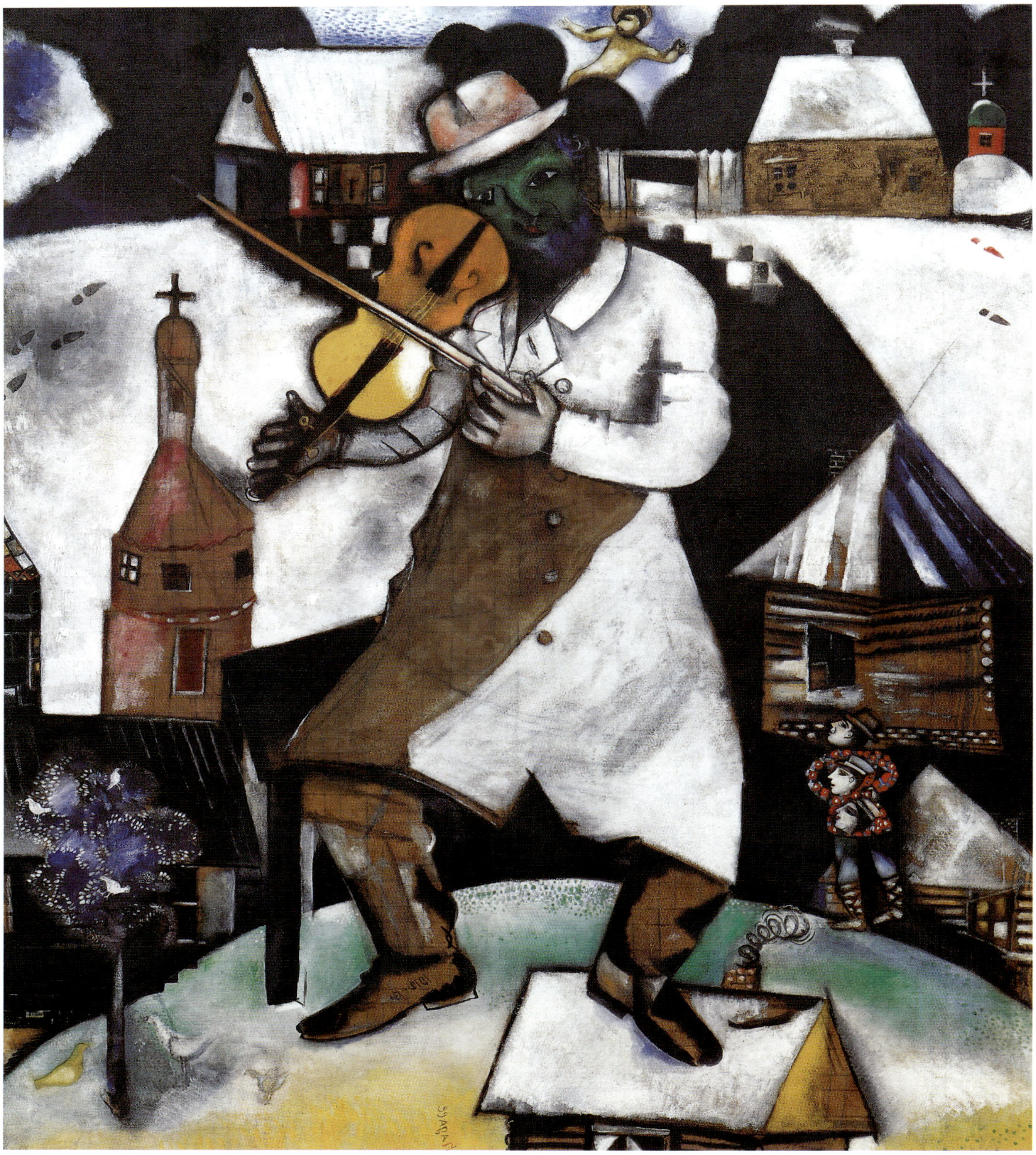

112. ***The Fiddler.*** *1912–13. Oil on canvas, 188 x 158 cm., Stedelijk Museum, Amsterdam, on loan from Netherlands Institute for Cultural Heritage*

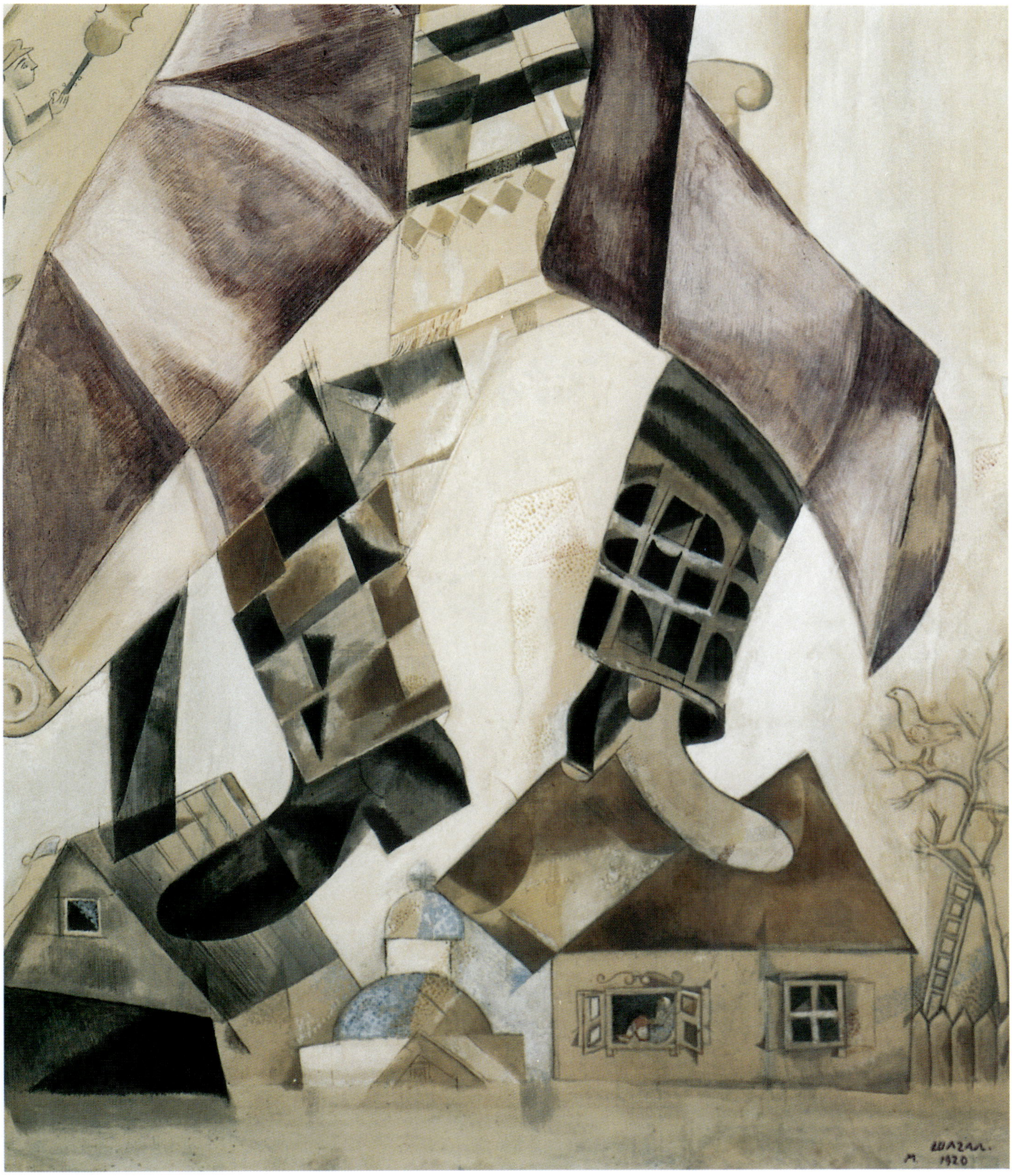

113. ***Music*** *(detail). 1920. Tempera and gouache on canvas, 212.4 x 103.5 cm. Tretyakov Gallery, Moscow*

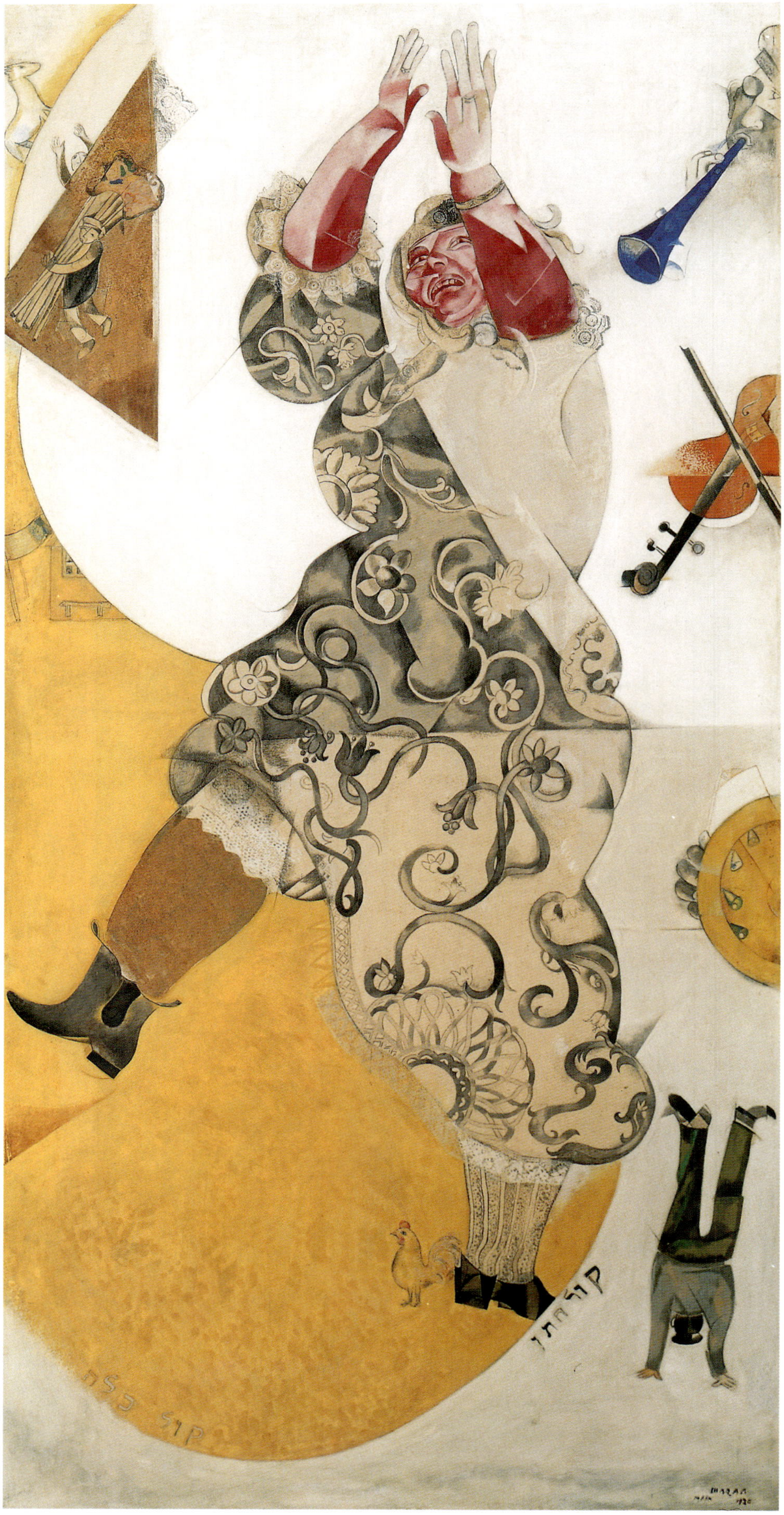

114. ***Dance.*** *1920. Tempera and gouache on canvas, 213.7 x 108 cm. Tretyakov Gallery, Moscow. On the margins of the circle:* ***Kol Kalah / Kol Hatan*** *["the voice of the bride / the voice of the groom"—from a Hebrew wedding song].*

shtetl scene. Yet it is not a continuous realistic event, functionally interrelated, but a kaleidoscope of autonomous anecdotes, a panorama of Chagall's *shtetl* world. The justification for the combinations of figures on this canvas can be found only intertextually, in the former theater mural. The vestiges of the formal elements (such as the green circle or the separated head and legs of the fiddler) add a surreal character to it all.

The acrobats on the righthand side of the *Introduction* received their reincarnation in *Three Acrobats*, 1923 (no. 124), in which their few remaining Jewish attributes are overwhelmed by a flood of ornaments. The list of major Yiddish writers multiplied into a mass of notes glued to several legs. These acrobats also appear in *Life*, 1964 (no. 125), in which they participate in a carnival of life, and in which the phylacteries of the clown on the right are barely preserved.

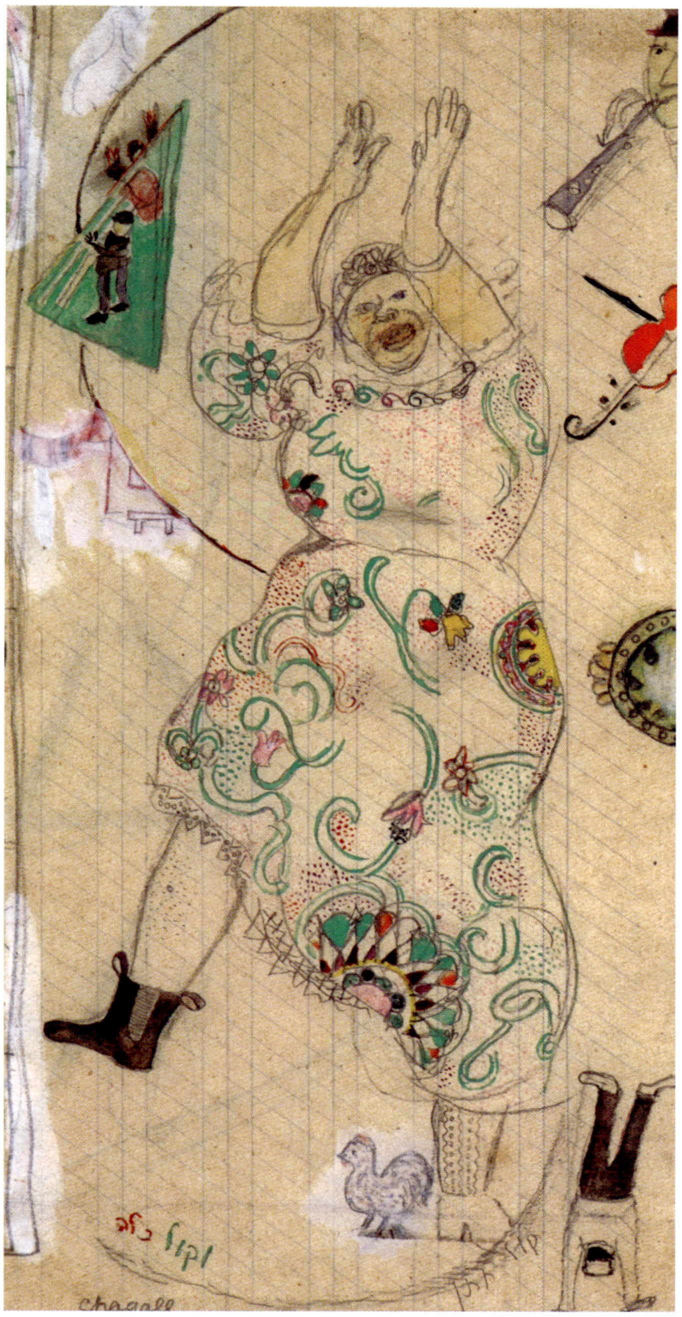

115. ***Study for Dance.*** *1920. Ink and watercolor on paper, 24.1 x 12.7 cm. Courtesy Comité Marc Chagall, Paris*

---

1. As suggested by Amishai-Maisels.

2. Amishai-Maisels has a far-fetched theory, that the cow represents Chagall's nemesis Malevich, because he also painted a cow and a fiddle; and it is green to indicate it is an immature style, because in Yiddish "green" means raw, immature (only in Yiddish?). But there is no similarity between the two cows and their situations. Green is a favorite color of Chagall's, and to assume that it means young and immature makes no sense for the old *Jew in Green* (no. 204) and Chagall himself in *I and the Village*. This interpretation implies a theory that colors have definite lexical meanings and painting is an encrypted message. And why would the hated Malevich be a central figure in the opening of the Jewish theater?

3. See *Marc Chagall and His Times*, p. 146.

4. The identity of the player as Mikhoels was recently questioned, but is recorded by Franz Meyer in Chagall's name and matches Chagall's memoirs on Mikhoels's puzzled admiration for Chagall and his conversion to the painter's Modern art, which carried the whole ensemble. Even if it is not Mikhoels, he fulfills the same function.

5. Inscriptions on the murals are rendered here in capital letters.

6. Chagall clearly wrote this long name from left to right, i.e., from the end backward, for in Hebrew a vowel marked under a letter comes after the consonant. Otherwise, if he had read it in the Yiddish direction, it would come out: ikisvonarag and would make no sense either way we read.

7. It could also be the acronym in Yiddish for "Yidisher Kamer Teatr." Indeed, the Soviet spelling of Yiddish at the time began with "A," and Chagall himself used it on the foot of the dancer in *Love on the Stage*, but this was an aberration: both the modern and the traditional Yiddish spellings are with "Y." For example, Sholem Aleichem's book *Stories for Jewish Children*, 1912, is titled: *Mayselekh far Yudishe Kinder*.

8. It seems that Chagall started to write this name from left to right, as he wrote it in the sketch, then stumbled for some reason (perhaps because, instead of *A*, he wrote *V*, as it would be in

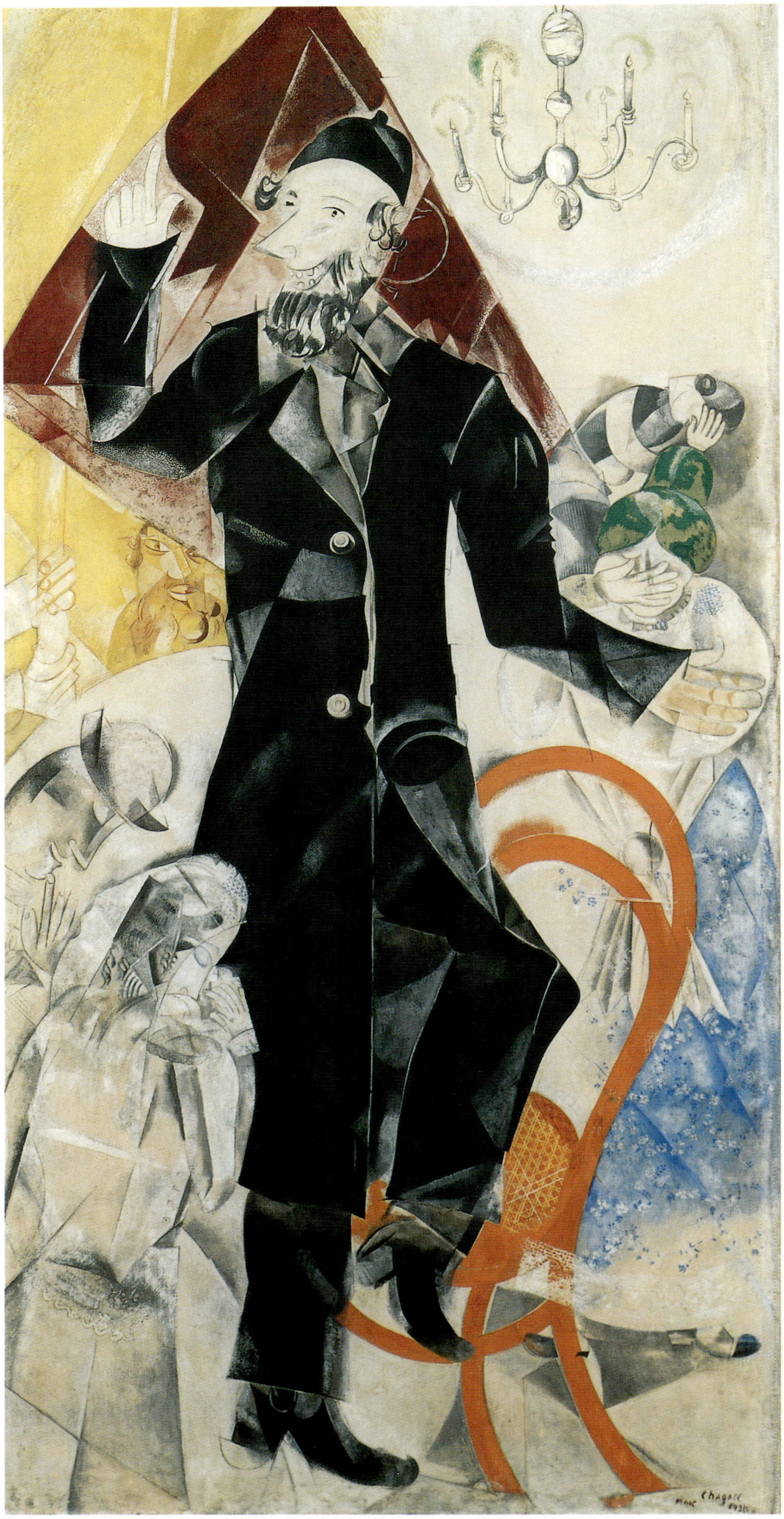

116. ***Drama***. *1920. Tempera and gouache on canvas, 212.7 x 107.3 cm. Tretyakov Gallery, Moscow*

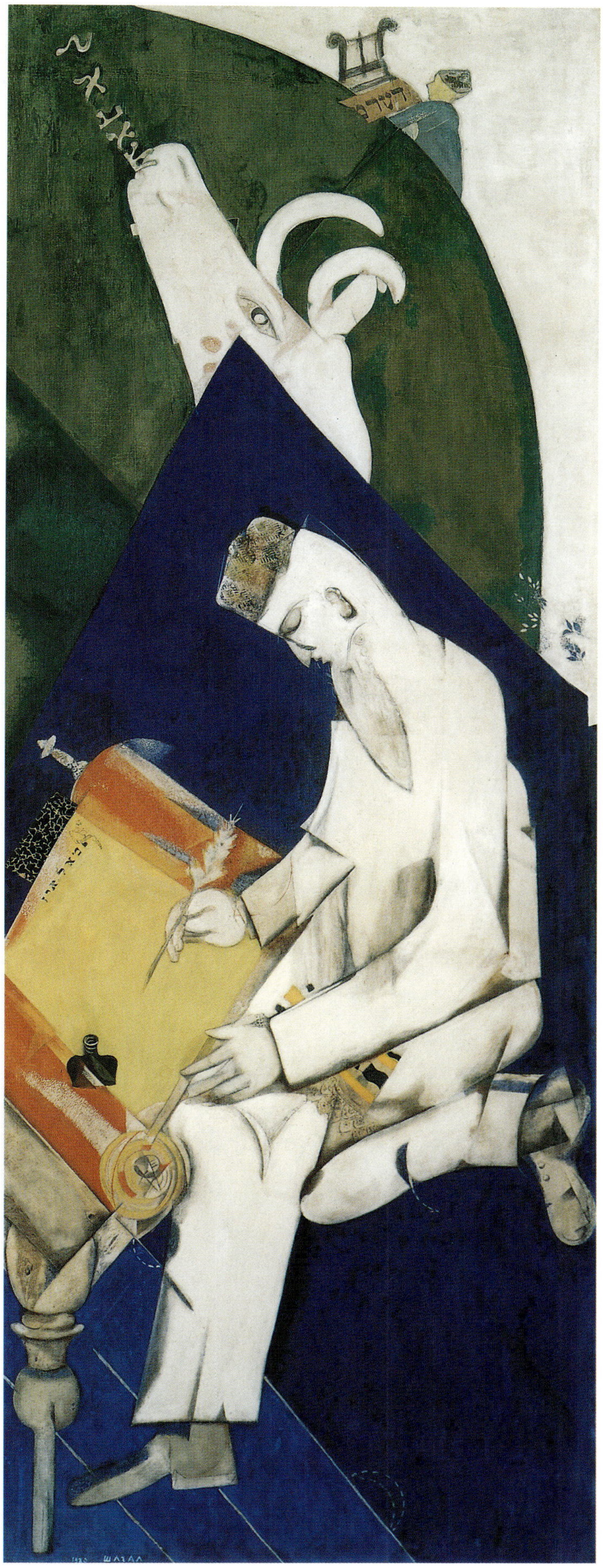

117. ***Literature.*** *1920. Tempera and gouache on canvas, 215.9 x 81.3 cm. Tretyakov Gallery, Moscow. On the torah scroll, the scribe writes in Yiddish:* **A Mol Iz [Geven]** *("Once Upon a Time"). The animal screams:* ***Shagal*** *(some letters are inverted).*

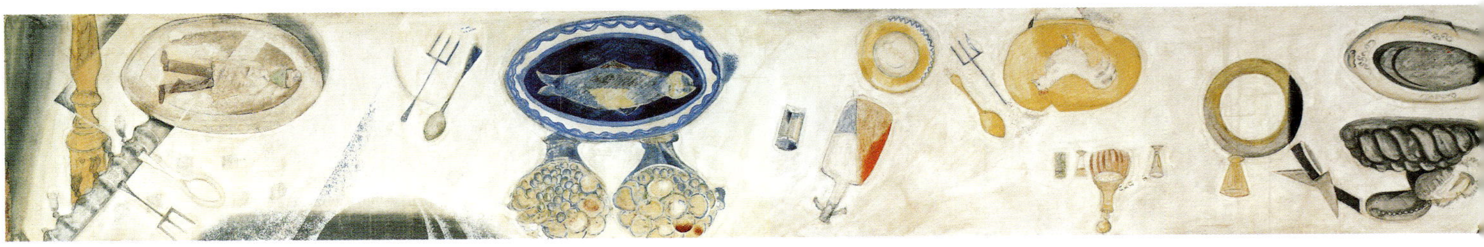

118. ***The Wedding Table.*** *1920. Tempera and gouache on canvas, 63.8 x 799.2 cm. Tretyakov Gallery, Moscow*

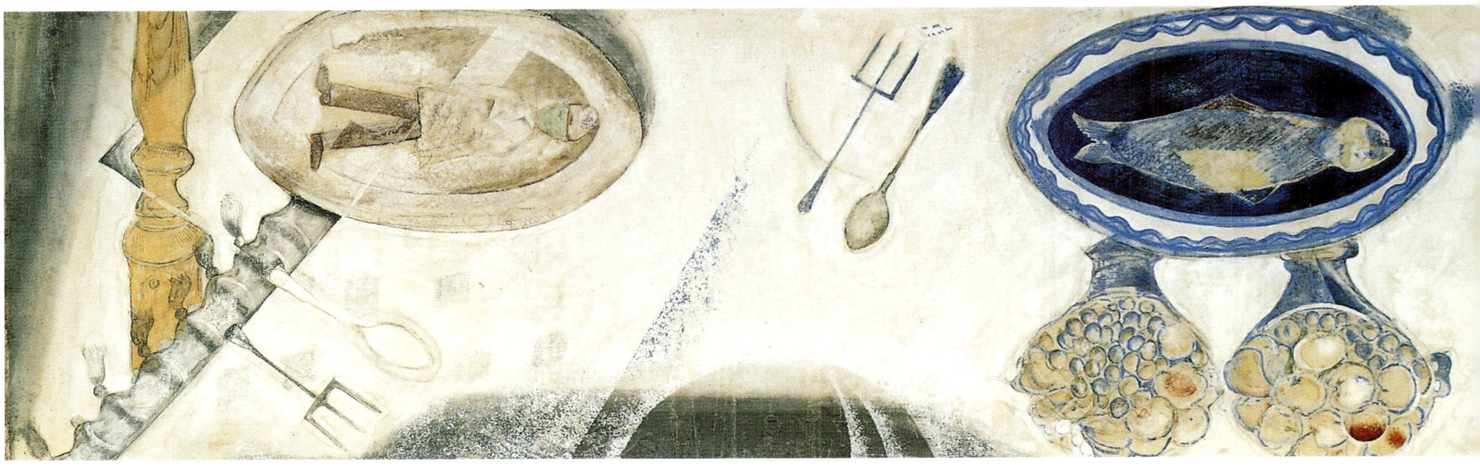

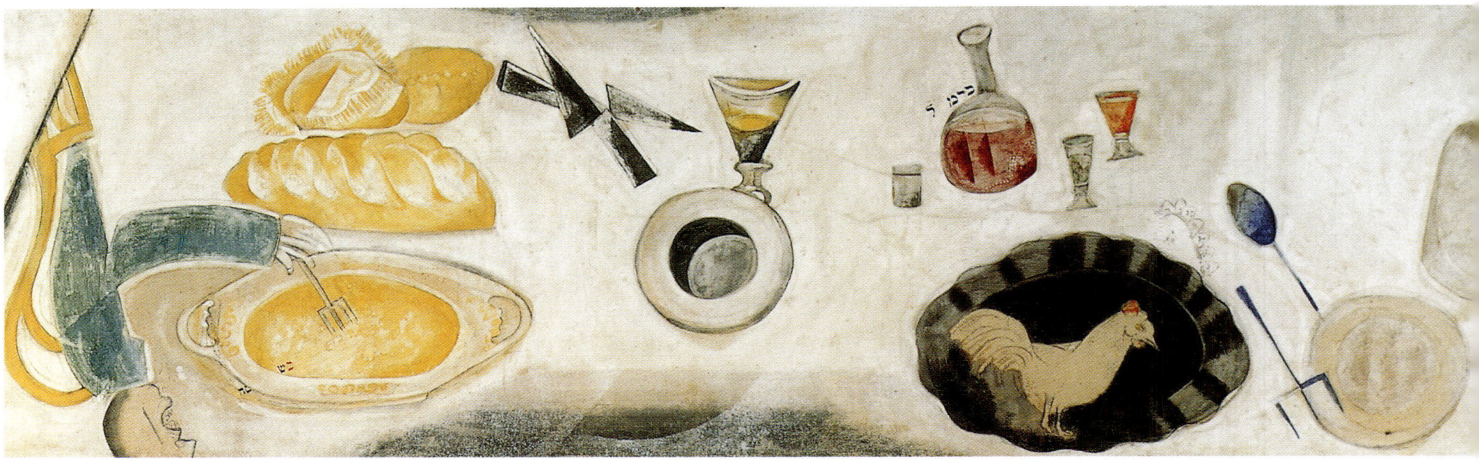

The Wedding Table *(detail). 1920. Tempera and gouache on canvas, 63.8 x 799.2 cm. Tretyakov Gallery, Moscow*

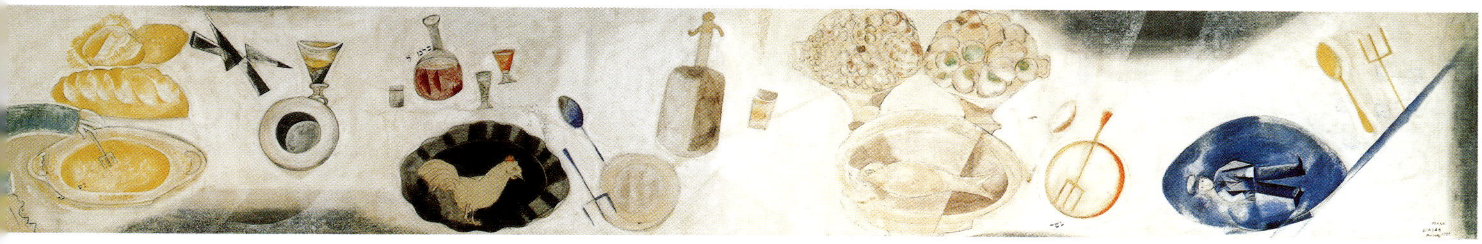

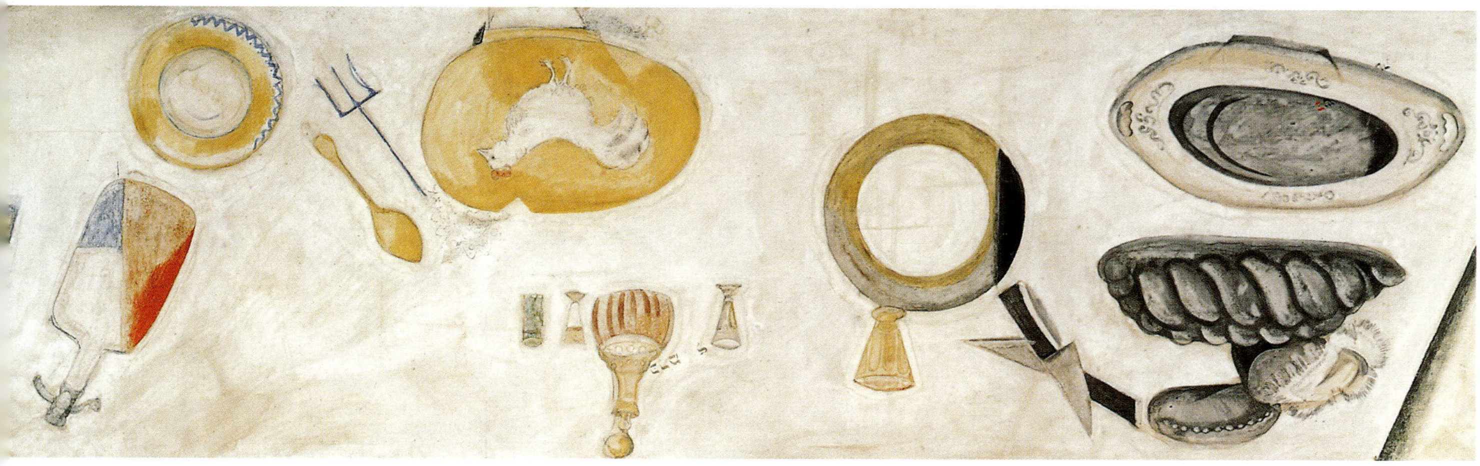

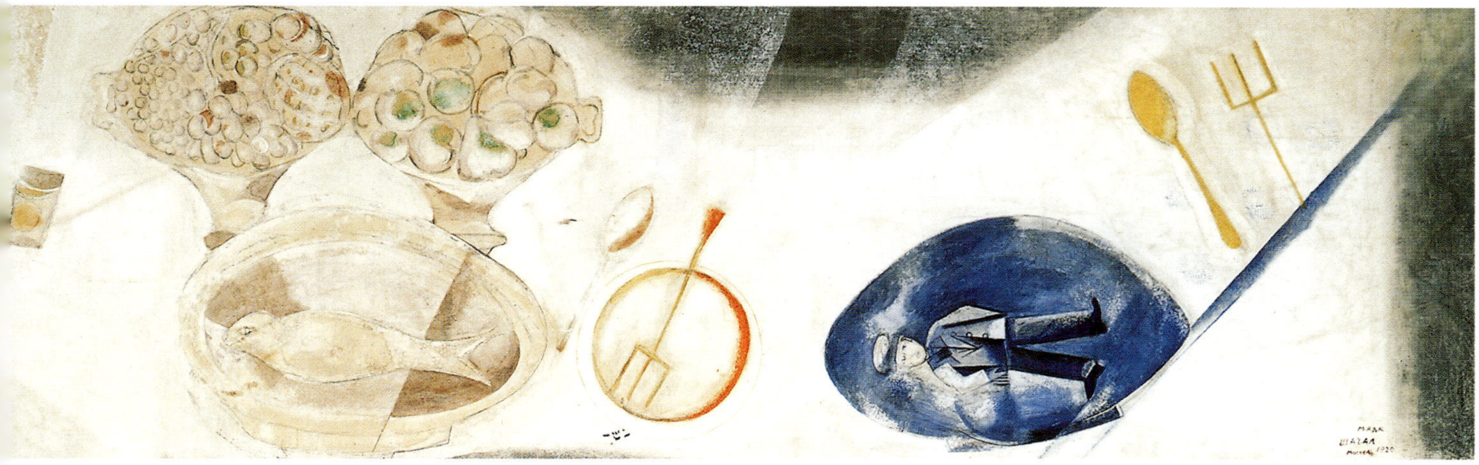

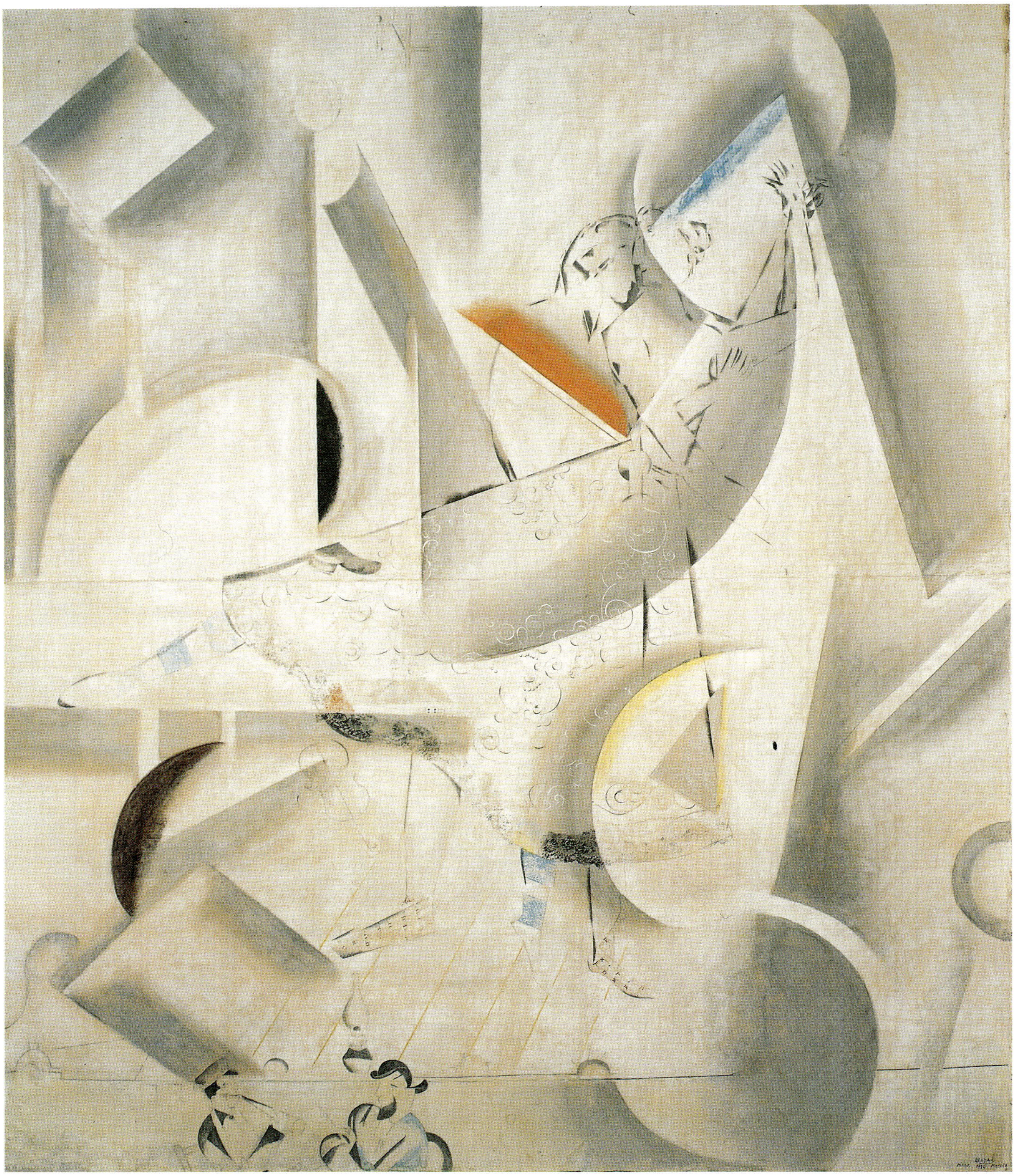

119. ***Love on the Stage.*** *1920. Tempera, gouache, and white clay on canvas, 283 x 248 cm. Tretyakov, Moscow*

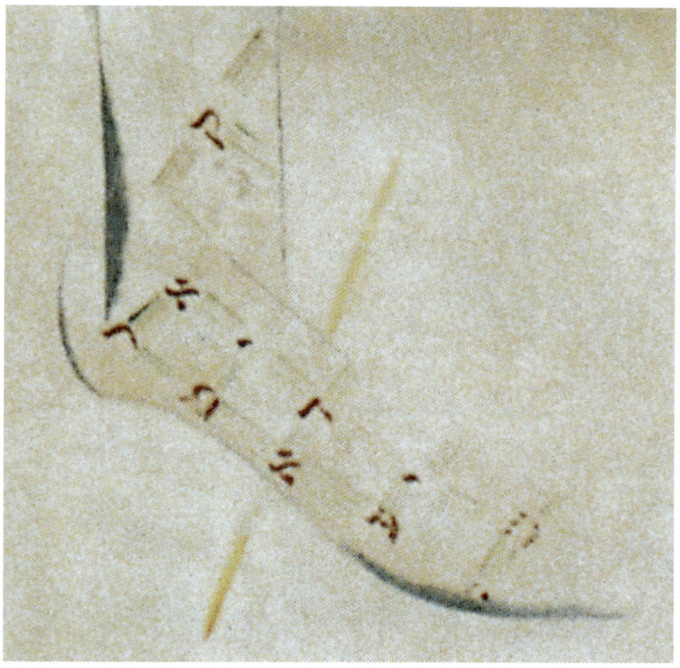

120. ***Love on the Stage*** *(detail). 1920. Tempera, gouache, and white clay on canvas, 283 x 248 cm. Tretyakov, Moscow*

Hebrew). Then he started with small letters from the right, slowly moving up toward the size of the left-side letters and intending to spell *IKS*, but discovered the graphically similar *IKT*, the name of the theater, and repeated it in order to fill the void. There is, clearly a leap upwards from the right side to the U on the left.

9. The Jerusalem catalogue describes this figure as a peasant, but why? Does a peasant blow a shofar? A peasant would have taken off his hat in this situation.

10. Amishai-Maisels thinks it is the character from *Sholem Aleichem*, but why would his beloved, living grandfather be missed from the list of the family? Menakhem-Mendl was a popular name in the area, as of the influential eighteenth-century proto-Zionist Lubavitsh Rebbe "Menakhem-Mendl from Vitebsk."

11. Some read this as "Yiddish Chamber Theater Movement," but this seems to me to be wrong: "*Yidishe*" here is feminine, while "theater" in Chagall's dialect is masculine: *teatr*, as in Russian. Here only "movement" is feminine, hence, if correct, it could only mean "the Yiddish movement of chamber theaters;" but there was no such movement, and a chamber theater with ninety seats makes hardly one. The trap lies in the letter "K" which elsewhere alludes to *K[amer]* ("Chamber") but may also allude to *K[ultur]*, as here, or to K[ultur-Lige], i.e., the Yiddish culture movement.

12. The Yiddish reflexive *ikh bàleve zikh* or, in colloquial Yiddish, *ikh bàlevezakh* ("I entertain myself," from the Russian *balovat'sia)* is written here in one word, as in Russian, yet another example of Chagall's use of Russian spelling habits in Yiddish. The repeated *ikh* (I) at the beginning and end of the phrase is a form of folk grammar, used emphatically, as in Menakhem-Mendel's speech in *Agents*. Amishai-Maisel's translation of this expression as: "I love you" has no basis in either Yiddish or Russian.

13. *Marc Chagall on Art and Culture*, p. 40.

14. Andre van Gyseghem.

15. The Pompidou catalogue *Oeuvre sur papier*, 1984, p. 102, mistakenly identifies the Hebrew word as *"Le grand sage,"* which would be in Hebrew *TsaDIK* (*tsadik*). It is in fact *TsDK* (*tsedek*), justice.

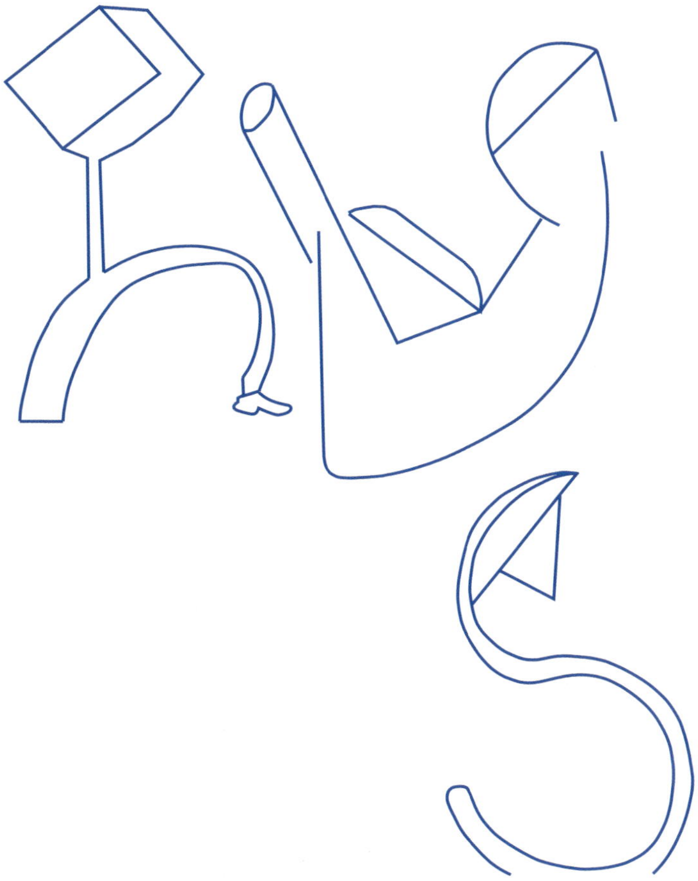

121. *Diagram for Chagall's signature in* ***Love on the Stage***

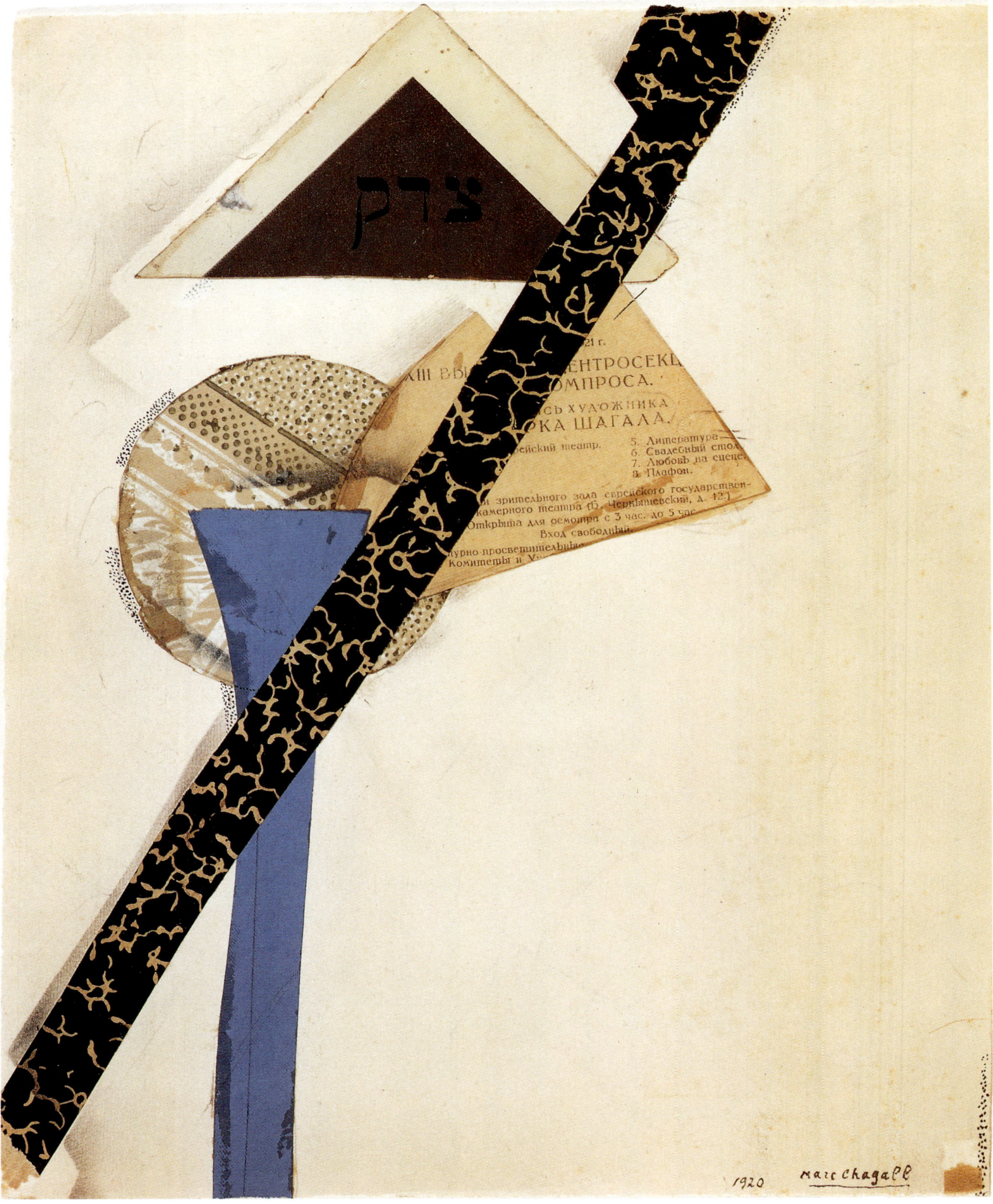

122. **Collage.** *1921. Colored paper, pencil, and chalk on paper, 34.2 x 27.9 cm. Musée National d'Art Moderne, Centre Georges Pompidou, Paris. On the brown triangle, like on a Jewish gravestone:* ***Tsedek*** *("Justice") not* ***Tsadik*** *("a Just man").*

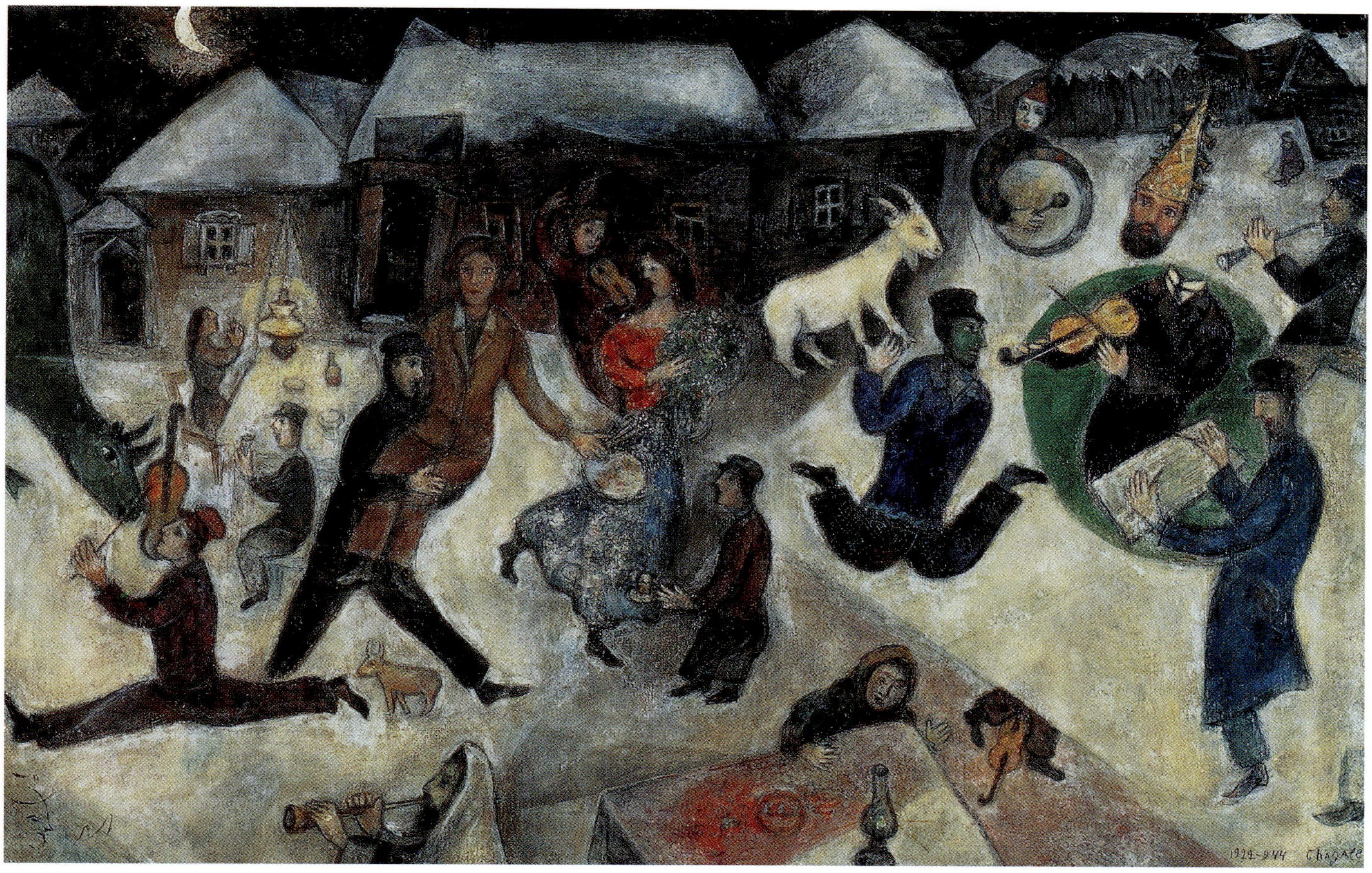

123. ***The Harlequins.*** *1944. Oil on linen, 56.5 x 86.8 cm. Musée National d'Art Moderne, Centre Georges Pompidou, Paris. This painting reinterprets the left side of the* ***Introduction.*** *The composition is preserved but the scene has changed: instead of the geometrical shapes we have a Jewish* ***shtetl.*** *The diagonal square shape up front becomes mother's table. Instead of to Granovsky, Chagall is brought to Bella.*

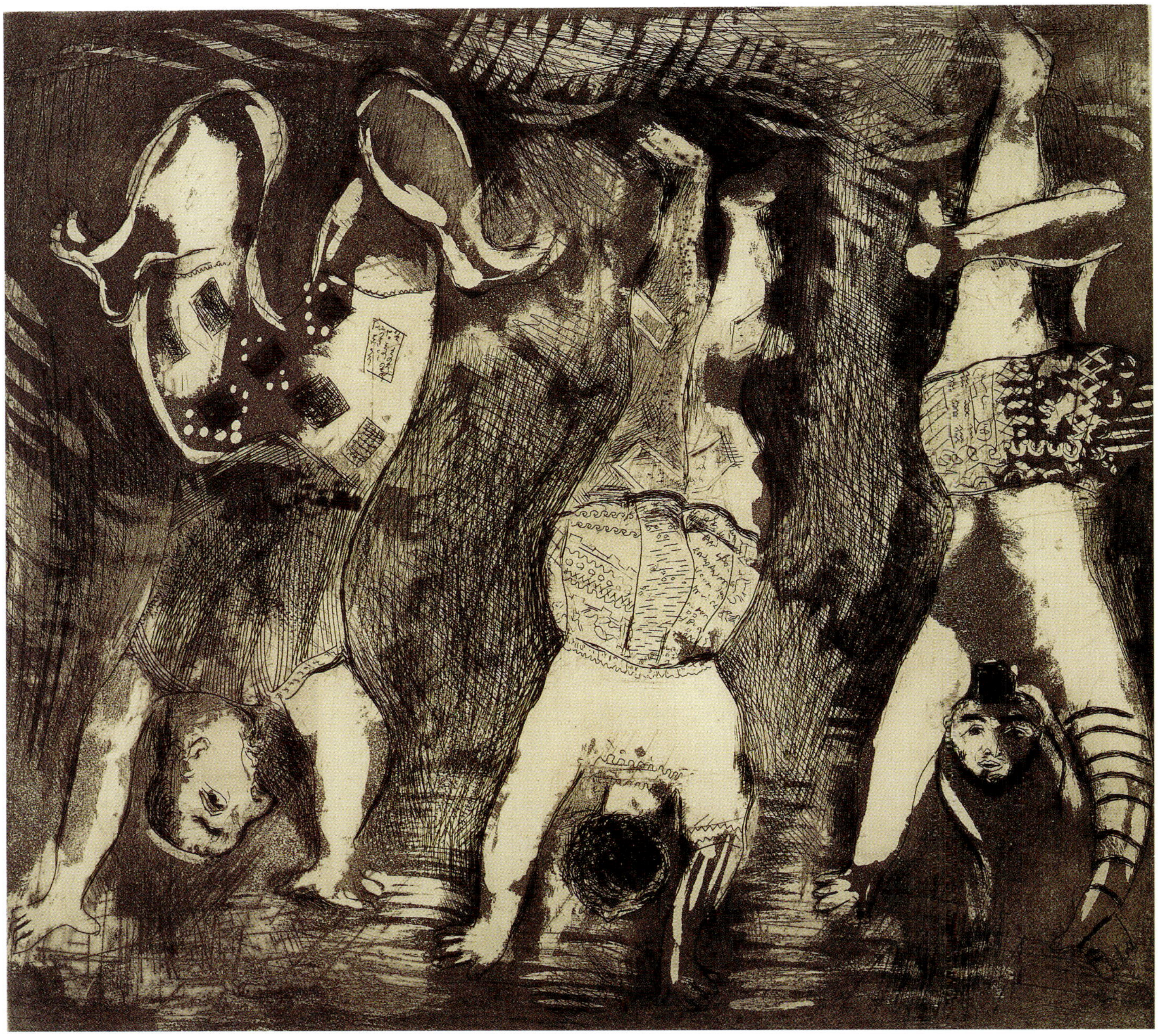

124. ***Three Acrobats.*** *1923. Etching and aquatint, 34.2 x 37.3 cm. Collection of E.W. Kornfeld, Bern*

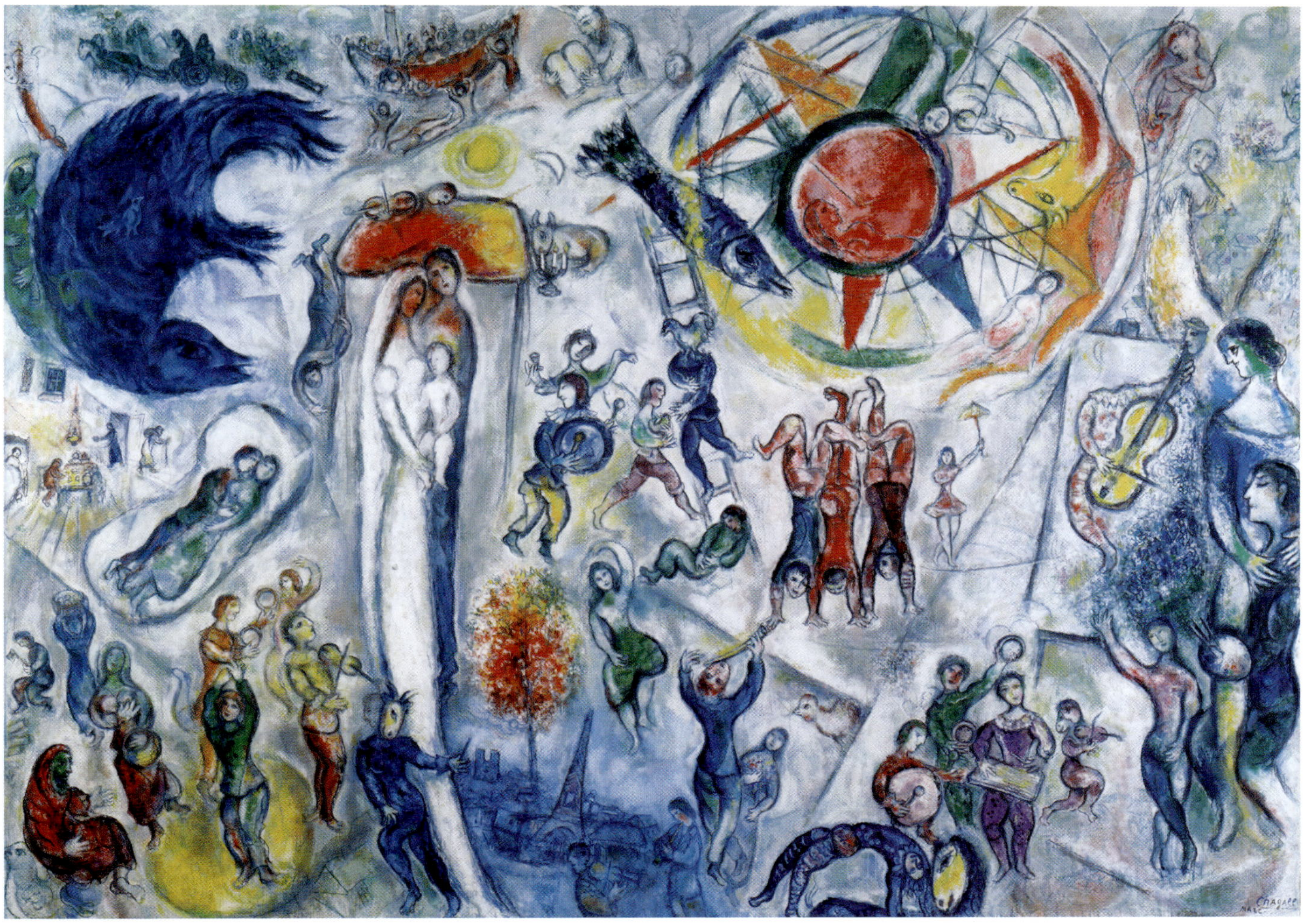

125. ***Life.*** 1964. *Oil on canvas, 296 x 406 cm. The Foundation of Marguerite and Aimé Maeght, Saint-Paul, France*

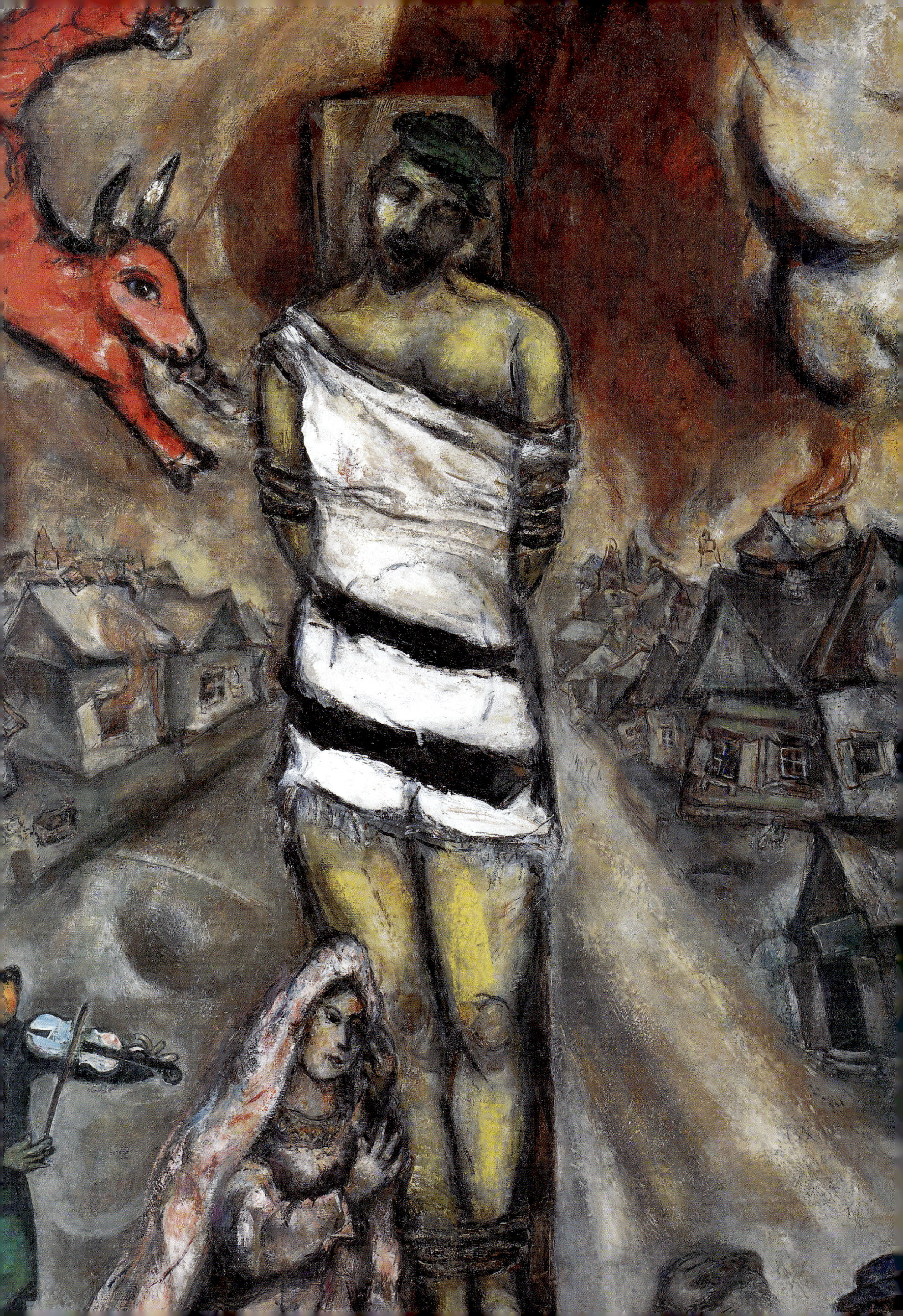

8. New Images—Revolution, Jesus Christ, Holocaust

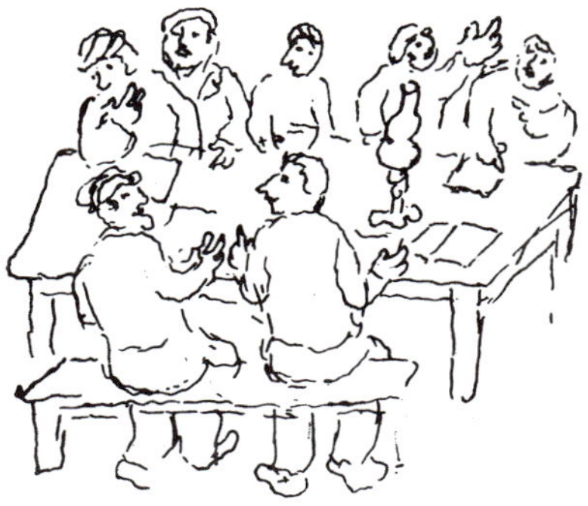

THE SECOND HALF OF CHAGALL'S CENTURY

The revival of interest in Chagall in recent years has focused on the dramatic rediscovery of his early work, 1908–23, from the seminal painting *The Dead Man* (no. 27) to his final settlement in France.[1] The first thirty-six years of his life laid the foundation of Chagall's art (thirty-six is a magical figure in Kabbalistic numerology and means "twice life"). As we have seen in this book, these so-called "Russian Years" are as much French as Russian: more precisely, their thematics derived mostly from Russia and Jewish life in Russia but the stylistic and formal problems were worked out in a dialogue with French painting.

In the years between the two world wars, Chagall tried to paint French landscapes and sights; he also absorbed the impressions of his travels in Palestine, Greece, and the Mediterranean. Some of his work of this period is mature, strong, and beautiful, but those images mostly did not enter the basic Chagallian repertoire. In the 1920s and 1930s, he rethought and reworked his kaleidoscope, notably adding the images of his wife Bella, a symbol of beauty and love. Now he ventured beyond his old fictional world (he was physically cut off from his symbolic "Vitebsk") into illustrating the poetry and fictional worlds of others. And he moved from an emphasis on painting to intensive work on etchings and lithographs. Here he got caught in the cultural wars of the thirties: he and his dealer Ambroise Vollard were viciously attacked because a Russian Jew was illustrating the French classical poet LaFontaine's *Fables*. Yet he also made new forays into Jewish culture, especially the early Bible etchings of 1930–31, perceived through Eastern European eyes. For his etchings he was awarded the first prize at the Venice Biennale in 1948, when he returned to Europe after spending the war years in America. Even Clement Greenberg, the guru critic of Abstract Expressionism, who didn't like Chagall (he was too figurative and too Jewish) wrote, "as an etcher and lithographer, Chagall belongs altogether in the first rank, unrivaled except by Picasso in this [the twentieth] century; and his book illustrations, together with that master's, make a last glorious burst in what seems to be an expiring art." (1953)[2] Thus Chagall expanded both, his rich but exhausted fictional world and his technical media.

In 1937 Chagall was fifty, a major event, called Yovel ("Jubilee") in the Jewish tradition. His paintings were displayed by the Nazis in the infamous exhibition "Entartete Kunst" ("Degenerate Art") in Munich. The Civil War in Spain in 1936–39 seemed like a last stand against the spread of Fascism, and Chagall wrote in the Parisian Yiddish Communist newspaper, *Naye Prese*, in support of the Jewish volunteers who went to Spain.[3] He also applied and received French citizenship.

But Chagall's later work was not merely repetitive. On the contrary, the extremely prolific production of the second half of his century turned out some beautiful masterpieces. His innovations proceeded in several directions.

First, under the pressure of both his self-examination and the ominous political situation in Europe, Chagall

OPPOSITE: ***The Martyr*** *(detail). 1940. Oil on canvas, 164.5 x 114 cm. Kunsthaus Zurich*

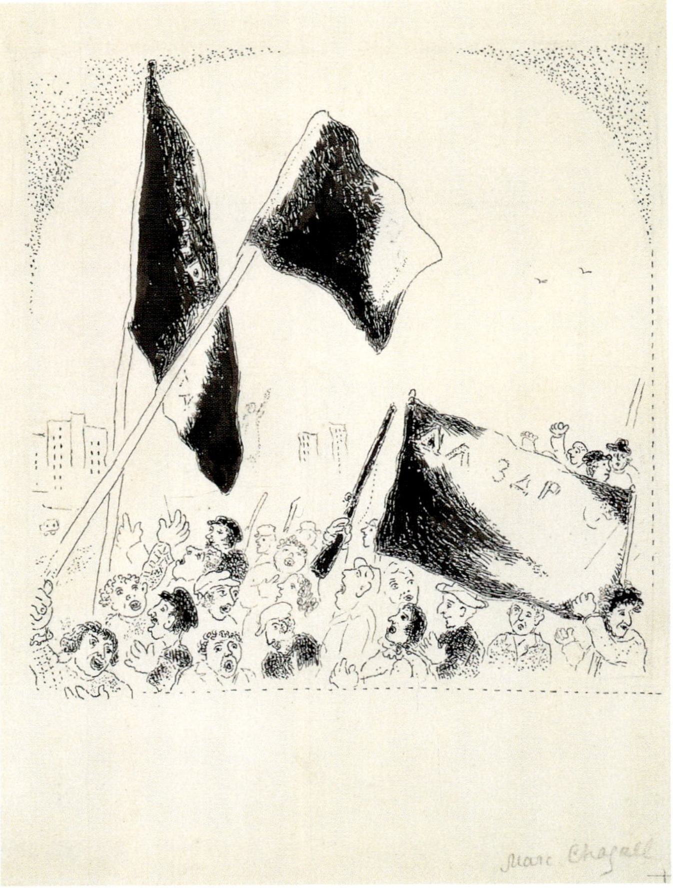

126. ***The Revolution**, from the series **Lider un Poemen** by A. Lyessin (Abraham Walt), with 34 drawings by Chagall. 1931. Ink on paper, 14.5 x 13.5 cm. Musée National d' Art Moderne, Centre Georges Pompidou, Paris*

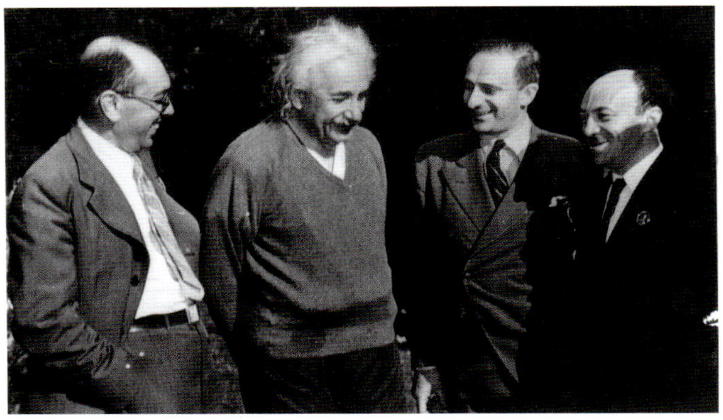

***A delegation of Soviet Jewry visiting American Jewry at the height of the Holocaust, September 1943.** Fom left to right: Itzik Fefer, Albert Einstein, Joseph Brainin, and Solomon Mikhoels. Chagall was a member of the Board of the American Committee of Jewish Writers, Artists, and Scientists and a friend of Mikhoels and Fefer from his Russian years. Courtesy of David Brainin*

renewed his repertoire by turning to new and more public cultural and historical images, including the Bible, for which the French government bestowed on him a national museum in Nice. And second, after his return to France in 1948, he expanded the scope of his media into stained-glass windows, ceramics, sculptures, tapestries, and mosaics. Now he accepted many commissions for public institutions and monuments and made hundreds of lithographs and mass-produced pictures that popularized and spread the Chagallian images around the globe.

A thorough study of Chagall's later work would require another book. I shall dwell on two examples of the directions he took later in his life: here, the new and interlocked imagery of Revolution, Jesus Christ, and Holocaust, and in chapter 9, the stained-glass windows of Jerusalem.

REVOLUTION

In 1936–37, after several years of procrastination, Chagall made thirty-four drawings for the three volumes of A. Lyessin's collected poetry in Yiddish. Lyessin (the pseudonym of Abraham Walt) was born in Chagall's Byelorussia, and in his youth he participated in the Socialist revolutionary movement in tsarist Russia. He became a major Yiddish cultural figure, poet, and editor in New York and wrote poems in rich meter and rhyme on themes of Jewish history and national spirit. Immersion in Lyessin's poetry greatly influenced Chagall, and instead of depicting Jewish types grotesquely and ironically, he began to present them in the endearing, sentimental, or even heroic mode that dominated his later Jewish and Biblical figures. In 1937 Chagall wrote a long poem in Yiddish, "My Distant Home," an elegy for the lost world of Vitebsk and his teacher Yury Pen, murdered in January 1937 by the NKVD (Soviet secret police). The poem was published in 1937 by Lyessin in New York in his journal *Die Tsukunft* ("The Future") and in several other places. Later it was broken up into small pieces, translated into French and other languages, and became a source for Chagall's basic conceptions of his family and his art.

Lyessin's poem "The Pioneers" was written in retrospect in New York in 1922.[4] It is a hymn to the young Jewish revolutionaries in Russia at the end of the nineteenth and the beginning of the twentieth century. It states (in a literal translation): "In the gray, clandestine dawn,/ You emerged with a red lantern;/ In the darkness you said:/ Let there be light!// You were heralding the Salvation that awakes and lifts up!/ And wherever this light appeared/ It tore through the lead and lit up/ Ever

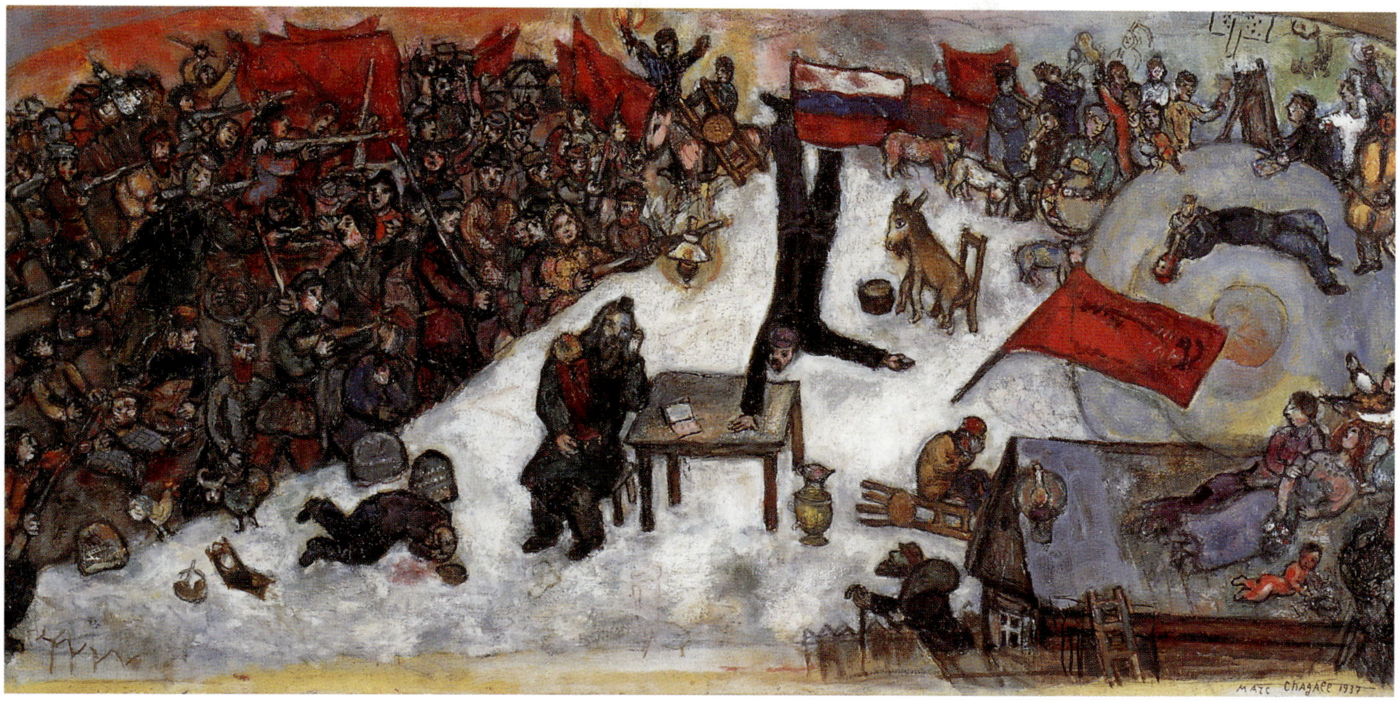

127. *Sketch for* ***The Revolution****. 1937. Oil on linen, 49.7 x 100.2 cm. Musée National d'Art Moderne, Centre Georges Pompidou, Paris*

wider and wider circles.// For me, the wonder of wonders happened,/ The change of millennia—/ With my own eyes I saw/ A new-born nation." This belief in the fusion of the Socialist revolution with the rebirth of the Jewish nation was shared by Lyessin and Chagall.

Chagall's illustration to this poem, later called *The Revolution*, 1937 (no. 126), is perhaps the first mass scene in his oeuvre. Indeed, the long mural for the Moscow Yiddish theater also had many figures, but each represented a specific person with a name, whereas now we have scenes with anonymous masses, although the drawing still distinguishes individual faces. The participants in the revolutionary demonstration raise their red banners, and the lower banner carries a slogan in Russian: *Da zdr[avstvuet svoboda]*, "Long Live [Freedom]." Yet behind the demonstration we can see Lyessin's observation point in New York with its tall buildings and the Statue of Liberty. The date of the drawing, written as "1931" is probably wrong. In 1931 Chagall began corresponding with Lyessin about the illustrations to his poetry, but from the correspondence it is clear that the bulk of it was done in 1936–37.

In September 1937 the First Yiddish Cultural Congress was held in Paris with delegations from around the world. It was a time of the French Popular Front, which included left and left-of-center political parties in the French government. In the face of rising fascism, the World Yiddish Cultural Alliance (IKUF) was established with the participation of leftist and centrist Jewish organizations and liberal writers and cultural figures. Chagall was elected to the Central Board of IKUF, as a member of the French delegation, and to the committee on art. At the same time a Jewish/Yiddish pavilion was built at the International Exhibition in Paris, showing Jewish books and manuscripts, modern Yiddish literature, and paintings by Marc Chagall and Chaim Soutine. The Spanish Civil War influenced Chagall to move more to the left. He saw the Jewish volunteers on the Republican side as the contemporary embodiment of the Jewish spirit, in the wake of "Spinoza, Freud, Einstein, Mendele, Peretz, Sholem-Aleichem, Bialik, Israels, Pissarro."

Such was the context of Chagall's ambitious painting *The Revolution*, 1937 (see sketch no. 127), which was intended as a blueprint for a major mural. Yet the Russians wouldn't accept Chagall in their pavilion, and there was no patron to pay for such a mural. It is not clear whether the painting was finished toward the twentieth anniversary of the October Revolution or whether it was exhibited with other Chagall paintings in the Jewish pavilion of the International Exhibition. Five years later, in November 1942, *The Revolution* was a centerpiece in the Chagall exhibition in the Pierre Matisse Gallery in New York. During World War II he divided the composition of *The Revolution* into three parts and made paintings for each that completely transformed the subject matter of the original (see below).

The Revolution has all the ingredients of a massive presentation of the historical world upheaval of the October Revolution, and the Jewish element in it. Lenin wrote that the Jews played a crucial role in the victory of

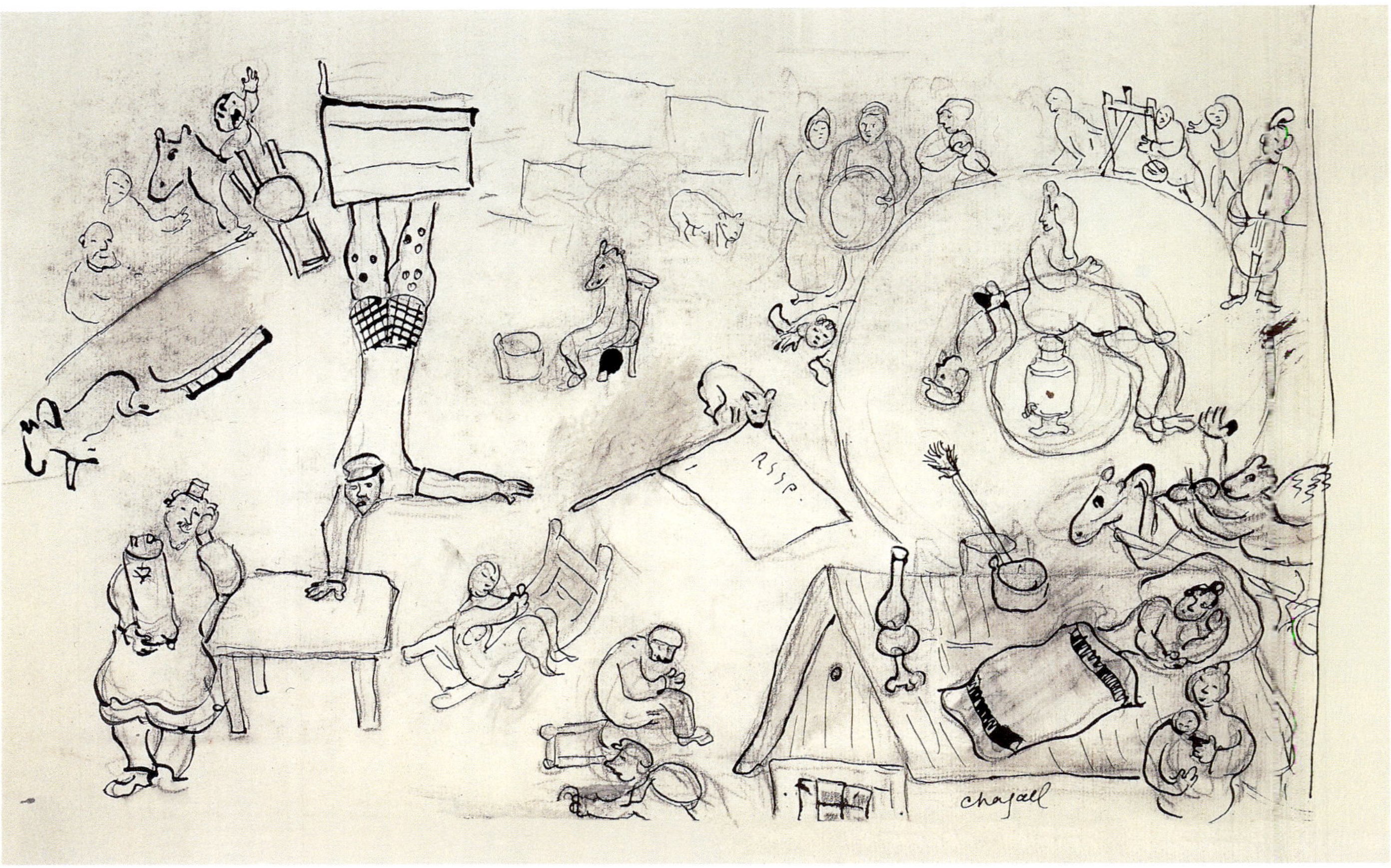

128. ***The Revolution.*** *1936–37. Ink, pencil, stump on laid paper. 27.7 x 42.2 cm. Musée National d'Art Moderne, Centre Georges Pompidou, Paris*

the October Revolution and the painting bears witness to it. Yet Chagall also remembered the paradoxical twins that were born together in Dovid Hofshteyn's *Troyer* ("Grief"): the futuristic world upheaval and the tragedy of the Jews. The snow and the samovar represent Russia. Sleds in the *Study for The Revolution* (no. 127) make this particularly obvious. In the snow on the lower left we can see the graves of children, which Chagall depicted earlier in an illustration to *Troyer* (no. 72), and to the right of the samovar a grieving boy sits mourning on an upturned chair. The lower right corner represents the Old World: a *shtetl* hut, a kerosene lamp, a pair of lovers on the roof, and the Eternal Jew going into exile.

Centerstage is shared by Lenin standing on his head and the sad, Eternal Jew with his Torah and phylacteries. Chagall wrote earlier, "Lenin turned Russia upside down, as in my paintings"—as if Lenin was influenced or foreshadowed by Chagall. Indeed, Lenin lifts the old Russian banner on his feet and turns the whole scene into a circus. The large triangle on the left side represents the massive armed revolt with its red banners, led by a torch and an oil lamp (placed as in the *Introduction to the Yiddish Theater*, no. 95). In the upper left corner we see a tilted church and little *shtetl* houses. Someone carries a bathtub, there is a wheel (with a baby carriage), and chickens can be seen up front. The revolutionary crowd includes young workers with caps, women, and some bearded Jews. At the upper right corner of the triangle there is a white donkey. According to Jewish legend, the messiah will come on a white donkey. One boy climbs the donkey, and another raises the torch of Revolution above it.

At the upper right there is a celebration, *klezmer* music, a painter with his easel, and a trumpeter bending backwards on the three circles of the circus. The narrative of this jolly painting can thus only be described as heroic.

JESUS CHRIST

Chagall was not an ideologue, and although at some points in his life he was close to programmatic Jewish art circles, he never joined them. Through the years he maintained contacts with both Jewish cultural circles and French intellectuals. Even in his most Jewish national statement, *Leaves from My Notebook*, published in Moscow in a Yiddish journal in 1922, he stated, "Beginning with the Renaissance, national arts began to decline. Boundaries are blurred. Artists come—individuals, citizens of this or that state, born here or there (blessed be my Vitebsk)—and one would need a good registration or even a passport specialist (for the Jewish desk) to be able to 'nationalize' all the artists."[5] He is proud of what the "little nation" of Jews has achieved: It gave the world Christ and Christianity, Marx and Socialism, and it will "show the world some Art." He and his generation considered Christ, Marx, and Einstein to be part of the Jewish contribution to world culture. There was no identity crisis here because in the minds of young intellectuals on both sides of the Modern Jewish Revolution, general culture and Jewish culture coexisted in one consciousness.

Because Christianity was central to the European cultural tradition, it attracted many Jews in the modern period: Edmund Husserl, Gustav Mahler, Alfred Döeblin, Roman Jakobson, and many others converted to Christianity. Chagall was not one of them, because he was deeply connected to Jewish folk sensibility; but culturally, the Christian world was a tangible reality in his work and life. His friends in the interwar period, Raïssa and Jacques Maritain, actively propagated conversion of the Jews. Raïssa, herself a Russian Jew who converted to Catholicism, also wrote a book about Chagall.[6] Hence the many fusions and confusions of Jewish, Russian, and Christian elements in Chagall's paintings; they interact, coalesce, and represent each other, just as other modular individuals—man and animal, or man and woman—do. He presented the sacrifice of Isaac in the form of a Michelangelo *Pietà*, and he portrayed the Holy Family with a little, bearded, "old" Jewish baby; he painted himself as a Christ-child along with his parents in *Golgotha* (see chapter 3, no. 40). Some Jewish critics were puzzled, even outraged by the use of Christian motifs in the works of Jewish artists such as Scholem Asch and Marc Chagall. But Christian art was the mainstream of the European art tradition and was part of Chagall's intellectual world, as Buddha and Zen Buddhism may appear in the writings of a Christian writer. Such, too, was the openness of modern Jewish literature in Hebrew and Yiddish.

A special case is the figure of Jesus Christ. Jesus was seen in secular Jewish culture as an historical figure, a Jew, attractive because like contemporary Jews he revolted against the religious establishment and its rituals, such as praying three times a day. Chagall saw him as a great poet. The historical or legendary Jesus was part of the modern gallery of Jewish literature. Dr. Yosef Klausner, a native of Russia, editor of the flagship journal of Hebrew literature in Europe, *Ha-Shiloah*, and the first professor of Hebrew Literature at the Hebrew University in Jerusalem (1925–49), devoted many years to the study of Jesus of Nazareth and his time. Uri-Tsvi Grinberg, the Expressionist poet who wrote prophetic poetry in Yiddish

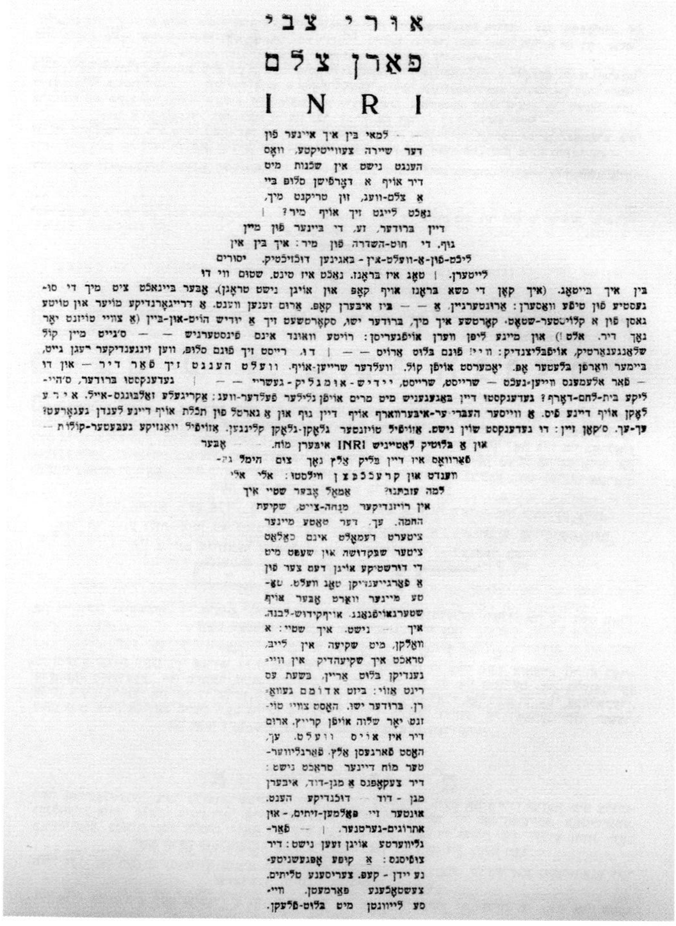
אורי צבי
פארן צלם
INRI

129. *Uri-Tsvi Grinberg.* ***Uri-Tsvi Before the Cross INRI [Jesus of Nazareth, King of the Jews].*** *In* ***Albatross: Journal for the new expression of poets and artists*** *(in Yiddish), no. 2, Berlin, November 1922, page 3. Courtesy Yivo Institute for Jewish Research, New York*

and Hebrew and who edited the avant-garde Yiddish journal *Albatros* in Warsaw and Berlin in the 1920s, used the figure of Jesus prominently in his work. There can be no doubt that Chagall knew *Albatros*, for it was a major organ of the *Khalyastre* ("Happy Gang"), a group of Yiddish Expressionist poets who also published the journals *Khalyastre* and *Literarishe revi*[7] in Paris, with many illustrations by Chagall.

Grinberg had been a frontline soldier during World War I, deserted, and lived in hiding in Serbia. After the war, having experienced a pogrom in his hometown of Lemberg (Lvov), he became an ardent Zionist who firmly believed (as early as 1924, in Berlin) that the earth was burning under the feet of the Jews in Europe, and that one day they would be gassed. In 1924 he left for Palestine, where he became a prominent Hebrew poet and extreme nationalist. In 1922 he wrote a Yiddish "concrete" poem in the form of a cross, which was entitled *Uri-Tsvi Before the Cross / INRI*, 1922 (no. 129) ("INRI" printed in large letters).[8] Chagall painted a similar image, *The White Crucifixion*, 1938 (no. 130), with the same letters "INRI" above the cross, and below it, in Aramaic: "Jesus of Nazareth King of the Jews" in Hebrew letters. In "Uri-Tsvi Before the Cross" and in the long poem "In the Kingdom of the Cross," Grinberg addresses Jesus as "our brother," symbol of Jewish suffering, who was hanging on crosses all over Europe for 2,000 years. I will quote a few lines pertinent to Chagall:

> At the churches
> Hangs my brother
> Crucified
> Frozen
> From his covered member
> Girls get pregnant [. . .]
> Why am I, one of the suffering caravan, not hanging next to you on a village pillar at a crossroad, sun drying me, night weighing on me? [. . .]
> Brother Jesus, a Jewish skin-and-bones shrinks (two thousand years after you. Old!) [. . .]
> Brother Jesus. You had two thousand years of calm on the cross. Around you, *no longer world* [. . .] At your feet: a heap of cut-off Jewheads [allusion to the pogroms]. Torn *tallises* [Jewish prayer shawls]. Pierced parchments. Blood-stained white sheets [...] Ancient Jewpain. Golgotha, brother, you don't see. Golgotha is here: all around. Pilate lives. And in Rome they sing psalms in the churches [...]
> The Jews! The Jews!
> When poisoned gas enters the temples
> *And icons suddenly scream in Yiddish* [. . .]
> On the wound-ridden body a torn *tallis*—the body
> Feels good in a Jewish *tallis*—Oh, good in a *tallis*:
> The wind cannot blow sand on the dripping wounds [. . . .]
> Oh-Ho, I am King in a wound-and-blood *tallis*! [Emphasis added.][9]

Such was the Jewish context of Chagall's *The White Crucifixion*, which included Jesus wearing a *tallis* to cover his genitalia while hanging crucified over the roads of Europe. And Chagall often mentioned "the two thousand years that we were crucified." A few days after World War II was over, Chagall wrote:

> Now is the time. No world conferences will be successful until the Jewish people are taken off the cross on which they were crucified for 2000 years.[10]

Just as Chagall borrowed images from Yiddish literature, so did his painting evoke responses from inside Jewish culture. Here is a comment about the painting *The Flayed Ox*, 1947 (no. 131):

> Look closely at the red, flayed calf, hanging as a crucifix over the whole city. As the true crucified, the father of all the crucifieds in the world, since the evil of a living creature wielded its power over a living creature. See how the red of its blood screams, see the brutal cut in its body split in two, see the purity of its face licking from the bowl—
>
> Does another crucified like this exist among all the crucifieds?
>
> Weren't we all stunned, trembling in our childhood, when we saw the neighbor butcher slaughter our beloved calf? Isn't Feierberg's *The Calf*[11] authentically Jewish for all time? And is there a more authentic feeling of pity for the lot of the powerless? And a stronger scream of rage at the brutality of the heartless? And isn't Chagall here like Feierberg? . . .
>
> Look closely and see the zenith of human Evil, emanating from an idyll that is clear purity and beatitude.[12]

This was written in Yiddish after the Holocaust by the President of the State of Israel, Zalman Shazar, a

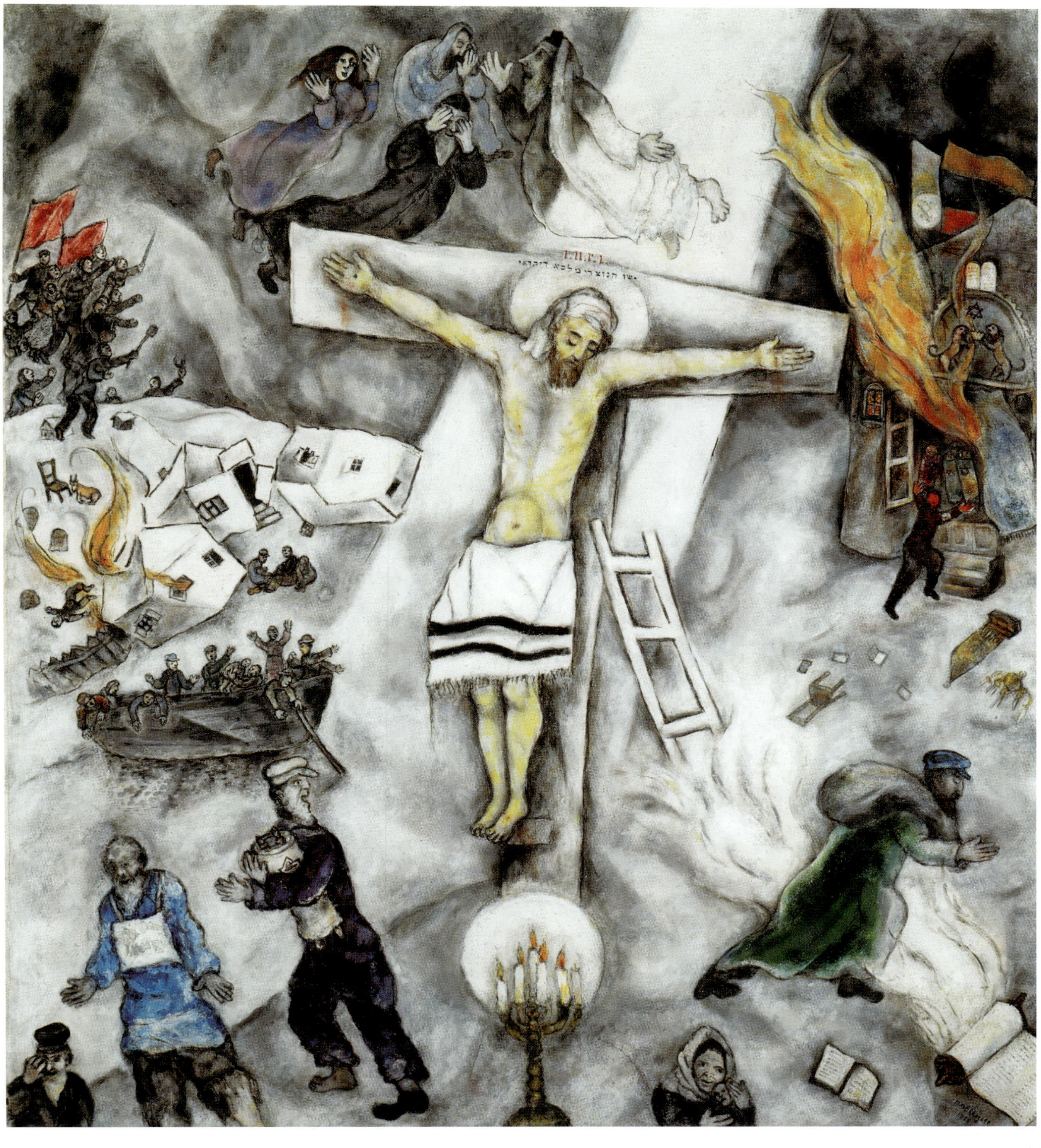

130. ***White Crucifixion.*** *1938. Oil on canvas, 154.3 x 139.7 cm. Gift of Alfred S. Altschuler, 1946.925, The Art Institute of Chicago*

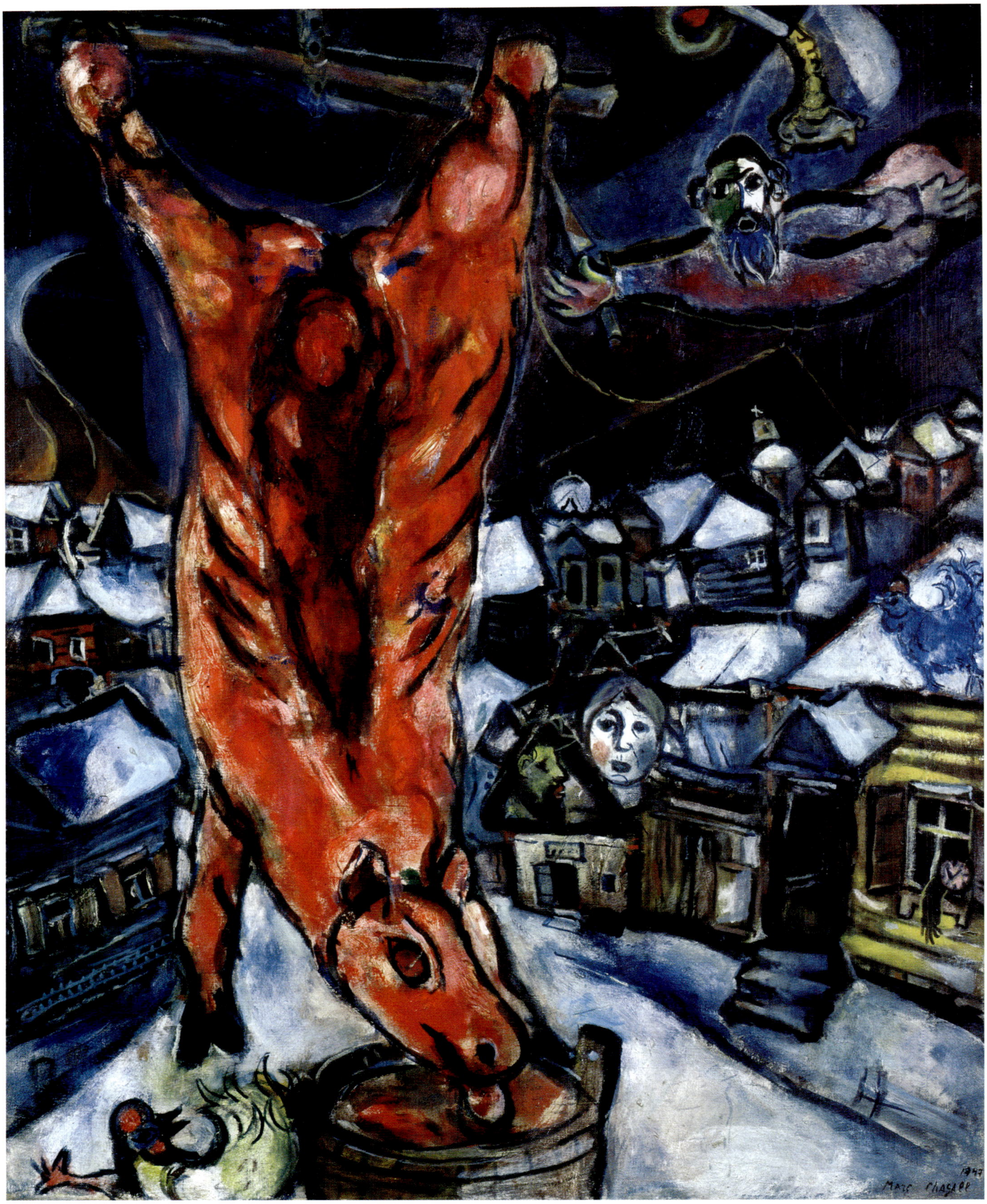

131. ***The Flayed Ox [or Calf?].*** *1947. Oil on canvas, 100 x 81 cm. Courtesy Comité Marc Chagall, Paris*

Hebrew scholar and former Israeli Minister of Culture, who was born in Byelorussia two years after Chagall. Given their shared cultural background, the calf may be more appropriate than the ox in the painting's title. Chagall's autobiography supports this: As a child, he witnessed the slaughter of a calf by his grandfather the butcher of Lyozno.

Naturally, Chagall had ideological hesitations about crossing religious boundaries in his paintings. As a young man of twenty, before leaving for St. Petersburg to study art, he went with his mother to Lubavitsh to see the head of the ChaBaD Hasidic sect and ask for his advice; characteristically for that time, the Rebbe told him he must judge for himself. And half a century later, Chagall wrote to the first President of Israel, Chaim Weitzman, invoking the traditional authority of the Rebbe, and asked for advice from "the highest Jewish authority" about whether to accept a commission for a Christian church. According to Chagall, who felt apologetic toward his Jewish friends, Weitzman, too, answered that Chagall must decide for himself. And he did.

The suffering Jew (Jesus) is placed at the center of *White Crucifixion*, and around him are references to Chagall's own times. The work was probably painted in 1939 or 1940, after *Kristallnacht*, November 9, 1938, when synagogues were burnt all over Germany. The vignettes around the central figure tell the story. At the top left we see a group of Jews in religious attire closing their eyes or puzzling over the events, much like the New York Yiddish poet Jacob Glatshteyn did in his poem "Here I Have Never Been." On the top right we see a pogrom in a German synagogue. Religious objects are being thrown out and the two tablets of law, the Star of David, and the images of lions over the entrance to the synagogue are on fire. Clockwise we proceed to the Eternal Jew going into exile; a Jew in a blue (Zionist) shirt, humiliated (in an earlier version there was the inscription "Jude" on his plaque); a ship overloaded, trying to escape overseas; a burning town in Eastern Europe, and the Red Army, approaching, as in *The Revolution* (no. 127), as a kind of savior, despite its weak and helpless appearance. The burning town on the left is an image taken from a song by Mordekhay Gebirtig sung all over the Diaspora in 1938, *Dos shtetele brent* ("The small town is burning"), a song now seen as foreboding the Holocaust to come.

RESISTANCE, RESURRECTION, LIBERATION

The link between Christ, Revolution, and Holocaust appears again in an ambitious triptych painted in America during the Holocaust. As the poet Glatshteyn wrote: "I cannot imagine six million deaths, I can only focus on one individual who was exposed to it, and there were six million such individuals." Chagall did not live through the Holocaust in Europe and had no personal experience of the suffering. For him, Jesus served as the individual who embodied the suffering in his own personal myth. He also served as the focal point of each painting. The first two parts were completed by 1948 and the third in 1952.

The triptych is clearly a response to the Holocaust but cannot be understood unless we read the Jewish Communist rhetoric of the first years after the Holocaust and Chagall's own writings in the Communist press. Instead of the prevalent religious and Zionist narrative that Diaspora leads to persecution and annihilation, hence the solution is a Jewish state, he uses the Communist narrative: Resistance leads to the Resurrection of the Jews and their Liberation by the Red Army, as part of the victory of Communism in eastern Europe.

The three parts of the triptych are based on the *Revolution* of 1937, now transformed. At the center of the middle panel, *Resurrection* (no. 132), a Jewish crucified Jesus takes Lenin's place. This time it is the painter in blue who stands upside down, alongside Jesus's body. Jesus, of course, is the universal symbol of resurrection, and here the resurrection being referred to is that of the Jews in Eastern Europe after the Holocaust. His role as a symbolic martyr is also made clear by his wreath of thorns (see detail, no. 133). And on the left, we see the liberating red partisan crowd, including the Wandering Jew with a sack on his back. A young partisan carries the torch, and Jesus stretches his fingers toward it (see detail, no. 135). The red banners are all but suffused in the large red area; even the Messiah's donkey is red. And at the lower right, a mother and child calling for help take the place of the Wandering Jew. The yellow loin cloth and the halo around the lamp as well as the long, pale, effeminate body of Jesus provide a focus, bridging and unifying the red and blue areas of the painting. It is a powerful resurrection, rising from a hut drowned in the dark over the whole height of the picture. Yet it is a martyr's rise.

In the first part of the set, *Resistance* (no. 136) (on the left), Lyessin's revolutionaries of 1905 who became Lenin's revolutionaries of 1917 are transformed into the partisans of World War II. Women and children are part of the motley crowd of surviving partisans. The *shtetl* falls into a dark abyss and the old clock falls into the river. The Messiah's white donkey takes over the torch

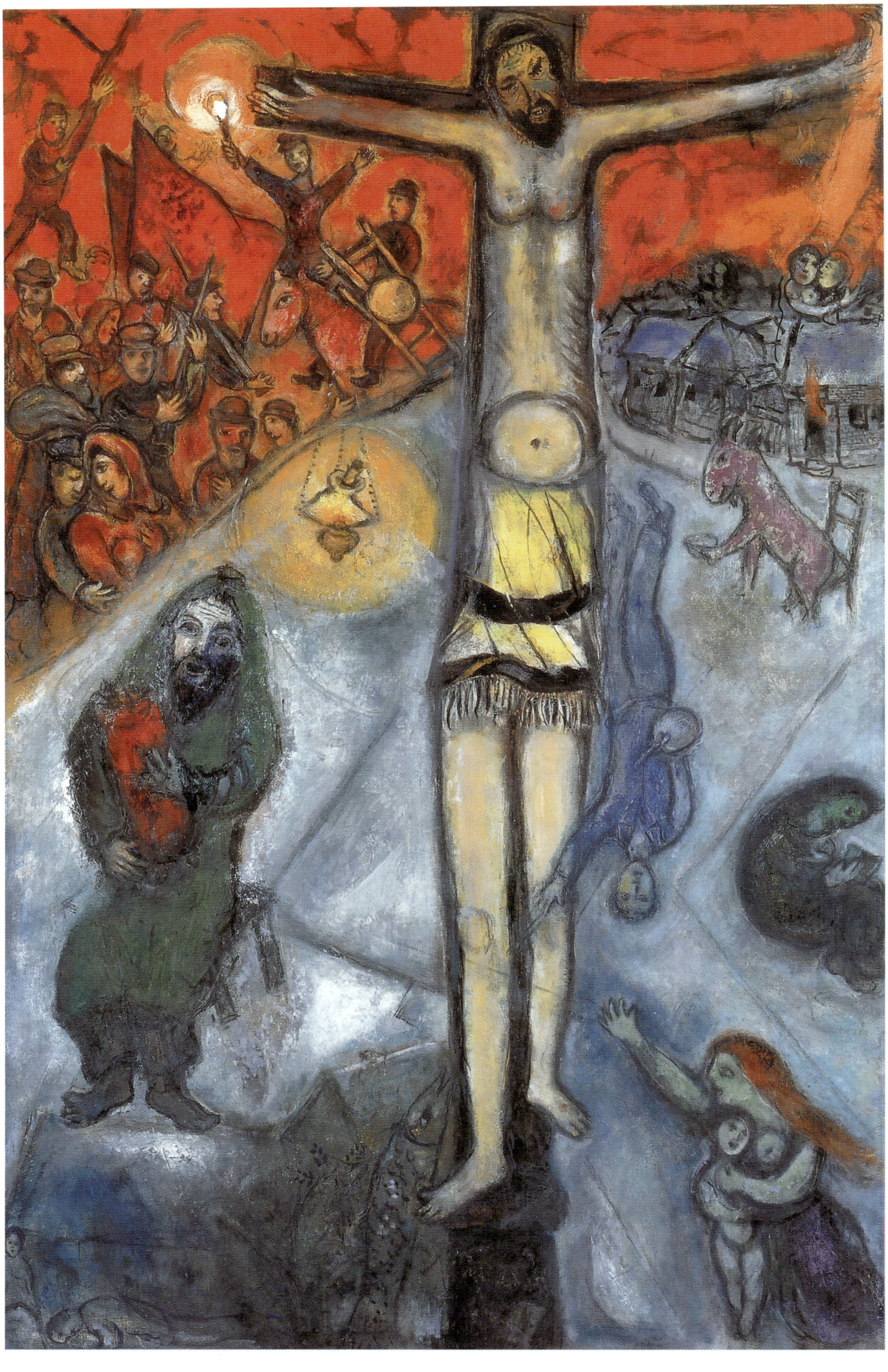

132. ***Resurrection***. *1937–52. Oil on canvas. 168 x 108 cm. Musée National message biblique Marc Chagall, Nice, France*

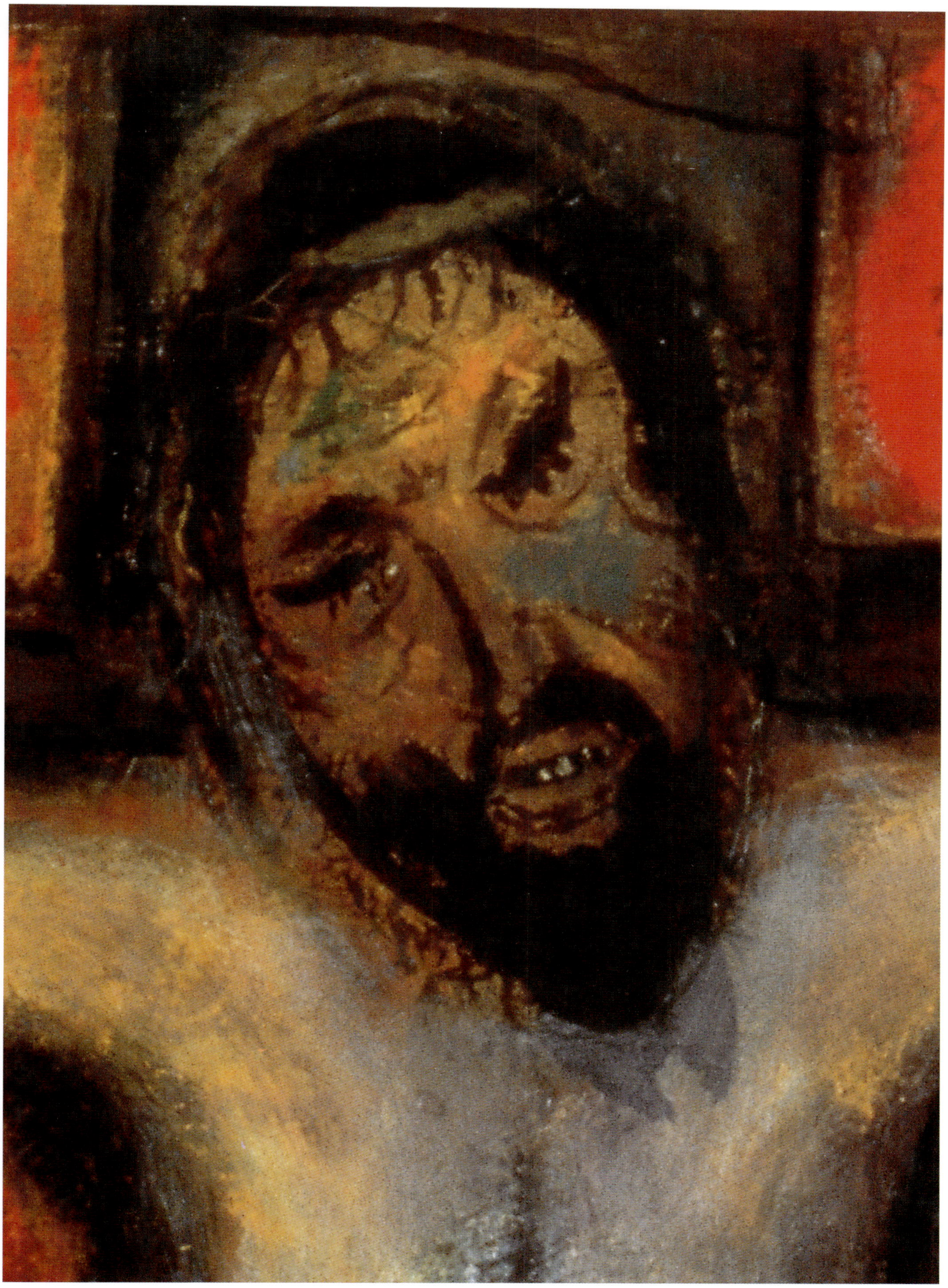

133. *Detail from* ***Resurrection****. 1937–52. Oil on canvas. 168 x 108 cm. Musée National message biblique Marc Chagall, Nice, France*

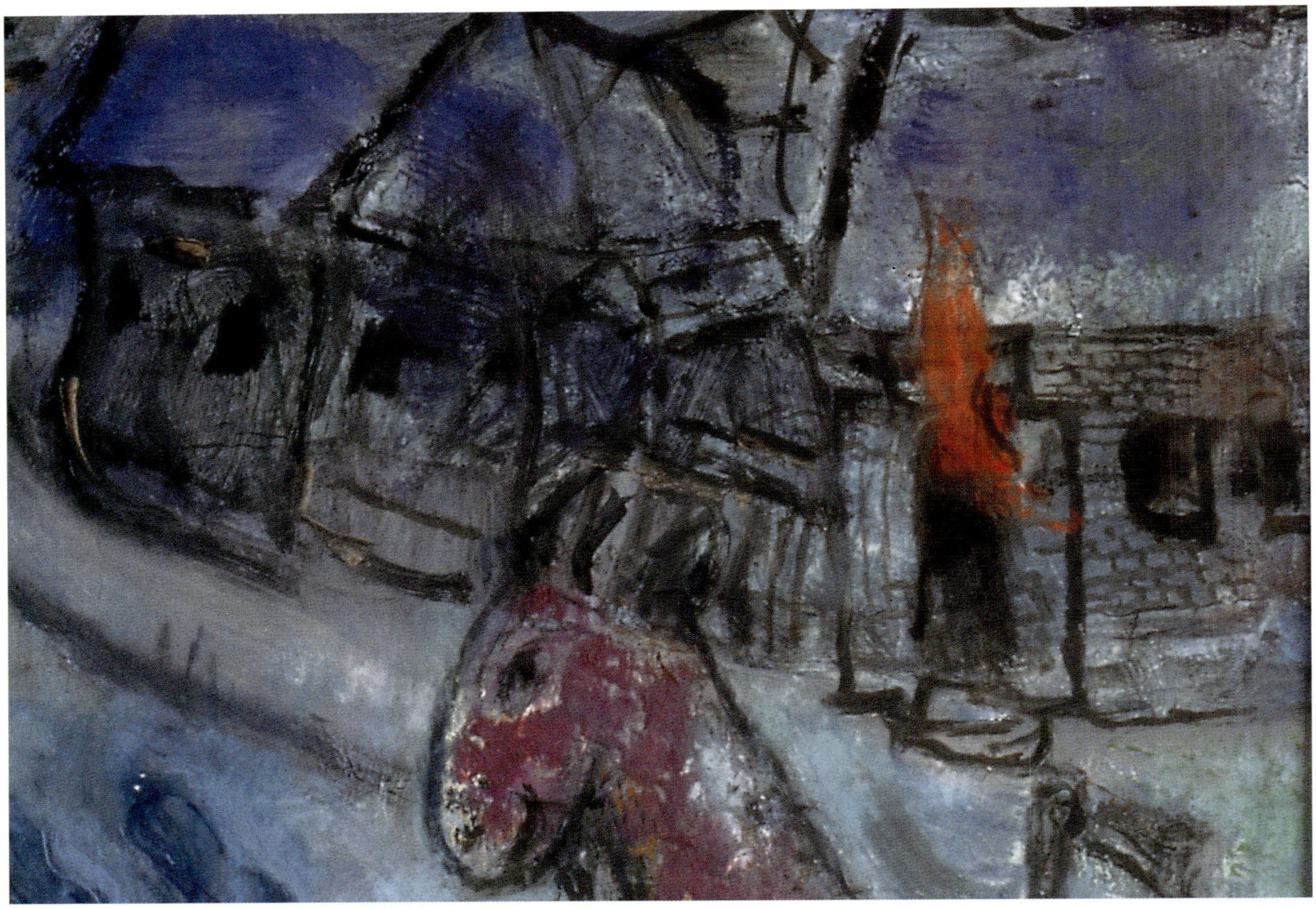

134. *Detail from* **Resurrection**. *1937–52. Oil on canvas. 168 x 108 cm. Musée National message biblique Marc Chagall, Nice, France*

and Jesus, in a *tallis*, unifies the composition. Note also that Chagall's rooster watches closely behind Jesus's head (see detail, no. 139).

The third panel is *Liberation* (no. 140). According to the optimistic Communist view the title alludes to liberation by the red army. It restores the old happy symbols of joy in a folkloric manner of Eastern Europe. A circus of daily life and joy captures our attention, as if all had returned to the beginning of the century. Many of Chagall's modular units take part in the celebration.

Chagall included the motifs of the seminal paintings *Revolution* and *White Crucifixion* in many paintings throughout his life. In certain works he even included the very figures that appear in these paintings, although he changed their hierarchies of importance. *The Martyr*, 1940 (no. 141)—close in time to *White Crucifixion*—is a response to the Nazi invasion of Poland in September 1939 and the destruction that ensued (prior to the actual Holocaust). The Jesus figure is not crucified but tied by his phylacteries to a pillar. He wears a simple cap, and the *tallis* covers his white torso. And the town goes up in fire. Expanding on this image, *The Burning Village*, 1940 (no. 142), shows a family's fear and horror at the burning of their town.

Christ with Clock, 1956 (no. 143), juxtaposes two tall, major images: a grandfather's clock, representing Time (here, in the sense of history), and the swaying crucified Jesus. The moon and the sun (below and above the Jesus figure) keep their light in the sky, and the clock lights a home candle to illuminate the scene: the dark shtetl and the mother and child fleeing into exile.

A more drastic scene of exile is *War*, 1964–66 (no. 144), which depicts a town enwrapped in a conflagration, a horse and wagon packed with children, and the Eternal Jew walking behind it in the snow. The Messiah's white donkey becomes a surface for another image, a cluster of women and children huddling together in exile from the city.

Exodus, 1952–66 (no. 145), is influenced both by the book of Exodus in the Bible and the ship Exodus from Europe (in Hebrew and Yiddish, *Yetsiyas Eyrope*), which took 4,000 Jewish survivors to Palestine in 1946, was rebuffed by the British navy, and caused an outcry around the world. An anonymous mass is embraced by the resurrected Jesus figure who radiates a yellow light that dominates and symmetrically organizes the whole scene. Other motifs are repeated from Chagall's kaleidoscope.

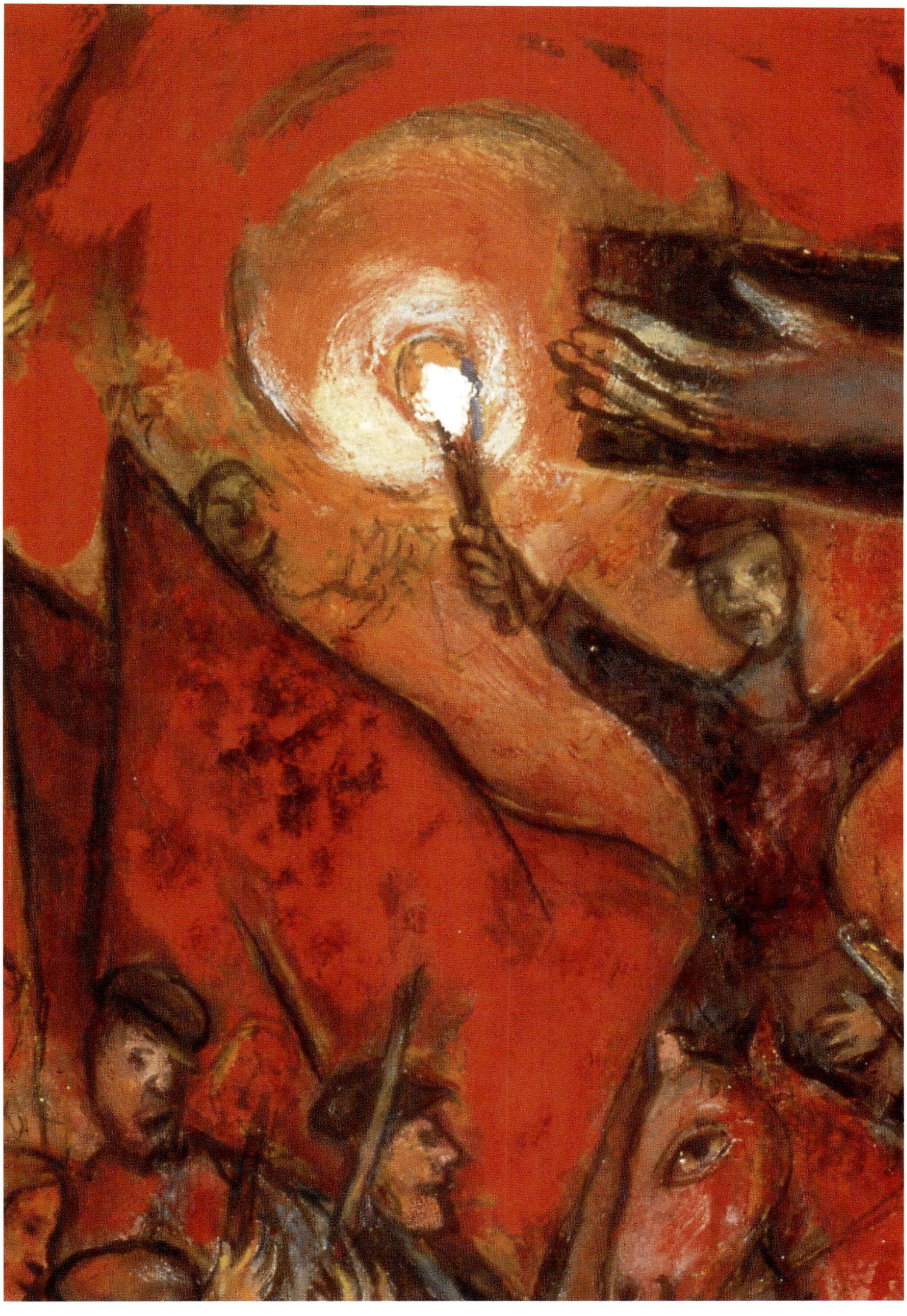

135. *Detail from **Resurrection**. 1937–52. Oil on canvas. 168 x 108 cm. Musée National message biblique Marc Chagall, Nice, France*

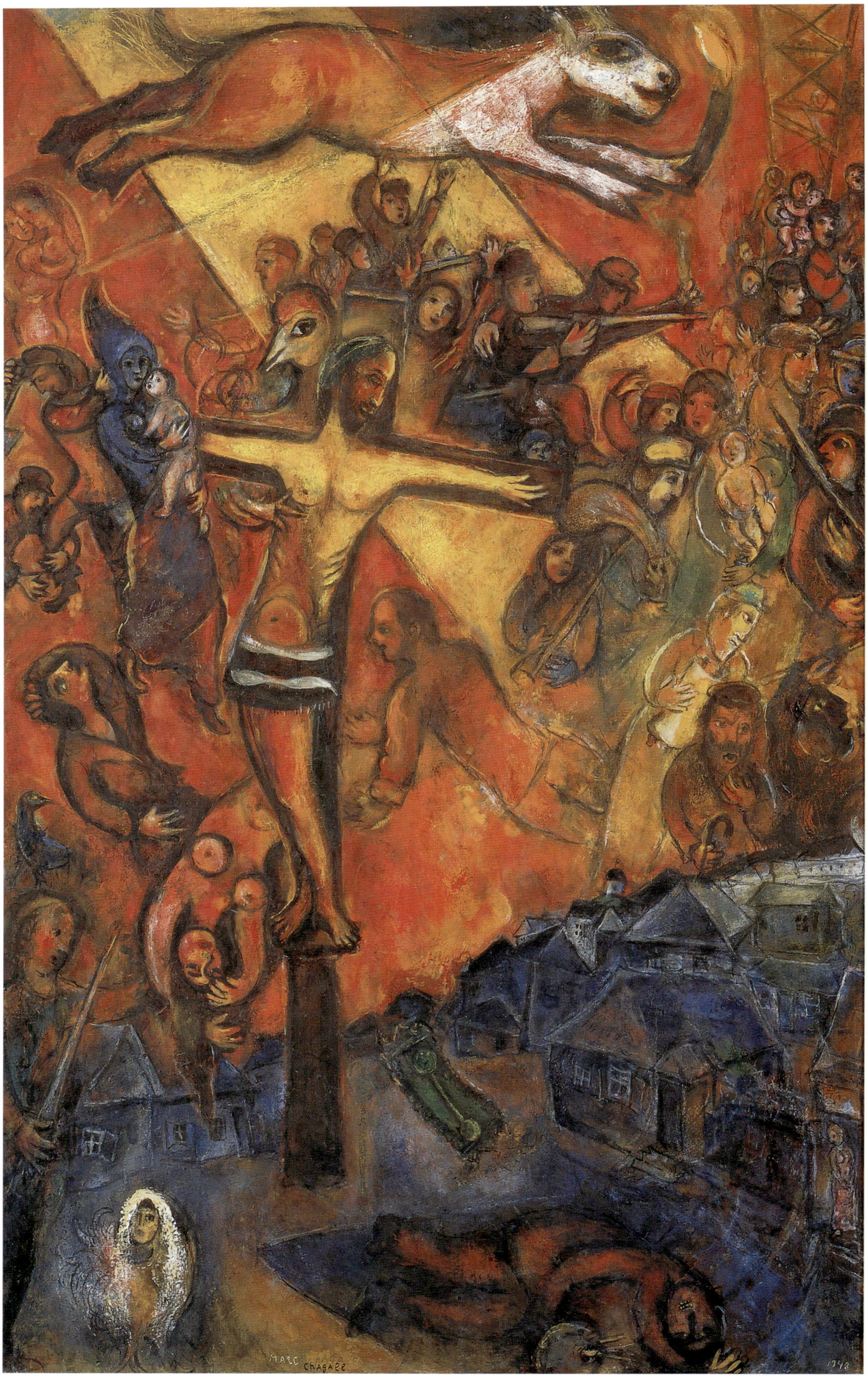

136. ***Resistance.*** *1937–48. Oil on canvas, Musée National message biblique Marc Chagall, Nice, France*

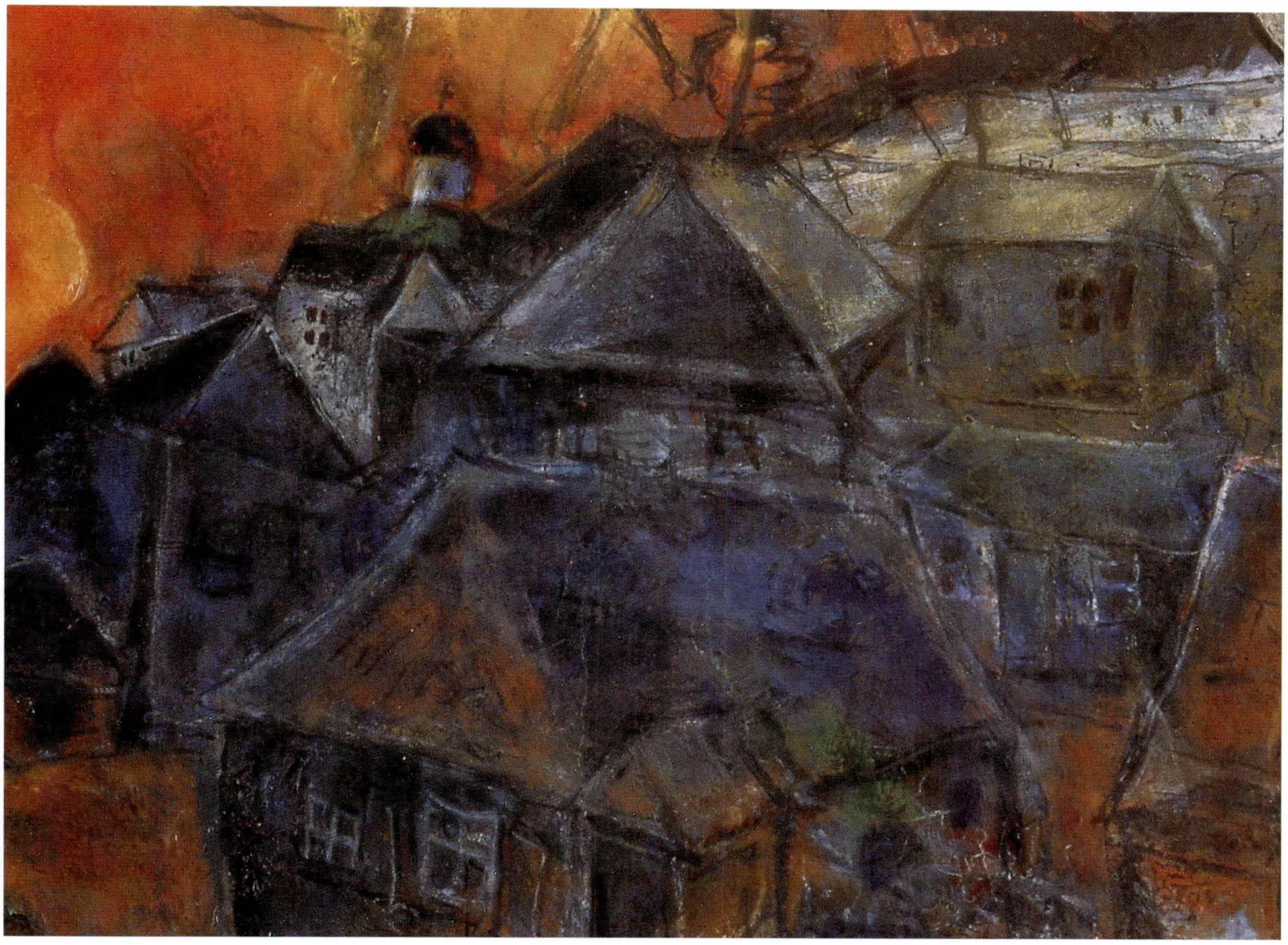

137. *Detail from* ***Resistance.*** *1937–48. Oil on canvas, Musée National message biblique Marc Chagall, Nice, France*

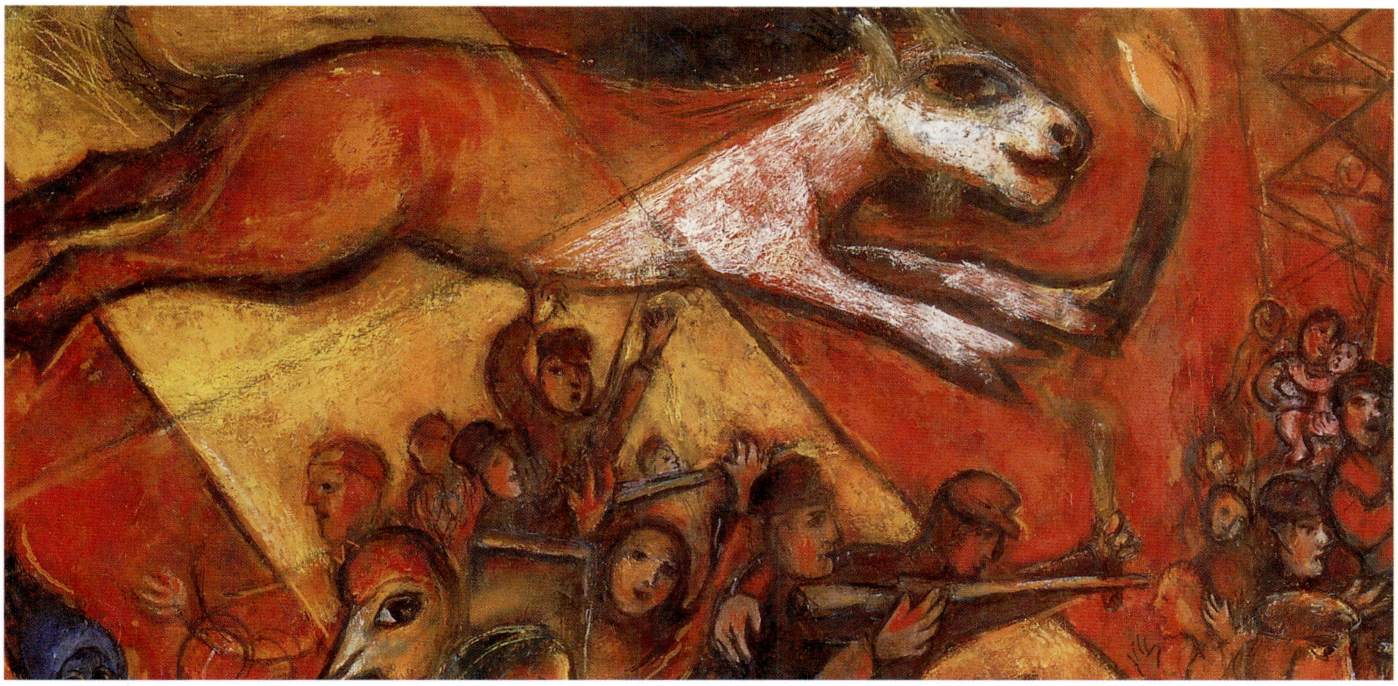

138. *Detail from* ***Resistance.*** *1937–48. Oil on canvas, Musée National message biblique Marc Chagall, Nice, France*

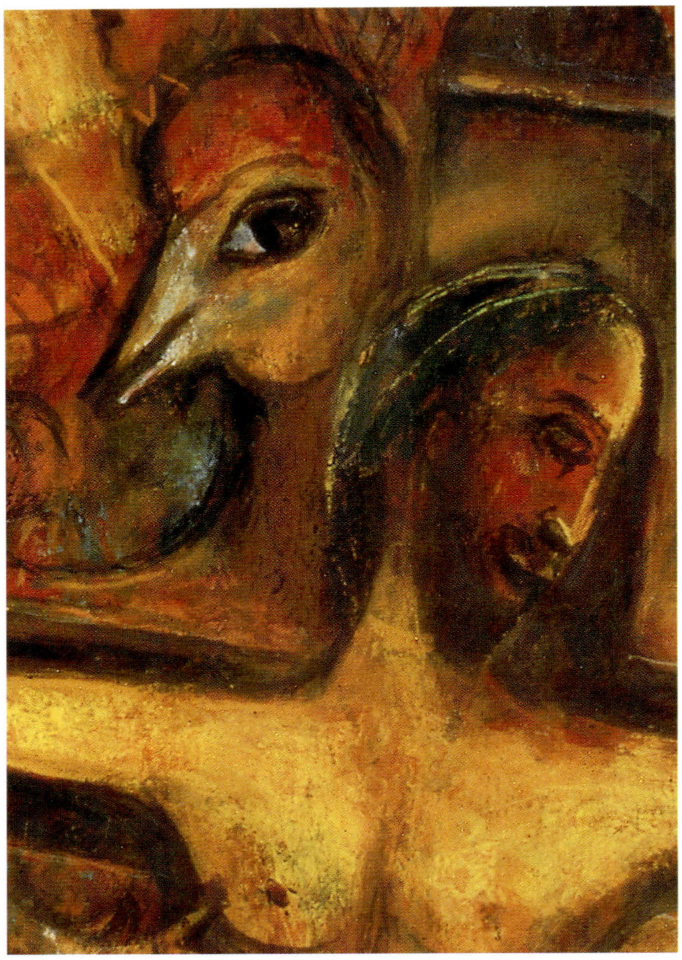

139. *Detail from* ***Resistance****. 1937–48. Oil on canvas, Musée National message biblique Marc Chagall, Nice, France*

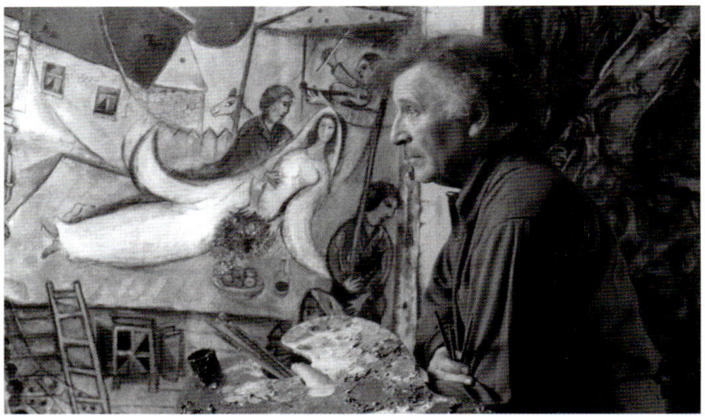

Chagall working on his painting ***Liberation****. High Falls, New York, 1948. Photo by Charles Leirens. Courtesy of Virginia Haggard*

At the age of ninety-four, Chagall painted *The Vision of King David*, 1981 (no. 146), in which lies a muted image of reconciliation: King David with a harp on one side; Jesus crucified on the other. The work was painted with oil on canvas, and the effect is as light as that of watercolors. The crowded *shtetl* with the little church at its peak is Jerusalem in the clouds. Mother and child, the reading donkey, the painter at his easel, young Chagall playing his violin to the children mingled with *klezmers*, little Chagall riding a rooster (as in *Introduction to the Yiddish Theater*, no. 95), and other various Chagallian images all float harmoniously through the white-blue fog of the painting.

---

1. Some accounts start from 1907, when he left his first teacher Yury Pen for St. Petersburg.

2. Clement Greenberg, *The Collected Essays and Criticism*. Chicago and London: The University of Chicago Press, 1993, vol. 3, p. 158.

3. *Marc Chagall on Art and Culture*, p. 145.

4. Abraham Walt (A. Lyessin), *Lider un poemen (1888–1938)*, with drawings by Marc Chagall in three volumes, New York: Forwards Association, 1938, vol. I, p.108.

5. See the English translation in *Marc Chagall on Art and Culture*, p. 40.

6. Raïssa Maritain, *Marc Chagall*. New York: Edition de la Maison française, 1943.

7. Edited by Peretz Markish and Oyzer Varshavski respectively; they also translated Chagall's autobiography from Russian into Yiddish in 1924–25, when all of them lived in Paris.

8. Uri-Zsvi Grinberg, "Uri-Tsvi Before the Cross/INRI," in *Albatros: Journal for the New Expression of Poets and Artists* (November 1922), no. 3.

9. Uri-Tsvi Grinberg, "In the Kingdom of the Cross," in *Collected Yiddish Works, Vol. II: 1922–1958*. Jerusalem: The Magnes Press, 1979, pp. 394, 431, 433, 459, 460.

10. See "The End of the War" (1945), in *Marc Chagall on Art and Culture*, p. 103.

11. Story written by M. Z. Feierberg in Hebrew in 1897 and published in 1899.

12. Zalman Shazar, *Di Goldene keyt* 60 (1967): 33.

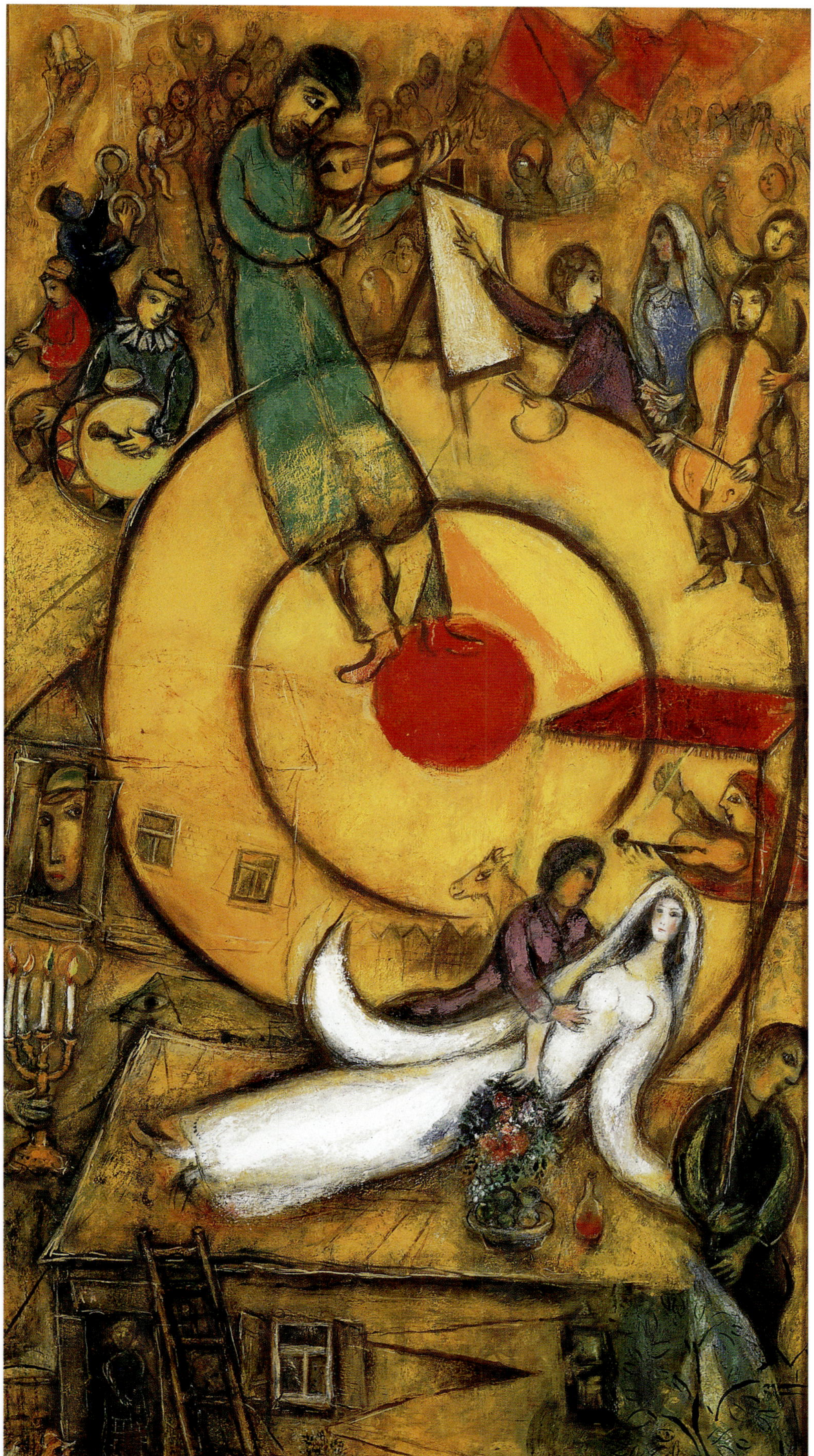

140. ***Liberation.*** *1937–52. Oil on canvas, 168 x 88 cm. AM 1988-72. Musée National message biblique Marc Chagall, Nice, France*

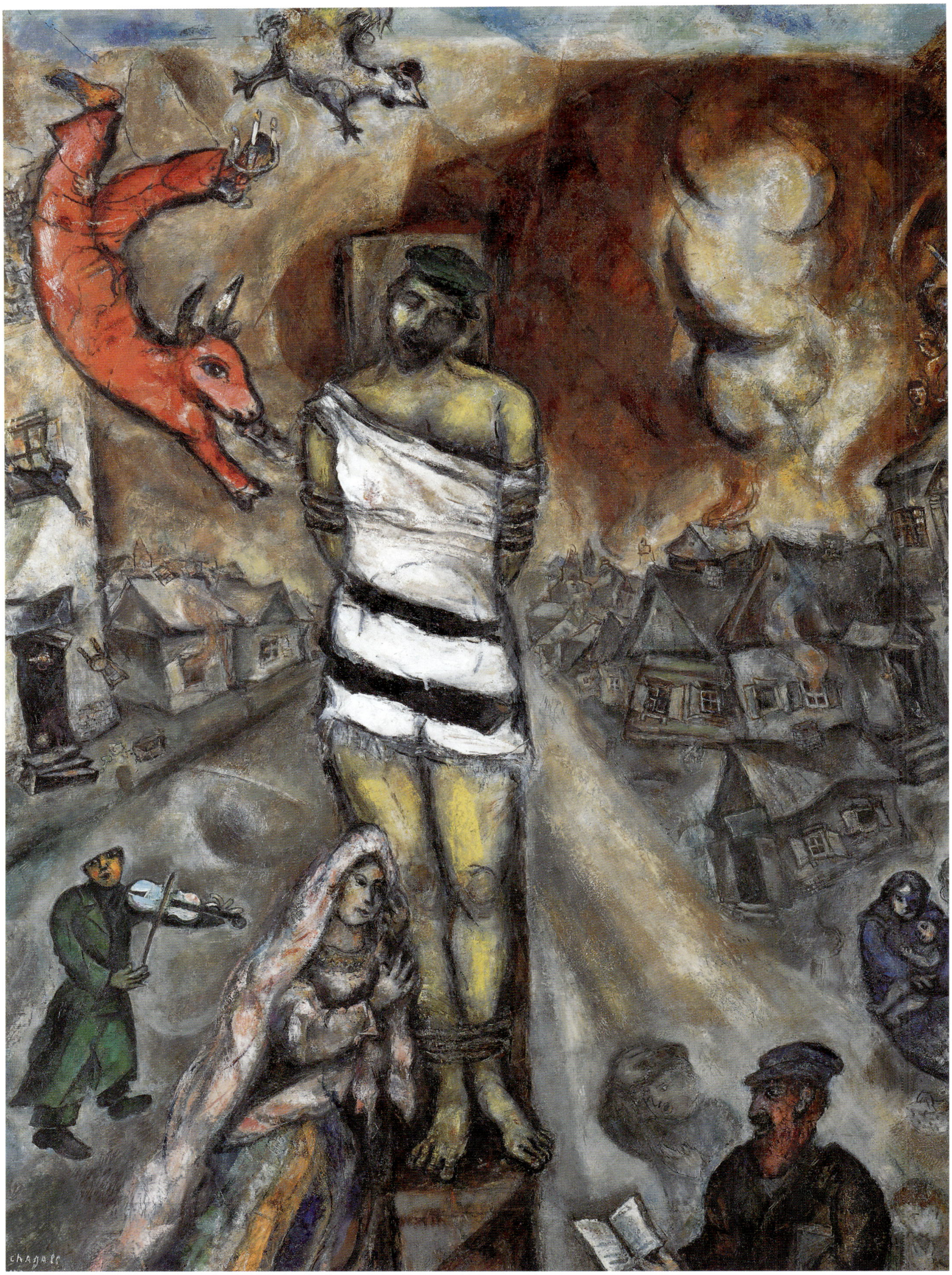

141. **The Martyr.** *1940. Oil on canvas, 164.5 x 114 cm. Kunsthaus Zurich*

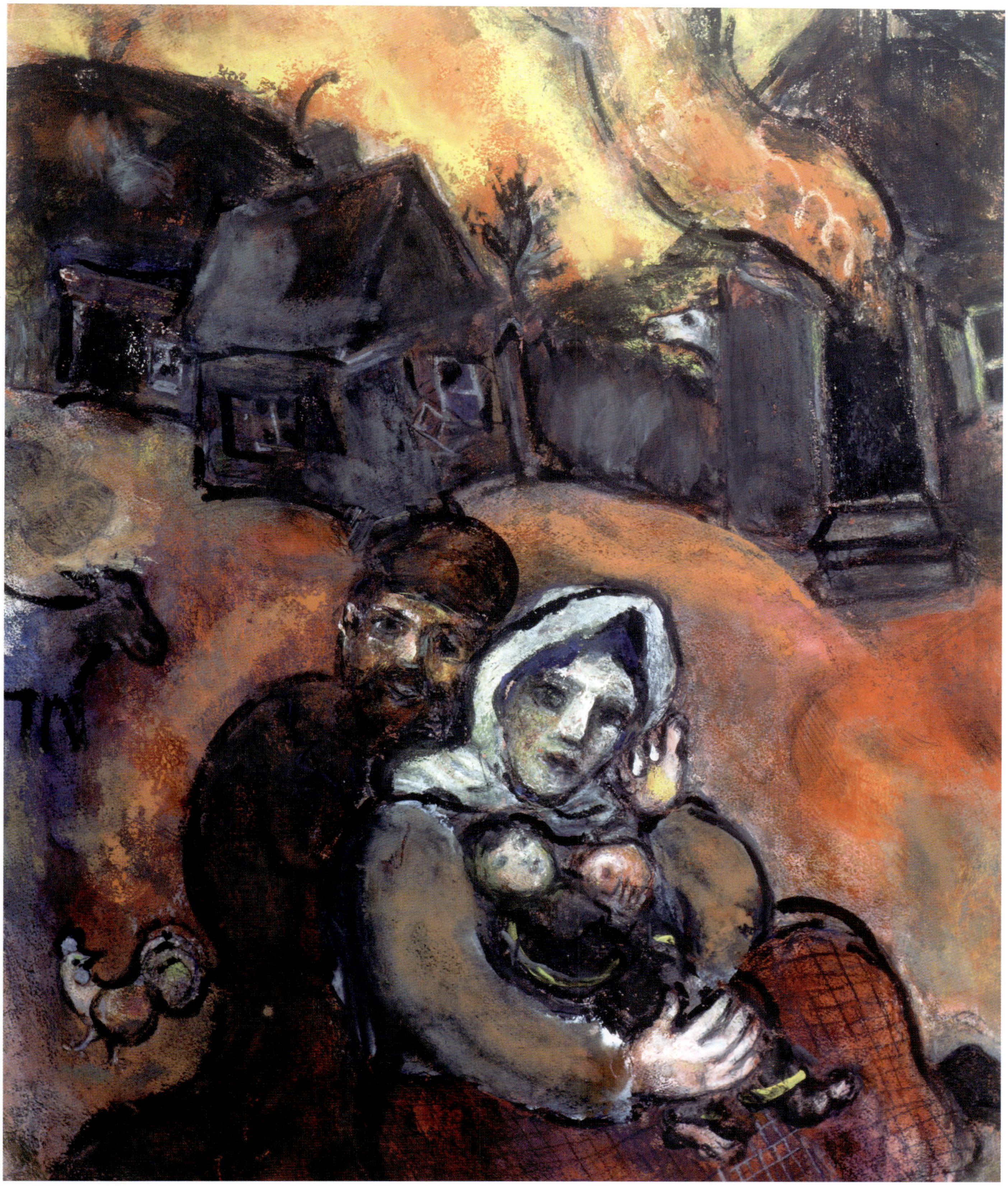

142. ***The Burning Village.*** *1940. Gouache on paper, 67.6 x 51.4 cm. Private collection*

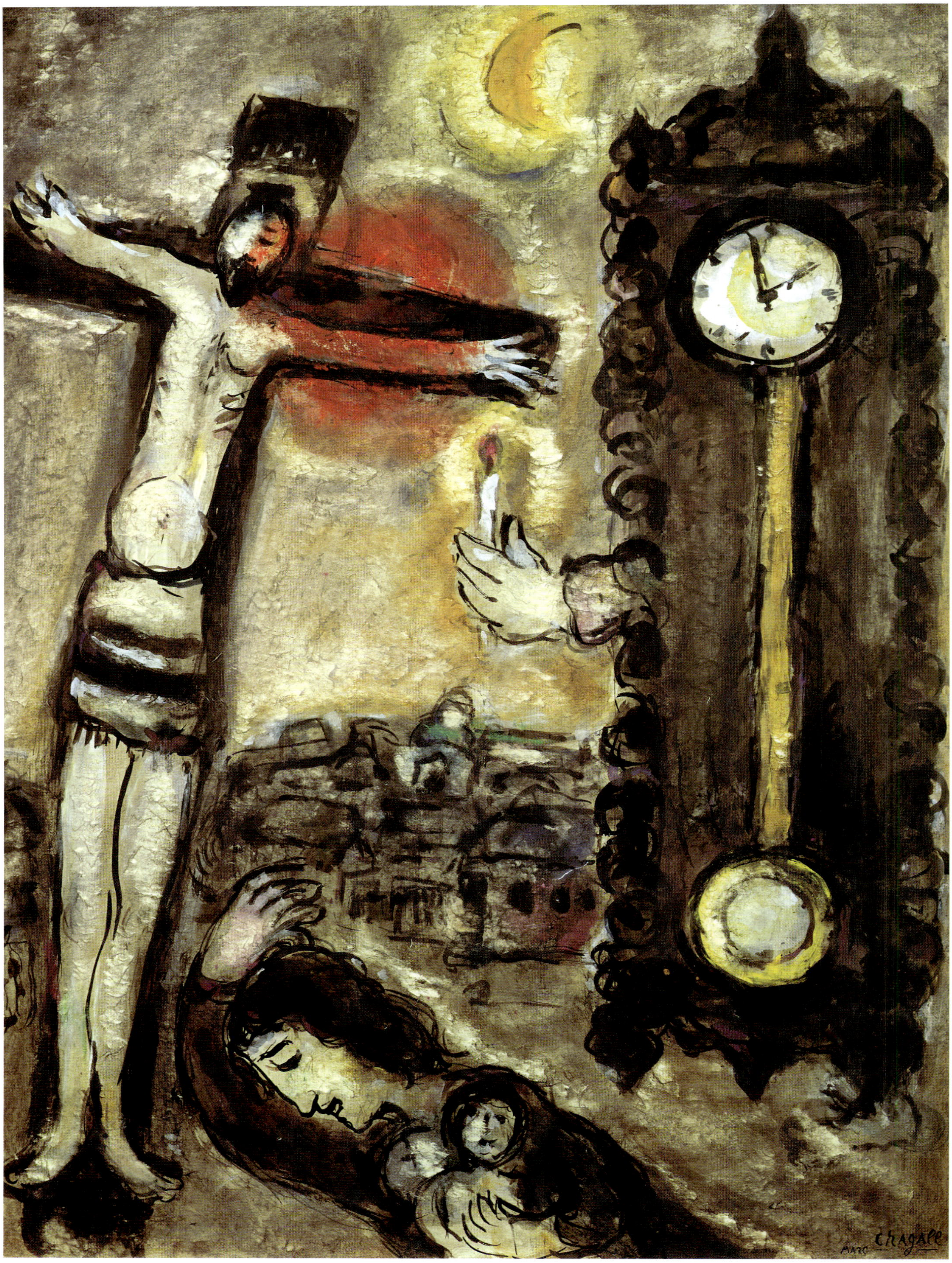

143. ***Christ with Clock.*** *1956. Gouache, 75.8 x 56.2 cm. Angela Rosengart Collection*

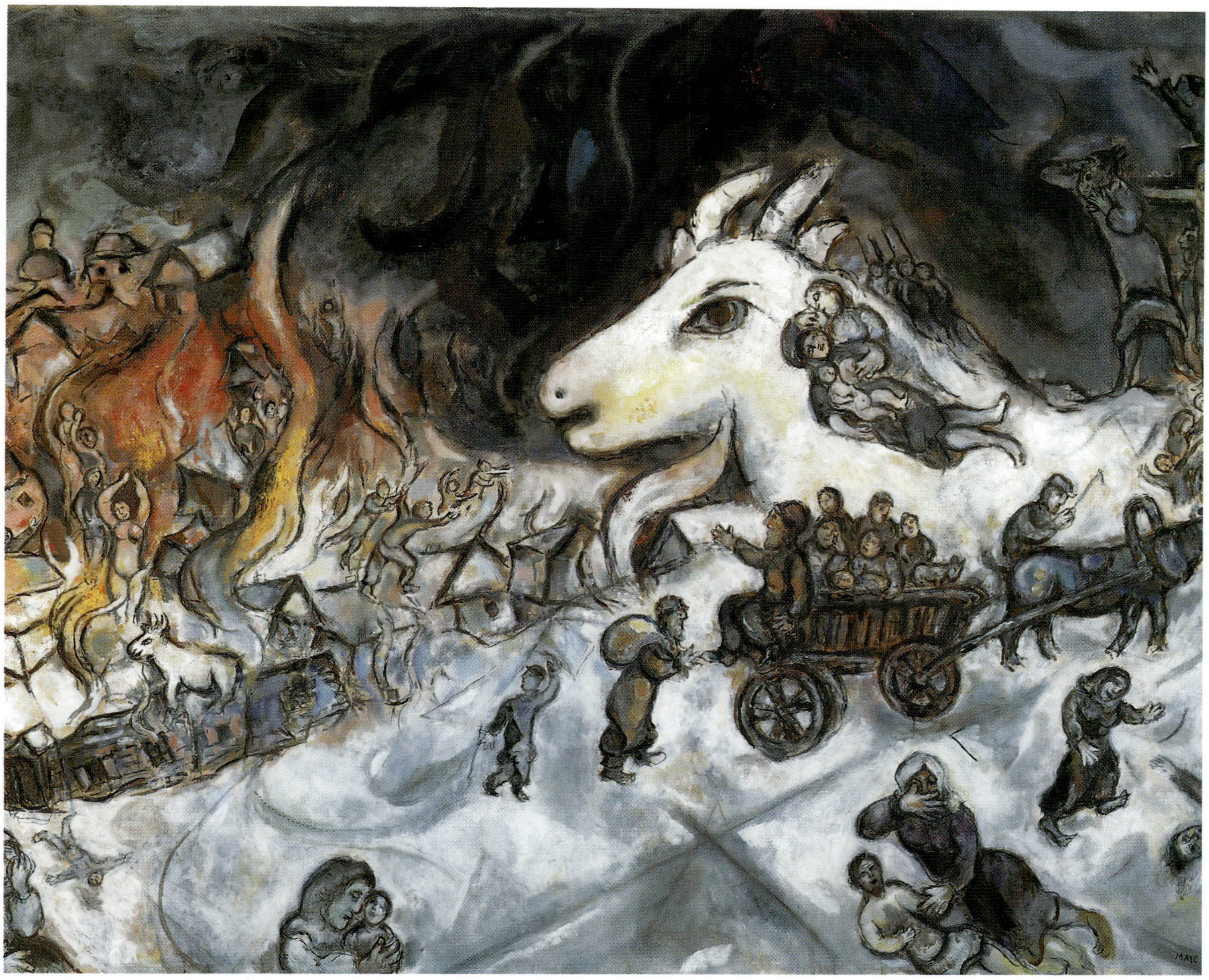

144. **War.** *1964–66. Oil on canvas, 163 x 231 cm. Kunsthaus Zurich*

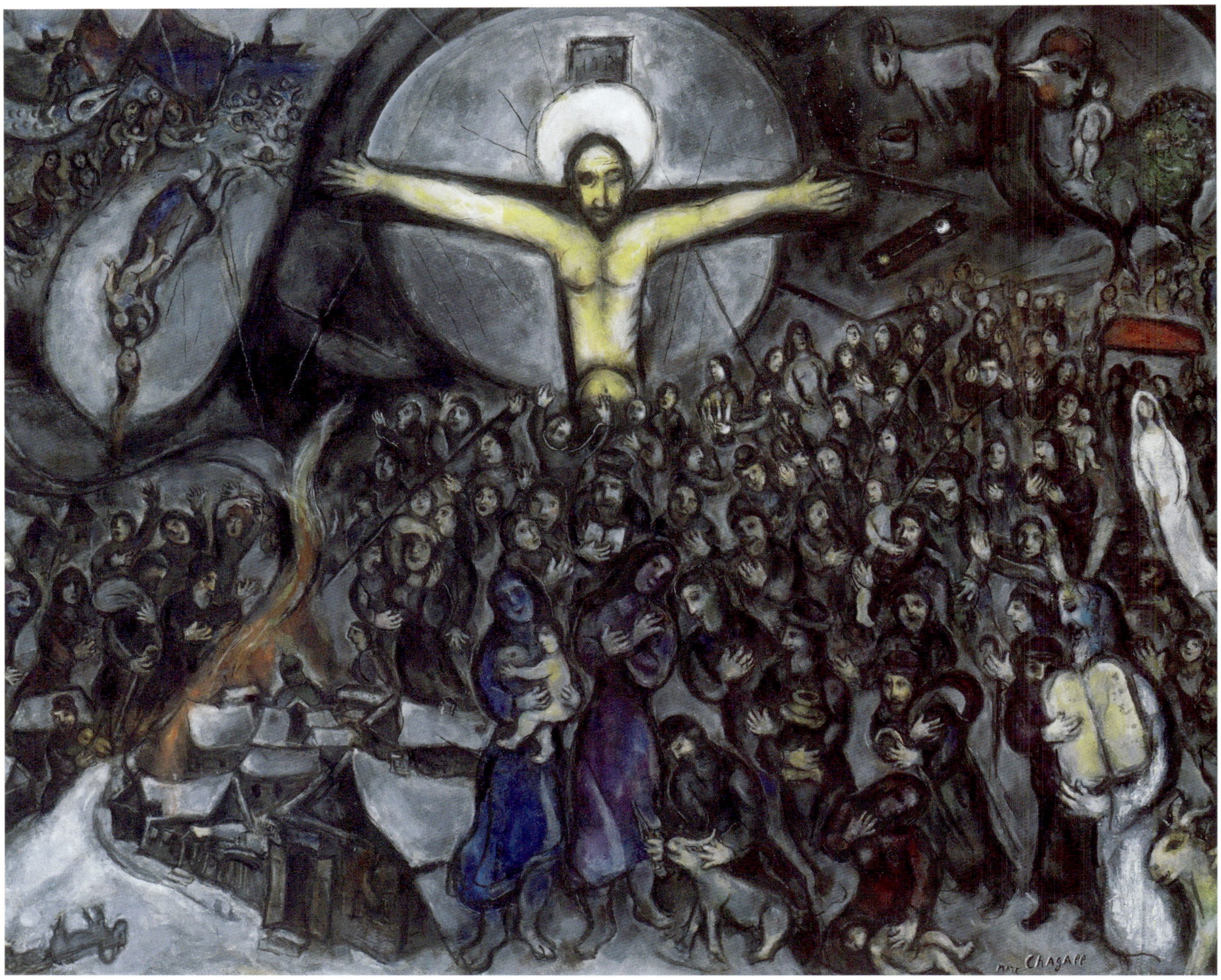

145. ***Exodus.*** *1952–66. Oil on linen canvas, 130 x 162.3 cm. Musée National d'Art Moderne, Centre Georges Pompidou, Paris*

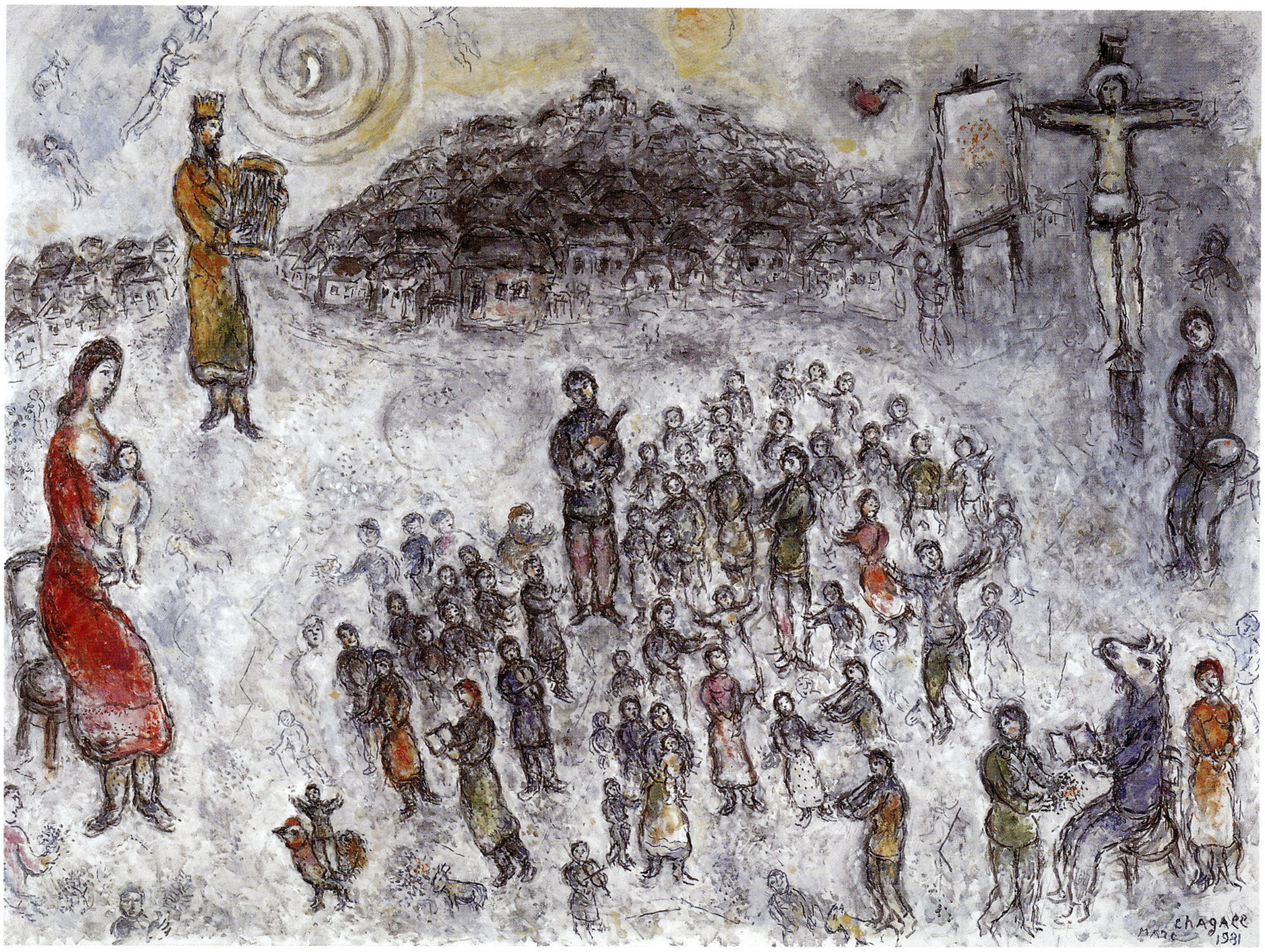

146. ***The Vision of King David.*** *1981. Oil on canvas, 114 x 146 cm. Private collection, Basle*

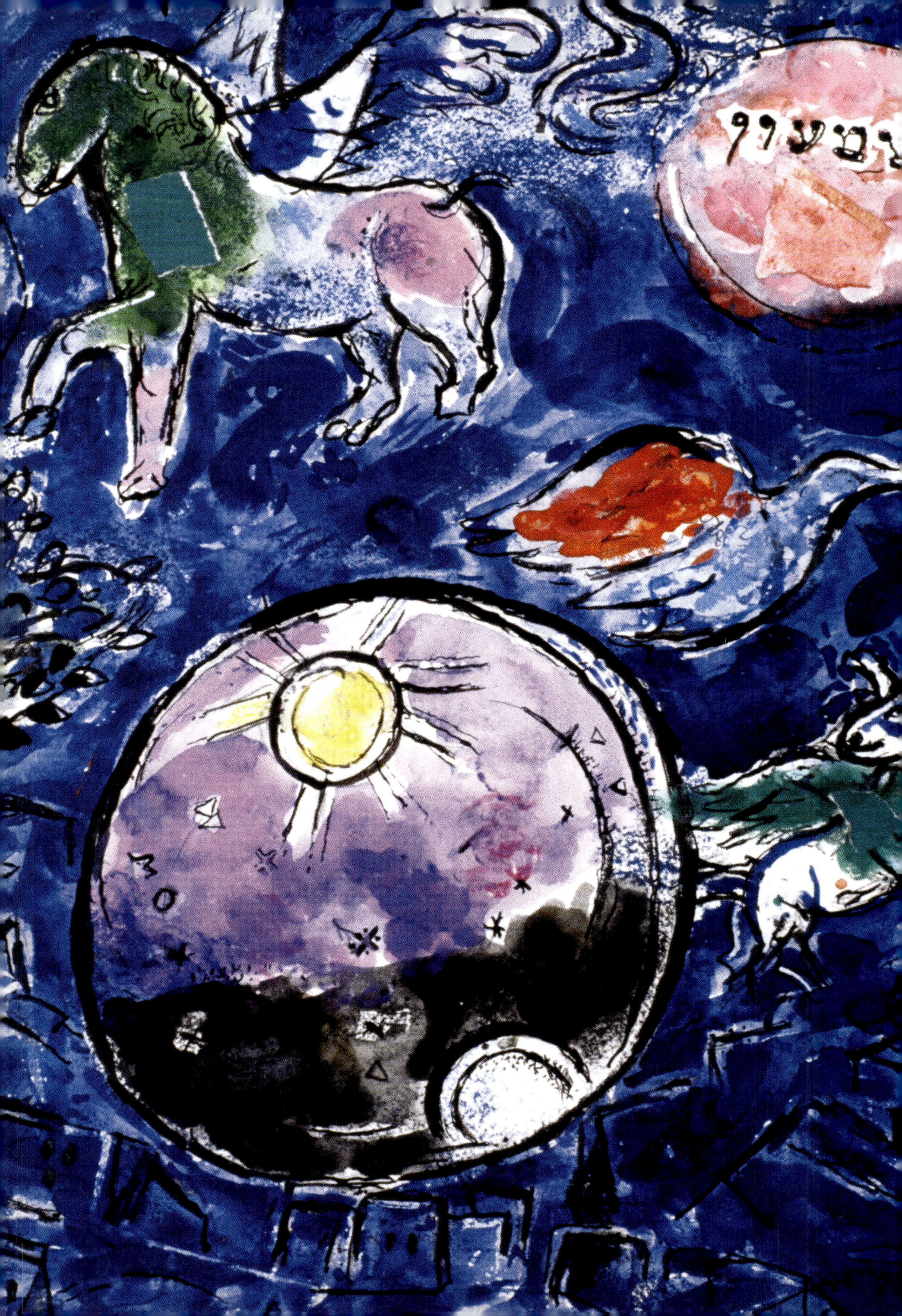

9. The Jerusalem Windows in the Perspective of Chagall's Poetics of Art

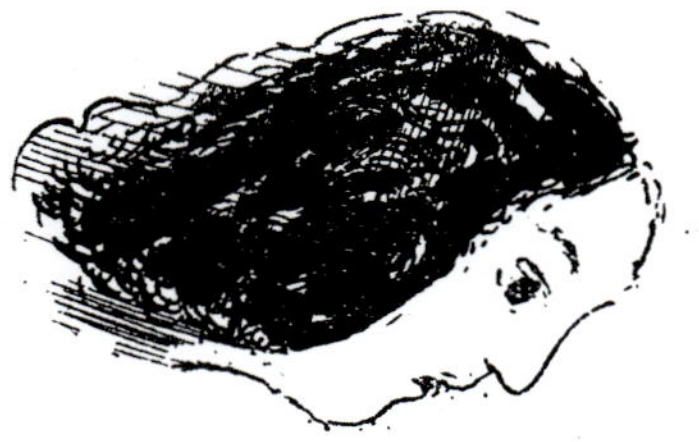

In his early work Chagall developed a fictional world of his own, which encompassed many individual works and was based on his mythologized city "Vitebsk." In 1922, before leaving Soviet Russia for good, he wrote: "Enough of Vitebsk. Its road is finished and its art came to an end." He was referring both to the death of his parents and the exodus of his sisters as well as to the dispersion of the avant-garde masters from the Art College he built there. When Vitebsk died and "the lost Jewish world" all but disappeared, he turned its elements into modular, emblematic units that reappeared in changing combinations throughout his oeuvre. From here, Chagall expanded in two directions: illustrating the fictional worlds of others, and transposing his personal vision and language of art into new media.

The first direction made him a prolific and brilliant illustrator of contemporary poetry and classical literary texts, culminating in the Bible. The absence of a new fictional world, even a landscape, of his own, channeled his creative energy into translating the canonized fictional worlds of others into his own language of art.

The second direction, expanding the gamut of media, led him from his early mastery of drawing and oil painting to making public posters in Revolutionary Russia (1918), stage sets for the Theater of Revolutionary Satire (1919), murals for the avant-garde Yiddish theater in Moscow (1920), etchings and other modes of reproduction that he studied with Herman Struck in Berlin (1922), and sets and costumes for theaters and operas in America (1942–46). After World War II and his return to Europe, he further expanded his media to lithographs, ceramics, stone statues, wall mosaics, tapestries, and stained-glass windows.

This expansion was fueled by two great impulses. One was Chagall's desire to create monumental art and reach a wider audience. This was a radical transformation of the introspective artist ("the crazy Russian" of the early Paris days) under the impact of the exuberant social rhetoric of the first two years of October. Little Chagall wanted huge walls; idiosyncratic and "solitary" Chagall (as a Communist writer called him) wanted to create public and accessible art. One of his manifestos as commissar of art in Revolutionary Vitebsk screams: "Give Us a Wall!" He repeated that craving in his murals for the Moscow Yiddish theater and expressed this wish ever since. When the cryptic and capricious Chagall became widely accepted and his recognizable modular language was naturalized and canonized, it became easy for him to achieve a mass appeal.

The other impulse was his lifelong romance with the Bible. From age four to thirteen, he attended *heder*, the traditional elementary Jewish school, conducted in the teacher's home. There he learned to read Hebrew texts (especially some chapters of the Pentateuch and basic prayers) but not to speak, write, or understand Hebrew. In his childhood milieu, the stories of the Bible were retold in Yiddish, and that retelling blurred the boundaries between the fundamental Biblical text and the stories, allegories, and imaginative explications that grew on it

OPPOSITE: ***Tribe of Simeon** (detail). 1959–60. Watercolor, India ink, pastel, pencil and paper collage, 20.4 x 15.1 cm. Private collection*

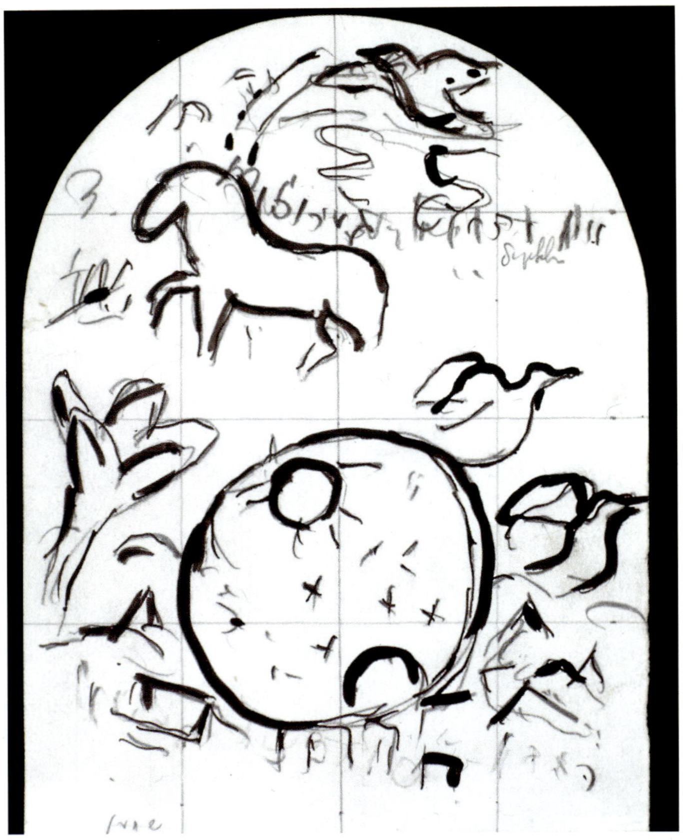

147. ***Tribe of Simeon.*** *1959–60. Pencil and India ink with brush, 20.3 x 14.9 cm. Private collection*

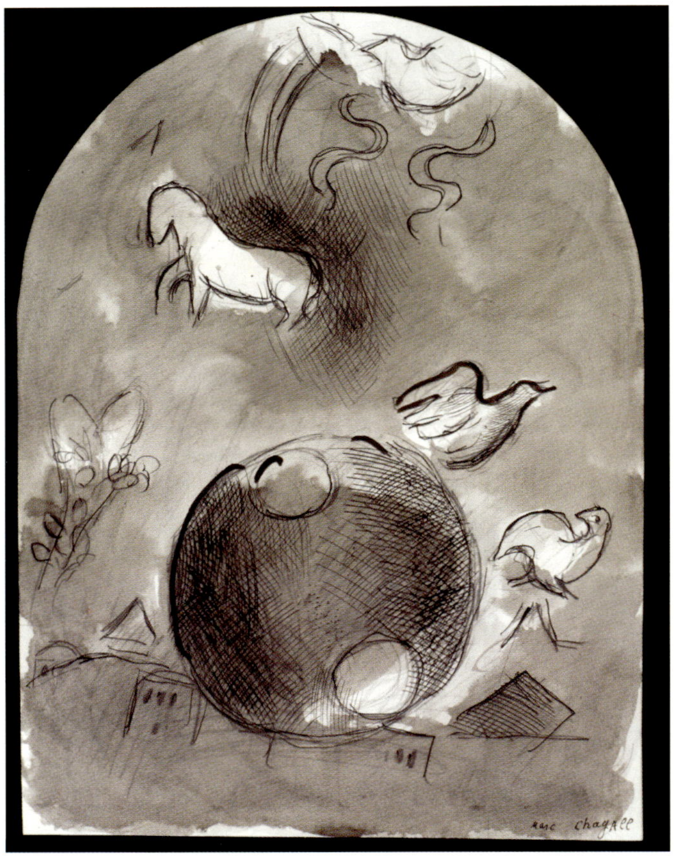

148. ***Tribe of Simeon.*** *1959–60. India ink wash, India ink with pen and pencil, 40.6 x 30 cm. Private collection*

throughout the ages, often summarized in the commentaries of the medieval French Hebrew commentator Rashi, which every child learned to read along with the Biblical text.

When Ambroise Vollard invited Chagall to Paris in 1923, he asked him to illustrate books based on the worlds of his homeland, notably Gogol's *Dead Souls* and the Bible. *Dead Souls* was read to him by Bella in Russian, yet Chagall could not understand the Hebrew Bible. In 1925, he asked his friend from LaRuche days, the Yiddish art critic Leo Kenig in London, and his lifelong friend, the American Yiddish novelist Yoseph Opatoshu, who was at the time in Poland, to buy him a Modern Yiddish translation of the Bible. Both sent him the first books of the Yiddish Bible. In the course of the years, Opatoshu got him volumes of the new, brilliant translation by the American Yiddish poet Yehoash as they were released. On November 8, 1928, Chagall wrote to Opatoshu in New York: "I received from you a marvelous Bible by the marvelous poet Yehoash." Yehoash was a modernist and wrote a poetic Bible in Yiddish using archaisms as neologisms, thus creating a rich Yiddish language in the guise of an archaic style. At first Chagall received the first published two books of the Pentateuch, and indeed his engravings of 1930–31 were almost all illustrations to the first two Biblical books. As the translation was completed, he received it all.

Vollard intended to extract from Chagall his knowledge of the parochial world of Russian provincial life and Russian Jewry, but with time Chagall inverted the direction and considered the Bible a gift of the Jews to all of humanity, the most universal book, as institutionalized in the National Museum Marc Chagall the Biblical Message in Nice. Finally he achieved a focal point whereby, as envisaged by his early critic A. Efros, past, present, and future all meet. The Bible filled the place of the mythological past, the present emerged as Chagall's omnipresent childhood, through which he first absorbed the Biblical figures, and the transhistorical, "spiritual" perception of Biblical images served as a message for the future. Furthermore, the Bible was as an intimate, familiar world, which could serve as a natural bridge between the Christian culture in which he was living and the Jewish culture of his childhood, and as such served as a symbolic "message" for all humanity. But Chagall's own Bible was the Yiddish translation; he thought about the Bible in Yiddish and conducted a dialogue with himself in Yiddish, as we can see it from a few Yiddish inscriptions in the mockups for the Jerusalem Windows.

•

I shall focus here on one example of Chagall's stained-glass windows, the windows he made for a little synagogue in the Hadassah hospital in Jerusalem.

The Jerusalem Windows are in many ways unusual in Chagall's work. They were made for a synagogue rather than for cathedrals or public places; they relinquished the use of human figures—an essential element in all of Chagall's work; and they don't tell a story or illustrate a preexisting narrative. His sensibilities and flights of imagination are conveyed not in flying figures but in flying colors.

In 1957 the French government bureau in charge of historical monuments invited Chagall to design two stained-glass windows for the Metz Cathedral. In the spring of 1958, upon his return from his first trip to the U.S. after 1948, Chagall met Charles and Brigitte Marq, the proprietors of the Jacques Simon Glass Works in Reims.[1] Marq caught the spirit and the intentions of Chagall, which were often expressed in gestures and feelings. The Marqs were impressed by Chagall's spirituality, thorough knowledge of the Bible, and meticulous attention to detail, and a close collaboration ensued. Charles Marq described his relations with Chagall as that of an actor to a scriptwriter, or of an orchestra conductor to a composer. Together they created a series of famous works, combining the effects of glass, light, and many shades of color.

In June 1959 Dr. Miriam Freund, President of Hadassah (the women's Zionist organization in the U.S.) and Joseph Neufeld, the architect who designed the Hadassah-Hebrew University Medical Center in the mountains near Jerusalem, saw the first Metz Cathedral windows exhibited in Paris and commissioned Chagall to produce twelve windows for the small synagogue in the new medical center.

Chagall's early art exhibited a demonstrative eclecticism. He absorbed various elements of several modernist trends (especially Fauves, Cubism, Suprematism) and confronted them with the dreamy images of a personal, multicultural subtext, as if he were juggling between art as innovative style and art as cultural representation. That tension created global contradictions and counterpoints: between representations and semi-geometrical forms or autonomous colors; between expressive semi-realism and irony; between grotesque and sentimental projections of situations; or between forces of gravity and movements defying it.

In the Jerusalem Windows, however, the taboo on human figures and absence of narratives shifted the emphasis to other counterpoints: between the depicted objects (spheres and animals) and formal forces sub-

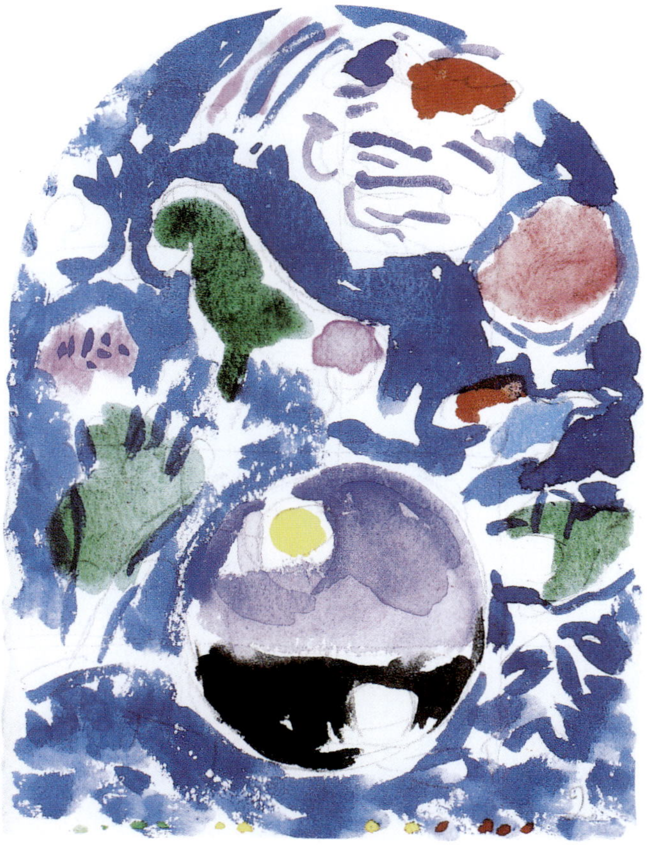

149. ***Tribe of Simeon.*** *1959–60. Watercolor, India ink and pencil, 20.3 x 15 cm. Private collection*

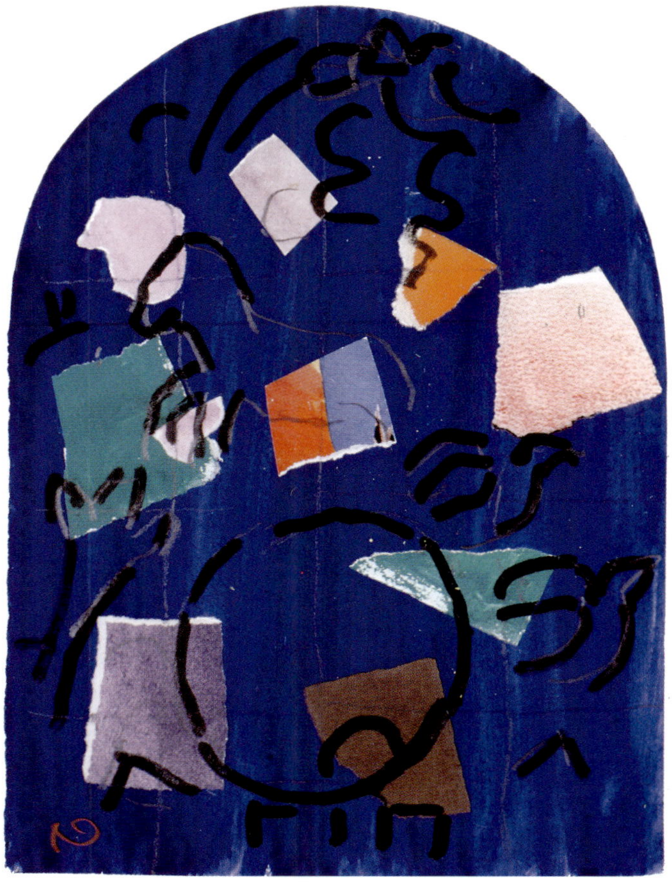

150. ***Tribe of Simeon.*** *1959–60. Watercolor, India ink, pastel, pencil and paper collage, 20.4 x 15.1 cm. Private collection*

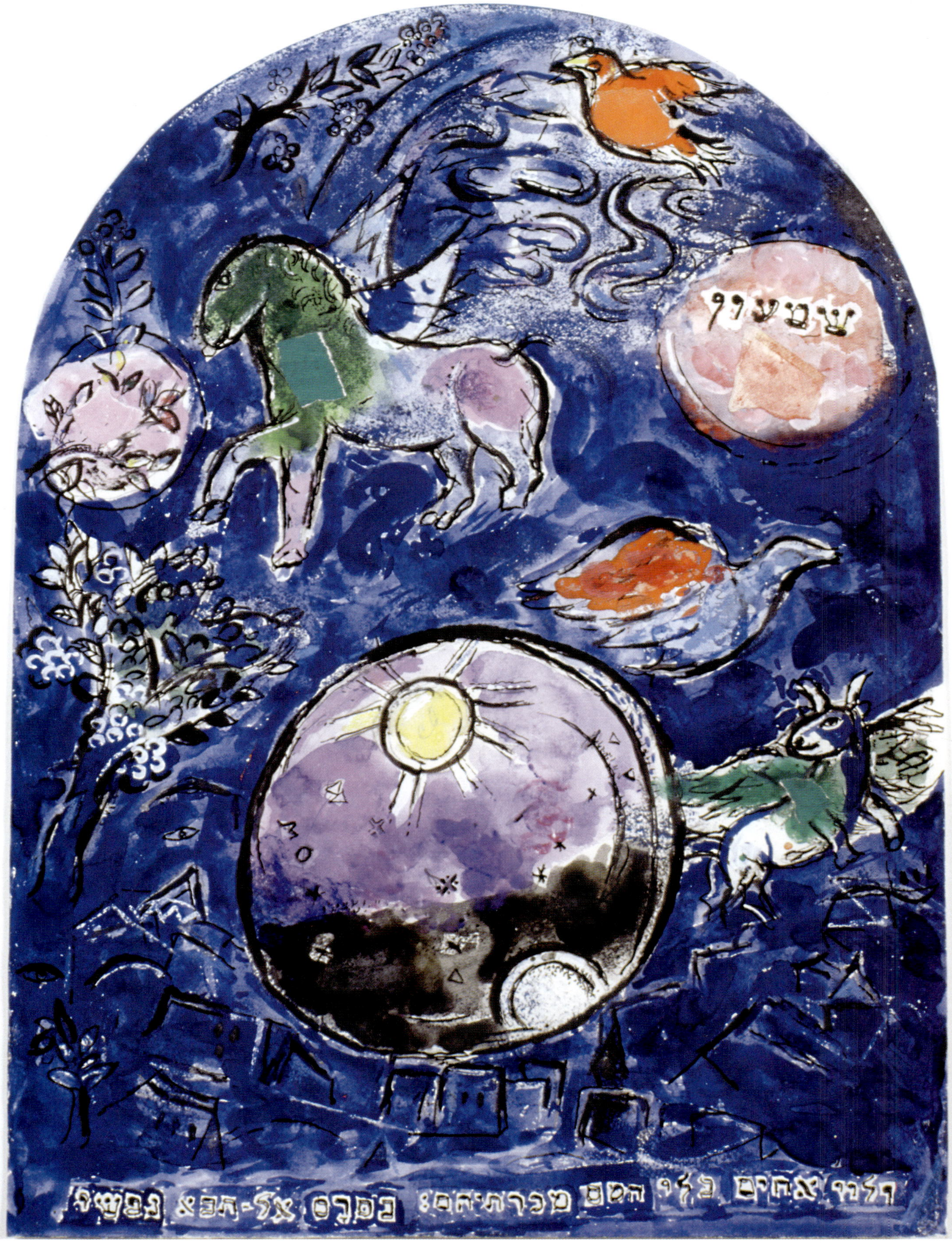

151. ***Tribe of Simeon.*** *1959–60. Gouache, watercolor, pastel, India ink, and paper collage, 40.7 x 30 cm. Private collection*

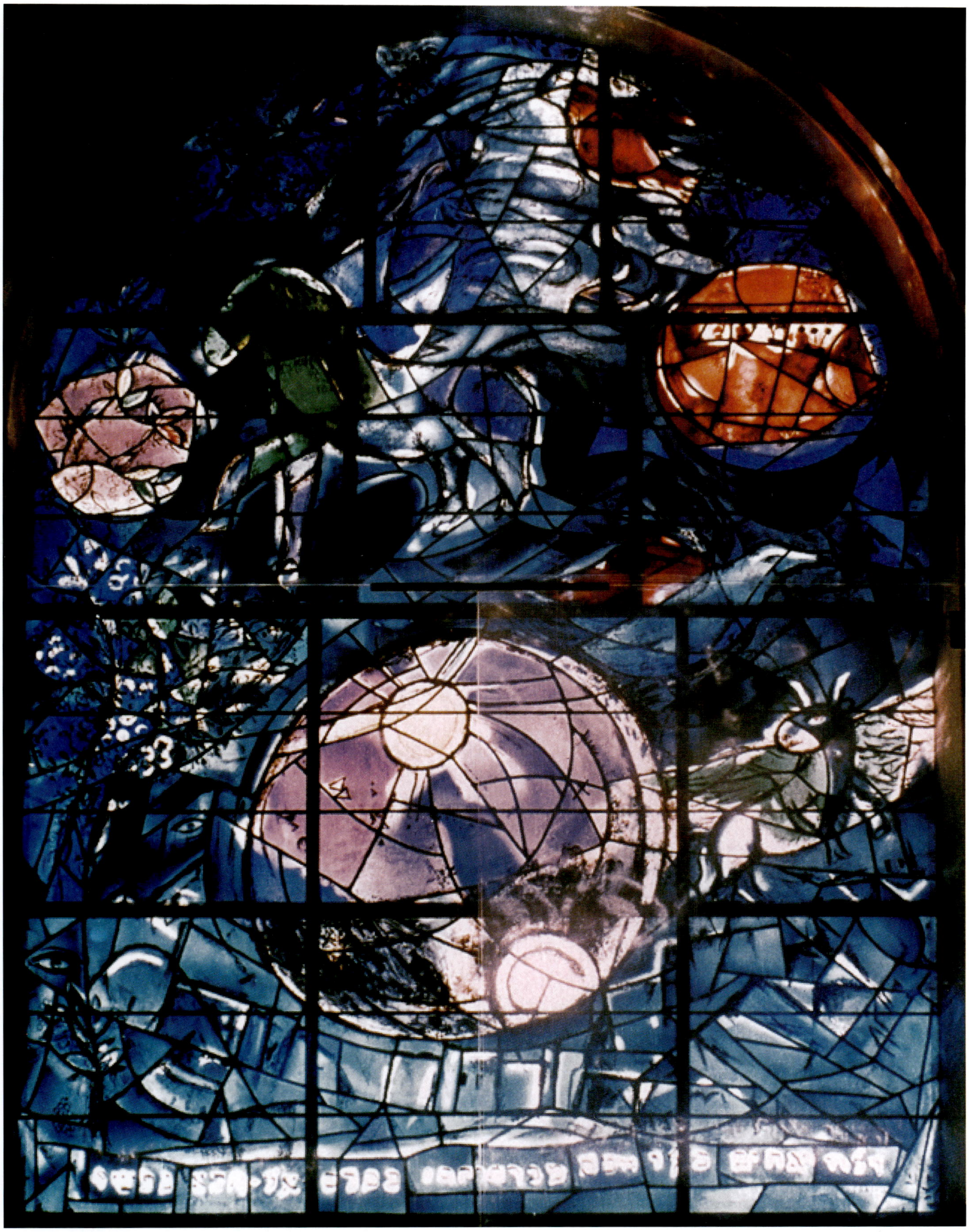

152. ***Tribe of Simeon.*** *1961. Stained glass window. Jerusalem, Hadassah hospital*

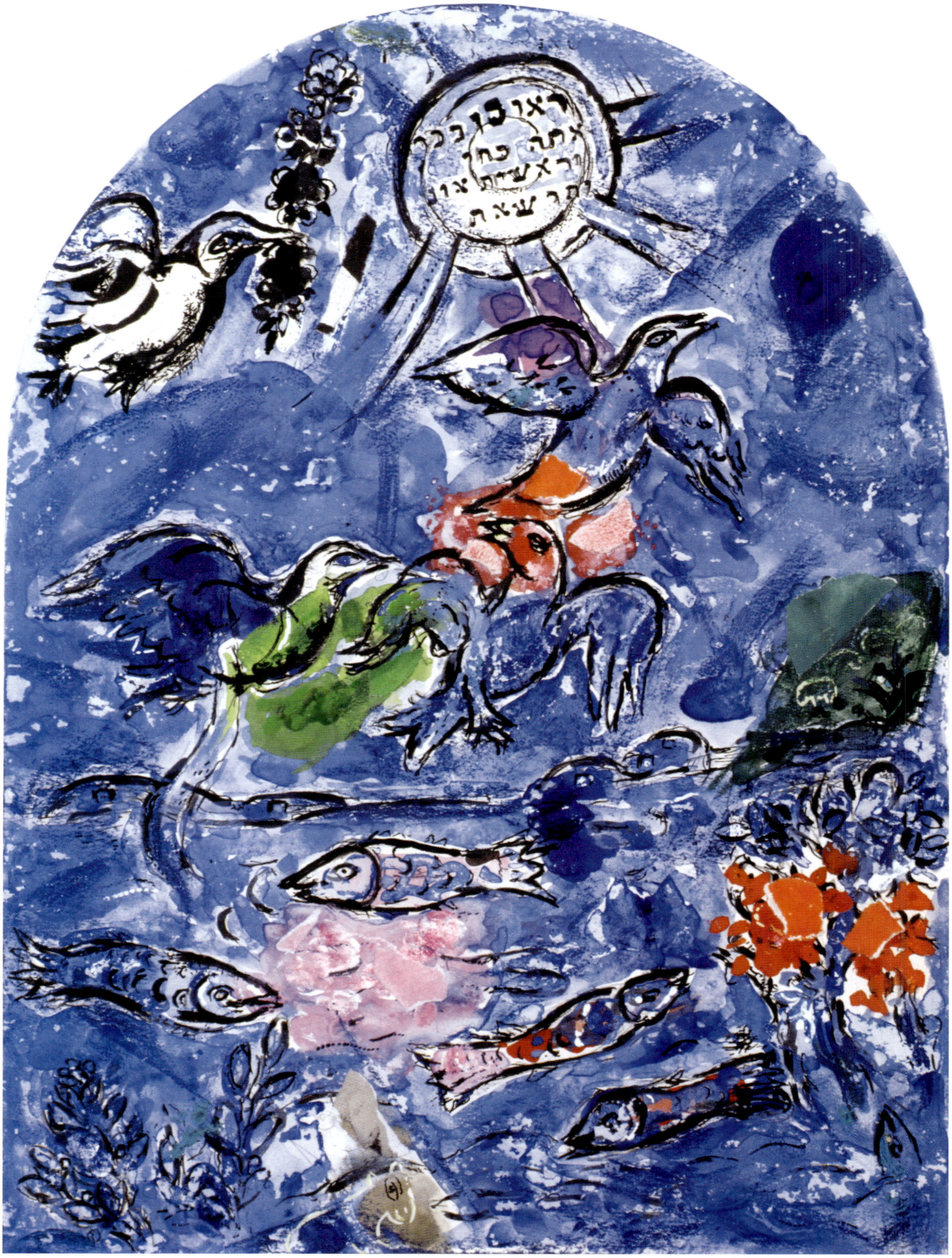

153. ***Tribe of Reuben.*** *1959–60. Gouache, watercolor, pastel, India ink and paper collage, 40.7 x 30 cm. Private collection*

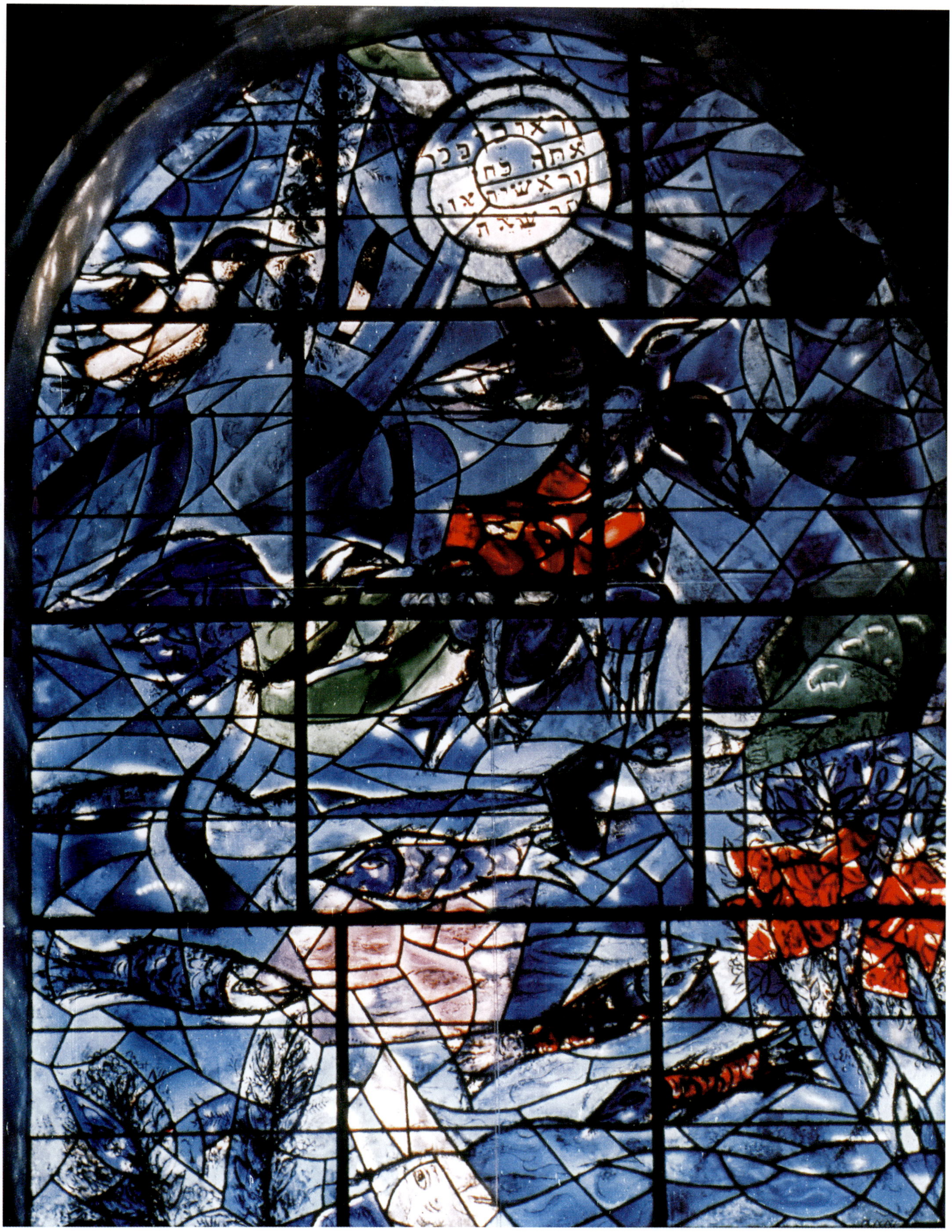

154. ***Tribe of Reuben.*** *1961. Stained glass window. Jerusalem, Hadassah hospital*

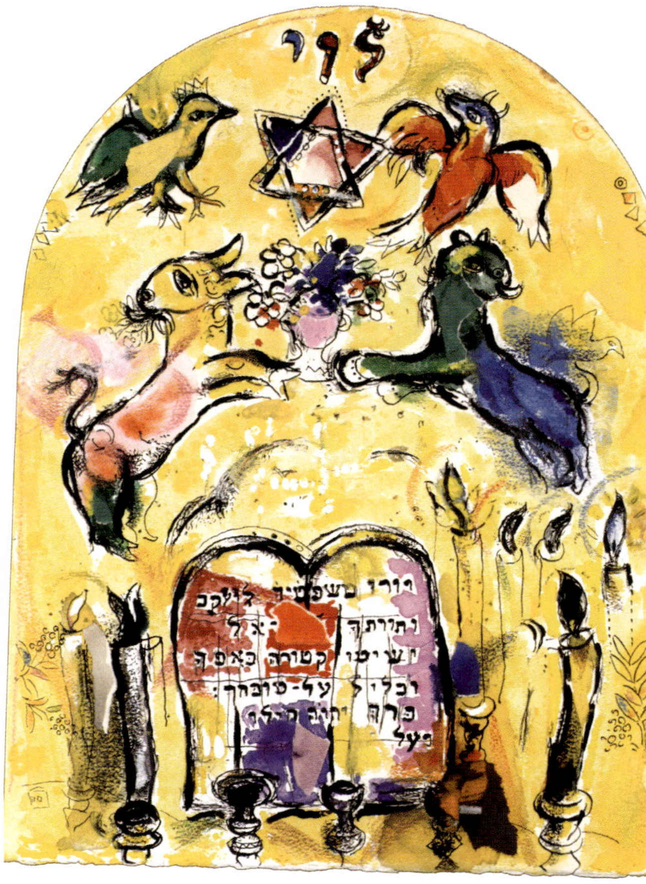

155. ***Tribe of Levi.*** *1959–60. Gouache, watercolor, pastel, India ink and paper collage, 40.7 x 30 cm. Private collection*

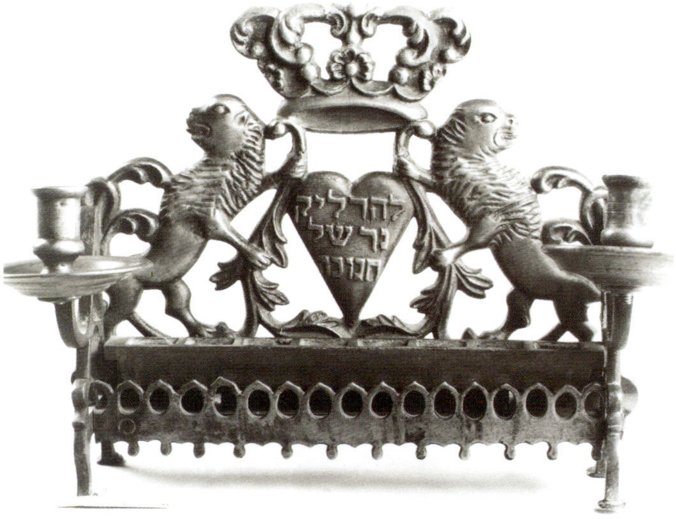

156. *Hanukkah lamp, Russia, nineteenth century. Courtesy of the author*

merging them (shapes and colors); between different dominant colors, and between those colors and transparent areas of light; between spreads of color and the semi-geometrical shapes and clusters created by the curvilinear tracery of the leading; and between the solid shapes of the grid or solid patches of color areas and the thin, lyrical twigs and flowers in grisaille. It is as close as Chagall ever came to abstraction or his own kind of "Abstract Expressionism" dependent on light and a spiritual communion. Chagall wrote:

> A stained-glass window has a different fate from a painting. Because of the setting, the eye does not look at it in the same way as a collection of paintings. The eye of a man at prayer is simply part of his heart. For me a stained-glass window is a transparent partition between my heart and the heart of the world. Stained glass has to be serious and passionate. It is something elevating and exhilarating. It has to live through the perception of light. To read the Bible is to perceive a certain light, and the window has to make this obvious through its simplicity and grace.[2]

Most of Chagall's illustrations to the Bible dwell on major Biblical figures, as mediated and domesticated in the oral transmission of his childhood, and are often depicted in terms of an East European milieu. The characters are perceived in what E. G. Lessing called "a pregnant moment," an image in space representing a crucial moment of a narrative in time. Yet the twelve tribes do not represent such a narrative. They are static characterizations, listed in Jacob's blessing to his sons and in Moses's benediction to the twelve tribes before entering the Holy Land. Moreover, they are hardly part of the folklore, the retelling of the exploits of the familiar Biblical heroes, which Chagall would have heard at home or in *heder* in his childhood. For the same reasons—lack of a symbolic narrative and absence of well-known heroes—the twelve brothers are rarely represented in the Christian tradition of Biblical iconography (although the twelve sons of Jacob can be seen as a prefiguration of the twelve disciples of Jesus).

This unusual choice of a serial, nonnarrative ensemble was clearly dictated by the occasion. The gathering of all the tribes in Jerusalem represents the Zionist dream of the "ingathering of the exiles" and the exhilarating experience of the young state of Israel that, indeed, all Jewish tribes from the ends of the world are coming back to their ancestral land.

When his stained-glass windows were installed in the small underground room of the Hadassah hospital synagogue—hardly the size of a cathedral—Chagall was furious; he broke chairs, as he had done in the Yiddish Chamber Theater half a century earlier. Chagall's perception of the place and weight of his windows had shifted from a parochial commission for a marginal prayer house (which he had accepted) to a sense of a contribution to the state of Israel itself and an expectation of a solemn reception. Yet, of course, he was aware in advance of the modest synagogue dimensions and made the windows so that they would almost cover the whole walls. Again, as in the Moscow theater, the spectators were enclosed in a "Chagallian Box," although this time above eye-level. But when his friends in Israel understood his grief and wanted to move the windows to a more central venue, he was against it. In a letter to M. Tsanin, editor of the Israeli Yiddish newspaper, *Di Letste Nayes*, who published Chagall's original Yiddish speech at the unveiling of the windows, Chagall wrote:

> I value the things you wrote and said to important persons about the twelve stained-glass windows in the Hadassah synagogue. But no matter what—I don't want it moved and a big synagogue built, where the stained-glass windows would be transferred. I think they should be in a more intimate place (with space, let's say, for about 200 people). Otherwise, they'll get lost or worse, be surrounded with various "art decorative." (December 13, 1967).

Chagall had a long-standing love affair with Israel, as attractive and ambivalent as all other ideologies he encountered (Communism, Surrealism). On his first trip with Bella and Ida, they spent almost three months in Palestine (they left Paris on March 1 and returned on June 4, 1931). They stayed in the house of the first mayor of Tel Aviv, Meir Dizengoff, and traveled to *kibbutzim* (collective villages) and to holy places. For Chagall, it was an extremely emotional trip. As he remarked, his father would weep whenever he mentioned "Jerusalem." Skeptical about the vitality of Jewish life in the Diaspora, Chagall admired the new Jewish presence in Palestine, the building of a modern Jewish city, and the new class of Jewish workers in the communal settlements. And beyond all that, echoes of the Bible—especially Genesis and the Prophets—spoke to him from the desert landscape. In January 1933 he wrote in a postcard from Palestine to Opatoshu in New York: "You want to travel to Eretz Israel. There you will see real Jewish workers and the settlements [underlined by Chagall] as you feel them in the Bible. This was my strongest impression of the new Palestine."

The windows were prepared in six stages as can be seen in the *Tribe of Simeon*. Stages 1 and 2 (no. 147, no. 148) are sketches in pencil, pen, and India ink. Stage 3 (no. 149) is the first color sketch, in India ink and watercolor. Stage 4 (no. 150) is a map of colors and figures. Stage 5 (no. 151) is the final model in gouache and collage. Stage 6 (no. 152) is the actual window, divided into geometrical squares and crisscrossed by a network of intricate curvilinear lead tracery. As the final product it subsumes, yet deviates from, all the previous stages. Jean Laymarie described the iconography of each window, relating it directly to the Biblical description,[3] and recently a thorough comparison was made in the book *Marc Chagall: Hadassah: From Sketch to Stained Glass Windows*.[4] From the monolithic stages of work in the twelve windows, it is clear that Chagall worked on all of them simultaneously. Thus, in the window of *Gad*, the Yiddish quotation from the Bible reads: "Simon and Levi are brothers." Chagall cross-referenced the two, perhaps because of Gad's similar violent nature, or just as a private reference to the earlier window, so as not to confuse the warrior imagery of the two.

Furthermore, in addition to the several epithets of the specific tribe in each window, there is a varying but repetitive imagery throughout. Because the blessings are in the book of Genesis, the first two windows depict creation (echoing what Chagall called the Genesis of modern Israel). Stage 5 of *Tribe of Reuben* (no. 153) shows the separation of water from sky (in Hebrew, *máyim/shamáyim*), divided by the "firmament." This is reinforced by the division of fish and fowl (four of each), underlined by the alliteration *fish/foygl* in Yiddish. We may see here also an allusion to his early painting *Time Is a River Without Banks* (no. 77), where a winged fish flying with a grandfather clock hovers above the water, thus raising the theme of the infinity of time. In Stage 6 of *Tribe of Reuben* (no. 154), the actual window, these divisions are all blurred by the play of colors. In *Tribe of Simeon* we have the earlier separation of heaven and earth within a transparent globe, and the creation of day and night.

Beyond the specific topic of each window, all windows are filled with animals, sketches of towns in the lower part, and religious objects. The animals include serpents and lions, which are not part of Chagall's regular bestiary or childhood memories but part of traditional synagogue ornaments, and—interestingly enough—do not include Chagall's personal, beloved cow, which he wanted to place on his calling card. In the window *Tribe of Levi* (no. 155), Chagall makes use of the traditional two lions crowning a Chanuka menorah or the tablets of the law, facing each other but with their heads turned backward.

His lion is a domesticated Chagallian animal (who saw lions in Vitebsk?) with no mane on its head, as we can find in the folklore tradition (see the photo of a menorah from nineteenth-century Russia, no. 156). Yet the lion on the left is amazing: He has turned into a lamb, such that the lion on the right can be seen as a wolf, as in Isaiah's prophecy, "the wolf shall dwell with the lamb." But the left animal also resembles a goat, the ubiquitous, milk-bringing animal of Eastern European Jewish life and Chagall's paintings. Be that as it may, it is a conflation of two different sources and a little Chagallian joke. Culturally, it is like the holy scribe in *Literature* (no. 117) copying not a Torah but a Yiddish folktale.

All those animals and objects are floating on the surface of the window, with no realistic continuity, no perspective, no ground, and no gravity. In a sense, most of them are ornaments, off center, or part of a multicentered balancing act.

In the final windows, however, it is not as easy to discern the figures and objects as one could do in the drafts: They are broken up by the metal grid, divided in a counterpoint by the lead tracery, and overruled by the color areas. This is why there are two schematic plans for each window in color: One is a map of the figures and the other a map of hard-edged color areas. Those are the two competing forces in the composition of the window. Thus, in Stage 5 of *Reuben's Tribe* (no. 151), there are four fish and four birds, but in the final window (no. 152) the lower right bird has all but disappeared, while its head is separated from the body and included in a strong red area.

The organized force of color appears on two major levels: the background of each window or the dominant color, especially prominent in the drafts, and the balancing local color areas superimposed on it. The dominant colors of the twelve windows are arranged in asymmetrical triads: three on each wall, so that only two are parallel in some way and the third is out, like a rhyming scheme *aam*, where *a* and *a* rhyme and *m* has no rhyming partner. This style is typical of the Prophets: whereas the dominant mode of rhythm in Biblical poetry is the parallelism of two adjacent versets, the Prophets often use the triad. Thus, Isaiah 1:2 begins:

> Hear, O heavens,/ and give ear, O earth/ for the Lord hath spoken.[5]

The first two versets are parallel to each other, the third stands alone. This structure embeds the poetic parallelism in a wider, more prosaic or more sweeping move. The organization of the whole ensemble can be seen in the diagram (no. 157).

The parallel windows have a basic background in the four basic colors of the windows: blue, red, green, yellow. As in Biblical parallelism, the second verset (here, window) on each side does not repeat the first but presents a variant or gradation of it: light/dark or different hues of red or yellow. He starts blue on the east and comes full circle (clockwise) to an odd blue window, linking the end of the series with its beginning. Thus, the circularity and the unity of the whole ensemble are emphasized.

On top of this background a second level of internal colors is articulated which, as seen in the schematic plan of stage four for each window, follows the same principles: hard-edged patches of color, each of which has a counterpart of a different shade or dark/light variation in the same window, although totally unrelated to their neighbors. An asymmetrical harmony is achieved, although not immediately discernible by the naked eye, because in the final product many boundaries have melted into each other: outlines of bodies and outlines of colors, blue and green, red and pink, and so on.

The same poetic principles determine the fate of the Hebrew letters. The traditional Hebrew letters are highly modulated and curvilinear. Chagall was one of the modern masters who introduced Hebrew geometrical letters (see chapter 4). Here he reverts to the traditional shape, yet somehow sloppy and soft, melted in the color world. It is hard to tell the difference between the Hebrew letters "b", "k," "n," or "z." Often the sentence is unfinished, or the text goes beyond its boundary. The reader is supposed to know the text by heart, and the letters serve primarily as an evocation of the Book of Books and as one more graphic element.

In the absence of human figures, the force of color—and color tensions, echoes, and contradictions—is overwhelming and takes us back to Chagall's roots. Under the influence of the Russian reception of the Fauve painters, Chagall early on impressed his contemporaries by the force of his colors, expressed in two ways: the fantastic or shocking use of color, unrelated to any realistic representation of figures or objects, and the flow of colors across the boundaries of objects and figures, as we saw in his early painting, *I and the Village*. The major influence in this direction came from Chagall's first real teacher of art, Léon Bakst. Bakst inspired in his students an expressive emancipation of color. Chagall's fellow student Yuliya L. Obolenskaya wrote:

> The ability to juxtapose contrasting colors, balancing their mutual influences and embodying them in the simplest forms—all that helped especially those of us

> who later worked on murals. . . . We trained not so much our hand as our sensibility. . . . We were preoccupied with the world of bright, sonorous, contrasting colors, the life of a color in its unfolding, in its clashes with other colors.[6]

This is still fresh and valid when we look at the Jerusalem Windows.

In a lecture in Chicago a year after the inauguration of the Jerusalem Windows, Chagall equated Color with Love—a diffuse, mystical concept, pervasive in his sensibility of those years. Love is the only force that can save the world in the Atomic Age, and its equivalent in painting, Color, must be "authentic," for the "moral crisis is also a crisis of color" ("A Crisis of Color," 1963). Elsewhere, he stated, "I have always painted pictures where human love floods my colors ("On the First Day of the War," June 6, 1967).[7]

Now, after a long detour dominated by "dreamlike" and "surreal" scenes or historical pageants—where color was secondary to the dominant, representational force—barred from depicting human figures, he came back to a celebration of color and light. As Jean Leymarie wrote:

> The essence of the Jerusalem Windows lies in color, in Chagall's magical ability to animate material and transform it into light. Words do not have the power to describe Chagall's color, its spirituality, its singing quality, its dazzling luminosity, its ever more subtle flow, and its sensitivity to the inflections of the soul and the transports of the imagination.[8]

1. I am grateful to Charles Marq for the two interviews he granted me and my son and putting Chagall's letters at my disposal.

2. The quotation is from *Marc Chagall on Art and Culture*, p. 145.

3. *Marc Chagall: The Jerusalem Windows*, text and notes by Jean Leymarie. English translation, New York: George Braziller, third edition, 1996.

4. Musée d'art et d'histoire du Judaïsme. *Marc Chagall: Hadassah: From Sketch to Stained Glass Windows*. Paris: Société Nouvelle Adam Biro, 2002.

5. The diagram comes from my article "The Jerusalem Windows in the Perspective of Chagall's Poetics of Art," in Musée d'art et d'histoire du Judaïsme. *Marc Chagall: Hadassah: From Sketch to Stained Glass Windows*. Paris: Société Nouvelle Adam Biro, 2002, pp. 119–30.

6. Y. L. Obolenskaya, "In the School of E. N. Zvantseva, Directed by L. S. Bakst and M. V. Dobuzhinsky (1906–10)," lecture at the Academy of Art Sciences, Moscow, 1927 (Russian typescript in the Chagall family archives). English translation in *Marc Chagall and His Times*, pp. 183–85.

7. Both lectures are translated in *Marc Chagall on Art and Culture*.

8. See Jean Leymarie. *Marc Chagall: The Jerusalem Windows*. Transl. from French by Elaine Desautels. New York: George Braziller, 1996, p. xi.

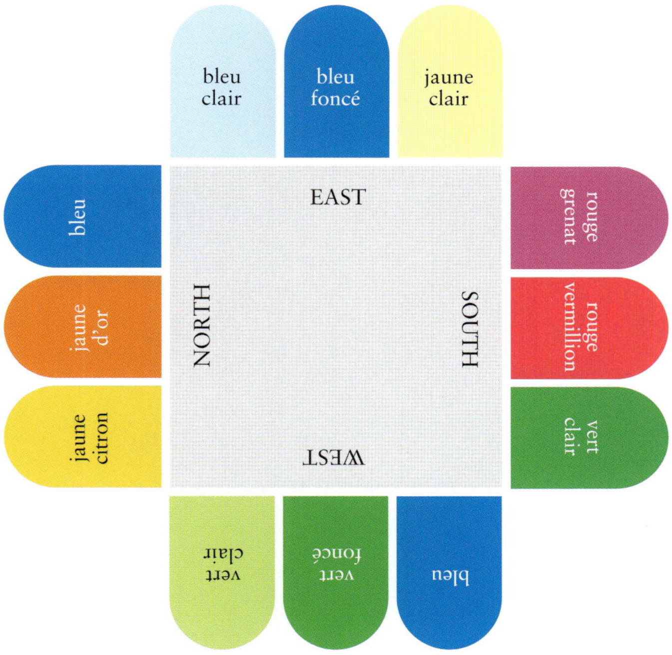

157. *Diagram of the placement of colors dominating the windows in Chagall's Hadassah Synagogue. Courtesy of the author*

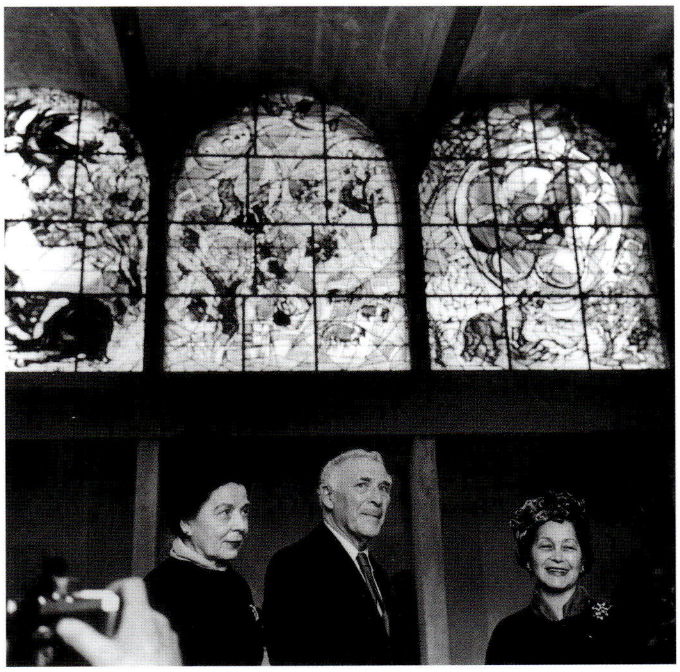

***Vava and Marc Chagall with Miriam Freund, President of American Hadassah** under Chagall's windows in the Hadassah Hospital synagogue in Jerusalem. Photo by Boris Carmi. Courtesy Rubin House, Tel Aviv*

Bibliography

Key to Languages: [E] – English; [F] – French; [G] – German; [H] – Hebrew; [I] – Italian; [S] – Spanish; [Y] – Yiddish.

Abramowicz, Dina. "Marc Chagall's Memoirs of His Youth in *Tsukunft* and His Letters to A. Leysin," *Tsukunft*, vol. 95 (1988), nos. 5–8, pp. 58–63. [Y]

______. "Marc Chagall," *Tsukunft*, vol. 95 (1988), nos. 9–12, pp. 123–28. [Y]

Alexander, Sidney. *Marc Chagall: An Intimate Biography*. New York: Paragon House, *1989*. [E]

Altman, Natan. "The State Yiddish Chamber Theater (After the Premiere)," *Der Emes*, Sept. 29, 1921. [Y]

Altman, Natan, Marc Chagall, and David Shterenberg. *Kultur-Lige*. Moscow: Kultur-Lige, 1922. [Y]

Amiard-Chevrel, Claudine. *Le Théatre artistique de Moscou (1898–1917)*, Paris: Centre national de la recherche scientifique, 1979. [F]

Amishai-Maisels, Ziva. "Chagall's Jewish In-Jokes." *Journal of Jewish Art*, vol. 5 (1978), pp. 76–93. [E]

__________. "Chagall and the Jewish Revival: Center or Periphery?" In Apter-Gabriel, pp. 71-100. [E]

_________. "Chagall's Murals for the Jewish State Chamber Theater." In Vitali, 1991, pp. 107–28. [E]

___________ "Jüdische Tradition in der Kunst Marc Chagalls" ["The Jewish Tradition in Marc Chagall's Art"]. In Chiappini 49–68. [G]

Antonova, Irina, Andrey Voznesensky, and Marina Bessonova. *Shagal: Vozvrashtshenie Mastera* [*Chagall: Return of the Master*]. Moscow: Sovietsky khudozhnik, 1988. [R]

__________ *Chagall Discovered* (trans. from the Russian by John Crowfoot and Alex Miller). New York: Hugh Lauter Levin, 1988. [E]

Apter-Gabriel, Ruth, ed. *Tradition and Revolution: The Jewish Renaissance in Russian Avant Garde Art 1912–1928*. Jerusalem: The Israeli Museum, 1987. [E]

__________ ed. *Chagall: Dreams and Drama: Early Works and Murals for the Jewish Theatre*. Jerusalem: The Israeli Museum, 1993. [E]

Arnheim, Rudolf. *The Genesis of a Painting: Picasso's Guernica*. Berkeley and Los Angeles: University of California Press, *1962*. [E]

Aronson, B. *Mark Shagal*. Berlin: Petropolis, 1923. [R]

______*Marc Chagall*, trans. From the Russian by R. von Walter. Berlin: Razum-Verlag, 1924. [G]

________ *Marc Chagall*, trans. from the Russian by Ben-Baruch. Berlin: Idisher literarisher ferlag—Petropolis, 1924. [Y]

__________. *Sovremennaya evreiskaya grafika* [*Contemporary Jewish graphic art*]. Berlin: Petropolis, 1924. [R]

Atkinson, J. Brooks. "The Play" (review of *The Dybbuk*). *The New York Times*, Dec. 14, 1926. [E]

B. "The Opening of the Yiddish Chamber Theater," *Pravda*, Oct. 5, 1923. [R]

Baal-Teshuva, Jacob. *Marc Chagall: 1887–1985*. GmbH: Benedikt Taschen Verlag, 1998. [E]

Bablet, Denis. *The Revolutions of Stage Design in the Twentieth Century*. Paris: Léon Amiel, 1977. [E]

Ben-Ari, R. *HaBima*. Chicago: L. M. Shteyn, 1937. [Y]

Berezkin, V. I. *Sovetskaya stsenografiya* [*Soviet Stage design*]. Moscow: Nauka, 1990. [R]

Bergelson, Dovid. "Dovid Bergelson On the Theater". *Literarishe bleter*, April 27, 1928. [Y]

Bernstein, Ignaz. *Yudishe shprikhverter un rednsartn* [*Yiddish proverbs and expressions*]. Collected and edited with B. W. Segal. Warsaw/Frankfurt: J. Kaufmann, 1908. [Y]

Beyder, Chaim. "Marc Chagall Returned to Russia." Unpublished. [Y]

Bir., O. "The Al'tman, Chagall, and Shterenberg Exhibit." *Teatral'naya Moskva*, no. 35 (April 17–23, 1922), pp. 13–15. [R]

Bojko, Szymon. "Three Waves of Emigration." In Charles Coria, ed., *Russian Samizdat Art*. [E]

Bowlt, John E. *The Silver Age: Russian Art of the Early Twentieth Century and the "World of Art" Group*. Newtonville, Mass.: Oriental Research Partners, 1978. [E]

_________. *Russian Stage Design: Scenic Innovation. 1900–1930*. Jackson: Mississippi Museum of Fine Arts, 1982. [E]

_________. *Khudozhniki russkogo teatra 1880-1930: Sobraniye Nikity i Niny Lobanovykh-Rostovskikh* [*Artists of the Russian theater 1880–1930: The Nikita and Nina Lobanov-Rostovsky Collection*]. Moscow: Iskusstvo, 1990. [R]

Bozo, Dominique, ed. *Marc Chagall: Oeuvres sur papier* (Marc Chagall: Works on paper). Paris: Centre Georges Pompidou, 1984. [F]

Brockett, Oscar G. *Modern Theatre: Realism and Naturalism to the Present.* Boston: Allyn and Bacon, 1982. [E]

Buber, Martin. "Jüdische Renaissance." ["The Jewish Renaissance"], *Ost und West* 1901; in: Die jüdische Bewegung. Berlin: *Jüdischer Verlag*, 1916. [G]

_________. "Von jüdischer Kunst." ["On Jewish Art"], *Die Welt*, January 17, 1902; in: *Die jüdische Bewegun*. Berlin: Jüdischer Verlag, 1916. [G]

Burko, Faina. *The Soviet Yiddish Theater in the Twenties.* Ph.D. diss., Southern Illinois University, Carbondale, 1978. [E]

Burrus, Christina, ed. *Marc Chagall.* Martigny, Switzerland: Fondation Pierre Gianadda, 1991.

Cain, Julien. *The Lithographs of Chagall.* Monte Carlo: Andre Sauret, 1960.

Carter, Huntley. *The New Theater and Cinema of Soviet Russia.* New York: International Publishers, 1935. [E]

_________. *The New Spirit in the Russian Theater: 1917–1928.* New York: Benjamin Blom, 1970. [E]

Cendrars Blaise. "Portrait," Oct. 1913, from *Selected Writings of Blaise Cendrars.* Ed. by Walter Albert. New York: New Directions, 1966.

Centro Cultural/Arte Contemporaneo. *Chagall en nuestro siglo* [Chagall in our century]. Mexico City: Centro Culutral/Arte Contemporaneo, 1991. [S]

Chagall, Bella. *Brenendike licht* [Burning candles]. New York: Book League of the Jewish Fraternal Order, 1945. [Y]

_________. *Di ershte bagegenish* [The first encounter]. New York: Book League of the Jewish Fraternal Order, 1947. [Y]

Chagall, Marc. "Eygns" ["From My World "]. *Tsukunft*, vol. 30 (1925), pp. 158–62, 290–93, 359–61, 407–10. [Y]

_________"From My World" [English translation of above, in Harshav, *Marc Chagall and His Times*, 2003, Chapter 2]. [E]

_________. *My Life* (trans. From the French by Elizabeth Abbott). New York: Orion Press, 1960. [E]

_________. *Angel nad kryshami* ["Angel above the roofs"], Chagall's poetry, translated from the Yiddish by L. Berlinsky. Moscow: Sovremennik, 1989. [R]

_________. *Die Bibel Gouachen. Aquarelle, Pastelle und Zeichnungen aus dem Nachlass des Künstlers.* Bundeskanzleramt Bonn: Landesmuseum Mainz, 1990. [G]

_________. "Two Letters of M. Chagall", *Shagalovskiye dni v Vitebske* (special issue of *Vit'bichi*), July 3–5, 1992. [R]

Chagall, Marc, and Klaus Mayer. *Der Gott der Väter: Das Chagall-Fenster zu St. Stephan in Mainz.* Würzburg: Echter Verlag, 1978. [G]

Charney, Daniel. *A yortsendlik aza* [Such a decade]. New York: CYKO, 1943. [Y]

Chiappini, Rudy, ed., *Marc Chagall*, Museo d'Arte Moderna, Città di Lugano, Skira 2001. [G]

Chipp, Herschel B., with Peter Selz and Joshua C. Taylor. *Theories of Modern Art: A Source Book by Artists and Critics.* Berkeley and Los Angeles: University of California, 1968. [E]

Compton, Susan. *The World Backwards: Russian Futurist Books 1912–16.* London: The British Library Board, 1978. [E]

_________. *Chagall.* London: Royal Academy of Arts, 1985. [E]

_________. *Marc Chagall: My Life—My Dream.* Munich: Prestel-Verlag, 1990. [E]

_________. "Chagall's Auditorium: 'An Identity Crisis of Tragic Dimensions'" in Guggenheim Museum, 1992, pp. 1–13. [E]

Däubler, Theodor. Marc Chagall. Rome: Ed. Valori plastici, 1922. [I]

Deytsh, Aleksandr. *Maski evreyskogo teatra* [Masks of the Yiddish Theater]. Moscow: Russkoe teatral'noe obshtshestvo, 1927. [R]

_________. "The Paths of GOSET." *Teatral'naya dekada*, no. 5 (1935), pp. 4–10. [R]

Dobrushin, Yikhezkel. "From Cloud to Fire". *Der Emes*, Jan. 21, 1923. [Y]

_________. "The German Press About the Guest Performances of the Moscow State Yiddish Theater." *Der Emes*, May 10, 1928. [Y]

_________. *Mikhoels der aktyor* [Mikhoels the actor]. Moscow: Der Emes, 1941. [Y]

Doria, Charles, ed. *Russian Samizdat Art.* Essays by John E. Bowlt, Szymon Bojko, Rimma, and Valery Gerlovin. Now York: Willis, Locker and Owens, 1986. [E]

L'École de Paris 1904–1929, le part de l'Autre. Musée d'Art moderne de la Ville de Paris : Paris musées, 2000. [F]

Efros, Abram. "Remarks about Art: Chagall, Al'tman, Fal'k". *Novy put'*, nos. 48–49 (1916), pp. 58–64. [R]

_________. "The Artist and the Stage." *Kul'tura teatra*, no. 1 (1921), pp. 11–12. [R]

_________. "Before the Opening Curtain: The New Season at the Jewish Theater". *Teatr I muzyka*, no. 9 (Nov. 1922), pp. 110–11. [R]

_________. "On the Rise: The Jewish Chamber Theater." *Novaya Rossiya*, no. I (1924), pp. 18–19. [R]

_________. "The Artists of Granovsky's Thater". *Iskusstvo*, vol. 4 (1928), books 1–2, p. 74. Reprinted in *Kovtsheg: Almanakh evreyskoy kul'tury* ["The Ark: Almanac of Jewish Culture"]. Moscow/Jerusalem: Tarbut/Khudozhestvennaya literatura, 1991.) [R]

_________. *Profili* (Profiles). Moscow: Federatsiya, 1930. [R]

Efros, A., and Y. Tugendhold. *Iskusstvo Marka Shagala* ["The art of Marc Chagall"]. Moscow: Helikon, 1918. [R]

_________. *Die Kunst Marc Chagalls* (trans. from the Russian by Frieda Ichak-Rubiner). Potsdam: Gustav Kiepenheuer Verlag, 1921. [G]

Erben, Walter. *Marc Chagall.* New York and Washington: Frederick A. Praeger, 1957. Rev. ed. 1966. [E]

Evreyskaya entsiklopediya ["Jewish encyclopedia"]. St. Petersburg: Brockhaus and Ephron, 1915. [R]

Evreyskoe shtshast'e ["Jewish luck," brochure for the film]. Moscow: Kino-petshat', 1925. [R]

Felitsin, Y. "The Moscow State Yiddish Chamber Theater: On Its Fifth Anniversary", *Literarishe bleter*, no. 12 (1924). [Y]

Fischer, Yona, "Le désir de Paris," in *L'Ecole de Paris 1904–1929: le part de l'Autre.* Musée d'art modern de la Ville de Paris, 2000–2001. Paris musées. pp. 103–13. [F]

Fletcher, Valerie, ed. *Crosscurrents of Modernism: Four Latin American Pioneers*, Washington, D.C.: Smithsonian Institution Press, 1992. [E]

Foray, Jean-Michel, ed. *Chagall: Surréaliste?* Paris: ADAGP, 2001. [F]

Forestier, Sylvie. *Résistance, Résurrection, Libération de Marc Chagall.* Rennes: Édition Ouest-France, 1990. [F]

Forester, Sylvie and Meret Meyer. *Les céramiques de Chagall.* Paris: Éditions Albin Michel, S.A., 1990. [F]

Frost, Matthew. "Marc Chagall and the Jewish State Chamber Theater." *Russian History*, vol. 8 (1981), parts 1–2, pp. 90–107. [E]

Gay, Peter. "Sigmund Freud: A German and his Discontents." *Freud, Jews and Other Germans: Masters and Victims in Modernist Culture.* New York: Oxford University Press, 1978. [E]

Geyser, M. *Solomon Mikhoels.* Moscow: Prometheus, 1990. [R]

________ *Mikhoels: Zhizn' i Smert'* [Mikhoels: Life and Death]. Moscow: Journalist Agency "Glasnost" of the Union of Journalists of the Russian Federation, 1998. [R]

Gnessin, M. *Darki im ha-teatron ha-ivri* [*My road with the Hebrew theater*]. Tel Aviv: Hakibuz Hameuchad, 1946. [H]

GOSET (State Jewish Theater). *Moscow State Jewish Theater* [playbill for GOSET's *1926* tours to Minsk, Kiev, Homel, Odessa, and Leningrad; includes short play reviews]. 1926. [R+Y]

Granach, Aleksander. "Granovsky, Mikhoels, and Zuskin—Congratulations!" *Literarishe bleter*, no. 20 (1928), p. 390. [Y]

Granovsky, A. "The Yiddish Theater." *Zvezda*, Minsk, July 31, 1923. [R]

_________. "Our Theater." *Literarishe bleter*, April 27, 1928. [Y]

Green, Christopher. "Les cubismes de l'École de Paris" in *L'Ecole de Paris 1904–1929: le part de l'Autre.* Musée d'art modern de la Ville de Paris, 2000–2001. Paris musées., pp. 58–70. [F]

Gregor, Joseph and René Fülop-Miller. *Das russische Theater* ["The Russian theater"]. Vienna: Amaltheat-Verlag, 1927. [G]

Grinbal'd, Ia. *Mikhoels.* Moscow: OGIZ, 1948. [R]

Güse, Ernst-Gerhard, ed. *Marc Chagall: Druckgraphik.* [Works on paper; a collection of articles], Landesmuseum Münster / Mittelrheinisches Museum Mainz: Hatje 1984. [G]

Guggenheim Museum. *Marc Chagall and the Jewish Theater.* New York: Guggenheim Museum, 1992. [E]

Haftmann, Werner, *Marc Chagall*, New York: Harry Abrams, 1973.

________. *Marc Chagall: Gouaches, Drawings, Watercolors.* New York: Harry N. Abrams, 1975. [E]

Haggard, Virginia, *My Life with Marc Chagall* (New York: Donald I. Fine, 1986). [E]

Harshav [Hrushovski], Benjamin. "Fictionality and Fields of Reference: Remarks on a Theoretical Framework." *Poetics Today*, vol. 5 (1984), no. 2, pp. 227–51. [E]

_________. *The Meaning of Yiddish.* Berkeley and Los Angeles: University of California Press, 1990. [E]

_________. "Chagall: Postmodernism and Fictional Worlds in Painting," pp. 15–64, 200–204; and "Texts and Documents," trans. from Russian and Yiddish by Benjamin and Barbara Harshav, pp. 133–99, in Guggenheim, 1992. [E]

_________."Marc Chagall: Painting, Theater, World," *Alpayim* No. 8, Fall 1993a, pp. 9–97. [H]

_________. *Language in Time of Revolution.* Berkeley and Los Angeles: University of California Press, 1993b. Stanford University Press, 2000. [E]

_________."The Role of Language in Modern Art: On Texts and Subtexts in Chagall's Paintings," *Modernism/Modernity* Vol. 1, No. 2, April 1994, pp. 51–87. [E]

__________."Le postmodernisme et l'art du carnaval," pp. 18–39, and "L'Introduction au Théatre juif," pp. 200–23, in *Marc Chagall: Les années russes, 1907–1922.* Musée d'Art moderne de la Ville de Paris, 1995. [F]

_________ "Les vitraux de Jérusalem à la lumière de la poétique chagallienne," in: *Marc Chagall, Hadassah : de l'esquisse au vitrail*, Paris: Musée d'art at d'histoire du Judaisme, 2002, pp. 119–29. [F]

_________ "The Jerusalem Windows in the Perspective of Chagall's Poetics of Art," in: *Marc Chagall, Hadassah, From Sketch to Stained Glass Windows*, Paris: Musée d'art at d'histoire du Judaisme, 2002, pp. 119–29. [E]

_________ *Marc Chagall and His Times: A Documentary Narrative*, Stanford, Calif., Stanford University Press, 2004, p. 1026. [E]

_________ "On the Poetics of Chagall's Art," in *Marc Chagall: Bonjour, La Patrie!"* State Tretyakov Gallery, Moscow, 2005, pp. 110–23. [E]

Harshav, Benjamin, ed., "The Moscow Yiddish Theater," special issue of *Di Pen*, No. 28–29, Nov.–Dec. 1996, including: Benjamin Harshav, "The Flourishing of the Moscow Yiddish Theater" and publication (with Yoseph Schein): "Mendele Moykher Sforim," *Masoes Binyomin Ha-Shlishi*, literary theater script by Yikhezkel Dobrushin. pp. 1–40. [Y]

Harshav, Benjamin, ed., *Marc Chagall On Art and Culture*, translated from several languages by Barbara and Benjamin Harshav, Stanford, Calif., Stanford University Press, 2004. [E]

Harshav, Benjamin and Barbara, eds. and trans. *American Yiddish Poetry: A Bilingual Anthology*, Berkeley and Los Angeles: University of California Press, 1986. [E]

Hofshteyn, Dovid. *Troyer* ["Grief"], Graphic design and illustrations by Marc Chagall. Kiev: Kultur-Lige, 1922. [Y]

Hume, Samuel A., and Walter Rene Fuerst, *XXth Century Stage Decoration* (Vol.1), New York: Alfred A. Knopf, 1929.

Dos Idishe Kamer Teatr [The Yiddish Chamber Theater], On its opening in July 1919. Pertograd: Jewish Theater Society, 1919. [Y]

Idisher Kamer Teatr [The Yiddish Chamber Theater]. Kiev: Kultur-Lige, 1924. [Y]

Jakobson, Roman. "Linguistics and Poetics." *Language and Literature.* Cambridge, Mass.: Harvard University Press, 1987, pp. 62–94. [E]

Jencks, Charles. *The Language of Post-Modern Architecture.* New York: Rizzoli, 1987. [E]

_________. *Post-Modernism: The New Classicism in Art and Architecture.* New York: Rizzoli, 1987. [E]

Jiddisch: Monatsschrift für jüdische Kultur in Wien [special issue on the Moscow Yiddish Theater], vol. I, nos. 5–6 (Aug.–Sept. 1928) [including "Biographical note on the Moscow artists"]. [Y]

Jouffrey, Alain. "Theater and Revolution." In G. di San Lazzaro, ed., *Chagall Monumental Works* (special issue of *XXe siécle Review*). New York: Tudor Publishing Company, 1973. [E]

Le Juif un Témoin du temps Errant. Paris: Musée d'art et d'histoire du Judaïsme. Paris: Société Nouvelle Adam Biro, 2001. [F]

Kamensky, Aleksandr. *Chagall: The Russian Years 1907–1922*, trans. from the French by C. Phillips. New York: Rizzoli, 1989. [E]

Kampf, Avram. "In Quest of Jewish Style in the Era of the Revolution." *Journal of Jewish Art*, vol. 5 (1978), pp. 48–75. [E]

__________. "Chagall in the Yiddish Theatre" in Vitali, 1991, pp. 94–106. [E]

___________. "Art and Stage Design: The Jewish Theaters of Moscow in the Early Twenties" in Apter-Gabriel, pp. 125–42. [E]

__________. *Chagall to Kitaj: Jewish Expreience in Twentieth Century Art*. London: Lund Humphries, with the Barbican Art Gallery, 1990. [E]

Kann, E. "Music at GOSET" (in Russian). *Teatral'naya dekada*, no. 5 (1935), p. 10. [R]

Kasovsky, Grigori. "Chagall and the Jewish Art Programme" in Vitali, 1991, pp. 53–60. [E]

Kerr, Alfred. "The Moscow Yiddish Teather (1928)," *Mit Schleuder und Harfe: Theaterkritiken aus drei Jahrzehnten*. Berlin: Henschelverlag, 1981. [G]

Keshet, Yeshurun. "Marc Chagall". *Di goldene keyt*, no. 60 (1967), pp. 34–53. [Y]

Kloomok, Isaac. *Marc Chagall: His Life and Work*. New York: Philosophical Library, 1951. [E]

Kornfeld, Eberhard W. *Marc Chagall: Catalogue raisonné de l'oeuvre gravé*, vol. I: 1922–1966. Bern: Kornfeld und Klipstein, 1971. [F]

Kornhendler, Yikhezkel. "About the Moscow Yiddish Chamber Theater", *Fraye Arbeyter Shtime*, 1928. [Y]

Kovaliev, Aleksei. "Report on the Restoration of the Murals for the Jewish Kamerny Theatre in Moscow" in Vitali, 1991, 134–39. [E]

Kultur-Lige: A sakh-hakl [The Culture League: A stocktaking; publication of the Central Committee]. Kiev: Nov. 1919. [Y]

Lassaigne, Jacques. *Chagall*. Paris: Ediction Maeght, 1957. [F]

Levy, Emanuel. *Ha-teatron ha-leumi Ha-Bima: Korot ha-teatron ba-shanim 1917–1979* ["The National Theater HaBima: History of the theater in the years 1917–1979"]. Tel Aviv: Eked, 1981. [H]

Leymarie, Jean. *Marc Chagall: The Jerusalem Windows*. Trans. from French by Elaine Desautels. New York: George Braziller, 1996. [E]

Lirov, M. "The Jewish State Chamber Theater." *Prozhektor*, Dec. 31, 1924. [R]

Lissitzky, El. "The Synagogue of Mohilev." *Milgroym*, no. 3 (1923), pp. 9–13. [Y]

Lissitzky, El, and Hans Arp, eds. *Die Kunstismen. Les Ismes de l'art. The Isms of Art*. Erlenbach-Zurich: Eugen Rentsch Verlag, 1925. [G]

Litvakov, M. "Of the October Miracles." *Der Emes*, April 13, 1922. [Y]

__________. "*The Sorceress* in the Yiddish Chamber Theater." *Der Emes*, Dec. 16, 1922. [Y]

__________. Sholem Aleichem in the Yiddish Chamber Theater." *Der Emes*, Jan. 21, 1923. Also in *Literarishe bleter*, no. 4 (1924). [Y]

_________. *Finf yor melukhisher yidisher kamer-teater*, [Five Years of the State Yiddish Chamber Theater: The Revolutionary Theater], Moscow: Shul un bukh, 1926. [Y]

Lozowick, Louis. "Moscow Theatre, 1920s." *Russian History*, vol. 8 (1981), nos. 1–2, pp. 140–44. [E]

Lukach, Joan. *Hilla Rebay: In Search of the Spirit in Art*. New York: George Braziller, 1983. [E]

Lyesin, A. [Walt, Abraham]. *Lider un poemen (1888–1938)* [Poems and long poems, 1888–1938], vols. 1–3. With illustrations by Marc Chagall. New York: Forwards Association, 1938. [Y]

Lynton, Norbert. "Chagall 'over the Roofs of the World.'" In Susan Compton, *Chagall*, pp. 20–29. [E]

Lyubomirsky, Y.O., *Der revolutsyonerer teater* [The revolutionary theater], Moscow: Shul un Bukh 1926. [Y]

_________ *Mikhoels*, Moscow: Iskusstvo 1938 [R]

Mandelshtam, Osip. "Mikhoels (1926)." In G. P. Struve and B. A. Filipoff, eds. *Sobraniye sochineny v trekh tomakh*, vol. 3, p. 106. New York: Inter-Language Associates, 1969. [R]

___________. "On the Nature of the Word (1922)." In G. P. Struve and B. A. Filipoff, eds., *Sobraniye sotshineniy v trekh tomakh*, vol 2, pp. 241–59. New York: Inter-Language Associates, 1972. [R]

Manteyfel, A. N. "The First Theater of the Revolution." *Moskva*, no. I (1968), pp. 192–94. [R]

___________. "The Theater of Revolutionary Satire (TEREVSAT)." *Teatral'noe iskusstvo*. [R]

Marc Chagall: Les années russes, 1907–1922. Musée d'Art moderne de la Ville de Paris: Paris musées, 1995. [F]

Marc Chagall: Hadassah: From Sketch to Stained Glass Windows. Musée d'art et d'histoire du Judaïsme. Paris: Société Nouvelle Adam Biro, 2002. [E]

Marés, Antoine. "Pourquoi des estrangers à Paris?" in *L'Ecole de Paris 1904–1929: le part de l'Autre*. Musée d'art modern de la Ville de Paris, 2000–2001. Paris musées, pp. 138–47. [F]

Margolin, S. [S. M.] "Tragic Carnival: 'A Night at the Old Market' at the Jewish State Theater." *Vsemirnaya illyustratsiya*, no. 3 (1925). [R]

___________. "The Artist and the Theater: GOSET Performances." *Teatral'naya dekada*, no. 5 (1935), pp. 8–9. [R]

Markov, P. A. *The Soviet Theatre*. New York: G. P. Putnam's Sons, 1935. [E]

Mayzel, Nakhman. "Five Years of the Yiddish Chamber Theater in Russia." *Literarishe bleter*, no. 46 (March 20, 1925). [Y]

____________. "The Great Miracle of the Stage." *Literarishe bleter*, April 27, 1928. [Y]

Meyer, Franz. *Marc Chagall: Life and Work*. New York: Harry N. Abrams, 1963. [E]

Mikhoels, S. "The New Jewish Comedian." *Der Veker*, Minsk, July 19, 1923. [Y]

__________. [Vofsi-Mikhoels]. "Our Comedians' Parade in the Ukraine." *Idisher Kamer Teatr* [The Yiddish Chamber Theater]. Kiev: Kultur-Lige, 1924, p. 10. [Y]

__________. "Mikhoels Vofsi On the Theater" [interview]. *Literarishe bleter*, April 27, 1928. [Y]

__________. "What a Question!" [interview]. *Jiddisch*, vol. I, nos. 5–6 (Aug.–Sept. 1928). [Y]

__________. *Stat'i, besedy, retshi* ["Articles, conversations, lectures"]. Moscow: Iskusstvo, 1965. [R]

Mikhoels: 1890–1948 [Collection about Mikhoels, on his death], Moscow: Der Emes 1948. [Y]

Mikhoels, S., and Y. Dobrushin. "Yiddish Theater Culture in the Soviet Union." In S. Dimanshteyn, ed., *Yidn in FSSR* [Jews in the USSR: A symposium]. Moscow: Mezhdunarodnaya Kniga and Emes, 1935, pp. 149–62. [Y]

Milhau, Denis. *Chagall et le Théatre*. Toulouse: Musée des Augustins, 1967. [F]

__________. "Chagall and the Theater." In G. di San Lazzaro, ed., *Homage to Marc Chagall*. New York: Tudor Publishing Company, 1969. [E]

Moskovsky Tsentr Iskusstv [Moscow Center of Art]. *David Shterenberg: 78 stolov* [*David Shterenberg: 78 Tables*]. Moscow: Logos / Gnosis Publishing, 2000. [R]

Musée National Message Biblique Marc Chagall Nice: Catalogue des collections. Nice and Milan: Ministere de la Culture, 1985; Paris: Editions de la Réunion des Musée Nationaux, 1990. [F]

Neklyudova, M. G. *Traditsii I novatorstvo v russkom iskusstve kontsa XIX-natshala XX veka* ["Tradition and innovation in Russian art from the end of the nineteenth to the beginning of the twentieth century"]. Moscow: Isskustvo, 1991. [R]

Norman, Itzhak, ed. *Be-reyshit Ha-Bima: Nahum Zemach meyased Ha-Bima be-hazon u-ve-ma'as* ["The beginnings of HaBima: Nahum Zemach, founder, HaBima in vision and practice"). Jerusalem: Ha-Sifriya ha-Zionit, 1966. [H]

Orshansky, B. *Teater-shlakhtn* [Theater battles]. Minsk: 1931. [Y]

Osborn, Max. "Marc Chagall." *Zhar-ptitsa* no. II, Berlin 1923a. [R]

__________. *Jüdische Graphik* [Jewish graphic art]. Berlin: Petropolis, 1923b. [G]

Pavel, Thomas G. *Fictional Worlds*. Cambridge, Mass.: Harvard University Press, 1986. [E]

Payne, Darwin Reid. *The Scenographic Imagination*. Carbondale and Edwardsville: Southern Illinois University Press, 1981. [E]

Petrow, Wsewolod, and Alexander Kamenski. *Welt der Kunst: Vereinigung Russischer Künstler zu Beginn des 20. Jahrhunderts* (trans. By Hans-Joachin Grimm and Galina Bajeva). Leningrad and Helsinki: Aurora-Kunstverlag, 1991. [G]

Petrova, Evgeniya, and Jürgen Harten, eds. *Pavel Filonov i ego shkola* [Pavel Filonov and his school]. Cologne: Buchverlag, 1990. [R]

Picon-Vallin, Béatrice. *Le Théatre juif sovietique pendant les années vingt* [The Soviet Jewish Theater in the nineteen-twenties]. Lausanna: La Cité, 1973. [F]

Reifenscheid, Beate, *Chagall und die Bühne*, Kerber Verlag 1996. [G]

Rischbieter, Henning, ed. *Art and the Stage in the Twentieth Century* (trans. from the German by Michael Bullock). Greenwich, Conn.: New York Graphic Society, 1978. [E]

Romm, Aleksandr. "Marc Chagall." Unpublished. [R]

Ronch, Itzhak Elchanan. *Di velt fun Marc Shagal* [The world of Marc Chagall]. New York: YIKUF, 1967. [Y]

Roose-Evans, James. *Experimental Theatre: From Stanislavsky to Today*. New York: Universe Books, 1970. [E]

Rudnitsky, Konstantin. *Meyerhold the Director* (trans. by George Petrov). Ann Arbor, Michigan: Ardis, 1981. [E]

__________. *Istoriya russkogo sovetskogo dramatitsheskogo teatra* ["history of the Russian Soviet dramatic theater"], vol. I: 1917–1945. Moscow: 1984. [R]

__________. *Russian and Soviet Theater 1905–1932* (trans. from the Russian by Roxane Permar). New York: Harry N. Abrams, 1988. [E]

Russian Painters and the Stage: 1884-1965. [a loan exhibition of stage and costume designs from the collection of Mr. And Mrs. Nikita D. Lobanov- Rostovsky] Austin, Texas: University of Texas Art Museum, 1978. [E]

Sandrow, Nahma. *Vagabond Stars: A World History of Yiddish Theater*. New York: Harper and Row, 1977. [E]

Schein, Yosef. *Arum moskver yidishn teater* [Around the Moscow Yiddish Theater]. Paris: Les éditions polyglottes, 1964. [Y]

Schneider, Pierre. *Marc Chagall*. Paris: Flammarion, 1995. [E]

__________ "Chagall and Stained Glass." In: *Marc Chagall, Hadassah: From Sketch to Stained Glass Windows*, Paris: Musée d'art at d'histoire du Judaisme, 2002, pp. 13–19. [E]

Shatskich, Alexandra [Aleksandra Shatskikh]. "When and Where Was Marc Chagall Born?" In Vitaly, 1991, pp. 21–22. [E]

__________. "Chagall and Malevich in Vitebsk," in Vitali, 1991, pp. 62–67. [E]

__________ "Marc Chagall and the Theater," in Vitali, 1991, pp. 76–89. [E]

__________. "Marc Chagall and Kazimir Malevich." *Shagalovskie dni v Vitebske* [special issue of *Vit'bitshi*], July 3–5, 1992. [R]

__________. "Aleksandr Romm and His Memoirs of Marc Chagall." Unpublished. [R]

__________. "Copies of Mark Chagall's Theatrical Sketches in the Bakhrushin Museum." Unpublished. [R]

__________. "Mark Chagall and the Jewish Chamber Theater." Unpublished. [R]

__________. "The Theatrical Phenomenon of Mark Chagall." Unpublished. [R]

__________ *Vitebsk: Zhizn' Iskusstva 1917–1922* [Vitebsk: The Life of Art 1917–1922], Moscow: Yazyki Russkoy Kultury, 2001. [R]

Shazar, Zalman. "Homage to Chagall". *Di goldene keyt*, no. 60 (1967) pp. 27–33. [Y]

Shklovsky, Viktor. "Jewish Luck." In *Evreiskoe stshast'e*, 1925. [R]

[Shmeruk] Szmeruk, Ch. *Ha-kibutz ha-yehudi ve-ha-hityashvut ha-khaklayit ha-yehudit be-byelorusya ha-sovietit (1918–1932)* [The Jewish community and Jewish agricultural settlement in Soviet Byelorussia 1918–1932]. Ph. D. diss., Hebrew University, Jerusalem, 1961. [H]

Shtempfer, Shaul. "Population Growth and migration in Polish/Lithuanian Jewry in the modern age." In: Israel Bartal & Israel Gutman, eds. *The Broken Chain: Polish Jewry Through the Ages*. Jerusalem: Zalman Shazar Center 1997, pp. 263–86. [H]

Sorlier, Charles, ed. *Chagall by Chagall* (trans. from the French by John Shepley). New York: Harry N. Abrams, 1979. [E]

_________. *Mémoires D'un Homme de Couleurs*. Pré aux Clercs: NOE, 1985. [F]

_________. *Marc Chagall: The Illustrated Books*. Paris: André Sauret/ Michèle Trinckvel, 1991. [E]

Spencer, Charles. *Léon Bakst*. New York: Rizzoli, 1973. [E]

Sutzkever, Abraham. *Di fidlroyz* [The fiddle-rose]. Tel Aviv: Di Goldene Keyt, 1974. [Y]

_________. *Selected Poetry and Prose* (trans. by Barbara and Benjamin Harshav). Introduction by Benjamin Harshav. Berkeley and Los Angeles: University of California Press, 1992. [E]

Sweeney, James Johnson. "Art Chronicle: An Interview with Marc Chagall." *The Parisian Review*, no. II (Winter 1944), pp. 88–93. [E]

_________. *Marc Chagall*. New York: Museum of Modern Art, 1946. [E]

Swett, Herman. "German Jews, German Press, and the Granovsky Theater." *Literarishe bleter*, April 27, 1928a. [Y]

_________. "The Theater World in Berlin." *Literarishe bleter*, no. 41 (1928b). [Y]

_________. "Meyerhol'd and Granovsky." *Literarishe bleter*, no. 19 (1930), p. 344. [Y]

Tairov, Aleksandr. *Zapiski rezhisera* [Notes of a theater director]. Moscow: Kamernyi Teatr, 1921. [R]

Tarabukin, Nikolai. "Art Exhibitions: Al'tman, Chagall, Shterenberg," *Vestnik Isskustv*, no. 5 (1929), pp. 27–28. [R]

Tarenne, Viviane. "Chagall et la fortune critique, la presse des années dix et vingt." In *Marc Chagall: Les années russes, 1907–1922*. Musée d'Art moderne de la Ville de Paris: Paris musées, 1995. pp. 150–56. [F]

Teatral'naya Moskva [a guide to theater, music, and film, includes entries on the Moscow State Yiddish Theater and HaBima], 1926. [R]

Teatral'naya zhizn' [special issue on GOSET], no. 10: p. 764, 1990. [R]

Toller, Ernst, Joseph Roth, and Alfons Goldschmidt. *Das Moskauer Jüdische Akademische Teater* [The Moscow Jewish Academic Theater]. Berlin: Verlag Die Schmiede, 1928. [G]

van Gyseghem, André. *Theatre in Soviet Russia*. London: Faber and Faber, 1943. [E]

Van Norman Baer, Nancy, ed. *Theater in Revolution: Russian Avant-Garde Stage Design 1913–1935*. New York: Thames and Hudson/The Fine Arts Museum of San Francisco, 1991. [R]

Venturi, Lionello. *Chagall: A Biographical and Critical Study* (trans. by S. Harrison and J. Emmons). Paris: Editions d'Art Albert Skira, 1956. [E]

Vetrov, A. [Arkin, David]. "On Chagall." *Ekran*, no. 7, 1921a. [R]

_________. "Exhibition of Three." *Ekran*, no. 28, 1921b. [R]

Vevyorke, A. "A Jewish Theater Style: On the Sholem-Aleichem Evenings in M.Y.C.T. [Moscow Yiddish Chamber Theater]." *Der Emes*, no. 78, 1921c. [Y]

_________. "A Holiday," *Der Emes*, April 13, 1922. [Y]

Vitali, Christoph, ed. *Marc Chagall: The Russian Years 1906–1922*. Frankfurt: Schirn Kunsthalle, 1991. [E]

Vlasova, R. I. *Russkoe teatral'no-dekoratsionnoe iskusstvo natshala XX veka* ["Russian theatrical design of the early twentieth century"]. Leningrad: Khudozhnik RSFR, 1984. [R]

Vofsi-Mikhoels, Natalia. *Avi Shlomo Mikhoels* ["My Father Shlomo Mikhoels"]. Tel Aviv: Hakibutz Hameuchad, 1982. [H]

Walden, Herwarth. "The Moscow Yiddish Chamber Theater". *Der Sturm*, vols. 2–3 (1928–29), p. 229. [G]

Weinreich, Uriel. "Problems in the Analysis of Idioms." *On Semantics*. Philadelphia: University of Pennsylvania Press, 1980. [E]

Worrall, Nick. *Modernism to Realism on the Soviet Stage: Tairov-Vakhtangov-Okhlopov*. Cambridge: Cambridge University Press, 1989. [E]

YIVO. *Barikht fun der konferents fun dem yidishn visnshaftlekhn isntitut, opgehaltn in vilne 1929* [Report on the conference of the Yiddish Scientific Institute in Vilna, 1929]. Vilna: YIVO, 1930. [Y]

Yudovin, Sh. *Idisher folks ornament* [Jewish folk ornament]. Vitebsk: 1921. [Y]

Yudovin, Sh., and B. Malin, eds. *Idishe ornamentale folks kunst* [Jewish ornamental folk art]. Vitebsk: 1921. [Y]

Zagorsky, M. *Mikhoels*. Moscow and Leningrad: Kinopetshat,' 1927. [R]

_________. "Mikhoels." *Teatral'naya dekada*, no. 5 (1935), p. 7. [R]

Zingerman, B. "Russia, Chagall, Mikhoels, and Others." *Teatr*, vol. 2 (1990), pp. 35–53. [R]

_________. "About Mikhoels." *Moskovsky nablyudatel,'* no. 2 (Jan. 1991). [R]

Znosko-Borovsky, Evg. *Russky teatr natshala XX veka* ["Russsian theater in the early twentieth century"] vol. I. Prague: Plamya Press, 1923. [R]

Zrelishtsha (special issue on the fifth anniversary of GOSET), no. 89 (1924). [R]

Zuskin, B. "Actor B. Zuskin On the Theater" [interview]. *Literarishe bleter*, April 27, 1928. [Y]

Zylbercwaig, Zalman. *Leksikon fun yidishn teater* [Lexicon of the Yiddish Theater], vol. 2. Warsaw: Elisheva, 1934 [includes entries on Granovsky, pp. 516–17, the Moscow State Yiddish Theater, pp. 1227–1239 (with extensive bibliography), Mikhoels, pp. 1312–1314]; vol. 4. New York: Elisheva, 1963 [includes Sholem-Aleikhem and descriptions of all stage productions, pp. 3309–3578]. [Y]

List of Illustrations

This list is arranged alphabetically by title. Numbers at the end of each entry correspond to plate numbers.

WORKS BY MARC CHAGALL

Thinking About Picasso. *1914. Black ink on paper, 19.1 x 21.6 cm. Musée national d'art moderne, Centre Georges Pompidou, Paris. Photo: CNAC/MNAM/Dist. Réunion des Musées Nationaux/Art Resource, N.Y.* **no. 19**

Three Acrobats. *1923. Etching and aquatint, 34.2 x 37.3 cm. Collection of E.W. Kornfeld, Bern* **no. 124**

Time Is a River Without Banks. *1930–39. Oil on canvas, 100 x 81.3 cm. Private collection. Photo: Copyright © Christie's Images Limited* **no. 77**

To My Wife. *1933–34. Oil on canvas, 107 x 178.8 cm. Musée national d'art moderne, Centre Georges Pompidou, Paris. Photo: CNAC/MNAM/Dist. Réunion des Musées Nationaux/Art Resource, N.Y.* **no. 9**

To Russia, Donkeys and Others. *1912. Oil on canvas, 157 x 122 cm. Musée national d'art moderne, Centre Georges Pompidou, Paris. Photo: CNAC/MNAM/Dist. Réunion des Musées Nationaux/Art Resource, N.Y.* **no. 41**

Tribe of Levi. *1959–60. Gouache, watercolor, pastel, India ink and paper collage, 40.7 x 30 cm. Private collection* **no. 155**

Tribe of Reuben. *1959–60. Gouache, watercolor, pastel, India ink and paper collage, 40.7 x 30 cm. Private collection* **no. 153**

Tribe of Reuben. *1961. Stained glass window. Jerusalem, Hadassah hospital. Photo: The Granger Collection, New York* **no. 154**

Tribe of Simeon. *1959–60. Pencil and India ink with brush, 20.3 x 14.9 cm. Private collection* **no. 147**

Tribe of Simeon. *1959–60. India ink wash, India ink with pen and pencil, 40.6 x 30 cm. Private collection* **no. 148**

Tribe of Simeon. *1959–60. Watercolor, India ink and pencil, 20.3 x 15 cm. Private collection* **no. 149**

Tribe of Simeon. *1959–60. Watercolor, India ink, pastel, pencil and paper collage, 20.4 x 15.1 cm. Private collection* **no. 150**

Tribe of Simeon. *1959–60. Gouache, watercolor, pastel, India ink, and paper collage, 40.7 x 30 cm. Private collection* **no. 151**

Tribe of Simeon. *1961. Stained glass window. Jerusalem, Hadassah hospital. Photo: The Granger Collection, New York* **no. 152**

Uncle Zusya's Shop in Lyozno. *1914. Oil, gouache, and colored pencil on paper, 37.1 x 49 cm. Tretyakov Gallery, Moscow* **no. 3**

The Village Fair. *1908. Oil on canvas, 68 x 95 cm. Private collection, New York* **no. 30**

The Vision of King David. *1981. Oil on canvas, 114 x 146 cm. Private collection, Basle* **no. 146**

War. *1914. India ink and opaque white with pen and brush on paper, 22 x 18 cm. Kovalenko Art Museum, Krasnodar* **no. 49**

War. *1964–66. Oil on canvas, 163 x 231 cm. Kunsthaus Zurich* **no. 144**

Water Carrier by Moonlight. *1911. Watercolor, gouache, crayon and fountain pen on paper, 24.1 x 31.1 cm. The Metropolitan Museum of Art, New York, Bequest of Scofield Thayer, 1982 (1984.433.56) Photo: © 1989 The Metroplitan Museum of Art* **no. 84**

The Wedding. *1911. Oil on canvas, 99.5 x 188.5 cm. Musée national d'art moderne, Centre George Pompidou, Paris. Photo: CNAC/MNAM/Dist. Réunion des Musées Nationaux/Art Resource, N.Y.* **no. 35**

The Wedding Table. *1920. Tempera and gouache on canvas, 63.8 x 799.2 cm. Tretyakov Gallery, Moscow* **no. 118**

White Crucifixion. *1938. Oil on canvas, 154.3 x 139.7 cm. Gift of Alfred S. Altschuler, 1946.925, The Art Institute of Chicago. Photo: Reproduction, The Art Institute of Chicago* **no. 130**

ILLUSTRATIONS FROM BOOKS

Cover of **The Art of Marc Chagall** *(1918) written by Abram Efros and Yakov Tugendhold, Moscow* **no. 66**

Drawing. *Published in Sturm Bilderbücher, Berlin, 1923* **no. 39**

Illustration across from page X, **TROYER.** *Courtesy Yivo Institute for Jewish Research, N.Y.* **no. 72**

Illustration across from page XIV, **TROYER.** *Courtesy Yivo Institute for Jewish Research, N.Y.* **no. 73**

Page XI, **TROYER.** *Courtesy Yivo Institute for Jewish Research, N.Y.* **no. 71**

What do I need it, the transparent lucidity [that leaks into the cracks of ruins]? *or* **The Walking Village.** *1921. Illustration for* **Grief (Troyer)** *by D. Hofshteyn. Ink on vellum paper, 32.6 x 29 cm. AM 1988-217. Musée National d'Art Moderne, Centre Georges Pompidou, Paris. Photo: CNAC/MNAM/Dist. Réunion des Musées Nationaux/Art Resource, N.Y.* **no. 70**

ILLUSTRATIONS

Illustration for the cover of **Grief** *by D. Hofshteyn. 1919. Ink on paper, 47.2 x 33.7 cm. AM 1988-213. Musée National d'Art Moderne, Centre Georges Pompidou, Paris. Photo: CNAC/MNAM/Dist. Réunion des Musées Nationaux/Art Resource, N.Y.* **no. 87**

Cover illustration of **Khalyastre.** *1924. Courtesy Yivo Institute for Jewish Research, New York* **no. 88**

The Revolution, *from the series* **Lider un Poemen** *by A. Lyessin (Abraham Walt), with 34 drawings by Chagall. 1931. Ink on paper, 14.5 x 13.5 cm. Musée National d' Art Moderne, Centre Georges Pompidou, Paris* **no. 126**

Page 35 from **Seder Avodat Israel,** *edited by Yitzhak ben Ayre Yosef Dov, Seligman Baer, new edition, Schocken, Berlin. 1937. Courtesy of the Leo Baeck Institute, New York* **no. 86**

Cover illustration of **Shtrom.** *1922. Courtesy Yivo Institute for Jewish Research, New York* **no. 85**

THEATER AND SET DESIGNS

The Agents *by Sholem Aleichem. 1919–20. Pencil, gouache, ink on paper, 25.6 x 43.2 cm. AM 1988-253. Musée National d'Art Moderne, Centre Georges Pompidou, Paris. Photo: CNAC/MNAM/Dist. Réunion des Musées Nationaux/Art Resource, N.Y.* **no. 99**

Photo of actors from **The Agents.** *Courtesy Natalia Vofsi-Michoels and the History of Theatre Archives, Tel Aviv University* **no. 100**

It's a Lie, *set design. 1920. Pencil and gouache on paper, 22.5 x 30 cm. Collection of Ida Chagall, Paris* **no. 102**

Mazel-tov, *set design. 1920. Pencil and watercolor on paper, 25.5 x 34.5 cm. Collection of Ida Chagall, Paris* **no. 101**

WORKS BY OTHER ARTISTS

Uri-Tsvi Grinberg. **Uri-Tsvi Before the Cross INRI [Jesus of Nazareth, King of the Jews].** *In* **Albatross: Journal for the new expression of poets and artists** *(in Yiddish), no. 2, Berlin, November 1922, page 3. Courtesy Yivo Institute for Jewish Research, New York* **no. 129**

Kazimir Malevich (1878–1935). **Cow and Violin.** *1913. Oil on wood, 48.8 x 25.8 cm. Russian State Museum, St. Petersburg. Photo: Valery Kuner* **no. 103**

Kazimir Malevich. **A Non-Stop Station: Kuntsevo.** *1913. Oil on canvas, 49 x 25.5 cm. Tretyakov Gallery, Moscow* **no. 25**

Masaccio (1401–1428). **Expulsion from Paradise,** *Brancacci Chapel, S. Maria del Carmine, Florence. Photo: Scala/Art Resource, N.Y.* **no. 46**

Henri Matisse (1869–1954). **Portrait of Mme. Matisse.** *1905. Oil on canvas, 40.5 x 32.5 cm. Statens Museums for Kunst, Copenhagen, J. Rump Collection. © 2006 Succession H. Matisse, Paris/Artists Rights Society (ARS)/N.Y.* **no. 4**

Pablo Picasso (1881–1973). **Guernica.** *Paris, June 4, 1937. Oil on canvas, 349.3 x 776.6 cm. Museo Nacional Centro de Arte Reina Sofia, Madrid. © 2006 Estate of Pablo Picasso/Artists Rights Society (ARS)/N.Y. Photo: Erich Lessing Art Resource, N.Y.* **no. 98**

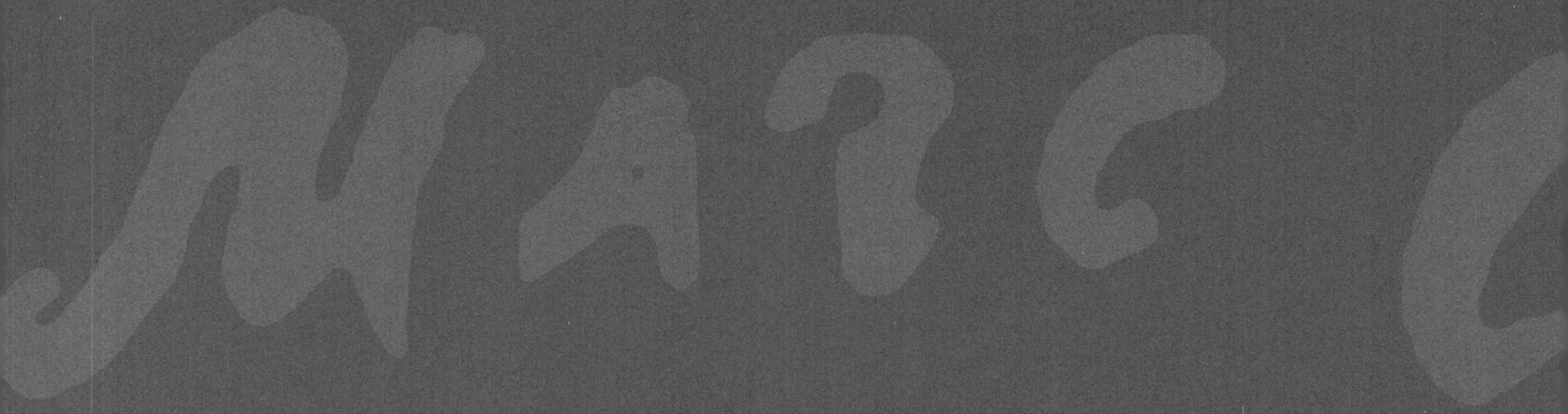
Marc

40 YEARS
at the Heart of
our Community

Celebrating 30 years of care
Caring for future generations

St Luke's Hospice

Art Exhibition & Auction

Moor Park Golf Club, The Orangery

A showcase of assorted artwork including paintings, ceramics, prints and pottery

Celebrating 70 years of local hospice care

Friday 10th February (open 10.00am-7.00pm) FREE ENTRY

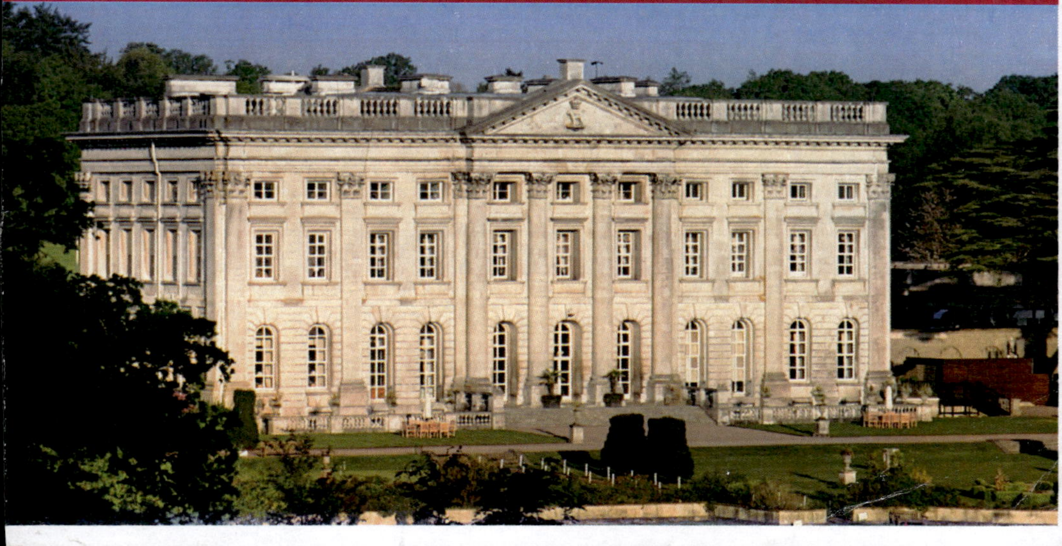

Welcome to our Art Exhibition & Auction

We very much hope you will enjoy visiting our wonderful 'pop-up' exhibition. Throughout the exhibition you will find individual items available for sale via a 'silent auction' which will be in operation throughout the day. All artwork has been kindly donated by the artists meaning monies raised can immediately start to make a difference. It is thanks to this kind of generous support we can commit to delivering our vision of expert care and support to those who need it, now and in the future.

2017 is a very poignant year for both hospices and provides a wonderful opportunity for us to come together to mark this special occasion in the wonderful setting of Moor Park. We are hugely proud of the care both our hospices provide to the local community, and it is amazing to think that together we have provided a total of 70 years care and support to local families and their loved ones.

If you would like to place a bid on any of the artwork please complete one of the slips available with your best bid and contact details. The highest bid will win the Lot and will be notified by Monday 13th February when we will take payment and arrange collection.

Thank you for joining us,

Lindsey Fealey
CEO Michael Sobell Hospice

Robin Webb
CEO St Luke's Hospice

LOT: MSH01

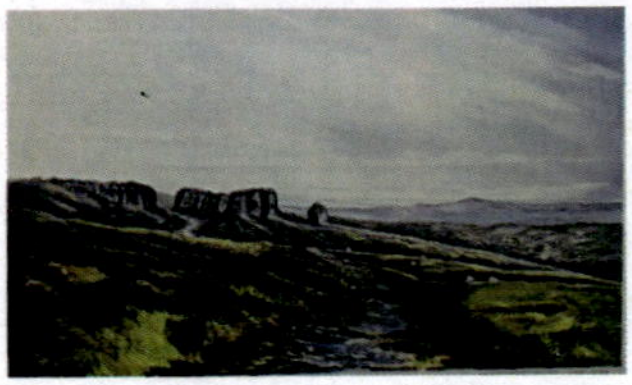

The Cow and Calf Rocks on Ilkley Moor

Ashley Jackson

Framed, Limited Edition print
26" x 20"

www.ashley-jackson.co.uk, www.yorkshiresociety.org.uk

Ashley Jackson is one of the country's leading and most successful landscape watercolourists. His unique evocative and distinctive paintings of brooding moorlands have become synonymous with Yorkshire, and more particular the moors above and around his Gallery situated in the heart of the Pennines, Holmfirth.

His works have been exhibited worldwide, and adorn the walls of many successful and famous people, from politicians to actors, from Tsars to Princes. Ashley was honoured when the former President of America, Bill Clinton, an avid art collector was presented with an original watercolour.

Ashley throughout his career has always been an ambassador for the arts. He has strived, through his life to encourage people not just to take up art, but to appreciate the beauty of the landscape around us. 'The Cow and Calf Rocks on Ilkley Moor' is kindly donated by the Yorkshire Society and is a limited edition mounted print.

LOT: MSH02

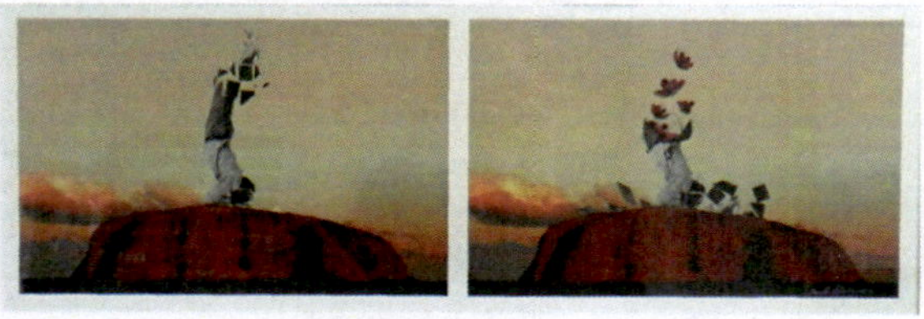

Uluru Face Plant In Bloom

Gareth Halliday

Framed 31.5" x 16.5"
Collage art

Gareth was first inspired to create art by a visit to the Picasso Museum in Paris as a teenager in 1992. Gareth admired Picasso's work that used collage and assemblage from abandoned sources and his rebellion against traditional art. Gareth graduated with a degree in Fine Arts at The University of Northampton in 2000. Throughout his degree he explored image making with collage, painting, photography and printmaking.

Gareth has been collecting and re-appropriating vintage printed media and ephemera for over 20 years. He is fascinated with the otherworldly qualities of images from a forgotten time or place. His collage and photomontage work tries to exert control over the flood of images we are confronted with daily; playing with relationships between scale and perception and disparate pop culture associations. Often these works end up as subversive commentary on the society we live in.

Gareth has been a part of several group and solo exhibitions nationally and had his first solo exhibition with Lazarides in 2014. He has sold work worldwide.

To contact Gareth or view more of his work please visit:

- garethhalliday@msn.com
- www.garethhallidaycollageart.com
- www.instagram.com/garethhalliday

LOT: MSH03

Summer Border

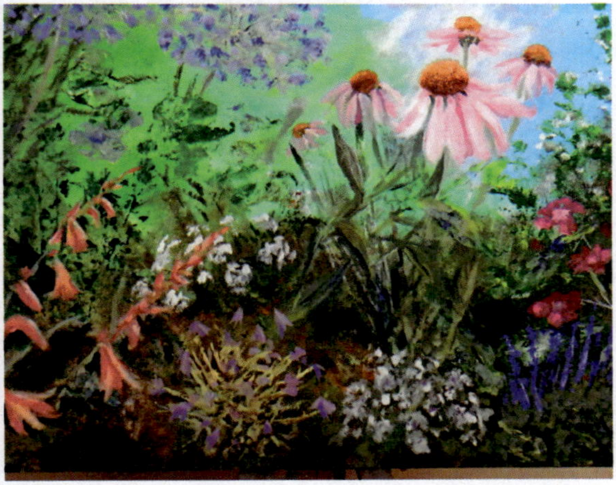

Ruth Hallet

Acrylic on canvas
20" x 16"

Born in the first few weeks of the war Ruth's best loved subject at school was art. Art has remained a constant pleasure throughout her life.

Ruth's sister spent her last days in Michael Sobell Hospice which inspired Ruth to become a volunteer, working regularly in the hospice's Northwood Shop.

Ruth's picture 'Summer Border' has been donated in memory of her sister.

LOT: STL01

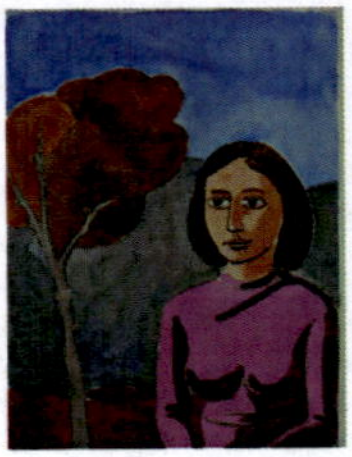

One Sunny Day

Shanti Panchal

Watercolour (22cm x 30cm)
www.shantipanchal.com
Reserve: £500

Shanti Panchal is a leading London-based Indian artist with an international reputation.

He has won the 1991 National Portrait Gallery/BP Portrait Award, was Artist-in-Residence at the National Gallery in London in 1994, and was a 2003 nominee for the UK Asian Achievers Awards.

Born in 1951 in Mesar in the state of Gujarat, Shanti Panchal studied art at the JJ School of Art in Mumbai where he also worked on a fellowship for a year. Further study at the Byam Shaw School of Art in London a British Council Scholarship directed his future track that included a stint as artist-in-residence at the British Museum in London. For over twenty five years Panchal has worked solely in watercolour not prepared to accept the conventional limits he pushes the boundaries of his medium, developing a unique way of using watercolour that is close to the art of fresco, building layer upon layer almost in a meditative state of being.

LOT: STL02

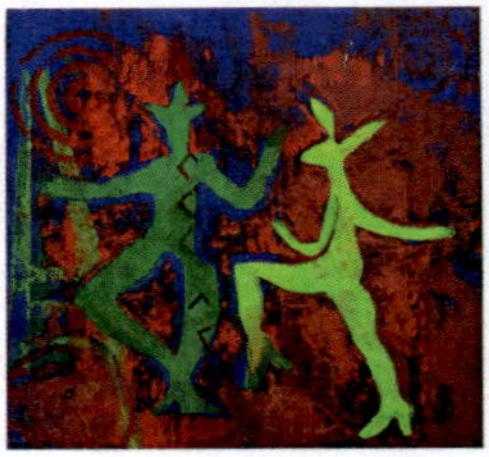

Escapade

Cheryl Gould

Monoprint + block printing
Framed (17.5" x 17.5")
www.cheryl-gould.com
Reserve £95

The framed print 'Escapade' is part of a series loosely based on Judith Kerr's novel "When Hitler Stole Pink Rabbit", which conjured up images that made a strong impact on me. So in this work the forgotten toy is now in disguise and being led to new adventures with her mischievous friend the Jester

Cheryl Gould is a member of the Royal Society of British Sculptors. She lives and works in Harrow. As a longstanding independent provider she tutors life drawing classes at the Harrow Art Centre and runs creative drawing workshops. She has exhibited widely including The Royal Academy Summer shows and has work in both private and public collections .She was recently commissioned to design and execute a 5ft Holocaust Memorial sculpture for the memorial garden in the grounds of Edgware and District Reform Synagogue.

Cheryl is a founder member of the Harrow Open Studios and is President Elect of Harrow Art Society as from February this year.

LOT: STL03

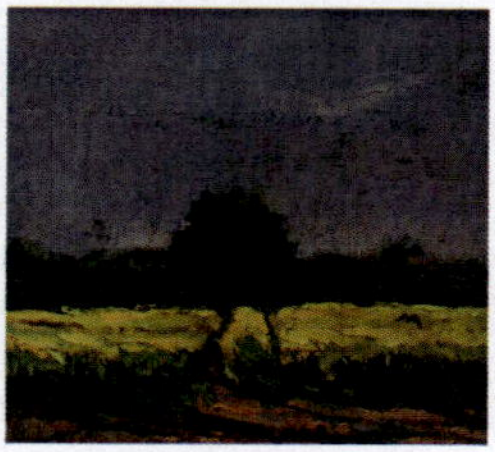

Suffolk Rape Field

Roy Rodgers

Oil on canvas
(19.5" x 19.5")
www.royrodgers.co.uk
Reserve: £350

ROY RODGERS studied at Kingston School of Art and the Royal Academy Schools. He gained the Landseer Painting Scholarship, two David Murray Landscape Prizes, & two medals for his painting.

A Senior Lecturer at Harrow School of Art until 1985 when he left to work in the film and T.V. industry on major productions until 2009, and is now painting full time as well as teaching, lecturing & exhibiting, with work in many private & major public collections including Rothschild Bank, R.S.C. City of London Author of "Starting in Oils" by Swallow Books edited by Ken Howard O.B.E. R.A. " Kenneth Clarke once said, "the most important thing about painting is that it must be life enhancing. "

To live with a painting by Roy Rodgers is a life enhancing experience, as he always shows us his way of seeing the world. He reveals the world to us, he celebrates the world and he communicates that celebration to us " KEN HOWARD O.B.E. R.A.

LOT: STL04

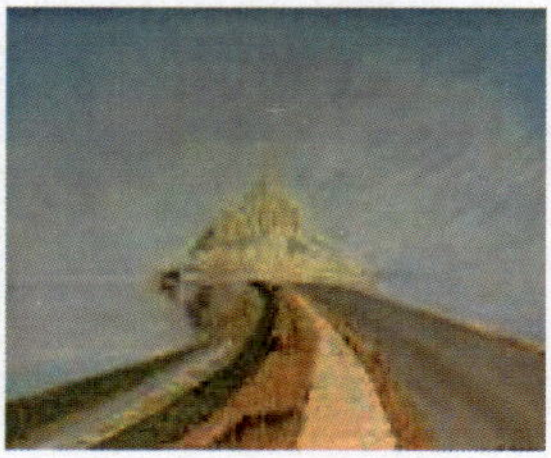

Mont Saint Michel

Gloria Moleman

Framed(23" x 27")
Reserve: £150

Gloria Moleman (nee Aizen) was born in the East End of London in 1934, the only child of a tailor and a seamstress. Gloria's childhood was disrupted when World War 2 broke out and at only five years old she was evacuated to the countryside. During the war years she was moved around a lot while her parents remained behind in London. It was during this time that she developed a love for literature, writing, poetry, art and painting. She especially loved Impressionism.

Gloria continued to paint all her life but after suffering strokes when she was 48 and 53 (which affected her right side) it became more difficult. She joined the Wembley Art Society where she was an active member when her health permitted. Gloria loved painting out in nature. Her earlier works were in oil on board but in later years she turned more towards water colour and soft pastels.

In 2006, Gloria was diagnosed with breast cancer which metastasised. She passed away on 13th January 2015.

LOT: MSH04

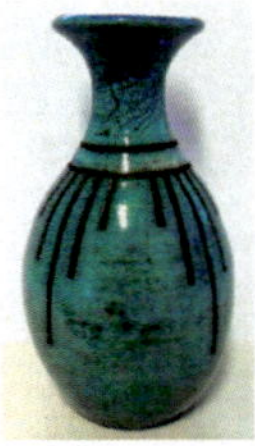

Raku

Sarah Crickmore Ceramics

scrickmore64@gmail.com

LOT: MSH05

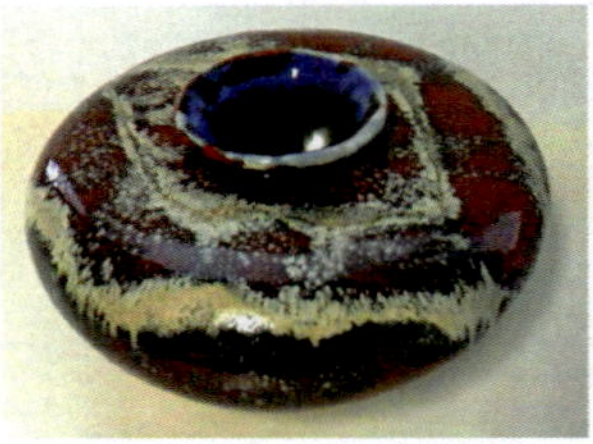

Original Red Stoneware Vase

Cobridge Stoneware

Cobridge Stoneware was set up by the owner of Moorcroft factory in 1988

LOT: MSH06

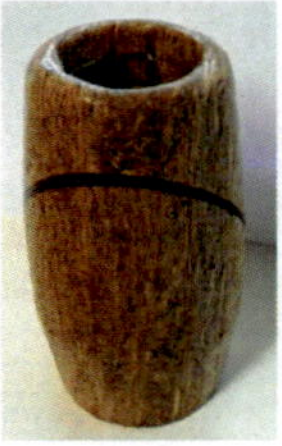

Vase

Gordon Cookson

Vase made from recycled OSB
www.middxturners.com/gordoncookson
gordoncookson1@btinternet.com

LOT: MSH07

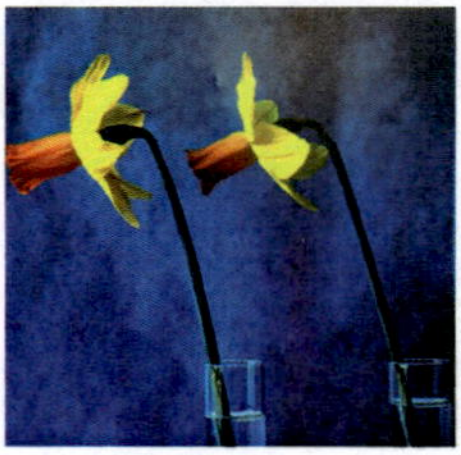

Narcissia

Hugh Harkness

31" x 31"
Canvas printed pigment inks meaning colour will stay vibrant for a lifetime

LOT: STL05

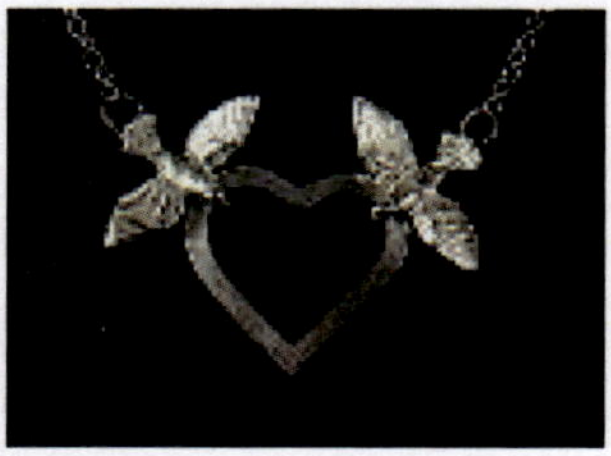

Sterling Silver Chain

Jane—Designed by JPP

Sterling silver heart with 2 doves and integral chain

www.designedbyjpp.co.uk

Reserve: £350

Jane developed a passion for working in gold and silver, precious and semi-precious stones and pearls, after taking several City and Guild courses at Sir John Cass College. She loves colour and texture, and her pieces often include hammer marks, oxidation and etching. Jane is inspired by nature and casts and forms naturalistic pieces.

Her collection comprises a variety of jewellery, spoons and other small pieces, and includes intricate jewellery design and techniques, both traditional and modern. Based in Pinner, Jane designs both to commission and for her own pleasure.

http://www.designedbyjpp.co.uk

LOT: STL06 LOT: STL07 LOT: STL08

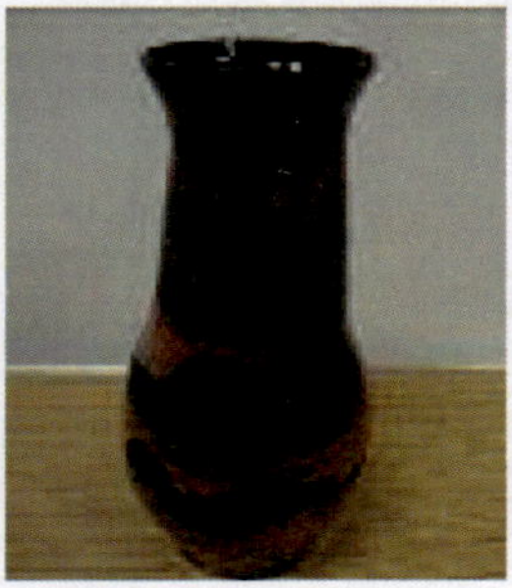

Reserve: £300

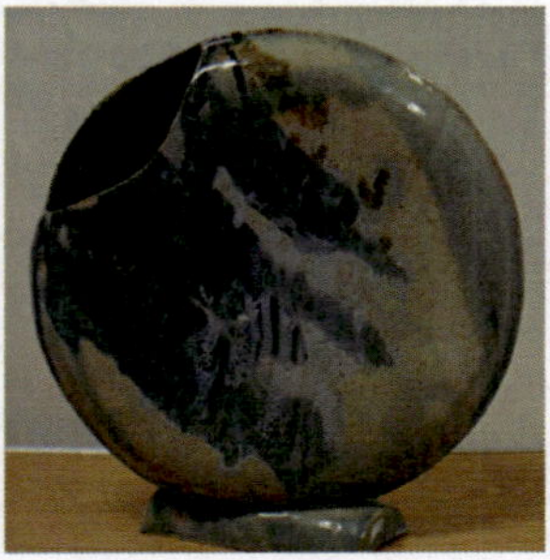

Reserve: £300

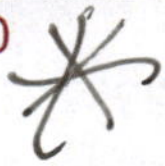

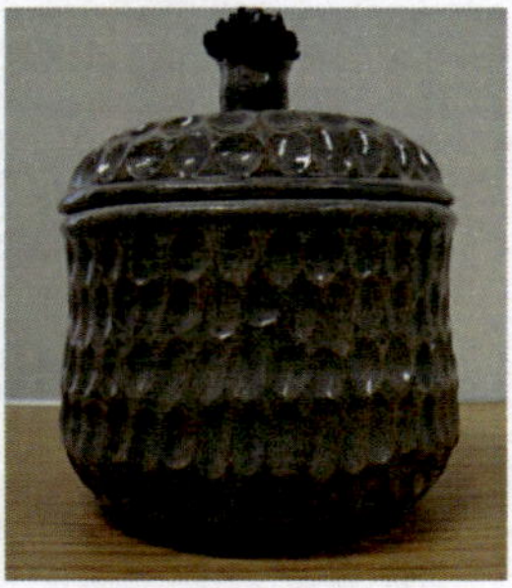

Reserve: £300

Ceramics - Zalina Dewan

Zelina creates contemporary ceramics using stoneware clay, incorporating smoked/raku firing. All pieces are handmade, functional, decorative and unique.

http://www.harrowopenstudios.com/wp/artists/zalina-dewan

LOT: MSH08

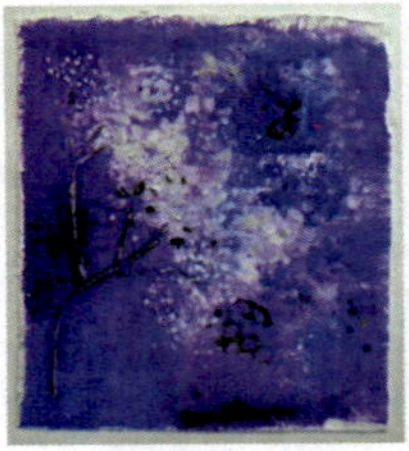

Hedgerow

Jil Baker (Creative Arts Lead MSH)

Framed
Mixed media
18" x 22"

LOT: MSH09

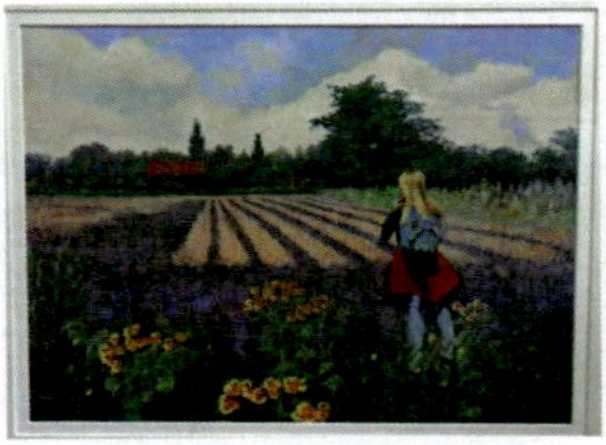

Across the Fields

Margaret J Morley

Acrylic
21.7" x 18"
margaretjmorley@gmail.com

LOT: MSH10

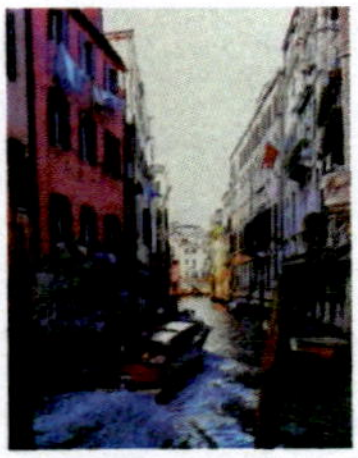

Venice Picturesque Scene

Marty Berg

Framed
Artistic photo effect
17" x 21"

LOT: MSH11

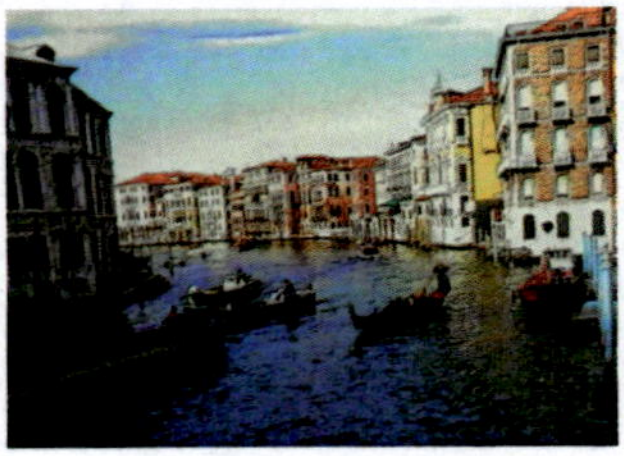

Venice Goldolas Scene

Marty Berg

Framed
Artistic photo effect
21" x 17"

LOT: STL09

In A Tranquil Place

Ann Kopka

A view of Pinner Memorial Park
Acrylic on deep edge canvas
(61 x 76 cm)
Reserve £150

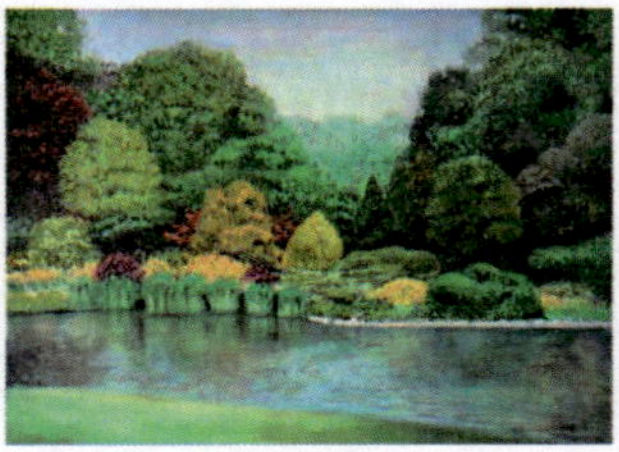

Ann studied Fine Art at The City Lit London and Central St Martins College of Art and Design, and Museum Curating at The Tate Modern.
She has exhibited in the UK, Germany and USA, including a solo exhibition at the Barbican Centre London.
www.artcontemporary.co.uk

LOT: STL10

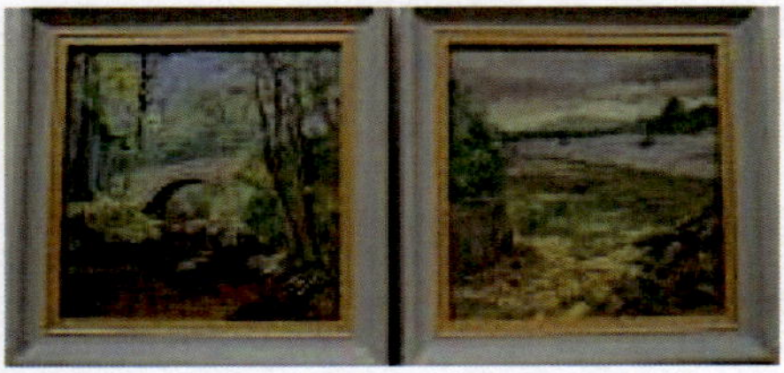

Estuary Devon/Country Side Devon

Marjorie E Torr

Oil
Two Framed 10" x 10" paintings
Reserve £70

LOT: STL11

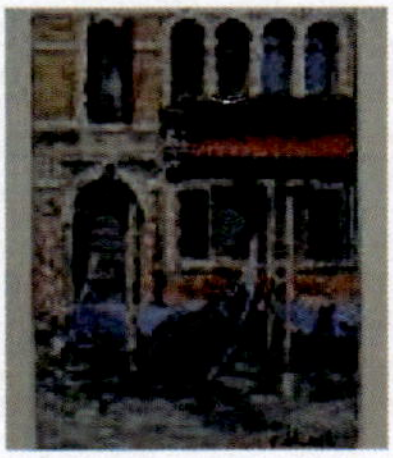

Venice

Vivien Wichel

Acrylic
Framed 10.7" x 8.6"
Reserve £100

LOT: STL12

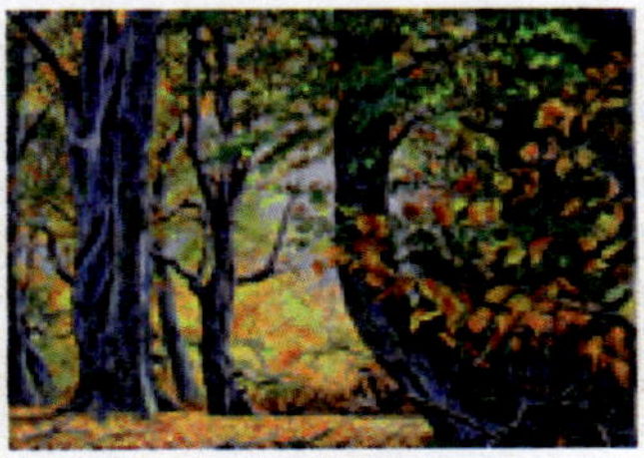

Reserve £100

Autumn in the Ashridge Forest

Gabriella Hargrave

Gouache on paper, framed (23" x 28")
Paintings inspired by nature, poetry & myths
gabriellahargraveart.co.uk

LOT: MSH12

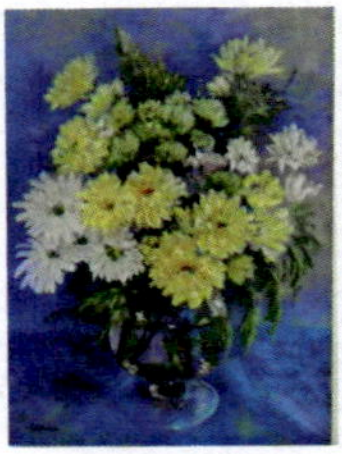

Yellow & White

Pam Adsley

Framed pastel
18" x 22"

LOT: MSH13

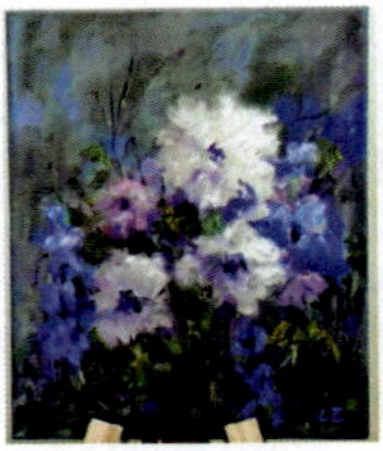

Flowers

Linda Zelin S.W.A.

Oil on canvas
9.5" x 12"
bernzelin@yahoo.co.uk

LOT: MSH14

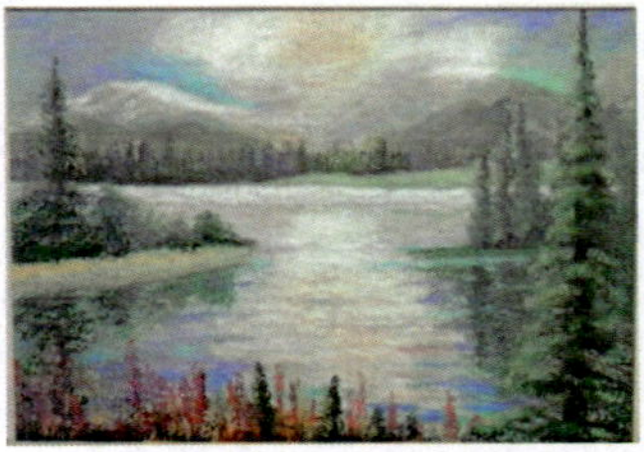

Lake Scene

S P Holme

Framed pastel
21" x 17"

LOT: MSH15

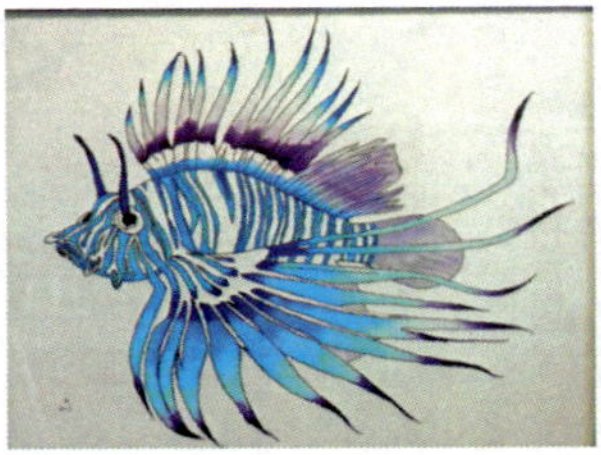

Funky Fish

David Brown

Framed, 20.5" x 16.5"
Original - painted using brusho - a vibrant but little used painting medium
www.art-uncle.com

LOT: STL13

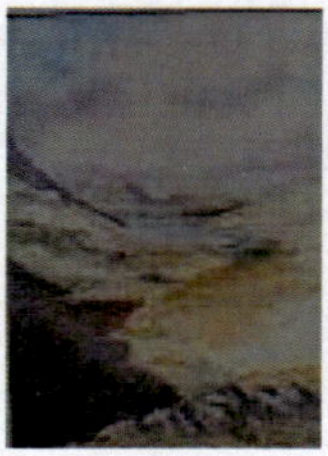

Buttermere 'View from Greencrag'

Peter Jackson

Watercolour
Framed (18" x 14")
Reserve £50

LOT: STL14

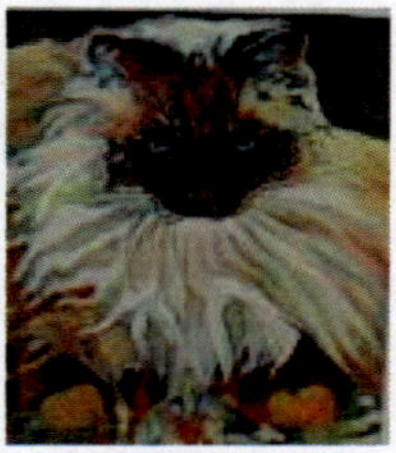

Abstract Cat

Dow Pichaiwatkomol

Acrylic
Framed (19" x 15")
Reserve £50
www.facebook.com/dow.pichaiwatkomolartist

LOT: STL15

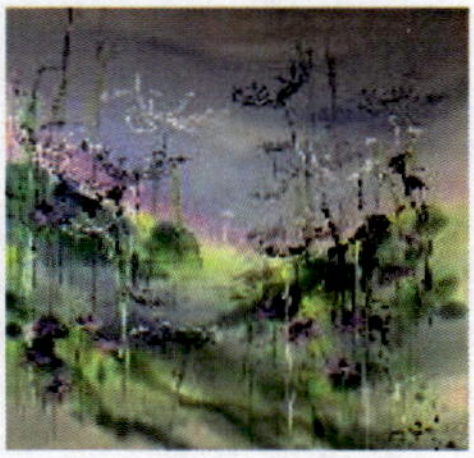

Canvas Flower

Judy Bywater

Canvas
1m x 1m
Reserve £200
judybywater.uk

LOT: STL16

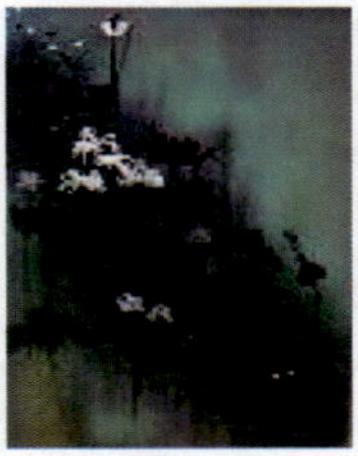

Flowers

Judy Bywater

Canvas
18" x 24"
Reserve £100
judybywater.uk

LOT: MSH16

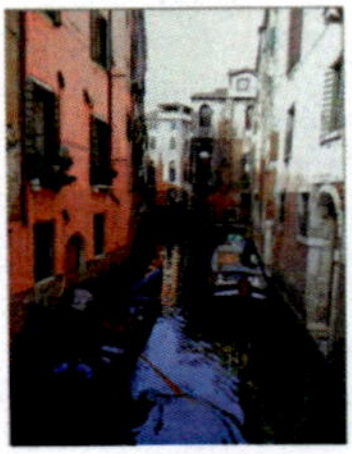

Venice Grand Canal

Marty Berg

Framed
Artistic photo effect
17" x 21"

LOT: MSH17

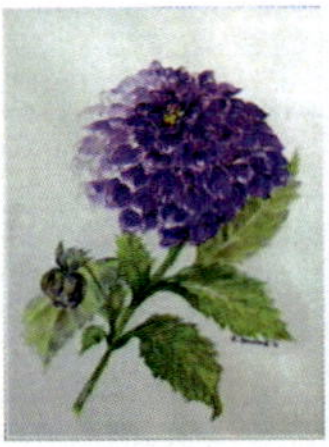

Purple Dahlia

Joanne Dawrant

Framed watercolour
16" x 20"

LOT: MSH18

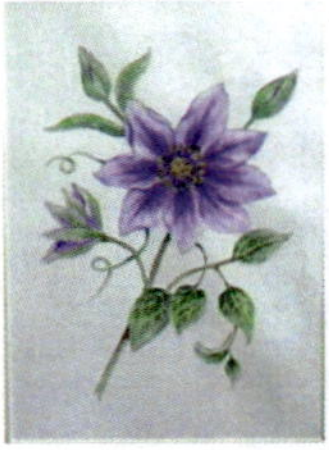

Purple Clematis

Marion Patterson

Framed
13" x 16"

LOT: MSH19

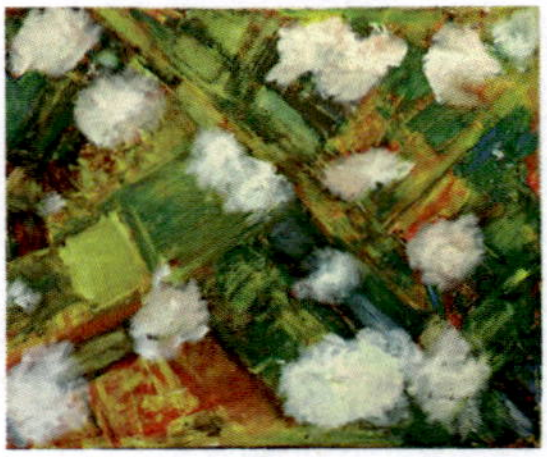

Coming Home

Bridget Sebastian

Canvas 24" x 20"
www.bsebastianartist.moonfruit.com

LOT: STL17

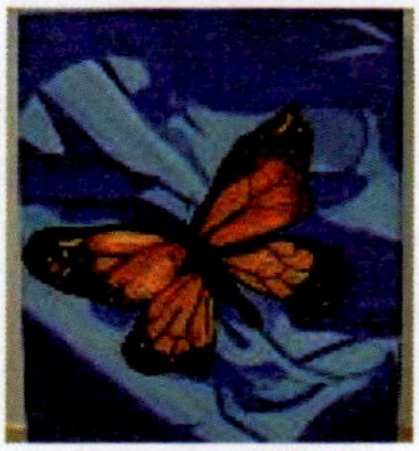

Reserve £30

Spread your Wings and Fly

Mira Saisha Patel

Acrylic on Canvas (18" x 22")
Mira is an art student and an aspiring artist.
mspvcxo.wixsite.com/mira

LOT: STL18

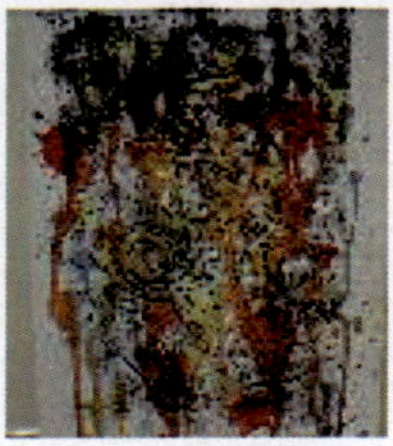

Reserve £50

Lord Ganesh 2

Mira Saisha Patel

Acrylic Paint and Drawing inks (9"x11.7")
Mira is an art student and an aspiring artist.
mspvcxo.wixsite.com/mira

LOT: STL19

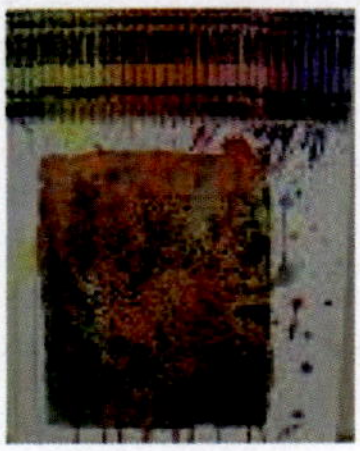

Reserve £50

Lord Ganesha

Mira Saisha Patel

Acrylic Paint, Drawing inks and crayons (11.7" x 15.7")
Mira is an art student and an aspiring artist.
mspvcxo.wixsite.com/mira

LOT: STL20

Abstract Sunset

Sue Varley

Framed (16.5"x16.5)
Reserve: £50

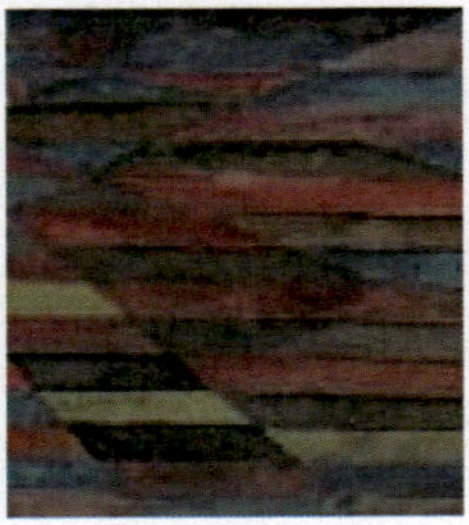

Sue Varley trained at the Bath Academy of Art and has taught at institutions including Godolphin and Latymer and North London Collegiate and exhibited extensively in Britain and Europe.

LOT: MSH20

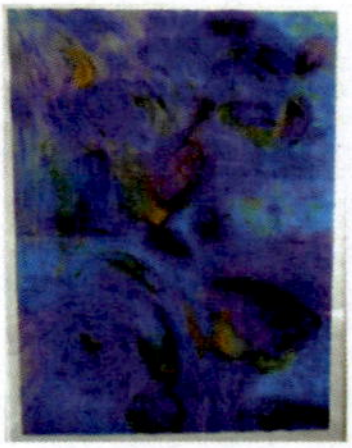

Storm

Group Painting

MSH Day Therapy Unit
Framed oil/rag
24″ x 32″

LOT: MSH21

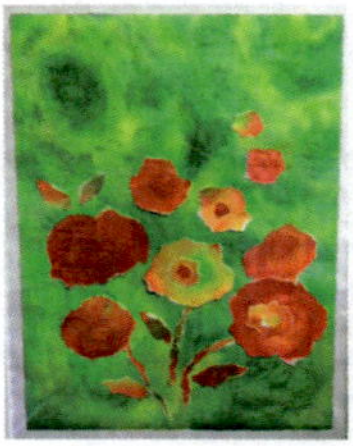

Floribunda

Group Painting

MSH Day Therapy Unit
Framed oil/rag
24″ x 32″

LOT: MSH22

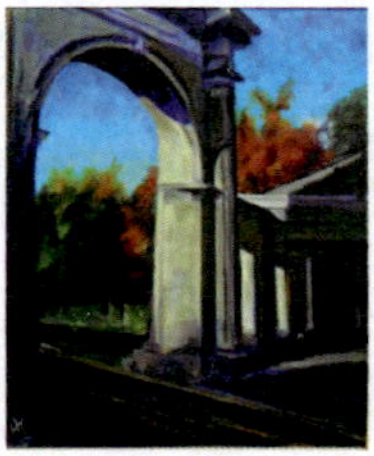

Moor Park Arch

Hazel Gammage

Framed
Oil on canvas
22″ x 26″

LOT: MSH23

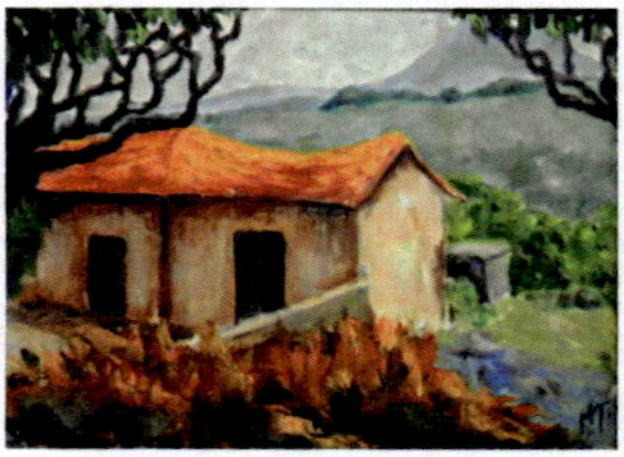

Crete 2000

Hazel Gammage

Framed
Oil
18″ x 14″

LOT: STL21

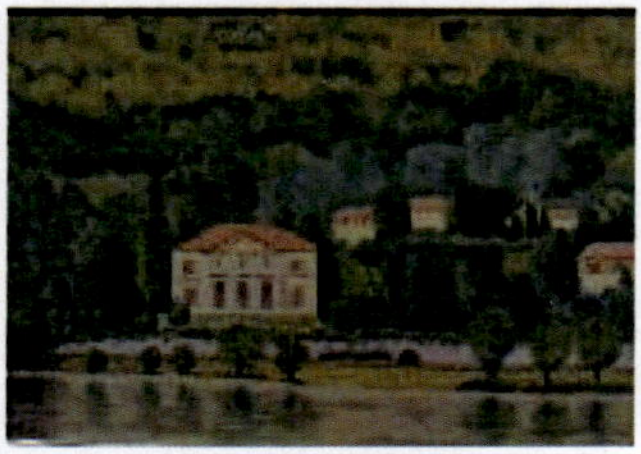

From Lake Maggiore

Pam Edkins

Oil on board
Framed (11.1" x 14.4")
Reserve: £70

LOT: STL22

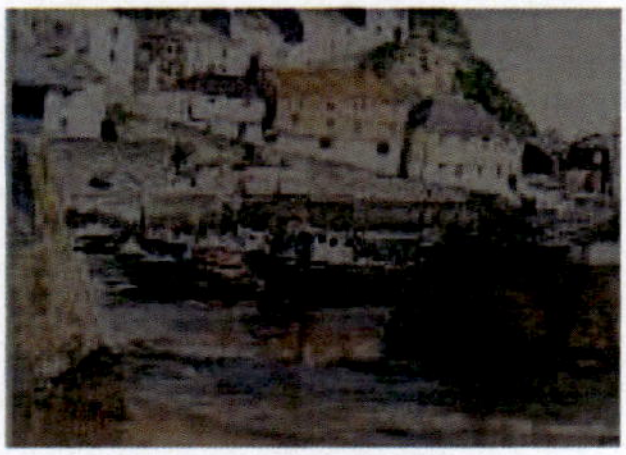

Isle of Man

Jean Massey

Watercolour, Framed (11.3"x13.3")
Harbour on the Isle of Man where I spent so many happy times.
Reserve: £50

LOT: STL23

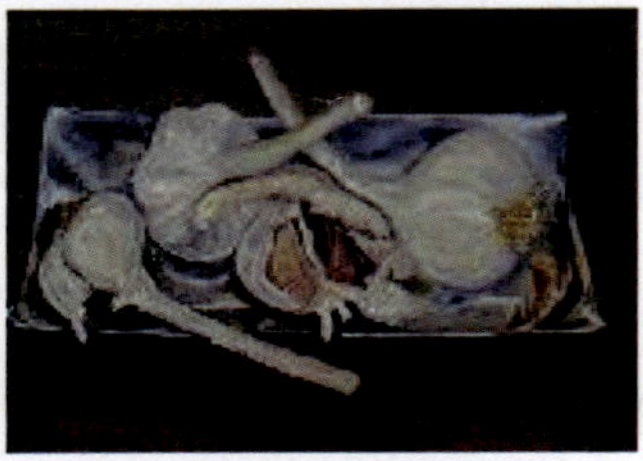

Garlic Bulbs

Enoka David

Oil Painting
Framed (11.3" x 15.3")
enokadavid@gmail.com
Reserve: £50

LOT: STL24

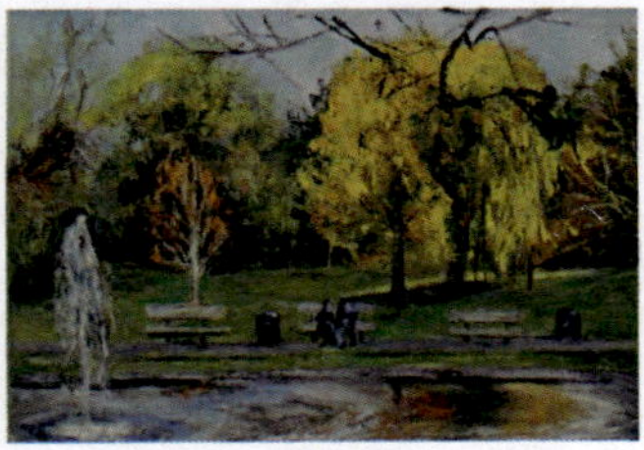

Golden Evening

Enoka David

Oil painting
Framed (10" x 14")
enokadavid@gmail.com
Reserve: £50

LOT: MSH24

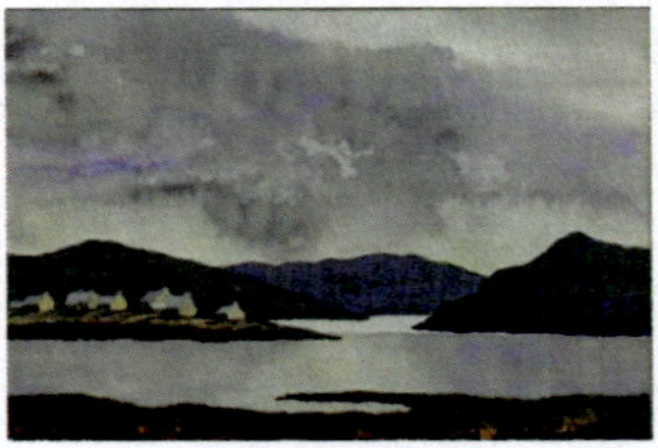

Scottish Loch

Julia Chipperfield

Framed watercolour
17" x 13"

LOT: MSH25

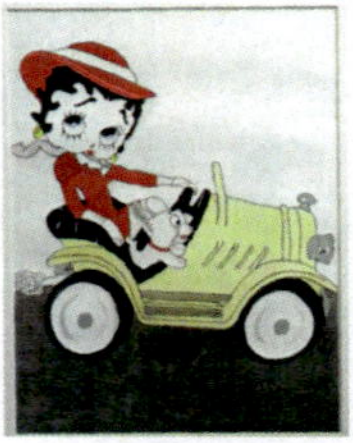

Betty Boop

David Brown

Framed, 19" x 22.5"
No.2 in limited print run of 100
www.art-uncle.com

LOT: MSH26

Iris
'Wedding Candles'

Brenda Paddy
(1936-2015)

Framed watercolour
17" x 22"

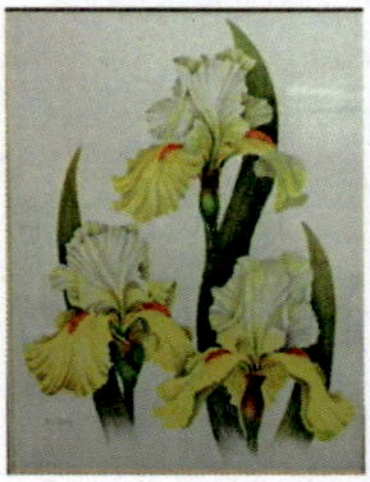

Brenda painted mainly flowers and plant subjects in watercolour. She was a members of the Society of Floral Painters and also exhibited regularly at the Society of Botanical Artists' Westminster shows. She was a member of the Hillingdon Artists' group and also acted as a tutor to the Ickenham Group of Disabled Artists (SODA). A collection of Brenda's paintings were generously gifted to Michael Sobell Hospice by her husband Michael following her death in 2015.

LOT: MSH27

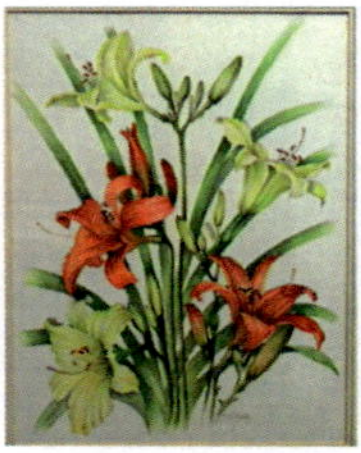

Hemerocallis Hybrids

Brenda Paddy (1936-2015)

Framed watercolour
18" x 22"

LOT: STL25

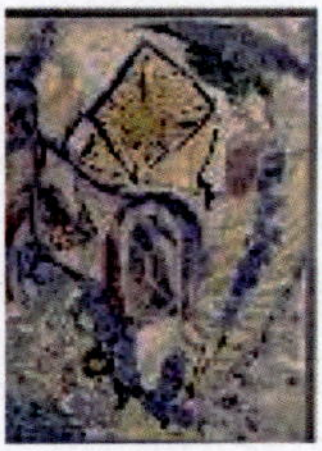

Cyprus

Mary Clark (1943-2015)

Acrylic on Paper
Framed (16.5" x 21")
Reserve: £60

LOT: STL26

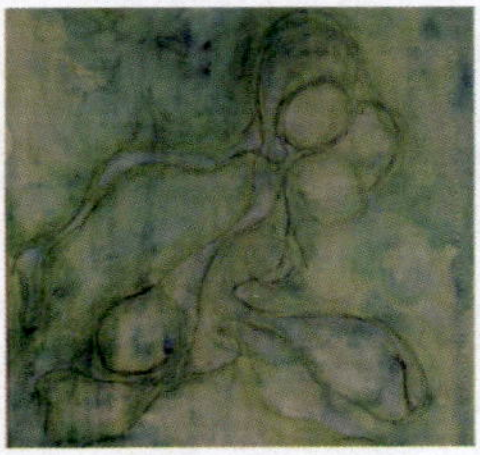

The Dialogue of 3 Companions

Mary Clark (1943-2015)

Canvas (23.5" x 23.5)
Reserve: £150

LOT: STL27

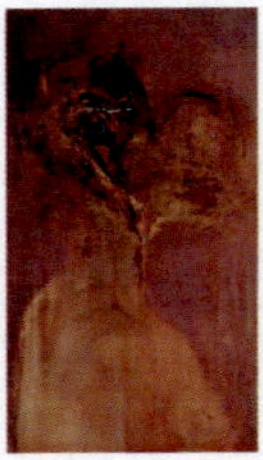

Breath

Mary Clark (1943-2015)

Acrylic on Canvas
19.5" x 35.6"
Reserve: £250

LOT: STL28

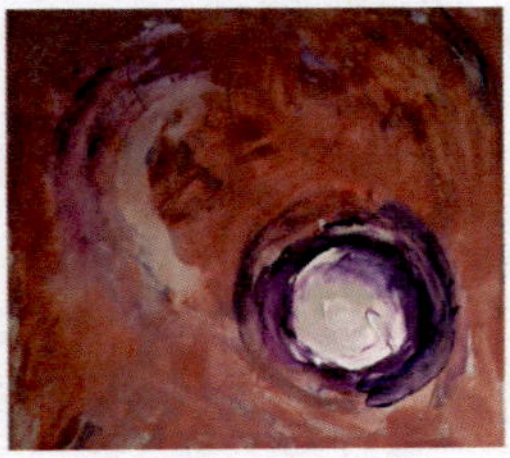

Chaos

Mary Clark (1943-2015)

Canvas (23.5" x 23.5")
Reserve: £80

LOT: MSH28

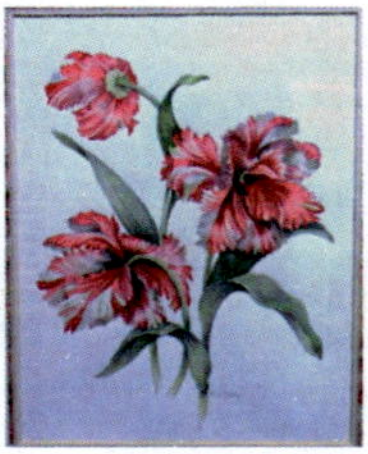

Tulip 'Estella Rynveldt'

Brenda Paddy (1936-2015)

Framed watercolour
17.5" x 22"

LOT: MSH29

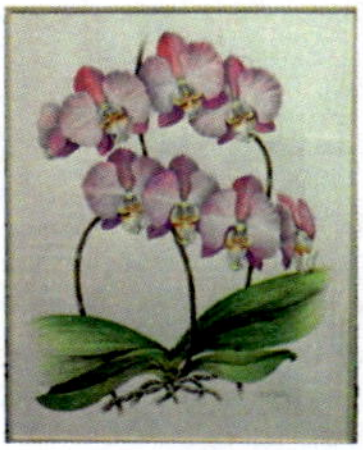

The Lilac Orchid

Brenda Paddy (1936-2015)

Framed watercolour
17" x 21.5"

LOT: MSH30

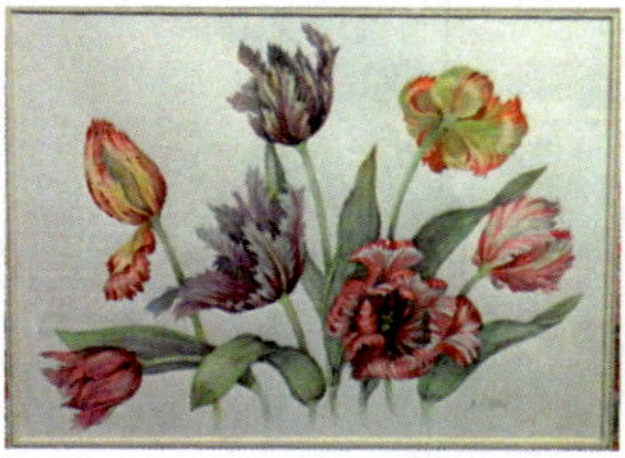

Bouquet of Parrot Tulips

Brenda Paddy (1936-2015)

Framed watercolour
22" x 18"

LOT: MSH31

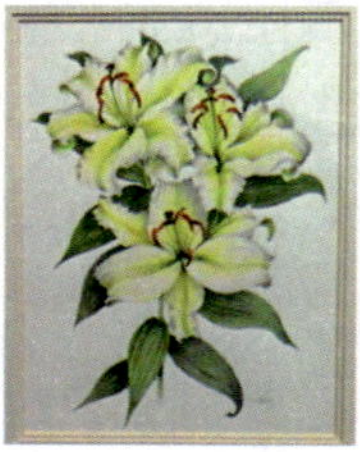

Lilium Aubade

Brenda Paddy (1936-2015)

Framed watercolour
16" x 20"

LOT: STL29

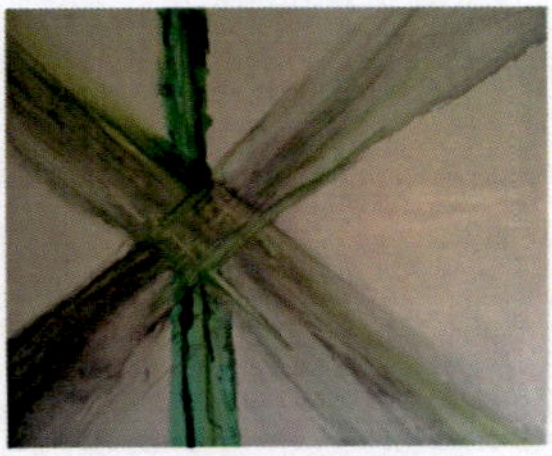

Crossroads

Mary Clark (1943—2015)

Canvas (31.4"x 27.4")
Reserve: £200

LOT: STL30

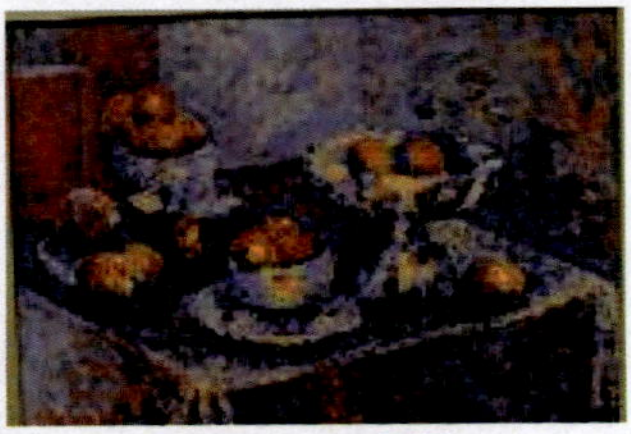

Reserve: £50

Bowls of Fruit on a Table

Susan Rabin

Framed (18.4" x 24.3")
Still life painted in acrylic on canvas in complementary colours with small loose brush strokes in the manner of The impressionists.

LOT: STL31

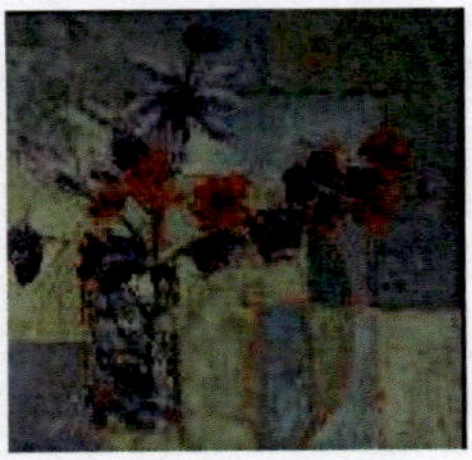

Vase with Flowers and Tray

Susan Rabin

Framed (25" x 25")
Still life painted in oil on board in a semi abstract style.
Reserve: £50

LOT: STL32

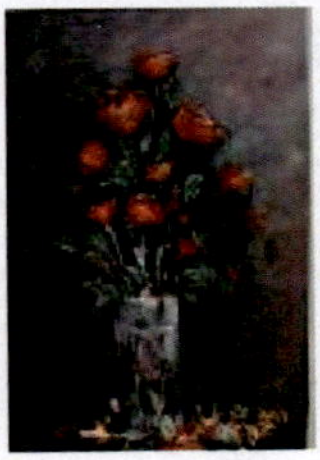

Still Life

Dow Pichaiwatkomol

Acrylic
Framed (24" x 18")
Reserve: £50
www.facebook.com/dow.pichaiwatkomolartist

LOT: MSH32

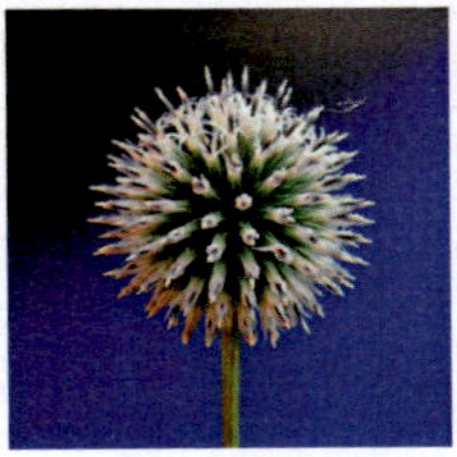

Echinops

Hugh Harkness

27.5" x 27.5"
Canvas printed pigment inks meaning colour will stay vibrant for a lifetime

LOT: MSH33

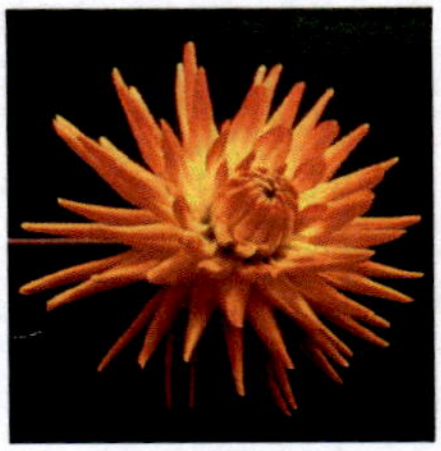

Ruskin Marigold

Hugh Harkness

28" x 28"
Canvas printed pigment inks meaning colour will stay vibrant for a lifetime

LOT: MSH34

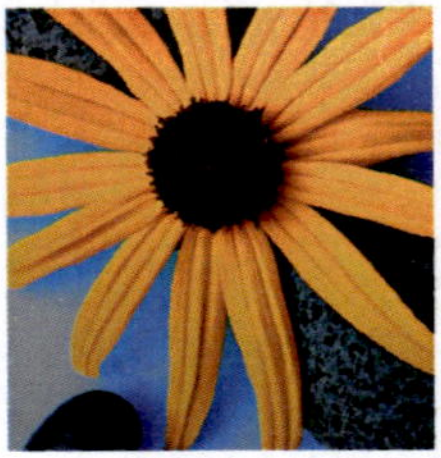

Rudbeckia

Hugh Harkness

27.5" x 27.5"
Canvas printed pigment inks meaning colour will stay vibrant for a lifetime

LOT: MSH35

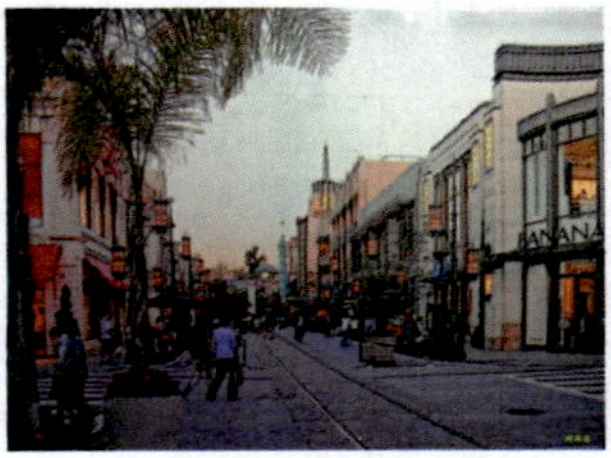

The Grove

Martin Berg

Artistic Photo Effects
Canvas
39.5" x 29.5"
www.hillingdonartists.org

LOT: STL33

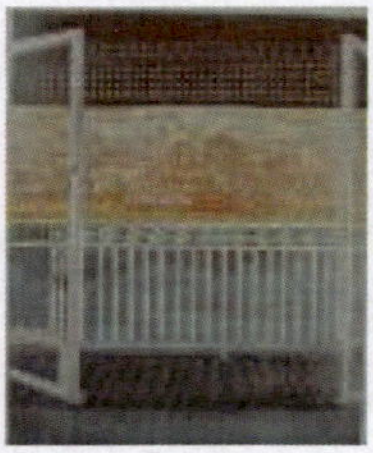

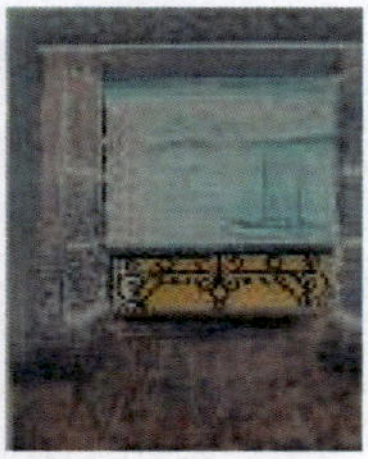

View from the Terrace &
View from the Balcony

Sue Kavanagh
Water Colour/Etching
Two framed paintings 18.2" x 22.2"
www.suekavanagh.co.uk
Reserve: £150

LOT: STL34

Tribute to Mary Delaney

Robin Tatham
(Owl Art Studios)

Lino cut print
framed, (22" x 30")
Reserve: £80

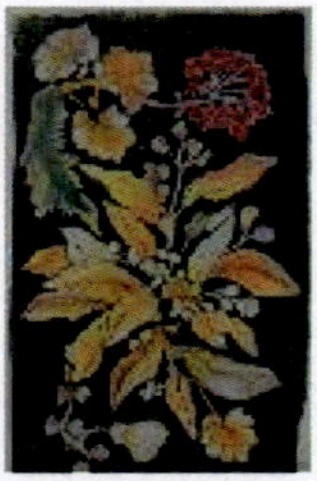

Commissioned to accompany the verse of the Canadian poet Robyn-Marie Butt; the poetry and the illustration are based on the decoupage work of Georgian artist Mary Delaney.
www.owlartstudio.net

LOT: STL35

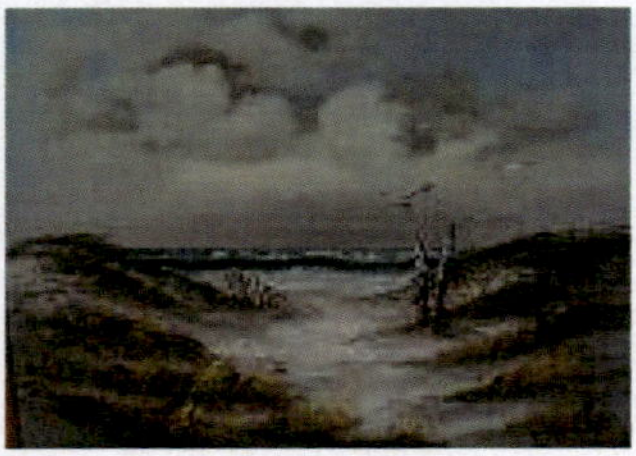

Seaside Scene

Whiteman

Framed
23" x 27"
Reserve: £50

LOT: STL36

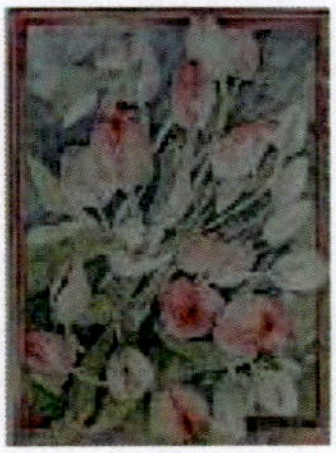

Tulips

Madeline Brennan

Watercolour
Framed (16.6" x 20.4")
Reserve: £90

LOT: MSH36

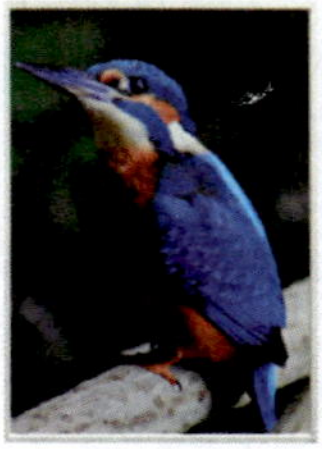

Male Kingfisher

Unframed photograph
12" x 16"

LOT: MSH37

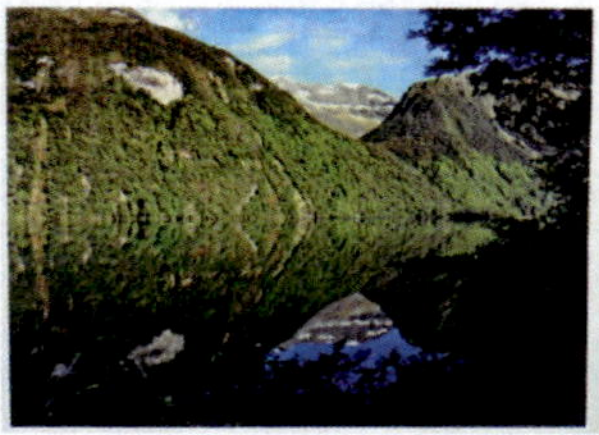

Mirror Lake
Fiordland, New Zealand

Phil Stone

Unframed photograph
19" x 13"
www.philstone.zenfolio.com/catalogue

LOT: MSH38

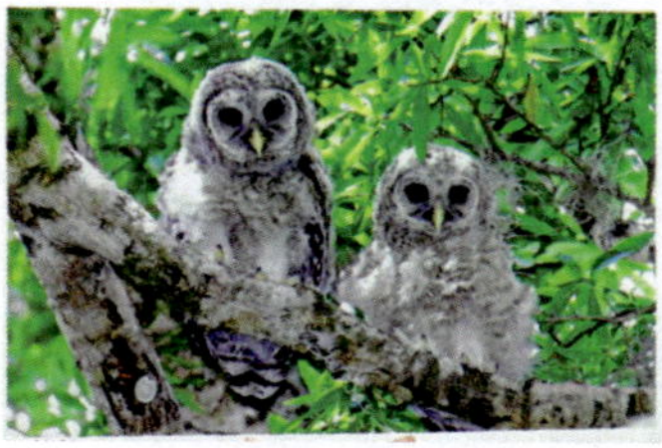

Barn Owlets, Florida

Phil Stone

Unframed photograph
19" x 13"
www.philstone.zenfolio.com/catalogue

LOT: MSH39

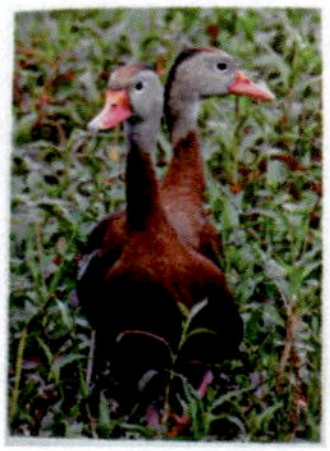

Black-bellied
Whistling Duck, Florida

Phil Stone

Unframed photograph
13" x 19"
www.philstone.zenfolio.com/catalogue

LOT: STL37

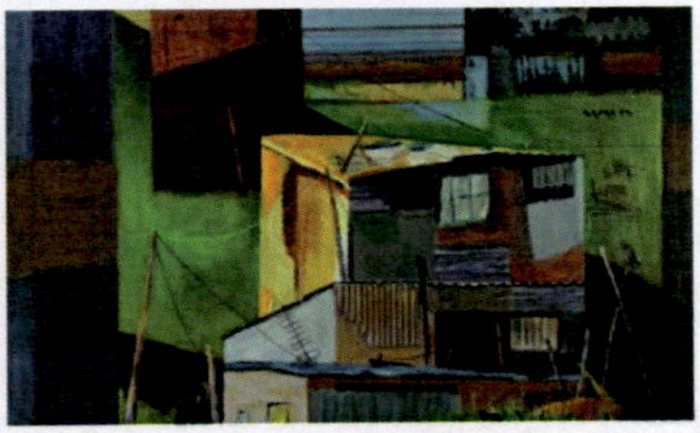

Shanti Town (1 of 3)

Pauline Heginbotham

Acrylic on board
Framed 23" x 32.3"
Inspired by a holiday in South Africa
Reserve: £50

LOT: STL38

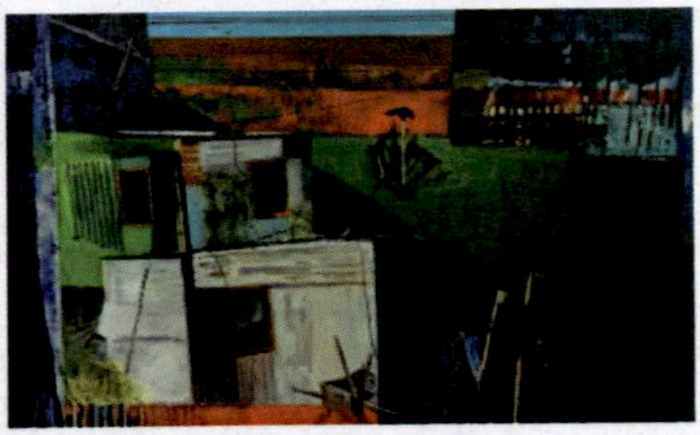

Shanti Town (2 of 3)

Pauline Heginbotham

Acrylic on board
Framed 23" x 32.3"
Inspired by a holiday in South Africa
Reserve: £50

LOT: STL39

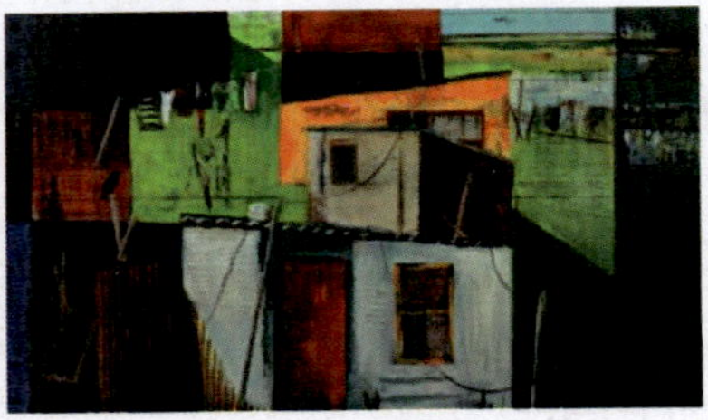

Shanti Town (3 of 3)

Pauline Heginbotham

Acrylic on board
Framed 23" x 32.3"
Inspired by a holiday in South Africa
Reserve: £50

LOT: STL40

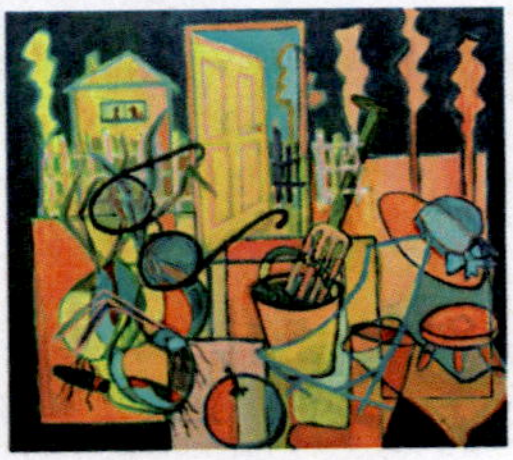

Reserve: £50

Summer Gardening

Veronica Lansman (Vero)

Canvas 23.5" x 23.5"
Veronica produces semi-abstract works in a variety of media, sometimes with added collage.
www.artbyvero.co.uk

LOT: MSH40

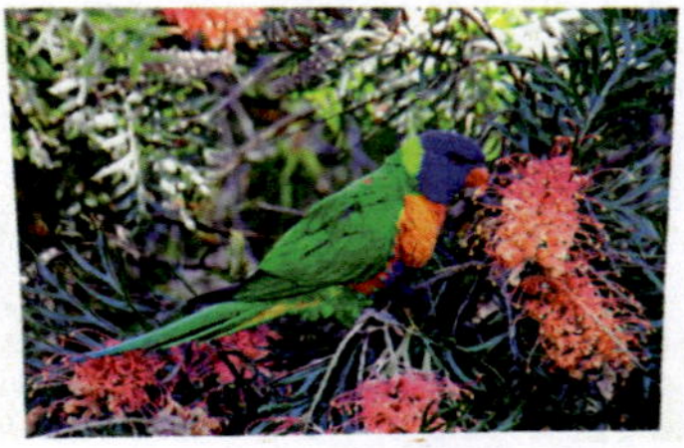

Rainbow Lorikeet
Sydney, Australia

Phil Stone

Unframed photograph
19" x 13"
www.philstone.zenfolio.com/catalogue

LOT: MSH41

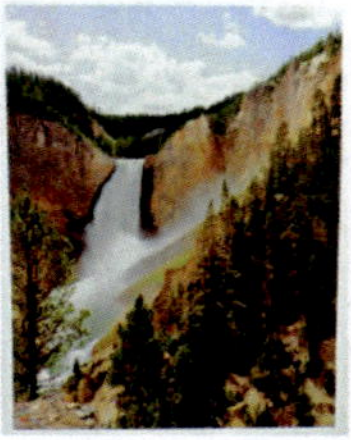

Lower Falls
Yellowstone National Park

Phil Stone

Unframed photograph
13" x 19"
www.philstone.zenfolio.com/catalogue

LOT: MSH42

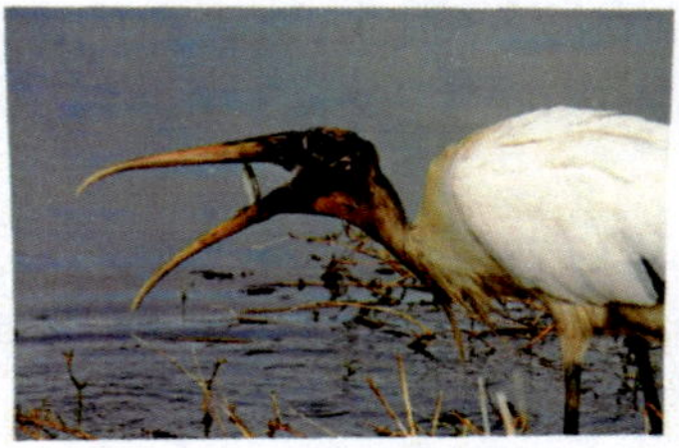

Wood Stork
Ackerman Lake, Florida

Phil Stone

Unframed photograph
19" x 13"
www.philstone.zenfolio.com/catalogue

LOT: MSH43

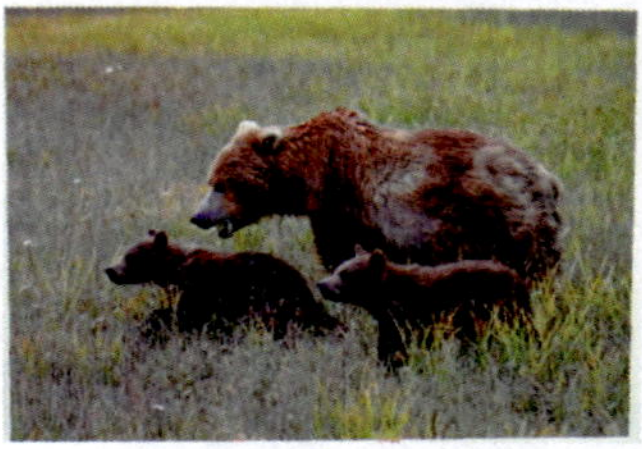

Brown Bears & Cubs
Alaska

Phil Stone

Unframed photograph
19" x 13"
www.philstone.zenfolio.com/catalogue

LOT: STL41

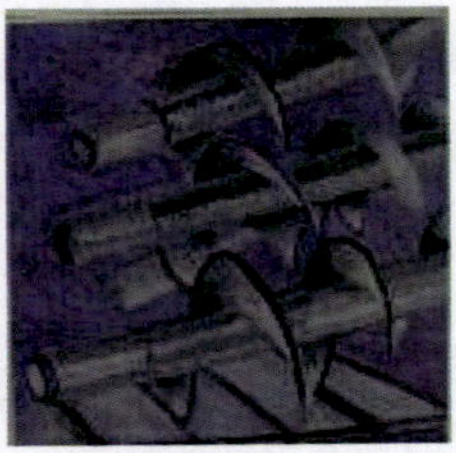

Industry

Sara Sabel

Soft Pastel, Framed 23.3" x 24.4"
Sara is interested in the interaction of shapes and marks made by soft pastel
Reserve: £50

LOT: STL42

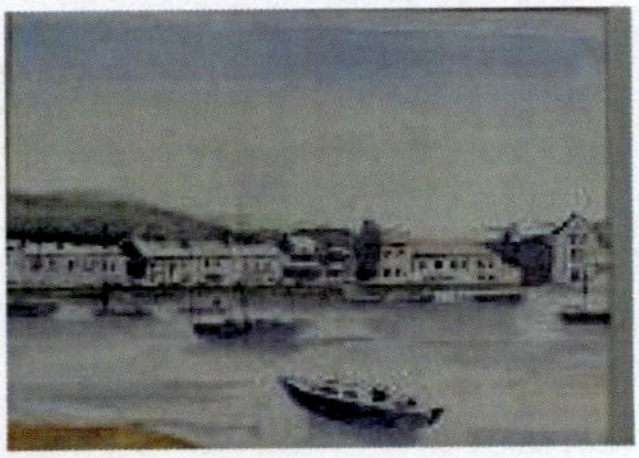

Safely Home. A Harbour Scene

Jean. I. Smith

Watercolour, Framed (11.1"x13.1")
Jean has been a member of Wembley Art Society since 1994
Reserve: £50

LOT: STL43

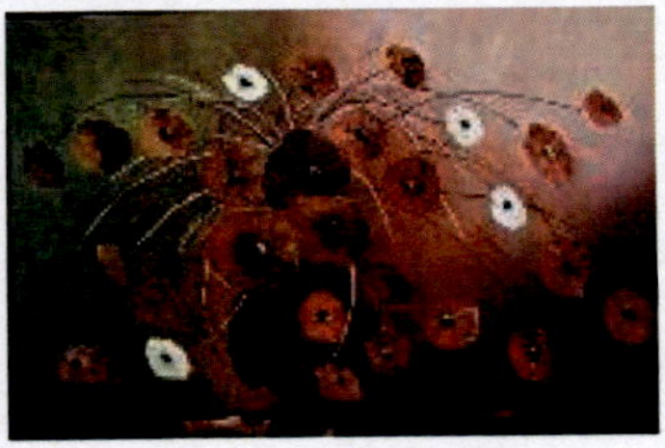

Abstract Flowers

Dow Pichaiwatkomol

Oil
Framed 21.2" x 31.2"
www.facebook.com/dow.pichaiwatkomolartist
Reserve: £50

LOT: STL44

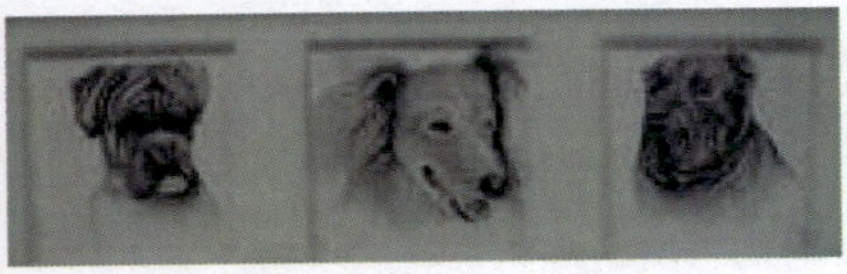

Dog Portrait

Dow Pichaiwatkomol

Pencil
Framed 12.2 x 28"
www.facebook.com/dow.pichaiwatkomolartist
Reserve: £50

LOT: MSH44

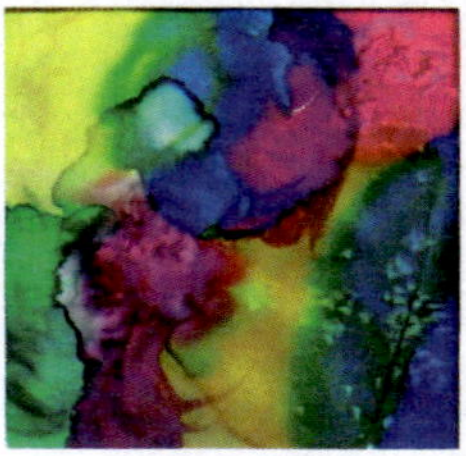

Colourful World

MSH Day Centre

Framed
Silk painting
9.5" x 9.5"

LOT: MSH45

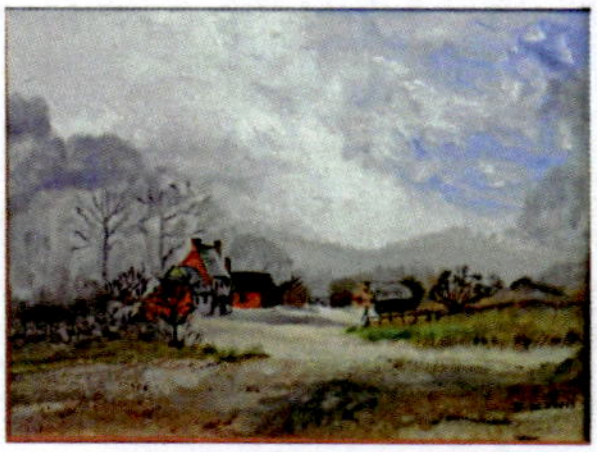

Farm Scene

Doris Davis

Framed oil on board
12" x 15"

LOT: MSH46

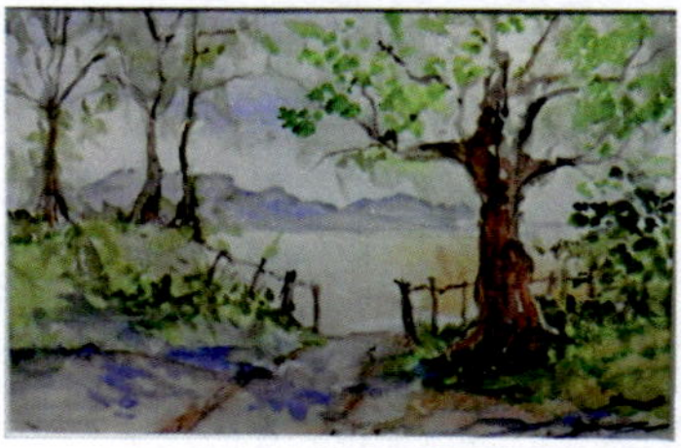

Country Scene

MSH Day Centre

Framed watercolour
17" x 13"

LOT: MSH47

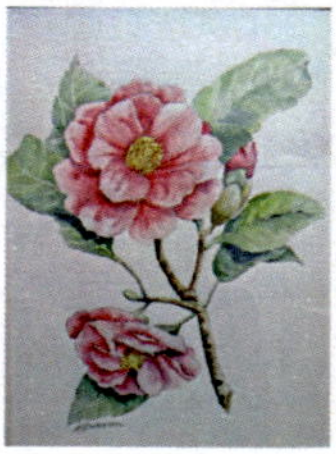

Camellia Japonica

Marion Patterson &
Maria Silverwood

Watercolour, Framed, 13" x 16"
Original by Aldeline Fletcher

LOT: STL45

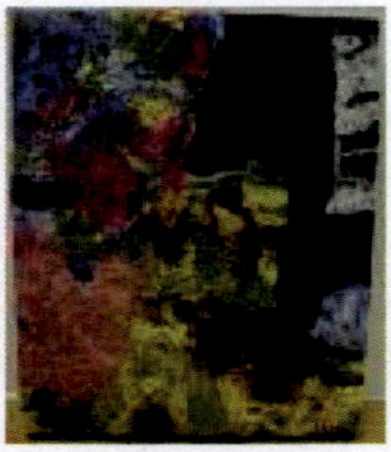

Felted Landscape (1 of 2)

Pauline Heginbotham

Felted Canvas
14.4" x 11.2"
Inspired by the South African Landscape
Reserve: £50

LOT: STL46

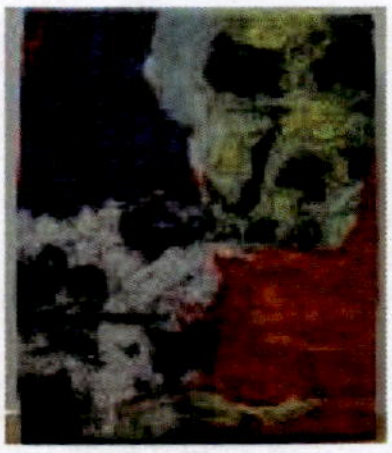

Felted Landscape (2 of 2)

Pauline Heginbotham

Felted Canvas
14.4" x 11.2"
Inspired by the South African Landscape
Reserve: £50

LOT: STL47

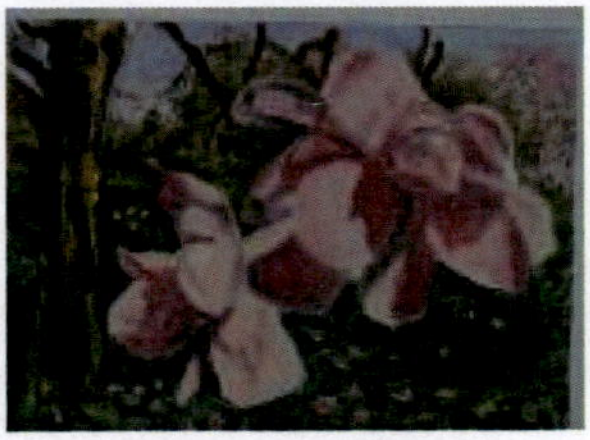

Reserve: £50

Magnolia Blossoms

Jacqueline Gerry

Acrylic, framed (11.3" x 9.3")
Jacqueline started painting 20 years ago. After a stroke in 2014 she has struggled to regain her former expertise

LOT: STL48

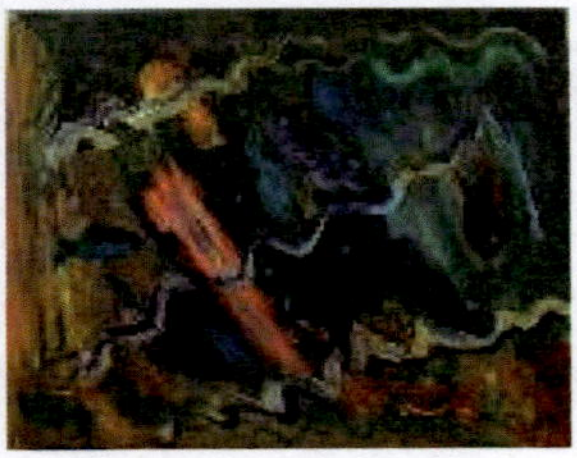

Something Fishy

Jacqueline Gerry

Oil on Canvas
13" x 16"
Inspired by a sense of fun
Reserve: £30

LOT: MSH48

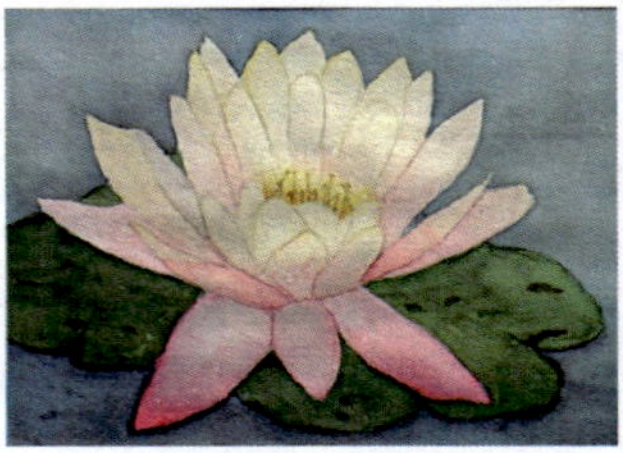

Pink & White Waterlily

Terri Conway

Watercolour, Framed, 17" x 12"
tc@terryconway.co.uk

LOT: MSH49

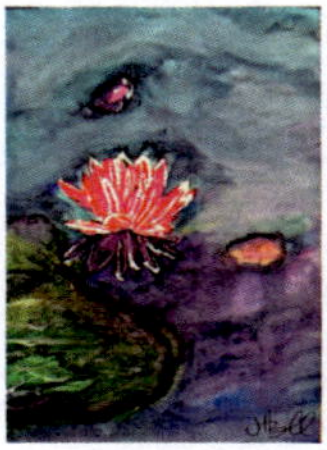

Vibrant Waterlily

Jacqui Hazel

Watercolour, Framed, 13" x 16"
glamorousgranny@yahoo.com

LOT: MSH50

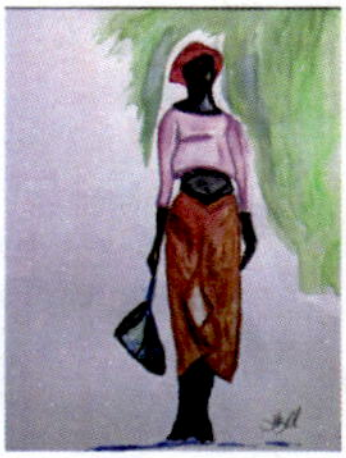

African Woman

Jacqui Hazel

Watercolour, Framed, 19" x 23"
glamorousgranny@yahoo.com

LOT: MSH51

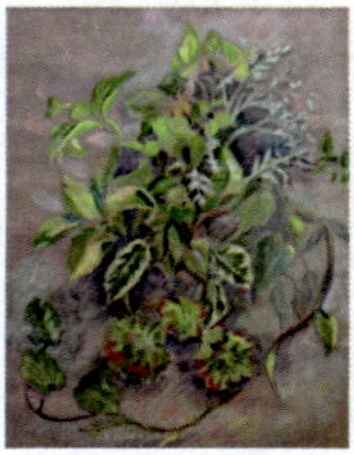

Still Life

Sheila Hulme

Framed, pastel
17" x 21"

LOT: STL49

Hellebores

Moon Kuan

Framed
(14" x 18")
Reserve: £50

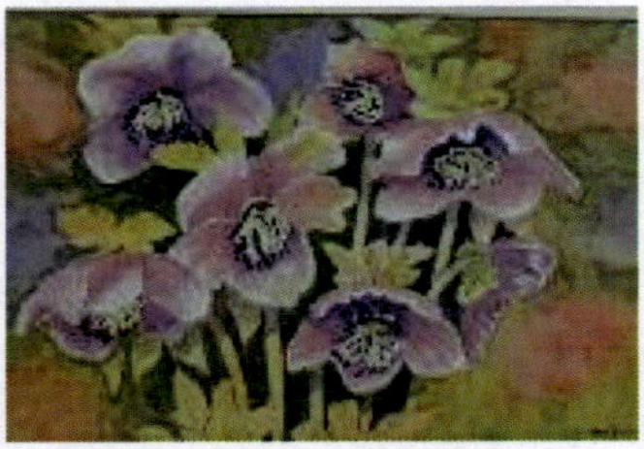

Watercololour painting of hellebores which grow in my garden at home, bringing colour to a sleeping garden at winter time.

LOT: STL50

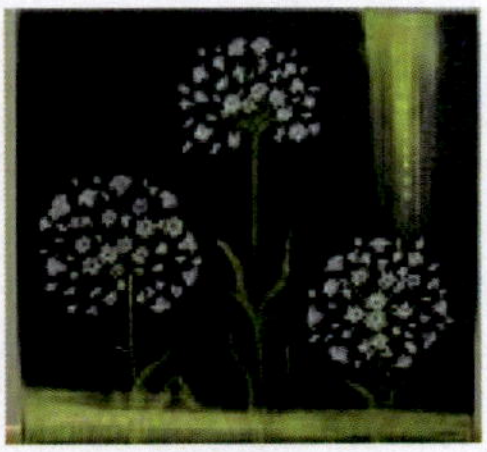

Flowers

Julie Davda

Acrylic on Canvas
15.6" x 15.6"
Reserve: £50

LOT: STL51

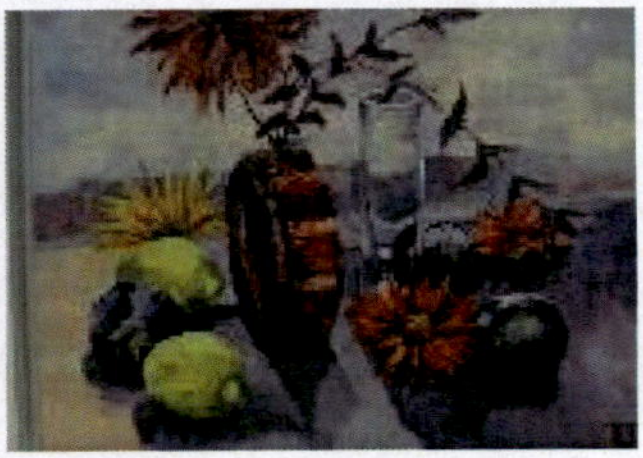

Still Life

Elizabeth James

Oil on Canvas
Framed 16" x 20"
Reserve: £50

LOT: STL52

LOT: STL53

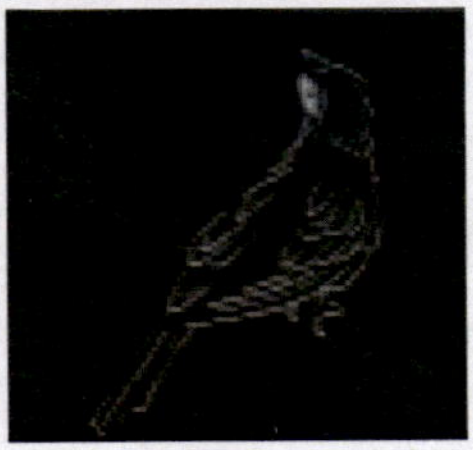

Framed 9.5" x 9.5"
Reserve: £50

Hannah Macdonald

Split stich sticked with silk thread onto silk dupion fabric. Hand embroidered by Hannah MacDonald, qualified apprentice of the Royal School of Needlework and one of the embroiderers of the Duchess of Cambridge's Wedding Dress.

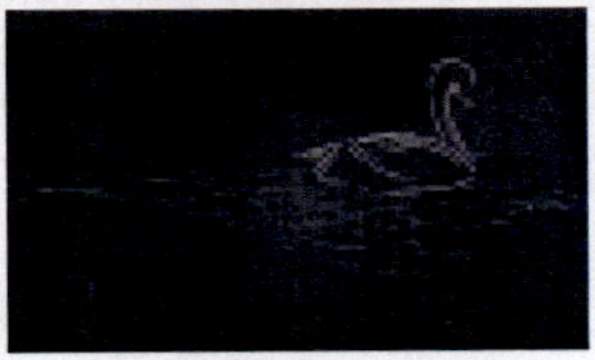

Framed 10.2" x 13.6"
Reserve: £50

LOT: STL54

Pick Up Sticks

Deni Lillian Art

Digital signed print, framed (16" x 15")
Reserve: £150
www.dla-luxury-art.com

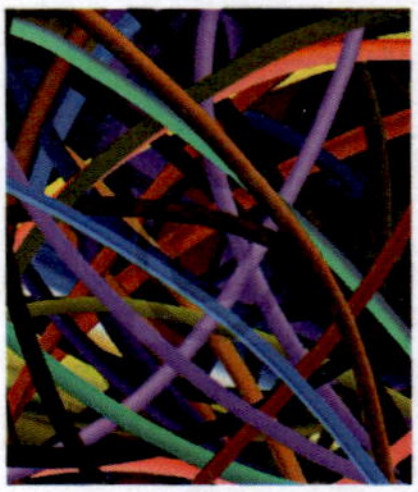

Deni Lillian Art was established in 2010. The art is contemporary, abstract, vibrant, and relevant to the surroundings of the commission whether it is residential, commercial or corporate.

Deni was also the only artist shortlisted for an award in the Contract Product category in the Society of British and International Design Awards 2015.

LOT: MSH52

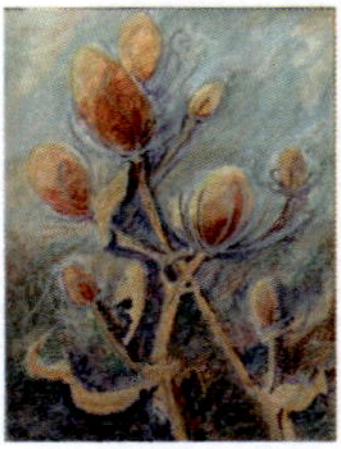

Still Life

Sheila Hulme

Framed, pastel
17" x 21"

LOT: MSH53

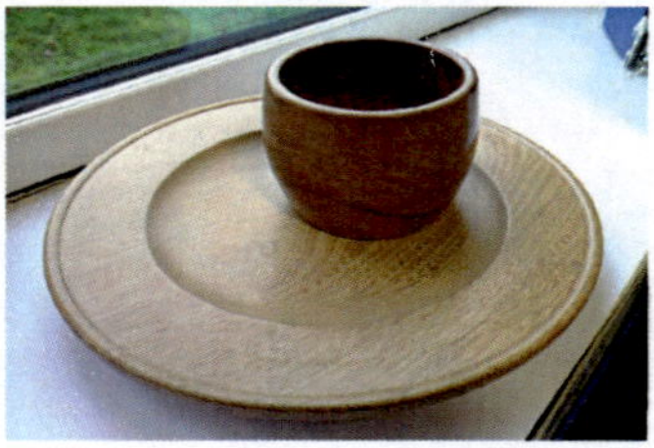

Wooden Bowl & Plate

Malcolm Gane

10.5" diameter

LOT: MSH54 LOT: MSH55

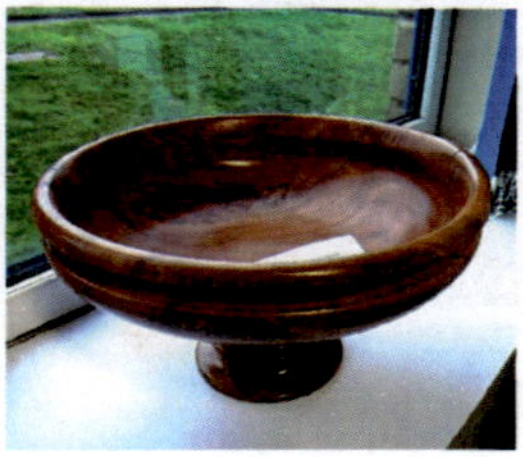

Wooden Art

Giancarlo Ciuffardi

gciuffardi.wordpress.com

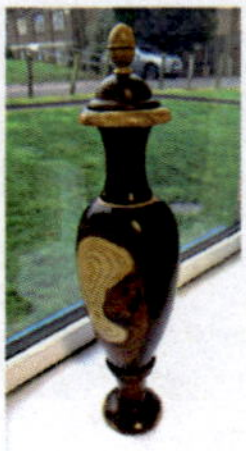

LOT: MSH56

LOT: MSH57

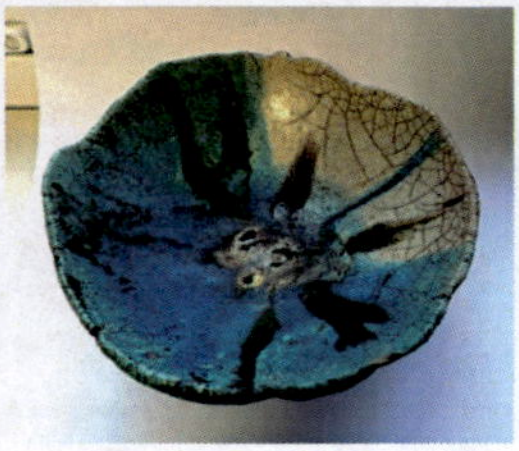

Handmade Art

Natalie Tolbert

Delicate glass and ceramic art

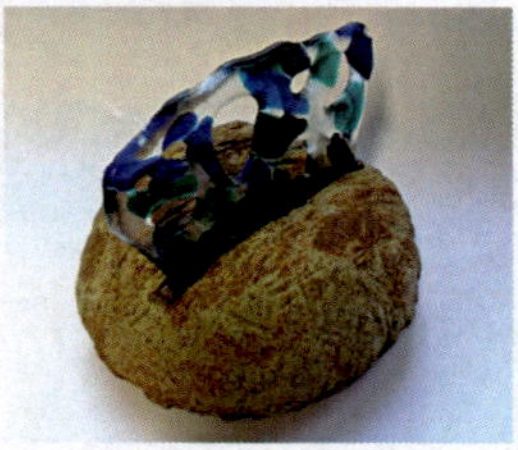

Huge thanks to all the artists listed who have individually donated their wonderful creations exhibited today.

We invite you to place a bid on any of the items displayed and ask you to remember that every pound you spend will help us to continue to provide amazing care to thousands of people each year – please be as generous as you can!

Placing a bid is simple but please do not hesitate to ask a member of the events team if you need any help. Bidding slips are available at the welcome desk and we will notify you by Monday 13th February if you are successful in securing a Lot.

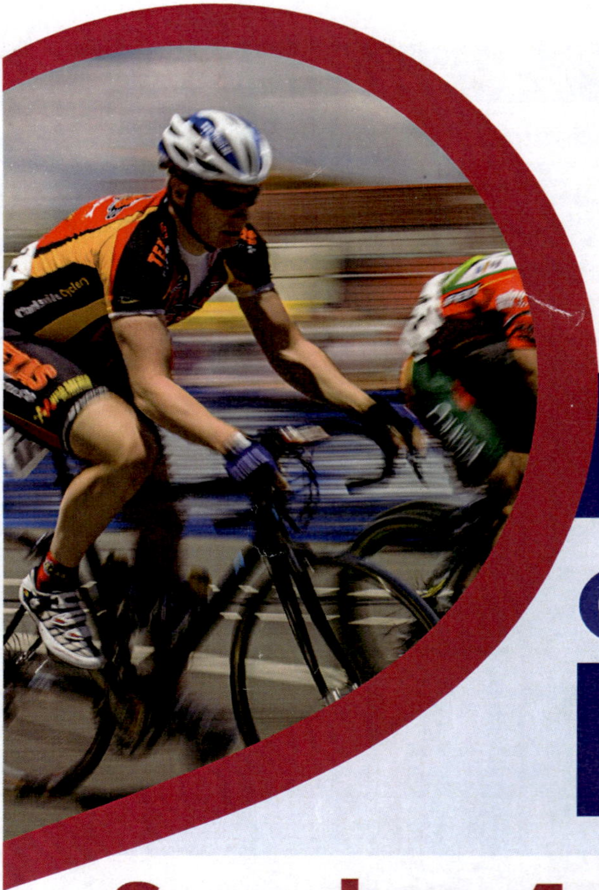